29. 36
Sm 4
20 Jan 2004

Jerry Wiesner: Scientist, Statesman, Humanist

In MIT's Killian Court. (Photo by Calvin Campbell. Courtesy of the MIT Museum.)

Jerry Wiesner: Scientist, Statesman, Humanist
Memories and Memoirs

Edited by Walter A. Rosenblith

The MIT Press
Cambridge, Massachusetts
London, England

This book was set in Sabon by SNP Best-set Typesetter Ltd., Hong Kong.

Printed and bound in the United States of America.

Library of Congress Cataloging-in-Publication Data

Jerry Wiesner—scientist, statesman, humanist : memories and memoirs / edited by Walter A. Rosenblith.
    p. cm.
  Includes bibliographical references and index.
  ISBN 0-262-18232-7 (hc.: alk. paper)
  1. Wiesner, Jerome B. (Jerome Bert), 1915–2. Electric engineers—United States—Biography. 3. Scientists—United States—Biography. I. Wiesner, Jerome B. (Jerome Bert), 1915– II. Rosenblith, Walter A.
  TK140.W54J47 2004
  621.3′092—dc21
  [B]
                                                                    2003051288

10 9 8 7 6 5 4 3 2 1

A work

conceived and initiated by Walter A. Rosenblith

completed by Judy F. Rosenblith

Contents

JERRY IN HIS OWN WORDS   189

You asked why I chose my profession. I guess I was one of those lucky people who has always been interested in the thing he ended up doing. From my earliest childhood I was interested in electricity and I used to experiment with motors, batteries, telephones, etc. I had the good fortune of having a neighbor at a later time who was a radio amateur and he stimulated my interest in wireless broadcasting. As I've grown older my interests have broadened, but I regard myself as lucky because most of the important problems in the world are really communication problems and my early background has served me extremely well as I have aged and I've become interested in more general things.

—Jerry Wiesner, in a letter to John D. Buchanan, September 7, 1967

Foreword

Edward M. Kennedy

One day in the Oval Office, President Kennedy was involved in a meeting on the issue of one of his greatest concerns—slowing down the arms race. Once again he was listening to arguments from Pentagon representatives warning him about the dangers of disarmament, and especially of any ban on testing nuclear weapons. And once again, Jerry Wiesner was vigorously countering their arguments with the vast scientific knowledge stored in his brilliant mind.

Afterward, Jerry told Arthur Schlesinger that he feared he had talked too much and was wearing out his welcome with the president during these very emotional discussions. Later, Arthur had the opportunity to mention Jerry's concern to the president. My brother smiled and said, "Sometimes I think Jerry talks too much, but I didn't think so yesterday. Tell him that I thought he made a series of excellent points and that I want him to keep it up."

Jerry kept it up. In fact, Jerry kept up his passionate involvement to make this a better world, and a safer world, throughout his entire life. During the years of World War II, he used his enormous ability to help protect our nation with vital work in the field of defense-related research on radar and microwaves. Later at Los Alamos, he helped develop electronic components used in the testing of atomic bombs at Bikini Atoll. Jerry knew firsthand the devastating power that was unleashed, and I think that very personal awareness motivated him to want to rein it in.

Edward M. (Ted) Kennedy has represented Massachusetts in the U.S. Senate since 1962, when he was elected to finish the term of his brother, President John F. Kennedy. Since then he has been reelected to six full terms, and is now the second most senior member of the Senate. Among his legislative priorities are health care, educational reform, civil rights, the minimum wage, and the environment. He has served on a number of key Senate committees, including the Labor and Human Resources Committee, the Judiciary Committee, and the Armed Services Committee. He is a trustee of the John F. Kennedy Center for the Performing Arts in Washington, D.C.

So it was that after many productive years at MIT, attendance at the Pugwash Conferences on Science and World Affairs, and election to the National Academy of Sciences, Jerry took a leave of absence to become President Kennedy's Special Assistant for Science and Technology and chaired the President's Science Advisory Committee. In Jerry my brother found, as he wrote to Arthur Krim, a remarkable man who was "a good friend and trusted advisor . . . one of those rare individuals who can work effectively to relate the complexities and the opportunities of science to the needs of a nation, to its culture, its security, its influence and its humanity."

Together they worked to establish an Office of Science and Technology in the executive office of the president. It enabled President Kennedy, and all future presidents, to have unfiltered access to the cutting edge of scientific information, and to promote the importance of science and technology in our society and throughout the world. But most important of all, Jerry was part of the committed team of strategists and determined negotiators who assisted President Kennedy in making the partial Nuclear Test Ban Treaty a reality. Few things mattered more to my brother, and few achievements gave him more satisfaction. He knew it would have been a lot harder to accomplish—without Jerry Wiesner.

For Jerry, the signing of the Test Ban Treaty launched him even more forcefully down the path of leadership on nuclear disarmament issues. After 1963, he commented that it could "inspire us to persist in the efforts to avoid the nuclear holocaust that so haunted" President Kennedy after the Cuban Missile Crisis. Although Jerry returned to his work at MIT, he continued to be a part of the public discourse on disarmament. In 1965, he became the head of the Citizens Committee on Arms Control and Disarmament. He carried on the effort he had started with President Kennedy, and also became an invaluable adviser and friend to me.

In 1969, I asked Jerry and Abe Chayes to help the Congress with its crucial deliberations on the deployment of the ABM missile system by providing an independent nongovernmental evaluation of the issue. They enlisted 15 other eminent scientists and produced an in-depth study that became an indispensable book, *A.B.M.: An Evaluation of the Decision to Deploy an Anti-Ballistic Missile System*. It gave members of Congress the other side of the story, and helped to pave the way for the 1972 ABM Treaty with the Soviets.

I was very proud to have Jerry as a friend and especially pleased to have him as a constituent. He brought innovation and integrity to all he did. His academic colleagues recognized his great ability and chose him to be the president of MIT. As president, he pointed out to the faculty and students that science must not become isolating and needed to be complemented by the arts. He supported the establishment of the Program in Science, Technology, and Society as a way to bring human-ities into the education of engineers and scientists. Now there are a student art gallery and a media laboratory and visual arts center in campus buildings named in his honor. He was also fascinated by the way people related to machines and technology and championed that field of study, because Jerry knew that a better future depended on it.

Perhaps most impressive is the fact that Jerry took the role of "citizen" seriously. Despite all his many responsibilities, he made the time to be on the local Watertown School Committee in his own community. He was also in the forefront of raising questions about the inequities of education when racism was apparent. Doing what he could, he organized conferences on the subject and recruited minor-ity professors for MIT. He urged the MIT faculty to be part of the exchange of "vis-iting scholars" at historically black colleges and universities because, as he said, "it is important to help these struggling institutions as much as we can." It was yet another instance of his great sense of civic responsibility.

As this volume demonstrates so clearly, Jerry was a brilliant scientist, an innov-ative educator, a devoted public servant, and a man of genuine caring and endur-ing courage. He left everything he touched the better for it, and all who had the good fortune to know him were the better for it too. His own country, and many other nations, recognized his contributions and honored him with their highest awards. Jerry Wiesner honored us with his warm and loyal friendship, and his mag-nificent example.

Preface

Joshua A. Wiesner

For many years, my father had in mind that he would like to write a book chronicling his involvement in the U.S.-Soviet arms race from its postwar inception to the demise of the USSR in the late 1980s. Over time, as he thought about the scope of the book, he began to realize there were other parts of his career he would like to discuss as well, and he started envisioning a somewhat broader kind of memoir. In the years that passed before he found the time to start working on it, the form of the book continued to change and evolve, but the core remained his perspective on U.S.-Russian relations.

By the time he finally sat down to put his memories on paper in a sustained way—he had made a couple of brief efforts in the mid-1980s—my father's life had changed considerably as the result of a stroke he suffered in 1989. Though he made considerable progress in his recovery, there were things that would remain difficult for him to do. Quite early on he resumed writing on the book, as a way to take his mind off his troubles and also to make the cognitive and manual dexterity exercises he had to do more stimulating to him. It was slow going for quite a while. One day during this time I asked him if he would like me to help him with his work. He was enthusiastic and immediately began planning things for me to do.

What I did was a combination of research, writing, and editing. Also, I did with him a series of taped interviews in which I questioned him about different aspects of his work, covering the whole of his career from the early 1940s to the 1980s. The initial purpose of these interviews was twofold: to familiarize me with areas of

---

Joshua A. (Josh) Wiesner, a resident of Cambridge, Mass., helped his father in writing and editing a number of the autobiographical pieces included in this book. Several years ago his interest in nineteenth-century photography evolved from a hobby into a business involving the researching and selling of early photographic works.

his work I didn't know much about so I could help him write about them, and to aid him in remembering details of the past he hadn't thought about for a long time.

We conducted these interviews off and on over a three-year period, 1991–94. We did more than fifty of them; transcribed, they came to over six hundred pages. After getting over some early awkwardness, the conversations became quite interesting for us both. They helped him to remember things and also to clarify in his mind how he had thought about issues and events over time. For me, they filled gaps in my knowledge about his work and also gave me insight into how he had approached various issues in his life. Frequently, too, we would stray onto more personal matters, digressions that were interesting in a different kind of way. A lot of the material from these tapes was incorporated in his writing and added a great deal to it.

Something my father and I discussed quite frequently while I worked with him was how he felt reading other people's accounts of events he had taken part in, and how different their memories could be. I think he saw this as an inevitability of time and perspective, and although he would sometimes make a remark or two, he generally refrained from criticism, even when people's views diverged substantially from his.

In the fall of 1993, because of his health, he had to stop working on this writing. There existed, by then, quite a bit of material, some of it fairly polished but more of it in something like a first-draft state. Unfortunately, he was never able to get back to it and eventually I gathered it together to consider, at a later time, what to do with it.

After his death I spent some time trying to pull together what had been done, hoping that I might be able to get it into publishable shape. I worked for a while with a professional writer. We organized the material into sections and tried to decide what would need to be added to create a readable narrative. In the end, it seemed that there simply was not enough finished writing and that we would be creating a final product that was not enough my father's work. So in the spring of 1996, I put away the papers with the hope that some time in the future they would find their way into print one way or another.

In the early part of 2001, my father's friend Walter Rosenblith called me to say that he and some other people at MIT were discussing putting together a book about him. Their idea was to ask a number of people who had known and worked with dad through his career to contribute remembrances of him, and to combine these with excerpts from his memoir and other written material and information from his life. I said I was pleased to hear about it and was happy that some of the auto-biographical writing would finally be published.

The book that has resulted is a very nice tribute to my father. Those who knew him know well the appreciation he would have felt that such a collection had been dedicated to him and that so many friends and colleagues were a part of it. The book shows the range of his interests and involvements and also, through the eyes of the contributors, the person who got so much from the varied work he did and the many personal relationships it brought him.

Introduction

Judy F. Rosenblith

This book was conceived by Walter A. Rosenblith, my husband. Unfortunately, he did not live to see it to completion.

Walter was a long-time friend and colleague of Jerry Wiesner. They became friends in the late 1940s. Both belonged to Norbert Wiener's supper seminar held at Joyce Chen's restaurant near MIT. Walter always credited Jerry for inviting him. True or not, these meetings helped build a close friendship based on what they had learned about their shared interests and values. I might note that they were both strong optimists.

A few years after Jerry's death, Walter started to worry that no one was writing a biography of Jerry, and that people who had known and worked with him were growing old and dying. Josh Wiesner, one of Jerry's four children, had consulted with Walter about his own efforts to write a biography using some of Jerry's writings and the interviews he had taped with his father. But at that time, Walter was not well and could not help Josh.

Then came the summer of 2000, when we were on Cape Cod and seemed to be reliving the past. Though Walter was 87 years old at the time, he was in excellent shape mentally and felt really well. He was interviewed extensively about his history

Judy F. Rosenblith, developmental psychologist and educator, taught at Simmons College, Harvard Graduate School of Education, and Brown University, and headed the Laboratory of Human Development, Massachusetts General Hospital (1961–64), before joining the psychology faculty of Wheaton College in 1965. At Wheaton, she was the first A. Howard Meneely Professor (1972–74). She held research appointments at Brown University (1961–77). A member of the Maternal and Child Health Research Advisory Committee, National Institute of Child Health and Human Development (1974–78), she is also a fellow of the American Psychological Association, where she was chosen for responsible roles such as membership on its Board of Social and Ethical Responsibility. She is a long-time member of the Society for Research in Child Development, and was its secretary (1965–69) and chair of the History Committee (1993).

in relation to MIT, as part of an MIT oral history project. Our daughter Sandy and I videotaped him and his brother Eric about their early life in Europe. In the same period, Sandy and some colleagues were working to map out a documentary about rural community development, the field she pursues. There was a discussion one evening in which Jerry's name came up, and it turned out that the film makers knew of his efforts on behalf of educational television and his service as a trustee of the John D. and Catherine T. MacArthur Foundation. Walter pointed out that Jerry never had a chance to finish the autobiography he had begun, and no one had yet written a biography of him. They were astonished and said that someone certainly should.

Their reaction and Sandy's enthusiasm strengthened Walter's desire to rectify this situation. Walter had said something in his remarks at Jerry's Memorial (December 1994) that may have presaged his interest in this project: "Even today's entire panel cannot expect to do more than highlight a few of his unique contributions and only touch on his unique human qualities."

After thinking some more and with some help from Sandy and me, Walter decided on a format he thought he could manage. He would ask colleagues from some of the many facets of Jerry's life to each write a brief general reflection on Jerry as they had known him. He also realized that someone should determine which of Jerry's writings existed that might be used to provide a portrait of Jerry "In His Own Words." With encouragement from Sandy and myself, he discussed the whole concept with Larry Bacow when he visited us at Cape Cod. Larry, then chancellor of MIT, was delighted with the idea.

Clearly, Walter was uniquely qualified to undertake such a project. Not only had he known Jerry for a long time, but Walter had always credited Jerry with his being hired by MIT as an associate professor in the Department of Electrical Engineering in 1951, when Jerry was a professor and associate head of the Research Laboratory of Electronics. After Jerry became provost in 1966, he watched Walter's two years as the elected chairman of the MIT Faculty (1967–69). Then in 1969 Jerry appointed Walter as his associate provost. And when Jerry became president of MIT in 1971, he made Walter provost.

Thus, Walter was in a particularly favorable position to appreciate Jerry's contributions to MIT. In fact, we have found little evidence of correspondence between the two men (except when Jerry was in Washington), and deduce that they were so close they must have communicated orally most of the time. I know they discussed political matters as well as Institute matters. They jointly led the way in a number of major changes at MIT. Then, too, Jerry was a political activist, and Walter was then and had always been very tuned to the political scene. Both were even involved in practical politics, as in the formation of Scientists and Engineers for Johnson and Humphrey in 1964.

After talking to Larry Bacow, we contacted Josh Wiesner to see how his biographical project had fared. As noted in his preface, he had not continued and was delighted that someone else might. He also told us more about what Jerry had written and about his tapes with his father.

Larry, Walter, and I then talked with Frank Urbanowski, director of the MIT Press, who was enthusiastic about publishing such a book. Before Larry left MIT to become the president of Tufts University, he arranged funding for the project and persuaded Philip Khoury, dean of the School of Humanities, Arts, and Social Sciences, to oversee it.

Walter's concept for this book included providing an opportunity for people to go beyond the limited remarks that they might have made at a memorial service. But it was more. He very much wanted to do Jerry justice, but also to help others find Jerry's faith that one person can make an enormous difference. He even hoped the book would provide some lessons about how.

Although Walter had developed a list of potential contributors, he decided that there should be an advisory panel (he refused to call it a committee) to discuss possible invitees. The panel included Walter, me, Paul Gray, Carl Kaysen, Philip Khoury, Ken Manning, Gene Skolnikoff, Lou Smullin, Josh Wiesner, and Philip Alexander, who had been hired to do the research for the book. This panel worked well because not only did Walter and the panelists discuss possible contributors, but those who knew a potential contributor best ascertained his or her interest informally before formal invitations to write an essay were sent. Panelists also frequently followed up with their contacts about deadlines or edits. Every potential contributor was enthusiastic about the project, although not all were able to write an essay.

The fact that Philip Alexander was in on the book from the very beginning and familiar with all the panelists was very important—this was a very fortunate (even lucky) circumstance. He has proved to be invaluable. In the period between the panel's meeting and Walter's death in Miami, there was a great deal of dialogue between Walter and Philip. Philip frequently sent copies of archival materials and forwarded draft essays. A rather vast e-mail, fax, and telephone "correspondence" developed between them, in which every aspect of the book was discussed—what should be included in a chronology of Jerry's life, etc. I participated in most of these discussions with Walter prior to his "discussions" with Philip.

Walter was very pleased by Philip's diligence and thoughtful views. In short, he was happy about *their* work. As the essay drafts, Jerry's materials preliminary to a memoir of his own, and copies of his speeches and letters continued to arrive, Walter became happier and happier about the book. In part, his pleasure was due to the content of the essays, and in part to the amount of material that Josh had and that Philip was able to ferret out. Philip, incidentally, has been largely responsible for my being able to fulfill my promise to Walter to see the book through to completion. Not only did we both edit the materials, but he wrote the preambles for the memoir pieces. Also, he not only found the photographs but wrote their captions.

While Jerry's draft chapters, meant for inclusion in a memoir, were not ready to be sent to a publisher, the material they contain is fascinating. We trust that readers will understand our feeling that it was more important to make them available than to worry about their lack of polish. We also hope that the contributed essays—along with Jerry's memoir drafts, speeches, and letters—will stimulate interest in this remarkable man, as well as in the wide range of themes and issues that captured his attention and that remain so relevant today.

MEMORIES

Brothers[1]

Walter A. Rosenblith

Memorial[2]

It is, of course, impossible in the time available to do anything resembling justice to Jerry's multifaceted influences on the people and institutions with which he had contact. Even today's entire panel cannot expect to do more than highlight a few of his unique contributions and only touch on his unique human qualities.

It was my good luck that Jerry and I met in the late 1940s and not only found each other "simpatico" but somehow resonated to each other. I suspect that it was Jerry who got me invited to the Norbert Wiener supper seminars, thus giving a chance for more glue in our relationship. Around the mid-century there were several

Walter A. Rosenblith (1913–2002), a pioneer in the use of computers and mathematical models in brain studies, was a member of the physics faculty at the South Dakota School of Mines and Technology (1943–47) and a research fellow at Harvard University's Psycho-Acoustic Laboratory (1947–51) before joining the MIT faculty in 1951. He was chair of the MIT faculty (1967–69), associate provost (1969–71), and provost (1971–80). One of a small number of scholars elected to all three of the U.S. National Academies—the National Academy of Sciences, the National Academy of Engineering, and the Institute of Medicine—he served as foreign secretary of the National Academy of Sciences (1982–86). In recognition of his role in global science and technology issues, the National Academy of Sciences inaugurated an international lecture series in his honor in 1993. The Walter A. Rosenblith Professorship in Neuroscience was established at MIT in 1994. MIT founded the Rosenblith Fellowships in 1997, awarded over three years to 50 graduate students spread throughout the Institute.

1. Excerpts from several documents that Walter had planned to use as a basis for his own essay on Jerry, as an introduction to this book. The resulting collage may be somewhat overlapping—not quite the polished, unified piece that Walter would have crafted for this book—but we hope it conveys at least a part of his vision of Jerry.
2. From Walter's remarks at the MIT memorial for Jerry, December 2, 1994.

occasions for the Wiesners (Jerry *and* Laya) and the Rosenbliths to discover that they shared many interests and outlooks (e.g., at the 1950 meetings of the Acoustical Society). Though we were both communication engineers of some kind, our approaches were complementary, not carbon copies of each other, so our resonance was one of complementarity, not one of cloning.

Actually, I think that despite the fact that Jerry was a few months younger than myself, he played the role of my academic older brother. Having grown up in America, he had a deeper understanding of American institutions, had been involved in World War II, and had scientific and technical achievements far beyond my own. As elder brother, he played a major role in my career.

But there are big brothers and big brothers. Jerry was not the big brother against whom one had to compete or who competed with you, but the big brother who helped you achieve your own goals. He was the big brother who made you feel so equal that you might have thought he saw himself as your twin—except for the many ways in which you were complementary rather than alike, albeit with a very largely shared value system.

Jerry had the ability to work with people who were in subordinate roles without ever making them feel they were playing second fiddle. He was the epitome of a supportive superior. He would designate me to stand in for him in situations where he could have kept his own name foremost by accepting and sending me to meetings when he was too busy—but no, he asked them to appoint me instead of him. Much of our work on the MIT Centennial Committee fit the same model.

Jerry was not only an excellent team player, he was an imaginative composer and conductor of teams. As such, he worked with many different teams at many levels of public life. Thus, during the "years of trouble" the team of Howard Johnson, Jerome Wiesner, Paul Gray, Constantine Simonides, and myself "kept the lid on" most of the time. Jerry worked with and largely animated teams in the domain of arms control, and was an effective member of "the White House team."

How can one endure the loss of such a brother? One can take some comfort in knowing that his contributions to MIT, to the United States, to Boston, to his home community of Watertown (Mass.), to the international community, and to so many of you here today were so great. One's own grief thus is shared by many, and in sharing it we can hope that we will be inspired to continue Jerry's work to the best of our more limited abilities.

Science in the Public Interest[3]

Jerome B. Wiesner's career is distinguished by the fact that his contributions to science and engineering have been matched by his contributions to the welfare of our society.

He came of age, scientifically, during the period when nuclear weapons were first being developed and advanced technology was being exploited intensively for military and defense purposes. His leading role in the establishment of ionospheric and tropospheric scatter propagation circuits led to the only high-reliability long-range radio communications until the advent of satellite communication in the mid-1960s.

By the mid-1950s, Wiesner was drawn more and more into national policy questions that derived from new technologies, particularly questions bearing on national security. He became a member of the President's Science Advisory Committee in 1957, and in 1958 he served as staff director of the United States delegation to the Geneva Conference for the Prevention of Surprise Attack. During that same year, he first became associated with the "Pugwash" group of scientists whose activities were directed toward improving communications and relations between intellectual leaders in the Soviet bloc and those of the Western world.

In 1961, he took a leave of absence from MIT in order to serve as Special Assistant for Science and Technology to President John F. Kennedy and, simultaneously, as chairman of the President's Science Advisory Committee. One of the ancillary effects of his accomplishments in Washington was to stimulate the development of science and public policy as a field of research and education in American universities. A substantial number of universities have since established formal programs in science and public policy, and many of the graduates of these programs are in key positions in the public and private sectors today. Dr. Wiesner is not the father of the field, but his activities in Washington gave it an impetus that greatly changed its scale, character, and significance.

In the over thirty years in which he has devoted himself to public service as a scientist, educator, and academic statesman, Jerome Wiesner has always generated the vision of research as a profoundly human activity—a natural consequence of our innate curiosity and a fulfillment of our most unique potential as human beings. He has always felt that the fruits of academic research should enrich the life of the nation and the lives of individuals. In his various public service assignments, he was

---

3. From Walter's nomination of Jerry for the first Vannevar Bush Award, National Science Board, 1992.

deeply involved in technical problem solving at both a national and an international level; as a witness before Congress and as a spokesman on higher education, he had the opportunity to articulate elements of a national science and educational policy. In all these roles, his personal commitment to fostering science and technology as essential components of society's progress carries the mark of deep humanity.

Scientific Statesman[4]

As presidential science adviser, Dr. Wiesner's scientific statesmanship ranged beyond defense-related problems to include such issues as the threat to natural resources in the form of water and air pollution, the development of marine resources, the protection of agricultural productivity, and the development of nuclear power for civilian use. He recognized that research and development on such issues did not often promise sufficient financial return to be of interest to the private sector, which had produced many scientific and technical successes, and he argued that the research needs underlying these problems would need to be met, in part, by public as well as private effort. His approach was always to integrate the technical aspects of issues into the broader political and social framework. At the same time, he and his colleagues were able to show how technical choices often presented other policy options, and how real understanding of the interaction of the technical and social factors could lead to clearer policies to serve specific objectives. In effect, he demonstrated the breadth of the field that came to be known as science and public policy.

. . .

During the four decades that Jerry Wiesner has been an imaginative scientist and educator, an academic statesman, and a public policy maker, he has been an international spokesman for the humane use of technology, and he has articulated his sense of the role of science in harmony with our cultural, historic, and artistic values.

---

4. From Walter's nomination of Jerry for the first Japan Prize, 1984.

The Wiesner Years: A Retrospective View of the Future[5]

The years up to about the mid-1940s were the prelude for Jerry Wiesner. Then came the overture. I don't know how many among you are really Wagnerian fans (like my father was), but it turns out that in the overture all the leitmotivs occur. The word leitmotiv is not one that is easily translated into English, and the best I can do is to say that it's something like a theme song, but it isn't quite that.

But what happened during those first five years was that, having been a staff member of the Radiation Laboratory and having been to Los Alamos, Jerry came back and quickly joined the electrical engineering department at MIT. And, he got involved with Norbert Wiener and the Lewis Committee. In some sense these two major influences on his first five years have left a mark—not only upon him, but, I think, upon the institution.

You must remember who sat on the Lewis Committee. There were Jay Stratton, Viki Weisskopf, and Elting Morison, and there were all those people who in some ways had already absorbed (some of them for quite a few years) the essence of MIT—its commitment to excellence, to the real world, to the best of the new knowledge, and, yes, its commitment to education above all. Jerry's work on the Lewis Committee told him what was essential, it told him what needed to be attacked in educational reform.

Now, what if you look at the other decades with the exception of what Jerry called the Washington interlude? Those other decades were something in which that overture was worked out, acted out, and, as I will dare say at the end, it was more than that because it isn't finished yet. I'm not going to give you a detailed biography of what he has done, but I will try to show you how MIT's evolution into a modern university found in Jerry one of its most effective builders and indeed architects.

Let me just say that modern universities have repeatedly been compared to the cathedrals of an earlier period, in the sense that they are never finished. At Pittsburgh they call it "the cathedral of learning." I think that in each of these cathedrals there are periods that mark the institution, that give it its basic character, during which important changes are taking place because there are people of vision, architects, master builders, contributors from the whole institution who come together and who, in a very strange way, feel their way towards the future.

---

5. From Walter's speech at Technology Day, MIT, June 3, 1980.

What I'm going to try to talk about is: how, in retrospect, did we feel our way towards the future, and how did the institution do what it has done in the last fifty years? Fifty years, which in terms of its total lifetime, have been as seminal a period as when MIT was founded by William Barton Rogers.

. . .

It is often said of MIT that we would rather invent the future than look at the history of our inventions. And yet, it seems to me that we are an institution so unique in the world (the Romans would have said "sui generis") that we have an obligation to humanity to also try to understand how we became what we are. I trust that doesn't sound too boastful.

In some sense Karl Compton set the style, call it scientific-Gothic. And then the towers were built. The influence of the Second World War on this building of the towers was enormous—the new schools, the new departments, the new interdepartmental laboratories. And so we come to the mid-century convocation, Dr. Killian becomes president, and Winston Churchill, no less, comes to celebrate with MIT what we had become.

This is a period when Jerry became director of the Research Laboratory of Electronics and in which he entered into a variety of what were then called "summer studies" (even if they took place in winter). The summer studies dealt with great problems of the outside world. It was a sobering counterpart to what Jerry said was the optimistic mood of the Lewis Committee. There was the air defense problem, the problem of communication in a world that no longer looked so friendly, and then Jerry was involved in the institution building that came out of these summer studies—the Lincoln Laboratory, the Center for International Studies, and others.

But it wasn't just the question of institution building. What did these summer studies develop as a style? They developed beyond what the Radiation Laboratory had done—the style in which people from fields outside of science and technology came to look at military options, at political options or foreign policy options, and at different aspects of communication. It is important to understand that when these people came together and worked so intensely on these matters, they had to break through the barriers of the jargons of their disciplines, they had to recognize constraints that their fields had never taught them. I'll never forget how Elting Morison said to me, "I got a very different view of foreign policy after Jerry Wiesner explained scatter communication." Because then we knew that we could communicate through the troposphere in a way that we previously didn't know. One of the most profound challenges of technology is that it creates possibilities for human beings that they didn't know existed.

Out of all of that came the feeling that you can create an intellectual pressure cooker, which is what the summer studies were. One outcome of such activities was that Jerry could see alternative ways for packaging learning (e.g., quantum physics taught intensively, night and day). More broadly, not every problem can be solved in the same mode. I think that later on when the "Independent Activity Period" came, to some extent out of Wiesner's fertile brain, there was a chance to say— Monday, Wednesday, Friday, or other class schedules are not really God-given. There are other ways in which one can package intellectual enterprises.

In those early years, the influence of Norbert Wiener on all of us was great. Norbert and Jerry got together on a project called Felix. It came out of the desire to use modern electronics that had come out of the Second World War in order to allow people who had trouble hearing to hear through their skin, through a prosthetic device using the skin senses. Later on, we (including Jerry) were also interested in what one could do in terms of allowing blind people to use modern technology in order to be able to guide themselves. In some ways, this has remained a theme—a leitmotiv—which comes back later in the partnership with Harvard in building a health sciences and technology college.

In the late 1950s, a period in which Jerry was already very much involved outside of MIT, what became so very clear at MIT was how pervasive communication really is. One of Jerry's students used the techniques and the electronics that Norbert Wiener and the Research Laboratory of Electronics had developed to work in astrophysics and radio-astronomy. This is another of the things that Jerry kept a permanent interest in. If today you look at the Haystack Observatory, at the way in which astronomy and astrophysics have become a field at MIT; if you look at what happened in the earth sciences, in which the application of communication theory and information theory came together; and, if you look at Jerry's interest in the way in which nuclear events need to be detected, you can see this coupling of the real world with what the Institute had to contribute. So, it was in the 1950s that we conceptualized the idea of a Center for Communication Sciences at MIT.[6]

---

6. One of the few surviving pieces of correspondence between Walter and Jerry (as close friends and colleagues, they preferred to communicate orally) is a memo from Walter to Jerry, "Summary of Discussion Concerning an Institute of Communication Sciences," February 19, 1954, MC 420, box 1, folder 5, MIT Archives.

However, that was the period in which Jerry had already gotten very much involved in dealing with problems on the national or international scene. Then he went to the White House from 1961 to 1964. It's interesting to look back at what he did at the White House as a successor to Drs. Killian and Kistiakowsky as science adviser. Obviously, he worked on problems of great military and defense importance, and he had a major role in the whole question of the nuclear test ban treaty, but he also got very interested in the problems of energy. If this nation had listened to the report that had come out at that time, we might not be in the trouble we are in today. After Rachel Carson had written her book *Silent Spring*, Jerry formed a panel on pesticides and the problem of the protection of natural resources.

While at the White House, he didn't look only at problems. He also had panels on graduate education and on the needs in this nation for a scientifically and technically trained work force. He became very much convinced of the fact that all of these efforts to solve problems—be they at the level of institutions such as MIT, or at the level of the nation, or at the level even of international relationships—depend, for their solution, on better public education. This theme of public education is one that has come back time and time again. Even today, when Jerry reads the program that some of our colleagues have put together in Science, Technology and Society, he asks: "What are they thinking about if they leave out public education?" Of course, not only has he been active in public education in an abstract way, but he was twice elected to the Watertown School Committee and has been involved in the public broadcasting system, including as a member of the board of WGBH. In the latter role, he led what I can say is a continuing battle to have science and technology fairly and interestingly represented.

When he came back to MIT as dean of the School of Science in 1964, it was a time in which there was a good deal of educational turmoil here and elsewhere. As you remember, Sputnik did something to high school education in this country. It got people very much interested in the whole problem of how we teach physics. How do we teach the new math? How do we teach biology? Professor Zacharias, who was the head of the Physical Sciences Study Committee (PSSC), played a pioneering role in trying to answer these questions. When you looked at these issues, you became convinced of the fact that if all of these educational reforms were happening in high school, we at MIT had to adjust if we were to provide an effective interface.

At that time, MIT had a Committee on Curriculum Content Planning, euphoniously called "Triple-CP," chaired by Professor Zacharias. It looked at the freshman year in particular, and left a lasting imprint on the way in which this year was structured at MIT. But Jerry's concern with the problem of science teaching led him to help create the Science Teaching Center, which was first directed by the late Professor Friedman in physics, then by Zacharias, and later by Bob Hulsizer. So I think that what I am trying to persuade you is that these seminal experiences, these leitmotivs of the overture, come back again and again.

The years when Jerry was provost were not only years of unrest, they were also years of educational advances, of improvement in the learning environment. I remember a good number of meetings with Jerry, Paul Gray, Zacharias, Ben Snyder, and Ed Schein (who was then the planning professor), in which we were searching for new ways to bring what we had learned about teaching, about curriculum structure, and so on into a new environment—one that would be more responsive to what young people of that period needed. I think, however, that we didn't do much more than prepare the terrain.

One concern was with getting students to work together and not always compete. Paul Gray, who was assistant provost for educational innovation and curriculum development, will remember those days when the freshman year had experimental programs that came out of the imagination of the faculty. This was also the period during which the institution faced seriously for the first time the questions of minorities and women at all levels—undergraduate, graduate, postdoctoral, and faculty. At the graduate level, a joint program that continues today evolved with the Woods Hole Oceanographic Institution. A committee (called Engineering in Living Systems) was formed that worked together with members of the Harvard Medical School, and then there was the joint Harvard/MIT Program in Health Sciences and Technology.

This type of effort continued during Jerry's presidency. The interest in prosthetic devices continued, and the interaction with Harvard in relation to health became the Whitaker College. The energy study of the early 1960s became the Energy Laboratory of the early 1970s. Jerry's concern with relations to industry made him the best traveling salesman for MIT's Industrial Liaison Program. During the MIT Campaign, when he and Howard Johnson were so much on the road trying to appeal to new donors and organizations, Jerry conceptualized new ideas that had to do with brain sciences and cognitive sciences. He thus became an extraordinary resonator for the ideas and initiatives of the faculty in these areas.

Also as a spokesman for higher education in the country and an internationally respected statesman of science, he has time and again tackled the kind of problems that the Program in Science, Technology, and Society (STS) is trying to address. He was concerned that some of the best young students—students who do not want to become scientists or engineers, but lawyers or other professionals—should attend MIT in order to get the discipline of a scientific and technical education. In some ways he is still searching for what he has called "a liberal science education," or "a liberal education for the 21ˢᵗ century."

I think that Jerry and I, maybe in different ways, have shared the experience that most of the time it isn't really a chore to do what we have done. Most of the time it's fun, it's exciting, it's something that opens up perspectives that you didn't know you had.

. . .

In some ways, we have the seed kernels of the future—a future in which our knowledge of ourselves and of nature will play an ever increasing role, in which alumni will look back time and again to their alma mater and ask: How well did I learn from what you gave me? How well did it serve my future? How did it make me more effective in my own life setting? Did we learn together more than beginner's science, technology, human nature, society? Are we committed to continue with something that is a very long feedback loop? When you are here, you don't really know what it is that you are going towards. And when you come back twenty or thirty years later, you then say: "Well, you failed me here, but you helped me there."

It is this long feedback loop which frequently makes for poor performance in certain mechanisms. It takes people of the stature and of the willingness to stay with it that the Comptons, the Killians, the Strattons, the Johnsons, the Wiesners, and the Grays have brought to this institution, that have given it a continuing personality, a continuing motivation, a continuing desire to be better and more effective as a human institution. Whenever I read or hear on the radio or television something about futures, I'm always thinking that the only institution that really deals with futures is us. Let me close with a quote from one of my favorite French authors, Valéry, who said: "The future isn't what it used to be, but then it never was."

Technological Visionary[7]

As I interpret my assignment today, it is to try to present a personal, in other words, necessarily sketchy and selective interpretation of some of the doings of Jerry and

---

7. From Walter's speech at the dedication of the Wiesner Building, MIT, October 2, 1985.

Laya that led to this splendid Wiesner Building, also called the Arts and Media Technology Building. (By the way, media is a term that Jerry calls "nicely vague, as it ought to be.") Let me also make a guess as to where the activities in that building may fit on MIT's intellectual map. My task is not to sing paeans of praise, nor to assess objectively, nor to analyze critically from a dogmatic vantage point, but to do all of these in moderation, and from the perspective of three and a half decades of friendship.

The Wiesner story starts out, as Laya confirmed to me again last night, at the University of Michigan, where both Jerry (a budding electrical engineer) and Laya (a student in mathematics) get acquainted in the university's radio broadcasting studio. They get entranced with each other and with music, the recording thereof, and the use of these techniques in speech correction and in the teaching of music students. They learned quickly to live in worlds different from engineering and mathematics alone.

In 1940, the Wiesners moved to Washington, D.C. Jerry became chief engineer for the Acoustical and Record Laboratory of the Library of Congress, and the Wiesners became friends with the librarian and poet Archibald MacLeish, who later wrote the magnificent "Speech on a Public Occasion" for Jerry's inauguration as president of MIT. Jerry also developed advanced sound recording equipment and traveled with ethnomusicologist Alan Lomax through the South and Southwest recording folk music.

World War II brought Jerry and Laya for the first time to MIT, where Jerry contributed significantly and with originality to radar development in the Radiation Laboratory, that multi-disciplinary pressure cooker that changed MIT forever. After a short excursion to Los Alamos, Jerry and Laya returned to MIT, where Norbert Wiener was pulling together mathematics and the new technology into a synthesis called *Cybernetics.* The three C's—communication, control, and later computers—became the leitmotiv of the dawning information age. Together with the particles of high-energy physics and the complex molecules of life, they were to dominate the subsequent scientific and technological agenda.

MIT—not yet a hundred years old, born in the Civil War, and with the oldest school of architecture in the country—had been irreversibly transformed by the Compton presidency in the 1930s and 1940s, with its emphasis on science and research, and by its service to the nation during World War II. Jim Killian coined the formulation of "a university polarized around science, engineering, and social technology," and both he and his successor, Jay Stratton, returned to William Barton Rogers's fundamental educational principles with emphasis on "usefulness" and "a large, general cultivation" in the post–World War II context. The mid-century Convocation at which Winston Churchill was present saw the emergence of MIT as a world institution.

At MIT, Jerry got involved immediately with educational reform—with the Committee on Educational Survey (also known as the Lewis Committee) and with the "summer studies" of the Cold War that led to the creation of the Lincoln Laboratory. Given his original contributions to radar, in particular his work on transmission of scatter techniques from the ionosphere, it is clearly understandable why this came about.

In the 1950s, he became director of the Research Laboratory of Electronics, the follow-on organization to the Radiation Laboratory. The progress reports of that laboratory bespeak the range and grasp of Jerry's fertile imagination. There was research in microwaves, in electronics, in signal processing, in plasma physics, in circuit theory, in radio astronomy and radar—it goes without saying—but there was also research on speech analysis, hearing, and vision. All his life Jerry has been concerned with the blind and the deaf, looking for prosthetic devices that would come out of the new technology to make life more livable for these people. There was Jerry's work with Wiener on the problems of the deaf through a project called "Felix"—"Felix" didn't mean here the lucky cat; it was an attempt to get information into the human organism through the skin, to feel sound. There was also work on the beginnings of a theory of patterns of human communication. There was even a study of artistic style by that incredible Mexican surrealist, Manuel Cerrillo. There was support for machine translation and for linguistics. Out of this concern with communication—human, animal, and machine—emerged the concept of the communication sciences.

By then, Jerry had also become involved with public policy. During the 1950s, he was an adviser to various departments of our government. He was in Geneva for the conference on the prevention of surprise attack. In the 1950s, Jim Killian was science adviser to President Eisenhower, and MIT people played a significant role in the creation of a new institution, the President's Science Advisory Committee (PSAC). Jerry became a PSAC member in 1957.

In 1961, the Wiesners went for their second Washington interlude. This time Jerry was science adviser, first to President Kennedy and later to President Johnson. In that role Jerry dealt not only with technical aspects of defense (e.g., the nuclear test ban) and space, but also with energy, graduate education, and the environment. After Rachel Carson's book *Silent Spring* was published, he got a panel of PSAC to worry about it. He played an important part in the preservation of the famous monuments of Abu Simbel on the upper Nile, interacting with UNESCO in this matter very forcefully. We shouldn't imagine that in those years Washington was the cultural capital it is today. But both Laya and Jerry supported many of the local activities that helped make it that way today. The many friends they made there and on Martha's Vineyard further broadened their views of culture, of the arts, of the world.

In 1964, Jerry returned to MIT as dean of science, after which he became provost in partnership with Howard Johnson (as president), and later president in partnership with Paul Gray (as chancellor) and myself (as provost). Jerry extended and above all deepened his commitment to understanding how we as a species learn (not just how we reform our curricula), and how society learns. He was especially concerned with urban problems, problems facing minorities, and how humanity protects itself against nuclear war. While strengthening MIT's disciplinary fabric, he made a major effort to put its strength in science and technology into the service of humanity in areas ranging from cities to health.

But he and Laya did not stop there. Building upon the steps the Killians, Strattons, and Johnsons had taken, they made participation in arts activities more accessible to students. In 1971, Jerry created the Council for the Arts. What he wanted to achieve was an institutional framework involving students. There were historical precedents: Gyorgy Kepes, who gave MIT an example of how to relate science, technology, and the visual arts; and Klaus Liepmann, who did so much for the development of music here. While Jerry was provost, Professor Kepes founded and became the first director of MIT's Center for Advanced Visual Studies. Hence, in announcing the formation of the Council for the Arts, Jerry referred to it as "a catalyst for development of a broadly based, highly participatory program that is firmly founded on teaching, practice, and research in the arts." "We hope eventually," he said, "to transform MIT into a large multi-purpose arts center. . . . I happen to believe that the arts are in fact useful knowledge, and that imagination, the mental muscle of man's spirit, atrophies if it is not used." We do not yet have the facts and figures to prove that the arts are useful, but I suspect it is susceptible to proof, and I think it will probably need to be proved if society is to take cultural development seriously. In some sense, this all reminds me of Robert Oppenheimer's phrase about the impact of the sciences—exhilarating, but oh, so useful.

. . .

Before concluding, I would like to make a few remarks that are not entirely serious. Yesterday afternoon I listened to a discussion of the word "media" in a meeting of the Council for the Arts. Afterwards, thanks to my assistant Jerilyn Edmondson, I decided to look in the *Oxford English Dictionary*. What about *arts and media*? It's clear that what Jerry said about the term *media*, that it was "nicely vague," is an understatement. Definitions for the arts are legion, filling more than two pages in the dictionary. Media started out as the plural of medium (in the nonspiritualistic sense). Medium refers to a go-between, to acting through an intervening agency; in that sense, medium would describe a substance in which fish swim and electromagnetic waves are propagated. That Jerry Wiesner, who contributed so much to the study of techniques of radio, should become involved with the more contemporary meaning of media may strike one as a bit ironic. But I think it is important that this ability of his to come to grips with new definitions, without being hampered by what was meant in the past, is one of Jerry's strengths.

To digress a bit here, Jerry and I have often discussed the question of whether age really makes you less imaginative. Jerry, in terms of the classical, traditional definition of age, has reached the biblical age, but as a friend of mine said the other

Jerry with Vannevar Bush, Howard Johnson, Julius Stratton, and James Killian on the occasion of Jerry's inauguration as MIT president, October 7, 1971. (Photo by Sheldon Lowenthal. Courtesy of the MIT Museum.)

day, that's only on the Fahrenheit scale. If you took the Centigrade reading, he would barely have reached maturity—twenty-one—and I think those of you who know him, know that that is so true. One can even see in his behavior something of what Nietzsche said, that in every man there is a boy who wants to play. To see Jerry with computers is to see how right Nietzsche was.

So, to end my digression, he and Laya have contributed to all of us a vision neither monochromatic nor narrow, but a multi-splendored vision that enriches those whose life and work it touches. His technological savvy has inspired several generations of scientists, engineers, and indeed humanists in a way that has encouraged them to address challenging problems and to penetrate into unknown territories.

The Wiesner Building is not only an aesthetic milestone; it promises to be anything but an esoteric academic structure. It is hard to foretell how soon it will be part of MIT's heartland, but it is already a bold experiment at MIT's endless frontier (to use Vannevar Bush's phrase). Let there be tolerance at that frontier for a multitude of approaches, for a multitude of outcomes, and even for the traditions of the past. That would be in keeping with Laya's and Jerry's human qualities, their deep intuitive yearning for taste, for justice, for peace.

Abiding Optimist

Louis D. Smullin[1]

Jerome Wiesner—"Jerry" to almost everybody—led an exciting and productive life and, more than most, he made a difference. He went from an "electronic warrior" during World War II, to a "cold warrior" during the early days of the "Missile Gap," and finally to a leading spokesman for the nuclear test ban and a worker for nuclear disarmament.

Jerry and his younger sister, Edna, were the children of Joseph and Ida Wiesner, each of whom had come to the United States at about the turn of the century. To escape having to take violin lessons, at age nineteen, Joseph had run away from his parents in Vienna in about 1892 and had shipped out to places as far away as Alaska and the California gold fields before landing in New York. (Edna remembers her

Louis D. Smullin, electronics engineer and educator, joined the MIT faculty in electrical engineering in 1955, served as department chair (1966–74), and held the Dugald C. Jackson Chair of Electrical Engineering and Computer Science (1974–86). During World War II, he was a staff member of Group 53 (Radio Frequency) at MIT's Radiation Laboratory, and, in the postwar period (1948–50), headed the microwave tube lab at the Research Laboratory of Electronics. In 1962, he conducted Project "Luna See" (with Giorgio Fiocco), using high-power optical maser technology to bounce a laser beam off the moon's surface, the first time space had been spanned by laser light. He is a fellow of the Institute of Electrical & Electronics Engineers and the American Academy of Arts and Sciences, and was elected a member of the National Academy of Engineering in 1970.

1. Excerpted and edited from Louis D. Smullin, "Jerome Bert Wiesner, May 30, 1915–October 21, 1994," *National Academy of Sciences Biographical Memoirs* 78 (2000): 335–353. The editors hoped that Lou would write an original essay for this book, focusing on Jerry's family background and relationships, their years together as students at the University of Michigan in the 1930s, Jerry's wartime work, and his experiences as a young MIT faculty member in the 1940s and 1950s. Unfortunately, Lou was unable to carry out the assignment because of illness. Instead, we print here parts of his memorial to Jerry, with a few additions.

Joseph Wiesner (1874–1954), Jerry's father. (Courtesy of Josh Wiesner.)

Ida (Friedman) Wiesner, Jerry's mother, at age 47—from her certificate of citizenship issued in Detroit, Michigan, January 11, 1932. (Courtesy of Josh Wiesner.)

Little Jerry with Aunt Jennie (Eugenie), his mother's sister, ca. 1915. (Courtesy of Josh Wiesner.)

On horseback with sister Edna, ca. mid-1920s. (Courtesy of Josh Wiesner.)

High-school portrait, ca. 1932. (Courtesy of Josh Wiesner.)

father telling stories about meeting and drinking with Jack London in Alaska.) Ida had come from Romania to New York with her younger sister. She worked in the garment industry and then as a housekeeper until she and Joseph met and married in 1914. Shortly thereafter, they moved from New York to Dearborn, Michigan. In the early days of their marriage they helped Ida's four brothers immigrate to the United States. Sometime during the 1920s, Ida and Joseph opened a small "mom and pop" dry goods store in Dearborn, and the two children—Jerry and Edna—grew up and went to the public schools there.

Jerry went on to study electrical engineering and mathematics at the University of Michigan in Ann Arbor, where I first got to know him. While there, he met Laya Wainger, a fellow student majoring in mathematics. They married in 1940, and developed a deep and abiding lifelong partnership. Besides being the mother of their four children—Stephen, Zachary, Lisa, and Joshua—Laya was one of Jerry's primary intellectual companions. Together they explored issues and ideas. She critiqued many of his most important documents (beginning with his Ph.D. thesis). Laya was very active in community and national civic affairs, and they entertained and worked with leaders from the academic, arts, media, business, civic, and governmental arenas.

Throughout his life, Jerry's glass was always at least half full, as is illustrated by his sister's recollection of his teenage efforts as a radio ham in Michigan. Just after he got his first receiver working and on the air, he burst out of his bedroom to announce that he had picked up a station from a foreign country. Not much later, he came out to amend his announcement. He had, in fact, tuned into a Polish language station in Hamtramck, a small city about ten miles from Dearborn.

The story illustrates his abiding optimism about the power and possibilities inherent in technical things, and in his later years about the possibility of saving the world from a nuclear disaster.

World War II and the Postwar Years

Jerry's life, as for so many engineers and scientists of his generation, was shaped by his World War II experience in the MIT Radiation Lab, where he worked on the development of radar, and by his work at Los Alamos directly after the war. Through these experiences, he learned new scientific and engineering ideas and techniques, he learned about the needs of the military, he learned how to deal with the military, he learned how to manage large group projects, and he met the people who helped shape his career.

In the Radiation Lab, he began his weapon systems work on a 3-cm radar for a Navy night fighter. This was followed by his taking over the job of directing the final stages of development of Project Cadillac, an airborne early warning (AEW) radar for the Navy. It was a very big and complex system that brought him into close contact with the highest levels of the Navy command structure. The AEW system played an important role in the Battle of the Pacific.

At the end of the war, Professor Jerrold Zacharias was recruited from the Radiation Lab to set up a new nuclear weapons engineering group at Los Alamos; among those he brought with him was Jerry Wiesner. In his autobiographical notes, Jerry indicates that because of the postwar letdown at Los Alamos, he was not very gainfully employed, but he was able to attend many of the heated discussions about the future peacetime control of atomic weapons and of atomic energy. These made a deep and lasting impression on him: "In later years I realized that the understanding I gained, both about the bomb and the controversy surrounding its use, had provided me with a valuable education on issues that were to occupy a large part of my life."

In September 1945, as MIT was moving into its peacetime mode of operation, Professor Harold Hazen, head of the Department of Electrical Engineering, recommended to MIT vice president James R. Killian that Jerry be appointed to the faculty:

As I told you yesterday, Mr. J. B. Wiesner says he would very much like to come to this Department. He had earlier explained to me that Dr. Zacharias had strongly urged him to join him to do a badly needed job out West for a period of perhaps ten months.[2] Wiesner had asked whether this would be incompatible with his accepting the appointment. I told him that it would probably cause some temporary inconvenience but from the long-term point of view, familiarity with that project would probably be substantially more of an asset than his immediate absence would be a liability. Consequently, I thought that he had better go.

It would appear appropriate to write a letter to him offering him the opening which is for an Assistant Professorship for three years at a salary of $5,000 per year on the annual basis. Mr. Wiesner may leave as soon as Friday, September 21, and I think it might be desirable to have an exchange of letters before that time, if practicable.

Jim Killian wrote Jerry a day later:

I wish to confirm the offer which Professor Hazen has discussed with you, a position in our Department of Electrical Engineering. We take pleasure in inviting you to join the Institute staff as an Assistant Professor for three years at a salary of $5,000 a year on an annual basis.

---

2. Referring to the Los Alamos assignment.

The date at which this appointment starts may be determined mutually by you and Professor Hazen; but it is understood that your acceptance of the assignment in the West will in no way conflict with this appointment, although naturally we hope that you will be free to take up full-time duties as soon as convenient.

We look forward with much pleasure to having you join us at the Institute. We believe that opportunities here over the coming years in your field of interest will be of ample scope to your work.

Jerry accepted the invitation and returned to MIT in 1946 as a faculty member in electrical engineering, conducting his research in the Research Laboratory of Electronics (RLE), the peacetime successor to the Radiation Lab.

After his return to MIT, Jerry was a participant in many of the summer studies on military problems (anti-submarine warfare, the distant early warning [DEW] line, etc.). In these studies, a selected group of scientists and engineers from industry and academia were briefed by appropriate military officers and civilians on the detailed nature of the problems, and various solutions were proposed and discussed. Many important recommendations were made and implemented. In this way, Jerry (and his colleagues) began the move from purely technical matters into the broader domain of policy making.

The beginnings of the Cold War were symbolized by a number of important technical events. Among these were the race between the United States and the Soviet Union to copy the German ballistic missile technology, the explosion of the first Soviet atomic bomb, and the successful launching of *Sputnik*.

Faced with the threat of the Soviet atomic bomb, the MIT Lincoln Laboratory was established in 1951 to work on the problems of air defense of the continental United States. One of its projects was to set up a distant early warning chain of radar stations to warn of an attack by Soviet bombers coming across the North Pole. To get the maximum warning time, the line would be located along the shore of the Arctic Ocean. However, radio communication in these high latitudes was uncertain and could be blacked out for long periods because of intense electrical activity in the ionosphere. In about 1953, Jerry and some of his colleagues proposed the use of forward scattering from the troposphere for reliable (but narrow band) communication. (For many years, these systems provided secure communication from the DEW line to the North American Air Defense Command in Colorado.)

In 1952, Jerry became the third director of RLE, succeeding professors Julius A. (Jay) Stratton and Albert G. Hill in that role. Under their successive leaderships, RLE developed into a multidisciplinary, interdepartmental center. The joint services (Army, Navy, and Air Force) contract under which RLE was organized specified that it should "do research in the field of electronics, physics, and communication, and publish."

Inspired by Professor Norbert Wiener, Jerry recognized that communication included psychology, language, and sensory physiology. Thus it was that from its earliest days RLE brought in linguists, psychologists, and neurophysiologists, as well as information theorists, radio engineers, and physicists. Much later, when he became provost and then president of MIT, Jerry played a similar role in stimulating the growth of the humanities and the arts at MIT. As president, he pursued educational reforms and the cultivation of fields not previously represented at MIT, or represented up until that time at less than their potential level of excellence.[3]

Jerry's Lifelong Partner

Laya Wiesner (1918–98) was an important partner in all these activities, particularly in broadening the scope of life and work at MIT. She provided the inspiration and leadership for the MIT Workshop on Women in Technology that took place in May 1973 with grants from the Carnegie Corporation, the General Electric Foundation, and the Alfred P. Sloan Foundation. This led to the WITS Project (Women in Technology and Science), a program that recruited MIT faculty members and engineers and scientists from Massachusetts industry to speak to high school students on science and technology careers. Subsequently, the project worked intensively with Boston schools to foster minority participation in scientific and technical education endeavors.

In civil rights Laya's activities covered much ground, but two of them bear special mention. She was one of the original organizers of METCO, a system for busing black students from Boston to schools in the more affluent suburbs. She was one of a group of women from around the country who went to Mississippi in the 1960s to observe and report on voter registration activities in that state. They hoped that their presence would lessen the danger of police violence, and it did.

Starting in about 1970, a progressive muscular disease—polymyositis—began to seriously affect Laya's ability to travel and even to move around. At the time of Jerry's death she was already confined to a wheelchair, but she continued to main-

---

3. Omitted here is Lou's account of Jerry's "Washington years," fully covered elsewhere in this book. Also omitted is the summary of his role as MIT provost and president, with the exception of comments on Laya Wiesner, which follow.

tain a lively interest in her family and in world and public affairs. When Laya died in September 1998, Catherine N. Stratton, widow of MIT's eleventh president, Jay Stratton, said: "Laya Wiesner was a remarkable woman with an indomitable spirit. She was incredibly courageous, allocating her energy to the causes which mattered most to her—civil rights, mentoring MIT women students in the fields of science and engineering, and being a sparkling, creative partner to her husband." And Jerry, too, knew how lucky he was to have her caring support throughout his career.[4]

---

4. Omitted here are Lou's brief comments about Jerry's final years and his summary of Jerry's role in the MacArthur Foundation. The MacArthur period is covered by Ruth Adams in her essay.

Ace Communicator

Alan Lomax[1]

The First Job

I first met Jerry Wiesner in 1940 when he came to build the Acoustical and Record Laboratory of the Library of Congress. It was his first job. We were the same age, both young marrieds, and we had great fun together, Jerry and I, and Elizabeth and Laya—Laya, the beautiful, dark-haired girl with an infectious laugh and a keen mind that was quite the match for her husband's. Jerry, of course, was on the homely side, but had slathers of charm. He had a leprechaun curl to his lip, a way of doubling up with silent delight at something that pleased him, and of laughing silently. And he was always so eager, so enthusiastic, so all-out to get the job done, to get everybody together toward a decision.

Jerry had been chosen for his job at the library because of his brilliant accomplishments as an acoustician, but also because he had made a wonderful

Alan Lomax (1915–2002), legendary folklorist and musicologist, was for several years (1937–42) in charge of the Archive of American Folk Song of the Library of Congress. He made collecting expeditions for the library, produced a seminal series of documentary folk music albums entitled *Folk Music of the United States*, interviewed performers such as Jelly Roll Morton, and introduced audiences to an array of folk musicians. After leaving the Library of Congress, he continued his career as a musicologist, author, radio broadcaster, filmmaker, concert and record producer, and television host. He was awarded the National Medal of Arts from the National Endowment for the Arts in 1986, and in 1993 received the National Book Critics Circle award for nonfiction for his book *The Land Where the Blues Began*.

1. Edited and excerpted from a talk given by Alan Lomax at "A Gathering to Honor and Celebrate the Life of Jerome B. Wiesner," Massachusetts Institute of Technology, Cambridge, Mass., December 2, 1994. The editors had hoped to ask Mr. Lomax for an original essay on Jerry, but his health did not permit; he died on July 19, 2002.

A long-time fan (and occasional performer!) of American folk music—Jerry at the "steer roast," an annual community-building event at MIT's Senior House since 1964. (Courtesy of the MIT Museum.)

communications station out of the University of Michigan radio station. He was an ace communicator, concerned from the beginning about both communication and the technology of communication.

The first thing he did at the library was to create the laboratory. It didn't take him long; he could cut through the Library of Congress red tape as if it wasn't even there. And he created a wonderful laboratory, the like of anything in New York City. We could record, we could broadcast, we could make records.

So we set out to make the first releases from the archive of folk song, and I want to play you some of those songs, because these recordings are one of Jerry's first pieces of actual published work. I think you'll know the first voice—Woody Guthrie! And then next is the sound of the banjo, which was then almost unknown in America, but which now of course is as familiar as a drink of water on every communications system. All these sounds became part of the Wiesner emotional repertory. He loved this music and he worked with it beautifully. Now, here's a black work song. He also made the first master recording of that great man of the blues, Muddy Waters. You can see why Jerry took such pleasure in remembering the years of his first job with the library.

Such was Jerry's legacy to the Library of Congress, a part of the New Deal, a government that for the first time was taking interest in the thoughts and feelings of all its people. I believe Jerry remained a New Dealer all his life, as I have.

A Career Recognized

In 1993, near the end of his life, I had the chance to see the qualities in this man which had made him such a power for good in the counsel of Washington. The National Academy of Sciences was honoring him, awarding him a medal for his work for public welfare. All the scientists of Washington were there, and after the banquet and all the speeches in his honor, it was Jerry's turn to speak.

He went to the lectern. And then one of those terrifying incidents occurred which affect the speaker at the lectern sometimes. There was not enough light for Jerry to read his speech, as his eyes had been weakened from the stroke he had suffered a few years before. They had candlelight, sentimental candlelight, for the occasion. He tried again and again, but he simply couldn't read it. And then I saw something, an act of tremendous courage. He stuck his speech in his pocket, stuck his jaw out in the way that he had. He blushed with excitement, and gave it ad lib—a tense, passionate review of the world situation and what needed to be done to move toward peace. It electrified his audience.

When he finished, there was a pause before the rousing round of applause. He looked around at the crowd and said, "There are people right here in the room who, if they took action tomorrow, could help slow down the crisis that we're in." That's the way he was, always challenging himself and others to think and act in the public interest.

Scientist, Educator, Sailor

Robert I. Hulsizer, Jr.

My friendship with Jerry spanned 52 years. He and I both arrived at MIT in May of 1942—he at age 27, I at 23. We both came to MIT to work on radar development at the Radiation Laboratory. Among the senior scientists in the lab at that time were two physicists who were to have lifelong influences on both of us: Jerrold Zacharias from Columbia University and Wheeler Loomis from the University of Illinois. Jerry's work focused on aircraft radar systems and I worked, in another building, on electronic circuits for processing radar data. Totally absorbed in our separate crucial projects, we saw little of each other during the war. Afterwards, Jerry went to work at Los Alamos and I stayed at MIT to get my Ph.D.

In 1949, Wheeler Loomis, who had returned to the University of Illinois, offered me an assistant professorship there, which I took. In 1951, when the country got into the Korean war, a group in Urbana under Loomis's direction and a separate group at MIT, aided by Zacharias, each took on the job of learning how to use the emergent electronic computers to handle naval and continental air defense. During this time, I visited MIT a lot and saw Jerry often. This continued until 1955, when the war ended.

Shortly thereafter, Jerrold Zacharias organized the Physical Sciences Study Committee (PSSC), a program to improve the teaching of physics in high schools. I joined

Robert I. Hulsizer, Jr., physicist and educator, joined the MIT physics faculty in 1964, after a period of teaching and research at the University of Illinois (1949–64). He also became a member of MIT's Laboratory for Nuclear Science, specializing in elementary particle physics. During World War II, he was a member of Group 63 (Precision) at MIT's Radiation Laboratory (1942–46). His deep interest in science teaching led to his involvement in the educational reform efforts of the Physical Sciences Study Committee (1958–60), and while at MIT, he was active with the Education Research Center, serving for a time as its director (1964–68). He was elected chairman of the MIT faculty (1977–79), and retired as professor of physics emeritus in 1986.

that effort, which brought me frequently to MIT, but I only saw Jerry occasionally, since he was increasingly involved in national and world affairs and largely based in Washington.

The high-school physics program was so effective that Jerrold started a similar project to improve physics teaching for college freshmen. A new MIT center to study the techniques and strategies of science teaching was soon established in the School of Science, directed by Francis Friedman. After Francis suddenly died in 1962, I was invited to join the MIT faculty and replace him as director. By that time, Jerry had returned to the Institute as dean of the School of Science, and I reported to him. Jerry was strongly interested in the challenges of science education and hoped that MIT would play a leading role in developing new and better methods. The current (2002) plan to put all of MIT's course work on the internet is an example of the kind of thing he would have encouraged.

As an administrator, Jerry bubbled with energy, yet he always considered decisions circumspectly and carefully. Later on, I became chairman of the MIT faculty and sat on the academic council with Jerry presiding. Over and over again, issues that had very vocal supporters and opponents would come up for decision by the council. It was impressive to watch Jerry listen to all the arguments and then come out with a solution that satisfied each faction.

The MIT campus during that era was hardly tranquil. There was much dissension among both faculty and students over the Vietnam war. So many confrontations took place that Jerry appointed a committee of four faculty members, of which I was one, and a second committee of four students to advise him on how to respond. If the discord began to get out of hand, we would be called to go to wherever trouble was brewing and try to ameliorate the situation. Many of us had to learn to swallow the shock of being called "ass-hole" by some of the students before we could even start to negotiate. Jerry's mediation skills provided a good model for "getting to yes."

I remember on one occasion I was standing near a large crowd of unruly students in the stairway leading to the corridor where the president's office is located. Several students were sticking posters on the stairway wall near where I was standing. Jerry came down from his office, went directly to the students, and asked them to take the posters away. He explained that he had worked for years to get enough money to paint those walls and he didn't want them defaced. I fully expected that one of the tough, hulking protesters was going to attack him physically, but Jerry stood his ground and the protesters began to giggle. The sight of a middle-aged man taking

"A middle-aged man taking on a mob of shouting 20-year-olds" (Robert Hulsizer)—Jerry, as MIT provost, confronting members of SDS (Students for a Democratic Society) outside the MIT president's office, November 4, 1969. (Courtesy of the MIT Museum.)

on a mob of shouting 20-year-olds was ludicrous. Several other faculty members and the campus police soon showed up and things quieted down.

There were many other incidents during that period which sorely tested Jerry's patience, but he never lost his cool. Once a student claimed he was pushed down some stairs by a professor. Jerry did not dismiss the charge out of hand, but asked us to hold a hearing to determine what had happened and who, if anyone, was at fault. On another occasion, a professor was accused of handing out marijuana before his final exam. Jerry requested that we adjudicate to determine whether the professor's behavior had violated his tenure standing. Life around Jerry in those days was rarely dull. He always gave the impression of being calm and collected, but at what cost we will never know.

Jerry and I had warm relations with Wheeler Loomis, whose family had long been summer residents of Martha's Vineyard where the Wiesners also vacationed. The Loomises rented a farmhouse which still stands on a piece of the property that the Wiesners ultimately bought. In 1960, Wheeler had a heart attack and was unable

Martha's Vineyard—a stroll on the beach. (Courtesy of the MIT Museum.)

to use his sailboat, a classic sloop. He offered to loan me his boat for the summer, a gesture that led to my own choice of Martha's Vineyard as a holiday retreat and many years of delightful sailing with Jerry. As composed as he appeared to be in his professional life, Jerry was never so visibly relaxed as when he was on the Vineyard, and especially when he was on the water. He truly adored sailing under all kinds of conditions and beamed with pleasure when the wind picked up and salt spray started coming over the rail.

His nautical interests extended beyond seagoing adventures. Based on his sailing experience on Menemsha Pond and Vineyard Sound, Jerry collaborated on a Martha's Vineyard Shipyard project to build a 29-foot Vixen class sailboat, specifically adapted to local waters. He and I had many discussions about the design and made frequent trial runs in the first model before the boat went into production.

Jerry loved taking people out on his boat and was often on the phone trying to round up a crew for an afternoon of sailing and schmoozing. I recall one particular day when the wife of an eminent writer was his guest and I went along for the ride. Jerry let her take the tiller, and at one point she became so intent on the discussion that she didn't pay attention to what the boat was doing. I was sure she was going to swamp us. I can't remember what we were talking about, but I'll never

Through an arch of crossed oars—racing shell christening ceremony at the Pierce Boathouse, MIT, May 1974. (Courtesy of the MIT Museum.)

forget my fear that she would put us all in the drink. Jerry, as usual, was unfazed and we returned to the mooring damp but safe.

The Vineyard brought out the environmentalist in Jerry. He was always keenly aware of the island's beauty and fragility. He went to great lengths to cultivate his own property wisely and to protect abutting lands on Menemsha Pond. The result was a vista of colorful gardens and open pasture land that delighted the eye and attracted a multitude of birds.

A word must be said about Jerry and Laya's roles in the lively summer community. Many of the Vineyard's resident luminaries gravitated to the Wiesners' hospitable Chilmark home, to mix there with family members, close old friends, and neighbors from all walks of island life. One might meet Lillian Hellman, John and Barbara Hersey, William and Rose Styron, Mike Wallace, James Taylor, or any one of a stream of famous off-island visitors—Ann Landers, Leonard Bernstein, and James Watson are a few who come to mind. Jerry's genuine and abiding interest in the accomplishments of his talented guests from the worlds of arts and letters, music, theater, and politics was matched by his guests' pleasure in his explanations of science for nonscientists and his whimsical commentary. Chez Wiesner, the conversation was always fascinating, and the charm and warmth of the host and hostess were memorable.

I think still of those pleasant outings in Jerry's boat, gliding out into the pond from the edge of his beautiful meadow. We would chat about nothing more cosmic than how our children were faring or how to preserve the Vineyard landscape and quality of island life that he and Laya loved so much. Sometimes we wrestled with MIT issues or questions about whither science, and Jerry in his quiet, thoughtful way seemed to gain new, satisfying perspectives while at the helm, peering toward the horizon. It was always a privilege to be in his company.

A View from the White House

Theodore C. Sorensen

Not since Merlin has any head of state made greater use of, or relied more upon, his chief science adviser than John F. Kennedy relied on Jerry Wiesner. Kennedy's secretary of defense Robert McNamara, national security adviser McGeorge Bundy, and I also relied upon Jerry's wisdom. Whether the issue on the table was food, drugs or medication, arms control (especially a nuclear test ban), the efficacy of new weapons systems, the rate of scientific discovery, the administration's relations with academia, or a wide range of other topics, JFK often turned to Jerry, who was at home with these and virtually any other topic.

I came to know Jerry during the years preceding the 1960 presidential campaign, when he was the mainstay of our "Academic Advisory Committee"—a group of university professors in the state of Massachusetts, including Harvard and the Massachusetts Institute of Technology—whom JFK and I consulted on a variety of major problems facing the Senate and nation. Our relationship with him increased during the postelection, preinauguration transition when he chaired a task force study on specific scientific issues facing the new president, especially space exploration. The task force's report dealt with the cost of developing a space program, the political embarrassment that would attend any highly publicized failures, and the best way to organize that effort within the federal bureaucracy. Jerry warned that the United

Theodore C. (Ted) Sorensen, lawyer, was an attorney for the Federal Security Agency and a U.S. Senate staff member before becoming an assistant to Senator John F. Kennedy in 1953. He remained a close confidant throughout Kennedy's Senate term (1953–61), and went on to be President Kennedy's special counsel in the White House (1961–63). He has authored a number of books on issues in American politics, including several on the Kennedy years— *Decision Making in the White House*, *Kennedy*, and *The Kennedy Legacy*. After returning to private law practice following President Kennedy's assassination, he remained active in public affairs. He served in the Carter administration as a member of the President's Advisory Committee on Trade Negotiations, and was later a member of the Democratic National Committee's task forces on political action (1981–82) and foreign policy (1986).

States was not likely to win the competition with the Soviet Union for space pre-eminence. The group's burden (and Jerry's) was not made any lighter by my request on JFK's behalf that it "focus on those matters which lend themselves to early action . . . would not do serious damage to the president's budget goals or economic stabilization program, required significant steps on which you think the next Administration must decide in its first 60 days . . . which can be successfully acted upon during the first months [and] which the Congress is most likely to approve . . . [all] ranked according to priority."

Simultaneously, Jerry provided us with a list of key names for possible presidential appointment. By late November 1960, he had sent to me a long confidential letter listing a large number of names for those positions that he thought were essential for the effective implementation of the president-elect's new approach to foreign policy, including arms control: secretary of defense, deputy secretary of defense, secretary of the Air Force, chairman of the Atomic Energy Commission, national security adviser to the president, and director of the U.S. Information Agency. Most of his lists for each position contained the usual names prominent in arms control and peace circles, although Walt Disney for head of USIA, and Paul Nitze, Stuart Symington, and Richard Bissell for some key positions showed Jerry's consistent willingness to think outside the box. A great many of the names he listed ended up in the administration, but these were mostly names that also appeared on a number of other lists, and it would be hard to prove that Jerry's recommendation was determinative. Nevertheless, I am certain that his letter was studied by the president and his personnel team with respect. It is particularly notable that Jerry took pains to advise JFK that the prospects for real control on atomic weapons depended upon his obtaining a sympathetic chairman of the Atomic Energy Commission and halting the "four-front" effort to sabotage arms control from within the Administration and the NATO Alliance.

Jerry then moved with us into the White House as science adviser to the president and chairman of the President's Science Advisory Committee (PSAC). Before taking up his official duties, he unofficially and on his own initiative resumed his personal contacts with Soviet scientists and lower-rank officials. These conversations, which continued for some years, were necessarily delicate as well as sensitive, and on more than one occasion JFK expressed some question as to whether his own efforts were being furthered or compromised by such contacts. Nevertheless, they continued throughout Jerry's years in government and proved on balance to be valuable sources of information and understanding between the two superpowers.

Matters of state—the White House office, August 4, 1961. (Courtesy of the MIT Museum.)

In his official capacity, Jerry played a particularly important role in the small meeting convened in my office after the Gagarin flight in 1961 had given the Soviet Union an apparently insurmountable lead in the conquest of space. That was the meeting that spelled out for the president the next likely breakthroughs in the "space race," and the possibility that the United States could be the first to land an astronaut on the moon and bring him back safely.

Jerry and I also worked together on a number of budget issues, including those posed by the Defense Department. At a time when the Pentagon seemed already stuffed full of both money and redundant weapons systems, Jerry consistently opposed spending taxpayer funds on proposed new weapons systems that he or his committee had concluded might not work. (In fact, he was opposed to proposed new weapons systems that would work, although there he and JFK sometimes parted company.)

With all due respect for those who preceded and followed him in the science adviser position, it is my conclusion, after reading extensively about the others, that none enjoyed the access to the Oval Office that Jerry enjoyed; nor did any of the others have more respect from their contemporaries in the scientific community. It was Jerry's stature as well as his access to the president and White House staff that enabled him to attract to the PSAC some of our nation's best minds in those fields.

Despite the surface differences between Jerry and America's first Catholic president, a millionaire war hero who had devoted his career to politics and government, they shared more values than one might have thought, assuring a comfortable and compatible working relationship, especially after Jerry learned, and adapted his own style to, JFK's need for brevity in briefings, both oral and written. Those common values were the key: both had inquiring minds, curious about almost everything; both shared a particular concern about the prospects for nuclear conflict and fallout; both hated war; both enjoyed public service; both loved sailing. When the press overplayed a sailing accident in which Jerry was injured, the president called him at home to cheer him up, offering tongue-in-check to give him advice on both sailing and press relations.

Jerry Wiesner's service as science adviser to the president is a precedent worthy of emulation. Too many presidents are slow or even reluctant to fill that position, and seem unaware of the importance of recruiting a top, broad-gauged scientist to that post, and the value of consulting him or her frequently on the widest range of issues. Admittedly, there was only one Jerry Wiesner; and his like will be hard to find.

International Perspectives

Michael Sela

I first got to know Jerry through his connections with the Weizmann Institute, some of which occurred prior to my meeting with him. He was a devoted friend of the Weizmann Institute of Science, situated in Rehovot, Israel. His role here began with his friendship with Meyer Weisgal, the colorful and remarkable personality who was instrumental in building the Institute and crucial in making an imprint on the aesthetics and beauty of the campus. While not a scientist, Weisgal was very keen on advice from leading scientists.

The director of the Weizmann Institute in the late 1950s and early 1960s was the physicist Amos de-Shalit, and it was at his invitation that Jerry Wiesner came to the Weizmann Institute in June 1959 to a meeting attended also by Isidor Rabi, Viki Weisskopf, Philip Sporn, and the then young Alex Rich, among others. The invitation was really issued on behalf of the Prime Minister of Israel, David Ben-Gurion, and these scientists were asked to evaluate the scientific capabilities of Israel.

The group reported its findings to Ben-Gurion at a session that took place in the San Martin guest house of the Institute. Alex Rich had come on another mission, as the guest of the Katzir brothers and myself, but Amos de-Shalit invited him to join the illustrious group. Alex was kind enough to give me a summary of his recollections, which I present here in slightly modified form:

Michael Sela, immunologist and chemist, is the W. Garfield Weston Professor of Immunology at the Weizmann Institute of Science, Rehovot, Israel. He joined the Weizmann Institute in 1950, and served as its president (1975–85). The author of more than 700 medical and scientific research articles, he is the recipient of the UNESCO Albert Einstein Gold Medal (1995) and the Wolf Prize in Medicine (1998). He is a member of the Pontifical Academy of Sciences and the U.S. National Academy of Sciences. He has been a visiting professor at a number of American universities, and was a founding member and board member of the International Foundation for the Survival and Development of Humanity (1988–92).

On the evening of June 21st, we met in the San Martin with Ben-Gurion and his group, which included a young Shimon Peres. In that discussion we commented on the fact that, although the natural resources available to Israel were quite limited, the intellectual resources were considerable. Our strong recommendation was that the government try to invest in science-based industries so that it could utilize this intellectual capital. Similar advice, I am sure, was being offered by the Israeli scientists, but as is usually the case, when the recommendation comes from outsiders, it is viewed as serious and less likely to be self-serving.

The meeting held in the San Martin dining hall was well attended by a number of senior scientists from the Institute, who listened to our comments with great interest. Our small group had strong representation in experimental and theoretical physics and both electrical engineering and power engineering, with my being able to make some judgments on chemical and biological aspects. Ben-Gurion impressed me as a sensible person who listened carefully and asked a number of questions that were very much to the point.

In this group, it was clear that Jerry very much played the role of the leader. He was very active in initiating questions and making suggestions. We all looked to him as the natural spokesperson for the group. I think it reflected the fact that he was so easily at home with people in both science and engineering, and was fully coupled to business activities as well. I believe he made the major contribution to the effort.

In 1961, Jerry became an Honorary Fellow of the Weizmann Institute. This was at a time when we did not yet award doctorates *honoris causa*, which started only in 1973. Since then, the honorary fellowships have been discontinued and their recipients have become "vintage." Jerry became a member of our board of governors in 1964 and was an active member until 1990, when he became a governor emeritus and remained so until he died in 1994.

It is interesting to recall his comments at various board meetings. At the first meeting he attended, in April 1964, he was paraphrased as follows:

Prof Jerome Wiesner noted that problems of growth at MIT and at the Weizmann Institute were basically the same. It was characteristic of all academic institutions that things turned out more costly than Management anticipated. Commenting further on the question of the rate of growth, he said that the cost of research in the United States had been growing faster than the gross national product. Therefore, either the rate of increase of the gross national product ought to be accelerated or there would have to be higher selectivity on what research is taken up. He felt that there was bound to come a moment when growth began to slow down naturally to a lower annual rate. It was up to scientific managers to determine which research and which scientists to support, and what was most worth doing or discarding. Finally, he warned that the transition from intensive growth to a period of consolidation and stability must be accomplished without doing harm.

As for Israel, it seemed that one of the factors needed was more technically-oriented industry—by deliberately creating industries in which research and technology come to bear. Prof Wiesner cited the examples of such industries which developed around Harvard and MIT, and the Japanese electronics industry.

In December 1965 Jerry arrived in Rehovot, heading a Survey Commission, which—in the Life Sciences—included Renato Dulbecco, Alex Rich, and Gordon Tomkins. I think it was around that time that I first met him. I remember mainly two things from the work of the Commission. Jerry was told that the Department of Physics functioned splendidly as one big unit, and was asked whether we should not unite all our biology departments into one big entity. Jerry's answer was typical: if it works well, do not try to improve it. The Wiesner Committee, as we used to call it, made some remarks about a single Department, and these were taken into consideration, leading to personnel changes in leadership.

Jerry's general comments were very positive, and I shall give some excerpts which exemplify his approach to problems. They are taken from the Minutes of the Executive Council of the Weizmann Institute of Science in October 1967 (a few months after the Six-Day War):

When you come to a turning-point in history (and I think there's no question that this is a turning-point in Israel's history), you don't tighten your belt and slow down. You ask yourself instead how the hell you can move forward! How can you give an extra impulse; how you can do more, not less. I think we should be doing more; we should be asking ourselves how can we take advantage over the next two or three years of this tremendous opportunity both to help the country and to build the Institute, to push it up one more notch. This may mean extraordinary measures to get a little extra money; but then we must all work a little harder.

I must say that, as a member of the Survey Commission, I'm very gratified by what has happened already—I think it's all really quite amazing and the people concerned ought to be congratulated. There is still more to do, of course. . . .

I don't suppose that there is any human activity that can't be badly organized—if you try hard enough. I might say, in my own experience of visiting committees that they are either ineffective or very effective. They rarely do any harm, particularly if they're chosen with a certain amount of discretion. Maybe some of you have had bad experience with visiting committees. In my own institution, I inherited the system of visiting committees—they occupy about twenty days a year of my time and periodically I ask myself, particularly after I've dealt with an ineffective one: Is this thing sensible?

Generally it turns out that the ineffective visiting committees are those that we've paid no attention to. I'm quite serious, you don't worry about the selection, you don't worry about being prepared, and you don't ask them questions—and what you get back from them is just what you put into them. Generally this happens in the case of departments we're not really concerned about. If a department really worries me, I talk to the Chairman of the visiting committee (and this is one of the advantages, incidentally, of continuity). You can't, and you normally shouldn't, expect to change a department and its character, or solve its problems overnight.

I went on to serve as president of the Weizmann Institute between 1975 and 1985, and saw Jerry several times in New York and Boston during that time. When I finished my term, I enjoyed a sabbatical year in Boston—1986–87—and one of my hosts was Professor Herman Eisen in the Cancer Institute at MIT. The Wiesner Building was close by, and I enjoyed visiting Jerry in his office on several occasions. A short while later, Jerry visited me in my office in Rehovot. He signed my guest book on March 24, 1988.

An International Foundation

A few months earlier, Jerry had called me on the phone to discuss a new idea—a joint American-Russian Foundation, which he initiated with his Soviet counterpart Professor Yevgeniy Velikhov. Velikhov and Wiesner decided to include as members scientists of other nationalities, and Jerry suggested an Israeli. Velikhov asked him whom he had in mind, and when he mentioned my name, Velikhov—says Jerry—enthusiastically agreed.

And so, at the beginning of January 1988, I was in Beltsville, Maryland, attending a meeting on agricultural research cooperation between the United States and Israel, when Jerry called and told me to go immediately to the Soviet embassy in Washington, D.C., get my visa, and come straight to Moscow. I left Beltsville in a snowstorm, got the visa, took the plane, and met Jerry and the other participants in Moscow.

At our inaugural meeting, it was decided that the name would be the International Foundation for the Survival and Development of Humanity, with Velikhov as chairman and Wiesner as vice chairman. The purpose was to promote collaborative international research on global problems such as environmental pollution, arms control, and economic development.

The next day we arrived at the Kremlin on a very special occasion, when Sakharov, just permitted to leave Gorky (today called again Nizhni Novgorod), joined us on a visit to Gorbachev. We were actually present when Sakharov was introduced to Gorbachev. A long discussion around a table ensued, and at some point Sakharov spoke about the need to release many more political prisoners. He caused a stir when he stood up and went to Gorbachev to present him personally with a list of such prisoners. When we left the building, Jerry said to Sakharov, "If you are not careful, they may send you back to Gorky." To which Sakharov retorted, "I have been in Gorky before, I am ready to go back there again."

The International Foundation had a meeting at the National Academy of Sciences in Washington in November 1988. This was at the time of the first and only visit of Sakharov to the United States, and we joined him not only at the meeting of the

A committed internationalist—Jerry enjoying a break from a conference of the International Union of Radio Science, Paris, late August 1954. (Courtesy of the MIT Museum.)

Foundation in Washington, but also as his "groupies" at several social events, both in Washington and at the Metropolitan Museum in New York. There is no doubt that Jerry enjoyed being both host and guide for Sakharov during this visit. I also remember a dinner we had in Teddy Kennedy's home in honor of Sakharov. A short while after Velikhov visited me in Israel in May 1991, the Foundation disbanded and discontinued its activities.

Having a chance to know Jerry was for me a privilege, both for the issues we shared a common interest in and for the sheer enjoyment of his company.

A Man for All Seasons

Eugene B. Skolnikoff

It is not easy to encapsulate my impressions of Jerry Wiesner in a brief essay, not only because of the incredibly broad range of his interests and activities, but even more because of the special role he played in my professional life. I first came to know him, slightly, when I was a student in electrical engineering at MIT in the late 1940s. Then, he was a congenial but remote figure to me, clearly a star of the department, but not a professor with whom I had much interaction.

That changed in 1958 when I joined the staff of the Science Adviser's Office in the White House under Jim Killian, with Jerry serving as an active and prominent member of the President's Science Advisory Committee (PSAC). What was most striking about Jerry at that time was the unfailing energy and innovative ideas he committed to almost any issue that came before the committee, but especially anything to do with Cold War relations with the Soviet Union. I watched with astonishment, and some trepidation, the often virulent discussions of the committee on central issues of war and peace. This was during the first incarnation of the White House science office, when it had the ear of the president and very considerable clout in the government as a whole on any issues involving science and technology, particularly defense issues. Jerry's views were always central to the debates, and as time went on increasingly skeptical of an unbridled focus on strate-

Eugene B. Skolnikoff, political scientist and educator, joined the faculty in political science at MIT in 1966, serving as department chair (1970–74) and director of the Center for International Studies (1972–87). Before coming to MIT, he served as a systems analyst for the Institute for Defense Analyses, Washington, D.C. (1957–58), and as a staff member in the Office of the Special Assistant for Science and Technology during the Eisenhower and Kennedy administrations (1958–63). In the Carter administration (1977–81), he was a consultant to the White House Office of Science and Technology Policy. Over the years, he has consulted for several government agencies, including the U.S. Department of State, the Office of Technology Assessment, and the Agency for International Development. He has been professor of political science emeritus at MIT since his retirement in 1996.

gic forces. Most of the PSAC reflected that view as well, but Jerry was often ahead of the others and frequently in disagreement with the more conservative members of PSAC.

In particular, what impressed me at the time, and even more so as I worked over the next several years with Jerry in Washington and later back at MIT, was his quite genuine commitment to making a real difference in major issues that affected people, nations, and institutions throughout the world. He started with the simple assumption that his actions would make a difference, that he could really move mountains. He rarely, if ever, discussed an issue without at the same time asking what ought to be done about it and what he or we could do. The result was a never-ending string of ideas and proposals—some unrealistic, most innovative, and many brilliant, but almost all of which he attempted to put into action. These covered the spectrum from issues of war and peace, to domestic matters, to innovations he could make at the institution he loved best—MIT.

This characteristic of Jerry's was in fact novel in my experience, but made an enormous impression. At first I was overawed by the self-confidence and commitment it implied, along with the wide-ranging intelligence behind it. Inevitably, it became something more to me. In a pattern that I suspect affected many others who came in close contact with Jerry, he in effect set a personal goal that might be unrealizable but provided a standard of what a career in public life ought to try to achieve.

It had its downsides, of course. Among others, it meant that his staff, when he became Kennedy's science adviser, was constantly being pressed into action on new ideas and initiatives. The already substantial pace of work picked up in the transition from George Kistiakowsky, Eisenhower's last science adviser, to Wiesner and Kennedy. I found myself catapulted into a variety of new initiatives, one of the more pressing being developing ideas for outer space cooperation with the Soviet Union in the face of significant opposition from NASA. The president was seeking areas for possible cooperation with that nation to begin to move back from military confrontation, and space seemed both the most dramatic and potentially politically useful. Jerry was a strong proponent, and actively proposed and explored a range of ideas. He was influential in persuading Kennedy to raise, in his September 1961 address to the UN General Assembly, the possibility of joint U.S.-Soviet ventures in space. These eventually materialized in the early 1970s, with the Apollo-Soyuz Test Project (ASTP), the first human space flight mission managed jointly by two nations.

There were many other subjects, while Jerry was in Washington, that showed the same sense of his seeking ways to make that difference in the lives of everyone.

Meeting to plan a history of the Harvard-MIT Division of Health Sciences and Technology, November 1992—*front row*: Irving London, Jerry, Walter Rosenblith; *back row*: William Beck, Robert Ebert, Derek Bok, Walter Abelmann. (Courtesy of Judy F. Rosenblith.)

Many of the military and arms control initiatives of the Kennedy years involved Jerry centrally, especially the test ban negotiations started in the Eisenhower Administration with a partial test ban signed in 1963. Jerry was an ardent advocate of a comprehensive test ban, and almost succeeded in negotiating an acceptable comprehensive treaty with the Soviet Union, finally scuttled by opposition in the United States, not Moscow. His active leadership of the PSAC and the Science Adviser's Office led the White House science policy operation into an increasingly broad range of subjects, including—among others with which I was involved—education, foreign aid, relations with Japan, and U.S. science policy.

On his return to MIT, and in the later years as I worked under his leadership, Jerry never lost his determination to change the world. Within the Institute, the faculty found itself having to deal with a series of Wiesner ideas that materialized at a steady rate. MIT may be less of a status-quo university than most, but change still comes relatively slowly and with difficulty for a university structure. While Jerry was dean of science, provost, and then president, a host of new initiatives emerged, such as the Harvard/MIT Division of Health Sciences and Technology, the Education Division, the Program in Science, Technology, and Society (STS), and the Center for Policy Alternatives (CPA). Jerry was not solely responsible for these initiatives; in particular, his close colleague over many years, associate provost and then provost Walter Rosenblith, played a critical, symbiotic role. But most, probably all, would not have happened without Jerry's commitment.

My own trajectory after returning to MIT in 1963 to seek a PhD in political science, and then joining the faculty in 1966, was again influenced directly by Jerry and indirectly by his fertile imagination. The direct influence was clear, for when Jerry, while still provost, visited me in Switzerland in 1969, where I was on a year's leave of absence, to ask me to become head of the political science department, I put up a show of resistance, but there was no real chance I would refuse him. Similarly, when he asked me to take over the Center for International Studies (CIS) in 1972, I found I had little psychological choice. How could you say no to someone who occupied that space in your psyche?

Jerry's commitment over the years to the role of science and technology in policy issues showed itself repeatedly both in practice and in attempting to enhance MIT's already substantial, but diffuse and sporadic, institutional capability for contributing to policy. One of his motives in asking me to head political science and then CIS was his knowledge that I had worked with him on such subjects. He believed that MIT should be doing deliberative analysis of policy issues in a more sustained and focused way than it already was. The result was proposals for further innovations. One of those was the idea of a department or program (originally conceived as a "College") devoted to analysis and teaching on the interactions of science and technology and human affairs, with a strong leg in science-related policy issues. That became the STS Program; with Jerry's strong support to attract high-quality faculty, it quickly developed into a leading, nationally recognized educational endeavor.

Another proposal directed toward the study of policy was the idea to create a center devoted entirely to policy studies. Jerry asked me in 1968, while he was still provost, to chair a seminar series that would consider the kinds of subjects for which MIT might have a distinctive capability for analysis and recommendation. We were then supposed to advise the president (Howard Johnson) and provost whether or not the Institute should proceed to establish such a center. The seminar series was a bit of a sham, since it was clear from the start that Jerry and the leadership of the Institute wanted to go ahead. But, we gave him the evidence he needed; moreover, it was a good and justified idea. In the end, it took several years to create the CPA

In the MIT president's office, under a portrait of Karl Taylor Compton (MIT president, 1930–48). (Photo by Calvin Campbell. Courtesy of the MIT Museum.)

because of some false starts, but it finally came into being in 1972, and exists today in somewhat altered form in the School of Engineering.

Notwithstanding his determination to change all he saw for the better, Jerry never lost his sense of the importance of quality and excellence, especially at MIT. As one example, after assuming the presidency he made a point of insisting that new department heads should be intellectual and scholarly leaders in their field, not appointed on the basis of their administrative skills. He saw that as a means of setting a standard for the rest of the faculty, even when such a policy might create administrative problems—not all intellectual leaders prove to be adept at administration.

I experienced Jerry's commitment to excellence many times while I was head of Political Science and director of the CIS. Just one incident illustrates the atmosphere he fostered. A significant member of the science faculty, probably on his way to a

Nobel Prize (at a time when MIT had few Nobel laureates), proposed that a family member of his be appointed to the faculty of the department I chaired; if not, he said he would move to another university. Before responding, I thought I should consult with Jerry, for I knew how important the individual was to him and to MIT. His response was quick and unequivocal: we should decide ourselves, according to our criteria, whether the family member was appropriate for us. If not, case closed.

There are innumerable incidents and examples of that commitment and all the others that Jerry exemplified. He was a unique individual who left profound legacies in every institution with which he was involved, as well as on the larger world stage. He worked hard and tirelessly, even after his stroke, to improve the lives of us all. At the same time, those larger goals did not crowd out his interest in the lives of friends, family, and colleagues. I can personally attest to the enormous influence he had on my own life and career. He is greatly appreciated, and deeply missed.

An Enlightenment Man

Philip Morrison

Jerry Wiesner and I were born only a few months apart near the end of 1915, he in Michigan and I in New Jersey, to live as parallel but distinct witnesses, event by event, to the surging growth of science and technology, to deep changes in the American polity, and to wars great and small. We first met casually in 1945 just before the end of World War II, at busy Los Alamos, where the final links in the chain that led to atom bombs were forged.

Wiesner

A prewar graduate thrown into an unprecedented wartime career, Jerry was a gifted electrical engineer from Ann Arbor with a communications bent. He came to Los Alamos from the home of American radar, the redoubtable secret wartime Radiation Laboratory at MIT, a successful young engineer in system design. He came to bring new electronics to the 1947 Bikini bomb test, and to refresh Los Alamos electronics by up-to-date instrumentation for the new weapons that would replace the improvised wartime bombs. (The nuclear flavor of the MIT lab name was a dis-informing hint, chosen as cover for its real microwave purpose.) Before his days at the Rad Lab, Jerry had spent a year or so as director of audio

Philip Morrison, physicist and educator, taught at Cornell University for twenty years before joining the MIT faculty in 1965. He was a member of the Manhattan Project for four years (1942–46), working at both the University of Chicago and the Los Alamos laboratory. At Los Alamos he participated in the Trinity test, the first test of an atomic bomb, and since the end of World War II has spoken out widely against nuclear war and the arms race. Over the years, he has written and published (often with his late wife Phylis) to broaden the public understanding of science, as in the film "Powers of Ten" and the PBS television series "The Ring of Truth." He is the recipient of the First Annual Hans Bethe Science in Public Service Award of the Federation of American Scientists, 2003.

recording technology at the Library of Congress, and went characteristically into the field himself to serve as recording technician for the library's folklorist Alan Lomax, using the new magnetic wire recorder to record folk singers.

Some say that the atomic bomb ended the war, but that radar—which made possible the U.S. Navy's success at sea against the Japanese—won the war. Jerry's work, in that sense, helped "win" the war. This robust, good-humored young engineer, known as both analytical and imaginative, soon found a post of leadership at the MIT Research Laboratory of Electronics (RLE), which grew postwar at MIT out of the Rad Lab. His extraordinary breadth and depth of mind became more and more evident with the years. Full professor of electrical engineering by 1950, he became director of RLE in 1952. Big RLE was never a starchy place, but not all lab leaders would have found a young linguistic revolutionary who got his start there, Noam Chomsky, now the most influential theorist of language, essential to its staff, among a wide spectrum of other scholars far from electronics but vital to the human activity of communication.

Morrison

A young quantum theorist with a penchant for applications, I earned my Berkeley Ph.D. under J. Robert Oppenheimer in 1940. Beginning in 1942 I worked in the Chicago laboratory where Fermi started the first chain reaction, coming to Los Alamos a full year before the climactic desert bomb test in July 1945. Before Pearl Harbor, I was a new physics instructor at Urbana; by the spring of 1942, I was at work there on the use of high-energy gamma rays for cancer therapy and for examining heavy armor plate. I joined the Manhattan Project in Chicago at the end of 1942.

Eager for peacetime after four years of following the bomb, I left Los Alamos in 1946 to join the Cornell physics department. A few of us had visited Hiroshima and Nagasaki, and many Japanese cities about as ruinous, wherein a cloud of hundreds of our heavy bombers had strewn flaming firebombs amidst the houses before a single fateful plane could set off one giant nuclear fireball. A number of other Los Alamos physics veterans came to rural Cornell, some to our postwar theorists' group led by Hans Bethe, so clearly an inspiring senior among a few new faculty members. Academic by taste, dissident from the warlike trend of the times, I spent more than a dozen postwar years there before I saw MIT, though even quiet Ithaca was not beyond all the turmoil of that decade. An outsider there could join public debate on war and its preparation.

Physics at War

The war had rapidly conscripted new branches of science and technology. By now that process is a commonplace, though it was not always so. Cannon-founders and shipwrights in wood were not often seen as scientists, though they were plainly skilled technicians essential for sea-going states. In the late eighteenth century, the Royal Navy managed free passage for its survey ships through the French block-aders; the French, gallant and rational as well, recognized that on occasion hostile ships that would collect astronomical and geographic data served the common good of all nations. Even the American firebrand Tom Paine rejoiced that a scientist could be at home in any country where he planted his foot. As World War I opened, one brave young pacifist, Albert Einstein, could find no guilt for any warlike uses of his new physics, yet in the next great war he wrote urgently in 1939 to FDR saying that the time had come for research on the explosive reaction of neutrons in uranium. New nuclear devices for war have been so assiduously developed during and since World War II that it is hard even today to talk of neutron physics without reawakening the faint echo of mass destruction.

Even the end of World War II did not slow for long America's arming to deter or to wage nuclear war. The Cold War had taken clear form with the 1946 Iron Curtain speech of Winston Churchill. Its political roots can be traced back to the ousting of visionary and conciliatory Henry Wallace from the 1944 FDR ticket, once it became clear that the ailing Roosevelt was unlikely to survive to term's end in 1948. The Cold War soon extended its harsh shadow of preparation for war over American political life, growing apace from mid-1946 to a high pitch in the early 1960s. It continued to wax and wane until the late 1980s, past two fierce American-led wars into Asia, with expanding military expenditures in the United States and in its poorer adversary, each furnishing an outrageous arsenal of inter-continental nuclear warheads, still stored by the tens of thousands in both places.

A Dark Day in the White House: JFK, Wiesner, and the Future of Nuclear War

I believe that the first clear voices from our government against the Cold War's perilous and enduring stance came from the Kennedy White House at mid-year of 1963. Jerry Wiesner served among the science advisers to three presidents—Eisenhower, Kennedy, and, briefly, Lyndon Johnson. He was an exemplary figure among insiders, the technically expert, often academic officials close to the political decision-makers they guided.

The narrative of that time still fascinates. One gloomy day, probably early in 1962, cold rain was falling hard on the White House lawn. Jerry often spoke of that time:

I remember one day when President Kennedy asked what happens to the radioactive fallout, and I told him it was washed out of the clouds by the rain and would be brought to earth by the rain. And he said, looking out the window, "You mean it's in the rain out there?" I said, "Yes." He looked out the window, very sad, and didn't say a word for several minutes.

U.S. and Soviet tests had been fired in the open air repeatedly for years, without plain purpose, often in showpiece crescendos of yield. Global fallout followed, as the seven winds slowly mixed the radioactive dust and gas. The two superpowers seemed to be playing a slow hand, trick slapped down on trick. The highest yield was that of the final year of the game, 1962, the largest single manmade explosion with a Soviet device yielding near sixty megatons, never since approached. Whether on the day described the easily measured activity of the lawn had come from an American test in the Eastern Pacific or from a Soviet one in the high Arctic is not clear, and matters little.

Recall also that in the late summer of 1961 the two heads of state had been caught up in a two-week melodrama, the Cuban Missile Crisis, a look into the Pit of Despond if ever there was one. But on June 10, 1962, the young president—his adviser Jerry was two years his senior—delivered an important commencement speech, indeed an unprecedented one, at the American University in D.C.:

Total war makes no sense in an age when great powers can maintain large and relatively invulnerable nuclear weapons and refuse to surrender without recourse to those forces. It makes no sense in an age where a single nuclear weapon contains almost ten times the explosive force delivered by all the allied forces in the Second World War. It makes no sense in an age when the deadly poisons produced by a nuclear exchange would be carried by wind and water and soil and seed to the far corners of the globe and to generations yet unborn.

In a time of tension, the president spoke firmly for peace and then acted against fierce domestic dissent. His reasoned views prevailed among the great majority, and the Treaty of Moscow, a couple of pages of text, was completed and signed after due consultations among the three first nuclear powers—the United States, Soviet Union, and United Kingdom. It was signed on August 10, 1963, only eight months after the Cuban Missile Crisis. No doubt Kennedy and Khrushchev bore their own fresh memories of that terrifying, uncertain fortnight, and sought a new path. (JFK died in November 1963.)

The Partial Test Ban Treaty banned nuclear explosions in the atmosphere, in outer space, and under water, and is of unlimited duration. That Treaty did not end the arms race—as Jerry, I, and others had hoped—nor even the steady competition for more and stronger nuclear weapons, though it did drive nearly all nuclear tests underground for good. Thus it improved the future public health of every nation. Above all, it was the first example of a broad, concrete agreement among uneasy powers, an agreement of mutual gain. The fallout phenomenon is complex, but the most important radioactive species decay slowly enough to affect the world for a lifetime or so, yet not so slowly as to tithe their damage across so many generations of the far future that the effects are lost within the natural causes of malignancies. The elements are spread out everywhere on land and sea where there is rain or snow to carry particles to the surface. Strontium and cesium simulate the elements calcium and potassium well enough chemically so that they are taken in by the body along paths more or less like those followed by natural elements of food.

Figure 1 records the ominous steep rise in fallout concentration on the ground during the 1950s and 1960s worldwide. At its peak, the radioactive deposit had increased the radioactivity of staple foods in the prenuclear weapons age by a factor of 100 or 200. The deposited activity falls steadily enough over the years, as the active nuclei decay and as airborne particles are washed to ground and sea. It never was abundant enough to claim a measurable fraction of all the human lives lost amidst the general toll we pay to cancer from many causes. Yet the Partial Test Ban Treaty stopped the rapid and disastrous trend while levels were still tolerable.

The Treaty is a legacy to the world from key people who fought and pushed for it, a geological monument chiefly to its initiator, President Kennedy, and to Jerry, his brilliant insider, among all the leaders who concurred. The global change cannot be ignored; it is indelibly signaled in the rocks and the sea bed. It cannot be forgotten even by posterity. This first real step to the eventual control of nuclear warfare gave rise to a subtle but ubiquitous geological fact.

That was clear by the mid-1970s. My wife Phylis and I were so much impressed by this tale that we prepared a presentation of the published data to the Wiesners on an occasion recognizing the close of Jerry's ten years as one of MIT's most effective reforming presidents. The years of his presidency yielded lasting student diversity (women now comprise more than 40 percent of undergraduates) and a widened range of opportunities for creative teaching and research, reaching the arts, spanning the humanities, and including the serious study of science and technology in their relation to society.

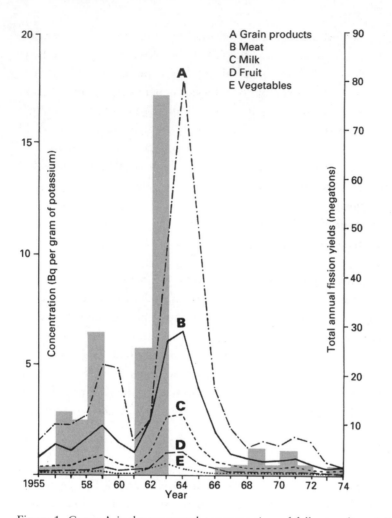

Figure 1. Curve A is the measured concentration of fallout radioactivity in the grain products consumed in Denmark. Year after year one of the top contaminants in fallout, the isotope cesium-137, is a beta-ray emitter. Half of any of these cesium atoms decay over thirty years. The gray bars mark the annual megatonnage yield of atmospheric tests, offering a demonstration of cause and effect. Once the tests stopped by agreement, the fallout peaked out. (From United Nations Environment Programme, *Radiation: Doses, Effects, Risks* [United Nations Environment Programme, 1991].)

The Enduring Illusion

Into the 1980s, Jerry and his wife Laya remained public citizens of weight. Good works, press recognition, and awards for merit continued from their Watertown home, at MIT, nationally, and internationally from as far away as Russia and Japan. But both were slowed by disabling illness, and they played less part in the great changes the 1990s brought to our country, the fading of the danger of catastrophe in the large.

In 1992, Jerry was continuing his recovery from a stroke that had kept him home-bound for some years. He worked with me and Kosta Tsipis on a publication that we hoped would get people thinking about the need to redirect government spending from military to social and environmental needs. Kosta and I are both physicists, old MIT friends of Jerry's and sharers in his concerns.

In January 1993, we published a booklet—*Beyond the Looking Glass: The United States Military in 2000 and Later*—for quick circulation during the first months of President Clinton's new term in office. Our title is an allusion to a frightening operation carried out for three decades by the United States Air Force. I paraphrase here a part of our prologue:

Looking Glass

Twenty-four hours a day in every season for thirty years without a break, one or another of a group of big jets was somewhere aloft high over North America on its random track. Aboard in unvarying rotation was a general officer of the Strategic Air Command and his crew bound to stay aloft long hours until confirmed replacement was airborne. These grave and anonymous officers were equipped, trained, and authorized as a surrogate command able to order the awesome nuclear retaliation of the United States should the White House, the Pentagon, and the SAC base in Omaha be destroyed by a sudden nuclear strike.

Looking Glass first took up its unending rounds in February 1961, and was brought to an end in July of 1991. The thread of thermonuclear confrontation is no longer drawn taut.

In our time, the actuality of September 11, 2001, has replaced the threat so seriously accepted for thirty years. Though the tragedy of 9/11 in 2001 ended the lives of some three thousand innocents, the sudden wider strike that Looking Glass sought to deter would have cost not fewer than a *thousand times as many* lives. Jerry's thoughtful preface, on the question of where we go in the post–Looking Glass era, is worth quoting in part here:

In these pages we outline a national necessity: prompt and radical reform of America's giant military enterprise. That reform can help us out of the economic muddle, and provide for our nation's safety in the long run. . . .

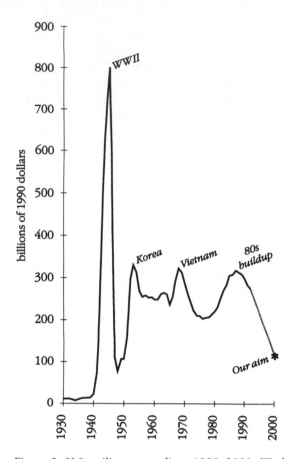

Figure 2. U.S. military spending, 1930–2000. We have added one data point for the year 2000, using the customary, if not very accurate, deflator from 1990 dollars to 2000 dollars, here 30%. (From Jerome Wiesner, Philip Morrison, and Kosta Tsipis, *Beyond the Looking Glass: The United States Military in 2000 and Later* [Program in Science and Technology for International Security, MIT, 1993].)

Military spending, so long fed by fear, outmatches the crooked Wall Street games and the bankers' disasters of the eighties. We undertook a huge debt to field weapons we didn't need, that even brought new dangers. To outspend and overawe the Soviets, we have more armaments than prudence could ever justify. . . .

There is a widespread feeling that the United States is awakening on the morning after. We can save half a trillion dollars and move towards a stabler peace. An opportunity has opened wide for change.

And our joint conclusion:

We believe that we Americans, along with the citizens of all the other nations who live with some degree of comfort and safety, will have step by step to replace mutual fear by mutual aid, or enter into a fiercely unstable world. The task is surely long, but it is worthwhile. In a stable world most persons, even the myriads of poor—many here in the wealthy USA— need to see some path that promises them safety, justice, and even well-being ahead. Those few who will not accept the promise must encounter high barriers against violent international change, barriers that will be well-guarded by the many.

We have perhaps five decades to nourish that outcome from our present world of bitter division and its implied conflicts. Certainly violent conflict will not disappear, nor will military forces, but both need to dwindle greatly in scale; the terrible weapons of mass destruction can sleep.

Great hope comes from one great fact: the economic, technical, and human resources now sequestered annually in the unproductive world of arms amount to the major part of a trillion dollars a year worldwide. In nature and size these resources are capable of bringing profound change to the lives of most of the world's people. Among those billions a working solution to our acute environmental and human problems rests, not less—and with good judgment not more—than one long lifetime ahead.

Figure 2 shows how little we knew in 1993 of the decade to come, how overly sanguine we were about the prospects for change.

Generous, optimistic, wise, with unmatched inside experience, Jerry Wiesner, writing as a senior, daring outsider far from the White House where he had worked decades earlier, grew less vigorous month by month and died of heart failure the year after our book came out. His views and my own seem those of the Enlightenment, as for Jefferson and Franklin, improved by recognition of the universal rights of all humans, and by awareness that reason itself requires constant advocates. In the optimistic style of old, I hope and believe that our current peace by fear will be replaced by a stable pattern of mutual aid among the nations. I think Jerry would have felt the same way.

Educator, Political Leader, Much Loved Friend

John Kenneth Galbraith

For many years, I have no close count, we journeyed of a Sunday afternoon to Watertown. There we spent the early evening with Jerry and Laya, the Wiesners. It was a precious part of the week. Our conversation ranged over the current political scene, with the inevitable enjoyment of errors and idiocy, of MIT and Harvard and the books that were holding our attention—in Jerry's case, what he was reading; in my case, too often what I was writing. Sometimes there were other guests, occasionally we were alone. It was the glorious time of the week.

My relationship with Jerry, however, was of a larger sort. He was my guide on many aspects of life. There was education—its administration and its purpose. With informed candor he spoke of the problems and goals at MIT; I cannot believe any university president in our time has been better informed. I heard of plans and problems in engineering, science, and the social sciences. Economics—its task, its problems, and its instruction—was a frequent topic. He presided over one of the most accomplished economics faculties in the country and, indeed, in the world. Jerry was interested, admiring, and informed. I do not think I ever offered any useful advice. Jerry was already there.

We dealt also with the current political scene. Jerry assigned, as did I, a vital role in civilized life to government. His concern was with everything from education to

John Kenneth Galbraith is the Paul M. Warburg Professor of Economics, emeritus, at Harvard University, where he has spent most of his academic life. He held a number of academic and government posts before joining the Harvard faculty as professor of economics in 1949; he retired in 1975. He was U.S. ambassador to India during the Kennedy presidency (1961–63). Among his many books, most of which relate to economics and social policy, are two that focus on the Indian experience—*Indian Painting* (1968) and *Ambassador's Journal* (1969). He was awarded the Medal of Freedom, by the U.S. president, in 2000. A fellow of several professional associations, he has served as president of the American Economic Association (1972) and president of the American Academy and Institute of Arts and Letters (1984–87).

John Kenneth Galbraith (right) holds the rapt attention of (left to right) General James Gavin, retired chairman of Arthur D. Little Co., Jerry, and Georgiy Arbatov. Arbatov, a leading Soviet expert on arms control and Soviet-American relations, had just delivered a lecture as part of MIT's "World Change and World Security" series, April 11, 1977. (Photo by Calvin Campbell. Courtesy of the MIT Museum.)

defense and to those who did not respond to the threat of nuclear accident or war. I wonder if sanity on these matters owed as much to anyone as it did to Jerome Wiesner.

We also shared an adverse view of our terrible misadventure in Vietnam, where I had once been sent by Kennedy. There were other meetings when I sought instruction from Jerry. I perhaps put too much emphasis on those meetings in Watertown. Jerry, more than anyone, helped originate and guide the politically effective Council for a Livable World and its campaign support for peacefully disposed legislators, free from dominance by the Pentagon and the defense industry. The council is still very much in this service.

In the Kennedy years, I was in India, he much in Washington. I had a well-remembered rescue by Jerry. One day an official telegram came in from Washington asking that I approach Nehru on a particularly idiotic venture relating to some collaboration between the CIA, the Pentagon, and the State Department on, characteristic of the time, a particularly weird Cold War venture. Indian approval was needed for, if I correctly recall, some airplane over-flights, or some other similar Indian tolerance of the insanities of the time. I was deeply troubled; Nehru would automatically refuse. Intelligent American initiatives might be damaged. Most notably, no doubt, I would have an assignment with the Indian government which I would very much dislike. After some thought, I telegraphed Jerry who had influence on such matters. Next day I got a lovely telegram telling me to ignore the whole business. He said it was all a lot of crap, or words immediately to that effect.

Many reading the words here, mine and all the others, will remember the memorial service for Jerry. It was wonderfully attended, beautifully staged. It never quite came to an end. That was because everybody, as they made their way out, wanted to tell of their affection for Jerry Wiesner, recall some compelling anecdote. Kitty and I took a lovely half hour to get out of the hall, perhaps more. Everyone had a remembrance. For the same reason, contribution to this volume and the memory so stirred will have been for all a pleasure. Assuredly, it was for me.

Memory of Jerry centered on Washington, MIT, and Harvard. A word on the latter. There was no member of the Harvard faculty who knew Jerry and did not wish that he were a mile up the Charles.

One should occasionally accept, even in the academic world, that he can lack originality. So I do here. With others I say: We will never see his like again.

Race, Education, and Community

Elma Lewis[1]

You told me that other people might have known Jerry better than you did, but that nobody loved him as much. How did you come to know him?

I came to know Jerry when he was the new president at MIT. For people of my generation, that was rather impressive, because Jewish people had to expect some road blocks, much as black people did, though certainly not to the same degree. We were no strangers to discrimination. Also, those of us who were Christian had studied Israel since we were born, so we knew how that went.

Jerry came to my attention partly because of his civil rights attitudes, and then, as I said, because of his presidency at MIT. I think one of my very good friends, Dr. Willard Johnson, was on the presidential search committee. I was, of course, interested because that was new at that point, students and young professors being on a search committee.

When Jerry was chosen to be the president, he actually cried, and he said to me, "I never thought a poor Jewish boy would get this opportunity." I said, "The difference, Jerry, is that I *knew* no black poor kid would ever get this opportunity, so you're sure ahead of the game. There's not going to be any time in the near future

Elma Lewis, an icon in the Boston arts community for more than half a century, founded the Elma Lewis School of Fine Arts in 1950 and the National Center for Afro-American Artists in 1968. In 1969, she staged the first local production of Langston Hughes's "Black Nativity" pageant, which became a local favorite. Among her numerous awards, she received the Presidential Medal for the Arts (1983) and the "Living Legend" award of the Black Arts Community (1988). She is a fellow of the American Academy of Arts and Sciences. In 1981, she was one of the first recipients of the MacArthur Foundation Fellowship, awarded to individuals who show exceptional creative merit and promise.

1. Edited and excerpted from an interview conducted on April 13, 2002, by Kenneth R. Manning, Thomas Meloy Professor of Rhetoric and of the History of Science, MIT.

when we'll be talking with equivalent experiences, but they are experiences which will help us understand and relate to each other."

Jerry was always an activist. In his science career, he wanted to "see it happen." He wasn't an abstract person; he didn't want to write everything down in a formal way. I was interested in his activities with the Kennedys. The Kennedys were my kind of political people. At that time, most black people who wanted to see progress made in this country were devoted to radical thought. What may not be radical thought today for a white male was very radical at the time, and for the Kennedys, and I could see that they would choose Jerry—that is, John F. Kennedy, particularly, would choose him to be in his intricate science program.

Jerry's relationship to the Boston black community was to make opportunity for youngsters to learn at the same pace and under the same conditions as white youngsters in the suburbs. Consequently, he was one of the original thinkers in METCO, the Metropolitan Council for Educational Opportunity. In METCO, Ruth Batson, who was the first director, was his personal friend and also my personal friend. We were collegial in that spirit. We were always at each other's houses or in discussions.

Then I had the good fortune to be a trustee of WGBH, for twenty-seven years, with Jerry, John Silber, and the nutritionist Jean Mayer, the president at Tufts. We always voted together—John Silber, Jerry, Jean Mayer, and I. We were always on the same side of issues and we were good friends. I could count on them to have the right civil rights position at all times. It doesn't sound sensible to young people now, but you would turn your television on and for a week, ten days, two weeks you wouldn't see a black face. In fact, it was so astounding that when a black came on to read the news or do the weather, you would call the whole family, "Look, look, look—that man is black!" Jerry, John, Jean, and I tried to change some of those things.

I'm very dissatisfied with progress, but it is overwhelming. If you come from another time, it wasn't common to do as we did—go to each other's houses, parties, meetings, or whatever. Jerry was not reluctant to be here at my house. He was a poor Jewish boy, and he knew just exactly what the pain was. He was at my school, the Elma Lewis School of Fine Arts, and he was in this community. Willard is proud to say now, "I was one of the ones who voted for him—I wanted him." And I always said, "Willard, that was a good choice, that was a *very* good choice!"

You and Jerry had a particular common interest in that Jerry was very much into the arts.

Very much. He was an incredible folklorist, and, more importantly, both he and I saw the arts not as entertainment but as cultural expression. The arts tell you who the person is. In opera, you know the difference between Verdi and Puccini and the German composers. You listen and their music tells you who they are, what they lived, and why. When you hear the music of black people, you know who they are and why. You can hear Africa just as strongly today as you could when we left Africa. It's right there.

People tend today to talk about gospel, but gospel is quite new, only since 1926 or so, with the coming of Dr. Thomas A. Dorsey. There were jewels for the transition into gospel, and you can hear them. When you go to South Africa, you hear a music more similar to that of black Americans than the rest of Africa's music, because South African blacks and American blacks have experienced the same quality of apartheid experience. The music comes out of your experience, the poetry comes out of your experience. When Leopold Senghor talked about negritude, for example, it had a similar expression to that of the South African poets. While we come from their derivation, our cultural experiences are both different yet make us the same kind of artistic beings. You hear Hugh Masekela play jazz and you hear jazz in New York City—it's the same sound.

Jerry recognized all this a long time ago, that art is not entertainment. It upset him and me to hear people think that it is. Art can be *entertaining*, but it's not *entertainment*.

I think you're right—he was looking for something deeper in art.

All the time, all the time. And he had a fortunate partner in Laya. They were quite the same kind of people; it was a fortunate marriage. Towards the very end of his life, I saw him at Spaulding Rehabilitation Hospital. He said, "Now I guess Laya and I will just have to take care of each other." They were then knowingly approaching the end of their time.

I am sorry that he didn't live longer to achieve even more. That which he did as a scientist was impressive, but his humanity was probably greater than his scientific knowledge. He had a great understanding and tolerance for young people. Much of the time when they were argumentative and abusive, he was not abused. He withstood that very well. He understood that it came to that, at that moment in history. While he would be winning on the side of the Kennedys and so forth, he was losing on the side of young black people and young Jewish people who did not understand that. I think we come from the less immediately fortunate generation. We do the work, we don't get the praise. The praise is coming later. So if praise is what you are looking for, well, then, you are in trouble.

One day I was at Northeastern. I don't remember what group of young people were there, but Jesse Jackson was among them. These young people were yelling and screaming, "Martin doesn't do anything—he just talks a lot about how the white people should stop!" And the other ones would say, "Well, Malcolm is my kind, Malcolm is my man!" Jesse was having a sickle cell attack at the time and had to sit down at the table. He raised his head and said, "What are you talking about? They both killed the same number of white people—none!" That made them stop and think. Martin and Malcolm had different tactics, but they were going down the same road.

That was the thing that Jerry understood always—people have different tactics, but they are going down the same road. One time he had a blazing argument with John Silber, and he never got over it. John came in yelling and screaming and got over it in ten minutes. I was always trying to patch that argument up—"Why don't you make friends with Jerry?" John would say, "I tried, but he doesn't want to be friends with me." When Jerry was through with someone, he was through. And the argument was quite nonsensical. They were arguing about who knew the most in the area of civil rights and who had contributed the most. But their contributions were so entirely different that it was an irrelevant argument.

So they were talking about whether Jerry had contributed more than John, or vice versa?

Right—"You don't know what you're talking about!" The fun part of it was that they both had blistering mouths. That was a side of Jerry that the public didn't see that much of. You saw that in John Silber all the time, but you didn't see it in Jerry. You didn't even know he could do that.

Tell me about the kind of support he gave your efforts in the Elma Lewis School.

He was very supportive. For one thing, I attribute the fact that I was a MacArthur Fellow largely to him. Young MacArthur was his student. When the father died, and he didn't want to leave his money to his children and didn't want to leave the money to the government, he left the money in that Foundation with Jerry and some others who would define what would happen to it. They decided that they wouldn't give awards to anybody for writing a paper or making a suggestion. Your award would be based on what you had done. The idea was that people who had been particularly creative would then be the people who would be apt to be creative in the future. Foundation officers just looked at people and decided—not that they were rich, not that they were poor, not that they were of any racial origin or anything—who would get awards on the basis of future promise.

You were among the first, weren't you?

Yes. At the time it came, I had been diagnosed as a level–2 diabetic and had taken that big plunge for the other side of the road. I was losing my eyesight and my legs were giving me a lot of trouble. In the summer of that season, I think it was 1982, John O'Sullivan Francis was the administrator of the NCAAA, the National Center of Afro-American Artists. On a Sunday morning he called up—I don't think I ever admitted to people that I couldn't read—and said, "I want you to read the *Globe* this morning. There's an article in there about a new foundation, and Jerry Wiesner is one of the trustees." He called me back about three or four hours later to see if I had read it, and I said no. He said, "Well, what does it take to get your attention?" Then he told me about it, saying, "I don't know how people submit for this, but I would like to submit your name."

So he called Jerry, because he'd call him about anything, and Jerry said, "Well, we're not supposed to interfere—they've got a search committee out there looking at the world at large, and they'll come in with various recommendations. I have to look at everything objectively." John said, "Okay, but I just want you to know certain things that you may not know." And Jerry said, "Well, I know all about Elma anyway—you shouldn't do that, because I don't need it." But John persisted and sent him a series of newspaper clippings.

I was therefore not totally surprised when I got the award. It was a day that I was sitting in the kitchen. I plopped down on a chair, going into darkness, and I knew I was about to receive thirty thousand dollars of medical bills on my eyes. I said, "What am I going to do with this in relation to everything else? I don't know where it's going." I am very religious—not churched, but religious. I was brought up in the Episcopal Church, which has served me well, but that is not really my theology.

A few days earlier, Tom Winship from the *Globe* had called me and said, "There are people around here asking questions about you." So I said, "Sure, answer them!" He said that maybe six hundred inquiries had been made on me. So few people who are political are like Tom Winship—I'll call Tom literary—or like my dear friend Ed Brooke. Tom said, "People are accustomed to helping others whom they want to be their friends—and they want it known." I knew something was up, but I didn't know what.

So that day I was sitting in the kitchen, the phone rang. It was a Friday afternoon, and I'll never forget it. It was dreary outside, so I really couldn't see. I always answer the phone, "Elma Lewis speaking." The voice said, "Is this Elma Lewis?" I grew a little testy and said, "I *said* 'Elma Lewis speaking'!" He said, "Have you ever heard of the John D. and Catherine T. MacArthur Foundation?" I said, "I've heard of it." And he said, "Well, congratulations! The trustees met this afternoon and you've been voted a Fellow." Well, somebody was always giving me a plaque or something, so that was not very exciting. Next I said, "How nice." But then he went on to describe the terms, and the award was irrevocable. If I went out and murdered a man, I'd *still* get the five years. And then the best part came—comprehensive health benefits!

Jerry was a large factor in the awarding of the MacArthur. When I got the call, it was a Friday afternoon around three o'clock. The man on the other end of the line said, "We would hope that you don't answer the press if they call you up. Let us make the announcement—don't say anything to anybody." One of the additional benefits of the award was a yearly grant of fifteen thousand dollars to the charity of your choice. It was all tax-free, though it has been modified greatly since then. I attribute the fact that I am still working at eighty years of age, and working steadily since 1980, to the MacArthur Prize Fellows Award. I received money for five years which allowed me to take care of my medical needs and to work quietly at home at my own pace, expanding on the thought which is the cornerstone of our new cultural center.

I have every reason to expect that this cultural center will become a reality shortly. Incidentally, I had two young men helping who were then approaching thirty—John Andrew Ross, musician, and Edmund Barry Gaither, an art historian—who were at the NCAAA at the time and are still there. Nobody ever left emotionally. This is the reward at the end of my life, and I expect that it will reward generations of world citizens to come. I am very grateful to Jerry for being involved in that.

He was a man of great integrity.

Great integrity. He would tell you he could do something, or he couldn't do it—and that would be true either way. I find that true of John Silber, too. He's more acerbic, but his integrity is the same, and you'll find that people of integrity usually find each other. Whether they are socially acceptable to each other or not, their thought processes coincide. I don't think I ever heard Jerry complain about anything. He would talk about things, but not complain about them—it was just that that's the way they had to go at that historic moment. I have accepted that, too.

My family is from Barbados. My father came here before 1920, and he lived until 1976. He was amazed by the social and economic transformations. His life experience had been so remarkable. Often we are discouraged when something doesn't happen when we want it to, but his and Jerry's view was that all good things come in their due time.

I was sorry that Jerry had to pass from the scene, but as determined by the Divine Providence, he spent his time, did what he should, and—hallelujah!—spent it on *what* he should. I think about black Americans from the South who tell me of the terrible things that have happened to them and their families, lynchings and whatever. I'm sorry for them as individuals, but that was called for to bring about change. I don't feel angry with God—it was necessary at that time. It was necessary for Nelson Mandela to spend that long period in confinement. Many things are necessary, and I feel that Jerry was a man of his time too.

You mentioned METCO. Can you say a little about that and the connections that Jerry and Laya had with it?

Laya was connected with anything Jerry was connected with, but he was really one of the main spearheads at the beginning of METCO. He saw it as something that Ruth Batson could do, and it gravely affected the whole outcome of her life. She lived about two blocks from here and we grew up together. She had three little children and a nonprofessional husband, and her career took that quantum leap because of Jerry. Jerry wanted her for the METCO directorship, and she became director. She has an organized mind—a mind that doesn't take flights of fancy, such as the art mind does. She's right on the money all the time: "Well, tell me what you want me to do and I'll get it done!" That was something that Jerry respected a lot, and he enjoyed her as a deep friend.

He even went further in this community. The reason that Ruth, Burt Lee, and others owned the TV station, Channel 7, was because of Jerry. I don't know if people know that. Burt Lee went to him with the proposition that he could break RKO. That didn't seem very likely, but Jerry funded him for two years to do it. That's the kind of concentration it takes that few of us can give to a project, because we have to eat. Jerry funded that, and every time RKO was in court, Burt Lee and the troops were there. Of course, you had to have a corporate structure, so Ruth and Burt and a few others set one up which melded with another corporate structure that included Mel Miller. Finally, those people took over RKO and got Channel 7. They raised the large amounts of money that were necessary to accomplish this. They also had the patience to wait for it because they had backing.

That's one of the things that I cherished about Jerry. Many people will help us to get welfare, but they won't help us to get "goodfare," like Jerry did. His activities with METCO were hands-on. Each of the communities had host families. I think it's changed a great deal now and I'm not sure for the better. It was a very trying experience. Many people in this community were against it, and still are, because they thought only the children who had privilege would be included. That's not true in one sense, but in another it is. Only the children who had parents with vision could be included, because it's strenuous.

Two children in my family were METCO children—I don't remember what town, it might have been Framingham. My niece, who was a single mother at the time, wanted her little boy to play in the school orchestra. They rehearsed before school in the morning, so it became her personal responsibility to get the child out there at the appointed time. At five o'clock in the morning, you'd look around and see all these children going to get the bus. That's a serious commitment, and that would not have happened without people like Jerry being as involved as he was. I'm not sure people understand how involved he was.

He was quiet. There are people who get involved and they are always letting you know they're involved.

And they're the front-runners, while black people take the back seat.

He wasn't like the ones out front.

And it wouldn't have been appropriate, because that was the whole complaint at the time—we wanted to direct our own destiny.

So he wanted black people to be in the front and to take control of their own decisions.

That's right, and nobody would have listened to him if he had tried to be the "big white father."

That's what I've heard in another context that really strengthens a point about him—that he really wanted black people to do it for themselves.

Right. That's why he became acceptable to people like Ruth or like me. I was a Garveyite, so it definitely would not have been acceptable to me to have a "big white father." I'm still a Garveyite, really.

I love to hear people say they are Garveyites, because I think Garvey was a man of vision.

A man of vision, and a great part of his demise came for that reason. The ruling class always denounces our heroes by accusing them of having feet of clay. When these same rulers decided that Martin Luther King was a womanizer, a communist, and so forth, he was a nobody. These accusations weren't true, but if they were, what difference would it have made? His principles were still correct, and they were principles that I believe Jerry understood and sympathized with.

Do you think your being a Garveyite had anything to do with your father?

Oh, yes. We couldn't escape it. We went every Sunday afternoon to the meetings. My brother sold the newspaper, *Negro World*, and I was a Girl Guide. We were strong in the movement. My father came here at the age of nineteen, and he read a lot—he was an omnivorous reader.

I think about people like my father and I'm very sad, because he was an unheralded giant. But he was a poor kid out of a poor parish in Barbados. He loved learning. He had heard of Booker T. Washington. He came to America specifically to relate to Booker T. Washington, but he couldn't, because Booker T. Washington wanted to please white people and come in line with their aspirations. But in looking around, he met Garvey, because that's the way he lived, and it was good for me.

Like my father, Jerry's parents were, I believe, immigrants looking for new opportunities—probably not the same ones my father was looking for, but new opportunities nonetheless.

How old was your father when he came here?

Nineteen.

Did he come straight to Boston?

He came to Boston.

And was this his home?

That I'm living in? Yes. It was my mother's and his house. I've been in this house fifty-nine years.

I remember once when I was an undergraduate at Harvard—you don't remember this—that I picked you up and brought you to Harvard and you had an evening with us. I remember you telling us the most wonderful story I'll never forget about a grand piano and how the white man sold it to your family.

For twelve hundred dollars, a dollar a week. It's down in that living room right now. That was my mother's doing. My mother was a different person from my father. He would have yelled and screamed at the white man and said some foolishness, but my mother said, "Alright." She knew that when she had a dollar she only owed him a dollar, and when she had twenty-five dollars, she would pay that on the piano.

If my mother's children wanted something, they had to have the best. Since her little boy was going to be a pianist, he was going to have a grand piano. The next boy went to Harvard, because if you're going to be a doctor, where do you go? You go to Harvard. He had to stay out of school one year because he didn't have the fee. She considered that he was going to be out another year, so she walked over to Harvard and said to President Conant, "This boy is too smart to be out of school! Let him in and I'll pay you some time," and that's just what she did. Black students didn't receive scholarships in those days, you had to pay.

That's a wonderful story.

I've had a wonderful life.

Have you written your autobiography?

I'm writing it now. Other people want to write their stories and embellish them. What I'm writing now is why I believe an international cultural center is of the essence, and I think Jerry would have related to my views on this. I probably will never see it. It will probably take us two or three years to break ground even if we begin right now.

But anyway, there *is* no "black culture" and we keep saying there is—there isn't. There are many black cultures. You come from something absolutely different than what I come from. One of my staff members is the product of an Irish mother and a black father who came from Canada—no doubt an escaped slave, and he is a very fair-skinned New England-type man. Another is from a small South Carolina town, others are from black urban communities, and still another is from a Yoruba community in Nigeria. All of us are part of the black culture, but differently expressed. The African element of us and the Caribbean elements of us, which embrace many cultures, are now refining themselves into something else.

For five thousand years, the Chinese have had a culture. They are a homogeneous people. We blacks are not—we are the most heterogeneous people. We have the most profound statement of all to make, but we have let other races tell us that their statement is more profound. We rate English literature at the top, but it isn't. We say Italian opera is the top, but it's not—it's a form of music. We lumped all that together and produced something new—it's in production right now. We'll take it and run with it. It's an example of art as cultural expression, the concept that Jerry understood so deeply.

With the little children, politicians make a big issue out of whether they should be taught bilingually or not. Children should learn in six languages! As you go abroad, when you go to Africa, they don't have porters at the airports. These children come out, meet the airplane, size you up, and when you speak English, they speak English to you. Another guy says, "What hotel can I take you to? Can I take you to this restaurant and that restaurant? I'll show you where to shop." They're having a dialogue with you in your language, be it in English, French, Spanish, or whatever. That's not that hard.

We just have foolishness written into the school curriculum here. I want to see a curriculum that teaches children by third grade to be trilingual. It's not hard in these communities—the Hispanics live here, the Haitians live here, the Southern blacks live here. They can speak to everybody, and they do. One of my young women who went to Germany to live took her six-year-old. He was totally English-speaking, and by eight he was German- and English-speaking. One particular Easter she went to Greece to do a project, and at one of the hotels the Greek kids started talking to her. But she couldn't speak Greek because she didn't get courses in that. Her child, on the other hand, was playing with Greek children outside, speaking their language. Her child, who had left America at six, was now trilingual.

I want to see the school system constructed differently, because the whole world is as large as they make it. And Jerry's values, I believe, were similarly focused on the importance of change, on social outreach, and on ways to seek and find our shared humanity across nations and between cultures.

The Search for Soviet Cybernetics

Spurgeon M. Keeny, Jr.

There is no better way to really get to know someone you have worked with professionally under demanding conditions than to take a leisurely trip abroad with him. My wife Sheila and I had the good fortune to vacation with Jerry and Laya Wiesner in the Soviet Union for two weeks in 1964. To give a little focus to our trip, Jerry decided that we should quietly inquire into Soviet progress in cybernetics, a subject in which he was particularly interested and which had become a matter of considerable concern in some inner circles in Washington. But first a bit of background is necessary to explain why I was on this trip in the first place and why we were interested in Soviet cybernetics.

My first real contact with Jerry was in 1956–57 on the Security Resources Panel, created by President Eisenhower to examine the need for civil defense in the wake of Soviet development of a thermonuclear weapons capability. The panel, which eventually produced the "Gaither Report," was initially intended to study fallout and blast shelters, but quickly expanded to include active defenses against aircraft and missiles as well. From there, it grew to include all aspects of Soviet capabilities and intentions, as well as U.S. vulnerabilities. Jerry was on the Executive Committee, but also participated in the active defense working group which was one of the first serious examinations of ballistic missile defense. I was on loan from the Office

Spurgeon M. Keeny, Jr., arms control specialist, began his career in disarmament as a staff member on the Panel on Peaceful Uses of Atomic Energy, Joint Congressional Committee on Atomic Energy (1955–56). He went on to serve the federal government in several capacities, including as technical assistant to the president's science adviser (1958–69) and as senior staff member of the National Security Council (1963–69). He was assistant director for science and technology (1969–73) and deputy director (1977–81) of the U.S. Arms Control and Disarmament Agency. After a period as scholar-in-residence at the National Academy of Sciences (1981–85), he became president and executive director of the Arms Control Association, Washington, D.C.

of the Secretary of Defense and was assigned to the working group on passive civil defense and eventually the vulnerability of the Strategic Air Command. The conclusions of the study were extremely alarmist and not only helped create the alleged "missile gap" but also made recommendations that would almost make the U.S. a garrison state. President Eisenhower, fortunately, did not buy the recommendations and was infuriated when the contents of the report were leaked to the press before he was briefed on it.

The experience with the Gaither Study had a profound effect on Jerry's thinking. It helped persuade him, and I believe many of the other distinguished scientists associated with the study, that an open-ended technological arms race was not the solution to the U.S.-Soviet confrontation and that diplomatic negotiations and arms control were imperative to avoid a catastrophic disaster. Meetings with General LeMay and debates with other members of the study, as well as the subject matter itself, brought home to Jerry how close we were to a thermonuclear holocaust that would certainly destroy civilization as we know it.

In response to the launch of Sputnik in the fall of 1957, President Eisenhower appointed James Killian, president of MIT, as the first full time presidential science adviser. Jerry was a member of Killian's initial President's Science Advisory Committee (PSAC), which was made up of a truly outstanding group of scientists most of whom had special expertise in areas related to national security. Killian immediately set out to pursue issues raised by the Gaither Report, but on the advice of Wiesner and others also explored the possibilities for arms control. With the encouragement of President Eisenhower, the group focused on the possibility of a comprehensive ban on nuclear testing, and concluded that such an agreement was verifiable and would be in U.S. interests. On the basis of these conclusions, Eisenhower proposed that a multinational conference of experts be convened in Geneva in July 1958 to see if agreement could be reached on the verifiability of such an agreement. I became the staff director for the U.S. delegation to the Conference of Experts and then a part-time delegate to the subsequent trilateral negotiations on the Discontinuation of Nuclear Tests. Jerry took on the broader task of organizing and serving as staff director of the U.S. delegation to the U.S.-Soviet Surprise Attack Conference that fall. Our paths overlapped in Geneva, but we were both much too busy to enjoy the leisurely diplomatic Geneva-style living.

When Jack Kennedy was elected, Jerry was named science adviser, as generally expected, although some thought he might be considered too radical. When Jerry asked me to continue as his technical assistant, I knew how fortunate I was to work with a friend who had an agenda I strongly supported and was close to the new president. Jerry greatly expanded the span of activities of his office and PSAC on issues of science and public policy, but his heart belonged above all to the problem of reducing the risk of war with the Soviet Union. It would be a major undertaking simply to summarize all the issues and problems that I worked with him on during the thousand days, which were the most exciting time of my life. And I should emphasize that I was involved in only a part of Jerry's activities.

A few examples capture the importance and diversity of those activities on which I worked with him. Jerry tried valiantly to breathe new life into the comprehensive nuclear test ban negotiations, which had collapsed after the shoot-down of the U-2 over Sverdlovsk. Although the negotiations resumed after the election, they were soon hung up over the annual quota of on-site inspections—with the U.S. demanding seven and the Soviet Union standing pat on three. Despite his persistent efforts, Jerry could not convince Kennedy to propose a compromise of five inspections and got into a bit of trouble when we informally suggested to the Soviets that they propose five. But his efforts were to no avail, since neither side was then really prepared to agree on a comprehensive test ban. He led a lonely but ultimately successful fight to kill a high-profile defense proposal to launch a costly massive nationwide fallout shelter program. With the help of an all-star scientific panel, he took on the intelligence establishment to achieve a radical technological breakthrough in satellite reconnaissance capabilities. He was at the center of the successful effort to improve nuclear command and control by installing Permissive Action Links (PALs) on nuclear weapons delivery systems, starting with the most dangerous forward-based alert aircraft with non-U.S. NATO pilots. Drawing on his own knowledge and the help of a strong panel of experts, he tried to bring some technical sanity to the ballistic missile defense research and development program, which even then—40 years ago—was growing out of control.

Then there was the overall defense budget on which we worked with the Bureau of the Budget to help eliminate or phase down technically unsound and militarily unnecessary programs. In this connection, one day in the fall of 1963, Jerry and I—together with McGeorge Bundy and Carl Kaysen—attended a meeting with Secretary Robert McNamara, Deputy Secretary Roswell Gilpatric, and a few of their senior staff at which the director of the Bureau of the Budget and a few of his senior staff reviewed major controversial issues in the fiscal 1964 defense budget which would be presented to the president for decision. We were in the midst of a heated discussion on some controversial issue when a military aide entered the room and whispered something to McNamara, who excused himself. Gilpatric took over the chair and the debate continued vigorously until Adam Yarmolinsky, McNamara's aide, entered the room and whispered something to Gilpatric, who left after asking Charlie Hitch, Defense Comptroller, to take over. Before the meeting could really resume, Gilpatric looked through the door and said to Bundy, "Mac, I think you should join us." There was then a dead silence that seemed to go on forever until the door opened again and Gilpatric said, "Gentlemen, we have just learned from Dallas that the president has been shot and is on the way to a hospital."

We were all in a state of shock, but driving back to the White House with Jerry I realized how deeply and personally he felt the loss. And with Kennedy's death he entered a period of depression, which as his friends know could be very deep, and decided to resign his post of presidential science adviser as soon as a suitable successor could be found.

As part of his transition from the heady world of the White House, Jerry decided to accept a long-standing official invitation to visit the Soviet Union and bring with him and Laya any friends he wished. I am sure his hosts expected him to include some illustrious member of the U.S. scientific community in his party. But Jerry never felt constrained to do the obvious. When he asked if Sheila and I would join him and Laya on the trip, my immediate response was that I would be delighted to go but that my wife could hardly accompany me because our third child had been born just a short time before. Jerry insisted, however, that I ask her, and I was surprised when she said of course she would go, and was on the phone with her mother making arrangements before I could reason with her. Jerry was not surprised.

Aside from relaxed tourism, Jerry decided it would be interesting to have a project in mind to give a little nonconfrontational focus to our activities. The status of Soviet work in cybernetics appeared to be an ideal topic on which Jerry had special insights. At the time, certain individuals in the CIA were advancing the remarkable theory that the Soviet Union was making gigantic strides in cybernetics and that in a relatively short time they would have automated their entire industrial complex with the objective of freeing up an immense pool of manpower with which it could ultimately control the world. The notion that there was not only an emerging "cybernetics gap," but that it presented a serious threat to the West, had resonance among at least some of the deep thinkers in Washington. While Jerry considered this notion ridiculous in the extreme, he thought it deserved some preemptive investigation since few people in Washington had any idea what "cybernetics" meant but could easily be persuaded that it sounded like an ominous clear and present danger.

On arriving in Moscow, Jerry made a point of paying his respects to the U.S. ambassador. We found the embassy in utter turmoil. It had recently been discovered that the entire building was bugged. The Soviets had found a very low-tech method of reading very high-tech cryptographic systems by acoustically recording the distinctive sounds of keys in the machine used to encrypt and deencrypt messages. The U.S. had facilitated the operation by placing the cryptographic machines in front of the unsightly radiators, which were built into the walls and provided effective shielding for microphones. The U.S. officials responsible for tearing the radiators out of the walls and digging wires out of spaces between the brick walls and outside stucco were not in a very charitable mood and had no knowledge or interest in Soviet cybernetic developments. Although Jerry had some interesting observations on some of the more esoteric aspects of the disaster, the topic of conversation was basically how to conduct business in the future from inside plastic "bubbles."

When we met to discuss the itinerary with our extremely cordial designated host, Dr. Jermen Gvishiani, deputy minister of the Soviet State Committee on Science and Technology, he suggested that in addition to Leningrad and Kiev we might like to see Novosibirsk, which was then still off the beaten track, or perhaps Tblisi, his hometown. To my surprise, Jerry chose Tblisi perhaps realizing it would involve fewer bureaucratic frustrations as well as much better weather. We then were given an extended briefing on the organization of Soviet nonmilitary research and development, a universally accepted bureaucratic device to fill up time and avoid substance. Gvishiani illustrated his lecture by sketching out an organizational chart that resembled a two-dimensional plate of spaghetti. When Jerry asked how decisions were made on assigning priorities to different areas, Gvishiani drew a small box totally disconnected from the tangle of lines and arrows and explained that such "policy matters" were decided by the Minister and himself in consultation with a few senior aides. Jerry then broached our interest in seeing some application of cybernetics in the industrial process. Gvishiani promised that arrangements could be made to accomplish that even in Tblisi, and that he himself was interested in the subject. In fact, he reported that he had recently written a book on cybernetics and management, although he confided it was really a rehash of material produced at MIT and that he had added "cybernetics" to the title to increase interest in the book.

Gvishiani was obviously delighted that he could show us his beautiful homeland, and he and his lovely wife, who turned out to be the daughter of Soviet Prime Minister Kosygin, did everything possible to make our trip enjoyable. When we arrived in Tblisi, arrangements had been made for us to visit an institute that was allegedly doing advanced work in cybernetics. We arrived at mid-morning and were greeted by the director, an elegant elderly gentleman who gave the appearance of being a holdover from a different era. After the usual organizational briefing, the director introduced a mechanical robot that ran around the room periodically sticking its tail into an electric socket to recharge itself. Jerry could not hide his boredom with this piece of undergraduate gadgetry and asked what else they had to show. The director replied, "We are not doing anything here that would possibly be of any interest to you." Then he went on to say that in honor of Jerry's visit they had arranged a modest reception, and opened the door on an adjoining room with a banquet table piled high with fruit and pastries and ample supplies of fine Georgian champagne and wines (we learned the vintages and numbers that Stalin preferred). The party was soon joined by a number of extremely attractive young ladies who sang lovely folk songs. Jerry had a great time, and we never asked whether the director had been informed about Jerry's long-time interest in folk music.

We arrived back at our luxury suites at the old Grand Hotel only to find that all of the fixtures had been removed from all of the bathrooms. Wringing his hands, the manager apologized saying, "I told them not to do it, but they did it anyway since it was called for in the five-year plan." That evening, Jerry's birthday was celebrated at a lavish party in a beautiful restaurant overlooking Tblisi. The party was attended by a large number of local officials, who I doubt had any idea who Jerry was but clearly did appreciate the opportunity for an open bar. Overhearing excellent singing coming from a nearby room, Jerry suggested that the seemingly endless series of incomprehensible toasts by strangers be interrupted to invite the unknown singers to join the party. The music turned out to be a quartet of mustachioed streetcar conductors with accompanying musicians and dancers who were attending a streetcar conductors' convention. After a long evening, we managed with some difficulty to recover sufficiently by the following morning to inspect a champagne bottling plant, which was the most efficient enterprise we saw in the Soviet Union. After amply sampling the product, we abandoned further efforts in our cybernetics quest in Georgia.

When we arrived in Leningrad, at Jerry's request one of our first stops was a visit to a radio astronomy installation that he knew was located somewhere in the neighborhood. Jerry thought it might give us some insight into the sophistication of Soviet instrumentation. The installation turned out to be an apparently ancient one-story building designed more as protection against the cold than as a home for modern research. We were greeted by a truly venerable director, who quickly showed us his radiotelescope that appeared to my inexperienced eye to be in desperate need of repair or at least a coat of paint. We then retreated to his office, where we were invited to sign a golden book of distinguished visitors dating back to the eighteenth century.

As the director rambled on about the long history of the observatory and Jerry asked some polite questions about present activities, I became increasingly troubled about the curious nature of the establishment. Finally, I asked how the installation had managed to survive the siege of Leningrad. The director, who seemed a little surprised at my question, responded that the laboratory actually marked the siege-line at that point and then produced some photographs that were reminiscent of pictures of Verdun during World War I—a maze of overlapping bomb and shell craters with absolutely nothing left standing. He remarked that they had been fortunate to find blueprints of the original building and had rebuilt it exactly as it had been before the war. The thought of taking advantage of the devastation to build a modern facility had apparently never been considered.

Then, on about the last day of our trip, we received word that special permission had been granted for us to visit a modern industrial plant exhibiting cybernetic innovation. Jerry was overjoyed that his persistence had finally paid off. We were taken on a long drive through parts of Leningrad dominated by dilapidated brick industrial buildings, evidencing little activity, to our promised destination, a similarly unimpressive structure that seemed more of a warehouse than an industrial enterprise. Our numerous hosts then escorted us through what appeared to be a back door up a dingy stairwell to a large room the size of a basketball court. The room was dominated by four moving belts, with rows of women seated on each side frantically assembling what appeared to be Leica-type cameras. The women, who were of all ages, were dressed in white smocks and caps and appeared somewhat traumatized. They took little notice of the distinguished visitors, since the production lines kept moving steadily along. At the end of the hall on a raised platform, a rather unkempt loutish young man lounged on a chair in front of a small console. At first glance he seemed strangely out of place, but his function quickly became apparent. As a camera came to the end of each of the moving belts, he pressed a button that registered a new total for the number of cameras credited to that production line. We never learned whether the winners of the continuing competition were given Stakhanovite awards or the losers were penalized.

Jerry's first reaction was to look on the unexpected scene in stunned amazement, but his expression soon relaxed into a wry smile. He thanked our hosts for their hospitality and fled the depressing spectacle as rapidly as propriety permitted.

With this adventure, Jerry's quest to discover the alleged Soviet cybernetic superiority was over. He could not, of course, disprove the existence of a parallel

Farewell to the White House—with Lyndon B. Johnson shortly before Jerry's departure as the president's special assistant for science and technology, January 1964. (Courtesy of the MIT Museum.)

universe in which the Soviet military-industrial complex might be successfully harnessing cybernetic concepts. He could, however, rest very confidently in his conviction as to the utter nonsense of the bizarre proposition that Soviet cybernetic superiority would allow it to subjugate and control the world.

With lots of wine and folk songs, Jerry's quest did not, of course, prevent him from having a good time along the way, and from making many new friends, all of whom would have been convulsed with laughter had they known why we were interested in the state of cybernetics in the Soviet Union.

A Passion for the Arts

Catherine N. Stratton

Jerry Wiesner had a passion for the arts, and among these, music occupied a special place. He delighted in it. His love of music and special professional combination of inventive engineer and skilled acoustician eventually led to "total immersion" in the summer of 1940 when he, a freshly minted college graduate, and Alan Lomax traveled to this country's South to record its music and folklore for the Library of Congress. There was music in Jerry's home, his office, and his boat. Music was his constant companion. His secretary Jarmila Hrbek recalls that in the early 1970s Jerry, as MIT's president, never wanting to waste a moment, would dictate from his sailboat. "Please turn Beethoven down," she would plead, "I lost that last word."

I first met Jerry sixty years ago. At the outbreak of World War II, he joined MIT's nascent Radiation Lab, and my husband Jay Stratton and I had the pleasure of sharing our Christmas dinner with the delightful young Wiesners—Jerry, his wife Laya, and infant son Stephen—in 1942. It was the beginning of a long and close friendship.

Jerry's brilliant success as an engineer and scientist in the war effort led to his appointment to the MIT faculty and steady rise in rank. His first tangible opportunity to have an impact on the arts and humanities at MIT may have come when he and my husband were both appointed to the Warren Lewis Commission in 1947.

Catherine N. (Kay) Stratton, civic leader, arts patron, and "first lady" of MIT (1959–66), is the widow of MIT president Julius A. (Jay) Stratton. She has been active in promoting the arts at MIT, playing a key role in the early Arts Committee, which she cofounded in 1960, and in helping to establish MIT's Council for the Arts in 1971. She has also devoted considerable energy to women's issues, serving in leadership positions on YWCA national committees, on the board of Lesley College, and with the MIT Women's League. She inaugurated the Annual Aging Successfully Series at MIT in 1988, and in 1994 a lecture series—the Catherine N. Stratton Lecture on Critical Issues—was established in her honor by the MIT Women's League.

Norbert Wiener, Kay Stratton, and Jerry at a dinner meeting, ca. 1960. (Courtesy of the MIT Museum.)

This group was charged with examining the Institute's educational environment, and its recommendations in 1949 led to a sweeping overhaul of the status of the humanities and social sciences at MIT and to the establishment of what is now the School of Humanities, Arts, and Social Sciences.

Jerry became dean of science in 1964, and two years later, President Howard Johnson, another keen supporter of the arts, appointed him provost. As chief academic officer, Jerry had more opportunity to influence all of the five schools that comprised MIT at the time. His enormous energy, concentration, and wide range of contacts went partly into broadening and building "teaching and research in the humanities and the arts," in order, he said, to balance the analytic curriculum concentration in science and technology.

And building blocks in the arts there were indeed! The Art Committee, founded in 1960 by my husband Jay when he was MIT president, rapidly evolved into the

Art Collection Committee, with the acquisition of contemporary sculpture as its goal. A charter member was Ida Ely Rubin, art historian, conservator, and consultant. Through Ida's friendships, persuasiveness, and the generosity of a number of people, the sculpture collection saw the addition of works by some of the twentieth century's most significant sculptors. Jay also initiated the "2% for Art" program—that is, 2% of the cost of any new building should be allotted for the arts (since reduced to 1%, with a cap of $250,000). Both Jerry, as provost, and his associate provost, Walter Rosenblith, later continued their support for this program. There was also a faculty committee on the visual arts—under the chairmanship of art historian Wayne Andersen—that was active in directing the Institute's art programs. Ida recalls Jerry's enthusiasm for the art forms springing up around the campus:

The Art Committee made its first acquisition in 1963 with the sculpture entitled "Elmo" by Dimitri Hadzi, given by Samuel Marx. The same year a sculpture by Henry Moore was donated by Eugene and Margaret McDermott. In 1966 the McDermotts made an even more memorable gift, a monumental sculpture by Alexander Calder, "The Great Sail," that rose in the plaza in front of I. M. Pei's Earth Sciences building, a gift of Cecil and Ida Green. As the five soaring black forms took their places, Jerry Wiesner and crowds of faculty and students watched the superb demonstration of esthetic engineering that was to become an MIT landmark and icon.

When Howard Johnson became MIT president in 1966, he continued the beautification of the campus and the outdoor sculpture project. Among other developments was the establishment in 1967 of the Center for Advanced Visual Studies by Gyorgy Kepes—MIT professor, painter, and designer—who served as director until 1972. The center was interested in affecting the shape and vision of the environment, and it sponsored a broad range of sculptural and design activities. Later, initiatives by Walter Rosenblith, Angus MacDonald, and Margaret McDermott led to the establishment of the Kepes Prize that annually recognizes individuals who reflect Kepes's "vision and values."

So when Jerry became president in 1971, he was in a position to carry on a rich tradition with his usual gusto. Jerry saw the Art Committee as a good foundation for a larger dream. In a year of work with all of the MIT constituencies (administration, faculty, and alumni), his dream became a reality. The Council for the Arts was launched in November 1971, with a splendid reception at the Metropolitan Museum in New York. Jerry introduced Paul Tishman as chair and Roy Lamson as faculty liaison. As chair of the acquisitions committee, Ida continued to aid in getting donations of very important pieces by Jacques Lipchitz and others. Three Lipchitz sculptures were given for the music library courtyard by his wife, Yulla Lipchitz.

Jerry, Juliet Kepes, Gyorgy Kepes, and Angus MacDonald at the establishment of the Gyorgy Kepes Fellowship Prize by the MIT Council for the Arts in 1982. The Kepes Prize is awarded annually to individuals at the Institute whose creative work reflects the vision and values of Gyorgy Kepes, particularly the relationship between art and science, and art and the physical environment. (Courtesy of the MIT Museum.)

Jerry was ecstatic. "I believe even more strongly than I did at the Council's outset," he later wrote to Ida, "that its positive effects on education at MIT are of the greatest importance."

At the first meeting of the council in October 1972, Jerry set forth goals in a rousing speech: "Our basic goal," he said, "is to enhance the richness of the educational opportunities for MIT students, complementing the outstanding offerings in science and technology with the equally distinguished and exciting activities in the creative arts." He went on to outline in detail new fields for humanities and social studies, and informed his audience of the establishment of a Corporation visiting committee for the arts, with former president Jim Killian as chair. This was the first time a visiting committee had been created with such a broad charter.

The formation of the council was a huge step forward in integrating the creative arts with science and technology, and we all went home from the first meeting in heady anticipation of further developments. The council would go on to highlight the diverse and scattered existing offerings in the Departments of Humanities and of Architecture, and in shared offerings in the Departments of Metallurgy and Materials Sciences. And it would become actively involved in the emergence of the new fields for humanities and social studies that Jerry envisioned.

Developments came fast and furious during the first year. An executive committee was appointed, the council's goals were outlined, an executive director was hired, and working committees were appointed. We were off and running! Distinguished members joined enthusiastically. Among the first were Archibald MacLeish, Luis Ferré, I. M. Pei, Harold Edgerton, and Stanley Kunitz, whose statement "there are many disciplines but only one imagination" became a council mantra.

The second annual meeting foreshadowed another leap forward. The Grants Committee's first grant showcased the MIT student orchestra on a national tour, which drew great acclaim. After that triumph, on Jerry's request, an advisory commission was named to study the possibility of constructing a new building to meet the scientific and technological needs of the arts—in essence, an arts and media building. This would establish the interface between the creative arts and technology that Jerry so clearly envisioned and went on to pioneer.

The arts and media building became a reality, in part, through major donations by Vera and Albert List and the National Endowment for the Arts. Designed by architect I. M. Pei, in collaboration with Ken Noland and Richard Fleishner for decorative enhancement and plaza design, the building was named in honor of Jerry and his wife Laya and finally dedicated in 1985. The atrium held the List galleries, which became a model in Boston for the best, the newest, and often the most controversial in contemporary art. Kathy Halbreich, former director of the List Gallery, recalls Jerry's ongoing presence:

My memories of Jerry start with the fragrance of pipe tobacco that preceded him. I always was startled by his unannounced appearance in my office; it was as if this extremely busy world leader had nothing in the world to do and was simply walking the halls, looking for a place to stop for a few moments. I've come to realize these seemingly impromptu visits were probably quite considered; he had a keen sense of how to make all of us feel important enough to continue burning the midnight oil for the institutional good. . . .

Jerry knew how his own love of music, art, and architecture made him both a more sensitive person and evocative thinker, one who critically assessed the social implications of innovations while marveling at the intellectual leaps which made them possible. . . .

There were times when MIT's needs didn't dovetail perfectly with my own professional standards. For example, I remember Jerry and I had a terrific argument about a monumental, outdoor sculpture that was being offered as a gift by a particularly successful graduate. It was an atrocious work that I knew would require more than I was capable of to convince the students to accept as a new element in their environment. Jerry tested and tortured me until I finally whimpered, "But didn't you hire me to make these sorts of decisions?" He

"The fragrance of pipe tobacco . . . preceded him" (Kathy Halbreich). (Photo by Yousuf Karsh. © Karsh, Ottawa.)

immediately stopped interrogating me, took a deep draw on his pipe, and smiled his crooked smile, seemingly proud that we had parsed the possibilities and happy to allow me the final decision. Jerry was like that: quizzical, demanding, ethical, and, finally, respectful. I adored the guy.

With Jerry's support, Kathy helped continue the tradition of the Art Lottery as part of the List Gallery's projects. Originating in 1966, the Art Lottery is unique to MIT. For thirty days, 350–400 contemporary works are displayed on the gallery walls. Students wander through the gallery marking cards with their first three choices. On the final day, cards are drawn at random and smiling winners walk away with their prizes—works of art to keep in their rooms for the academic year.

As a break from his international responsibilities, presidential job pressures, and even town government concerns, Jerry would spend time away with his family at their place on Martha's Vineyard. Here, he and Laya held open house for their friends and neighbors. And it was an intriguing collection of intellectually challenging artists to work and play with. Among them were Lillian Hellman, Beverly Sills, and Leonard Bernstein. Then there was summer theatre, sailing the "Beetlebung," jazz concerts, and clam bakes. Life was good!

Besides music, Jerry had another obsession: the newest gadgets—electronic, computerized, or digital—particularly those with a communications focus. He was always among the first to try them out. Cheryl Morse, his last secretary, lifted the phone one day to hear Jerry say, "I'm trying out this cell phone, Cheryl, sing to me." "French, German or Italian," she asked. "French!" So Cheryl trilled a phrase from *Carmen*, and to her embarrassment loud applause erupted from a carload of testers.

It was always a delight to have a reason to visit Jerry in his corner office. On one wall was a large Calder tapestry. Another was filled with photographs: JFK and Jerry, Jerry with his colleagues from Science, Defense, Arms Control, the National Academy, smiling, earnest, or grave. And on his desk an amazing collection of maquettes and a small wire mobile from John Kennedy. Jerry was intrigued with Picasso and once told an interviewer, "I negotiated with him for a number of years to do a piece for us, but he never did. He was into his erotic drawing period, and he couldn't get his mind off that work." Eventually Carl Nesjar, who worked with Picasso, created a piece which stands at the entrance to the Hermann Plaza of the Sloan School.

The Wiesners gave wonderful parties in their big white house in Watertown. Guests overflowed, band music played, guests danced, talked art, ate sizzling hot shrimp, and toasted their genial hosts with chilled wine. At home, Jerry and Laya

"My father loved art [and] was particularly fond of sculpture" (Zachary Wiesner). (Courtesy of the MIT Museum.)

took particular pleasure in their eclectic art collection. I asked their son Zack about those early days, which he recalls this way:

My father loved art, and he and my mother filled their house with paintings and sculpture. Dad was particularly fond of sculpture. There were at least a half dozen Eskimo carvings at the house, including a whale vertebra with two beautiful faces, one on each side, like an Arctic Janus. When Dad retired as president of MIT, the faculty gave him and Mom a black steatite Eskimo carving of two owls back-to-back. They kept it in the front hall of their house, and it always reminded me of them, an inseparable pair.

The faculty gift reflected Dad's commitment to increasing the presence of art at MIT. I believe that the Calder stabile, Lipchitz Sculpture Garden, and one if not two Henry Moore's came to MIT in no small part due to Dad's efforts. He made several visits to Moore's studio and told me at length of how impressed he was with Moore's creative process. Moore started with small maquettes and iteratively increased the size and form of his pieces, reworking, refining, and enlarging. The final form was executed in large styrofoam blocks which could then be cast in bronze.

My own interest in sculpture started the summer I was nine, when I went to Europe with Mom and Dad and my older brother. I remember the stonework and stone sculpture perfectly. Dad and I went by ourselves to Greece and I was very excited about the chance to see the Parthenon as well as other temples and sculpture. When we got to our hotel in Athens, Dad had a message waiting for him at the hotel. A man he had met through MIT had invited us to spend the weekend on his yacht. I would have been the only child there, and Dad knew how much I was looking forward to a trip to Mykonos and Delos we had planned, so he turned down the invitation. He found out after the weekend that Ingrid Bergman, his favorite movie star, had been on the yacht for the weekend. This became a favorite "family story" of my mother's, and it makes me smile when I think of it and Dad's support for the arts.

Zack's younger brother Josh added his recollection of art in the family's Watertown home:

[My parents] were quite modest art purchasers. By the end of their lives they had several works by well-known artists, but all of them were moderately valued and had been originally purchased when they were inexpensive. They had two Picasso ceramic vases, one of which my father bought for a hundred dollars in the early 1970s. Hard to believe, but that's what they cost then. They kept it on their dining room table. They had a Miró and a Chagall lithograph in their living room. I now own the Chagall and my sister has the Miró. They are both nice but unexceptional.

The other well-known artist whose work they had was Escher. I think they must have bought the two prints they had in the 1950s and I'm sure they cost very little then. One of them is the classic ducks and fish wood print and the other is a mobius strip with mounted soldiers going around it. They are very cool. I think they probably reflect my father's technical/scientific side.

Two other things come to mind. One is that they were both very fond of Eskimo art and had a number of carved pieces around the house. They continued buying those through the years. The other is that my father and I got interested in a Martha's Vineyard wire/metal sculptor in the 1960s and he bought several of these small, sort of humorous pieces, which he had in his home office. As much as any other art he owned, these simple, amusing wire characters, seem characteristic of his taste.

Jerry helped bring art to life in his home and at work. He expanded, in both depth and breadth, the role of the arts, humanities, and social sciences at MIT, partly through his own exploration of the relationship between the arts and computer technology. He brought MIT a long way. He established a culture that changed the Institute's vision, as well as people's vision of the Institute.

Peace Became His Profession

Carl Kaysen

When I call the image of Jerry to mind, I think of the always energetic, always active man, busily improving the world about him. Near the center of his agenda for much of the time I knew and worked with him were the tremendous questions of war and peace in a world of possible nuclear war. Like many scientists and engineers of his generation, he had first helped to create that world, then devoted himself to seeing that the possibility never turned into a reality.

I first encountered Jerry in the summer of 1950, in the context of Project Charles. This was an early example of what became a typical MIT activity—government-sponsored summer studies to explore the feasibility or possibilities of finding a new technology for dealing with an urgent problem. In the particular case, the problem was the defense of the United States against what was seen as the rapidly increasing threat of a nuclear attack by the Soviet bomber force. The leaders of the study were mostly veterans of the MIT Radiation Lab's experience of World War II: in addition to Jerry Wiesner, there were Al Hill, Jerrold Zacharias, Frank Wheeler Loomis, and George Valley, among others. My own part was small, and of no consequence. Paul Samuelson had recruited Jim Tobin and me to analyze what could be done to reduce the vulnerability of the U.S. economy to air attacks with nuclear weapons and to measure the economy's capacity for recovery after an attack.

Carl Kaysen, economist and educator, began his career as a researcher for the U.S. National Bureau of Economic Research (1940–42). After serving in the Army during World War II, he became a faculty member at Harvard University (1946–66), associate dean of Harvard's Graduate School of Public Administration (1960–66), and director of the Institute for Advanced Study at Princeton (1966–77). During the Kennedy administration, he served as deputy special assistant for national security affairs (1961–63). He joined the MIT faculty as David W. Skinner Professor of Political Economy in 1977, retiring in 1990. He was director of MIT's Program in Science, Technology, and Society (1981–87). A fellow of the American Academy of Arts and Sciences and the American Philosophical Society, he has held numerous prestigious lectureships at universities both here and abroad.

The center of the study was an examination of how to build an effective air defense. Its first result was the creation of Lincoln Laboratory as an MIT-managed government-funded research and development center, initially focused on air defense. Soon it led to the creation of a number of defense systems: 1) the Distant Early Warning (DEW) chain of radars in northern Canada; 2) the Semi-Automatic Ground Environment (SAGE) system of communications facilities and computers that linked the radars, and processed and integrated the signals they received; and 3) the North American Air Defense Command (NORAD), the joint U.S.-Canadian headquarters to manage the system and direct the defense aircraft and missiles. The creation of SAGE involved many important innovations in computing with wide applicability in the civil as well as the military world.

All this was characteristic of the first phase of Jerry's engagement with the nuclear dilemma. The weapon-building phase had started with his participation in the Radiation Lab during World War II, and included work on nuclear testing in 1945–46.

The second, longer-lasting phase of Jerry's engagement with the fateful issues of war and peace—that of directly promoting peace through arms control, disarmament, and political negotiation—was evident in our next encounter. This was in 1959–60, when we were both participants in an informal MIT-Harvard faculty seminar on arms control, organized by Tom Schelling. The seminar's deliberations were crystallized in a special issue of the journal *Daedalus* (Fall 1960) on "arms control," which put these issues before a broader academic public.

In February 1961, Jerry went to Washington as Special Assistant for Science and Technology to the new president, and thus chairman of the President's Science Advisory Committee (PSAC), of which he had been a member for some time. In the Cold War atmosphere of the time, questions of nuclear weapons testing, of weapons research and development, especially of delivery means for nuclear weapons, and of how and how well we understood Soviet actions in these arenas formed a major part of Jerry's agenda and that of the committee. I joined the administration in the late spring of 1961 as a senior member of the national security staff in the White House (that fall I became the deputy special assistant for national security affairs) and worked closely with Jerry on many of these issues. Jerry's weight was on the side of caution and restraint in all of them. Ever mindful of the awful consequences of nuclear war, ever attentive to the shared interest of the United States and the USSR in avoiding it, he scrutinized every proposal and possible action in the light of these concerns. Let me mention four instances in which I participated with him in seeking the more peaceful path—two successfully, two not.

In the public eye—Jerry captured, in a candid AP snapshot, disembarking at Idlewild Airport, New York, on a flight from Boston, January 11, 1961, the day his appointment as President Kennedy's special assistant for science and technology was announced. (Courtesy of the *Boston Herald.*)

First was civil defense. My first task for the White House, on which I had begun to work even before I came to Washington, was to frame the administration's civil defense program. President Kennedy, responding to criticism from Republicans, especially Governor Nelson Rockefeller of New York, pressure from the Pentagon, and his own deeply felt concern for his duty to do what he could to lessen the impact of war on the American people (since he felt that he could not rule out its possibility), decided he had to do something about civil defense. My assignment was to draft a program that was technically feasible, not provocative in the sense of appearing to the Soviets as preparation for initiating war, not requiring spending on a grandiose scale, and promising useful results on a relatively short time scale—two to three years, not five to ten. I worked closely with Jerry and two members of his staff, Spurgeon Keeny, Jr., and Vincent McRae, on the project. Jerry's role was that of skeptical critic, pointing out how little effect on saving lives anything we were likely to be able to do would have. Any program promising a substantial result would have violated the constraints the president had set. In the event, the unenthusiastic Congressional response to the ultimate proposal of creating fallout shelters in the basements of existing public buildings, and equipping them with radiation detectors and stocks of food and water, led to a very modest program indeed.

From September through Thanksgiving 1961, Jerry and I worked together to slow the pace of the buildup of U.S. missiles targeted on the Soviet bloc. Our aim was to cut the following year's budget request for building new solid-fueled missiles, land-based Minutemen and submarine-launched Polaris, by nearly half. We rearranged the recent intelligence data that showed the non-existence of a missile gap, questioned the damage criteria which military planners had set up for allocating warheads to targets, and urged the consideration of probable Soviet response to our programs—all in an effort to show that the smaller program was ample. We failed totally. The secretary of defense convinced the president that his original proposal was the minimum politically acceptable in light of the president's campaign criticism of his predecessor and pressures from the military services.

My third example was an equally clean-cut success, one that was particularly Jerry's own: the installation of permissive action links (PALs) on nuclear weapons. Jerry had long been concerned about the possibility of an unauthorized or accidental launch of a nuclear weapon. It was particularly troubling in the case of the "alert" weapons in Europe, nuclear bombs carried by Allied as well as American aircraft sitting on runways in Germany, Holland, and Greece, ready to take off immediately in response to a Warsaw Pact attack. The planes of our NATO allies were nominally guarded by U.S. airmen who were in practice unable to exercise any useful control. Jerry pushed hard against NATO and Air Force resistance to introducing effective controls on these weapons. To overcome arguments that such were possible only by negating the capacity to launch these weapons in a timely way, Jerry in effect designed electronic locks that could be unlocked only on receipt of an appropriate coded radio message, and showed that they could easily be procured and installed. In time, PALs were incorporated into most of our nuclear weapons.

The final example of Jerry's abiding concern for reining in nuclear weapons involved their testing. Here again I was directly involved, and the result of our efforts was the Limited Test Ban Treaty of 1963, ending tests in the atmosphere, under water, and in outer space. Beginning in the summer of 1961, there was a year-long argument about the military need for the U.S. to resume testing. The Soviet Union in our view had broken the moratorium on testing, on which Eisenhower and Khrushchev had agreed; on their own it was the French, members of NATO, who had broken it and thus justified their own resumption of testing. Jerry saw no military need and pushed hard for negotiating a treaty outlawing all testing. The ensuing discussion lasted more than two years, during which we did resume testing. The discussion involved complicated technical questions about the possibility of monitoring compliance with such a treaty and the relative advantages of continued testing to the U.S. and the USSR. Again the military services, particularly the Air Force and the weapons laboratories, strongly resisted any treaty, putting up a barrage of arguments that Jerry and the PSAC had to shoot down one by one.

After both of us had left Washington, I again found myself in alliance with Jerry in the interests of peace, this time in Vietnam. Toward the end of 1965, Secretary of Defense Robert McNamara had begun to doubt that the U.S. could win the war in Vietnam, and to believe that only negotiation provided a way out. Jerry Wiesner, George Kistiakowsky, his predecessor as the President's Science Adviser at the end of the Eisenhower administration, and I were among many in Cambridge who had, either earlier or more recently, come to that view. We also assumed, as did McNamara, that stopping the bombing of North Vietnam was a sufficient condition for productive negotiation. In retrospect, that was a false assumption. At the time, in late 1965 and early 1966, Jerry, George Kistiakowsky, and I persuaded McNamara to support a summer study in Cambridge with the purpose of finding more effective ways than bombing to slow or stop the infiltration of men and materiel from North to South Vietnam. The study took place the following summer, resulting in a design for an "electronic fence" also known as the "McNamara line." But the idea was never properly implemented, and had negligible effect on the course of either the war or diplomacy in Indochina.

In the following decade, when Jerry became successively dean of science, provost, and president of MIT, and I was in Princeton, I saw him or talked to him only infrequently. A few times it was about recruiting matters. The physicists at both the Institute for Advanced Study and MIT were trying to lure Murray Gell-Mann from Caltech, as was Harvard. I remember Jerry's predicting correctly that none of us would succeed, and saying that Murray "enjoyed practicing job-hunting interruptus." We saw each other at an occasional Pugwash meeting and once or twice on the Vineyard.

In 1976, when I left the Institute for Advanced Study at Princeton, Jerry, through Bob Solow, offered me a professorship at MIT in the School of Humanities and

The Corporation of the
Massachusetts Institute of Technology
has the honor to present

JEROME B. WIESNER

the following resolution
on his retirement as
Thirteenth President of the Institute

RESOLVED:

That the Corporation of the Massachusetts Institute of Technology unanimously acclaims with deep appreciation the superb leadership of Jerome Bert Wiesner as Thirteenth President of the Institute, and records MIT's lasting debt to him, as he concludes his term as President.

His association with MIT began thirty-eight years ago, when he entered as a staff member of the Radiation Laboratory. From the beginning he brought rare qualities of scientific insight, analytical style, and presence which have left their mark on the Institute.

As Professor, Director of the Research Laboratory of Electronics, Head of the Department of Electrical Engineering, Dean of the School of Science, Provost, and President, he has cultivated and helped to fulfill MIT's highest aspirations. By his gift of lucid exposition he has made clear complex problems and policies and conveyed the objects, aims and spirit of MIT to a wider audience. This quality manifested itself fully in his role as Science Advisor to Presidents Kennedy and Johnson and in his national advocacy of research universities in their relations with government. His catholicity of mind has given him the qualities of a humanist as well as those of an engineer and scientist, those of administrator as well as those of a scholar. His perceptive concern for the individual, especially the individual student and junior colleagues, has prompted warm appreciation as shown by the numerous student and faculty tributes. The establishment of an endowed Professorship named in his honor bears testimony to the regard of his fellows as teacher and scholar.

His administrative career at MIT has been a period marked by innovation in teaching and undergraduate research with more choices open to the student, with a more flexible curriculum, deepened by science and broadened by augmented resources in the health sciences and technology, energy research, arts, and humanities. His administration has been a period when the bonds of our corporate fellowship have been tightened and a shared sense of purpose enhanced. It has been a period of great building, both physically and intellectually, with wider opportunities for women and minorities. The Institute has grown bigger, but more importantly it has grown better.

In all this, Dr. Wiesner has played a central and inspiring role. So, too, has Mrs. Wiesner, and we honor both as a team which is greater than the sum of the parts. Her zealous contribution to the expansion of professional opportunities for women in science and technology is a matter of record.

In recording these achievements we also honor those qualities of his which no formal curriculum vitae can capture—his gift for leadership, his dedication to the successful completion of an unprecedented capital campaign, his good judgment, his sensitive, warmly understanding relations with his colleagues, and his demonstration that one man, and his spouse, can indeed make a difference.

BE IT FURTHER RESOLVED:

That the Corporation express its very great satisfaction that Jerome Bert Wiesner will continue his association with the Corporation as a Life Member, and that it express the hope and anticipation that he will find the next chapter of his career as Institute Professor also happy and rewarding.

AND BE IT FURTHER RESOLVED:

That these resolutions be spread upon the permanent records of the Corporation and that a copy be sent to President and Mrs. Wiesner.

Howard W. Johnson
Chairman

Vincent A. Fulmer
Secretary

Adopted at the meeting of the Corporation of the Massachusetts Institute of Technology on June the second, nineteen hundred and eighty, and presented to Jerome B. Wiesner on the same day.

Social Science. I accepted and joined the Program in Science, Technology, and Society (STS), then newly created on the initiative of Jerry and Walter Rosenblith. Later I became its second director, and especially after Jerry's retirement from the presidency in 1980, I saw and talked with him regularly. Worrying about nuclear weapons, the possibility of nuclear war, and finding cooperative paths in international relations that would eliminate the possibility remained at the center of his concerns. In one form or another, they occupied many of our conversations, although his interests in the problems of the "third world" had risen in salience. I fear he was in the end a bit disappointed in his creation: STS had become too much an academic program in the history and sociology of science, too little the forum for bringing many minds from many disciplines to bear on the world's problems.

To sum up my reflections on nearly half a century of interaction with Jerry: he was imaginative, broad in his interests, generous in dealing with the ideas and views of people he worked with, extremely energetic, at once persistent in the way he pushed for what he thought should be done and impatient to see it done, ready to think and act unconventionally—a direct and personally simple person with no "front." He wanted to use his intellectual talents to change the world for the better, and he did.

Excellence in Action

Paul E. Gray

Jerry and I first met in 1964, after he had returned to MIT from his years as science adviser to President Kennedy. It was at the Faculty Club, where he was giving a talk about his experiences in Washington. I was struck by his observation that "In Washington, one learns that the Congress really is representative of the people." That comment said a great deal about Jerry—that he cared as much about the people as he did about the science. In many ways, I think he was the embodiment of science in service to society, and this outlook informed his influence on MIT in countless ways.

Our paths crossed again as we both moved into academic administration. In 1965, I—a young member of the electrical engineering faculty—began to serve part-time as associate dean for student affairs, with responsibility for the Freshman Advisory Council and for implementation of the new Institute Requirements that had grown out of Jerrold Zacharias's Committee on Curriculum Content Planning. In 1966, Jerry became provost, and the next year asked me to move to the provost's office as assistant provost, still with a primary responsibility as a faculty member in electrical engineering, but with responsibility to Jerry for oversight and improvement of the core undergraduate programs of the Institute.

At about this time, a close friend of Jerry's, Edwin H. Land, founder and chief executive of the Polaroid Corporation, made a substantial gift to MIT, with the

Paul E. Gray, educator and university administrator, has spent over half a century at MIT, where he earned his bachelor's (1954), master's (1955), and doctoral (1960) degrees. He joined the MIT faculty in 1960, became professor of electrical engineering in 1967, and served successively as dean of the School of Engineering (1970–71), chancellor (1971–80), president (1980–90), and chair of the MIT Corporation (1990–97). He returned to the faculty as professor of electrical engineering in 1997. Among his numerous board memberships, he served as a trustee of Wheaton College (1971–97) and as board chairman for more than a decade. He is a fellow of the Institute of Electrical & Electronics Engineers, among other professional organizations, and is a member of the National Academy of Engineering and a fellow of the American Academy of Arts and Sciences.

In consultation with MIT chancellor Paul Gray, ca. 1971. (Courtesy of the MIT Museum.)

understanding that it would be used to improve undergraduate education at the Institute. Dr. Land must have expected some of these resources to be used to build on the ideas in his Arthur D. Little Memorial Lecture at MIT, delivered in May 1957 and entitled "Generation of Greatness: The Idea of a University in an Age of Science." In that lecture, he deplored the regimentation in the way students were introduced to college, which he felt drove out much of the innate creativity of young people just as they were entering higher education.

Jerry created and chaired an informal planning group comprised additionally of: Walter Rosenblith, associate provost; Ben Snyder, director of MIT psychiatric services and leader of a seminal study on the adaptation of students to the Institute (published in book form as *The Hidden Curriculum*); Jerrold Zacharias, physicist, Institute Professor, and "the man who leads the bull into the china shop"; and myself. This led to the development of the Undergraduate Research Opportunities Program (UROP), one of the most profound changes in the nature of undergraduate education at MIT. We invited a new postdoctoral instructor in physics, Margaret L. A. MacVicar, an MIT alumna, to devise a program that would implement Land's idea that each entering student should have, as early as possible, a "faculty guide" who could serve as mentor. The idea, as it developed, was to find ways in which undergraduates could participate with faculty members and graduate students in cutting-edge research, a perfect instance of learning-by-doing. The late Professor MacVicar's genius in creating UROP as a low barrier, nonbureaucratic activity—voluntary for faculty and students alike—rapidly made it the central experience of an MIT education for many students, one that now engages over three-quarters of MIT undergraduates and a large fraction of our faculty. Widely copied at other institutions but never cloned, UROP has become a hallmark of MIT.

Jerry's interest in exploring new ways for students to learn did not end there. His committee was instrumental in creating several alternative first-year programs, including the Experimental Study Group, Concourse, and the Integrated Studies Program, which add richness and variety to the learning experience available to our entering students.

September 1968 marked the start at MIT of protests against the war in Vietnam and against the Institute's involvement with the U.S. defense establishment. In the week before the term started, a lecture in the Stratton Student Center was disrupted by a small group of students, led by the president of the Undergraduate Association, Michael Albert. The level and significance of the protests increased in the months that followed.

Jerry was conflicted by the antiwar protest at MIT. He was opposed to our nation's involvement in the war, and demonstrated that opposition by marching with the protestors to an antiwar rally on the Boston Common. At the same time, he was also very concerned that the protest focused on MIT would develop in a manner that would damage the integrity or the coherence of the Institute. He spent hours in discussion with Michael Albert and other students and faculty who were prominent in the MIT antiwar movement, and was clearly frustrated by his inability to persuade them that their intense focus on MIT was misplaced and dangerous.

The 1969–70 academic year saw a dramatic intensification of protest activity at MIT. There were large-scale marches on the Draper Laboratory (an integral part of MIT at that time) and at the Hermann Building, which housed the Center for International Studies. There were disruptions of classes and, in January 1970, the occupation by a group of students and faculty of the offices of the president and the chairman of the MIT governing board.

The occupation infuriated Jerry, who in its first minutes mounted a table in the president's office to demand, through a bullhorn, that the occupiers leave. Soon after that, with about a hundred highly emotional and hostile protestors in the offices, he calmly walked into the suite and unobtrusively removed the memory plug-in units in the primitive word processors used at the time. I marveled both at his calm courage and at the fact that he knew exactly what to do to prevent compromise of the records in these offices.

In February 1971, the search committee appointed by the governing board (the MIT Corporation) to seek a president to succeed Howard Johnson concluded that the times required more than one person to serve as the chief executive of the Institute. They asked Jerry to serve as president and me to serve as chancellor, the president's deputy.

Thus began the next chapter in our extended close relationship. Neither the search committee nor the Corporation itself chose to be specific about how the tasks were to be shared, and our efforts to explore those questions with the search committee led to the comment, "Just work it out together." So we did.

Jerry was, of course, the senior leader of MIT. As such, he was the principal shaper of strategic new directions, the principal spokesperson, and the point of contact with federal agencies and the Congress. I was primarily concerned with finances and with ongoing operations of the Institute. We were in near-daily contact and effectively provided, I believe, the focus and the functions expected by the Corporation. This arrangement, which lasted until Jerry's retirement in 1980, was my first real experience as a full-time administrator. It was therefore a time of intensive learning—learning from a wise and compassionate colleague and mentor.

Jerry had strong convictions, but it was his nature to be soft-spoken and collegial in his relationships with all. Once, he delivered a speech in Washington in which he said the government was treating research universities as "battered children." That phrase was widely reported. Soon afterwards we were in a conversation with Jerrold Zacharias, who asked: "Jerry, why is it that you can make the most inflammatory statements and have them accepted, while when I make similar comments I get in trouble?" Jerry, after a puff or two on his pipe, replied with a smile: "It's easy—I mumble."

During all his years as president, Jerry served as a freshman adviser. With his advisees as with most people, he exhibited a full measure of patience. But that patience could quickly disappear if someone seemed to him to be particularly obtuse or dim concerning things that really mattered to him. I learned—the hard way—

that I should usually delay a day or two before acting on a command that had grown out of Jerry's anger with someone or some part of the Institute.

On one occasion early in our time together, Jerry told me to instruct a vice president of the Institute to summarily discharge a senior individual who reported to that VP. I did so, only to learn the next morning that Jerry had had second thoughts and did not want the individual fired after all. I rushed to the vice president's office and pulled him out of a meeting with the individual in question, just as he was about to deliver the bad news.

Sometimes Jerry's impatience was with an individual, sometimes with a group. Once, he returned from a meeting with the faculty of a certain department, thoroughly infuriated by their lack of understanding of the context in which their grand plans for expansion had to be assessed. He asked me to determine how much MIT would save if the department were to be closed. Fortunately, it took a day or two to ponder the analysis, by which time Jerry had reconsidered and withdrew his request.

In 1980, when Priscilla and I were planning our transitions to our new roles in the leadership of MIT—and to a new residence on campus—Jerry was wonderfully helpful. His advice, concerning the importance of protecting time for family and having some place to which we could "escape" when necessary, was exactly right.

Nearly a decade after Jerry retired as president, he suffered a serious stroke that affected his ability to speak, read, and use his left arm and leg. When Priscilla and I visited him in the early days of his hospitalization, we were most encouraged by his obvious intention to treat all these consequences as strictly temporary. He refused to accept the conventional medical wisdom that there was no benefit in continuing rehabilitative therapy beyond a year or two, and he was right. He continued to regain capacities almost to the time of his death. I have a vivid memory of his showing me, following a meeting in the Bartos Theater, that he could now operate his cell phone with his left hand while using his right to manage the cane.

Very little slowed Jerry down. Throughout his later years, he continued to give us the benefits of his wisdom, his sparkling wit, and his deep caring for the welfare of MIT and the world.

Jerry was for me a splendid colleague, a trusted and reliable friend, and a marvelous mentor. He was, as Archibald MacLeish put it, one who "asks not what you know, but what you have not thought of." And his greatest gift to me was that he made it possible to serve as his successor.

A Lesson in Wisdom

Shirley Ann Jackson

My first impressions of Jerry Wiesner were about as clear as those most students have of their undergraduate university administrators. Throughout my four undergraduate years at MIT, I was focused, appropriately, on courses and grades, professors and mentors, fellow students and friends. The Institute appeared to run itself, and although I occasionally thought some changes were needed, I was not particularly concerned with the provost. I knew Jerry Wiesner had done many great things, but I did not really know him as an individual, although I remember him with his pipe. He always had a pipe.

In April of my senior year, however, my life was transformed. I had been in the process of deciding which of several graduate schools I would choose. I had visited the University of Pennsylvania, where I had received a fellowship, and I was deciding which professors I might want to work with. A sorority sister was driving me back to the airport. The car radio was on. And suddenly, we heard that Dr. Martin Luther King, Jr., had been shot in Memphis, Tennessee, and shortly thereafter that he had passed away. We were so shocked that the car nearly ran off the road.

A major portion of the civil rights movement had taken place during my childhood. I was a child of the King era, when Dr. King came into his own, led the

Shirley Ann Jackson, physicist and university administrator, earned her undergraduate and graduate degrees at MIT (SB 1968, Ph.D. 1973). She was a research associate at the Fermi National Accelerator Laboratory (1973–74, 1975–76) and a visiting scientist at the European Organization for Nuclear Research, Geneva, Switzerland (1974–75) before becoming a member of technical staff at AT&T Bell Laboratories in 1976. After fifteen years at Bell Labs, she became professor of physics at Rutgers University (1991–95) and then chairperson of the U.S. Nuclear Regulatory Commission (1995–98). She was appointed president of Rensselaer Polytechnic Institute in 1998. Active in a number of professional societies, she has sat on several committees concerned with the role of women and minorities in science. She has served as president of the National Society of Black Physicists.

Montgomery bus boycott, and organized the March on Washington—all before I graduated from high school. I knew from personal experience that the movement Dr. King had led so ably and nonviolently had made it possible for those previously shut out to begin to participate—fully—in American life.

Dr. King's death had an enormous impact on me, and afterward, graduate school took on new meaning—meaning beyond my own academic development. I had been pretty quiet as an undergraduate, but when Dr. King was assassinated, I decided that I had a responsibility to stay at MIT to try to stimulate change there, because MIT was an important institution, and because I was familiar with it.

So I attended graduate school at MIT and became one of the cofounders of the Black Students' Union there, along with Jim Turner, a graduate student in physics like myself, and others. Like many such groups at that time, we drew up a list of "proposals" that we presented to the administration—things that we believed we wanted the administration to do to recruit more black students and to make the school more hospitable to black students and to others. In response, the administration—and this was Howard Johnson, Jerry's predecessor as president—set up a Task Force on Educational Opportunity chaired by Paul Gray, who later succeeded Jerry as MIT president. This group met every week, sometimes several times a week, and often for hours at a time, all afternoon or sometimes all day—thrashing out issues and developing policies and processes. We had formed the Black Students' Union at the end of my senior year, and so it was during my first year as a graduate student and a large part of the following year that I met with the administration on these issues, and got to know Jerry, who was provost at the time.

But there was another way I came to know Jerry. One of the early leaders of the Black Students' Union was a young man who served with me as cochairman during the first year of the organization. I was a first-year graduate student, he was a first-year undergraduate—a freshman. He was very committed to the Black Students' Union and to black people overall, and he spent a lot of his time on the development of policies to benefit the lives of black students at MIT and to enhance the Black Students' Union.

As it turned out, Jerry Wiesner was this young man's faculty adviser. When a student arrived at MIT, each was assigned a faculty adviser who guided the student on course selection, major, preparation, and so forth, although the freshman adviser could differ from the adviser assigned once the student had selected a major. One day, Jerry and I had a falling out about this young man. Jerry told me he felt that I was wrong to have involved him as cochair of the Black Students' Union, because he was a freshman. I defended the young man's right to make his own choices, but

Lunching al fresco with students in Project Interphase, summer 1974; at left is incoming MIT freshman Margaret L. Smith. Interphase was established in 1969 to ease the transition of minority students to MIT, providing an introduction to academic and social life on campus in the summer just before the start of their freshman year. (Courtesy of the MIT Museum.)

Jerry felt that, because I was a graduate student, I should have known better than to involve a freshman, at such an early stage, in some fairly heavy issues. Of course, I thought that Jerry was a "stick-in-the-mud" who wanted us to just do calculus or physics problem sets and not deal with the important issues of the day. I felt that he betrayed us, that he did not really support our goals and was trying to weaken the leadership of the Black Students' Union.

Jerry usually was a very nice, very quiet, and unassuming individual, but that day we had a pretty sharp exchange. He said something to me like, "You should know better. How could you ask this young man to do this kind of thing? It's wrong and you're going to hurt him." And, of course, I did not want to hear it. I believe I was taken aback as much by the way he said it as by what he said, because he was being accusatory. I had never heard him use such a sharp tone. My feelings were hurt, and I was angry with him for quite a while—several months.

But then I thought about it and finally went back to him, and together we talked it through. He let me know that he was totally committed to what we were trying to do, and that his greatest desire was to have more black students come to MIT, but that it was also very important for overall progress that those who came did well. I think Jerry respected me and felt that I had more influence than I realized on the young black students who were coming to MIT at the time, and that with such respect and influence I had a responsibility to understand the need not to involve a freshman in these matters. He said that those of us who were the older students had a responsibility to set an example for the younger ones, and that our example was important for expanding the number of black students at MIT in the future.

And in the end, upon reflection, I agreed. As this young man's adviser, Jerry could see the risks to him that I could not, because I was wrapped up in what we were trying to do. I recognized that what Jerry was really letting me know was how much he cared about the young man and about his success, particularly when he started to falter. And, I felt very guilty.

The whole episode showed me what kind of person Jerry was. His greatest care was for this young student, and he was hurt that this young man was wound up in all of these nonacademic issues to the neglect of some of his studies. And, the exchange was not about me per se, but about his worry about this particular young man, and also about what it meant in terms of the future success of black students at MIT.

I have chosen a number of unwitting mentors throughout my life—people whom I have watched and emulated, learned from, and after whom I patterned myself— who never knew I had privately designated them a mentor. In some cases, some of these individuals were unknown even to me at the time! Upon reflection, I believe that Jerry Wiesner was one of those: an unwitting mentor from whom I learned to require not only excellence of myself and those around me, but excellence mellowed by kindness, caring, humanity, a greater vision—in other words, wisdom.

Three Glimpses

Robert M. Solow

Since I am neither an electrical engineer, nor any other kind of scientist or engineer, nor an expert on science policy, nor an academic administrator, my picture of Jerry Wiesner is necessarily limited in scope, and perhaps more personal and less professional than it ought to be. But we shared three quite different contexts. We were friends and colleagues at MIT for a very long time. We were both in Washington during the administration of John F. Kennedy (in my case at the Council of Economic Advisers). And we both had summer houses in the town of Chilmark on Martha's Vineyard, and loved to be there. That is enough to help round out the picture. It goes without saying that, like everyone else participating in this book, I was truly fond of Jerry and Laya, and admired them both enormously as people, as colleagues, and as citizens, cut from the same cloth in all three respects.

As President Kennedy's science adviser, Jerry had (at least) two distinct functions. One of them, of course, was to see that the president understood what the best available science had to say that was relevant to any important policy questions that had some scientific content. The other was to play a part in the making of federal policy affecting the scientific enterprise and the scientific community.

It happens that long ago—but not long before the Kennedy administration—I did some work that led to the conclusion that technological progress in a broad sense

Robert M. Solow, economist and educator, joined the MIT economics faculty in 1949, retiring as Institute Professor in 1995. He created the modern framework for analyzing the effects of investment and technological progress on economic growth, which has greatly influenced economics and economic policy worldwide. He was senior staff economist on President Kennedy's Council of Economic Advisers (1961–62) and a member and chairman of the Federal Reserve Bank of Boston (1979–80). A fellow of several professional organizations, he has served as president of the Econometric Society (1964), the American Economic Association (1979), and the International Economic Association (1999–2002). Among his numerous awards, he is the recipient of the Nobel Prize in Economics (1987), for his "contributions to the theory of economic growth," and the National Medal of Science (1999).

was surely an important contributor, and probably the most important contributor, to the long-term growth of the U.S. economy. One way of putting this point, both accurate and attention-grabbing, is to say that public and private spending on science and technology functions rather like other, more conventional investments. That is, a current expenditure yields tangible returns over some future interval of time. In principle, one could calculate a rate of return on an investment in science as one would calculate a rate of return on an investment in a bond or other security. In practice, it is incomparably more difficult, and the uncertainty attached to those calculations is great, for fairly obvious reasons.

Measures of the return to particular investments in science and technology exhibit a wide spread, as one would expect, but usually come out pretty high, and often higher than the rates of return on more conventional capital investments. People with an interest in federal support of science like these results; they suggest that both public and private spending on research pays off, and perhaps more amply than alternative expenditures. If that is so, then increasing investment in science and technology would be a good idea, from the national point of view.

I am often asked by friends in the business to cite chapter and verse that will provide reinforcement for their campaigns to expand federal support for science and technology. Jerry understood the argument clearly, and he welcomed this kind of evidence for the big-time social utility of science. We talked about these ideas during our overlap in Washington, and after. What I want to emphasize is that Jerry was always less insistent, less narrowly focused, less impatient with the uncertainties, less ready to ignore the error bands than the average seeker after good things to say about the national importance of science. He was more laid back, in other words.

I do not think that he was any less fundamentally devoted to the goal of bringing more science, better science, and more useful science into being. Instead, I draw a couple of different implications about Jerry's character. The first is that he was more tolerant of ambiguity than most of his peers. Nobody—at least nobody in his role—likes ambiguity, but Jerry had learned to accept its inevitability and to deal with it. Maybe this is a matter of temperament, or maybe it is a habit that can be learned. Jerry would never have been a good prosecuting attorney. (By the way, that very valuable capacity can sometimes lead to bad decisions; understanding that fact is part of the capacity.)

The second implication is that, in the circumstances described, Jerry had in him some empathy for the problems of his interlocutor. Trying to extract from a mess of (non-experimental) data a measure of the social return to scientific effort is a dirty job. (Does somebody have to do it?) A person who just wants the end-product and wants it now is likely to think of the tentative provider as a mildly incompetent obstacle to progress. Jerry had too much fellow-feeling to take that view, and too much intelligence about the search for knowledge. He felt your pain, to use a later locution. He would have made a terrific science adviser for William J. Clinton.

Now I want to tell a quite different tale out of school, as a vignette of Jerry Wiesner as president of MIT. One day during his tenure he turned up in my office wearing a look of supreme embarrassment. Anyone who knew him will remember the look. He told me about a close personal friend of his who was also a very good friend to the Institute. This man had a son who had applied for admission to the Ph.D. program in economics at MIT, and had his heart set on it.

Jerry explained with great seriousness that he would never dream of using his office or a friendship to obtain preferment for someone he knew. He understood completely that the admissions process had to take its majestic course. Decisions of that kind were the province of each department and no one could or should interfere with the department's vital prerogatives. He had only felt obliged to tell me what the situation was.

I knew exactly how he felt. In the first place it was written excruciatingly all over his face, not to mention the rest of the body language. In the second place, the same thing had happened to me several times, in a smaller way of course. So I immediately wrote a note to the chairman of the department's Graduate Admissions Committee. I told him in enough detail what the story was. Needless to say, I went on, I would not dream of interfering in the majesty of the committee's deliberations and decisions. "Still," I told him, "I think you should know that, if this young man is not admitted, I am going to sit down in the doorway of your office, pour gasoline on myself, and set myself on fire."

The rest of the story is exactly what you expect. The committee admitted the young man, paying absolutely no attention to my report, I am sure. He came; he delighted everyone who taught him, was an excellent student, and wrote a fine Ph.D. thesis. It could not have been otherwise. Jerry felt the tug of friendship, and he respected the rules of the game. He was visibly torn. But he would never have spoken up if he had not been convinced that he was acting on behalf of a very able person. There are many ways to go wrong; in dealing with human situations, Jerry usually found what was right.

Finally, I come to Martha's Vineyard. The Wiesners had discovered Chilmark before it was newsworthy enough to drive up land values. They had acquired a lovely piece of land on the shore of Menemsha Pond (which is tidal). The family summered in the moderately ramshackle Vineyard house that was already there when they first saw the land. "Up-island" has a large academic summer population;

Jerry in "Beetlebung"—thrilling to the wildest elements. (Courtesy of the MIT Museum.)

A relaxed moment—Jerry and Laya in "Beetlebung." (Courtesy of the MIT Museum.)

even after Laya's health had begun to deteriorate, she and Jerry could still hold court with a large and interesting circle of friends.

Naturally, Jerry loved to sail. (You will appreciate the force of that "naturally.") He was able to invest a little in the local family-run shipyard, when that was needed. When the yard designed and built a class of 29-foot canoe-stern fiberglass boats, called Vineyard Vixens, Jerry bought one and named it the Beetlebung. (Beetlebung is the New England name for a species of gum tree; and one of the two intersections in Chilmark is called Beetlebung Corner.) He sailed it happily around Vineyard Sound with a crew of devoted friends—some of them MIT people, some not. But not with me; we had a boat of our own, docked just two slips down from Beetlebung in Menemsha Harbor. It seemed right with the world when, on the water in Vineyard Sound, we could spot Jerry and the familiar profile of the Beetlebung.

I want this to sound idyllic, because that is how it seemed to me and, I think, to Jerry. And that made it all the sadder when, after his stroke, he could get out in Beetlebung less and less often, needing more and more help. Jerry and Laya spent less and less time in Chilmark, and eventually Beetlebung sat there alone.

A Man of Courage and Integrity

Willard R. Johnson

First Meeting

I think I first met Jerome Wiesner at his Watertown home in the mid-1960s, when he was still dean of the School of Science at MIT, or had just been named provost. It was not long after his wonderful wife, Laya, had joined a group of persons (some of whom were friends to my wife, Vivian) to start the METCO program that provided access to suburban schools for a significant number of inner-city students. I think Laya was hosting that party. She was a rather shy, somewhat frail person, with a very ready and warm smile and an at-ease demeanor that may have belied her strongly progressive political convictions. My wife and her friends had great respect for Laya.

I remember Jerry as a person with a direct approach to people and a penetrating gaze. He was often puffing on his pipe or had it in hand. For me and for most of my African-American colleagues, he was approachable and friendly but not really close. I remember his broad smile, but I do not remember him laughing. I always felt that he had the demeanor of someone who was to be taken really seriously.

Willard R. Johnson joined the MIT faculty in 1964, a year before earning his doctorate in political science at Harvard University. He retired as professor of political science in 1996, becoming professor emeritus. While at MIT, he was connected to the Center for International Studies as well as the Department of Political Science. He served as director of the center's Business Management for Economic Development Project. Among his outside activities, he was executive director and later board chairman of both the Circle Inc. and New England Community Development Corporation, community organizations based in the predominantly black neighborhoods of Boston. He founded the Boston chapter of TransAfrica (1980) and was its president (1980–85, 1989). He has been a board member of TransAfrica and TransAfrica Forum since 1977.

Jerry and Laya, all smiles, at the entrance to the MIT president's official residence. When Jerry became president in 1971, the Wiesners decided to continue living in their Watertown home. "The official residence is magnificent for entertaining," Laya observed, "but not ideally suited for family living." The residence was used for special events during Jerry's time, such as the popular Sunday evening dinners (inaugurated by Laya) when students and faculty came together on a more informal, sociable basis than usual. (Courtesy of the MIT Museum.)

My Sense of the Man

Jerry Wiesner was among the most courageously principled persons I have ever had the pleasure to know—a person of complete integrity. Of course, he was brilliant and extremely accomplished, attributes for which he was very widely known. For me, however, what set him apart from most other white Americans in the New England environs was his capacity to understand the perspective of all victimized peoples, and his willingness to put his understanding and his principles to work, even if that led to conflict and disagreement with his colleagues, others in his own ethnic group, and occasionally even with friends. In this regard I would put him in the very rare company of Noam Chomsky, but unlike the latter, Jerry kept—and perhaps even cultivated—his ties to the academic and liberal Democrat political establishments.

Among my fellow African-American faculty and staff at MIT, he was widely appreciated for these qualities. On several occasions I have heard some of them say that Jerry was the white person among those they knew who best understood all the ramifications of the issue of race in American life, institutions, and culture. Several of them have said that Jerry was the only white they had met in these environs who seemed to understand their perspective, and more often, they would say that he consistently and openly recognized and honored their humanity. To me, that was the most important of his attributes—far more important than his engineering and scientific contributions, or even than his public policy and public service contributions. Such people are still sorely needed throughout our society, *if America is ever to be.*

Candidacy for MIT President

A new president was being selected for MIT in 1970–71 at a time of great turmoil throughout the country. This had affected MIT and, even more so, Harvard in the late 1960s. The civil rights struggle had been succeeded by the "Black Power" and "community control" and "Black Nationalism" movements, and the Black Panther Party, Revolutionary Action Movement, and Weatherman organizations. The antiwar struggle was heating up. Youth and students were among the leaders of these movements, and they were not impressed with the attributes even of a Jerry Wiesner. There was a searching for meaning, a testing of academic traditions and practices against new standards of relevance—to address the exclusions, the oppressions, the hypocrisy in the society at large.

It was inevitable that in this context there would be considerable discussion about the purpose and governance patterns of "the university," and at many leading institutions, including MIT, a concern for recruiting black and minority students and faculty (or at least the willingness to "study" it). There had been major studies at Harvard under President Nathan Pusey about the governance and mission of the university in American society. These concerns were evident at MIT as well—under President Howard Johnson, when Jerry was provost. They had fostered an open discussion of and preparation to accommodate these historic trends.

In 1967, as chair of a subcommittee on teaching in the Department of Political Science, I had expressed concern that we "make our scientific skills relevant to our judgments and our judgments relevant to our convictions, and these to our involvements. This means at least greater exploration of issues, and continued freedom for activism." That concern would frame my understanding of the significance of the Wiesner candidacy for president of MIT, when I was later appointed to the Institute's Faculty Advisory Committee for this selection.

Jerry was a controversial candidate, not only because he would be the first president of Jewish background, but, I believe, because he had demonstrated the courage of his convictions in the political and public policy arenas. At the time, I had heard commentary about his support for arms control and the nonuse, if not dismantling, of the nuclear arsenals of both the Soviets and the U.S. I sensed that, in a quiet, responsible, yet firm way, he supported the search for a fair peace in Vietnam, and opposed prolonging and escalating the U.S. war against the Vietnamese. As provost, he had already shown visionary leadership in promoting the expansion of opportunities for African Americans and other groups historically denied any but token access to economic and political power, and to social standing in the general American society. Also, he had promoted an open grappling with issues of academic reform not only to prepare these venerable institutions to fit into an open society, but to foster access to and a capacity for ample use of the new information technologies by the nontechnical and nonprofessional public.

I sensed that these factors had created strong currents of support as well as opposition to his candidacy among the faculty and staff. I had little sense of student reaction to his candidacy, nor was I very aware of the currents of opinion about his candidacy among the members of the MIT Corporation, the body with the ultimate authority and power to make this appointment. I have heard, and can easily imagine, that many were opposed to his appointment.

The Selection Process

I felt privileged to be asked to serve on "The Faculty Advisory Committee on the Presidency" (FAC). Our search happened at the same time as the search for a new president at Harvard, which itself came in the context of what outgoing President Nathan Pusey called "a shameful state of affairs," where the traditions of that and other universities were under "attack" from within as well as outside academe. But he had admitted that, despite his profound disagreement with the tactics of most of the protesters, the blame had to be shared by the academic and

A "pride of presidents and first ladies," ca. 1980—*left to right*: Julius Stratton, Margaret Compton (widow of Karl Taylor Compton), Elizabeth Killian, James Killian, Catherine Stratton, Elizabeth Johnson, Howard Johnson, Laya Wiesner, Jerry, Priscilla Gray, Paul Gray. (Photo by Calvin Campbell. Courtesy of the MIT Museum.)

societal establishment for not moving as rapidly as they could "to correct obvious abuses and shortcomings which have festered too long among us . . . [and for failing] to enliven courses which have ceased to speak to the condition of the new young."

I think that many of the faculty members on our advisory committee were deeply concerned about changing this pattern, too. But, it might have been that the MIT faculty at large was either not so caught up in these issues or they believed that our role in the selection process was not very consequential, because only about 12 or 13 members responded to the advisory committee's solicitation for advice about "the kind of person we should have as President, and . . . one or more names that fit your ideas."

In our deliberations, several suggestions came to us from the existing administrative leadership and corporation members that disturbed me. One was the idea that the position should be offered for only a rather short period of time, and also divided into two parts, with a chancellor added to assist the president. This seemed to me, and to others, to reflect hesitancy to risk having a person with as strong a personality as Jerry Wiesner, with such readiness to express criticism of national arms and nuclear policies. Yet strangely enough, these suggestions came from people who asserted that their leading candidate was Jerry.

I was even more perplexed by the suggestion that the job would not be good for Jerry. One very prominent MIT leader said that he thought Jerry would quickly become frustrated—"He'd last about two years and then he'd say to hell with it." I spoke up immediately, saying something to the effect that it reminded me of my own experience in college when I applied for a summer job selling automobiles and was turned down with the admonition that they were doing me a favor, because the job would not be good for someone with such a record of accomplishment and with such a bright future. I thought we ought to let the candidate speak for himself on that question. I said: "The man's reactions to the job should not be guessed at . . . the only reliable guide is the man himself at the time when the job is actually offered." Neither I nor any other member of our advisory committee had heard that Jerry was not interested, although there had been no formal interview with him, and thus this idea was probably only hearsay. However, one faculty member did assert that he had heard that Jerry had stated that the job would "cramp his style."

Our committee held one meeting in conjunction with the corporation's Joint Advisory Committee (CJAC)—a permanent committee that included some corporation members, faculty, and students. Some of these issues surfaced again, and I responded saying that I interpreted suggestions that the MIT Corporation would not want either of our two committees to come in with a strong endorsement of a particular candidate—but rather a list of four or five persons, or even a list of people that could be considered an alternative to Jerry—as veiled opposition to appointing Jerry. I said that there seemed to be two reasons expressed in these deliberations against our clearly recommending Jerry to the corporation: "1) that the Corporation wants to make certain that there should be no collision . . . [with our] Committees [this interpretation was immediately objected to] and 2) . . . [some] questioned Wiesner's desire to take the job and remarked on the likelihood that Wiesner would not keep it." I said that neither of these arguments was convincing, and I recommended "that CJAC join the FAC in the latter's statement to the Corporation committee adopted at [its] meeting of December 11, in which Wiesner was termed the most desirable candidate." That vote of our committee had been by a margin of six for, none against, and two abstentions. I then urged the joint CJAC/FAC committee to conclude our deliberations and, before we broke for Christmas vacation, to recommend that the corporation make the offer to Wiesner in short order. Only three of the nineteen persons participating in this joint meeting did not include Wiesner among their top four choices, but they were not at that time ready to conclude the matter.

Just before Christmas 1970, the FAC conveyed to the corporation its own clear preference for Jerry among all the internal candidates (those already at MIT) and indicated six leading outside candidates (which we listed only in alphabetical order) among the persons the committee had evaluated up to that point. The corporation selection committee was not scheduled to meet on the matter until after the holidays, and it sent back several additional outside names for us to consider, which were researched but which did not change our opinion.

I think that, in the end, a deal was cut. I do not know the behind-scenes maneuvers that went on within the corporation. I am sure that it took continued advocacy for Jerry's appointment by his corporation supporters, but the stage had been set over several years. Jerry had been an effective and respected provost (and his appointment to that post also took courage, for which Howard Johnson must be given credit). There were strong blocks of support for his candidacy among the faculty. He was a highly respected and visible person, although a controversial one, and a feared force in some quarters among the more general society and in government circles. Within the next six weeks, the MIT Corporation went on to offer the position to Jerry (without limiting the term of this appointment), which he accepted. At the same time, the new position of chancellor was offered to, and accepted by, Paul Gray.

The Wiesner Presidency

During the early phases of Jerry's presidency, he continued to show a concern for global issues and for charting a role in them for MIT. I had a personal exposure to Jerry's efforts to discern the broad trends of society, the problems they would pose, and the way in which MIT and its people might address those problems.

Not long after his taking office, I was invited by him to join a relatively small group of faculty and officers to discuss his idea of MIT's sponsoring a major convocation in 1975, regarding "possible directions for society in the next half century." His invitation letter spelled out some of his concerns: "the role of science and technology," but also broader issues such as "the conflict between growth and a satisfying society, the conflict between efficiency and individuality in a heavily organized, communication-rich society, the proper use of technology in education, the creation and use of resources, how to make choices in a complex society, career and work patterns for the future, the moral dilemmas of contemporary society, etc." It was an ambitious vision of addressing the fundamental challenges facing our society in the coming decades, and would have produced only the third convocation to address such issues in MIT history. The group invited to think this through with Jerry was made up mostly of stellar intellectuals, including Noam Chomsky, Salvador Luria, Donald Schon, Sheila Widnall, and Edwin Land.

At a dinner meeting to plan the convocation, I had the experience of Jerry immediately understanding my point of view, and being willing to back me up before anyone else did. I had a brief clash with Edwin Land of the Polaroid Corporation, a personal friend of Jerry's, around the issue of whether he—or anyone for that matter—could fully understand the perspective, needs, and aspirations of *everyone* else. Is there really a human understanding or persona so common and basic as to be universal and yet relevant to such high order challenges? If not, then we cannot speak of "mankind's" appreciation of or challenges by technology. Would we—or any small group of intellectuals and leaders, regardless of how smart they were— be able to frame such issues and challenges in a way that would be shared by every normal adult person? I did not think so. I posed it as a question of whether the "we" (as in Land's query about "what difficulty do *we* have in sloughing off old skins, and harnessing change?") is really ever a "we." Some people have the power to make their view dominate the situation, I said, but that does not reflect or create commonality of perspective.

Land looked baffled. What was I talking about? He looked furtively around the table for some clue. Wiesner seemed to get my point, and quickly spoke up to explain to Land that people do not all see things the same way. There might not be particular characteristics of human nature that are universal enough, and yet robust enough, to produce a common perspective on such questions despite markedly different circumstances of life or experiences. In such a quest to chart the trends in technology and their significance for human society, we would have to have a convocation that involved people whose framework for understanding the issues reflected quite different circumstances.

I do not know if the convocation ever happened, but it was clear to me then that Jerry's appreciation for diversity was broadly philosophical as well as practical.

Wiesner's Concern for Diversity at MIT

Jerry was not so wrapped up in the truly global challenges of importance to world survival that he was not also concerned about more local issues. I was particularly impressed with the range of his vision for MIT itself, especially with regard to issues and areas of concern to a person like myself—from a "minority community" that had not traditionally been well represented at MIT or at most other prestigious aca-

With Herman Branson, president of Lincoln University and a member of the MIT Corporation, February 26, 1979. Branson delivered the first lecture in MIT's Minority Graduate Students Spring Lecture Series, speaking on "Availability, Barriers, and Solutions in Generating Scholarship in Black Students." (Photo by Calvin Campbell. Courtesy of the MIT Museum.)

demic institutions as well. He was concerned to promote diversity at MIT and opportunity for blacks, and for other groups historically "underprivileged" in American academia and in society.

He also took the time to attend to external requests and to deal with minor issues that might be of concern to me or other African-Americans on campus. For example, he forwarded to me several inquiries made to him, or to others at MIT, from Africans on the African continent or elsewhere who wanted to have the institutional support of MIT or collaboration with our faculty. I also received MIT support to complement external resources to bring several African Research Associates to work with me in my "Business Management for Economic Development Project." Earlier, the Sloan School had developed a major Research Fellows in Africa project.

During his years as provost, Jerry had been concerned to bring in black faculty at all levels of MIT. One of the early recruits was Frank Jones, whom Howard Johnson had initially recruited from the Scott Paper Company. Johnson and Wiesner collaborated to turn this rather quickly into a tenured appointment—one of the first, if not the first, black tenured at MIT, not long before my own achievement of tenure (although I had followed the normal route up through the ranks—probably the first instance of that as well.) It took leadership at the highest level for Jones's appointment to succeed, as it did not originate within a department.

Clarence Williams came a bit later as a result of the work of the Task Force on Educational Opportunity that Howard Johnson had established and Jerry kept going. Clarence came initially as an assistant dean, but not very long thereafter he was asked to serve as a special assistant to the president for minority affairs. A similar special assistant position already had been created for women.

Jerry's personal leadership as provost had also brought in the noted sociologist, Dr. Kenneth Clark, who had played a key role in presenting the scientific evidence for arguing that "separate schools were inherently not equal schools" in the 1954 Supreme Court case outlawing racial segregation in U.S. public schools. Dr. Clark came to MIT first as a speaker, and then stayed on as a visiting professor.

In all of this, Jerry did not neglect the more ordinary ways of connecting with local social needs. He had helped to expand, if not initiate, "Tutoring Plus" and other tutoring programs which used MIT students and resources in the surrounding communities. He had facilitated support for the MIT Upward Bound program. He also spoke out publicly as president to support national "affirmative action programs" and policies in 1973, when they were coming under serious attack.

Yet another example of Jerry's vision and willingness to try something really new was the quick and enthusiastic support he gave to Mel King's idea to offer a sabbatical-type experience for persons who were leaders in neighborhood and community-level improvement and service organizations. This became the Community Fellows Program, likely the first of its kind in the nation, where the administrators and leaders of community development corporations, neighborhood associations, "settlement houses," civic and civil rights organizations, and the like could come for a year, refresh and retool themselves, and rethink their programs and prepare proposals for future funding and program direction.

One project that I had expected would get more MIT support had arisen out of the longstanding efforts of Mel King and other African-Americans in Boston—such as Calvin Hicks, Trish Willis, and Archie Williams—to have a "Community University" in Roxbury. An early manifestation of these efforts was the inauguration in 1968 of an Adult Education Center at the New Urban League, which Mel was heading. Draft by-laws were then written for an "Afro-American Community College." Serious discussions about such a project were conducted with Harvard's School of Education, the University of Massachusetts, and the Mass Bay Community College. I wrote a seven-page memorandum to Walter Rosenblith, then chairman of the MIT Faculty, backing their suggestions that MIT turn over the Lowell Institute School to this effort in the black community. I recounted all these efforts and outlined the possibilities.

A couple of months later, in June of 1968, a close associate of Jerry's, Constantine Simonides, started to work on plans for the Lowell Cooperative Program that would meet some of the needs we had outlined, but did not foresee turning over these or any other significant facilities to a community-based group. However, by then Boston College had entered into a functioning collaboration with the Urban League, establishing a Joint Center for Inner City Change. Subsequently, the Roxbury Community College did develop as part of the state-supported system. And, the Community Fellows Program was developed at MIT. But MIT did not really go into an alliance with community-based organizations or people to develop these instructional and educational resources "out there," and with community-based people and institutions playing a guiding role in determining their mission, their clientele, and their impact. Although not surprising, it was disappointing to me. I then took a leave of absence for two years to run a community-owned economic development complex called The Circle Inc., based in Roxbury.

Racial Fairness and Depth in the Media

In 1968, Henry Hampton, the noted founder and CEO of Blackside Films, and several African-American associates filed a challenge to RKO-General's license to operate Boston's Channel 7 TV station, which at that time was the ABC affiliate in Boston. A Roxbury businessman, Bertram Lee, was also a principal organizer of this group, named the Dudley Station Corporation. Ruth Batson, Hampton's associate with the Museum of Afro-American History, was also a member. Over many years, a number of groups had challenged the renewal of RKO TV licenses, for having failed to meet public affairs programming standards and for media monopoly as well as faulty business practices.

One day Jerry stopped me as our paths crossed while walking across campus to ask me if I thought it would be a good thing for him to join the Hampton group. He did not hesitate to express his admiration for Henry Hampton, who was a good friend of mine. Hampton's company would later produce the internationally acclaimed "Eyes on the Prize" TV documentary series on the civil rights movement, and many other award-winning documentaries. Henry had also been, with Ruth Batson, the chief force behind the acquisition and rehabilitation of the African Meeting House by the Afro-American History Museum, on the board of which my wife, Vivian, served.

Jerry had already come to know Henry and most of the other African-Americans with whom he did become partners. He had probably met Ruth Batson through his wife, Laya, when she was involved in creating the METCO Program. He knew Bertram Lee, who had come to Boston from Chicago to run the Opportunities Industrialization Center (OIC) and had asked Jerry and others at MIT for advice and support. After leaving OIC, Lee continued to promote business and job creation development in the Roxbury area, which is the context in which I met him, when he joined my board of directors in The Circle Inc. Jerry may also have interacted with Lee, Batson, and others, especially Mel King, in the early efforts to fight the displacement that Boston's urban renewal programs were causing, and to promote access to housing in the city that poor people could afford. Thus, when Jerry entered into this media partnership, he had already established a friendly and effective working relationship with the principals involved.

I suspect Jerry stopped me and posed his question not for information he did not have, or in order to really corroborate the project's appeal and significance, but, rather, to let me know that this was something he cared about and was involved in.

In 1981, the Channel 7 franchise finally was wrested from the RKO and awarded to New England Television, a company headed by the supermarket magnet, David Mugar, whose New England Television Company had also challenged the RKO license shortly after the Dudley Station Corporation had done so. Mugar also had established a relationship with Boston's black community by including among his partners Melvin Miller, a prominent lawyer and publisher/editor of a black-owned and black-focused newspaper, the *Bay State Banner*. By then, the Dudley Station Corporation had merged with and become incorporated into the more richly endowed New England Television Company (NET). So there were several African-Americans involved in this operation when NET actually took over the station in 1982. I understand that Jerry distinguished himself from other nonblacks on that board by his willingness to take a rational and dispassionate approach to controversial questions that sometimes had produced confrontation between members of the Jewish and the black communities. Jerry did not carry "extra baggage" into those meetings.

In 1986, Jerry, along with many other shareholders, including all the African-American partners, decided to sell most of their shares in NET to Mugar, who probably wanted more direct control of the operation. It was widely assumed at the time that most of the shareholders simply wanted to cash in their investment, as the reputation and value of the station deteriorated along with that of other such stations. Instinctively, I suspect that the politics of media representation of blacks and other nonwhite people and causes were also part of the motivation for this change, because I know that the policies and politics of ethnically sensitive media representation can be quite contentious.

I also had occasion to interact with Jerry around the programming of Boston's PBS station, WGBH, on the board of which he sat, *ex officio*, while MIT president. In 1978, I wrote to him about the station's refusal to air in a time slot of broad appeal, or release to others to air, anything but a substantially pared down and politically neutered version of a show called "Blacks Britannica." The show was produced in Britain following the outbreak of urban violence in black ghetto areas such as Brixton. It pointed to the roots of such problems in British practices of recruiting cheap labor from its colonies and then neglecting, if not abusing, those workers and the families who had subsequently joined them. WGBH had acquired all rights to air the show in the United States.

In my letter to Jerry, I urged that "every consideration be given . . . to the release for wider viewing of the film Blacks Britannica. I have seen this film in its original, unaltered version and I think it is an important, truthful treatment of an issue that we need to have understood among thoughtful Americans. I hope that the Board will . . . permit circulation of this film, or the sale for some reasonable sum of money of its copyright back to its producer." Jerry did take the matter up with the WGBH board and management, and in his response to me pointed out: "There seems to be two issues here: first, whether the film was weakened or improved by WGBH, and second, how much responsibility for its programming the station must exercise. In the case of certain programs, viewers charge that the management has failed to exercise enough control over their content. In the case of others, viewers complain that the management has engaged in 'censorship.' There are some no-win situations in life. This seems to be one of them." This was an occasion when Jerry did not fight for the position that I believe most black media specialists would have supported.

There were other occasions, however, when Jerry took special precautions to let the African-American faculty and staff know that his own sentiments (and behind-scenes actions) did not always synchronize with those that might prevail among the

MIT leadership. He would send one of the media partners to talk with me, or other faculty and staff, to signal his own position on issues or actions that might be of concern to us. There were, no doubt, many such issues, especially as we at MIT continued to fail to really change the overall diversity picture in terms of faculty appointments, and especially tenured ones.

Jerry also took a personal hand in seeking to advance and enhance the professional careers of several African-Americans on the MIT faculty. He was among the earliest persons to encourage Hubie Jones to become dean at Boston University, and to support his candidacy. Once, not long after Jerry became a board member of the MacArthur Foundation, he asked for my résumé. I did not and still do not know for what reason. Perhaps he knew of some MacArthur Foundation program that would support my work with community economic development programs in Boston, or my efforts to assist with the launching and leadership of Trans-Africa ("the African-American lobby on foreign affairs"), or my efforts to help build the American anti-apartheid movement. Neither I nor these projects received any support from that particular Foundation, but I am sure that if my résumé or projects got considered in their processes at all at that time, it was because of Jerry.

In 1980, when he retired from the presidency, the faculty tribute to him recognized and praised him for the fact that he wanted MIT to "be a refuge for people who have the courage to seek truth and speak out." In that quest, he had set the example. I feel privileged to have known him, and to have been known by him.

Giving Women a Break When Few Men Did

Carola Eisenberg

Jerry was a wonderful human being. Getting to know him was one of the great adventures of my life. I welcome this opportunity to honor his memory by sharing some of my memories with his friends, colleagues, and interested readers.

It all began when I moved to Cambridge in 1967. I found myself unemployed for the first time since I was an adolescent. I had been an Assistant Professor of Child Psychiatry at Johns Hopkins, maintained a substantial practice, and ran a bustling household with two adolescent sons (marvelous young men, of course, but nonetheless adolescent with all that entails). Being a lady of leisure and serving as honorary president of the Harvard Neighbors (which offered monthly afternoon teas for the spouses of newly arrived faculty) soon lost its charm. In looking about for a position, I sought advice from Grete Bibring, the first woman to be a professor at Harvard Medical School and, as it happened, a good friend of Jerry and Laya Wiesner. Grete said there was only one place worth my while to explore, given my interests: the psychiatric service at MIT. She sent me to Ben Snyder, then its chief; I was taken by Ben (and he apparently was taken by me) because I had a job offer within days, an offer I accepted with great enthusiasm.

The students at MIT were quite extraordinary. Those who consulted me had problems all right, but they had so many personal assets and such high intelligence that

Carola Eisenberg, psychiatrist and educator, held several positions at Johns Hopkins University before moving to the Boston area in 1967. After five years as a psychiatrist in the MIT Health Services, she was appointed dean of students at MIT in 1972. In 1978, she left MIT to become dean of student affairs at the Harvard Medical School, where she had already been a lecturer in psychiatry since 1970. She served as dean at Harvard until 1990, and in 1992 was appointed lecturer in social medicine. Throughout this period, she was active in a number of organizations concerned with women's and human rights issues. She has been vice president of Physicians for Human Rights, and is a life member of the Council on International Affairs, as well as a member of its human rights committee.

On the steps of the MIT Student Center (Julius Adams Stratton Building), with director of admissions Peter Richardson and dean of students Carola Eisenberg, ca. 1972. (Courtesy of the MIT Museum.)

working with them led to tangible and satisfying results. I had never felt more effective as a psychiatrist (or happier fulfilling my maternal wishes; my own sons were away at college; MIT undergrads filled the empty nest). It wasn't all fun and games. Students on bad trips, students drinking too much, students who attempted (and sometimes "succeeded" in) suicide, the depressed student and the (very uncommon) psychotic student, led to emergency night calls and kept me awake worrying from time to time.

But even such difficult and distressing problems were easier to respond to because of the caring environment at the Institute, an environment that reflected Jerry Wiesner's priorities first as provost and then as president. An unlisted fringe benefit of the job was coming to know Laya and Jerry and their children, first through official events and then privately as our friendship prospered. We couldn't—and didn't—discuss my patients, but we could—and did—discuss what could be done to enhance the quality of campus life away from the classroom.

Cake, effigy, and celebration—with Walter Rosenblith and Benson Snyder, ca. 1975; possibly an office party for Jerry's 60th birthday. (Courtesy of the MIT Museum.)

Such was my professional life when I got a message one day in 1972 that President Wiesner would like to see me sooner rather than later. What had I done wrong? Perhaps a patient or a patient's parent had complained. Perhaps I had parked my car in his parking place. I went to his office with some anxiety; but I was promptly reassured by his warm greeting.

Jerry as a River Boat Gambler

I was entirely taken aback when Jerry asked if I would like to be the dean for student affairs. Could he really mean me? Could someone else be in the room? But there were only the two of us. I had never seen myself occupying so important a role as an academic executive in so illustrious a university! I blurted out, "Why me?" His response was direct and to the point—"We need to do more to humanize this environment; I think you're the person to do it."

I was moved by his confidence in my abilities, but I felt obliged to point out the huge gamble he was taking. I had never managed anything larger than my own medical practice and my family. True, I had had years of experience teaching medical students and seeing patients, but I was entirely without administrative experience or training. That cut no ice with Jerry. What he cared about, he said, was people skills and commitment to students. On both counts he had no doubts. After mulling it over for a week, I decided, anxious and all, to take a flier.

I have never had a better job in all my life. I owe it to Jerry's willingness to take a risk on a novice. Not the least of the rewards of the job was reporting to Paul Gray and getting to know him, and turning to Paul as well as to Jerry for advice and counsel. In retrospect, Jerry had been a bit too dismissive of the importance of administrative knowledge. To cite but one example, my role as dean made me a member of the Academic Council. One of the council's duties was to review budgets. I was perplexed. Why would such a high-powered group of people sit around raising questions about spending a few thousand dollars? When I finally got the courage to ask, a colleague pointed to the notation at the top of every budget sheet—"omits three zeros." The amounts were in millions and hundreds of thousands. I remembered the quote attributed to Senator Dirksen of Illinois: "You spend a billion here and a billion there and before you know it, it adds up to real money!" It was no coincidence that I was offered "an opportunity" to take a course in the summer of 1974 given by the Institute for Educational Management at the Harvard Business School. It did help remedy my ignorance, but I would still not pass muster as a budget officer.

I flatter myself that I did make a small difference at MIT. But that was only because Jerry Wiesner gave me a chance I never would have had from a more cautious or more bureaucratic president.

Is It Really True What They Say about MIT?

On April 28, 1977, the underground newspaper *Thursday* carried a front-page story headlined "Confidential Guide to Men at MIT." The headline was no hoax. Under a by-line of two women undergraduates, it named names and gave ratings to the sexual performance of male MIT students with a short descriptor to validate the zero- to five-star rating awarded! All hell broke loose. Women on campus were outraged. The story was picked up by the wire services and published in the United States and abroad. MIT offices were deluged with complaints from alumni who protested against the negative publicity. Surely, the MIT that had molded their characters and their careers had not been allowed to become a sexual zoo!

In my role as dean for student affairs, I called the young women in; their (male) editor came with them. Yes, indeed, the by-lined students had written the story. True, the women were on pot and hilarious when they wrote it, but they insisted that the facts were as stated. The ratings and descriptive comments were based on participatory "field investigations."

Jerry was under tremendous pressure to close the newspaper. He was so infuriated by the disregard of common decency on the part of the editor and the writers (several of the students named in the story as poor performers were humiliated) that he was itching to shut it down. I don't remember ever seeing Jerry so angry. I entreated him not to convert a case of bad judgment and poor taste into a battle over freedom of the press. Referring the matter to the Discipline Committee was the appropriate step to take. Jerry reluctantly agreed.

When the case came before the committee, its members ascertained the sequence of events. The coeds were high on pot when, as a lark, they prepared the rating chart. They were giggling about it to each other the following morning when their editor came to their dorm room, read their essay (he, by the way, was one of the students named as a disaster in bed!), and talked them into letting him print it. He was identified as the major culprit, but the committee was unable to identify a forceful response. The editor was in his last semester, had all the credits he needed to graduate, and had already been accepted at an excellent law school. The report of the Discipline Committee was sent to that law school. So far as I know, the law school took no action.

One of the "journalists" did suffer a personal misfortune. An anonymous correspondent cut out the news story and sent it to her parents, who were a church-going rural family. Enormously distressed by their daughter's licentious behavior, they withdrew their support for her college education (MIT became the lender of last resort). MIT had had its 15 minutes of fame on the national scene. The campus was soon preoccupied with other issues. *Thursday* was no longer a collector's item.

The following year applications to MIT were more numerous than they had been the year before. Was this merely coincidence? Had applicants decided that MIT students weren't all nerds and that MIT wasn't quite the grim campus it was supposed to be? Was Caltech envious? We'll never know.

Partings

Being dean for student affairs at MIT was often demanding, never boring, almost always rewarding, and gave me many opportunities to appreciate Jerry's wisdom and integrity. Even though I knew that Jerry's term as president was due to end in 1980, I was ambivalent when I received an offer of a similar position at Harvard Medical School. Returning to medicine was appealing; the job at HMS was bound to be less demanding, if only because the student body was one-fifth as large. Giving up the best job I had ever had was painful. My difficulty in deciding was compounded by the fact that no one knew who was going to succeed Jerry; the next president ought to have the opportunity to appoint his or her own candidate. Had I known it was to be Paul Gray (to whom I had reported as dean and for whom I had the highest regard), I would have remained in office until Paul pushed me out!

As I dithered about what to do, I went to see Jerry, whose judgment I knew would be fair to me and fair to the Institute. I began by telling him I had a problem I was uncomfortable about discussing. He encouraged me to tell him about it no matter how upsetting. I had trouble speaking because I was afraid I would break into tears. When I described my dilemma, Jerry's response was unequivocal: "Of course, we want you to stay, but the decision must be yours. What counts is where you think you'll be more productive and happier." I thought about it for some days. The uncertainty of the succession together with the opportunity to work with medical students finally made the decision for me. Jerry was sad about my leaving, but made it immeasurably easier for me by his personal support.

My friendship with Jerry and Laya remained close in the years that followed. My husband Leon and I were their guests many summers at the Vineyard. Like their other friends, we visited them often during Jerry's cardiac difficulties, his stroke, and Laya's chronic illness. Jerry never gave up. His response to each setback was to look for what constructive steps could be undertaken. To the very end, he worked on computer programs for patients with aphasia, not only in the effort to combat his own residual symptoms, but to help others.

Many more good things can be said about my years at MIT. The most wonderful of them all was the chance to become Jerry's friend.

Campaigner for Urban Justice

Melvin H. King

In 1971, I happened to be on my way back to Boston from Washington, D.C. As I boarded the Eastern Airlines flight and walked through the first-class cabin, I saw Jerome Wiesner sitting in the first row with a vacant seat beside him. I promptly took that seat and began what turned into a most important conversation.

I had first met Jerry in the early 1960s when he and Jerrold Zacharias were working on PSSC (Physical Sciences Study Committee) physics. They were both part of this extraordinary effort to improve and expand science education in high schools across the country, in the aftermath of Sputnik and in an effort to compete with the Russians. Jerry was concerned about equity and full distribution of the science curriculum, especially in underserved communities that might not ordinarily receive such materials.

My next involvement with him was a few years later in connection with the struggles around the desegregation of Boston public schools. Jerry was involved with the METCO Program, where his concern centered around a similar theme—access for students who had been traditionally shut out. METCO, the Metropolitan Council for Educational Opportunity, took African-American high school students from inner-city Boston and enrolled them in school districts in the suburbs. The idea was that through exposure to schools with greater resources, these students would be

Melvin H. (Mel) King is a community activist with extensive experience in the design and implementation of vocational education programs. As executive director of the Urban League of Greater Boston (1967–71), he led a number of efforts to develop programs for minority youth and professionals in the Boston-Roxbury area. He joined the MIT faculty in 1971, serving as lecturer in urban studies (1971–76) and adjunct professor (1976–96). He helped organize and direct MIT's Community Fellows Program, which brings minority activists and public officials to MIT for study and research. Recipient of the NAACP Man of the Year Award (1966), he served five terms as senator (9th Suffolk District) in the Massachusetts state legislature, and was a candidate for mayor of Boston (1979 and 1983).

given a chance to advance their chances for academic success. It was Jerry's wife Laya who had actually taken a lead in METCO, but he followed as an equally staunch supporter of these efforts, organized and led by Ruth Batson. Jerry had also been involved in struggles over housing discrimination and fair housing, among the same issues that I later raised in my campaigns for mayor of Boston in 1979 and 1983. In short, he had taken deep, personal stands on racial justice some years before assuming the presidency of MIT.

No doubt these recollections crossed my mind as I briefly talked with him on that flight from Washington to Boston. I mentioned how a few years back, while I had worked on a Jobs Corps proposal for Sanders Associates, an electronics firm in Nashua, New Hampshire, and while driving there several times a week, I had noticed new electronics firms springing up along Route 128—firms that MIT graduates and faculty had started. These MIT people had taken advantage of institutional resources to zero in on and develop ideas that would emerge as state-of-the-art, cutting-edge businesses. Their special relationship to MIT had given them a competitive edge, I told Jerry, and I wanted to give people involved in community struggles the same opportunities as those who had developed these businesses. I wanted African-Americans to build on an MIT relationship that would forge expertise and contacts for civil rights activists interested in community development. Many of these activists were potentially burning out, in need of some kind of sabbatical—a period of reflection, research, and development of ideas that they could use in their struggles, but that they had never had the time to work out as they carried on their campaign to overcome the impact of racism and discrimination on individuals and communities.

Jerry listened nonstop for over an hour, until our plane landed at Logan. He was completely sold on the whole idea.

The next thing I knew he had set up a meeting with me and Lloyd Rodwin, head of the Department of Urban Studies and Planning at MIT, to start talking over what later became the Community Fellows Program. Larry Susskind, another professor in the department, joined me to write the initial proposal. Also included in the planning stages were Charlie Miller and Frank Jones, both senior professors in the department.

There was discussion about where the program would be housed. At first the idea was that it should relate to the institution as a whole and be located in the central administration. Jerry's wisdom held sway in the long run, however, for he felt strongly that the program should be connected with a school or department. He knew the Institute well and warned against an arrangement outside the departmental structure, which he sensed would compromise its legitimacy. It was decided, in the end, that the program would be located in the Urban Systems Laboratory within Urban Studies and Planning. When efforts to have James Farmer, a national civil rights figure, direct the program failed, Frank Jones and I were enlisted for the job. Frank had a closer and more personal relationship with Jerry than I.

Once the Community Fellows Program got under way, Jerry continued to be involved in several ways. First, he was instrumental in placing direct sources from MIT—in the form of seed money—at our disposal. Outside support came from the Mellon and Rockefeller Foundations, as well as Reebok and the Ford and Kellogg Foundations, through contacts of mine, Jerry's, and others. Jerry and Laya were especially gracious in opening their home to the Fellows and their families as a way to welcome them to the MIT community. Jerry was adept at mingling with community activists and politicians, much as he had done earlier during his days in Washington.

He was never one to be deterred by political opposition. From the beginning, he had to take a firm stand to establish the Program at MIT and to maintain ongoing support for it. He had to convince not only the MIT administration, but also the governing board—the corporation—about the worthiness of the Program and about my suitability for its leadership. As an activist during the 1960s, in my earlier days at the Urban League, I had run across MIT officials while pursuing support from the United Way. One particularly dramatic occasion involved our delegation attending a fancy luncheon, where we carried around garbage bags from table to table picking up crumbs and thereby symbolizing the pittance the Urban League was receiving from the United Way. News of the event spread around MIT and stuck in the minds of many. But Jerry dealt effectively, with integrity and conviction, to get around such situations.

Most importantly, he took special pride in the Community Fellows Program. The Program brought to campus talented African-Americans who made valuable contributions to our curriculum, our students, and our community. Several went on to elected public office. Some, like Chuck Turner and Mary Burros, became Boston city councilors; Gloria Fox and Byron Rushing were elected to the State House; Hubie Jones joined the Urban Studies faculty, later led the Community Fellows Program for a year, and ended up as dean of the School of Social Work at Boston University. All these Fellows crossed Jerry's path, and his office was always open to them and to me during his decade as MIT president.

The Origins of the Media Lab

Nicholas Negroponte

I met Jerry Wiesner when 300 baud[1] was considered fast. As president of MIT, he was provided with 9600 bps (bits per second) by a device the size of a refrigerator; I must admit to modem-envy at the time.

In the 1970s, computers were not for people. Research in computer graphics or music was for sissies. Acceptable research was about networks, operating systems, and programming languages. In fact, the food chain of computer "science" started with basic materials, moved to integrated circuits, on to operating systems, programming languages, applications, and turn-key solutions—getting progressively less scholarly and scientific along the way. Keep in mind, this was before personal computers and in a period when multimedia meant nightclubs.

At the time, I was running something called "The Architecture Machine Group," named after a hastily written (1968) book at the dawn of my own research in computer-aided design. In the early 1970s, it was clear that no self-respecting designer would use any of this stuff, for a variety of reasons, one of which was the sensory deprivation of the computer environment.

To put this into context, in 1972 we built a color computer display system driven by racks full of solid-state memory (256 k bytes at the time, which today represents

Nicholas Negroponte, a pioneer in the field of computer-aided design, joined the MIT faculty in 1966 and is currently the Jerome B. Wiesner Professor of Media Technology. In 1968, he founded MIT's Architecture Machine Group, which conducted innovative research on the relationship between humans and computers. He cofounded (with Jerry Wiesner) and chairs the MIT Media Laboratory, a leader in the use of digital technologies and interdisciplinary research to explore modes of thought, expression, and communication. Author of the bestseller *Being Digital* (1995), he has also been general partner in a venture capital firm specializing in digital technologies for information and entertainment.

1. The speed at which data are sent over a phone line.

much less than 1% of a common memory chip). This work was highly criticized at the time as being wasteful of a scarce resource (memory) and careless about perception (color was considered gratuitous if not misleading). When we started to combine image and sound, and integrated video, the work was widely regarded as cuckoo. Many people on campus, according to *Fortune Magazine*, considered us "charlatans."

Not Jerry.

By contrast, Jerry's life had deep parallels in computers and audio. As part of his early work as chief engineer of the Library of Congress Radio Research Project, he toured the South with Alan Lomax and others recording traditional American folk music. His later work, especially at MIT's Research Laboratory of Electronics (RLE), was at the core of communications and computer science. His love and knowledge of the arts made him totally amphibious in the sea of science and on the land of art.

Nascent Period

It is not surprising that Jerry would be the president of MIT most engaged in non-traditional forms of learning and research in science and technology. On campus, institutions like the Division for Sponsored Research in Education, the Health Sciences and Technology Program, and the Program in Science, Technology, and Society were all outside the normal bounds of church-and-state departments and labs, as we knew them. These were extremely controversial programs.

Perhaps none was more so than Arts & Media Technology (the original name of the Media Lab program). I recall one heated campus-wide meeting when I was asked if I really meant newspapers, movies, television, and so forth. The tone of the question was, "Yuck." And I said, "You better believe it." We were then told unequivocally not to use the words "computer" or "communications" in our name, whatever it might be, which was fine by me.

Late in 1977, Abe and Vera List approached Jerry with the idea of building a gallery. The gift was very much the result of Jerry's Arts Council, founded in 1971, composed of some of the world's greatest art connoisseurs and patrons. Jerry accepted a $3 M gift, which felt like real money at the time, and used it to leverage his plans to make MIT a more humane place.

I had a different idea.

On the last Friday of August 1978, I arranged a lunch with Jerry and Provost Walter Rosenblith—a pretty intimidating appointment. I explained, with immature

A festive spirit—Evening with the Arts at MIT, November 7, 1974: *left to right*, Walter Rosenblith; Jerry; Laya; Roy Lamson, special assistant to the president for the arts; and Susan Knight, associate director of the Council for the Arts. (Photo by Calvin Campbell. Courtesy of the MIT Museum.)

polemics, that building a gallery was to the mind what a tennis court is to the body. I called it "occupational therapy." Surely we at MIT could do much better, something at a more Olympic level, something that was at the cutting edge of both art and technology, something that would be less like chamber music and more like science fiction. Jerry said, "Okay, have a proposal to me by Tuesday," and I did.

The idea appealed to Jerry, for reasons I did not completely understand. At the time, Howard Johnson (seven years younger than Jerry) was chairman of the MIT Corporation and doing a splendid job. For this reason, Jerry decided privately not to become chairman, as some former presidents had done. Instead, he planned to make a reentry into research, to pursue ideas of his own. Not surprisingly, these ideas were a concatenation of his life interests, and there was no ready place to do the work. "Let me build you a Lab where you can do this." That was the deal.

The changing face of MIT—Jerry discusses plans with I. M. Pei and Vernon Alden, November 1979. Among the MIT buildings designed by Pei are the Cecil and Ida Green Building (1962), the Camille Edouard Dreyfus Building (1969), and the Wiesner Building (1984). (Photo by Calvin Campbell. Courtesy of the MIT Museum.)

The Media Lab

The name Media Lab was the idea of then dean of the School of Architecture and Planning, John de Monchaux. I had all sorts of other more complex names. John's was simple and clean. It forced us to squarely face the negative connotations of the word "media."

In 1979, we started fund-raising for the Lab and Jerry asked his dear friend I. M. Pei to design it. There was little pretense of due process in selecting the architect, which was just fine. To some degree Pei was the campus architect, having just completed three new buildings on campus.

Many of my colleagues and close friends thought I was nuts to drop day-to-day research for fund-raising, a process which took two years. But in hindsight it was the most educational experience of my life, for two reasons. First, Jerry and I spent more time together than we did with our respective wives (which we both heard about at home). Secondly, we met extraordinary people, almost all of whom were friends of or contacts through Jerry. It is obvious when you say it: people in a position to give serious money are leaders, achievers, and very interesting people.

Fund-raising

A deal was struck when the MIT Corporation blessed the Media Lab as a project. The agreement was to raise money from "new friends," not tapping into the traditional channels of MIT endowment. Philanthropy is very much a zero-sum game. And to some people, Jerry doing this Media Lab project was in itself an opportunity cost to MIT, as he could have put his well-known fund-raising skills anywhere else he wanted.

New friends were found in three places: Hollywood, Japan, and the personal computer industry (itself nascent).

Hollywood was by far the most amusing and star-studded. *Variety* referred to us as Batman and Robin (guess who was who) and Jerry was accused of looking like a beagle. We were invited by Liz Taylor and Rock Hudson and had dinner with George Lucas. We had one breakfast with Robert Redford, who turned the tables on us by asking Jerry for money (Jerry was on the MacArthur Foundation board) and getting it. The most memorable moment of all was when Lew Wasserman (MCA) deducted interest, because he did not want to "mortgage philanthropy." He gave us $182,600 up front, instead of the $250,000 we asked for over five years.

For me, Japan became the beginning of a period of many trips (no less than six times a year for the next fifteen). I had ties with Matsushita, but Jerry had even deeper ones with NEC, through his old friend and then CEO, Koji Kobayashi (KK, as he was called by his close friends). Both companies stepped to the plate and subsequently, in good Japanese tradition, Hitachi, Toshiba, Sony, NTT, and Mitsubishi followed suit. A notable exception, not a huge company, was a medium-sized TV station in Osaka, Asahi Broadcasting. ABC's director of international affairs, Jihei Akita, orchestrated a gift and has remained a close colleague since. To this day, he is the Japanese Representative of the Media Lab, a role he has continued to play since his retirement from the company.

Personal computers were so new. We cheated a bit and asked IBM, which could not participate in the building owing to a board-level policy against giving to bricks and mortar. Apple *was* different. A strong friendship grew with Steve Jobs, who pledged half a million dollars when Apple could ill afford it.

Finishing the Project

By agreement between MIT and ourselves, we set December 31, 1981 as the deadline. If we raised the $20 M needed, we would begin the new building; if we did not, we would quit. I cannot imagine the latter, but that is what we told ourselves. Apparently, I believed it.

I have never told this story before. It was at the beginning of December, while in Tokyo alone. I called Dr. KK and asked if we could have dinner alone. He brought Dr. Yasuo Kato, his trusted associate, an MIT alum, and by then a good friend. They asked what I wanted.

Without any permission from MIT, I explained the following. We needed $2 M to complete the project and if NEC would give $1 M, Jean Riboud (chairman of Schlumberger, on whose board Jerry sat) would match it. I went on to say (it is hard to imagine the gall, now that I am older) that MIT would name the building after Jerry if this all happened—the Wiesner Building. Obviously, I had no such permission.

KK agreed, out of love and loyalty to Jerry. When I went back to my room and realized what I had done, I called Jean Riboud in France and, to my astonishment, he came to the phone and agreed to his million. By this point I was into this so deep that I called MIT. Neither Paul Gray (president) nor David Saxon (chairman of the MIT Corporation) was available, but John de Monchaux was. I explained to John that I had just named the building after Jerry. He later took this idea to David Saxon, who reportedly said he wished he had thought of it.

But, it was unclear how Jerry would feel. In fact, it took about two months for the name to officially become the Wiesner Building. Once or twice during that period Jerry mumbled (he was a mumbler) something about hoping I was not naming the building after him. In the end, I think he was delighted.

Salon des Refuses

In January 1985, the building was completed (sort of) and some of us started to move in. We opened officially in October, with a huge event catered by Martha Stewart and keynoted by Michael Crichton. I have since reminded both how their careers started at the Media Lab.

In the time between breaking ground and opening, I took a sabbatical in France (learning how *not* to run a Lab). The following year a group coalesced around some of the most interesting figures at MIT. I am thinking of Marvin Minsky (AI),

Seymour Papert (learning), Ricky Leacock (film/video), Muriel Cooper (graphic design), and Barry Vercoe (music). Later, we attracted Steve Benton (holography) to the MIT faculty from Polaroid. The group also included some hardcore Architecture Machine folks still at the Media Lab: Walter Bender (currently director), Andy Lippman, and Chris Schmandt.

What these people had in common were varying degrees of rejection from their home disciplines. Each was considered a bit too extreme and had been rebuffed. While some people may not see it exactly this way, you get my point.

Jerry delighted in the composition of the original group, because he clearly saw that the fringe was becoming central. When we started this project, nobody was interested in the human computer interface. By the time we finished the building, the look and feel of computers was advertised in full-page spreads in the *Wall Street Journal*. The periphery rapidly became the center. This *salon des refuses* was at the right place, at the right time.

The Early Years

By the time the Media Lab was funded as a building, Jerry turned to some of his other interests, notably disarmament. He worked out of the corner office of the Lab (now called the Wiesner Room, again without permission). Nonetheless, he kept a steady interest in communications and was a great advocate of spread spectrum, which he tried to explain to me many times. I just did not get it then, but I do now, long after. He continued his interest in satellites, and was particularly fond of Minsky's work in common sense and Papert's in learning. My job was to grow the Lab.

Because we had "rain checks," like IBM's pledge to fund us if we ever got the building finished, I turned to industry, even though all my own research (when I did it) was funded by government: the Defense Advanced Research Projects Agency (DARPA), Office of Naval Research, and, to a lesser degree, the National Science Foundation. I thought I knew industry better than government, and found decisions could be made quickly. On occasion Jerry would join me, a bit like sport fishing or a habit hard to kick. What started as opportunistic—that is, corporate funding— became a tradition, even a trademark of the Media Lab. Until the end of 2001, it represented 95% of our research budget.

Once again, many of my MIT colleagues told me in the early 1980s not to focus on industry, because it was shortsighted, controlling, and oriented to quarterly results. Terms like "compromising academic freedom" were used to portray what might happen if we became an industry-focused Lab. Well, just the opposite happened and Jerry encouraged me to continue down that path.

Over the next twenty years, because of government cutbacks and the general decline of federal funding, many of these same colleagues started to find that government agencies were looking at the shorter term, wanting more specific results, and needing things that looked to me more like business plans. By sharp contrast, the comment I get most these days from our industrial partners is "be crazier." In fact, the value to corporations is very much at the lunatic fringe, going out on a limb as much as possible, doing things they might not. Jerry would be proud.

Thereafter

The last years of Jerry's life were hard. After one illness, I visited the hospital and the first thing he said to me was, "The exit has been designed badly." Shortly afterward he had his stroke, but by no means was he about to exit.

I visited every day when I was in town and watched him recover, learn to walk and talk, and return to the Lab as an active participant. By this time we had over 300 people and 80 sponsors, dealing with all sorts of students and new faculty. Keep in mind we were still not 100% respectable and, as a consequence, any student or faculty member who applied had to be slightly mad. I saw this as a wonderful character test. In a very real sense, Jerry was a role model for everybody.

Jerry was as close to being a father, and I a son, as any two could be without being either. His patience with the stupid things I said and did was a real education. He taught me many things. But the one that sticks out most in my mind, the one I practice as best I can, is: put up with people who are a real pain in the ass, as long as and only if they are exceptionally brilliant.

Jerry, I have not forgotten.

Continuing Communication

Emma Rothschild

"My metamorphosis," Jerry Wiesner wrote in the notes he prepared for his first lecture in the undergraduate course on arms races that he started to teach at MIT in 1981, the year after he retired as president. His arms career, he wrote, could be divided into three parts. From 1946 to 1957, he was a "military technologist." From 1957 to 1964, he was both a military technologist and a "technology policy participant." In the third phase, since 1964, he turned to "concentration on activities directed at halting the arms race." His metamorphosis, he wrote, came from the "realization that U.S. was running an arms race with itself."

Jerry Wiesner never published a memoir of his own life. But the succession of courses that he taught at MIT for most of the 1980s constituted an extended, unconstrained, sometimes poignant conversation about his relationships to technology over forty years. There was "Arms Races in Industrial Society," beginning in 1981, as the United States and the Soviet Union confronted each other over nuclear missiles in Europe; there was "Science, Technology, and Social Change"; there was "The Arms Race: Ways in and Ways Out," in the spring of 1988, the epoch of glasnost and perestroika. I taught these courses together with Jerry (in a duo much commented on, in the students' evaluations of the "senior male colleague" and the "junior female member"); I had an extraordinary opportunity over the decade to see how he thought, and how he had lived.

Emma Rothschild, economic historian, has written extensively on economic history and the history of economic thought, including *Economic Sentiments: Adam Smith, Condorcet and the Enlightenment* (2001). In the late 1960s, she was a Kennedy Scholar in Economics at MIT, and later served on the faculties of the Writing Program and the Program in Science, Technology, and Society (1978–88). She has also taught at the École des Hautes Études en Sciences Sociales in Paris. Since 1991, she has been a fellow and director of the Centre for History and Economics, King's College, Cambridge. She is chairman of the Kennedy Memorial Trust, the United Nations Research Institute for Social Development, and the United Nations Foundation Board Executive Committee.

The students' comments depict a slightly disorganized, discursive, and exhilarating classroom. "Dr Wiesner anecdotes were tremendous," one student wrote. "Fascinating subject matter, thought-provoking," said another. "Take it before you graduate especially if you are considering working in the defense industry," said a third. All these (anonymous) observations about Jerry's classes are in the Institute Archives at MIT; to read them is to find oneself in the midst of a conversation about, among other things, how to organize conversations.[1]

"One suggestion I have for increasing the exchange of ideas is to have people sit closer together in class," a student writes in 1983. "Personal recollections by J. Wiesner" and by "guest lecturers P. Morrison, L. Thoreau [Lester Thurow] were fascinating," writes another. There was "too much pious rhetoric about the stupidity of the arms race," said one; "*no discussion about morality of the arms race, too much discussion in regard of the economy!*" said another. There is a certain impression of a flux of words, memories, opinions. "Lectures were prepared but not organized real well. Should start and stop on time," one student wrote. The strengths of the teaching were described as "diversity of views; excellent detail—use of humor—relaxed class." The weaknesses were not unrelated: "instructors sometimes interrupting each other." Or, "Both talked too much."

The students in the courses wrote term papers—one student conducted a long interview with Jerry as a project in a different course—and many of these papers, too, are in the Institute Archives. ("I found the written assignment of a long term paper to be ideal for this kind of course," one student wrote in the evaluations; "this allowed me to explore the complex issues fully, yet not become overworked, a rather common MIT symptom which I find negates true learning." Others had a different view; "I generally do not like writing long papers, nor am I especially good at them," wrote another student in the same year.) One student prepared "A Survey of American Military Advertising and Propaganda," from 1930 to 1980. There is "Eisenhower and the New Look: Military-Economic Policy from 1953–55." There is "Insecurities of a Doctrine of Deterrence"—"What are our ideals? They should cover a broad range of issues," Jerry writes in the margin. There is "Onward Christian Soldiers: Ethics and the Arms Race," and "Choosing the Lesser Evil: A Comparison of the Bishops' Pastoral Letter on Nuclear War and the Conservative Response."

1. The student evaluations and other class materials are in the Institute Archives, MIT, MC420/Boxes 129 and 133, and in a box of papers which I deposited in the Institute Archives in 2002. I am most grateful to the Institute Archives for permission to quote from these papers.

A lecture, casual-style. (Photo by Roger Goldstein. Courtesy of the MIT Museum.)

The students were eager, apparently, to study one another. There is a note in the files: "Dr Wiesner: remember me? I am the student in your STS 540 class last term who did a survey of the MIT physics faculty and students regarding the arms race." Another student, the one who in a different class wrote the paper on insecurities of deterrence, submitted a paper called "The MIT Student and Defense Work: What Do Future Engineers Think?" She had conducted interviews and a survey of students in one of the MIT houses, and she included copies of 34 completed questionnaires; Jerry responds with a handwritten note, "We would like to have you work w/ us—ER JBW." The occasional moments of disorganization recur: "Paper got lost by instructor: that's why this is so late," reads another note in Jerry's handwriting on a grade sheet in the spring of 1984. So does the exhilaration: "The sense

Picnicking with incoming freshmen, September 1972—MIT students, he said, would need both "a sense of duty and a sense of humor." (Courtesy of the MIT Museum.)

of responsibility the class received from the lectures far outweighed the amount of credit handed out," a student writes in 1983; "Dr Wiesner is an extremely interesting man to listen to."

How did I come to teach these courses with Jerry? I first met him in 1967, when I arrived at MIT as a student in economics. I was a "Kennedy scholar," and Jerry took a continuing interest in the program which sent students from Britain to MIT and Harvard, in commemoration of President Kennedy, his friend. Jerry also knew my father Victor, who was himself a scientist and involved in science policy. When I returned to the faculty in 1978, it was against Jerry's advice—I remember him sitting on the grass outside a class reunion in Kresge Auditorium, trying to dissuade me from doing anything so imprudent. I was interested, by then, in the economic history of military expenditure, and in the history of military doctrines.

When Jerry retired as president of the Institute in 1980, he and I decided to experiment with a new course on political and economic, contemporary and historical aspects of arms races. One course led to the next, in an engagement with undergraduates which Jerry valued. I knew him well, I think, for more than 25 years. But

I came to know him in a different way during these extended, discursive conversations of the 1980s.

The arms race, which was the principal subject of the courses Jerry and I taught together, was one of his consuming interests over much of his life. He compared the understanding of science, in the interview he gave to the student in our class, to the understanding of art: "Those who understood it appreciated it like they did poetry or music." His descriptions of the early part of his arms career, starting in 1942 when he joined the Radiation Laboratory at MIT, were full of poetry and purpose. "New ways of thinking: almost like optics: signals flowed in pipes not through wires: could do that too but too lossy," he wrote in his lecture notes, of the information science of the 1940s. ("Lossy" was, I think, one of Jerry's not infrequent neologisms, at least in the sense of an extended simile about the loss of information in the course of communication, with optics, acoustics, and the life of the mind.)

Jerry dated his metamorphosis, or the last part of his arms career, to 1964, the year in which he returned from Washington, D.C., to MIT. But his view of the arms race was deeply influenced, as he described it, by discussions within the Eisenhower administration in the late 1950s, as well as by the disputes over the "Missile Gap" in the 1960 presidential campaign, and their aftermath once he had moved to the White House as President Kennedy's science adviser. It was influenced even more profoundly by the worldwide protests of the early 1960s about nuclear tests in the atmosphere, and by his own involvement in the negotiations that led to the Partial Test Ban Treaty of 1963.

The Test Ban Treaty was for Jerry a great achievement, and a great failure (because it was only partial). He returned frequently, in the arms race courses at MIT, to the details of the negotiations over nuclear testing—with the Russians, and within the United States government. There was an inside of military policy, in his description, in which a Comprehensive Test Ban Treaty was occasionally almost within reach. And there was an outside, of public and political movements. The public was sometimes in favor of the arms race (as in 1960) and sometimes in favor of arms limitation. The movement to stop nuclear testing in the atmosphere "was driven largely by women, by the Women's Strike for Peace," he told our student who interviewed him in 1981; "they had the confidence to do what they were doing because a number of scientists like Linus Pauling were giving them the scientific information about the dangers of strontium–90 in milk . . . [they were] confident that what they were demanding was reasonable."

This conception of the inside and the outside of science was one of Jerry's continuing preoccupations. There was a potential universe of reasonable people (of reasonable women, in particular) and the responsibility of scientists was to "give people some understanding of the issues and some confidence that they're not demanding irrational things." Jerry used to recall, a little ruefully, the time in the mid-1950s when he and his colleague Jerrold Zacharias, having studied classified reports of nuclear fallout in the Pacific, decided to buy land in New Hampshire, selected because it was on the other side of a mountain from Boston, and secluded from the main roads which would be used by millions of people in the event of a nuclear strike. But he gave the land away, eventually. He came to think of himself as an outsider, or a semi-outsider, for much of the rest of his life. There was no security from a nuclear conflict, he came to believe. His role was to explain, and to instruct. The effort to reduce nuclear (and biological) weapons was his consuming interest in the 1980s and 1990s—the reason, always, to write one more op-ed article, stay one more year on a committee, go to one more meeting of the MacArthur Foundation, returning late and cold to Watertown.

But Jerry was also, throughout his life, and even at the period of his greatest preoccupation with military questions, someone who wanted to construct. Science is an inquiry into the nature of our existence, he said in his 1981 interview; it is "humanistic." When science was unimportant, he said, "people would appreciate scientific discoveries for the essential beauty and knowledge." When it became important, "people thought it could make possible any kind of miracle." He was captivated, himself, by both sorts of beauty. His foreboding interest in military technologies coexisted, always, with a delight in practical, entrepreneurial, and industrial research. His and Laya's life in Watertown was accompanied by an incredible series of new, experimental, and semi-disconnected machines. He drove one of the earliest cars with electric windows (it broke down on the way back from Logan Airport); he had one of the earliest "facsimile" machines; there was always a newer computer in his study, in various states of disarray; he tried, with rather little success, to persuade his much younger colleagues on various committees of the 1980s to attach themselves to something called a "net."

Jerry's life was intertwined, since his earliest days as an itinerant acoustical engineer and in his collaboration with Norbert Wiener, with the development of the information industry. He was fascinated with communication, entertainment, computation. It is difficult, now, to describe the imaginative world of the 1950s and 1960s, in which information was only one among many incipient leading industries. There is an exchange of letters in Jerry's papers from 1970, in which my father wrote to Jerry for advice about a "new computational possibility." Jerry was unimpressed by the particular project, and he sought to convey the extent of the developing industry: "there are going to be a number of major improvements in computer hardware and computer software in the near future . . . I would guess that the research effort on computer hardware and machine structures exceeds two hundred million dollars a year." (One of my own part-time jobs, as an MIT student in the late 1960s, was as a highly inexpert research assistant to a young law professor who had been commissioned to reflect on whether new developments in the computer industry might have consequences, eventually, for privacy.)

Science and information, for Jerry, were always international. He was intrigued, towards the end of his life, by his own family's European past, and by their European politics. But he was also connected in countless ways to friends and colleagues, scientists and inventors and politicians, in Europe and around the world. He had a remarkable capacity to think himself into the minds and feelings of other people—a capacity for sympathy—and his view of the Soviet Union was influenced in a very important way by his friendships, starting in the late 1950s, with Russian scientists. His interest in economic development persisted for much of his life, and he saw in science (as in his own work on agriculture in Pakistan in the 1960s, and on the African Academy of Sciences in the 1980s) the possibility of a different and less impoverished world—with a "Department of Development," as he suggested in the last class he taught in 1988 ("Ways In and Ways Out"), to substitute for the Department of Defense.

The future of MIT, for Jerry, was to be a world university. His office, like our classroom from time to time, was filled in the 1980s with visitors from almost everywhere: French oil exploration engineers, Soviet generals (to the occasional surprise of the local office of the FBI), Indian environmentalists, and Pakistani political leaders. It was also filled with Jerry's friends from Japan. He loved visiting Japan, and he was entranced with Japanese television, ceramics technology, ceremonies, designs, architecture. He had an extraordinary talent for elective affinities, and the affinity he chose, towards the end of his life, was to a great extent Japanese. "Life is a continuous experiment in all dimensions," he told our student, and one of the most important of freedoms—a freedom of which the Soviet Union was deprived—was the "freedom to experiment and evolve."

Science, for Jerry, was not a profession, or a responsibility of public life. It was a part of almost everything in his daily existence. It was also a source of strength, and unending curiosity. All of Jerry's friends, over the last three decades of his life, must have been struck by his fortitude. Laya's illness, his own sudden onset of diabetes, his stroke in 1989—he was beset by devastating events. But he tried to understand all these events, and all the ways in which they might be mitigated (the ways out). His extraordinary recovery of speech following his stroke had a great deal to do with his endless interest in the world. He observed his own words and sounds; he theorized; he thought about his own work, half a century earlier, as a sound engineer; he put together experiment and theory and the will to communicate.

Jerry's life in the 1980s, as I have tried to recollect it, was an extended, inquiring conversation, with students, visitors, friends. But it was also, above all, a conversation at home, and with his family. His conversation with each of his children and grandchildren ebbed and flowed, but never ceased. His continuing conversation with Laya was quite simply the heart of his life. In the correspondence with my father, there is a letter from 1971 in which my father writes to Jerry about a dinner with Laya and my mother: "Thank you both so much for such an enjoyable evening—just the sort which Tess and I enjoy." What they seem to have been doing, the four of them, was talking about risk: Jerry had made "a qualitative distinction between the probability of an event when comparable events have occurred before, and the probability of an event when there have been no comparable events before." Among all of Jerry's multiple gifts, he was transcendently endowed with the gift of friendship. One of the things he gave to his friends, until the very end, was the opportunity to be part of his and Laya's life.

Commitment to International Peace and Security

Ruth S. Adams[1]

Where did you first meet Jerry?

My first encounter with Jerry was through the *Bulletin of the Atomic Scientists*. Working with editor Eugene Rabinowitch, I was often the one who corresponded with potential authors or telephoned them. Jerry was a valued contributor to the *Bulletin*.

But when I first really got to know Jerry and watch him speak in a public arena was in 1960, at the important and timely Pugwash conference in Moscow. The meeting was in December following the November election of President Kennedy. Jerry had been appointed his science adviser. To that meeting in Moscow came two or three other people who were going to be members of Kennedy's Cabinet. Khrushchev was then the premier of the Soviet Union. It was hoped that progress would be made in arms control and that agreement would be reached on a test ban. Jerry played an effective role in bringing these issues to the table and often led the discussions.

Ruth S. Adams has been active in a number of efforts relating to arms control, the public understanding of science, and other social and educational issues. She served in several editorial capacities with the *Bulletin of the Atomic Scientists* (1955–68, 1978–84), and in the intervening period (1969–78) was a research associate at the American Academy of Arts and Sciences. She joined the staff at the newly established Program on International Peace and Security, John D. and Catherine T. MacArthur Foundation, in 1985, and was its director until 1992, after which she was appointed senior adviser to the Foundation. She has played a key role in the Pugwash Conferences on Science and World Affairs since their inception in 1957, and has served on the boards of the International Centre of Insect Physiology and Ecology, Nairobi, Kenya (1971–79) and the Council for a Livable World (1962–91).

1. Excerpted and edited from an interview conducted on October 4, 2002 by Adele Simmons, president, John D. and Catherine T. MacArthur Foundation, 1989–1999.

These contacts cemented a friendship which then continued, and our paths would cross in other interesting ways before we became still more closely associated at the MacArthur Foundation. I worked in Africa for ten years on the development of a research center in Nairobi, the International Centre of Insect Pathology and Ecology (ICIPE). The United Nations Development Programme and the Ford Foundation were early supporters. I recall when Carroll Wilson, professor of management at MIT, and I went with Jerry to discuss the project with McGeorge Bundy, then president of the Ford Foundation. During the initial fundraising, Jerry opened many doors for us.

Our paths crossed at American Academy of Arts and Sciences meetings and at conferences on arms control or peace issues. Then, in February 1983, I had a phone call about ten o'clock at night. On the phone was Rod MacArthur, whom I had known vaguely in Chicago. He said, "I've got a friend of yours here—I'm going to put him on." That was Jerry, and he said, "We're having a meeting here." The meeting included Jonas Salk, Murray Gell-Mann, Rod, and Jerry, I think that was it. They obviously had all been having many glasses of wine and had finished their dinner at a little French restaurant. Jerry said, "Hop in a cab and come down—we have some ideas we want to share with you."

That was the beginning of efforts to establish the international peace program at MacArthur. At the time, I think there were two programs under way—one in health and, of course, the so-called "genius" or MacArthur Prize Fellows program. Peace was to be the third one, and Jerry was determined that the Foundation should take the leading role in identifying ways to lessen the danger of a nuclear war and to make progress in arms control and U.S.-Soviet relations. Rod agreed with him, as did Jonas and Murray.

From the beginning, we understood the Foundation's wish to maintain bipartisan programs, and we needed to keep all directors informed of our activities and in essence to bring them along with us. So what we did was consult specialists from different fields and professions, and these discussions were shared with other directors. We invited McGeorge Bundy as the chair and approached the Carnegie president, David Hamburg, to cosponsor the project. Both accepted.

What was Mac Bundy doing at that time?

He was not tied to a schedule other than his own. Preparing his memoirs, he was a professor at NYU and living a life of the gentle intellect, if you will, having retired from public service. Fair to say that he was much intrigued by the challenge of assisting a new foundation to establish a peace and security program. So we worked with him for nine months and convened numerous meetings with numerous people. It was really great fun. Jerry was always present. His enthusiasm was infectious, his careful articulation of the issues admired. At the finish, we had a report—"To Make a Difference: A Report on Needs and Opportunities for Philanthropic Action in the Field of International Security."

Backing up a bit, when Jerry first came on the MacArthur board, he, Rod, Murray, and Jonas formed an early committee to explore new programs for this very new foundation.[2] As I recall from informal conversations with Jerry, it was clear that he was consumed by three needs—or three reasons, I should say—for the Foundation to invest in a new program on international security. In the first place, Jerry had always been passionately interested in the U.S.-Soviet relationship and how that defined the Cold War. He particularly wanted to understand how these nations perceived and misperceived each other. Then he thought there was a great deal of important research that should be done so that the two governments and their civil servants could more effectively handle the relationship. He also understood and would talk at length about the difficulties that were presented to two nations with such conflicting political systems. On the one hand you had the openness and liberties of a democracy, on the other hand the restraints and constraints of a bureaucracy.

Secondly, through his whole life, Jerry expressed his concerns about weapons of mass destruction, particularly nuclear—how these weapons themselves defined military strategies, defined political strategies. As these weapons threatened the very survival of humankind, I think he saw in this area the greatest need for clarity, for research, and for involving the public in thinking about weapons of mass destruction. Finally, with those two—the Cold War and the weapons of mass destruction—there remained his concern for what were known at that time as the "third world countries," the countries of poverty, the countries without technology and education.

I know that Jerry believed and hoped to find some way of expressing all these convictions of his in a new program on international security at the MacArthur Foundation. Writing on behalf of the committee, he said—"We have been guided by the recognition that political and social stability and the evolution toward a global order in which democratic ideals and associated rights of individuals could

---

2. Jerry was elected to the board on May 18, 1979, and served until his death in 1994 (information provided by Richard Kaplan, director, Grants Management, Research, and Information, MacArthur Foundation).

survive and progress are globally important. The attached proposal and its appendices present our recommendations and document our work."

Jerry thus argued that the MacArthur Foundation could make a difference, and the board approved the proposal in November 1983. He thanked his colleagues and commented—"in making this investment of such significant size and intelligent design at this very unusual moment, the MacArthur Foundation can reasonably expect to have a major impact over the course of the next decades."

From the beginning, Jerry, Murray, Jonas, and others on the board played a role of collective leadership. Each director had an interest in one of the programs of the Foundation, and indeed helped to develop programs. The structure was such that each program had a committee of interested board directors who played a very important role in the implementation of these programs, guiding policy and so on. Typically, the president proposes the grant program and funding strategy. In the case of the early years of the MacArthur Foundation, however, it was in a sense many smaller foundations, each having its board of directors, namely, a program committee. I found that the arrangement worked well, but only because the individuals involved were talented and committed.

What were some of the issues you were struggling with or talking about early on, and who were some of the other people involved?

We talked to everybody we could think of, including Warren Buffett and Bill Perry, later to become secretary of defense. The issues were how to train the next generation and how to do it through established institutions—that was one point—and secondly, how to really begin to build a public that understood these issues. Since the end of World War II, the public had become traumatized by the fear of a Soviet attack, by fear of nuclear weapons, so that many felt helpless. It was Jerry's strong feeling that we had to find a way to embrace the public so that they could begin to see where the risks were and how we could make a choice between certain risks that still in the end would yield great improvement over the present Cold War situation.

Briefly, the program's primary purpose was to broaden and strengthen the field of international security and to do so within traditional educational institutions and the public-interest community. To accomplish this goal, the plans envisioned grants for institutions and fellowships in support of independent thinkers and policy studies, with the overall mission of furthering international understanding.

Jerry believed that the world was in a crisis of vast dimensions brought on by the scientific and technological revolution. He thought about future scenarios, about ways to lessen the danger of violence and destruction. What would be the steps toward a more stable world? What kinds of arrangements or engagements could you make with nations such as the Soviet Union where you did not share the same values? How could you learn to build bridges whereby confidence and trust began to shape international discussions? And what of the role of the United Nations and other international institutions?

That was a huge project to take on. In January 1984, the board approved a five-year program. If I recall, in those days we had a very large budget. I think it was 15 or 20 million a year, which was a major investment for the Foundation. Through all the deliberations, Jerry was the force that propelled us all. His intense interest in the problems and new ideas that developed out of this program has been recorded in many different ways.

As staff, together with the supporting board committee, began to put into effect the Program on International Peace and Security, it was clear that the difficulty would center on the educational institutions. MacArthur had requested that ways be found to create interdisciplinary programs, which in most cases went against established practices. So Jerry conceived of what he called "the wise council." The basic purpose of this group would be to test the idea that research efforts integrated across disciplinary specialties could produce "practical, consequential improvements in prevailing conceptions of security." The hope was to put together a group of perhaps twenty individuals, selected first for their interest in security and second for the special experiences and studies they brought to bear upon the matter. This effort on Jerry's part, to issue a mandate for a group to review the most promising and most important conceptual issues underlying the problems of international security, tells us how passionate and concerned he was about the threats to humankind and the earth itself from weapons of mass destruction.

But I think Jerry always was in some conflict with himself. He had to find a way to balance his ideals and hopes with the reality of the world he faced. I sense that this conflict probably was with Jerry for most of his life.

He gave his full attention to the program. People often asked, why did members of the MacArthur board act and spend time as if they were staff members? It's true they did. Since I was there during those days, I must say I really enjoyed it. The board members became colleagues. We would organize seminars and bring people there, and the board would come and the staff would participate. Of course, there wasn't much of a staff in those days. But it is certainly true that the board members played a major role and were excited about it—Murray, Jonas, Jerry, and later, Gaylord Freeman, CEO of the then First National Bank of Chicago, and Elizabeth McCormack of the Rockefeller Associates.

Another characteristic of Jerry's was his belief in a participatory role for all directors. He expected everyone to understand the nonpartisan nature of the security field. So if some of his more conservative colleagues would challenge, he would respond that peace and security were not partisan issues—they were fundamental for the long-term survival not only of the United States but of the world itself. I believe he would be deeply saddened to see how far his country has moved away from firm international agreements and multilateral negotiations.

At the time that the planning was going on, the Cold War was beginning to unravel a bit at least.

It was a key time, although we didn't really recognize it then. The changes that were taking place in the Soviet Union were in part economic, and a few people in the United States began publishing articles saying that the Soviet Union could not afford to continue to keep up with the United States in the arms race, that they had to have arms control.

There were other signs. New international scientific meetings were taking place in the Soviet Union in those days—in biology, for example. Then, of course, one saw changes in the top leadership. People were asking—what does it mean, where is it going? Nobody really knew, but this program of MacArthur's was in place at a key moment. Importantly, the Foundation had the interest and cooperation of a generation of young people whom we would probably not have had if this program had started ten years earlier.

After you set up the program, how did you and Jerry go about making it work?

He would come to Chicago and we would be on the phone constantly. So it wasn't as if the board approved a program and the program officers—namely, me and some wonderful young people who came to work for us—then just went about doing it. Jerry was part of it from the word go, as was Murray. Once the program got going, Rod went on to think about other things, so he didn't play much of a role. It was Jerry, Jonas, and Murray who were involved. I would also pay tribute to the advisers who came from the research and educational communities we were supporting. In many respects, they provided both sensitivity and intellectual discipline to the program.

When you think about the program, how did it evolve and what is your sense of its impact?

Assessing impact is always problematic for protagonists, but the program did evolve in ways that I think strengthened its role and influence. To begin with, what became clear in this relationship with Jerry and the program was that he saw more clearly than almost anyone else at the time the need to be interdisciplinary. He knew that we couldn't just have physicists negotiating test bans. He knew that we had to have economists, that we had to have sociologists, that this was highly political. So the program was interdisciplinary from its very beginning, and it's really rather unusual that it was a scientist—an engineer—who led the way and insisted that it had to be interdisciplinary.

The unfortunate aspect of it—and I know it always bothered Jerry—is that there was no way to make a physicist who wanted to do security issues succeed in physics at the same time that he worked on security issues, whereas in the social sciences there were options for young people in the research field. That was always a problem. We tried very hard to involve people in the natural sciences as well, but I can't say that we really succeeded.

But Jerry did it at MIT, too. He started the Program in Science, Technology, and Society, and supported people like Kosta Tsipis, who directed MIT's Program in Science and Technology for International Security. He did this many times against the feelings of senior scientists at MIT, but he persisted because he felt these kinds of things were very important.

Was there ever any ongoing debate within the MacArthur board about the direction of the program after it got started, and if so, how did Jerry manage that?

I didn't often sit in on those discussions. We were called in when they discussed the program, but I was never a part of the discussions that occurred when they looked at the Foundation as a whole. Jerry would sometimes report on the meetings. I think many people felt that too much money was being spent on the program, point one; point two, that we didn't have enough control over it; and point three, that we didn't have very good evaluation procedures. The other issue that used to come up—and it troubles foundations to this day—is, what do you take risks for, how do you take them, and how do you evaluate them?

Jerry was uniquely suitable—and suited, I should say—to say, "Hey, that's risky, let's do it!" That was really what was unique in many ways about MacArthur in those days. It was also Jerry who would look at what the students were doing and say, "You know, if we just had five-thousand-dollar grants, we could change this whole college campus." And he was right. That was the other aspect of the program that was good, the small grants. Again, Jerry was the one who I'm sure persuaded his colleagues on the board to go along with that.

I think of the research and writing program, too, which was not just designed for academics. Was Jerry part of thinking that this needed to have a broader reach?

That was part of it, yes. It was to give people from all fields—they could be journalists, they could be scientists, they could be good writers—the chance to take on some of these issues, if they wanted to. We got an amazing group of people through that program. It took a while for it to get off the ground because it had a big review component. We would get all these requests and the question was, how are we going to review them and decide? But once we got going on it, I think it was probably one of the more successful of the programs.

On the issue of wanting to change educational institutions, I think of Paul Doty's program at Harvard, for example, which was beginning just at that time.

You can certainly see the results of all these efforts today at Stanford, at Berkeley, at Minnesota—security studies have become more widely a part of educational curricula. For me, and I'm sorry Jerry isn't around to witness it, it's a pleasure to see that so many people who are now becoming not senior but middle-range in their careers, so to speak, came out of the MacArthur program. Some are in academe, others in government; many elected to work in think tanks and public-interest organizations. We used to bring them together for an annual conference. They would meet in different parts of the world, and it clearly was a major educational experience.

There were meetings in Mexico, Turkey, and India.

Yes, also in Eastern Europe and Africa.

Jerry was passionate about young people. He had always helped Pugwash. I don't think he attended that many meetings, but he was always supportive. When Student Pugwash was organized, he helped to raise money and encourage campus organizations. He liked to be in the know, to be involved. He spoke of shaping and influencing young minds.

Sometimes he was difficult—arbitrary and impatient. As president, you must have witnessed this during board meetings.

That's absolutely true. I felt sometimes that he had a sense—particularly when I became MacArthur president—that time was running out, that his time was running out. He was the person who argued most for spending down the endowment. The problems then seem to pale compared to the ones we have now, but his view was, "We have these horrible problems—let's address them, let's use the money we have."

But the point is, too, that he had faith in education and he had faith in the capacity of the human species to produce wise people. He felt we could solve these problems.

He had a sense that the Cold War was going to end not through competitive throw weights but through political solutions. It seems so easy for us to say now, but I think it's hard to understand that it was not conventional wisdom at the time.

It certainly was not, but you have to remember that for American intellectuals and Russian intellectuals there was a common pattern of discourse, they read the same books, they knew the same history. They were divided by political systems, but among the scientists—and musicians and artists—there was a great font of commonality. In fact, what made Pugwash so successful in the early days was that it really became an international community. One of the big decisions that helped this community to become special was that everybody was invited to bring a companion, probably a spouse. It became, in addition to a very serious meeting on very serious problems, a marvelous holiday. For reasons which I've never quite understood, the Russian government never put a stop to it.

When we thought of Russia, we thought of the Russians we knew. It gave confidence to thinking we could do something in the society. I think in large part we were all very naive, but on the other hand, what really influenced Jerry and helped MacArthur to seriously consider setting up its Russian office was the faith he had in education, intelligence, and rationality.

What did he hope the Russian office would accomplish?

I think it was the same hope that he had for the office in Chicago, and that was that we could help people become independent and we could support independent minds who were working on problems that were important to solve. He often said, "A foundation has two important contributions to make—one is money and the other is independent judgment." He fervently believed that. That carried him, I think, to really taking the establishment of an office in Russia very seriously.

Jerry's activities early on in the transition of the Soviet Union to Russia took the form of cooperation with some of his scientific colleagues in the Soviet Union. Primary among these was Academician Velikhov. With Velikhov and Senator Mathias, Jerry proposed a private foundation to be incorporated in Moscow. The title that the three of them gave to this new venture was the International Foundation for the Survival and Development of Humanity. An office was set up, grants were raised from several private U.S. foundations, and for about a year this foundation operated in Moscow as the very first private foundation. It failed, however, and with its failure Jerry became very much interested in assisting the MacArthur Foundation to establish an office in Moscow.

This was achieved in 1992. Unfortunately, Jerry's health at that time did not permit him to travel to Russia and to be on the scene, so to speak, with the new Foundation branch. But needless to say, it quickly became a success and it was an achievement, I think, for which Jerry could rightly share the responsibility and personal pleasure.

It was clear to me that if I didn't go forward with setting up a Russian office, Jerry would be deeply disappointed and very distressed. He was the motivation behind it and he had the vision. I believed in it, but I didn't have the kind of experience he had.

It was very exciting in those days. Jerry became very close to Gorbachev and Sakharov, in addition to other scientists. It certainly was his vision and his spirit that led the way. He wanted MacArthur to be there first, and MacArthur was.

As you look back over Jerry's remarkable work in peace and international security, is there anything you would like to add?

Jerry had been devastated by the Kennedy assassination. I think he thought that the two of them could really find ways of using science and in a sense reach new heights by putting science seriously into politics. Those dreams crashed when Kennedy was killed. It was almost eighteen years later that Jerry got involved with MacArthur.

Do you know who asked him to join the board, or how that happened?

Jerry, Jonas, and Murray were nominated by Rod and approved by the board, part of a deal in which Rod successfully lobbied to revitalize the board by adding subject experts who would be valuable in the grantmaking process.

There was enough money so that each one of them could have their own program. There was a kind of understanding that one did not overly interfere in the program of the other.

That's true. Murray was certainly very close to the fellowship program, the Prize Fellows. In fact, talking about being a staff member, he certainly was one in every sense of the word. At the same time, he was very faithful to the international committee and he wanted his say on that committee. Jonas was both health and international issues. I think everybody was concerned about the program on peace and security and cooperation. Some were very suspicious of it, others were really very supportive, but it couldn't be ignored. Murray and Jonas and Jerry would always jump to its defense.

Jerry, probably because of his own background, was very sensitive to what he called the bureaucracy of people who don't know what to do. Because he came from a university community, he also was willing to let grantees have a great deal of freedom to develop programs. He never insisted, as happened a bit later, on very strict rules of reporting or sending people out to supervise. He also would argue, and I think persuasively, when people said you couldn't give so many small grants because you couldn't really make them accountable, "Well, when you give small grants away, you just have to take a risk—period." He used to argue that, and I think in many respects that was one of his great contributions: to keep the Foundation more open and innovative and less bureaucratic.

At that point the board was meeting once a month, so there was constant interaction.

Yes, they really developed cohesion as a result of being together so often and with a very heavy schedule. I think almost everybody enjoyed it.

It was a huge time commitment.

Yes, it was. The Foundation became part of their lives. They thought MacArthur, they acted on behalf of MacArthur, and they loved it. They really felt they were doing great things, and they were.

I thought they were pretty terrific as a group. I don't know what went on in those board meetings over a relaxed dinner or a bottle of wine, but it was clear they made the board work. As far as I know, at least for the years when I was close to the board, it was very effective.

And Jerry's commitment to the issues provided momentum. In 1988, in an address to the centennial symposium of the National Geographic Society, which he entitled "Survival, the Moral Equivalent of the Arms Race," Jerry laid out his concerns for what was happening to the world around him. He considered that we were facing global chaos. He argued that the extent of global disarray was only dimly perceived, because individuals everywhere tended to regard the troubles they faced as local or national. But his philosophy, which determined his role at the MacArthur Foundation, was expressed very clearly in this speech. He said: "The challenge is for us, those now alive, to mobilize, to start building a world that is in ecological and human equilibrium."

Jerry's last years at the Foundation were marked and shaped by the momentous events taking place in the former Soviet Union and Eastern Europe. He was well aware that he was living through a transformative era in human history. The breakup of old alliances and political systems outpaced, he felt, the capacity to think and design programs to meet these new challenges. First and foremost, he was concerned with reduction of military budgets in both the former Soviet Union and the United States, and then the question of dismantling armaments and the role and cooperation of the United States in the process. He spoke often of the need to think of ways to help in a reconstruction which had to take place in every dimension of society—in politics, the social system, the health system, and so on.

Jerry's tenure at the Foundation lasted a little over a decade. In those years, not only did he have a profound effect on the program strategy of the Foundation, he also influenced those people who worked directly with him, including myself. If the Foundation achieved a reputation as an innovative, caring, wise foundation, we credit Jerry for much of that.

As I reflect on the years of cooperation with Jerry, there were times when our anxieties—our lack of confidence—as to whether we were doing the right thing dominated. We had many discussions on the very nature of grantmaking and how one could achieve an independent and fair assessment of potential grantees. Often the grants we made were to individuals or institutions who were new, or at least unknown and untested. We supported people whose ideas were unpopular. We defended their rights to have those ideas. In the end, we used to say that grantmaking was clearly for the young and for the soon-to-be retired who were already freeing themselves of linkages to their former bureaucracies.

The MacArthur Foundation provided Jerry with an extraordinary opportunity to encourage new thinking and direction in the field of peace and security. I believe the years he spent at the Foundation gave him an opportunity to extend to others his values and his visions of a better world.

A Voice of Reason

Anthony Lewis

It is May 2002 as I write, and I have never felt the absence of Jerry Wiesner more acutely. How his voice is needed today, the voice of reason, of humanity, of faith in the open mind. We can imagine him warning against the scrapping of treaties—against the notion that the unilateral exercise of America's enormous military power will make us, and the world, safe. We can imagine him speaking to the medieval-ism that mars America now: the rejection of science because of fundamentalist religious doctrines, the rejection really of the open mind.

Jerry Wiesner brought his acute intellect and humane character to bear on the problems of this country and the world for forty years. He went to Washington, a much less sectarian Washington than it is today, as a member of President Eisenhower's Science Advisory Committee in the 1950s. He was there as science adviser to President Kennedy in the 1960s, a time that was probably the peak of Washington's openness to science and the life of the mind. (Jerry did the seating for the 1962 dinner for Nobel prize-winners at which Kennedy quipped, "I think this is the most extraordinary collection of talent, of human knowledge that has ever been gathered together at the White House, with the possible exception of when Thomas Jefferson dined alone.")

We have a vignette that suggests the crucial part Wiesner played in alerting President Kennedy to the dangers of radioactive fallout and, more broadly, to the need

Anthony (Tony) Lewis, one of America's best-known journalists, began his career as a newsman in 1948. He was a reporter with the *New York Times* and *Washington Daily News* before serving as U.S. Supreme Court and Department of Justice correspondent for the *New York Times* Washington Bureau (1955–64), then chief of the *New York Times* London Bureau (1964–72), and *New York Times* op-ed columnist (1972 until recently). He taught at Harvard Law School and Columbia University, wrote a mystery novel—*Gideon's Trumpet*—that earned him the award for best fact-crime book from the Mystery Writers of America in 1965, and won the Pulitzer Prize for National Reporting (1955 and 1963).

for the 1963 Soviet-American treaty barring nuclear tests in the atmosphere. In a film shown to visitors at the John F. Kennedy Library in Boston, there is a scene in which the young president looks silently out the windows of the Oval Office on a rainy day. A voice—Jerry's voice—says, "I remember one day when he [Kennedy] asked me what happens to the radioactive fallout, and I told him it was washed out of the clouds by the rain and would be brought back to earth by the rain. And he said, looking out the window, 'You mean it's in the rain out there?' And I said, 'Yes.' He looked out the window, very sad, and didn't say a word for several minutes."

But Jerry Wiesner's commitment to public life was not limited to the time he was in Washington. Justice Louis D. Brandeis used to say that the highest office in a democracy is the office of citizen. Wiesner lived that principle. In or out of official positions, he never stopped caring or working for the public good. He never thought it was not his problem. Like James Madison and the others who created the United States, he thought citizens of a republic have a duty to be involved in the fate of their country.

He really believed that one man or woman could make a difference in this complex world, with all its aggregations of power. He believed, even at the time when the United States and the Soviet Union were engaged in a spiraling, irrational nuclear arms race, a time when someone like Henry Kissinger was confident that MIRV'ing our weapons would give us the edge, only to find—predictably, if one's mind had been open to reason—that the Soviets followed suit and both of us were less secure.

"We seem absolutely trapped in a delusional system that grips us more year by year," Wiesner wrote in the *Boston Globe* in 1984. "My message is that piling up weapons erodes security rather than builds it." It was characteristic that he set out his warning in a magazine piece for the general public. "This article is aimed at nonexperts on nuclear war," he began. "That means everybody—including those supposedly in on the secrets—because there never has been a true nuclear war of the sort the United States and the Soviet Union have been equipped to fight for the last 25 years and there is no way to rehearse one." He went on to warn, compellingly: "We must understand the extent to which the United States has been running an arms race with itself, and in the process become a military culture."

Five years later Mikhail Gorbachev opened the Berlin Wall, and the Cold War was over. It became a truism that the United States had won. But Jerry Wiesner said—he was the first to say it—that both sides had lost.

"World security is not simply a question of military balance . . . it is a question of how causes of conflicts can be eliminated by economic equilibrium and the organization of peaceful cooperation"—German chancellor Willy Brandt speaking at MIT, March 9, 1977, as part of the "World Change and World Security" lecture series. (Courtesy of the MIT Museum.)

And delusion did not stop with the end of the Cold War. President Reagan's colorful dream of an impervious shield in space lives on in the form, now, of a distant defense against ballistic missiles fired by rogue states in the "axis of evil." We need Jerry Wiesner to explain the folly of giving up the security we had in the Anti-Ballistic Missile Treaty for the will-o'-the-wisp of missile defense that will cost endless, useless billions.

It must be painfully hard to know the reality of a situation as well as Jerry did and see the holders of power ignore that reality. Most of us would burst out in frustration, or give up. Jerry remained calm. He acted, with modesty, humor, patience. He never gave up. There was not a trace of personal ambition in his public stands—of the zest for power that drove, say, Edward Teller. As Viki Weisskopf said at the Wiesner memorial service, he was "a man of extraordinary virtue." There was a purity in his commitment; it was unaffected by personal interest.

Nor did he assume, as so many of us tend to do, that those who disagreed were evil. "The leaders of the military-industrial complex are not evil," he wrote in his *Globe* article. They just were not willing to open their minds and see that ever more weapons made us less, not more, secure.

Jerry knew, personally, all three corners of the military-industrial-scientific complex. But the knowledge did not daunt him. He believed that reason could overcome the follies and cruelties of mankind. When someone called him an optimist, he replied: "I don't know whether I'm an optimist or not, but I'm a realist. I realize this is the only world we've got. We have to use our intelligence, our reason—and work just a little bit harder."

Thinking of that optimism, if that is what it was, after Jerry's death, I remembered Robert Kennedy's speech at the University of Cape Town in 1966. In the bleakest days of apartheid, he told the audience that we have to resist the feeling of hopelessness. We have to dare to make a difference.

When we look at the world today, or at our own country, the temptation to give up is strong for many of us. Jerry would never have accepted that. Surely if South Africans could resist, and eventually overcome, the repressive power of the apartheid system that gripped them for so long, he would say, we should not turn away from the responsibility of caring.

Jerry cared—about issues, about people, about institutions. His caring was not affected by where he was or what he was. As a scientist, as a White House adviser, as president of MIT, as a private person, he was always a citizen.

Someone who never knew Jerry Wiesner might imagine him as ferociously intense, even humorless in his devotion to public matters. He was not like that at all. His manner was easygoing; he loved the curiosities of life; he loved jokes. He seemed happiest at his home on Martha's Vineyard, sailing on Menemsha Pond or just living a life of beauty and repose with his remarkable wife, Laya.

When I wrote about him after his death, I had a letter from a woman in Riverdale, Maryland. She said she had not started to vote until she was 30 years old. Now, she said, "I could imagine Mr. Wiesner approving that I had started voting. . . . I will take Mr. Wiesner's spirit to heart in future."

He was a citizen not of this country alone but of the world. The transparency of his devotion to humanity made it possible for him to work with people of different cultures, notably with Soviet scientists at the worst of times in relations between our countries. I remember him sharing a platform with Andrei Sakharov, whom he greatly admired. "Other civilizations," Sakharov said, "perhaps more successful ones, may exist an infinite number of times on the preceding and following pages of the Book of the Universe. Yet we should not minimize our sacred endeavors in this world where, like faint glimmers in the dark, we have emerged for a moment from the nothingness of unconsciousness into material existence. We must make good the demands of reason and create a life worthy of ourselves."

That is what Jerry Wiesner did.

Coda

Howard W. Johnson

All of us, in these essays describing Jerome Wiesner, see him through the prisms of our own experience and our own times. Each of us sees him more clearly than ever in these years since his death. He was, no doubt, a world citizen with an uncommon mix of quality, integrity, commitment, and ability. He was an intensely complex man with a wide range of interests. And yet, the preceding essays from his colleagues who best knew him produce a singularly unified picture of this man who had such large effects on all of us.

The central description of Jerry Wiesner, I believe, must settle on his character and his belief in the country. He believed in the fundamental quality and worth of the United States as a democracy. He would exercise his great gifts to encourage and advance our democracy in its responsible role as a member of the world community. He was, in a word often devalued, a patriot. He loved the country and felt he owed it the full strength of his powerful abilities.

My own close view of Jerome Wiesner came during his 14 years as an MIT administrator, first as provost, the chief academic officer (1966–71), and then as president (1971–80). Those years were, perhaps, the most critical in American higher education in the last century. During all that time I saw him almost every

Howard W. Johnson, business educator, corporate executive, and university administrator, served in the U.S. Army in Europe during World War II (1943–46). He began his career in teaching and research at the University of Chicago (1948–51, 1953–55), with an intervening period (1952–53) in personnel administration at General Mills. He was appointed an associate professor at MIT's Sloan School in 1955, and professor and dean in 1959. After a brief time as executive vice president of Federated Department Stores (1966), he became MIT president (1966–71), chairman of the MIT Corporation (1971–83), and honorary chairman (1983–90). He has served on numerous committees and boards, including as chairman of the Federal Reserve Bank, Boston (1968–69) and president of the Museum of Fine Arts, Boston (1975–80). His autobiography—*Holding the Center: Memoirs of a Life in Higher Education*—was published in 1999.

Howard Johnson and Jerry, 1966. (Photo by Steven A. Hansen. Courtesy of the MIT Museum.)

day. I saw him in his greatest days, and I saw him on those rare occasions of defeat and depression.

He was, initially, very reluctant to take on the provost post in 1966. He knew it would limit his time and flexibility in the fields where he most wanted to put his weight, especially nuclear disarmament, information theory, and civil rights. Not surprisingly to those who knew him best, he took the job and he performed it superbly well. When he considered taking on the presidency in 1971, he was again ambivalent in his conversations with me about the prospects. Again, he accepted the responsibility and he would go on to become an outstanding president, surely one of the best among his peers anywhere in all-around effectiveness. At the end, he came to believe that those years as president were the most important of his life. He brought to the job the full force of his ability, his energy, and his philosophy.

Jerry had the basic qualities of a good leader, developed over the preceding years of momentous experiences. He had a high personal standard and an exceptional

A painting by Chinese artist Liu Haisu, "The Roc Wings Fanwise, Soaring 90,000 Li"—commissioned as a gift to MIT by Ching T. Yang (class of 1930). Standing with the painting in the President's House, June 5, 1980, are Jerry, Ching T. Yang, Mrs. Yang, and Howard Johnson. (Photo by Calvin Campbell. Courtesy of the MIT Museum.)

intelligence, a record of accomplishment, a realistic and unfailing optimism, and an ability to act and follow through. Those abilities, required of the best, he had.

It was his style and his method that were more unusual. They were certainly not typical of the style and method of American leadership, political or corporate. His approach was not for everyone, and except in its broadest principles, not teachable in the ordinary sense. He would start with the big picture of where he wanted to go and the nature of the situation facing him. He used to say, often, "Let's clear our heads on this." He was open to all ideas. He had an easy threshold for new approaches, and his view was influenced deeply by a sense of compassion for the whole spectrum of humankind. He would deliberately pose an idea or embrace an approach that seemed to go well beyond the conventional. He was willing to take large risks if the possible gains were great enough. His standard greeting was to walk into an office or laboratory or a meeting of any kind and say with that characteristic, casual lift of his chin, "What's new?" He meant the question and he wanted answers. He would try constantly to probe, clarify, and press the new ideas with purposeful questions. I have never known anyone who could galvanize a meeting with short, clear questions better than Jerry Wiesner.

He interacted constantly with his closest colleagues, especially Walter Rosenblith, his closest collaborator, and an open-ended cast from around the community. He informally tapped the views of a very broad circle of his colleagues and friends in and out of MIT. His conversations with me usually included sessions at the end of the day and during our constant travels. He used the telephone more effectively and more consistently then anyone. It was always at his elbow or in his hand. There must be a hundred people who knew they were part of his close circle and, indeed, they were. His sense of humor, his easy, relaxed mode, and his general interest in people made dialogue easy.

He preferred to spend his time at the initial edges of problems. Once entered, once decoded, he expected that his colleagues in the process would carry the day, and he could move on to other topics. Because he was honest to the core, he was trusted and believed. He was usually even-tempered, but his rare bursts of wrath were monumental. He would willingly take on new problems, often unpleasant ones if the situation required it. He would enter these kinds of tasks with great enthusiasm.

As one example, it became clear during his term that we must go forward with a major effort to raise new and large amounts of money, perhaps the least attractive duty of any serving president. The educational institutions of the country had come through trying times in the 1960s and early 1970s, and the universities were no longer seen by many potential givers as great assets in the community. To him, successfully raising major resources for the Institute became a test for the country's renewing its confidence in higher education in general. He entered the lists with great enthusiasm. He wrote a major part of the book justifying MIT's fundraising cause. He made presentations to potential givers. He became extremely effective at it. He gave the MIT Campaign such priority that he took leave of his academic duties for six months to devote full time to it. He once told me, somewhat ruefully, that the most important thing we did in those years was raising funds to make it possible for MIT to go on successfully with a base of greater financial support for the faculty.

The task of fundraising, inevitably, put him in close contact with large numbers of corporate leaders with whom he could develop easy conversation and difficult agreement. His association with corporate America grew in his years as president of MIT. He learned so much about the management of companies, both in the

United States and abroad, that he was sought out by the best of his corporate colleagues as well as his political and academic colleagues.

Rightly, he is best remembered at MIT for his key role in initiating, supporting, and extending some innovative, important programs in education. They are described in many of the preceding essays, including the highly successful Undergraduate Research Opportunities Program, the Harvard-MIT Health Sciences and Technology Program, the new curriculum initiatives with emphasis on interdisciplinary work, the expanded MIT Council for the Arts, the Program in Science, Technology, and Society, and others.

His last years following his presidency were his most difficult, and as he put it, "the challenge of my life." A series of cardiac trials faced him with a difficult rehabilitation and recovery. His spirits constantly rebounded, providing an example for everyone. He was in this, as in everything, greatly supported by the love of his family and the support of his friends, but the main core of his strength was, as always, his character. It carried him magnificently through those final long chapters of his life.

With it all, he continued to be drawn to the hardest and most obdurate problems of our society. He devoted to these issues his intellect, his energy, and his heart during those final years, as he had during the years of his highest visibility. With a secure reputation in his original fields, and as a president emeritus of MIT, he took stands in those most difficult arenas that had always occupied him: among them, the advancement of the university as an ideal; the improvement in the relationships between old and powerful international adversaries; the improvement of the relationships between racial and ethnic groups in America, and the American dilemmas surrounding them; and the relationship of the arts and the sciences, one of MIT's most entrancing themes. And, in the end, he was deeply committed to education: the improvement of the process, the availability of quality education for everyone, and, always, the purity and power of the open mind.

We see him more clearly now. What a life! How fortunate the country, and all of us, were to have had him in our midst.

JERRY IN HIS OWN WORDS

MEMOIRS

Jerry began putting his rich, varied life in perspective quite early, at least as early as the period he spent in the role of science adviser to the U.S. president (1961–64). In a number of media interviews, for example, he reflected sometimes briefly—sometimes at length—on his own experiences, drawing connections between his personal background and his professional goals and activities. Profiles of Jerry, based on interviews and spanning the years from his childhood to the present, appeared in the *New York Times* (September 3, 1961), the *New Yorker* (January 19 & 26, 1963), and elsewhere. He was the subject of a number of oral history interviews, including one for the Kennedy Library (December 4, 1964) and one for the IEEE History Center (June 12, 1991), which, for all intents and purposes, were oral "memoirs" that helped him organize his thoughts for more formal autobiographical writing.

Jerry's first efforts to compose a memoir date from the mid-1980s. In a letter to Tom Wolf (April 14, 1986), he reflected on the growing urge to write about himself:

We must all be getting to that age when the desire to protect the record comes to the surface. I am working my way toward a book that will be a combination of personal experiences and historical interpretation. I have two embarrassments, however—one is that I have been involved in so many activities that I do not know how to filter them out, and the second is that I never kept notes and so my records are rather poor, and I am having to do a lot of research to fill them in.

A short time later (May 2, 1986) he wrote to David Bradley: "I have been slowly working my way to a decision to write the book you lobbied for. I am about 90% there but I am not quite sure which book to write. My head is so full of ideas that I have decided to start writing and see where it goes."

Sure enough, he began to work in June 1986 on something roughly titled *A Personal History of JBW and the Arms Race*. "I am having a rather difficult time," he noted in the preamble, "trying to decide where to begin this biographical/ autobiographical history of the arms race because so many pieces fit together and interlock." A fragment of the draft (17 pages) survives in his papers at the MIT Archives, apparently typed from 3 audiotapes not among the papers. It consists mostly of notes, anecdotes, and a rough narrative about scientists and the Cold War, especially Jerry's encounters with Jerrold Zacharias, I. I. Rabi, J. Robert Oppenheimer, Albert G. Hill, and others, as well as the work at Los Alamos, MIT's Radiation Laboratory, and (its successor) the Research Laboratory of Electronics.

Jerry appears to have put these notes aside, possibly because he was focused at the time on teaching, on speaking and publishing about issues uppermost in his mind (especially peace and disarmament), and on helping to establish the International Foundation for the Survival and Development of Humanity (1987). The notes were resurrected shortly after he suffered his debilitating stroke in 1989. His urge to write about his life and career reemerged, this time out of a keener sense of his own mortality and as a kind of therapy in the struggle to regain his physical and cognitive strength. He wrote again to David Bradley in July 1989:

The rumors are true. I have had a stroke which has slowed me down 95%. It occurred in January and I'm now beginning to do some useful work although I'm still very tired. The useful work consists of learning the alphabet and learning to spell and to walk, and I'm still trying to persuade my left hand to be part of the family.

. . .

I have just graduated from working on the spelling of single words which I sometimes get right to trying to write coherent thoughts. As a way of doing this, I have begun to write a few lines a day on that elusive autobiography which I never got around to, so when I get something that isn't too childish, I might send you pieces and get your reaction. It was your wonderful book that has both spurred me on to do this and made me feel not entirely incompetent to do a good job. But in any event, what I'm doing is exercise, and if it comes out more than that, great!

The book referred to is Bradley's *No Place to Hide*, an eyewitness account of the 1946 atom bomb tests at Bikini with an analysis of the dangers of nuclear weapons. It was first published in 1948, and Jerry had written a foreword to the revised edition of 1983.

The most systematic of Jerry's efforts to put together a memoir took place between 1991 and 1994, when his son Josh helped him edit drafts, interviewed him to supplement and enhance what Jerry was putting on paper, and occasionally composed drafts for Jerry to build on (see Josh's "Preface" and our introductions to each of the drafts for a more detailed account of how this process unfolded). Several of the resulting "chapters" are presented below.

The first chapter—"A Random Walk through the Twentieth Century," written in 1991 or 1992 and unfortunately incomplete—provides an overview of Jerry's goals in writing an autobiography, along with some highlights of his life and career. The remaining chapters are arranged chronologically and by theme:

Remembering the Rad Lab and RLE
Los Alamos
Technological Capabilities Panel
Up the Ladder to the White House
Kennedy
ABM
Gorbachev's Revolution

The coverage is incomplete—omitting many aspects of Jerry's career, most notably his role in academic administration at MIT—yet offers a tantalizing glimpse of how he viewed his contribution to the World War II research effort, to public policy in the federal government in the 1950s and 1960s, and to arms control and international peace initiatives from the 1960s to 1980s. Sadly, he did not live to continue working with Josh on this project. He died a few months after Josh's last recorded interview.

The "chapters" for Jerry's memoir are presented here essentially in their original form, with some excerpting; slight editing for grammar, style, and consistency; and occasional notes to clarify context or meaning. Some parts are more carefully crafted than others, some more polished in the writing, some more detailed—but all were part of a larger plan that, had Jerry lived to complete it, would have conveyed much about a life noted for its breadth, reach, and impact.

A Random Walk through the Twentieth Century

Part of a planned introductory chapter, written by Jerry in 1991 or 1992. In it he reveals when he first thought about writing an autobiography, outlines a rationale for the venture, describes the process of writing, and sweeps quickly over key events in his life during a fifty-year period—1940s to 1990s—with special attention to his role in scientific research, government science policy, arms control, university administration, and international affairs, as well as his struggle to recover from the debilitating stroke he suffered in 1989.

The structure is more thematic than chronological, as Jerry moves backward and forward in time depending on the topic under review. Working from rough notes typed on his personal computer, he polished only the portion presented here. He stopped midstream and somewhat abruptly, noting—"From here on in not usable without rethinking it. I have decided to skip it for now and work on the Rad Lab piece."

I have been considering writing this book, or at least some book, off and on for many years, but I have always been too intrigued and too busy with ongoing events to start writing seriously. In fact, this is still a problem, for I am unable to resist many of the commissions and committees which still seem to have a chance of making the world a better place. Now that the super-power arms race has collapsed, I hope that there can be some real progress toward a rational world order. I say "write some book" because, although I have been thinking about writing an autobiography since I returned to MIT from serving as President John F. Kennedy's Special Assistant for Science and Technology, I was not only busy, as I said, but also puzzled about what I wanted to write about, what would make a book useful to other people, for my life seemed to lack any coherence as I rattled between the university, government, and industry. So I did nothing about it beyond collecting and reading relevant magazines and hundreds of books on the arms race, world order, science and technology, trade, the environment, and the other things I found myself involved in at a given moment.

Formal portrait, July 19, 1946, shortly after assuming his first MIT faculty appointment, as assistant professor of electrical engineering. (Courtesy of the MIT Museum.)

As I grew older and became well known, I was invited to visit many countries, first in Europe and then to the Soviet Union, Pakistan, India, Japan, and China, a number of eastern European countries, Israel, Egypt, and Kenya. I saw their problems firsthand. While I was working for President Kennedy, he committed me to solving a serious agricultural water problem in Pakistan, and in the process I had my first serious look at what is now known as a "third world country," where poverty and illiteracy are endemic and hope is for most people nonexistent. I saw then that a little help from the outside in the form of economic aid and education could perform wonders, and since then I helped these countries whenever I could.

I began to try to understand how the many threads of science, technology, politics, religion, and human nature made every country that I visited be troubled but different. I slowly came to realize, too, that the world was living through the most dynamic, awesome, and dangerous period in human history, and that my trajectory through it via an interest in disarmament and science and technology gave me a special view of the dangers and a hope of helping a bit as well.

For a long time, I was not conscious of the fact that a special fascination about the intractable problems that were piling up all around us drove me to try to understand what was occurring. My life was too full of other challenges, and particularly my attempt to understand the dynamic of the nuclear arms race and my hope of stopping it, to realize the totality of the worldwide problems that I was seeing but not taking in.

There were other reasons than "busyness" for avoiding writing as well. First of all, writing didn't come easy to me. In addition, as I said earlier, until recently I did not understand even partially how the several strands that competed for my attention almost all of my life fitted together. I could not resist the call of any of them. A professor at the University of Michigan once warned me about taking on too much. He said I would end up a jack-of-all-trades and master of none. He may have been right, but his advice obviously fell on deaf ears.

I was particularly interested in communications and related computer technology, which I thought of as my profession long after it had passed me by. My years with Norbert Wiener gave me a cybernetic view of communications; I believed that the essence of all life—from the tiniest string of virus to the most complex society—was a communication process. This allowed me to fit many seemingly disparate issues and ideas together—including electronic communications, human behavior, education, and art—that have fascinated me all of my life.

As my life moved on and I had a chance to work in turn as scientist, technologist, science administrator, educator, "political" scientist, and observer of the international scene who was often at odds with the "establishment," particularly about arms and social policy, the thrust of the book I dreamed about changed and became more puzzling. As I said earlier, at first I planned to concentrate on the technical and strategic problems of the nuclear arms race, its driving forces, its myths and dangers. But my Washington responsibilities in the Eisenhower and Kennedy administrations and my subsequent life as one of the leaders of MIT—and what I learned from my ever-widening circle of associations around the world—convinced me that civilization had taken a disastrous, wrong turn. I began to worry about this more and more as I was falling asleep at nights. It was not just the arms race but also the plight of people and their environment that was getting worse all over the globe.

Jerry, daughter Lisa, and Eleanor Roosevelt during the taping of "The Scientist and World Politics," December 1960, part of the WGBH-TV series "Prospects of Mankind." (Courtesy of the MIT Museum.)

Finally, in 1979, as I was retiring from the presidency of MIT, I had the unbelievable good fortune of being appointed to the board of directors of the newly formed MacArthur Foundation, whose directors decided to apply the Foundation's considerable resources to what we believed to be among humanity's most vexing problems, and I had the freedom to puzzle about them almost full-time. As part of this new life, I became the chairman of the board's Committee on Peace and International Development, which caused me to focus even more on the arms race. The arms race remains one of the central themes in this book, because it has not only been what was driving me, it has also been the driving force of humanity in this century as the social, economic, and ideological fabric of societies around the globe has been warped by more than forty years of the nuclear arms race and the Cold War.

At the start of World War II, in 1942, I went to MIT to help develop radar, and I never escaped. This chance opportunity propelled me at a young age into the center of American scientific activities related to the war, and afterwards into both the Cold War and the social and technological upheaval that followed it. Later, my continued attempts to find a solution to the arms race made me an active participant in Gorbachev's attempts to reform the Soviet society. They also gave me the unusual experience of working closely with Andrei Sakharov for the last two years of his life, when I was exposed to his visionary views of a proper future for mankind.

In a real sense, I have experienced decades of cognitive overload and only recently, as illness has slowed me down, have I started to think of how the lessons I have learned might help set humanity on a healthy course.

Sixty years ago, as a boy, I lived through the Great Depression. People then thought that economic upheavals were in a real sense enormous natural disasters that were beyond the control of man. In the years since then, we have experienced the spectacular flowering of science, social science, and technology, with the promise of a decent life for all humanity. We have learned enough about the behavior of economic systems to believe that they can be regulated if people are just rational enough. Meanwhile, we have been forced to stand by helplessly as these triumphs of the mind were perverted to megakilling at the same time that a rapidly growing population was condemned to live illiterate, poverty-stricken, and increasingly bleak lives. And we can't blame an unyielding nature for this dilemma, except perhaps for man's nature itself. My hope is that by exploring these issues together I will find some ideas about what people of the world can do collectively to change the situation.

In 1989, I had a serious stroke which changed my life rather dramatically. First of all, my priority changed from an overwhelming and frustrating attempt to help halt the nuclear arms race to an intense regimen of therapy: learning the alphabet again, learning how to spell, how to talk, how to remember, how to walk, and how to use my left arm and hand which were totally useless. It was almost like being a child again. I am still learning to manage the many strands of my life that were unraveled. My longtime interest in human communication systems helped me through the frustrations of the long relearning regime.

Once my lifestyle destined me to have a stroke, I was fortunate in how and where it happened. In recent years, until I suffered the stroke, I had been involved in a hectic effort to create an International Foundation for the Survival and Development of Humanity, with headquarters in Moscow. The foundation work required many of the non-Soviet members to go to Moscow frequently, and the American members who were planning such a trip to Moscow had a preparatory meeting in Washington. I told one of the participants, Robert McNamara, that I was not feeling very well, and he phoned my wife to urge her to have me stay home. I took their advice, and the day after the others left, I suffered a stroke. It might otherwise have occurred in an airplane on the way to Moscow, and left me stricken and helpless thousands of miles from home. After a few days at Massachusetts General Hospital, as soon as I was stabilized, I was moved to the affiliated Spaulding Rehabilitation Center.

My daytimes were overflowing with relearning all of the cognitive and physical skills the stroke had knocked out, but my nights were long and full of memories of the many things I had been involved in as well as many questions about them. Then the shape of the book I wanted to write became clearer. I went home, but continued as an outpatient. By then I had learned to speak again, though not well, read and spell a little bit, and even walk a few hundred feet. As I began to regain my ability to spell and write, I started to use my computer's word-processor that has a built-in spelling checker. This made it possible for me to use words whose spelling I couldn't recall, which was most of them. At first I wrote laborious short notes to my therapist and a few friends, but as time passed and I became more competent, I found myself writing pieces about the memories that occupied my nights in the hospital.

Slowly, the pieces began to focus on the arms race and its aftermath. I suspect that this was due, at least in part, to the fact that I had been reading McGeorge Bundy's book on Eisenhower and Kennedy, and Andrei Sakharov's memoirs.[1] I read them out loud as a part of my speech therapy. Because of this it was slow going, and I had much time to think about their stories. The Bundy book is the work of a professional historian, while Sakharov's is the living journal of the life and times of one of the great scientists and humanists of our times, including much about science and technology, particularly about the creation of the Soviet nuclear bombs. I knew much of the story Bundy told from direct experience, and much that he didn't tell also. Sakharov told a new story, very interesting to me because I had spent many years trying to guess what the Soviets were doing and why, as I worked on the American side of the Cold War. Perhaps it will come as a surprise, but much of the time I had reason to question the actions and motivations of actors on the American stage as well.

---

1. Probably Bundy's *Danger and Survival: Choices About the Bomb in the First Fifty Years* (Random House, 1988); Sakharov, *Memoirs* (Knopf, 1990; translated from the Russian by Richard Laurie).

The most difficult part of writing this book is sorting out fact from memories and trying to understand the motives of the many people I had a chance to work with or observe during the Cold War years. Sakharov paints a vivid picture of growing up, working, and surviving in one of the biggest, most savage, and most failed experiments of all times. His stories were especially intriguing to me because in recent times I had worked with him. For several years after Gorbachev's rise to power, I had many talks with Sakharov about the Soviet H-bomb project and human rights problems in Russia. For two years, before my stroke and Sakharov's subsequent death, we were both members of the board of the International Foundation for the Survival and Development of Humanity, and of its human rights committee.

My need to keep on writing kept me going through many months. I was forced to look up almost every word, so that often I would write only ten lines an hour. Eventually, and to me miraculously, I learned to spell almost as well as I ever could. Meanwhile, the welling up of my memories led me to start writing seriously about some of those experiences, and this eventually led me to realize, perhaps for the first time, how involved I had been in science and technology and with more general world affairs in the last fifty years, especially issues relating to the arms race.

Looking back, I tried again to understand many events that completely baffled me when they occurred and for a long time afterwards. At the time, I could not understand how so many people—businessmen, politicians, military leaders, journalists, and even scientists—could do so many things that I regarded to be against the best interest of the United States and the whole world. For many years, I have believed that a combination of wrong or obsolete military doctrines continued into the nuclear age, vested interests of what President Eisenhower called the military-industrial complex, a consequent lack of support in recent years for many more urgent national needs such as schools, medical care, physical infrastructure, and housing—all exacerbated by extreme excesses of speculation, and the growing loss of competitiveness of technical industries that has put the United States into a downward spiral which we might possibly reverse if we understood better how we got into this situation in the first place. I believe that the Cold War gave President Eisenhower's military-industrial complex an uncontrollable grip on the nation, and that most of the other difficulties of the United States stem from this.

As I said earlier, I spent the war years at MIT helping to design and build microwave radars and working closely with members of the three military services to make certain that the radars would be used effectively. After that, I spent a year at the Los Alamos Laboratory of the University of California, where I learned about nuclear weapons and helped the laboratory get ready for the Bikini bomb tests.

I incidentally learned about the bitter but restrained arguments that were then brewing about whether or not a demonstration explosion off the Japanese shore would not have been adequate to make a nation already reeling from other blows surrender without a nuclear holocaust, whether the military or civilians should control the development of atomic energy, and the Oppenheimer-Teller feud over the thermonuclear bomb—disputes that were to split the scientific community in the years ahead.

After Los Alamos, I returned to MIT—to teaching, doing research and administration, consulting for industry, and serving as a technical adviser to the Defense Department and the Eisenhower White House. When John Kennedy succeeded Eisenhower as president in 1961, he nominated me as his Special Assistant for Science and Technology and chairman of the President's Science Advisory Committee (PSAC). Because he knew me well from our earlier associations, he gave me responsibility for almost all science and technology issues of the federal government, as well as many related problems. So with the members of PSAC, its consultants and the full-time members of the office staff, I became involved in many problems of higher education, civilian science and technology, the environment, science and technology for third world countries, as well as the innumerable problems relating to basic research, space, military technology, and disarmament that had been the principal preoccupations of my predecessors as science adviser, James R. Killian and George B. Kistiakowsky.

Because I had served on PSAC under the leadership of both of the former science advisers, I was familiar with the issues that occupied their time, but I gave increasing time to the country's disarmament efforts and the major space programs that were just beginning. It is now almost impossible for me to believe that our group was able to deal with the range of issues that we did, but somehow we did.

Quite naturally, the scope of this imaginary book continued to expand with the passage of time, since my exposure to new ideas didn't slow down when I returned to MIT after President Kennedy's death. I became dean of the School of Science, then spent two years as provost, and ultimately became the school's president, so I was assured of a continuing swirl of new problems, both scientific and administrative. I continued to be active in the American and worldwide search for ways to stop or at least slow down the nuclear arms race, as well as do research on the interface between communications and computing.

I have been involved in advanced technology for almost fifty years. In this short time, I have witnessed the metamorphosis of a world in which nature and natural forces dominated the character of human existence to one in which, in the technology-based societies, man's inventions dominate much of life. The consequence is a world in which human decisions shape the future, a world in which the forces available for good or evil exceed man's ability to manage them. Andrei Sakharov once said that we were living at a saddle point in history where many paths lead downward and so few up. I agree. The challenge of our time is to find those few that do lead upwards, away from the many man-made dangers and toward a better life for all of humanity. The challenge is to avoid the many traps that have been created and to learn how to maximize the potential of our modern world. I hope this book will make a contribution toward this goal.

For most of my life, I have lived in three worlds—academia, the world of industry, and the world of government science. In the latter, I focused heavily on space, military technology, and basic research. Sometimes my work focused largely on one or the other of these three fields, sometimes I shared time between them; sometimes the work overlapped, as when my teaching and research made it possible for me to conceive of new electronic systems for military use—the digital-computer-based air defense system, for example—or when I consulted on military technology for neighboring industries, or when I took off three days a week from MIT to work for President Eisenhower's Science Advisory Committee. When I served as President Kennedy's Special Assistant for Science and Technology, I was involved with science, technology, the intersection between science and policy, and from time to time with education at every level.

I think of myself as a communications engineer/scientist—engineer because I like to conceive and build things, scientist because of an abiding interest in the substance and processes of communications in living and man-made systems. This may seem like a dilettante's intellectual diet, and sometimes I have felt a bit guilty about my random walk from one problem to another, but as I look back I now realize that this diverse diet was involving me in the many parts of a giant jigsaw puzzle that remains a rather unfinished one, that may remain a puzzle and a challenge to humanity for a long time to come.

Two factors seemed to direct me. First of all, in a technological society there is a connectiveness between most of its parts, particularly when one's focus is on the substance of the connection, i.e., communications. The second factor was a characteristic of my mind that seemed unable to resist following those connections, ideas from different fields and worlds. This seemed to happen automatically, intuitively. For years this strange talent worried me. It worried me especially when these connections, insights, intuitions, whatever they should be called, made me uneasy about propositions stated with great confidence by wise, older authorities. For years I submerged these doubts and went along with the conventional wisdom.

In technical areas, letting things go unchallenged really didn't do much harm because nature rather quickly exposed the truth. But I look back with embarrassment and shame in the military/technical field at the "intelligence" estimates that for so long dominated the scope and direction of research and development efforts that I participated in. Ultimately, I began to pay serious attention to this unprovoked cognitive activity and to consciously explore the issues that it was bringing to my attention. Often this would lead me to conclusions that parted company with current views or goals, and ultimately has brought me in conflict with national policy. My transition from a worried acceptance of the conventional wisdom of the inevitability of an ever-growing arms race to a believer in the superiority of proper arms-control measures occurred while I worked for President Eisenhower. In fact, he gave me the courage to advocate disarmament measures in the face of enormous opposition and censorship. Then, as Special Assistant for Science and Technology under President Kennedy, I not only was concerned with military technology and space, but also, together with members of the PSAC, increasingly became involved with a myriad of civilian issues from medicine to the environment to lagging industrial technology.

My early postwar years with Norbert Wiener had conditioned me to think of all of life as interacting conglomerates, living and inanimate, as system problems whose scale depends on the problem in hand. For example, an engineer can study a complex system such as a telephone network or an electronic computer and simulate its performance completely. On the other hand, a biologist thinks of a single cell as a complex system with a myriad of interacting chemicals and, though the idea would be useful, the system is too intricate to model. Most living systems are of this nature, at least for now, although economists are able to make models of an economy realistic enough to yield useful predictions. A sociologist would regard the relationships among people as defining his system, and an environmentalist could regard the whole world—with all of its creatures, oceans, air, materials, etc.—as forming his domain, but neither can be quantitative. Nonetheless, the systems concept makes an important gift to understanding complicated interactions. This insight caused me to search for connections and hidden behavior patterns in many different situations.

I first used these concepts to help understand the many different forces that were propelling the arms race in both the United States and the Soviet Union.

Remembering the Rad Lab and RLE

Jerry joined the staff of the Radiation Laboratory (or Rad Lab, as it was familiarly called) in May 1942, and became a member of its successor, the Research Laboratory of Electronics (RLE), after the war. He served as assistant director of RLE (1947–49), associate director (1949–52), and director (1952–61). The narrative below outlines his experiences at the Rad Lab and RLE, with anecdotes and reflections on the research program, mission, goals, philosophy, and personalities that kept the Labs at the forefront of innovation in science and technology.

In October 1940, MIT was chosen as the site of an independent laboratory—staffed by scientists and engineers from many disciplines—to develop practical applications of microwave radar. The Rad Lab went on to design almost half of the radar deployed in World War II, created over 100 different radar systems, and constructed $1.5 billion worth of radar. At peak activity, it employed nearly 4,000 people working on several continents and evolved into an enterprise dedicated to understanding the theories behind experimental radar, while tackling its engineering problems.

The Rad Lab formally closed on December 31, 1945, and its staff members resumed their peacetime activities. The Lab's Basic Research Division continued for several months under the sponsorship of the U.S. Office of Scientific Research and Development. On July 1, 1946, its work was merged into MIT's new RLE, which became a major center for basic and applied research in four broad areas: electronics, optics, and photonics; communications and signal processing; atomic, molecular, and optical physics; and "living systems," particularly language, speech, and hearing.

Jerry entitled this draft "Remembering RLE," but it is as much about MIT's Radiation Laboratory as about the Research Laboratory of Electronics. In fact, it was written partly as a contribution to the Rad Lab's 50th anniversary celebration in 1991. Two surviving drafts are dated February 28, 1991, and March 1991; a third was edited by Josh Wiesner in 1995 or 1996. The present text is based on Jerry's March 1991 version, which was excerpted in RLE Currents 4, no. 2 (Spring 1991): 16–17.

✳

Laya and I first saw MIT on a sunny warm Sunday in May of 1942, having driven from Washington, D.C. where I had been the chief engineer of the Library of Congress (I was also the whole engineering staff). I had been invited to join the

Radiation Laboratory staff by a University of Michigan physics professor, Sam Goudsmit, whom I knew when I was a student there. I later learned that he had been reminded of my existence by Louis Smullin, who had been a fellow student. Goudsmit's letter didn't say what the lab was doing, but did say it was vital defense research.

I didn't know anything about the Rad Lab or what it was doing and almost nothing about MIT itself. MIT was a legendary place in the east that I knew about mostly because my smartest undergraduate classmate, Claude Shannon, had decided to go there for graduate studies. I knew vaguely, too, about Vannevar Bush's famous computing machines as well as research on the ionosphere which explained why my shortwave signals sometimes went halfway around the world. But I didn't have the foggiest idea of what I would be doing. Sam said that the lab was doing vital wartime research and desperately needed help. I could not imagine how my background in acoustics and recording, and particularly folk music collecting, which I had been doing at the Library of Congress, had much to offer the war effort. I had forgotten my years as a ham radio operator.

I almost didn't come. At that time I was busy helping Archibald MacLeish, the Librarian of Congress, set up a shortwave broadcasting system, and so I wrote a letter to Goudsmit saying that I was too busy and couldn't come. In fact, I dictated a letter to Sam telling him I was too busy helping Archibald MacLeish set up a string of shortwave broadcasting stations and studios for the "Office of Facts and Figures," the predecessor of the USIA,[1] and couldn't be spared. That evening I told Laya about my decision. She quietly reminded me that I had long been wishing for a more technical job and maybe I should find out more about it before I said no. The next morning I tore up the letter that I had written and wrote one saying I would like to learn more about what the lab was doing. Sam answered that the group was doing vital defense work and adding that he thought I would enjoy it. With this additional information, I asked MacLeish for a year's leave of absence, and Laya and I then drove to Boston.

On Monday morning I found the lab in a newly built temporary building behind the stately permanent MIT. After running a gauntlet of unsmiling guards, I found myself in the office of the deputy director, Wheeler Loomis, the head of the University of Illinois physics department, on leave for the duration. I also learned that the director was another physicist, Dr. Lee DuBridge from Cornell. After a few days I had the impression that most of the physicists in the United States were spending

---

1. U.S. Information Agency, established in 1953.

the war years at MIT, although I later learned that more than a few of them were at a Shangri-la in the mountains of New Mexico. Sometime later, I learned that while there were certainly many physicists, there was also almost every breed of scientist and engineer in the lab.

In spite of the hustle outside his office, inside Loomis was relaxed and leisurely. He at first seemed far too busy to be bothered by me, yet he shut the door to his office and spent about forty-five minutes first asking about my experience and then trying to explain microwave radar to me. Finally, he told me about the many working groups in the place. I was amazed by what he said and couldn't answer when, at the end of his story, he asked me where I might fit in. In the interview, I had described how in my university days I had built an FM transmitter, my expertise in sound recording, my university research on voice mechanisms, and my work with MacLeish—none of which seemed to qualify me for work at the Rad Lab. When Loomis heard that I knew something about broadcasting, he suggested that I see if Jerrold Zacharias could fit me into his section, Group 53, with responsibility for the RF Components used in all the radars. So I went to see him.

Zach, as he was known to everyone, was as friendly as Loomis had been, and I started to suspect that they were expecting someone else. He showed me a collection of the 3,000 megacycle (now called megahertz) coax and waveguide transmission systems that his group was engineering. He took great pride in the tiny silicon detectors that were being fabricated right on the spot. I met the young MIT electrical engineer who was making them, Nat Rochester, who typified the spirit of the lab—the liveliness, imagination, and freedom of the people, young and old, who were determined to help win the war by getting microwave radar into the field quickly. I didn't know it then, but my later work on this little gadget would set the direction of my life's interests.

After we left Rochester, I told Zach that these detectors looked very much like the galena detectors I had used when I built crystal sets, and he agreed and said that Nat's job was to make them sturdier and more sensitive. Then he made a remark I have never forgotten. Obviously embarrassed at having to use this primitive contraption, he said that they wouldn't have to use it long because the Bell Laboratories were designing a vacuum tube to take its place.

At the end of the tour Zach introduced me to Al Hill, his deputy, who was to be my supervisor. Al took me to a rabbit warren in Building 4 where he had taken advantage of the high ceilings by putting in an intermediate floor. My desk was on the temporary floor, which I accessed by climbing a ladder.

Zach and Al Hill had the same leadership style. They would assign a problem and expect you to get it done by yourself. They were ready to provide help if you wanted it, but you had to ask for it. At the time they both made it obvious, through continuous discussion, that they were very interested in your task. The four men I met on my first day at Rad Lab were to become lifelong friends and collaborators, Zach and Al two of my closest friends.

In a few days I was chosen to move the newly designed 10,000 megahertz components from Ed Purcell's research group to Zach's hardware group, so I moved out of my cranny in Building 4 to the spaciousness of Building 8, where Purcell's small group was located. I still remember fondly three people I worked with—Ed himself and a husband-and-wife team, Dorothy and Carroll Montgomery. They must have been horrified by my total ignorance, but they never showed it; rather, they set out to teach me about life at 10,000 megahertz.

The new system involved two kinds of components—the passive ones, waveguides and connectors, and the three active ones, the magnetron, a high-powered source of pulsed energy which was reflected from its target; a klystron signal generator which, along with Nat Rochester's crystals, formed the receiver; and a gas switching tube called the T-R BOX that was supposed to isolate the receiver from the large pulses made by the transmitter. Waveguides were new and fascinating to me, and I spent many hours poring over Maxwell's equations trying to understand them. The waveguides were completely designed so that I only had to transfer the blueprints for them to Zach's group. Of the more difficult active elements, only the klystron existed. It was fortunate that the klystron did exist, for it also served as a signal source which made it possible to work on both the waveguides and the other active elements.

When the magnetron didn't appear on schedule, Purcell made a sketch of one as he imagined it—complete with dimensions—and sent it to a magician, Percy Spencer at the Raytheon Company. In a short time it came back, and it worked. I was amazed—even the frequency was more or less right. That left the T-R BOX, and I soon discovered that it was my responsibility. I was to make that, under Dorothy Montgomery's supervision. The most important lesson she taught me was that I could think of distributed circuits like microwave cavities, just as one did discrete LC circuits with the cavity serving as the inductance and the capacitance as the area between two surfaces that could usually be identified. Soon I was using a file to change the frequency of a cavity that I was building. The first T-R switch I made worked, but it did not protect the crystals for very long. Neither did some that we received from the Bell Laboratories. This started me on a long search for the reasons

Some members of Group 53 (the "radio frequency" group) at MIT's Radiation Laboratory, September 8, 1945. Jerry is at far right in the middle row. Lou Smullin, a close friend and colleague of Jerry's (see his essay in this book), is at far left in the top row. (Courtesy of the MIT Museum.)

why it didn't work, which I eventually found but it would take a book to tell the story.

In the four years at Rad Lab, I did many other things, including helping Zach and Al run Group 53, serve as the head of a special project building an airborne early warning radar that was the predecessor to the present AWACS,[2] and serve on the lab steering committee. Most important of all, I found what I wanted to do with my life and even grew up a little.

It would take a book to even outline the many developments of the Rad Lab that included ground, shipborne, and airborne radars, an aircraft landing system, and countless pieces of test equipment needed to keep them all running. In fact, the last organized act of the Rad Lab was to author a set of books describing for posterity what had been learned.[3]

---

2. Airborne Warning and Control System.

3. Including *Five Years at the Radiation Laboratory: Presented to Members of the Radiation Laboratory by the Massachusetts Institute of Technology* (Cambridge, Mass., 1946).

The staff of Project Cadillac, 1945. Jerry is seated in the bottom row, sixth from the right. (Courtesy of the MIT Museum.)

As I write this, I see in my mind's eye the 584 air defense radar that was so important to the European ground war, the various shipborne and airborne fighter systems, including my own Project Cadillac, which literally saved the American fleet in the Pacific, and the systems H2S and H2X which made possible massed nighttime flights of allied bombers when they became too vulnerable to fighter aircraft and anti-aircraft on daytime flights. I see clearly, too, the hundreds of friends who worked night and day to have these complex and tricky machines ready on the impossible schedules that make all the difference in wars.

It is sometimes said that the Rad Lab was the first large interdisciplinary laboratory where people from very different disciplines used their special knowledge to work toward a common goal. I don't agree with that description, for although people with very different backgrounds, mostly scientists and engineers, worked together to develop microwave radar systems, most of them had to learn new disciplines and skills to be effective rather than practicing what they already knew. What the Rad Lab really showed was that well-trained, very bright individuals could quickly learn new disciplines and new skills. This obviously was not as difficult for physical scientists or electrical engineers as for biologists, medical researchers, or mathematicians, but it was not hard for the latter types either. In a situation where there were very few "experts," it was easy to get up to speed quickly. In a short time it was not possible to tell a person's background by skill that was exhibited in their work.

Even before the Rad Lab existed, there were many laboratories in which scientists and engineers with different backgrounds worked toward a common goal, usually an applied goal, but the range of disciplines found in them was usually rather narrow. Two good examples are the Bell Telephone Laboratories and those of the E. I. DuPont Chemical Company. A military laboratory, the Naval Research Laboratory, had a broader mandate and employed a wide range of scientists and engineers, but it was hardly an interdisciplinary laboratory in the true sense of the meaning. It was common for interdisciplinary teams to do medical research, but they were usually very small. After the war, engineers from MIT and doctors from the Harvard Medical School organized many such groups. Many academic arrangements were made in other areas, but most never reached their expected potential.

The Radiation Lab set a new style of collaboration. As far as I know, this was the first time that a large-scale collaboration was undertaken between an academic group, the military, and industry. The undertaking was a great success, and it set the pattern for postwar collaborations of a similar nature. The collaboration between academics and the military was facilitated by the fact that many of the military officers were really scientists and engineers who had joined the military for the duration. They were the unsung heroes because most of them had some reserve training before the war, and they understood military requirements. At the same time, they could communicate quite easily with most of the Rad Lab personnel, who were largely ignorant of military requirements and organization, to say nothing of being scornful of many of them.

As the Rad Lab started, it had much assistance from the researchers at the Bell Telephone Laboratories, one of the great laboratories of the world, whose early work on microwave components, radar systems, time measurement techniques, and many other aspects of electronics helped the Rad Lab people get a jump start on their task. With the passage of time, the help turned into true collaboration.

The wartime developments gave rise to a three-fold revolution in military systems and tactics that no one, military or civilian, understood or could cope with. Nuclear weapons had increased the explosive capacity of weapons thousands of times, aircraft and missiles increased the speed of warfare almost as much, and computers and feedback systems were better than men guiding the new weapons. But no one knew how to build these new systems reliably or how to use them in combat. So, after the war, there was a desperate need to continue the close collaboration that existed during the war.

Meanwhile, many of the wartime laboratories, including the Rad Lab, had been terminated, and the university faculties who had manned them had returned to their homes. Some collaboration continued, however, because some of the new war-trained experts took positions in the military and industry, and they in turn hired the returning faculty members as consultants. Also, many of the associations that had been developed between members of the armed services and individual professors continued after the war. People from universities and industry served on armed services committees like the Air Force and Navy Scientific Advisory Panels, and later on the Atomic Energy Commission (AEC) and the president's various advisory groups.

There was another reason for the continued collaboration between many of the faculty at MIT and the government—the creation of the Research Laboratory of Electronics (RLE), as a kind of successor to the Rad Lab. I say "kind of successor" because the new laboratory was supposed to concentrate on basic research and education, not military hardware. Professor John Slater, head of MIT's physics department, had early recognized how much new physics the Rad Lab's developments made possible, while at the same time many people responsible for the future of the nation's military technology recognized that it was essential to maintain a high level of research for security reasons. These complementary needs made it easy to agree on the new enterprise, and Professors Julius Stratton and Al Hill were chosen to create it. Luckily for me, the Electrical Engineering Department realized that a part of its future also involved microwave signals, so it became a sponsor of the new laboratory, and appointed me to be the guardian of their interests. The wisdom of this endeavor was seen first in the capacity that it provided MIT to handle the torrent of veterans who wanted a scientific education immediately after the war, and again in 1950 when an applied division of the RLE was easily spun off to support the Korean War needs.

My luck continued. While Jay Stratton, Al Hill, and George Harvey had to work out the details of the new venture, including the contracts with the three military services who were to be its sponsors, capture Rad Lab equipment needed to start the lab, and recruit faculty and students, I went to Los Alamos with Professor Jerrold Zacharias to start a new branch of that laboratory at Albuquerque that ultimately became the Sandia Laboratory of the AEC. When I returned a year later, my only job was to decide what we should do in the communications area, and I had a lot of help doing this. The RLE was only one, though the biggest one, of a group of university-based research laboratories that the Three Service Committee brought into being. There were eventually nine of them, and they were to play a major role in restarting research and higher education in the postwar period. Without this farsighted venture, there would not have been the continuity of research or the rapid reestablishment of education that took place in 1946.

The type of support that was available immediately after the war was very unusual and, unfortunately, it did not last for very long. The funds were provided as a lump

Whooping it up at the tenth anniversary of the Research Laboratory of Electronics, April 1956—at left are Walter Rosenblith, Robert Fano, and Helen Thomas; at right, Ann Serini and (seated) Miriam Smythe. (Courtesy of the MIT Museum.)

sum; the directors of the laboratories had the discretion to support research that they thought was worthwhile without having to justify it *a priori*, which would have been extremely difficult at the start of the new endeavors. This ideal funding mode continued for a number of years until the Joint Committee's funds were not able to meet the needs of the RLE, and additional support had to be sought from other agencies whose funding process involved providing individual grants in response to written proposals, a much more time-consuming process.

In the beginning, it was possible for the directors to make changes in or start new programs without appealing to Washington. Consequently, the money was used very efficiently. When major changes in direction were planned, we would seek the approval of the sponsors. For example, in the late 1940s, as associate director of RLE, I wanted to broaden the scope of the laboratory to include neurosciences by

RLE paperwork, ca. mid-1950s. (Courtesy of the MIT Museum.)

adding the work of professor Walter Rosenblith.[4] I asked Dr. Emanuel Piore, the Navy Representative on the Joint Committee which supervised the laboratory, whether it was alright to do this. He asked me, "Are there electrons involved?," and when I replied, "I'm pretty sure there must be," he said, "Well then, okay." And that was the justification for Walter's research in RLE.

The linguistics and speech research of professors Morris Halle and Noam Chomsky was another example of the breadth of the vision that guided the sponsors. These were clearly important aspects of human communication, not electrical engineering. The sponsors quickly saw that they were relevant and interesting, and gave their approval. Incidentally, their research at the start was goal-oriented. Professor Locke, chairman of MIT's Department of Modern Languages, wanted to explore the possibility of computer translation of language. It didn't take many months for him and his group to realize that we did not know enough about language to attempt computer translation, so we decided to take a detour and study

---

4. Walter came to MIT as associate professor of communications biophysics in 1951.

linguistics. The detour has taken longer than we expected, but I don't think anyone has ever regretted it.

At the start, the RLE had two quite separate tracks: *physics*, in which researchers set out to exploit microwave tools in search of information about the physical universe; and *communications*, which primarily involved electrical engineers at the beginning, then quickly broadened to include speech and linguistics, neurophysiology, psychology, and several other disciplines. Several joint programs developed, involving the two original sponsoring departments. They might otherwise not have happened. The RLE program in radio astronomy is a good example of this.

Much of the communications work was inspired by Norbert Wiener and his exciting ideas about communications and feedback in man and machines. Wiener's theories and those of Claude Shannon on information theory spawned new visions of research for everyone interested in communications, including the neurophysiology, speech, and linguistics investigations referred to earlier. The work was both theoretical and experimental, as well as basic and applied. For example, many of the early ideas about coding were developed in the RLE. So were broad-band communications systems and even much earlier work about digital systems, as well as interesting and exciting new ideas such as the use of correlation functions to enhance weak signals, random noise as the carrier of signals, and the use of noise to measure systems functions. This mix of the exploration of new ideas and their reduction to practice remains the hallmark of the present-day RLE.

In the winter of 1947, Wiener began to speak about holding a seminar that would bring together the scientists and engineers who were doing work on what he called communications. He was launching his vision of cybernetics in which he regarded signals in any medium, living or artificial, as the same, dependent on their structure and obeying a set of universal laws set out by Shannon. In the spring of 1948, Wiener convened the first of a series of weekly meetings that were to continue for several years. He believed that good food was an essential ingredient of good conversation, so these were dinner meetings and they were held at Joyce Chen's original restaurant, now the site of an MIT dorm.

The first meeting reminded me of the tower of Babel, as engineers, psychologists, acousticians, doctors, mathematicians, neurophysiologists, philosophers, and other interested people tried to have their say. After the first meeting, one of us would take the lead each time, giving a brief summary of our research, usually accompanied by a running commentary by Wiener, to set the stage for the evening's discussion. As time went on, we came to understand each other's lingo and to understand, and even believe, in Wiener's view of the universal role of communications in the universe. For most of us, these dinners were a seminal experience which both introduced us to a new world of ideas and new friends, many of whom became collaborators in later years. Wiener's theme that it was the organization of symbols, not their physical embodiment, bonded us together whatever our disciplinary origins.

Students came from all over the world to work in RLE's unique communications group in the 1950s and 1960s. Our intellectual reverie, exciting and productive as it was, made way for the realities of the developing Cold War and proved the premise that maintaining an academic laboratory would make it easier to mobilize science and technology in a future defense emergency. MIT took the lead in a new form of academic-military-industrial interaction—the "Summer Study," which brought together for relatively short times experts from many places to help some part of the government, usually one of the military services, cope with the growing threat that Soviet military power and belligerence were creating. These "studies" dealt with many problems, including nuclear-powered aircraft, submarine detection systems, continental air-defense, overseas transport, and shortwave broadcasting for propaganda purposes.

When the Korean War broke out, a part of RLE was transformed into an applied division which in turn formed a division of the Lincoln Laboratory when it was later created. The style and traditions of the Rad Lab were thus handed on to the Lincoln Laboratory when it was formed.

My overwhelming impression is really an emotional one: what a unique and wonderful experience to spend a major part of my adult life, and perhaps the most enjoyable period of it, in the MIT atmosphere—a sentiment that I gather is shared by most of my colleagues. Perhaps this is just the normal nostalgia of men grown responsible and proper from the free time of their youth. But I think that it is more, for we shared communication processes in man's universe and the hopefulness of the post–World War II period. Perhaps as seen from our present wiser perspective, we were over-excited and hoped for too much, but if so, we didn't know it.

Los Alamos[1]

Jerry worked for about nine months, September 1945 to June 1946, at the Los Alamos Scientific Laboratory—home to the Manhattan Project, the first nuclear-fission (atomic) bomb, and, in peacetime, research leading to the first thermonuclear-fusion (hydrogen) bomb. He helped develop electronic components used in the atomic-weapons tests conducted at Bikini, in the Marshall Islands, on July 1 and 25, 1946. Los Alamos, ironically, was also the place where Jerry was first exposed to heated debates over the control and uses of atomic weapons and atomic energy. The whole experience made a lasting impression on him: "[I]t was for me an interesting and sometimes even an exciting period," he wrote, "and in later years I realized that the understanding I gained—both about the bomb and the controversy surrounding its use—had provided me with a valuable education on issues that were to occupy a large part of my life."

In June of 1945, Robert Oppenheimer asked Jerrold Zacharias to come to Los Alamos to discuss the possibility of his taking charge of a special project there. In July, Jerrold left the Rad Lab to join the Los Alamos staff, taking the position of head of Ordnance Engineering. The job Oppenheimer asked him to do would involve assembling a group of scientists to come to Los Alamos, following the war's imminent conclusion, for the purpose of reengineering the bomb. The leaders of the Manhattan Project believed that the bomb, having been built in such haste, was not sturdy enough to be put into the hands of the military and needed to be reengineered before it was put into production.

Oppenheimer chose Jerrold for the job because of his work at the Rad Lab and because of his reputation for being both highly competent and extremely thorough

---

1. A draft written by Jerry in the early 1990s, with edits by Josh in 1995 or 1996 and additional edits and notes by editors of this book. Josh's edits include material incorporated from interviews about the Los Alamos period that he conducted with Jerry in 1991 and 1994.

in his work as an experimental physicist. In recruiting a group to work with him, Jerrold made a point of choosing people he felt would augment his own skills and would work well as a team. He hoped, with the support of such a group, to be able to justify Oppenheimer's faith in him.

After receiving Harold Hazen's permission, I agreed to take part in the project, as did Herb Weiss and several other Rad Lab members, and in September our group went out to join Jerrold on the project. The move to New Mexico was exciting for Laya, Steve, and me. We had never seen the mountains of the western United States and we were unprepared for the beauty of Los Alamos itself—a place apart from the world, where you woke every morning nested among the clouds, like my idea of what Shangri-la must look like.

Our first sight of the area was not quite so awe-inspiring. The train dropped us off at a small, isolated station a few miles from Santa Fe, where we were met by Zach in his Ford touring car, the right vehicle for a first glimpse of the desert. Bypassing the town, we began a climb up the San Juan mountains, following a dry river bed. We learned later that at certain times of the year, usually when the snow was melting in the mountains, the dry bed would become a roaring river and people who were unfortunate enough to be caught in one of these sudden torrents would have their cars swept downstream and would be lucky to escape alive.

As we traveled upward, we passed through a series of distinct and beautiful landscapes, each of them different from anything we had ever seen. At the lowest level was the yellow and red desert floor, where the only signs of life were the cactus, including the stately giant saguaros. Rising higher, sharp cliffs bordered the river bed on either side. Some of these cliffs had man-made caves in them. The hill dwellers who had lived in the caves had built long ladders to reach them, which they would haul up to protect against intruders. The caves were no longer inhabited but were maintained as historical sites, and we later visited them several times.

As we drove further, we did see inhabited Native American villages in the hills above the road. These were home to the San Ildefonso Indians, who were widely known for their pottery. On later trips we came to some of the villages for dinner and to see the work they did. Many of the things they made, particularly the dark red and black bowls and vases, were extremely beautiful. The most extraordinary pieces were by a woman named Maria, who was famous throughout the area.

From Jerrold's car we saw, too, those strange, hill-like mounts, rising almost vertically from the ground, as high as a thousand feet—the desert mesas. For some reason the mesas have not been leveled by the water coming down from the mountains, like the rest of the surrounding area, and they stand out like giant mushrooms dotting the landscape.

Though we didn't know it, our goal was an extremely large mesa, big enough to contain the village of Los Alamos, with its laboratories and the homes of the people who worked in them. We knew we had reached our destination when the road was suddenly blocked by a high fence and a gate manned by military guards. The fence ran across the plateau as far as we could see in either direction.

The guards were expecting us and the formalities were brief. After passing through, we were taken first to the Lodge, the social center of Los Alamos, where we were registered and welcomed by many of the scientists. I have a vague memory of speaking with Oppenheimer, whom I was to see frequently during our stay but only came to know at all well years later, when we would travel to Israel together to attend meetings at the Weizmann Institute.[2] I remember, also, Enrico Fermi, who had a room next to my lab; Hans Bethe; Willie Higginbotham, who was a leader in the drive for civilian control of nuclear energy; and Richard Feynman, whose sport, I was told, was picking the locks on the "top secret" and "most sensitive" files in the project offices.

After being introduced to these project members and speaking, as well, to a number of old friends who were also on hand to greet us, we were given a tour of the facility. The mesa was divided into two sections. The living quarters of the staff and their families occupied the eastern half, to which anyone who got past the outer guards had access. In the western half was the laboratory area, which was highly restricted and was surrounded by another tall chain fence. A second "division" immediately evident to the newcomer was the one that existed between the two different styles of architecture on the Hill. The first style was represented by the old, rather stately, log cabins, which had housed the students and staff of the exclusive boy's school attended by Oppenheimer in his youth. These solid dwellings had the feeling of belonging to their surroundings, fitting naturally into the landscape of the mesa. Almost all were occupied by the earliest arrivals to the project.

In sharp contrast to these older buildings were the newly erected structures put up especially for the project. These recent additions were unmistakably Army-issue—nondescript and box-like, the majority the same sand color as the ground, all laid out in neat, unvaried rows. These GI houses were mostly four-family units, and we were given a section of one of them. Sharing our house with us was a family

---

2. A research institution located in Rehovot, Israel. Jerry was elected an honorary fellow of the Weizmann Institute in 1961, and served on its board of governors from 1964 to 1990.

named Lavatelli, who had a daughter about the same age as Stephen. The two of them soon became close friends, a relationship which was to last through to their college years. The Lavatellis and the Wiesners were also very compatible, and we formed a friendship which lasted until Anna, the mother of the family, died in Boston many years later.

Once settled, our group spent the first few days acquiring some understanding of the work that had been done on the Project. Learning the details of how the bomb had been built was intriguing, and I was curious to discover what the various scientists who had left the Radiation Lab so mysteriously in 1943 had been doing. By the time we went to Los Alamos, the world knew the essentials of atomic energy and atomic bombs because Dr. Harry Smyth had published his surprisingly complete description of the two different types of bombs—one employing uranium, the other plutonium.

The uranium bomb was a simple linear device that was made to go critical by slamming two pieces of fissionable material together very quickly. The plutonium bomb, more complicated and also more elegant, was detonated by compressing the fissionable material to such a degree that its neutrons passed the critical point—two per atom—and it exploded, releasing the energy equivalent of many thousands of tons of normal high explosive. The bomb's extraordinary power is still hard for me to visualize, and when one considers how freely many people talked of using even the early, low-yield bombs, it is hard to imagine that many of them had ever truly visualized it either. This was before the arrival of the H-bomb, whose explosive power is normally measured in millions of tons. Dr. Smyth's book also described the enormous industrial effort that was necessary to make the small amount of fissionable material needed for the critical assemblies of the first bombs, and caused most readers to believe that only the United States had the industrial capacity to build them.

As things were to turn out, we Radiation Lab immigrants never came to fulfill the ambitious goal with which we had originally been charged. On our arrival, we were informed by Jerrold that for several months there had been an ongoing discussion about converting a section of the large Air Force base at Albuquerque into the Engineering Division of the Los Alamos lab. As it was Zach's understanding that our group had been hired to do the work it appeared this new lab was to do, much of his time, prior to when the rest of us arrived, had been spent trying to clarify where we fit into the picture.

Eventually, it was determined that the reason we had been hired was that Oppenheimer and the other project leaders believed our group would be able to execute the larger part of the redesign job in a relatively short period, and that we could then hand the work over to the Albuquerque lab for engineering and production. Unfortunately, this decision reflected an oversimplified view of the existing technical situation. Though the bomb's design was not quite as frail as had been feared, it was soon clear to us that a meaningful redesign would require a much larger effort than our small group was capable of and much more time than we had to spend on it. Indeed, we realized that, by itself, our group wasn't even adequate to complete the plans for the laboratory that would be needed to tackle the entire task, design as well as engineering.

In the event, Jerrold decided to join forces with Roger Warner, the Manhattan District engineer who had been charged with the continuing production of nuclear weapons, to begin to develop a program for the new facility. For the rest of us, we mostly just added our views to the arguments that had already taken place about the advantages and disadvantages of having the research and the engineering and design done at two different locations. Our consensus, finally, was that the two-site decision was the right one and we agreed to assist, as far as we could, in implementing it. In addition to this task, our group also did some work on those electronic components of the bomb that we had an understanding of. Herb Weiss and I formed a small group to work on the telemetering and timing systems.

In fact, it was rather hard to get a lot of work done because most of the Lab's staff was restless and eager to move on to their postwar careers, just as at the Rad Lab. In addition, most of the technician force consisted of GI's who had been drafted into the army and shipped to Los Alamos and who, even more than the scientists, had only one yearning—to return to civilian status and get on with their lives. Nonetheless, it was for me an interesting and sometimes even an exciting period, and in later years I realized that the understanding I gained—both about the bomb and the controversy surrounding its use—had provided me with a valuable education on issues that were to occupy a large part of my life.

So I spent my time simultaneously attempting to plan a sensible but limited program for our group on the Hill and going the ninety or so miles to Albuquerque to make my small contribution to the plans for the new laboratory. Jerrold and Roger Warner spent most of their time there, trying to give shape to their ideas for the new facility, often with more help than they needed from other people, including the top man, General Groves, who, competent though he was, had a special knack for annoying people.

The character of General Groves was one of the few things at Los Alamos about which there was a near unanimity of opinion among the project scientists.

Everyone had some story to tell. The members of our group referred to him by the rather sophomoric nickname, "Old Fatty."

When we first arrived at Los Alamos, we found most of the inhabitants incensed over a particularly ill-advised Groves economy. The town water system wasn't working because its sources had dried up and tank trucks had to be used to haul river water up the mountain to be dumped into the distribution system that fed the houses and labs. This arrangement had a number of drawbacks. First of all, there was always a shortage of water and the pressure was low, so houses at higher elevations often had no pressure and the water was frequently dirty or at least sandy. At times there was no water at all, usually during periods of high demand in the morning and evening. Once we had a fire in our laboratory and were only able to put it out by using water from a tank truck which I had to beg for. The rumor, which was generally believed, was that once, when Groves was in a foul mood, he had refused to approve a request for equipment needed to keep the water system operating.

In addition to problems with the water, the electrical plant, which consisted of a pair of old diesel-driven generators, had long been inadequate to accommodate the peak load which came at the dinnertime cooking hour. The solution that had been reached for this was to randomly cut off power to some part of the village every night. This, too, was blamed on Groves and was one more source of the project members' annoyance.

One of the most curious incidents I witnessed at Los Alamos was typical Groves. For some reason, he was very worried about a coming Congressional investigation of the money that had been spent building the bomb. He was particularly concerned about an enormous cylindrical drum called "Jumbo." Jumbo was about fifteen feet long, with sides a foot thick and open on one end. It had been ordered early in the project when confidence regarding a successful explosion was low. The plan was to have the first test set off inside Jumbo so that if it wasn't a high-level explosion the uranium could be scraped from its inside and used again. Jumbo was made from one large, solid cylinder of steel, turned to hollow its inside, the largest steel turning ever done. It was so big that it took a special effort to deliver it, rerouting it to bypass low bridges, etc. By the time it was delivered, there was much more confidence in the project and the scientists feared that using Jumbo would inhibit the explosion, so they decided instead to suspend the bomb from a tower. General Groves was very upset by this decision and classified Jumbo "secret."

The episode was forgotten by everyone but the company that had made Jumbo and the people who had transported it. Since the war was over, they wanted to show

A trio of "J's"—Jay Stratton, Jerrold Zacharias, and Jerry. (Courtesy of the MIT Museum.)

it in their advertising but Groves refused to declassify it, in spite of insistent and repeated requests from the maker. One day I happened to be present when a young colonel again gave the general a request for declassification. Half in jest, Groves said that if Jumbo was ever used it could be declassified. "Why don't you set off a charge in it?" he said. Taking Groves at his word, the colonel did just that, setting off an explosive inside it, but unfortunately he put the charge on the bottom of the cylinder instead of in the center where the forces were equal on all sides. Thus, pieces of the cylinder were scattered across the desert. Groves then had its classification upgraded to "top secret."

Zach and Groves often had disagreements, and the General usually had the last word. These differences generally had to do with money, too, for work on the new laboratory. Jerrold wanted to equip the new installation well from the start, while Groves preferred to build up more slowly. Their squabbles finally reached the breaking point when Zach wanted to have a small airport built on the Hill so that people working at both sites wouldn't have to travel the ninety miles each way by car every time they had to make the journey. Feeling that adequate liaison was going to be difficult, Zach believed a plane would make the frequent trips more bearable.

One morning I was standing near Groves's office when Zach came out, extremely angry. "I'm not going to work for that fat bastard anymore," he said. I asked him what had happened. "He won't let us have the airport." This was the final straw for Jerrold. He packed up his things and went home to Boston. This was in November. I might have left, too, but for several reasons, including the fact that our son, Zachary, was about to be born, I chose to stay for the duration of the time we had been hired.

Jerrold had used his spare time recruiting for MIT's physics department and his recruits—including David Frisch and the already internationally known theoretical physicist, Victor Weisskopf, as well as a half dozen others—were to give new strength to an already first-class department. Several of these scientists would be close colleagues of mine in the decades to come as we worked together on academic and social issues, particularly on efforts to control nuclear arms.

Many of the scientists at Los Alamos actually intended to make peacetime careers there, continuing to work on the development of nuclear weapons and related research. Most of those who were leaving expected to be gone by the summer of 1946, and though many did some work, only those people planning to stay on, plus a few very dedicated individuals, like Fermi, kept going with real zeal.

I had never met Fermi before coming to Los Alamos, but as his work area was next-door to mine, he was a frequent visitor to my office. He came in whenever he needed someone to hear one of his new ideas. Though I was rarely able to make any meaningful comments, it didn't seem to matter; he appeared simply to require a listener. I don't believe he ever realized that I wasn't a physicist.

Our group from the east discovered at Los Alamos something that had not existed at the Radiation Lab. This was the deep concern, shared by most of the scientists on the Hill, about how the future would be affected by the work they had done during the war. What the world would be like and how it would be managed now that the atom bomb existed were constant topics of conversation among the scientists who had taken part in its creation. The Rad Lab scientists did not have the same qualms about their work. They saw only positive things resulting from their new technologies: radar to make flying safer, relay systems to beam messages from one point to another, as well as a wealth of science made accessible by the newly developed microwave techniques.

During the period that they were working to build it, many of the Manhattan District scientists had not thought very much about the bomb's use. Then, after the initial euphoria that followed the Alamagordo explosion, a period of waiting and speculation had set in regarding whether or how the weapon would be used, followed by the horror of the destruction of Hiroshima and Nagasaki. There were some on the project who had not taken such a neutral stance and who, once construction of the bomb was accomplished, were definitely opposed to its use on what they saw as an all but prostrate Japan. These scientists felt that an off-shore explosion to demonstrate the bomb's power would have given the Japanese leaders adequate cause to surrender. The reason the bomb project had been initiated was that it was believed the Germans were working on one, too, and, if they succeeded first, would gain a decisive advantage over the allies in Europe. But with Germany defeated and Japan near to defeat, there were those who believed it was no longer possible to justify using the bomb against a populated target. Despite the esteem the majority of the project members felt for Oppenheimer, there were even some ambivalent feelings regarding his role in the decision to use the bombs. As it turned out, he had voted in favor of their use. Though there were complex reasons for his decision, it would come out that he owed his security clearance to General Groves and thus was under certain pressures as a result.

Although almost all the Project members were now deeply concerned about the future of civilization in the nuclear age, there was hardly a consensus about what should or could be done to mitigate the danger the world faced. For some, the political questions involved became the primary focus of their energies. Their concerns largely centered on two issues—what organization, military or civilian, would control the development and use of atomic energy in the United States; and what kind of agency would be required to oversee nuclear weapons, internationally, in order to avoid a nuclear arms race.

The debate on these questions had the effect of worsening the always strained relations between the scientists and the top military command, as personified by General Groves. These relations were exacerbated, as well, by what the scientists believed was the excessive secrecy still being enforced between the group on the Hill and the members at the other Manhattan District Labs, including Oak Ridge and the Metallurgy Lab at the University of Chicago—a situation that made it difficult for them to work together to lobby effectively on the issues that concerned them all.

Quite suddenly, in early October, a plan was proposed in which the War Department was to be put in charge of all atomic energy activities. The May-Johnson Bill, as the plan was called, was submitted to Congress by President Truman in a surprise move—in the hope, the advocates of civilian control believed, that it would pass before effective opposition could be mobilized. The legislation, if it had gone through, would have placed the responsibility for all atomic energy matters in the hands of a part-time commission appointed by the president, who could nominate anyone he chose. The introduction of the bill horrified the atomic scientists, who had expected a much more thought-out plan involving civilian control and a serious mechanism for international negotiations. Suddenly, no other issue seemed important to many of them, and they proceeded to apply the same energy and intelligence to the new cause that had earlier gone into the creation of the bomb.

When I arrived at Los Alamos, I knew as little about the politics of atomic energy and the problems of international control as I did about the weapons themselves. I was impressed by the intensity of the scientists' discussions and by the different viewpoints people defended with so much vigor. The arguments being new to me, almost all the speakers seemed to make good sense, even when they contradicted each other. I listened to innumerable hours of debate as the members of ALAS (the Association of Los Alamos Scientists) talked on, night after night, working their way toward a unified position.

The process of reaching agreement on the various issues was difficult for many reasons. First, much of the group changed from night to night and the scientists at the other sites forwarded papers that were read and discussed as well. In addition, Oppenheimer and other members of the staff made frequent trips back and forth to Washington, bringing additional news and information with each trip. Some of the scientists who went to the Capitol did so to meet with colleagues from the other sites. Others went to talk to senators, congressmen, and newspaper people, and to try to get a firsthand understanding of the emerging politics of the atom.

It took me several weeks to understand why most of the group was so upset by the May-Johnson bill. When I finally understood it, I realized that the bill did indeed have serious flaws. There was one clause, in particular, which appeared especially dangerous. This provision would have given the new entity the power to arbitrarily subject any scientific matter whatsoever to secrecy. This could have been catastrophic. Not only did it threaten to halt any effort to achieve international accords on atomic matters, it could also, in principle, have ended freedom of scientific inquiry itself.

As the scientists broadcast their message to Congress, to the newspapers, and, through the papers, to thousands of interested citizens, they built support for placing responsibility for atomic energy matters—both military and civilian—in a new agency of the government, the Atomic Energy Commission (AEC). The commission would have five members—including the chairman, who would be appointed by the president.

The mystique that surrounded atomic energy was so great that the Congress also created a rare joint committee, consisting of six members from the House of Representatives and six from the Senate, to oversee the new agency. The combination of the frightening and arcane subject matter and the secrecy that surrounded almost all nuclear issues resulted in the Joint Atomic Energy Committee having unprecedented power in the Congress, as well as what seemed like unlimited spending power. It also had nearly unlimited power to influence military and civilian uses of nuclear energy and to control decisions on international nuclear matters.

The committee would eventually become so powerful that it would constrain what presidents, including even Eisenhower, were able to do on military and international issues for decades. When the members made common cause with the chairman of the AEC, as was usually the case when President Eisenhower wanted to limit spending on weapons systems or limit nuclear testing, they almost always had their way. During the Kennedy Administration, the committee continued to oppose efforts to reach any kind of accord with the Russians, and when the terms of the Partial Test Ban agreement were being worked out in 1963, they forced Kennedy to agree to a number of foolish and unnecessary measures. Among other things, they insisted that he have the AEC stand ready to conduct further atmospheric nuclear tests at any time, at an annual cost of sixty million dollars.

As I have often contemplated the enormous price our country and the world have paid through the overbuilding of nuclear weapons, and as I personally saw the fear that the committee imparted, I have wished that we had developed a less powerful and less biased means of controlling nuclear energy. It was with great relief all around that President Nixon was finally able to abolish the Joint Committee.

Although I observed the successful political operations of the atomic scientists with fascination, I did not at that time know enough about the issues to become deeply involved myself. Despite the fact that Jerrold had left in a huff, it didn't affect the relationship of the rest of our group to the project. In the spring we were asked to take on a new assignment, designing and building the instrumentation system for the Bikini bomb test which the government had scheduled for that summer. The test was conceived by the Navy to study the effects of an atomic explosion on warships and submarines. They planned to take a group of ships they had left from the war and place them in a lagoon, at varying distances from the site of an explosion, and record the effect on the ships in relation to their proximity to "ground zero." There were to be, actually, two bombs—one an airdrop, which would be set off at about a thousand feet, and the other an underwater explosion detonated on the sea floor.

I was asked to be the leader of the instrumentation group. Our job entailed designing and having engineered the special devices that would detonate the bombs as well as those that would monitor the various effects—such as blast pressure, thermal output, and radioactivity—that the Navy wished to study. A large sea-plane tender called the Cumberland Sound was designated as the control ship for the tests. Since it was docked in San Diego, it was necessary for members of our group, including myself, to make frequent trips there, as different pieces of equipment became ready for installation and testing.

In those days, with the relatively slow flying speed of airplanes and the necessity of stopping to refuel, it was about a six-hour flight from Albuquerque to San Diego. Often when I made the trip, there would be just myself and an army pilot. The tediousness of the flight was such that one particular pilot, who flew the route regularly, frequently would put his head down on his hands and go to sleep. While he was napping, I would fly the plane for an hour or so. Having never operated an airplane before this made the trip considerably more interesting.

Although I was the head of the group, Herb Weiss actually ended up doing more of the day-to-day work than I did. He was responsible for most of the designing and the procurement of the special timers and radio links and the myriad other specialized pieces of equipment required for the tests.

By late spring, I was getting anxious to return to MIT and begin my new career there. As I had never taught before and was scheduled to begin with the summer session in July, I was beginning to worry that I wouldn't have adequate time to prepare my courses. Though I could have asked for an extension, my appointment at MIT was due to start at the end of June and I didn't feel it was a good idea to request more time. Because of this situation, it was clear that I wasn't going to be able to accompany the ships to Bikini or to take part in the actual tests. In the event, it was decided that I would go along with the flotilla as far as Hawaii and that Herb would then take over as leader of our group.

Thus, it turned out that I did not end up witnessing the explosions. I was, nonetheless, aware of the results, which were quite overwhelming and exceeded the Navy's expectations. In particular, they had not anticipated that those ships which were not destroyed outright would be rendered as powerfully radioactive as they were. From the measurements made by our group, it was determined that the levels of radioactivity were such that for anyone aboard any of the remaining boats there would have been no chance of survival.

Though my desire to return to MIT was the primary reason why I didn't go on with the group past Hawaii, there was another issue which caused me to be less than enthusiastic about taking part in the tests. Having become sensitized to the political issues surrounding the bomb, I had found objectionable a plan, which was ultimately discarded, whereby political leaders from around the world were to have been brought to Bikini to witness the tests and to receive, at first hand, a none-too-subtle demonstration of the new power of the United States. Though this exercise in political intimidation was, in the end, abandoned, it was clear that, notwithstanding some legitimate technical questions which the Navy wished to answer, one of the major purposes of the tests was to continue to impress upon the world the unassailable might of the United States.

On my last day at Los Alamos, there was a disastrous accident in which I was almost involved. A friend of mine, Alan Klein, invited me to join him and several others in witnessing the demonstration of a nuclear charge, in a test which Richard Feynman had named "tickling the dragon's tail." As I understood it, this entailed taking a ball of nuclear material which had a hole through its center, so that it was

MIT recipients of the President's Certificate of Merit for contributions to the war effort, October 4, 1948. Jerry is at far right in the back row. (U.S. Army photo. Courtesy of the MIT Museum.)

below critical mass, and very quickly dropping another piece through the hole, so that it went critical for a very brief period of time. I was tempted to join the group, but I had already taken the mandatory nuclear clearance to be checked for radioactivity and I didn't want to do it again, so I said I wouldn't go. As it turned out, something went wrong with the experiment and the insert didn't fall through as it should have. The result was a momentary burst of radiation that killed the physicist Louis Slotin and left Alan with serious medical problems for many years to come.

Thus it was in a rather somber mood that, the next morning, we packed up the last of our things and began the return trip East—back to Cambridge, where I would officially commence my affiliation with MIT, an association that would last, in varied form, for the next five decades.

Technological Capabilities Panel

A draft prepared in 1992 by Josh for Jerry's review and insertions, but which Jerry never got around to revising. It relates primarily to his membership on a secret government task force— the Technological Capabilities Panel (TCP), sometimes referred to as the Surprise Attack Panel—appointed by President Eisenhower in 1954 to undertake a thorough review of U.S. military and intelligence technology and to prepare a report for the president and the National Security Council. The report, issued in 1955 under the title "Meeting the Threat of Surprise Attack," underlined the growing influence of science and technology in national defense policy and led to the acceleration of the U.S. ballistic missile program, surveillance of the Soviet missile program by U-2 aircraft, and the gathering of key data for analysis of the so-called "missile gap" between the United States and the Soviet Union. Jerry's role on the TCP, as outlined by Josh, reflects a time when Jerry's focus was more on technical and administrative than social or political issues—a balance that shifted over the course of the next decade.

In 1954 Jim Killian, MIT's president, asked me if I would like to serve as a panel member for a study on the dangers of surprise attack that he had been asked to run for the Office of Defense Management (ODM). Killian was then a member of the science advisory group for ODM, along with both Jerrold Zacharias and I. I. Rabi.

The impetus for the study originated with concerns about U.S. preparedness and the efficacy of the technological systems underlying our defense. These concerns had originally been voiced by Trevor Gardner, then Assistant Secretary of the Air Force for Research and Development, in meetings with the science advisory group.

Gardner had become a close friend of Jerrold's and mine since Jerrold had gotten to know him in Washington, not long after Gardner had been appointed to the Air Force job. The issues he raised to the advisory group had already been on the minds of others, including Jerrold, for some time, and many of us discussed the different areas the study should investigate during the period that final plans were being made for its formation. We also talked about who might run the study.

Crêpes suzettes, 1959. (Courtesy of the *Boston Herald*.)

One night at our house, while fixing the kitchen stove, Jerrold, Trevor, and I discussed the possibility of having Killian, who had never headed such a group, take on the job. Although he had been president of MIT since 1949, Killian was at that time a man very restrained of speech who performed the president's job in an extremely understated—we sometimes even thought, undynamic—manner.[1] In discussing the possibility of his managing the study, we had in mind the increase in recognition and the distinction that would be afforded him by such a role. We did not foresee that he might possess exceptional abilities—which, indeed, it turned out that he did—to oversee and manage a large group of experts investigating a diversity of technical issues, and to organize the whole into a highly effective report that had extensive impact on everyone in the government.

---

1. Note by Josh to have Jerry recount memory of Killian attending but not saying a word in steering committee meetings of the Radiation Laboratory, 1940s.

After he had accepted the position to run the study, Killian and a group working with him began to hire people for the different areas that the panel proposed to investigate. I was asked to be the head of the Overseas Military Communications group. In addition to my group, there were four others: Nuclear Striking Power, North American Defense, Intelligence, and Military Manpower. I had already, at this time, taken part in several similar studies for the military, and many of my friends from MIT had also been involved in these. The situation was the same on this study, with many close colleagues working on different sections of the project.[2]

Of the people whom I asked to join the communications group, several were colleagues from MIT, like William Radford and Wilbur Davenport, who had worked closely with me and were both engaged on projects that had particular relevance for the study. Others, such as Harald T. Friis, who worked for Bell Labs and was an expert on high-frequency radio, I had known both professionally and personally for a number of years.

The intended task of the communications group was twofold. First, we were supposed to evaluate the current state of long-range military communications, and, secondly, to recommend ways of improving these capabilities, either through the upgrading of the systems then in place or by their replacement with more advanced and reliable systems. In regard to the evaluation of existing systems, the general information concerning these was familiar to all of us working in the group. Almost all overseas communication at the time, both military and civilian, was either by high-frequency radio or by telegraph cable. Both of these systems had considerable weaknesses. High-frequency radio, which carried the most information, was subject to natural interference and delay under the best conditions, and it was believed that in wartime it would be extremely vulnerable to enemy jamming and sabotage. Telegraph cable, besides its natural limitations in conveying information, was believed to be susceptible to enemy cutting or tampering.

Though the group members were familiar with the technical details of the systems in use, it was through briefings with the communications experts from the different services that we received specific information about the numbers of links to given areas, procedures for rerouting in the case of delays or link failures, the tests that had been run to gauge susceptibility to enemy jamming, and to what extent there was oversight and inter-service communication concerning the different networks. This last area, network oversight and cooperation between the different services,

---

2. Note by Josh to ask Jerry which friends should be mentioned here by name.

was one that we concerned ourselves with extensively and in which we found serious deficiencies. It was the subject of one of our most important and detailed recommendations in the final report.

In regard to the technical issues that we concerned ourselves with, we were, as I said, familiar with the features of the existing systems and with their weaknesses. Therefore, the largest part of our task was to evaluate and give recommendations concerning the most promising of a variety of new systems and procedures that were in various stages of development at different research facilities around the country. One reason I had been chosen to head the communications group was that a number of the new systems were being worked on in our lab at MIT, and I had, in the case of several of them, been personally involved in their inception and development. Of these, perhaps the most important was what was called "forward scatter communication."

Some years before the study, I had been working on what I hoped was an idea for a new kind of radar. In the process of this work, I went to England to talk with the men who had developed radar for the British during the war. Sir Robert Watson-Watt, who was one of radar's inventors, shared information with me and then he gave me over to one of his men for further discussion about their recent work. What they were then working on involved, as did my work, a process known as vertically polarized transmission. They were, at the time, experimenting with sending out electromagnetic signals and observing at what rate, in relation to distance, the strength of the signals fell off. The laws that were supposed to govern this rate were well known, but what was interesting was that after a certain distance the signals were no longer following the expected falling-off pattern. Instead, they were ceasing to fall off at all for a certain period and then falling off at a very slow rate, with the result that they were traveling much further than it was believed they would. The experimenters could not explain why this was happening, and the man who was filling me in on their work said that if I was interested in the related issues that we had discussed, I should try to understand this phenomenon.

I thought about what he had told me on my trip home, and although I couldn't see any way that this would fit in with the work on radar I was doing, it seemed to me that it might have possible significance as a means for long-range communication. When I got back, I had a discussion with a group of friends—among them Ed Purcell and Lloyd Berkner—about what I had learned. I told them about the English scientist's hypothesis that the signal might be scattering. They agreed that the phenomenon was intriguing and that it might hold potential as a communications process. During the discussion, Berkner suggested that if the process took place in the troposphere, it might also do so higher up, in the ionosphere. Eventually, we had this assumption tested and it turned out that it did. The result was that signals that I had hoped optimistically might travel 150 miles we were able to send up to 1,500 miles.

At MIT I got several people, including Radford and Davenport, working on the different aspects of this new process. We were able to develop a system that had many advantages over the current and most of the emerging intermediate and long-range communications systems. By the time of the TCP study, the Air Force had a few short scatter links in use and felt positive enough about their performance to be planning to extend and multiply their number. In the years following the study's report, this became for a time the most widely used and reliable intermediate-range communications system for all military communications, until it was exceeded by the increased use of telephone cable and then superseded, in the early 1960s, by satellites.

Of the other systems that were conceived at MIT and which I took part in developing, another very important one was a system called COZI, or the Communications Zone Indicator. This was a process that determined which parts of the ionosphere would reflect signals. Because of heating by the sun and other factors, there were certain times when parts of the ionosphere would not reflect a signal, and this system, which was essentially a radar that sent out a beam and waited for its return, would determine at any given time which parts of the ionosphere would function for communications purposes.

Besides MIT, other sources from which we got information regarding new systems included Bell Labs, which had developed telephone cables but were not as yet using them. We recommended their employment as a valuable process for military communication. At this time there were no transatlantic or transpacific telephone cables laid down, and though Bell Labs had the technology, they believed that there was not sufficient need for them. At our urging, they reevaluated this stance and decided to employ the first transatlantic cables, which we then arranged for the services to make use of.

Another source of new technology was RCA, which had developed a self-checking digital code that they used on some of their teletypes. This code worked in such a way that if the receiver did not record the correct number of digits, the received information would be returned to the transmitting end, calling for a repetition of what was left out of the message.[3]

---

3. Note by Josh for Jerry to elaborate on this explanation.

In addition to these systems, there were several more which we recommended in the final report, some of which held out more promise than others and which the group spent more time in considering. It is notable that one of the recommendations which we included, but which was not considered one of the most hopeful, was for the further investigation of artificial satellites. Only three and a half years before the Russians put Sputnik into orbit and the instigation of our own accelerated satellite program, our pessimism concerning the feasibility of functioning satellites was such that this was given only modest consideration in our report on overseas communications.

Besides the recommendations for new systems, we also spent some time considering ways to improve the procedures already in operation, including the employment of more powerful transmitters and improvement in antenna design. After evaluation of the technical processes, the group turned its attention to an area that it considered of nearly equal importance; this was the organizational structure for oversight and coordination of communications, both within the different services and military-wide.

As I mentioned briefly above, we found serious gaps in this area, concerning up-the-line communications in the different branches and with regard to the lack of any central coordinating entity for military communications as a whole. Because of this, we made a strong recommendation for a central agency to oversee all military communications. In making the recommendation, we stressed that the lack of such an agency hampered communications and made it impossible to coordinate plans and analysis, both under peacetime conditions and, more especially, in the event of war. Among the things that concerned us regarding the lack of central oversight was that, in the event of widespread enemy interference at the onset of hostilities—something which it was presumed would occur—it would be very unlikely, given the scattered and separate conditions under which the different facilities operated, for the awareness of such broad interference or jamming to become known and used as intelligence to alert the services to the fact of an attack. Even more importantly, it was our conviction that in the event of war it was imperative that there be a central authority to ensure the optimal functioning of communications, through combined knowledge of individual situations with the awareness of the larger, overall picture. Without a single entity commanding such an overview, the conditions obtaining during all-out war would quickly reduce communications to total disarray.

Although my work on the study was confined to the communications section, I was naturally concerned as well with the recommendations of the other sections, several of which had significant, long-term influence on American military policies. Of all the work that was done on the study, the group whose investigations probably produced the most wide-ranging impact on the area of its evaluation was the intelligence section. At the time of the study, much of what this group was working on was kept secret even from other members of the study, and its most consequential action—the planning of the U-2 spy plane—was totally unknown to the rest of us through the progressive stages leading up to its deployment.

The concept behind the U-2 was essentially the work of two people—Edwin Land, Polaroid founder and head of the intelligence group; and Kelly Johnson, who was an aeronautics expert from Lockheed. For a number of years Johnson, who ran a special section for military projects at Lockheed, had been trying to convince the Air Force to build a high-altitude plane which he had designed. The plane was extremely light, with outsized wings, and could operate at heights which made it exceedingly difficult to shoot down. This idea finally came to fruition in combination with a complementary idea of Land's.

In the process of the intelligence group's work, Land conceived of the idea of using special high-resolution cameras, which he believed he could build at Polaroid, to take detailed pictures of Soviet military installations. When the group began to consider this idea in depth, Kelly was asked to join them and the two ideas were put together to form the concept of the U-2. After the idea was formulated, it had to be presented to President Eisenhower. With a great deal of reluctance over the violation of Russian territorial rights, but believing that the necessity of gaining information on their military deployments overrode these reservations, Eisenhower gave his okay to the development and eventual deployment of the planes.

The U-2 gained a great deal of attention, owing to the Russians' shooting down of Gary Powers and the loud controversy that followed, but the work that the intelligence group did entailed much more than the U-2. At the time of the TCP study, the state of our knowledge about Russian military capabilities was extremely poor, with more conjecture than hard facts being the rule in almost all areas. The group felt it was mandatory that this situation be changed. A variety of far-reaching recommendations were made and acted on, with the result that our intelligence improved markedly in the period following the issuing of the study's report.

In addition to the recommendations of the intelligence group, there were significant recommendations made by the other groups as well. Of these, undoubtedly the most important was the endorsement of the building of long-range missiles. Other committees working for the Defense Department and the individual services had recommended their development, but it was largely as a result of the extensive

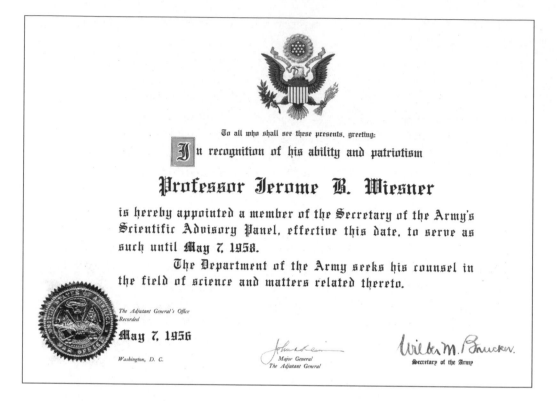

evaluation and backing of the idea as presented in our report that President Eisenhower decided to make this the country's number-one military priority.

As might be inferred by the impact of its recommendations, the study was considered one of the most successful of its kind ever carried out on defense development. It was received with the greatest respect—by President Eisenhower, who voiced the highest praise for it, and by virtually everyone else in government who was in a position to study and be influenced by it.

Up the Ladder to the White House

This chapter begins with Jerry's role on the so-called Gaither Panel, established in 1957 as part of the Eisenhower administration's consideration of a wide range of national security policy issues—particularly the strategic position of the United States relative to the Soviet Union. It continues with reminiscences of Jerry's early service on the President's Science Advisory Committee (PSAC) under Eisenhower, beginning in December 1957, a month after the Gaither Panel presented its report; attendance at the second Pugwash Conference on Science and World Affairs, March-April 1958, exploring international issues of nuclear disarmament and arms control; and concluding with his contribution to the Eisenhower administration's initial efforts to negotiate a test ban treaty with the Soviet Union.

The earliest surviving draft of this chapter, entitled "Working in the White House," was written by Jerry in 1991. The version presented here includes edits and additions by Josh, completed in 1995 or 1996.

✳

In the spring of 1957 I was invited by an old friend from Radiation Lab days, Rowan Gaither, to take part in a study for the White House that the Office of Defense Mobilization's Science Advisory Committee was running. The study was initiated at the request of President Eisenhower. The Administration had recently received a report from the Civilian Defense Administration proposing a 40-billion-dollar bomb shelter program and President Eisenhower, who was skeptical about the report, felt he needed an outside group to advise him as to the wisdom of the recommendation before making a decision about it. General Cutler, the head of Eisenhower's National Security Council staff, had suggested that a study group like the earlier Technological Capabilities Panel (TCP) be convened under the auspices of the ODM's Science Advisory Committee to look at the issue.

My involvement in this study—which was officially named the Security Resources Panel, but was known universally as "the Gaither Study"—would be a turning point in my work as a government consultant, and, in fact, in my whole career. Because of it, I went from being a part-time participant in military studies, welcomed for my technical contributions in spite of what was considered a personal quirk regarding the wisdom of depending so heavily on nuclear weapons, to being an "insider" whose concerns were taken seriously even when they were disagreed with.

Although I had worked on the TCP as a communications expert and done important work for it, I was a part-time participant and was not involved in its management. My work on the Gaither Study started me on a path that led, first, to membership on the White House Science Advisory Committee, and from there to the post of Special Assistant for Science and Technology under President Kennedy. I took part in the Gaither Study as a full-time participant until its task was finished in the winter of 1957. After that, I continued as a part-time adviser on military technology to President Eisenhower, working through his Science Advisory Committee. In 1958, I became a member of the committee.

The Gaither Panel had other antecedents besides the TCP. Perhaps the most important of these was a study that Eisenhower had had the Joint Chiefs of Staff conduct. This study was in the form of an ersatz nuclear war, whose outcome was unbelievably gruesome.

The realism of the study was amazing. Make-believe defensive systems were placed on desks in the Pentagon and simulated the area where the real defenses— the fighter planes, anti-aircraft missiles, radars, etc.—were expected to be. A make-believe air-defense missile had the effectiveness as a function of range that was found in the real-life situation. Make-believe fighter planes had a kill-effectiveness that was a function of their positions in relation to the incoming bombers, their relative speeds, the weather in the area, the locations of the ground radars, and the many other factors that might affect them. Men, functioning as enemy aircraft, would invade an area and the defenses would try to intercept them. The invaders would attempt to pick routes that avoided defenses, but their information was not perfect; also, some of the invaders would blunder into well-defended areas and be shot down. This game was repeated many times with different attack routes, bomber altitudes, and size of individual bomber groups. I was particularly intrigued because I don't think that any of the people involved in doing the simulation knew that they could have obtained the same result without the actual simulation by using a well-known statistical theory called the Central Limit Theorem.

The most important consequence of the Joint Chiefs' exercises was a heightened awareness on the part of the president of the utter catastrophe a nuclear war would constitute. Because of Eisenhower's concern, the Office of Defense Mobilization (ODM), under the leadership of Gordon Gray, began to look for ways of making a nuclear war less horrible. Although I was not concerned with this activity, I had some knowledge of the civil-defense field because of the earlier East River study done by Lloyd Berkner and the Associated Universities.[1] I had the distinct impression that people were not willing to spend money on making cities more secure, perhaps because they didn't think it was possible to do anything meaningful or because deep down they didn't want to think about nuclear war. The ODM had a similar problem. It did many studies and made some attempts to organize men and civil defense groups. I knew little about this, but I had the vague impression that its efforts were not held in high regard.

My familiarity with the power of programmable computers, plus the presence of Dr. Robert Prim from the Bell Telephone Laboratories as head of the Quantitative Assessments group and Norman Taylor of the MIT Lincoln Laboratory in my group, both of whom were very familiar with big computers, gave us the courage to wander into unexplored paths with very large computers. Much of this work was more useful in teaching us what we should have done than in helping us understand defense of the country. This work had an unanticipated lesson for me as well. After one of our briefings to the Steering Committee, I mentioned to Robert Sprague that I was surprised at how little the committee had quarreled with our findings, and he told me that the group realized that we had all of that computer-based information. In fact, we had not been able to decipher the computer output and had had to use old-fashioned hand calculations at the last minute for the presentation. I learned the magical power of the electronic computer.

The Gaither Panel, working in 1957, had to take into account aircraft attacks from Soviet bombers while realizing that in a very few years most of the damage in a nuclear war would be done to the United States by ballistic missiles rather than by aircraft, as the Eisenhower study had assumed. This double threat confused us because we didn't know the timing of the switchover from one to the other. The missile was clearly the weapon of the future, but was not yet in either the American or Soviet arsenals. But aircraft or missile, the result was always the same: nuclear war with a reasonably well-armed enemy would be devastating no matter how well the country prepared for it.

The Gaither Panel experience also convinced me of something I had long suspected, and in fact talked about before, that American intelligence about Soviet force levels was more often than not a reflection of our own plans. This experience also

---

1. *Report of the Project East River, Prepared Under Signal Corps Contract no. DA-49-025-SC-96* (New York: Associated Universities, 1952).

involved me forever after in attempts to understand and stop the nuclear arms race. It became an obsession for the rest of my life.

After the Gaither Panel completed its study, I continued to work as a member of the Eisenhower Science Advisory Committee, where I worked on missiles, warning systems, satellite communication, and, ultimately, on Eisenhower's efforts to reach safe agreements to achieve a less dangerous world, open skies, and many other plans. This in turn led President Kennedy to choose me to be his Special Assistant for Science and Technology, because of his own interest in these problems.

The Gaither Study marked a turning point, too, in my understanding of the forces that drove the arms race, especially the practice of using worst-case analysis on both sides, which was compounded by faulty intelligence information. This was fed by inter-service rivalries and the common practice of high-ranking military officers becoming, on retirement, high officials of companies that built much of the military equipment.

As I have already said, as a member of the Gaither Panel I saw firsthand what I had long suspected, that little solid information lay behind many—perhaps most—so-called intelligence estimates, which instead tended to reflect our own programs rather than those of the Soviet Union, but with time differences. At the start of the exercise, we thought that the Soviets trailed the United States by about two years in most military hardware; after the launching of the Russian satellite, Sputnik, which occurred just as the study was finishing in the fall of 1957, the imagined time lag went the other way with the Soviets now leading. When the facts became known, the Soviets had many fewer long-range bombers than American intelligence expected. Also, faulty intelligence caused the Panel to believe in the famous "missile gap" on which John Kennedy based his 1960 campaign, but which in the end turned out not to exist.

For many years after this, I speculated on why the Soviets didn't deploy their intercontinental missiles sooner. We saw the first flight of their five-thousand-mile missile in the summer of 1957 and could reasonably have expected an initial deployment soon after that. My best uninformed guess was that, soon after that, they had seen the American U-2 fly over Moscow with impunity, and realized that their missile took too long to launch, hence it was very vulnerable.

The Gaither Panel was to try to answer questions the president had about the contribution civil defense could play as a part of the nation's preparedness program in the event of a nuclear war with the Soviet Union. The question the president wanted answered, according to Gaither, was, "if one assumed that there was going to be a nuclear war, what civil defense measures should be taken to protect the

IN RECOGNITION OF PUBLIC SERVICE

The United States Department of State

Extends to

Jerome Wiesner

Its appreciation for assistance in the American program for the Brussels Universal and International Exhibition, 1958.

It was through contributions such as yours, generously and willingly made in the public interest, that the United States could present to the world, at Brussels, a representative picture of our land and our people.

It is my privilege to extend this official recognition to you on behalf of the Department of State.

Brussels, Belgium
October 1958.

Howard S. Cullman
United States Commissioner General
Brussels Universal and International Exhibition, 1958.

American people?" This seemed simple enough, but before we were finished with it we were to realize that it was a very complex and even loaded question—even the wrong question, because the very act of building a massive shelter system could probably make a nuclear war more likely, and there was no way of knowing how much.

I. I. Rabi, who chaired the Science Advisory Committee, did not like the study from the start because it was clear to him that there could be no adequate protection for the country in the advent of an all-out attack. He thought that even with the best defense system we could design and build there would be incredible loss of life and property. His view was that the nontechnical, nonquantitative issues—such as how much death and destruction the country was willing to accept—would be the most important ones, and he did not want to have scientists provide a cover for them. He was willing to help with the organization of the study and was a member of its Steering Committee, wanting to be certain the technical questions were properly answered. He even volunteered me to work on the panel, but he did not want to have the scientists be responsible for the study's outcome. Nonetheless, it was published under the aegis of the Security Resources Panel of the Science Advisory Committee. Moreover, when the final report was written it included not only an assessment of passive and active defensive measures, but also judgment of the deterrent value of the U.S. retaliatory forces, as well as the economic and political consequences of any significant shift of emphasis from offense to defense programs. As Rabi had feared, the Panel was charged with a very broad examination of the U.S./USSR confrontation rather than just shelter programs.

Rowan Gaither, who had been the president of the Ford Foundation in its formative years, had been persuaded to chair the study under the general direction of the head of the Office of Defense Mobilization, Gordon Gray, while a vague technical responsibility was retained by the Science Advisory Committee. I was recruited by Gaither, who asked me to take responsibility for the technical aspects of the study.

The organization of the study group was straightforward, consisting of a Steering Committee of senior people, chaired by Gaither. I was a member of this group. The substantive work was done by four working groups: the Active Defense group, which I headed; a Passive Defense or Shelter group chaired by an old friend, William Webster, president of the New England Electric Company; a Quantitative Assessments group headed by Dr. Robert Prim of the Bell Telephone Laboratories; and a Social-Economic-Political group chaired by John Corson of the consulting firm of McKinsey and Company. This was my introduction to this special brand of consulting, in which very good specialists substituted for competencies absent in corporate structures.

Gaither recruited most of the Steering Committee, but he was stricken with cancer soon after the study was started and his role was taken over by Robert Sprague, the president of the Sprague Electric Company, who one year earlier had undertaken a one-man review of the strategic balance for Eisenhower. He was all revved up, knew more than any other civilian in the country about the strategic bomber force and the air defense system, and consequently was almost the right person to substitute for Gaither. I say "almost" because he knew so much that it was sometimes hard to get him to listen to a new point of view. The study had a codirector, William C. Foster, who had previously been an Assistant Secretary of Defense for International Affairs. Although I had not met him before, we quickly became friends because he was a graduate of the MIT Electrical Engineering Department.

The Steering Committee, in addition to Sprague, Foster, and myself, included Corson; Prim; Dr. James Phinney Baxter III, president of Williams College; Dr.

Robert D. Calkins, president of the Brookings Institution; and Dr. Hector Skifter, president of the Airborne Instruments Labs. This was high-powered company for me, and it took a bit of getting used to.

This was not all. The study was really top-heavy. In addition to the Steering Committee, it had an Advisory Panel and a Science Advisory Subcommittee. The Advisory Panel was truly awe-inspiring, for it included the most illustrious military and political personages interested in international and military affairs, who wanted to have some relationship with the study. Conversely, the leaders of the study were anxious to have a broad base of strategists, officers, and scientists to validate the study's findings. And so, the Advisory Panel—chaired by Gaither—included a stellar roster including Admiral R. B. Carney, General James Doolittle, Robert Lovett, and John J. McCloy. This was my first acquaintance with all of these people, whom I was to see often in the years ahead.

There were many well-known military consultants as well. Two I remember best were Albert Wohlstetter and Herman Kahn. The latter was famous in nuclear bombing circles as the author of the book, *On Thermonuclear War* (1961), which I never thought made much sense because its fundamental premise was that two nations using nuclear weapons in a war would escalate gradually until one of them reached the limit of the risk it was willing to take and then quit. I never could be persuaded that a nuclear war would be that orderly or fought that rationally. In fact, that was not his mission at that time. He was a slob of a man who talked continuously and so fast that it was hard to keep up with him and often even understand him.[2] In the missile era, Kahn thought, safety required bomb shelters deep down under cities, as deep as a thousand feet down. I remember most vividly his plan to protect New Yorkers by constructing a labyrinth of blast shelters a thousand feet beneath New York City, which people would dive into when sirens warned them to seek cover. I never knew whether he wanted to be taken seriously or was trying to show us how absurd our assignment was.

Wohlstetter's urge was more sensible. He wanted us to recommend bomb shelters for the American bombers, something we did. This was not a new idea. On the contrary, Wohlstetter had been trying to persuade General LeMay to do this for a long time. We were just another way in for him to try. LeMay always said he would spend any additional money he received to buy more fuel so the fliers could practice more. These were but two of the hundreds of suggestions we

---

2. Josh notes here a reminder to look for a letter, date unspecified, that Jerry wrote to Herman Kahn, presumably on nuclear arms issues.

received while we were trying to build our staff and study what we thought was important.

My first assignment was to find people to work with me on the technical issues. Because the study was being done under White House auspices, the clearance procedures were thorough and slow. Our home was in the Old State Department building next to the White House. In spite of the difficulty of the clearance procedure, it was easy to recruit almost anyone we wanted for all of our groups, both as staff and as consultants, because we used the president's name freely when we had to, which was often. So all three groups were unusually able and experienced. Some of the members had worked with each other before, and as a consequence worked well together from the start. The working groups were expected to be involved full-time, and those individuals who did not live in Washington became temporary residents, most of us living in a single apartment hotel. This was very convenient because we usually continued our discussions late into the night.

I was joined at the start, as I have already said, by Dr. Robert Prim from the Bell Telephone Laboratories and Norman Taylor from the MIT Lincoln Labs, as well as many scientists, engineers, and military specialists from the Defense Department, experts from the Rand Corporation, the IDA (a captive think tank of the Joint Chiefs of Staff),[3] and many independent consultants too numerous to list. I note two people, however—Spurgeon Keeny and Dr. Vincent McRae—because they not only worked closely with me on the Gaither Panel, but we continued to work together for many years after that on the President's Science Advisory Committee (PSAC). We had help, too, from the Office of Science and Technology of the Central Intelligence Agency, whose head, Pete Scoville, was our most reliable source of information about Soviet technology and military deployment.

The CIA information was vital for us because the three military services always had widely different assessments of the strength of Soviet military systems, depending upon what best fit their parochial interests. For example, the Air Force told us that they expected the Russians would have approximately one thousand intercontinental ballistic missiles by 1960, the year that was thought to be the high point of danger for the United States. On the other hand, the Navy estimate was that the Soviet Union would have only sixty missiles at that time. Scoville's number was

---

3. The Institute for Defense Analyses, a federally funded research and development center established in the mid-1950s to assist the Office of the Secretary of Defense, the Joint Staff, the Unified Commands, and Defense Agencies in addressing important national security issues, particularly those requiring scientific and technical expertise.

somewhat higher than the Navy's. The Air Force was of three minds—LeMay's; Trevor Gardner and his group, including General Bennie Shriver and his Ballistic Missile Division; and the Air Force Intelligence group—so not only we, but they as well, were confused.

The consequence was that we often heard conflicting opinions about the value of the fighter aircraft and the computer system to direct them that we were building at the time. Even without the threat of missiles, I was beginning to get doubts about the worth of the fighter system we were working on. As we had it exercised by Strategic Air Command, we began to realize that the fighters had to be ready to defend all of the country, while the bombers could gang up on a few cities and overwhelm them. When missiles were added to the threat three or so years later, the fighter aircraft seemed to be totally unimportant. But the Air Defense Command didn't think so. Actually, a modicum of air defense had to be maintained to avoid giving the attacker a free ride.

As we studied anti-missile defenses, the same difficulty cropped up. An enemy could choose its targets, while the defense had to defend all of the nation's cities. This meant an effective defense cost much more than the offensive power to overwhelm it. The more I learned about nuclear weapons in the years ahead, the more convinced I became about this. We received ad hoc advice about this and many other issues from many sources, much of it interesting but often also impractical.

Our studies had several parts—assessing the capability of the many components of the strategic defense and offense systems, trying to estimate casualties from a variety of Soviet attacks against many different air-defense and missile-defense systems, trying to understand how much fallout or blast shelters could reduce the carnage. Finally, as if there would be even a minimally functional society after the nuclear exchange, I even designed a primitive anti-missile system. Now, thirty-five years later, it looks almost as good as the present battlefield systems.

I don't recall much of the detail of the studies after all of these years, but a few special events still stand out in my memory. First of all, as the study began to come together, we saw the horrors that had so upset the president several years before. We were all frightened, too. But different ones of us drew disparate conclusions from the same information. Some of my colleagues drew solace from the fact that casualties might be reduced from more than a hundred million people to sixty or eighty million. Either way there would be an incomprehensibly large number of dead or dying, and the nation's infrastructure would be demolished. In those moments, I wondered about the use of living. But I also realized that in many situations the damage and carnage would not be nearly so bad, and in the end I finally decided I would leave the decision up to the president. Later, I heard him say at a Science Advisory Meeting, "You can't have that war—there won't be enough bull-dozers to scrape all the bodies off of the streets." I eventually realized that since we couldn't know what happened until it had happened, we didn't dare let it occur. I still can't believe that I was so stupid.

Several different groups of us visited important installations like the Strategic Air Command headquarters and the Air Defense Command. I went to SAC with Robert Sprague and others to see whether they could perform as the president expected them to. In addition to the planes that were airborne, at all times SAC was sup-posed to have the capability of getting some part—I remember one third—of those on the ground, those in alert condition, in the air in less than one hour. We decided they would be lucky to get them off in 24 hours.

After the shock wore off, Sprague went to see Curtis LeMay, the head of SAC, and told him that we didn't understand what we had seen. It seemed to us SAC was not as ready to retaliate as we had been led to believe. "You're right," LeMay said. "We don't have to be. I will know a week before when they are planning to hit, and we will knock the shit out of them." "But that is not the President's policy," Sprague said. "It's my job to make it possible for the President to change his policy," LeMay said.

When we went back to Washington, Sprague reported the conversation to the secretary of the Air Force and the secretary of defense. The next afternoon Sprague, the two secretaries, and LeMay had lunch in the secretaries' dining room. Sprague sat between the Air Force secretary and LeMay. The Air Force secretary started the conversation by saying to LeMay, "Mr. Sprague has just told us a preposterous story." He proceeded to tell LeMay Sprague's story. When he finished, LeMay said, "Mr. Sprague is right."

I don't know what they talked about for the rest of the luncheon, but the next day the two secretaries and Sprague went to meet with the president to tell him the unbelievable tale. When Sprague came back to our office, I asked him what the pres-ident had said. The answer was, "Nothing—he just glowered." I waited to see what would happen to LeMay, expecting to see him fired or at least reprimanded. But nothing that I could see occurred, and I began to wonder whether Eisenhower didn't have two plans—one public, one private—between himself and LeMay. I tried to talk to Sprague about this idea, but he thought it was so ludicrous that I put it out of my mind.

But not completely. Many years later I asked General Andrew Goodpaster, who had been Eisenhower's closest aide. He recalled the fact that the president had been extremely angry about it, but said Eisenhower had learned to put up with misbehavior from individuals who were doing their jobs well. I remembered, then, that someone at the time had said that LeMay's value lay in the fact that he looked like someone who would easily carry out a bombing.

It was true. Everything about him, from his outspoken pride in SAC to the rakish angle of his ever-present cigar, made one—at least me—certain that he would have no hesitation to let the bombs roll if the president gave the word. If he had any inner doubts, there was no way I could have known about them, although he and I were partners several times in Pentagon war games later on when I was President Kennedy's science adviser. I often wondered how much of the intelligence he claimed to have was true and how much of it was part of the game he had played so long that it was no longer a game.

I had earlier seen LeMay's contempt for missiles. Nonetheless, our Panel believed that in the years ahead missiles would be the country's primary threat and they would change everything. The warning time went from many hours to a few minutes; the defense strategy for cities had to change from evacuation to local defense, active defense, fallout and blast shelters, and possibly even the preventive strike which LeMay was ready for. We did not study that option.

In July, as we began putting our report together, we had a reminder of the reality of our mission when the radar the United States had put in Turkey to watch the Russian missile tests was reporting flights of ever-increasing range—900 miles, 1,600 miles, and so on—until we saw one of intercontinental range. This was a piece of secret information, but it was known to the president and the leaders of our military group. This gave our report increased urgency, and we rushed to get it ready for presentation to the National Security Council.

At the same time, we asked ourselves and the CIA how many missiles the Soviets could make in a year and when their first ones could be operational. The answer we got to our first question was nonsensical—20,000—gotten by assuming that the Soviet Union turned all of its manufacturing capacity to missiles. As an answer to the second question, when would they have a few ready to field, two years more or less seemed reasonable, and that was where our "time of greatest danger" and the "missile gap" came from. Some of the Democratic members of the Senate were told about this situation. They were genuinely frightened by the situation, and their pressure eventually made it into Kennedy's main campaign issue. Meanwhile, Eisenhower ordered the Ballistic Missile Division to speed up its development of the Atlas, Titan, and Minuteman missiles, and waited for the Gaither Panel report.

Our groups worked on two distinct activities—measures to secure and augment the American deterrent power and measures to reduce vulnerability of people and industry. I will say little about the first, building up the deterrent power—even though the report had many things to say about the spending of 19 billion dollars over five years beyond the then current 38-billion-dollar a year defense budget—because it was mostly more of the same. And the president's concern was, as we knew from the start, what would happen if deterrence failed and bombs landed on the cities and countryside.

These additional defenses fell into two categories—active defenses (fighters, anti-missile systems, etc.) and passive defenses (shelters), items that were estimated to cost another 25 billion dollars over the next five years. When a nuclear bomb detonates, there are a number of effects that must be reckoned with, depending upon where it explodes—in the air, on the ground, or under water. These effects always include thermal radiation, blast and shock, initial nuclear radiation, and residual nuclear radiation. If a nuclear explosion is near the ground or water, it will also produce enormous amounts of radioactive fallout.

The amounts of energy released are almost impossible to imagine. There are two forms of nuclear explosion—fission, which occurs when an atom of uranium or plutonium breaks into lighter atoms and gives energy in the process; and fusion, in which a pair of light nuclei unite together to form a nucleus of a heavier atom and give off energy akin to what chemicals do when they burn, but much more energetically. An example is the fusion of the hydrogen isotope deuterium, or "heavy hydrogen," which forms a heavier element—helium—with the release of energy. The complete fission of one pound of uranium or plutonium releases as much energy as 8,000 tons of TNT. The fusion of one pound of deuterium releases roughly the same amount of energy as 26,000 tons of TNT.

Notice that the equivalent of one pound of nuclear explosive is thousands of tons of high explosive. When working with the effects of nuclear explosions, it is important to keep telling yourself this fact over and over again. Too many people lose sight of this fact and think of nuclear weapons as things that can be used in war. A one megaton bomb can totally destroy most major cities.

About the time that we did this study, the British simulated the bombing of Birmingham. Sir Solly Zuckerman gave me some top-secret photographs of what was left of the city, a sturdy city of brick and tile. The combination of fires and blast left it a pile of rubble. Zuckerman had given the file to me without permission, and I showed it to no one for a long time. But I see it clearly still when the talk turns to nuclear war. Something Zuckerman recently wrote gives the impression that Prime Minister Harold Macmillan showed it to both Presidents Eisenhower and Kennedy, but neither of them ever said anything about it in my presence. But then I never said anything about it to them either.

As we began to write the report, it became clear that a part of the group regarded its ingredients as recommendations they felt very strongly about, while others of us (certainly myself) found it impossible to differentiate between a war that had only 60 million casualties instead of 100 million at a cost of many billions of dollars. I also wondered whether such an increased spending for war preparations might not make a war more likely. I made the mistake of voicing these worries out loud in one of the writing sessions, and I was surprised by the number of people who disagreed with me. Incidentally, I didn't remember the final report being so strong or definite in its recommendations as it is, but I signed it. The Gaither Study just made me even more certain than I had been before that nuclear weapons were not usable weapons.

We were scheduled to give our report to the National Security Council in November. Before that, the U.S. radar in Turkey reported a successful flight of the Soviet 5,000-mile missile. This disturbing news was kept secret, so the world was not prepared for what seemed to be an inconceivable event—the Russian launching, October 4th, of a satellite, Sputnik, into an orbit about one hundred miles above the earth. This was not too surprising to the small group of us who knew about the earlier Soviet long-range rocket flight.

Some of us who, like me, had attended a July meeting of the International Geophysical Year, had received another warning as well. At the meeting, I sat beside the Soviet Union's representative for space activities. When an American reported on the Vanguard satellite, which was not going very well, the Russian said, "We are on the eve of launching our own satellite." I asked, "What does that mean? It could mean very soon, or it could mean a long night." To which he replied, "I don't mean a long night."

I reported this to Lloyd Berkner and a few other people, including in the CIA, who said that they already had heard his remarks. I was told that he had been saying this for some time now, and that the president of the Soviet Academy of Sciences had said it too—and his remarks had actually appeared in *Science* magazine, where they had gone unnoticed.

Since no one took this seriously, I went back to work on the Gaither Panel and forgot about the Russian's boast, until Sputnik began peep-peeping around the world. Then I remembered Eisenhower's brag of some years before that the United States intended to launch the world's first artificial satellite. The trouble was simply that Vanguard, which was to have its own rocket designed by the Navy, was under-funded by a factor of five to ten. The country had failed to back up the president's promise with what it would take to make it real. But the general public didn't know this, and to most of the world—in the United States and elsewhere—this surprise meant that the Soviet Union had equaled or even surpassed the U.S. in military technology. The fact that German war prisoners had helped build the Soviet rockets wasn't known and didn't change the fact of their existence. President Eisenhower tried to calm our frightened citizens by saying that a little grapefruit in the sky was hardly a threat, but for the first time in his career his prestige didn't work its magic.

This made our imminent secret report to the National Security Council even more urgent. The worldwide clamor, as well as the American anxiety, became too much for the White House to ignore. Many of us remembered how brilliantly Jim Killian, still the president of MIT, had managed the Technical Capabilities Panel, and urged that the president press him into service as his personal science adviser, with the assignment of making certain that everything possible was being done that needed doing to ensure the American security in missiles and space warfare, whatever that meant.

On October 15, the president met with the Office of Defense Mobilization's Science Advisory Committee, still chaired at the time by Rabi. (I was not yet a member of the committee and didn't know about the meeting; my information comes from Killian's book, *Sputnik, Scientists, and Eisenhower*.[4]) The president asked the committee whether American science was being outdistanced. The committee, through Rabi, told the president that while it thought that the United States had great strengths and many advantages, we must be aware that the Russians had gained momentum and were effectively mobilized to build their scientific and tech-nological strength. Rabi emphasized that unless we took vigorous action they could pass us, just as the United States had caught up with Western Europe and left it far behind in a period of twenty or thirty years. This discussion continued for some time, when Rabi made a specific proposal that there be a science adviser to the pres-ident. Killian recalls that, in an earlier lecture at Harvard, he had made a recom-mendation similar to the one that was being played back to him now, including transferring the Science Advisory Committee from the Office of Defense Mobiliza-tion to the White House, which was included in Rabi's proposal.

---

4. James R. Killian, Jr., *Sputnik, Scientists, and Eisenhower: A Memoir of the First Special Assistant to the President for Science and Technology* (Cambridge, Mass.: MIT Press, 1977).

After discussions with the president, General Bobbie Cutler, Sherman Adams, and others in and out of the White House, Killian agreed to come to Washington as Eisenhower's science adviser. The appointment was announced by the president in a radio and television address on the evening of November 7, the same day that we gave the Gaither Panel report,[5] but I didn't have any advanced warning of the president's speech. As if to punctuate the president's dilemma, the Soviets had launched a second Sputnik on November 3, this time with a dog—Laika—as a passenger.

I didn't know at the time that a subset of the Gaither Panel Steering Committee had a private meeting with Vice President Nixon, just before our report was released, to tell him how desperate they thought the American situation was, and to enlist his support for the Panel's recommendations. As far as I have been able to find out, none of the technical or staff members of the steering committee were present.

I didn't remember seeing Nixon in the audience when we gave our report. At least if he was there, he didn't say anything. We gave our report in the White House broadcast room, which seemed enormous to me at the time, although I have been in it since and I now realize that it is actually much smaller than it seemed then. It was crowded with people, including most of our Panel. I don't really remember much of what happened, although I do recall Gordon Gray introducing us to the president and the group. After Gray's introduction, Robert Sprague gave a short review of the threats the nation faced from the Soviet Union's bombers and missiles, and what we thought could be done about each of them to reduce the danger. Then several of us talked about our special area to improve the situation.

I have a copy of the report that tells what we said, more or less, but since only a small portion of it was ever implemented, I won't narrate it here. Some of the ideas that we talked about, like my quick-and-dirty anti-ballistic missile system, were not doable in the time available. In fact, as I continued to study the issue in the years ahead, I became more of a skeptic about its feasibility. Thirty years later a modern version of it—the Patriot—was used in the Gulf War, and unbiased assessments indicate it didn't do very well.

The entire report took about an hour and a half to present. When it was over, John Foster Dulles, the Secretary of State, quickly attacked it. "You can't do that," he said, "because you will frighten our allies, who will think you are getting ready for war. They will want the same protection, which you won't be able to give them,

---

5. *Deterrence and Survival in the Nuclear Age* (November 1957).

and they will desert us. And it will frighten the Russians as well." Others chimed in with variations of the same tune, and suddenly it was all over and everyone was leaving. I had never seen Dulles perform before and I was mighty impressed and also thankful, as I realized how much he had voiced of my many worries. He didn't say anything, however, about my main anxieties—the tens of millions of deaths and the ruined nation that were certain to result.

I was reflecting on this unexpected turn of events, as I slowly wandered down the hall from the broadcast room, when someone put his hand on my shoulder. I looked up and I was surprised to see the president. "I would do what you want," he said, "but the people won't let me." I said, "Mr. President, the people would let you do anything they thought you wanted to do." "In all modesty, I don't believe that," he said, "they would not give me last year's budget." "You let the Secretary of the Treasury contradict you in public when he said, 'If you pass this budget, you will have a depression that will curl your hair,' so the people didn't know what you wanted," I said—surprised, yes, even shocked, by what I heard coming out of my mouth. Then we walked silently for a while until I said, "I didn't want you to do this—we were just answering the question you asked." He just shrugged his shoulders in bewilderment and didn't say anything more.

Some weeks later (December 20, 1957), the *Washington Post* broke a story on the Gaither Panel by Chalmers Roberts, which was both accurate and, for its readers, chilling.[6] The article described the report as portraying the United States in the gravest danger in its history. It went on to say that it would require another 5 billion dollars a year on top of the then current 38-billion-dollar-a-year defense outlay, first for more retaliatory power and secondarily for fallout shelters as well as a sweeping reorganization of the command system in the Pentagon. It went on to say that the report also recommended a vastly increased research and development budget. The Roberts story had much detail about the National Security Council meeting, including the fact that McCloy and Lovett were present. It was clearly the story of the year, its impact being vastly amplified by the launching of the second Sputnik and the appointment of Killian.

Interestingly, the story did not talk about Dulles's very negative reaction that set the tone of the meeting and actually doomed most of the recommendations, except those that improved the warning systems and the bomber readiness. I decided that whoever gave him the story still believed that the president was going to subscribe

---

6. Chalmers M. Roberts, "Enormous Arms Outlay Is Held Vital to Research," *Washington Post*, December 20, 1957, pp. 1, 19.

to the main features of the report. I doubt that the president ever had any intention of following its script, but he was unhappy about the leak, as well as about Dulles's continued objections, and the charges made by Congressional Democrats that the defense budget was too small doomed it. I once asked Roberts who gave him the story, and he insisted that he had gotten it by talking to many people and laboriously patching it together.

The Roberts story, coming after the Soviet space triumphs and the Killian appointment in the White House, had a bitter-sweet flavor about it. It seemed to say that the country was in trouble, but at least the president realized it and was making very meaningful changes to do something about it. Killian quotes Eisenhower's memoirs as concluding, "In the final result, the Gaither Report was useful; it acted as a gadfly on any in the administration given to complacency, and it listed a number of facts, conclusions, and opinions that provided a checklist for a searching examination."

In my opinion, the most important result of the study was that it confirmed President Eisenhower's belief, based on his earlier Defense Department study, that a large nuclear war would leave the United States moribund, no matter how much money and effort he spent to prepare for it. This realization tended to make the president schizoid, for though he desperately wanted to reduce what he regarded as the terrible danger to the United States, this didn't make him trust Khrushchev and his peers any more. For the rest of Eisenhower's term in office, this problem was his most vexing. He was never quite certain that Khrushchev really wanted a test ban, but he was not willing to forgo the possibility he was sincere. There is some evidence that Khrushchev suffered from the same doubts and had his equivalents to Strauss and Teller.

With Killian's appointment and the reconstitution of the Science Advisory Committee directly under the president, Eisenhower now had a group of scientists who had a loyalty only to him. In contrast, there were some people high up in the system—such as some Cabinet officers—who had thousands of employees, big budgets to defend, and different views of what was in the country's best interest. Loyal as they were to the president, they also had other agendas to worry about. This went beyond the nuclear issue and could be seen, for example, in the failure to provide adequate funding for the Vanguard missile.

Killian's most difficult task was deciding among the myriad demands on his time—what was important and what was only a squeaking wheel, so to speak. Some things were obvious—anything the president wanted, whether a speech, a letter, just someone he trusted to talk to, or an organizational change such as bringing together the National Advisory Committee for Aeronautics (NACA) and the Army's Huntsville missile center into a civilian space agency to form the National Aeronautics and Space Administration (NASA). While both the president and Killian made a number of speeches emphasizing the defense issues and the importance of science and technology to the nation, the important reorganization was going on behind the scenes. The Science Advisory Committee, which before the crisis had not been called on very often in its Office of Defense Mobilization role, now had a central role in the new arrangement. Some of the committee members now worked full-time at the beginning of Killian's term, and most of them worked harder than they ever did before.

I can't really recall what I did with all of my time beyond finishing up the Gaither Study, talking to Killian about the members of the staff of the Gaither Panel who might work for him, and starting to work again on warning systems. Together with members of the Lincoln Laboratory and RCA staff, we decided to have three large ballistic missile warning radars—one in Scotland, another in Thule, and a third one at Fairbanks. In the years ahead, it became one of my PSAC duties to follow the progress of these installations. I joined other members of PSAC and members of the staff in starting to learn about the requirements of a test ban treaty, and I also had the pleasure of being home in Boston much more.

Killian, meanwhile, had to meet many demands on his time, including meeting dozens of new associates, some of whom resented his powerful new position— including some like Admiral Lewis Strauss, who could always be counted on for trouble. There was not much the rest of us could do to help him with these chores. By December 1, 1957, the president had his own Committee, with a number of new members, including myself. David Beckler, whom I had worked with on the ODM committee and was the chief of the staff, continued in the same role in the White House. The other members were Edward M. Purcell, Hugh Dryden, William O. Baker, Alan T. Waterman, George B. Kistiakowsky, Emanuel R. Piore, General James H. Doolittle, Lloyd V. Berkner, Herbert F. York, Hans A. Bethe, Albert G. Hill, Detlev W. Bronk, Edwin H. Land, I. I. Rabi, Robert F. Bacher, James B. Fisk, Jerrold R. Zacharias, and Caryl P. Haskins.

Our office was not actually in the White House, but rather in the old State Department building next to the White House. There was much more very elegant space than in the White House itself, with spacious rooms, marble floors, high ceilings, and high windows. It is the most beautiful building I have ever occupied, left over from an earlier time when, for some inexplicable reason, space was cheaper (it was scheduled to be demolished in the early 1990s, but was rescued at the last moment).

Killian's office was a particularly pleasant suite in the center of the main floor overlooking the White House, one I was to occupy briefly until Vice-President Lyndon Johnson dispossessed me when he decided to have a White House office as well as that in the Senate.

My new routine was interrupted by a letter from Lord Bertrand Russell, the famous British philosopher, inviting me to something called a Pugwash meeting at Easter time in Lac Beauport, Canada, a small skiing resort about ten miles from Quebec. It was the second of these conferences, his letter said, where scientists from many lands—including the United States, Great Britain, Russia, China, and France—gathered to see if they had any ideas about stopping the nuclear arms race. I was excited by the idea, but thought that because of the many secrecy clearances that I had, including those for intelligence information, I probably would not be allowed to go. I took the letter to Dr. Killian, who showed it to President Eisenhower. To our surprise, the president said it looked interesting and I might learn something useful. Then he added, Killian told me, that if I got into trouble they could always disown me. With that blessing, I wrote a response to Lord Russell saying that I would be delighted to come.

I received more information about the meeting and learned that it was entitled, "The Dangers of the Present Situation, and Ways and Means of Diminishing Them." The meeting was to be held from March 31 to April 11, 1958. In a most pleasant surprise, I learned that family members were welcome, so I made arrangements to have Laya and my eldest son, Stephen, go along.

When the time came, we flew to Quebec and were met by a chartered bus for the trip to Lac Beauport. There were about twenty people of various nationalities on the bus. Steve and I sat together and Laya sat with a Russian named Pavlichenko, whose opening gambit was, "Why do you have so much juvenile delinquency in the United States?" Laya's answer was that the last Sunday's *Times* had had an article on juvenile crime in Moscow, so it seemed to her that we had a common problem. "This is just capitalistic propaganda," he countered.

Laya wondered what we had exposed ourselves to. Later, we learned that Pavlichenko was not a scientist but the keeper of the Soviet scientists. He went to all of the Pugwash meetings for many years, and he and I became well acquainted. I got used to his boorish ways and found him useful to me on many occasions. For example, I once told him that Khrushchev was going to elect Nixon by criticizing him so much. Would he like that? He said he would see what he could do about this. After that, it seemed to me, Khrushchev was even-handed in throwing out his verbal darts. After the election, Pavlichenko asked me whether I was happy with

Mr. K's performance after our discussion, implying that he had changed the Premier's behavior. Many years later he became a member of the Soviet delegation to the United Nations, but I never found out what he did there. During that time, he came to see me at my summer house on Martha's Vineyard and once told Laya and me about his wife being robbed in Moscow, apparently his way of making amends for that trip years before. He also told me about his schemes to keep from being sent back to the Soviet Union. He had adjusted quite well to the American lifestyle.

The Pugwash meetings, I found, were an outgrowth of a public statement issued by Lord Russell, Albert Einstein, and nine other scientists in 1955, calling attention to the dangers that existed as a result of the development of weapons of mass destruction—a danger that grew ever more dangerous as the arsenals grew and weapons became more powerful.[7] By now I was in total agreement with their view. The statement called for a meeting of scientists which would make a true and independent assessment of the hazards.

An organizing committee that included Lord Russell and Prof. Joseph Rotblat began to make plans for the meeting and soon realized that they needed more money for it than the scientists could raise from within the group. They wrote letters to a wide range of philanthropic organizations and individuals, and received two replies. One was from Cyrus Eaton, a liberal Cleveland businessman, who offered to provide the necessary support if the group was willing to hold the meeting at his birthplace, Pugwash, near Quebec, Canada. After some negotiation, in which it became clear that Eaton had no agenda of his own, the originating Committee agreed to use his estate in Pugwash, and he agreed to meet all the expenses.

This was one of many things that Eaton did to foster better relations between the United States and the Soviet Union, for which he was frequently damned. In my opinion, he and the Pugwash group helped quite a bit to bring some sanity to the bilateral talks when the Cold War was at its worst. But clearly nothing anyone outside governments—or within governments, for that matter—could do was enough to overcome the deep suspicions that both sides harbored about the ill intent of the other. The Pugwash group did better than most for more than forty years, providing communications when little else existed, providing a cadre of people who had their science to sustain them when suspicions otherwise got too strong.

---

7. The so-called "Russell-Einstein Manifesto," issued in London, July 9, 1955; signed—in addition to Bertrand Russell and Albert Einstein—by Max Born, Perry W. Bridgman, Leopold Infeld, Frederic Joliot-Curie, Herman J. Muller, Linus Pauling, Cecil F. Powell, Joseph Rotblat, and Hideki Yukawa.

The Polish dictator, Gomulka, once told Khrushchev that he should be worried about his scientists because they were more anxious to talk together than they were concerned about affairs of state. In my experience, this was not true. While we—and both sides—often tried to find compromises, it was always interesting to me how much we stuck rather closely to the official line while we were looking for new routes out of the Cold War. I remember well a meeting in Moscow when I became upset because the Soviets were defending the party line, and then I realized that for two days I had been doing the same thing.

After a few years, Eaton and the Pugwash leaders parted company and the Pugwash group was financed by foundations and interested individuals. It is my opinion that this group was more important than any other in introducing scientists to the part they could play in making their countries conscious of the dangers of the nuclear confrontation.

I was rather anxious, as I went to Lac Beauport, for I had never met a Soviet citizen before, let alone talked to any of them about reducing the dangers of the present confrontation. But I knew that the president was interested in the subject from many chance remarks that he had made to the Science Advisory Committee after the Gaither Panel briefings.

We arrived at Lac Beauport at sundown, so we were confined to the hotel. We quickly settled in, met the many eminent scientists whom Lord Russell's letter had lured, read the papers that been prepared for us, and after dinner we had a surprisingly free-flowing discussion, after which, to my surprise, some of us agreed to work together to produce new papers for the next day. I personally knew about one-third of the participants from previous encounters and had heard about almost all of the others.

Now, almost forty years later, I think I am even more in awe of the group and their accomplishments than I was then. Many of the persons then unknown to me—such as Chou Pei-Yuan, the leading scientist in China, and Academician Topchiev, the Foreign Secretary of the Soviet Academy of Sciences—I got to know well in the years since. As I write this, I am aware of the fact that although I and my colleagues had been talking about Russian and Chinese threats to the United States, we for the most part had never seen or talked to any of them, and the threats were not greater than those that we, the United States, directed toward them.

I can't say what I expected to find at Lac Beauport, but I was not surprised to find that nuclear weapons frightened them as much as they did us in the West, and at least this group of scientists wanted to find a way to make sure that they would never be used. Inasmuch as the Russians had just been through the part of Hitler's war fought on their territory, leaving two of their most important cities in ruins, twenty million people dead, and countless more maimed and traumatized, this was not surprising. Their losses were something that I had realized long before, and that made me doubt the many claims of American warriors that Russian leaders were ready to see half their people dead if it allowed them to rule the world.

Topchiev and I agreed to write a paper on the monitoring of a nuclear test ban, which I remember as being good and that we were in complete agreement on. This is not surprising, since we didn't get down to numbers of inspections that would be permitted or the number of monitoring sites that would be allowed on each other's territory or all the other things that governments have been arguing about ever since. We were all impressed. There were many other interesting papers, and I'm sure that most of us were pleased with the conference.

Thinking about the meeting afterwards, I realized that each of us stayed close to the positions of our own countries. Recently I have tried to find the Topchiev-Wiesner paper, but so far I have been unsuccessful. Maybe it is just as well, for it probably has grown better in my memory.

The ambience was, for me, surprisingly pleasant, although in retrospect I don't remember what I expected, but still I was a bit worried. Eisenhower's offhand remark that they could always disown me carried more weight than his observation that it could be very interesting.

Chou Pei-Yuan turned out to have been a boyhood friend of an MIT colleague of mine, Dr. Wang, whom he had not heard from since the Chinese Revolution. He was interested in learning all about him and, as it turned out, vice versa, so I became a go-between, telling each of them about the other as well as their families. At a subsequent meeting at Kitzbühel, Austria, he gave me some booklets showing modern Peking to take back to Wang.

Because we had too much luggage, I sent a package home by mail and later, when it arrived, the booklets were missing. I called the post office, where I found a man I knew and told him about the situation. He told me it was illegal for me to have brought the booklets into the country, and so they had been confiscated. Then I challenged his right to do this, because I was an academic. He answered that I couldn't prove that they had been taken out of the parcel by the post office. After thinking about protesting for several days, I decided it was too much trouble, but it was for me just one more way in which the "land of the free" was being compromised. I did not like my decision to drop the matter either, but I realized that I couldn't take on too many issues.

Chou Pei-Yuan, who was for many years the head of the Chinese Academy of Sciences and the Rector of Peking University, over the years told me much about science and China in general, including the special difficulty of being an intellectual during the Cultural Revolution. I saw him in 1974 and again in 1980 on two trips to China, after Nixon made it legal to visit that forbidden land, and later he spent one summer at MIT as my guest. Through him, I learned much about science, culture, and survival under Chinese communism. Survival for prominent intellectuals was sometimes a full-time occupation.

I returned from Lac Beauport after a week of talking and skiing to find that the president and Killian had decided to hold a retreat for the Science Advisory Committee at Ramey Air Force Base in Puerto Rico to explore whether the group thought that the moratorium on testing that Eisenhower and Khrushchev had been flirting with would jeopardize the nation's security. I told the group about the Pugwash meeting I had just attended and my belief, formed long before the Pugwash meeting, that with the present perfection of the American nuclear weapons and the likelihood of the Russians being caught if they were to do a meaningful amount of cheating, a test ban would not put the country in any danger.

Many members of the committee agreed, but some had lingering doubts. Herb York, once the director of the Livermore Lab, had some worries, particularly whether it was right for a group of scientists to give advice on what he regarded as a political problem. After discussing the issue for almost a day, Herb and I were elected by the group to peel off and see if we could come back with an agreed-upon position. After a long discussion about all the issues we knew about, we reported to the committee that we believed that a test ban could be amply safeguarded.

In his book, Herb says that I won him over, so to speak, by telling him that—scientists or not—there was no other group as well positioned to make the decision for the country.[8] I don't remember that. I thought that my best arguments were technical, that no amount of Soviet testing would reduce the value of the American weapons. Inasmuch as we were not designing the seismic network, the United States could insist on one that satisfied our needs. In fact, as I saw it, our needs were more political than technical, for unless we could assure the nuclear conservatives in the Congress, the military, and the scientific community that the Russians were not testing clandestinely, any agreement to end testing would not survive for very long.

The committee used our informal report to have another wide-ranging discussion and, in the end, agreed to make a report to the president advising him that a

8. Herbert F. York, *Making Weapons, Talking Peace: A Physicist's Odyssey from Hiroshima to Geneva* (New York: Basic Books, 1987).

properly drawn and adequately monitored test ban agreement was in the country's best interest. It was the group's view, based on incontrovertible evidence from the debris obtained by our aircraft from Soviet tests, that the American nuclear weapons of all kinds were better at that time than their Soviet counterparts, for whatever that meant, and that a test ban agreement that was lived up to would preserve that advantage. It was also agreed that while the Soviets might successfully hide an occasional test, they could not make very much progress in that way and therefore were not very likely to cheat. My own view was that the greatest risk was that they would use the time gained by an agreement to get ready for a new series of tests, something we would probably do too as a precaution against a breakdown of the agreement.

The committee was critical of the lack of research on monitoring systems, and recommended that a group be set up to survey what was known about seismic detection and the ability to distinguish nuclear tests from earthquakes, because the Russian tests were conducted in Siberia where earthquakes were frequent. A continuing research program was included in the recommendations. With these assurances, President Eisenhower proceeded to negotiate with Khrushchev for a meeting of scientists to seek agreement on the design of a monitoring system. The same group, headed by Lloyd Berkner, began working on the seismic detection program, while another group, headed by Dr. James Fisk, began preparations for the meeting of scientists that was to take place in the summer of 1958. Berkner and Fisk were members of the PSAC. Several other members of the committee and its staff, as well as many other specialists, also joined in these tasks.

I should record an incident that took place during the early negotiation with Khrushchev, which seemed to be typical of the mode of communication between the American State Department and the Soviet Foreign Office. For reasons that I don't remember, Ed Purcell and I were chosen to check the letter that the State Department was to send to the Soviets saying that Eisenhower wanted to proceed with the Meeting of Experts. We were dismayed to see that it had a long preamble recounting a long history of Soviet misdeeds, before it came to the point where it said, in effect, that in spite of this the United States was prepared to join in a Meeting of Experts to see if a mutually satisfactory test ban monitoring system could be agreed to.

The two of us were appalled by the tone of the letter, and said so. We were told this was normal and the Soviets would not be offended by it. We showed it to Dr. Killian, he in turn called it to the attention of the Assistant Secretary of State, and we had the pleasure of seeing a civilized communication go from the United States to the Soviet Union. (Many years later, in 1963, at the height of the Cuban missile crisis, President Kennedy was waiting for Khrushchev's response to Kennedy's proposal for ending the confrontation. When it came, it contained a nine-page recital of American misdeeds before agreeing. As we listened to Khrushchev's wandering polemic, I imagined him pacing in his office getting all his frustrations off his chest before finally acquiescing.)

In any event, the Soviets agreed to the meeting in Geneva that included, as usual, both NATO and Warsaw Pact members.[9] Because of the study done by the Berkner Panel, the American group was better prepared than the others at the meeting and were able to convince the Soviet scientists to agree to what they believed was necessary. It included 140 seismic listening stations on Soviet territory and [?] searches for suspicious events.[10] The Soviet leaders quickly rejected this system as unnecessary and too costly, and there began a many-sided debate about numbers and, more important, a research program to improve the sensitivity of seismic detectors and ways of telling the difference between earthquakes and nuclear explosions.

The British military research laboratories, driven on by Lord Zuckerman, made important contributions to the technology. Later, Frank Press and I, using my knowledge of long arrays common in radar systems, started an analogous array for underground seismic detection. By 1963, when Kennedy and Khrushchev began negotiating about a test ban, so much progress had been made that we required no internal monitoring stations and could consider only five inspections per year in each country.

The Committee of Experts and President Eisenhower had long hoped for an "open sky" arrangement which permitted the United States and the Soviet Union to overfly each other's territory at will as a means of lessening the danger of a surprise attack. But the Russians would have none of it, maintaining that the real purpose was spying. Since I always thought the United States vastly over-estimated the size of the Soviet bomber force, I was skeptical of the Russians ever agreeing to the proposal.

---

9. Author's note to check whether this is correct.
10. Author's note to check figures for "suspicious events."

Kennedy

The first draft of this chapter, entitled "Backing into the Kennedy Administration," was written by Jerry probably in 1992. The version presented here reflects edits by Josh, along with substantial additions from interviews that Josh conducted with Jerry also in 1992. Notes here and there indicate plans to develop certain sections further.

Jerry's contact with President John F. Kennedy began in 1952 and continued for more than a decade, until JFK's assassination in 1963. The ties between them evolved from casual acquaintanceship into a close working relationship. They first met when JFK was a U.S. Congressman from Massachusetts. Then, as U.S. Senator from Massachusetts, JFK called on Jerry from time to time as an informal science adviser, especially in the period leading up to his successful U.S. presidential campaign; and finally, JFK selected Jerry as his "Special Assistant for Science and Technology," a post Jerry held throughout JFK's period as president.

The memoir below outlines the nature and development of their relationship, as well as key incidents, as Jerry saw them, in his role as science adviser to the U.S. president—the transition from the Eisenhower administration, particularly on issues of arms control; negotiations with the Soviet Union on a possible nuclear test ban agreement; relations among the Cabinet, White House staff, Congressional committees, and federal agencies; the role and makeup of the President's Science Advisory Committee (PSAC); directions for the space program; the Cuban Missile Crisis; and efforts to help Pakistan with a looming agricultural crisis. Such weighty issues are interspersed with delightful anecdotes—some humorous, some poignant—about a number of Washington personalities, the presidential inauguration, and the dynamic between Jerry, JFK, and others in the president's inner circle. The result is a richly woven tapestry of reflections on the workings of the White House, 1961–63.

The first time I met Jack Kennedy was in 1952, when he was a congressman from my home district in Massachusetts. Though I would come to believe that President Eisenhower was in some ways a man of considerably more substance than was commonly recognized, I was always a Stevenson Democrat and I worked for him on both of his presidential campaigns. In the early months of the 1952 election, the charge was being circulated in Massachusetts that Stevenson was sympathetic to communism, and someone in a position of power in the state was needed to refute the accusations. I was part of a group that went to meet with Kennedy to ask if he would make a public statement on Stevenson's behalf. Kennedy told our group quite frankly that he would have to discuss the matter with his father before he could make a decision. The lack of self-consciousness with which he told us this was striking to me. It seemed to me that most recently elected young congressmen would have gone out of their way to downplay any paternal influence on their decision-making, but Kennedy made no effort to mask it. The next time we met with him he told us his father didn't think that it was a good idea and he was sorry he wouldn't be able to help us.

Over the next few years I saw him only a handful of times, at political functions around Boston. We would exchange pleasantries and sometimes chat a moment about matters of public interest. I had little feeling for what his views were on the larger political issues of the time or for what he was like as a person, beyond a general amiability and an articulateness that seemed a cut above the majority of politicians I had then encountered.

Following his election to the Senate, several friends of mine began informally working for him. It was clear from the people he sought out that he was interested in getting the most competent advice he could in the areas he wanted to inform himself on.

It was about four years after that, around 1956, that he first initiated a telephone relationship with me, in which he would call from time to time to ask me about certain scientific and military issues that he had an interest in. As time went on, his calls became more frequent and occasionally we would meet to talk if there was an issue he wanted to learn about in more depth. We got along well personally. The more I saw of him, the more appealing I found him. I found him quick to grasp, in an intuitive way, the essential elements of the technical matters we discussed. Sometimes he would ask me questions about more general scientific matters, such as how radio worked. My answers never satisfied him, for an explanation of waves and frequencies would lead inevitably to how the waves themselves functioned and what was electricity.

I was quite surprised one morning in August 1960 when I received a phone call from *Washington Post* reporter Chalmers Roberts, who said he would like to talk with me about my role in Senator Kennedy's presidential campaign. I told Roberts I wasn't involved in the campaign and so had nothing to tell him, but he said he found that hard to understand, as the previous evening he had flown back from Milwaukee on Kennedy's plane and when he had asked Kennedy who his science adviser was going to be, he had given my name. I told Roberts that it wasn't true, that he must have misunderstood what Kennedy said, but he didn't believe me and told me so. The following morning he reported the story in the *Post*.

I was quite upset when I saw the story because of the awkward position it placed me in as a member of Eisenhower's Science Advisory Committee. I decided I'd better tell George Kistiakowsky what had happened, and when I did, he was even more upset than I was. "If you think I ought to," I told Kisty, "I'll resign from the committee." After we had talked it over a while, we decided he should tell Eisenhower what had happened—that I knew nothing about the matter, that I had not been asked by Kennedy, and that if I had I would certainly have informed George before giving any answer. I also agreed to phone Kennedy and see what he had actually said. Unfortunately, he was campaigning and I was unable to reach him.

The next day Kisty arranged to see Eisenhower. He returned from the meeting rather dumbfounded. "The President sees no reason for you to resign from the committee," he told me, "or to step down as chairman of the disarmament panel, as long as you don't use any classified information and don't campaign yourself." Both of these things were easy for me to promise, as I was not involved in the campaign and had at that point no intention of becoming so. I later learned that several writers, reporting on Eisenhower's decision, said they believed he made it in the hope that I would tell the Kennedy team the truth about the "missile gap," and that I was permitted to continue in the White House so I might communicate the true facts regarding the satellite intelligence. However, I never found this a plausible scenario because there wasn't enough time to hatch so complicated a plan. Eisenhower's response was given too quickly and spontaneously. In addition, I had several times talked to Kistiakowsky about having Eisenhower brief Kennedy on the intelligence situation, and the president had decided not to do so.

If Eisenhower was untroubled by my remaining on the committee after reports tying me to the Kennedy campaign, Vice President Nixon and his staff were not so indifferent. In fact, they were quite angry and they requested that Kisty terminate my appointment. However, Kisty informed them of Eisenhower's decision and, in addition, pointed out to them that it was probably better to keep me on board because of the inhibitions that were thus placed on me. This reminded me a little of Teddy Roosevelt's reason for keeping Bryant in his cabinet—that it was better to have him on the inside "pissing out" than on the outside "pissing in."

Meanwhile, the whole time I heard nothing from Kennedy and could only speculate on what had taken place in his conversation with Roberts. As I've said, he had for several years contacted me when he had questions about science, technology, or arms issues. He knew about the *Daedalus* magazine volume on disarmament that I had edited,[1] and occasionally he would ask me questions on nuclear issues. It had never occurred to me that I was his main source of information on these matters. Eventually, I concluded that in answering Roberts's question, he had simply been stating a fact, not making a campaign announcement. When I finally asked him about it, he confirmed my suspicion. He said that he or his staff always called me when they wanted an answer to a technical or scientific question.

Although I was never formally asked to join the campaign, Roberts's article gradually caused me to become involved, because a number of Kennedy's people, including several colleagues of mine, like Walt Rostow, saw the story and began asking me for advice on speeches they were writing. Soon I began, as well, to meet other members of Kennedy's staff whom I hadn't known before. One of his assistants, Deirdre Henderson, who was responsible, among other things, for disarmament speeches, began contacting me frequently. It was not long before I had the curious experience of hearing a number of my ideas voiced by the candidate as he spoke around the country. I supplied many of the ideas for Kennedy's position paper on disarmament, written by Rostow.

I was particularly pleased to have a chance to press once more for an official disarmament agency and even more pleased, after Kennedy was elected, to see that he actually intended to create the organization I had first envisioned after my disillusionment with the preparation and planning processes for the Test Ban and Surprise Attack negotiations. As I became more involved with Kennedy, I retained a reluctance to write on my own—maybe even more than normally—because of the awe in which I held most of the people who were writing for the candidate, though I did write bits to be inserted into larger pieces.

Keeping my word to President Eisenhower eventually presented me with a serious problem in regard to the "missile gap" issue. Although I was no longer privy to new secret information, it was apparent to me over the summer, from comments of other staff members, that the continuing satellite flights over Russia were not finding any missile installations and, as the coverage expanded, the missile gap was evaporating. In spite of later assertions that I was allowed to remain on PSAC so I would tell the Kennedy team the truth about the intelligence information, I was, in fact, unwilling to make any direct statements to them, as I believed that would breach

---

1. "Special Issue: Arms Control," *Daedalus* 89 (Fall 1960) No. 4: 674–1075. Jerry served as chair of the guest editorial board, which included as members Robert R. Bowie, Donald G. Brennan, John T. Edsall, Bernard T. Feld, William T. R. Fox, Stephen R. Graubard, Gerald Holton, Henry A. Kissinger, and Louis B. Sohn.

the guidelines given me by Eisenhower. I tried several times to hint at the facts to some of Kennedy's aides, but they seemed to have no interest in what I was telling them. After the election, when the truth came out, one of the people I had tried, indirectly, to apprise of the situation denied I had ever approached him on the matter.

Because of my inability to communicate with Eisenhower's people, I spoke once more with Kistiakowsky about having the president brief Kennedy. However, by this time Eisenhower was very angry about the Democratic claims that he had knowingly placed the country in jeopardy, and Kisty received no response when he approached him about it. In his book *Kennedy*, Ted Sorensen said that the candidate received some briefings from the CIA but that they were not very meaningful.[2] It is unclear to me whether anything was said about the missile gap issue.

There was another factor, besides Eisenhower's anger, that may have had an influence on why Kennedy was not given more information and why Eisenhower was not more forceful in refuting his assertions. This was the fear that the Russians might object to the satellite overflying if the United States was to make public how much information they were obtaining from it. In the minds of some decision makers, this possibility justified withholding the information from Congress as a whole and from Kennedy in particular, because his use of the information could not be predicted. It must be said that the possibility exists that Kennedy had more detailed knowledge of the facts than was ever admitted to, and that being kept officially in the dark, in fact, served his purposes quite well, as it allowed him to continue making political capital from the situation.

Despite my concern about this issue, I enjoyed the work I did on the campaign and I was, at times, sorry that I didn't feel free to be more publicly involved. Kennedy's apparent announcement of my role made many people aware of what I was doing, yet I remained unwilling to violate my promise not to take part in campaigning. In retrospect, I thought I probably leaned over too far backwards in honoring this promise. I even decided to skip the long election eve train ride through the Northeast, which ended in Boston in the wee hours of the night, a decision which I often regretted.

Kennedy won the election by a narrow margin, but he won. He soon began the task of assembling his staff and cabinet officers, his deputy cabinet officers, and the many politically appointed officials that make up an administration. His early mention of me as his science adviser caused people to assume I would be his first

---

2. Theodore C. Sorensen, *Kennedy* (New York: Harper & Row, 1965).

choice for the post of Special Assistant for Science and Technology. This may have been so, but I wasn't certain of it. In the beginning, I didn't think I wanted the position because I had been making plans for a new Information Science Center at MIT, for which I had been promised ten million dollars by President Stratton. Then, two things occurred that caused me to change my mind. First, I began hearing that Kennedy was being advised not to appoint me and, second, I was told by Stratton that the MIT Corporation had decided to use the money earmarked for the information center to raise faculty salaries, and that the center would have to wait. Suddenly, I had an urgent desire to be the new president's science adviser and I began anxiously awaiting some word from him.

After what seemed a very long time, but was in fact only about three weeks, I received a telephone call asking me to meet Kennedy at Arthur Schlesinger's house in Cambridge. On the day I was to see him, I arrived at Schlesinger's to find several other people there who had also been asked to meet with him. As I sat waiting my turn, I thought of various things I might say when we spoke. I felt, perhaps, I should tell Kennedy why I thought I was qualified for the job, but then I realized that he knew me too well for that.

After a short time, I was ushered into the library to talk to a smiling president-elect. Our discussion was brief. Kennedy simply asked me whether I was willing to be his science adviser and I replied, yes, if he wanted me. "I understand some people think I'm wrong for the job," I said, "because I'm too identified with disarmament and have a reputation for arguing too much." "The issue of your disarmament views is for me to worry about," he said. "Why do you think I want you for the job?" (In the years that followed, when I was not allowed to go to certain high-visibility meetings, such as those with British prime minister Macmillan, I would ruefully recall this conversation.) Our meeting ended with an agreement that I would see him in Washington later that week to discuss my responsibilities and to begin to make some plans.

That evening I received a gracious telephone call from McGeorge Bundy, who had already been selected to be Kennedy's national security adviser. "I want you to know that I was opposed to your appointment," Bundy said, "but now that the President has chosen you, I'd just like to tell you I'll support you completely and I'm sure we'll work well together." I had known that Bundy was one of the people advising Kennedy against picking me. I thanked him for calling and said, "I'm sure, too, that we'll work well together." Though I would have certain disagreements with Bundy, we did end up working well together.

Bundy was the only person to tell me of his opposition to my selection, but I received lectures on how to behave in my new, exalted position from several friends. The one that struck me most came from Jim Fisk, an old friend, who started by telling me how embarrassed he had been when I had interrupted President Eisenhower at the Advisory Committee meeting at Newport. Fisk said he hoped I would be more careful in my new post. Another old friend told me that I had to learn to be a "stuffed shirt." I told him that I doubted whether I could and, anyway, my behavior was known to the president, so he knew what he was taking on. The fact is, though, that I remembered the admonitions I received and couldn't help taking them somewhat to heart. Nonetheless, I don't believe I succeeded in becoming a stuffed shirt, or, for that matter, in managing not to argue too much when an issue seemed important to me.

My next meeting with Kennedy took place at his home in Georgetown. After talking rather informally for perhaps an hour on general issues, Kennedy asked me what I saw as my responsibilities. I described for him the things that Killian and Kistiakowsky had done, emphasizing the defense, disarmament, and basic research roles. I also said that Kisty had started to be involved in medical research at the National Institutes of Health, and told him I'd like to continue that if he agreed. Reciting the list of things the office was involved in, it seemed overwhelming to me, but Kennedy didn't appear surprised and said only that he would look to me for advice on all scientific matters, as he had in the past. After that, he asked about candidates for the chairmanship of the Atomic Energy Commission. We agreed that we should try to get Nobel prize winner Glenn Seaborg as the chairman and Leland Haworth to fill the other vacancy on the board.

He then asked me what I proposed doing about the Science Advisory Committee. I had already decided to ask his permission to continue the existing committee and staff, and this gave me the opportunity. The staff gave him no problem, but he challenged the wisdom of continuing with the same committee. Weren't they likely to have allegiances to the other side? I didn't think so, I said. Their allegiance was to the institution of the presidency. Ike never asked about the political affiliation of members. If he had cared, I said, I wouldn't have been on the committee. Nixon did worry about the membership of PSAC and thought all scientists were Democrats, anyway. I told Kennedy that Nixon's staff had wanted Kisty to fire me when he had told the *Washington Post* I was his adviser, but that Kisty, with Eisenhower's backing, had refused to do it. I then remembered that Killian had written a lengthy job description which Eisenhower had approved, and I said

I would try to find a copy of it. (When I later read it, I was pleased to see it was very comprehensive; in fact, it encompassed more than I could ever possibly do. Kennedy was impressed as well, and used it as the basis of a letter describing my responsibilities.)

Kennedy began asking me about what we could expect if we reopened the test ban negotiations with the Soviet Union, and I outlined for him the many opponents who had ganged up to confuse and frustrate Eisenhower. I ventured that most difficult for him would be his friends on the Joint Congressional Committee on Atomic Energy, particularly Senator Jackson. In response to this, he said, "Why don't we go see them?" I wasn't sure how to react to the suggestion, but a moment later he had gotten to his feet and was starting for the door. I got up and followed him, too surprised to say anything.

Outside, the two of us got into his car and with Kennedy behind the wheel we made our way through Georgetown, heading for Capitol Hill. Though it's difficult to believe now, we drove in an open car, just Kennedy and myself, with no visible security of any kind. At the time it didn't strike me as strange, though in retrospect it's hard to imagine.

The aim of our expedition gave me considerable worry because I knew how much Jackson opposed the test ban, but Kennedy made the decision so quickly that I didn't have time to express any reservations. I don't know if I would have said so if I had had time to think what a bad idea it might be.

When we entered Jackson's office, we were greeted warmly. Jackson frowned when Kennedy said we had come to seek advice on how to resume the test ban negotiations. "This is very dangerous," he said, "and I'm not in favor of it." I tried to be reassuring. "We will only consider it," I said, "if we're certain we can have adequate inspection which will leave the United States secure." Jackson's frown became a scowl. "I don't believe there's such a thing as adequate inspection when you're dealing with the Russians," he said. The more we spoke, the deeper became his displeasure. Finally, he said, "Let's talk to Clint about this" (Clinton Anderson, chairman of the Joint Committee). So the three of us took the underground Senate railroad to the building in which Anderson had his office.

I was extremely nervous as we made our way to see Anderson. Somehow, I felt, we had ventured into the middle of one of the most delicate debates that existed at the time, one that was to divide Kennedy and some members of the Joint Committee for his entire tenure as president. I had to wonder whether he had chosen deliberately to seek an early showdown on the issue, but it was hard to tell and he gave no clue on our later drive back to his house.

When we got to Anderson's office, we had a bit of good luck. In the outer reception area, we encountered a strikingly attractive, auburn-haired young woman working behind the desk. After we exchanged greetings with Anderson, Jackson asked him who the young woman was and then proceeded to disappear for the entire meeting. This left Kennedy and me with only one contentious senator to deal with instead of two.

Anderson was not sympathetic to our proposal to resume the quest for a test ban, either. He said he didn't think it could be monitored adequately and, in addition, he felt there was too much opposition to it, not only in Congress and the military but in the country as a whole. He said he didn't believe it was worth the trouble of trying. Kennedy responded to this by saying that his experience while campaigning showed him that the people desperately wanted to reduce the danger of nuclear war and that he believed this would be a good first step. We did not get any encouragement, but at least Kennedy learned the extent of the congressional problem, if he didn't already know it.

I don't recall how we left or what we talked about on the way back to Georgetown, but I don't remember any signs of discouragement on Kennedy's part. I don't think he was surprised by our reception and I never understood his motivation for the meeting. I've wished since then that I had asked him why he did it.

When we returned to his house, Kennedy asked me to wait before he drove me to my hotel, so that he could change suits. As he went up the stairs, I heard Bobby Kennedy asking who was downstairs. Kennedy said, "Jerry Wiesner—he's going to be my Science Adviser." With no attempt to keep his voice lowered, Bobby asked, "Is he any good?" Kennedy's answer was, "I think so."

President Stratton readily gave me a two-year leave of absence to join the Administration. MIT had had, from its founding, a generous leave practice for faculty selected for government service, and so, beyond meeting my classes, I was free, immediately, to be part of the informal team, suggesting appointees for posts such as the Atomic Energy Commission, chairing ad hoc panels on different defense issues, taking part in speculation on who would be named Secretary of State, and working with Kisty to ready PSAC and its staff for a more vigorous space program we knew Kennedy would want.

Presidential transitions are almost always turbulent, more so when the party out of power has won the election. Inevitably, there are bruised feelings left from the campaign. Also, a new administration that involves a change of party takes office with only a minimum of understanding of the problems it will face.

The Kennedy transition, in fact, went unusually well. This was due to Eisenhower's insistence, despite his anger about the missile gap accusations, that the new team should get all the help his people could give them. My position was somewhat unique because I was already ensconced in the office I was to occupy and, in addition, I would keep the same staff and committee assembled by my predecessors. One other department head whose situation was nearly comparable to mine was the director of the budget. When new administrations take over, it is usual to replace only the chief of the bureau and maybe a few of his assistants. The budget bureau was, in many ways, the strongest and most indispensable institution in the White House. Its large, permanent staff, whose duties gave them access to every nook and cranny in the government structure, was essential to every president. This group of self-effacing, scholarly people had only one constituent, the president— really the presidency—to whom they were fiercely loyal. And they had the power that comes with controlling the budget.

Dr. Killian had, early in his tenure, begun working closely with the budget bureau and they, in turn, developed the habit of calling the science adviser's staff—and sometimes the science adviser himself—about any technical program or incident that they found worrisome. David Bell, from Harvard, was Kennedy's budget chief, and his selection of Elmer Staats, deputy director in the Eisenhower administration, as his assistant, provided him a seasoned and very bright alter ego who personified the best qualities of the bureau.

I continued the practice of working closely with the bureau staff. This combination of support from the experienced staff that I inherited from Kistiakowsky, all friends of mine, and bureau staff, plus the fact that I had been working in the science adviser's office for several years, gave me a running start as the new administration began to take shape. Kistiakowsky and I made a list of defense research and development programs that he, backed by President Eisenhower, had tried, without success, to terminate, in the hope that Kennedy could get rid of them before their supporters in the military, Congress, and industry realized what was happening. This list included the B-70, which Eisenhower had canceled, only to be persuaded to resurrect it during the campaign; the nuclear-powered aircraft, which, as I've said, should never have been started; and the "Dinosaur," an early version of an air-breathing missile.

When Kennedy eventually followed our recommendation to terminate these programs, the Air Force accepted the cancellations with good grace. Not so, however, Congressman Melvin Price, a member of the Joint Committee, whose district housed the General Electric Company, one of two makers of the engines for the nuclear-propelled airplane. Price was very angry, and most of his ire was directed at me. He thought I was misleading Kennedy. He told him that he would be sorry when the Russians, who he claimed were building a nuclear-powered plane, had one and the United States didn't. The president wondered aloud what they would do with it, and Price answered that they would put neon lights on it that advertised "Made in Russia," and fly it around the world. Kennedy chuckled at this and said he was willing to take that risk.

Before the meeting, I had told Kennedy that in the ten years the project had existed the designers were unable to figure out how to make lightweight radiation shields to protect the pilots. I also told him that a nuclear-powered aircraft would turn every plane accident into a potential nuclear disaster. However, confronted by Price, Kennedy let the congressman do most of the talking. This tactic soon had Price saying many foolish things, ending with his telling Kennedy that his grandfather would turn over in his grave. He didn't say which grandfather.

Though the Air Force appeared to accept the termination of its programs, I quickly ran into problems with them when I wanted to get some information on one of their programs. I was sure their resistance was due, at least in part, to their resentment toward me for my part in the cancellations.

In December 1960, Walt Rostow and I had attended a Pugwash meeting in Moscow. During a lull in the proceedings, I suggested that the two of us pay a call on Deputy Foreign Minister Kuznetsov (who will be remembered as the head of the Warsaw Bloc delegation to the Surprise Attack Conference in 1958.) I telephoned Kuznetsov and he invited us to visit him at the Ministry. The three of us had a frank, broad-ranging talk, discussing the hopes we shared for a better relationship between the United States and Russia during the Kennedy era.

After we had been speaking for a while, the tone of Kuznetsov's voice suddenly changed. Pointedly he asked, "What can the Soviet Union do to show its eagerness for a better relationship with your new government?" With barely a second's pause, Walt replied, "Free the RB-47 pilots." He said it so quickly it appeared he had been waiting for the question. (In July, two American RB-47 bombers had been shot down by the Russians near the Arctic Circle. Following the downings there had been a dispute between the two countries about whether the planes had been over Russian territory at the time.) Kuznetsov did not hesitate long before responding. "We will free them," he said, "if you will promise to tell the new president what they were doing when they were shot down." Walt and I could see no problem with that, and we told Kuznetsov we would do so.

When we returned to Washington, both Walt and I told Kennedy about the conversation and then I forgot about it in the busyness of the transition. But Kennedy remembered, and he was careful not to say or do anything that might cause the

Russians to change their minds. The following month the Russians made good on Kuznetzov's promise and freed the pilots, timing the release for a few days after Kennedy's inaugural so that he, rather than the Republicans, would benefit from the publicity. At that point, I remembered that Walt and I had promised to have the president shown what the RB-47s had been doing. I asked the president if I had his permission to find out and have him briefed about it. He agreed, and I proceeded to ask the head of Air Force Intelligence to tell me what had happened. He refused, so I asked McNamara for help and he, the president, and I had an eye-opening review of what the RB-47s were doing.[3]

Their mission was to find out the location of a series of coastal radars, and they did this by flying a large group of RB-47 bombers toward the Soviet land mass at sea level, pulling up just as they passed the shoreline. The Russians would turn their radars on and the Americans would spot them. The planes would sometimes go quite a distance inland before Russian fighter planes could be scrambled, and then the RB-47s would quit and run. The annoyed Soviet fighters finally managed to shoot down two of the planes and their pilots were put in jail. The Air Force claimed the RB-47s were over international waters and protested the downings, while the Russians said that the planes were in their air space. There the issue had remained until Walt brought it up. Kennedy reacted with disbelief when he heard the story. "Jesus Christ, if they did that to us, we'd go to war," he said. (In fact, as I later found out, the Russians did do it to us in the Arctic area, but not so blatantly.)

Kisty, myself, and some PSAC members began, as I said, to conceptualize a more vigorous space program, with a number of options for Kennedy to select from, as we expected this to be an urgent issue for him, as it had been for Eisenhower. When Kennedy took over, we had to make many decisions about the space program quickly, a process I initiated with some trepidation as I was aware that Vice President-Elect Johnson intended to reinvigorate and head the Space Council, which he had created, but which President Eisenhower had ignored. I assumed, rightly, that it would take time for Johnson to assemble a staff, and I knew that we wouldn't be able to ignore what was called "the space problem" after Kennedy assumed office. The press, from the start, would want to know what he was going to do about it.

Amidst all the preparations, there was a time out from our work for the inauguration and the parties and celebrations that followed it. To attend the ceremonies, Laya and I had to buy new clothes. This was easier for her because she had more

---

3. Author's note to cite Arthur Schlesinger on the RB-47 incident.

practice buying the sort of things required for such occasions. I, like many of the other new appointees, had never even thought of owning a morning coat. Having never been to a presidential inauguration before, I wanted to do it properly. Luckily, I already had friends among the salesmen at Brooks Brothers, the clothing shop for academics, who were used to outfitting professors and perhaps even presidents to attend inaugurations, and soon they had me fitted with tails, morning coat, a new tuxedo, top hat, and gloves. They even had a booklet they gave to novices explaining what was worn when and how. The top hat, morning coat, and matching trousers haven't been worn again since.

Laya and I had, actually, witnessed an inauguration before—Franklin Roosevelt's, in 1942, which we viewed from a tree in front of the Library of Congress. Kennedy's inauguration was much more formal, more intimidating, and definitely colder. The night before, Washington had eight inches of snow, which slowed down but didn't dampen the ceremonies.

At the swearing-in, the members of the new administration were seated closely behind the president-elect on the stage erected on the Capitol steps. We could see all the activity from there and had an opportunity as well to speak with those future colleagues we hadn't yet had a chance to meet. In front of us, as far as we could see, were thousands of people—all, like ourselves, shivering. As we waited, we entertained ourselves identifying those persons we normally saw only in the newspapers—the members of the Supreme Court and its chief, Earl Warren; Kennedy himself and Jacqueline; many members of Congress; the craggy old poet from Maine, Robert Frost, who had written a poem for the occasion; President Eisenhower; and many others I have since forgotten.

Abruptly, the milling around came to a stop and we took our seats. Frost rose and read his poem, fighting the glare of the bright sun. Then Cardinal Cushing droned a prayer in a deep, sonorous voice that only he and perhaps Kennedy, who was used to him, could understand. And then, suddenly, there was a coatless, hatless Kennedy between the chief justice and President Eisenhower, repeating the Oath of Office.

Following the swearing-in was the inaugural address. It was an exciting speech, well crafted, primarily by Kennedy and Sorensen, combining parts of old speeches with many new ideas, both of their own inspiration and that of a number of other advisers. I can't recall much of it now, but it sounded presidential, if a bit too rhetorical and too tough. That was a result, in part, of Khrushchev's warning a few days earlier that, although the Soviet Union wanted to have better relations with the new government, so-called "wars of liberation" were nonetheless to continue.

That night we braved a blizzard to attend a ball and join the famous and the not-so-famous, like ourselves, celebrating and dancing and then cheering as the Kennedys and the Johnsons swept through the ballroom. At the end of the evening there was a crush for cars and we found ourselves seated in a limousine with the president of the International Union of Ladies Garment Workers, Sidney Hillman, who was made famous by Franklin Roosevelt's instruction to "Clear it with Sid." We had time to get to know him rather well, as it took our car more than an hour to find its way to the hotel.

During the first days of the administration, there were many vital—or at least noisy—issues all clamoring for the president's attention at the same time. Some, like the uproar over the Soviet space feats, were anticipated. Others—like the pending invasion of Cuba, that Kennedy didn't know about until just before taking office, or the need for immediate action regarding the situation in Laos—were major surprises.

Unlike previous administrations, there was no real Kennedy chief of staff. Kennedy preferred, in a sense, to be his own staff chief, though he was assisted at the task by a number of people. These included Ken O'Donnell, his political adviser; his secretary, Evelyn Lincoln; McGeorge Bundy and his deputy, Carl Kaysen, to whom were passed many of the onerous tasks given to Bundy by the president; Myer Feldman, who worked on domestic issues; the trio of general purpose intellectuals—Ted Sorensen, Dick Goodwin, and Arthur Schlesinger—who worried about everything and were almost always involved in Kennedy's speech writing; Larry O'Brien, the legislative liaison; Dave Powers, Kennedy friend and sometime court jester; Pierre Salinger, press secretary; and Fred Dutton and Lee White, who handled much of the substantive legislative work. Of this group, only Bundy and Kaysen were new to the Kennedy team.

Kennedy's comfortable manner, his self-deprecating humor, and his readiness to take on whatever hand life dealt were reflected in his staff's readiness to help each other and work tirelessly for him. It was a personal staff, mostly little known, except to each other—long-time colleagues who had cast their fate with Kennedy's and who had been swept into the White House with his victory.

I was pleased to find that, from the beginning, I was welcomed as a member of this group. I wasn't part of the innermost circle, but I never expected to be. But I rarely felt "out" either. Many of the long-time staff tended to treat me deferentially, or at least differently; some of them had never known a "scientist" before, and they seemed not to know how to deal with me. Some obviously believed I had much more knowledge than I did and weren't aware how much I depended on my staff and the Science Advisory Committee for facts and wisdom.

My relationship with Kennedy remained, in general, the same pleasant, informal one it had been previously, though I always addressed him as "Mr. President," even when working with him alone. I noticed that my colleagues and even his brother Bobby always addressed him this way as well. He was capable of being stern and even presidential if one omitted to do something he wanted done quickly, or failed to understand him correctly. Once, while I was working with Arthur Schlesinger in my office, Kennedy phoned for him. I told him that the president wanted him and before he answered the telephone, he put his suit coat on.

Kennedy was always puzzled when I told him I didn't understand an issue, and he was even more troubled when he discovered that there could be unresolvable differences between two factions of scientists, such as those that existed between PSAC and the group that surrounded Edward Teller. Facts are facts, he would say. And I would tell him that, in science, there were many more facts to be discovered than were now known. I'll always remember his dismay when Teller and his sidekick, Johnny Foster, and I differed by more than a factor of twenty on how large an explosion could be tested underground. Foster said 250 kilotons was the limit and I said it was probably at least 5 megatons. "How," Kennedy asked me, "could two people, using the same facts, come to such different conclusions?" When I replied that in this case the facts were what you wanted them to be, that we were both guessing, he shrugged his shoulders in disbelief. When I went on to tell him that much of my information actually came from Teller and Latter's theory on how the Russians could hide nuclear explosions in underground salt domes, it was too much for him.

As it happened, several members of the group who had lobbied Kennedy on behalf of Adlai Stevenson in 1952 eventually ended up working for him. One afternoon a number of us were sitting in his office having an informal chat. The conversation turned, after a time, to the writing of his book, *Profiles in Courage*. Kennedy began to speak with genuine feeling about the admiration he felt for men who were willing to take unpopular positions in the face of contrary public opinion. I couldn't help myself and said, teasingly, "I remember one time when you didn't have the courage." Kennedy laughed and said, "You mean that time with Stevenson in '52?" I said, "Yes." He said, "Well, you're right—but then, you notice, I didn't put myself in the book." When the group's laughter died down, he went on: "You remember I told you my father didn't think it was a good idea. Do you want to know what he really said?" And he proceeded to recount for us the scurrilous language employed by his father to characterize the members of our group who, he said, were out to destroy Kennedy's political career.

Things happened so fast right after the inauguration that they are a blur in my memory and, although I have a record of what happened, I can't completely sort them out in my mind. I can't believe that I was capable of doing so many things in parallel. We wanted to restart the test ban negotiations, revitalize the space program, stop some of the egregious military development programs, such as the nuclear-powered aircraft, speed up the Minuteman missile program, review all of the military and space programs, and be sure that all the other technical programs were being properly managed.

Because Kennedy had agreed to the retention of the Science Advisory Committee and its staff, I had a smoothly functioning organization with panels that had been studying most of the critical technical issues that we faced from the beginning. David Beckler continued as staff director, a position that he had held in the various incarnations of the Science Advisory Committee. Spurgeon Keeny and Vincent McRae managed the military, civil defense, and arms control panels. Nicholas Golovin worked with the space panel and Robert Kreidler dealt with international science. As in the previous administrations, each of the PSAC panels was chaired by a member of PSAC, with the general membership comprised of other PSAC members and independent experts; the staff member, an expert in the field the panel was looking into, served as the glue that held it together and kept me current on what the panel was doing and thought.

Kennedy and the White House staff tended to believe what our panels said implicitly, but it took a while to convince some of the new Cabinet members and other agency heads that our office had a useful, perhaps even important function. Secretary Robert McNamara's reaction, when I told him about PSAC, our staff, and my role, said, "If I am doing my job properly, none of this would be necessary." In spite of this, he didn't object to our studies of the Pentagon activities, and a few months later he told a reporter that if our office didn't exist, he would have invented it. He soon came to appreciate the value of our independent judgments, especially the fact that our panels often heard information that was being kept from him. He soon realized, also, that the president listened to me and the reports of our panels. This didn't mean that we always agreed. He had many more constituencies than I and his workload, as the head of the biggest department in Washington, meant that he was chronically overloaded.

PSAC's and my sole client was the president. McNamara's constituency started with the president, but included the Joint Chiefs of Staff, the four military services, the Congress, the press, and sometimes foreign governments as well. In expressing appreciation for us, I think that he was referring to our ability to act as an alternate route of information for him, which we provided by several means—our panel activities, information that we received from the staff of the Bureau of the Budget, and not infrequent tips about trouble that our staff was given by frustrated workers in the Defense Department itself. In time, McNamara and his two closest aides, Under-Secretary Roswell Gilpatric and Harold Brown, the deputy director for research and engineering, had lunch with me regularly and in that way they heard what our staff and PSAC panels were finding out.

During the Eisenhower term, I had seen the difficulty the science adviser's office had whenever it had to work with the different Cabinet secretaries, other than Defense, because there was no one at a high level in the departments who understood the technical issues that both their own people and PSAC were involved with. I therefore suggested to Kennedy that we appoint an assistant secretary for research and development for each of the Cabinet offices. He thought it was a good idea, but told me I would have to be responsible for selling it to the secretaries. I found that the plan appealed to all of them, but they, in turn, each gave me the task of finding a qualified person for their departments.

With the help of a PSAC committee, I was able to find extremely competent people for each of the positions. Doing this had two unforeseen benefits—I quickly became acquainted with the newly appointed Cabinet members, and the new assistant secretaries, people I had recruited, would now have places on the Federal Council of Science and Technology, a council that had done very well in the past.

Kennedy, more than Eisenhower, depended on his staff for more or less routine decisions, a fact that the Cabinet officers often resented but which freed him to concentrate on the few most important issues of the moment. He gave each staff person discretion about what he should bring to his attention and what the person might act on independently. I was never totally comfortable with this situation and I developed the habit of sending short notes, which Evelyn Lincoln would put into his nighttime reading and which he would either approve with an "OK" or, occasionally, ask for more information or, even more occasionally, write "See me" or its equivalent. I became quite practiced at summarizing the key points of an issue I wanted him to be aware of. After his death, when Johnson became president, he said one day in a meeting of the White House staff, "Why can't you guys all learn to write good memos like Jerry does?" The secret with Johnson, I discovered, was to keep my notes as brief as possible. I found that if I wrote a memo that was too long, he simply wouldn't read it, so I adopted the policy of never making a communication longer than one page, which was all he had the patience for.

When I was asked to come speak at the opening of East-West University in Hawaii, I wrote a speech in which I made a specific reference to Kennedy, so I decided I should clear it with him first. I went to see him and showed him the speech. As he read through it, he began making corrections to it, marking the pages and changing various parts. When he was all through, he said, "This is a poor speech." I said, "Why?" He said, "We should never make a speech where we don't propose something, and you don't propose anything in here." I said okay, and I took the speech back to my office. I wrote a new ending in which I proposed a five-million-dollar program to study the environment in Hawaii, and then I took it back to him. After he had finished reading it, he looked up at me and started to laugh. "This is fine, Jerry," he said, "only I hadn't planned for you to spend that much money."

I always tried to tell Kennedy what all his options were on an issue, even those choices I had doubts about, if reputable individuals put them forward. But I would also express my doubts about them. Sometimes this was hard to do, as in the case of the civil defense plan that Kennedy himself initiated after his meeting with Khrushchev in 1961. My earlier experience with the Gaither Panel left me with strong objections to it, and I told him so. It was an undertaking that I thought would frighten both Americans and our allies, cost billions of dollars, and not save many lives if a nuclear war should occur. I spelled out my reasons in a private memorandum which, I think, helped to change his mind on the plan.

The president often decided to disregard the PSAC's favored position, and sometimes even his own, if, in his judgment, a stand was not politically viable. I grew accustomed to having my advice at least partially ignored, particularly on nuclear and military procurement matters where I regarded it as my task to help him decide what was really necessary in the face of pressures to do much more. My role often helped McNamara in this regard as well, because it allowed him to take a middle position between my view of sufficiency and the military's requests for much more than was usually needed. In most administrations the Secretary of State could be counted on to have a moderating influence, but Dean Rusk was more of a hawk than McNamara.

For the most part, I didn't mind not having my way. I didn't expect to, and I felt I was allowing the president to have more freedom than he would otherwise have had. However, while I didn't believe he would always heed my recommendations, I did become annoyed by the continuing onslaught from people who told him that I was a danger to the country as a means of persuading him to do something I thought was not in the country's best interest. One day, Senator Symington came to my office with a letter written by a well-known person in the technical community which said how much harm my advice was doing to the Air Force. Symington said he was going to show the letter to the president and wanted me to know he was doing it. I was aware that the letter's author had a serious conflict of interest, being a large investor in a number of military suppliers, but I also knew that he was a good friend of Symington's, so I just said it was his privilege to show the president anything he wanted.

When Kennedy asked me about it later, I told him the facts as I knew them, and he said, "Don't worry about it." But I did worry, nonetheless, because I realized how often Kennedy or one of his staff was having to defend me. I often resolved to be more gentle in meetings with the president, but I was not able to do it for very long. I felt I was frequently the only one willing to state a moderate position, and in heated discussions I would often become impatient. It was a surprise to discover that Bobby Kennedy had written a letter defending me for my stand against allowing the Air Force to detonate a 50-megaton bomb after the Soviets had done so.

The one thing that President Eisenhower didn't tell Kennedy was the intelligence community's conclusion that the Soviets had not deployed any ICBMs, so I had to tell him about it. I concluded with, "There is no missile gap now." He told me to tell Bob McNamara. I did, and after a two-week look at the satellite and other kinds of information, he concluded that my information was right. He announced his discovery in a press conference where he said blandly, "There is no missile gap." Apparently, he hadn't warned Kennedy that he was going to do this, and so Kennedy was not prepared for the many claims that the president had known about this all along. But he didn't have much time to brood about it, because so many other things were hitting him at the same time.

For years since then, I have conjectured on why the Soviets took so long to have operational missiles after their successful long-range flight in 1957. I thought perhaps it was due to the fact that it took several hours to fuel, and when the United States began flying the U-2 spy plane, the missile was too vulnerable. I have asked many Soviet friends about this in the years since, and until recently have not received a totally satisfactory explanation. Not long ago, I was told that on October 24, 1960, on the anniversary of the October Revolution, there had been a terrible accident—an R-16 missile blew up on a test stand, killing 91 engineers and technicians and Marshal Mitrofan Nedelin, the head of the Strategic Rocket Forces. Of course, we didn't know of this and so, high on Kennedy's priority list, in which I had a hand, was countering Soviet space exploits.[4]

I was not very involved in the events of the Cuban Missile Crisis, although everyone in the White House, as in the nation as a whole, was preoccupied with the situation. Work on most other matters slowed as the hour-by-hour drama played out. Late one night, in the middle of the crisis, the White House line in my home office began to ring. It was Kennedy. The military had preempted *his* phone line. "Goddamn it," he said, "get down here and get me a line through to Guantanamo Bay."[5]

Kennedy's style gave each of us the freedom to act independently. It cost us dearly at least once, stopping our drive for a comprehensive nuclear test ban, but persisted throughout his term. We had the space problem on our hands at the same time. In fact, most Americans were much more worried about the country's lag in its performance in space than they were about a test ban. It seemed that they had become used to the dangers of a nuclear war, or at least didn't see any way out. Kennedy, early in his tenure, in his inaugural address and in his State of the Union message, proposed cooperative experiments with the Russians and, hoping that the Soviets might say yes, I had an ad hoc panel, chaired by Professor Bruno Rossi, a well-known x-ray physicist from MIT, planning experiments that we could do together. But the Soviets would have none of it. Their missiles, sorry as they were for combat, were ideal boosters for putting satellites into orbit, and they had no intention of sharing with us the best propaganda ploy that they ever had. I doubt that Kennedy really believed they would do it either, but it was worth trying.

Although I was deeply involved in military issues and in the strengthening of our country's defenses to protect against the threat from the Soviet Union, such an involvement was not incompatible with liberal leanings in other areas as would increasingly become the case in the decades that followed.

Kennedy often had ad hoc tasks for his staff as he sought to deal with a new problem, and he was in the habit of asking Mrs. Lincoln to get one of us on the phone, no matter where we were. It didn't matter to him. In May 1961, I went to a celebration of the hundredth anniversary of the founding of MIT, in Cambridge, Massachusetts. While I was there, I received a phone call from the president, who told me about a dilemma he had. Ayub Khan, the president of Pakistan, was about to make a state visit and the president was worried that he was going to ask the

---

4. Author's note to develop this section further.

5. Author's note to develop this section further.

United States to give him arms, something Kennedy was not willing to do because it would mean having to make a like commitment to India, thus helping to initiate an arms race between the two countries. After explaining the situation, Kennedy asked me if I know of anything he could offer President Khan which would be so important for Pakistan that he would willingly accept it instead of weapons, I didn't know much about Pakistan and had no idea whether or not there was anything that would be an appropriate substitute. However, quite fortuitously, I happened to have a meeting planned with Dr. Abdus Salam, President Khan's science adviser, who was to be a speaker at the MIT Centennial, so I told the president that I would see if Salam had any ideas that we could use.

When the two of us got together later that day, I asked Abdus whether there was anything that President Kennedy could offer Khan that would be particularly important to their country. At that time, Pakistan was having serious difficulties with salinization of their agricultural land. Salam told me that they were losing about a million acres of land each year, and that it was getting harder and harder for them to feed their people. In fact, the country was not able to feed itself and the difference had to be made up with both purchases and gifts of rice from many other countries, including the United States. We talked at some length about what might be done to alleviate the problem.

That evening, I called President Kennedy and told him what I had learned. In the course of the conversation I told him that I thought Roger Revelle, whom I had placed as Assistant Secretary for Research and Development in the Interior Department, would be a good person to discuss the problem with, and asked his permission to fill Roger in on the situation, to which he agreed. Roger's reaction, when I had given him the facts I had, was that the situation appeared to present an interesting challenge. This was typical. The tougher a problem was, the more interesting Roger found it. We agreed that the two of us and Salam should talk together and arranged to have a meeting the next day.

Early the next morning, Salam and I flew to Washington and the three of us spent about three hours going over the issue. After a few hours of discussion it was clear that, with enough pumping, such as the Pakistanis were already doing on a small scale, it should be possible to lower the level of the aquifer, and so stop the salting of the soil. The salinization problem was a result of a hundred years of irrigation in the Punjab, which had created a vast underground lake whose water was so close to the surface of the soil that capillary action drew it all the way to the surface, where it evaporated, leaving behind the salts that had been dissolved in it. The salt prevented plants from growing. We made some estimates of how many millions of

With Philip Noel-Baker at the MIT Centennial Celebration, April 1961. Jerry shared a number of interests with Noel-Baker, a British parliamentarian whose efforts on behalf of international peace and cooperation earned him the 1959 Nobel Peace Prize. (Courtesy of the *Boston Herald*.)

dollars the project would cost, but I can't remember what it amounted to. I am certain, though, that it was cheaper than the arms Khan wanted. In any event, it seemed to me that we had lucked out, because the problem that Salam told us about was so serious that if Kennedy proposed that we help with this dilemma, instead of agreeing to Khan's request for arms, he might be satisfied, particularly since Kennedy was not likely to agree to an arms deal.

The two presidents had a very satisfactory meeting, and the net result was that Roger Revelle and Abdus Salam started working together to alleviate the "water-logging" in the fertile fields of Pakistan. Roger's first task was to assemble an expert team who knew about agricultural irrigation problems. With my help, he gathered an unusually strong team from many parts of the country. The group he got from Harvard included Drs. Harold A. Thomas of the Division of Applied Sciences, Ayers Brinser of the Harvard Forest, and Robert Dorfman. Contributions were also made by the U.S. Geological Survey, specifically an engineer whose name, I believe, was Thomas Maddock. I also recall an impressive geologist named John Isaacs of the Scripps Institute. There were, as well, many experts from the Department of Interior's Water Resources Laboratories and Geological Survey, and other leading scientific organizations.

While Roger was bringing his group together, Abdus went back to Pakistan and assembled a briefing team of Pakistani experts who had the job of transferring all the existing knowledge to Roger's team when it got to Pakistan. The Harvard team did some pioneering modelings of aquifers with computers, so, for the first time, it was possible to show, with a mathematical model, what the effect of different spacing and well sizes would be. It turned out that the present wells were too far apart and too small; their only effect was close to the well, so that most of the land continued to be waterlogged. With this information it was possible to design a tube-well system, as it was called, that had some hope of solving the problem.

While this work was going on, Roger had another idea. He decided to look at the total food problem, instead of just the water problem. It was apparent to him that a given amount of money, using a combination of agricultural improvements as well as tube-wells, would provide more food. The agricultural practices in Pakistan were unbelievably primitive. Their farmers did not use water efficiently, they did not sow seed well, or plough deeply. More than that, the farmers had no access to fertilizers or pesticides and little thought had been given to the proper seeds for the climate and soil.

In October 1961, we went to Pakistan with a charter to investigate waterlogging and salinization. It took Roger something less than two days to understand (before anyone else did) that that was not the problem at all. The problem was a thoroughly incompetent, not to mention corrupt, agriculture establishment. The real problem with water was the Irrigation Department, which was arrogant, corrupt, and more interested in payoffs and keeping the distributaries free of weeds than in delivering water when the farmer needed it. The ignorant extension workers from the Pakistani Agriculture Department were nearly as bad. Deliveries of fertilizer and other necessary supplies arrived, if at all, after the crop had wilted.

These were the conditions that deflected Roger's attention from the technical problems of water use to his visionary million-hectare development scheme. In the end, his great schemes proved too difficult; they were never fully implemented, for the incompetent government could not carry them out. But his diagnosis was sound, and led to the brilliantly successful implementation of the many-faceted green revolution in the Punjab. Roger virtually singlehandedly revealed and led the way out of the horrible, though unrecognized, mess that Pakistani agriculture was in.

After very considerable study and discussion, Roger and his group decided to use a saturation technique employing the best agricultural methods that could be made to work at the hands of illiterate farmers. His plan was to do this on one-million-acre plots of land, doing one per year, as long as needed. The plan called for providing fertilizers and pesticides; roads to make it possible to move produce to market, tube-wells when necessary; and some simple education so that the farmers would use their water, fertilizer, and seeds more effectively, and also learn how to store their grain safely from pests. I watched this exciting project from time to time, as the team of Revelle and Salam, supported by all the help the two presidents could give, moved into high gear.

While the program was starting, President Kennedy was assassinated. I dealt with the shock and grief of the president's death, returned to MIT, and lost track of the program. Many years later, I met Dr. Salam at a third world conference at the United Nations, and he told the group how our insights had changed Pakistani agriculture from a grain-importing economy to one which had surpluses which could be exported. I had not realized this, and he gave me more credit than I deserved.

Kennedy preferred to deal with his Cabinet officers and Agency heads through his staff and, as a consequence, I was often concerned about problems that arose with one of them. This was particularly true in the case of the heads of the two agencies that dealt specifically with science—James Shannon of the National Institutes of Health, and Alan Waterman, the director of the National Science Foundation.

Shannon had not had a favored place with President Eisenhower, who objected to his plans to support birth-control research. When the new Administration's first budget was being readied, Shannon asked me whether I thought Kennedy would be opposed to having an item called "fertility studies" included in his department's budget. I said I didn't know, that I would ask him. When I approached Kennedy on the matter, he told me not to discuss it with him, that he didn't want to know about it. I took this to mean that I should handle it however I thought best. After thinking it over, I decided I would do nothing at all; I would simply allow Shannon to draw whatever inference he would from the fact that I never got back to him to say the president was opposed to it.

Knowing Kennedy's equivocal attitude about what he wanted me to tell him about a problem that might be embarrassing to him later led me into trouble with the Atomic Energy Commission's plan to give the Fermi award to Robert Oppenheimer. The chairman of the AEC, Dr. Glenn Seaborg, told me about the proposal and asked me if it would be all right with the president. In fact, he asked whether he or I should talk to the president about it. I didn't know how Kennedy felt about the Oppenheimer matter and decided I should talk to him to take the blame if he didn't want to do it, for he could put the responsibility on me for the decision if it later

With President Kennedy and Detlev Bronk at the National Academy of Sciences, October 22, 1963. (Courtesy of the MIT Museum.)

leaked out, as it was likely to do. When I mentioned it to Kennedy, he asked what the reaction to it might be and I told him that there would be two strong reactions—from those who were in favor of doing it, such as scientists; and from those, like the Joint Committee, who would not like it at all. He didn't say anything and changed the subject.

A few days later I brought it up again, with no better resolution. I began to think that he might prefer it if I made the decision. A few days later Seaborg asked me if I had talked to Kennedy about the issue, and I said something equivocal like I had, which was true, and it would be all right, which I was guessing.

When the award was announced, Kennedy's military aide, General Chester Clifton, complained to me that I didn't have the president's interest in mind. I then realized that I had never told Kennedy about my decision. I hadn't told anyone else either, so the word must have come from Seaborg, which was natural enough. Clifton said that they—whoever "they" were, including the president, I presumed—were going to have the award presented at the Germantown office of the AEC, with Seaborg making the presentation, while the president was out of town. I saw Kennedy several times after that, including at a party the Kennedys gave for the White House staff, and I waited for him to express his displeasure, but he didn't. I never saw him again after that because he left immediately for the trip to Dallas, where he was assassinated. Lyndon Johnson presented the award to Oppenheimer in the Oval Office, without knowing any of this background.

ABM[1]

This piece focuses on Jerry's contribution to the public debate over arms control from the mid-1960s to early 1970s, the period after he left the White House through the early years of his MIT presidency. It begins by outlining some key post–World War II context, especially how the arms race mirrored growing Cold War tensions, and then weaves a narrative around the complex technical and political issues tackled by the important players of the time— national leaders, legislators, policy makers, scientists, engineers, journalists, and, ultimately, ordinary citizens. The narrative ranges across four U.S. presidential administrations—Eisenhower, Kennedy, Johnson, and Nixon—with an emphasis on the Johnson and Nixon periods, when the debate over possible deployment of a U.S. anti-ballistic missile (ABM) system grew quite heated. Because Jerry was among the most highly visible opponents of ABM deployment—in particular, of the "Sentinel" and "Safeguard" systems then under discussion—he became a prime target for those on the other side. The Nixon administration, for example, considered slicing federal research grants to MIT as retribution; others challenged Jerry's accuracy, intent, even his ethical standards. Through it all, Jerry retained his characteristic blend of urgency and optimism, and continued to throw his energy into efforts to deal with what he called "the dilemmas of the nuclear age."

⚛

The first American thinking about anti-ballistic missiles began almost immediately after World War II, in response to the V2 bomb that the Germans had used to such lethal effect against England in the War. In 1946 the U.S. Air Force initiated two programs, called Thumper and Wizard, whose purpose was to investigate the possibility of building an anti-ballistic missile. These studies concluded that at the current state of technology, it would not be possible to construct a workable system

---

1. Written mostly by Josh Wiesner, in Jerry's voice, in the early to mid-1990s (the latest dated addition is June 3, 1995), with additional edits and footnotes by editors of this book. Josh based the piece on his interviews with Jerry, articles by Jerry, and congressional testimony, among other sources. There are notes here and there—"Dad fill in"—evidently for Jerry's attention and input.

for such a defense. Few of the important elements—including rocket propulsion, guidance, target acquisition, and high-speed data processing—were at a state of sophistication necessary to make such a complex system feasible. This remained the case throughout the 1940s and into the early 1950s.

Then, in 1953, a new development gave added impetus to the drive to create an ABM. American intelligence discovered that the Soviet Union had launched a major effort to develop an intercontinental missile. This prompted two reactions on the part of the United States: first, after study of the matter, a similar program was instituted here; and, second, renewed thinking was focused on developing means to intercept such missiles. At this time, both the Air Force (in its Wizard Project) and the Army (in its Nike air defense program, which was initially formed to work on problems of air defense against bombers) began to reinvestigate ideas for anti-missile defense.

For the next few years, there was intense competition between the two services to see which one could develop the most effective program. The necessary technology having developed to the point where many of the previous drawbacks could be overcome, both services were able to devise plans for apparently workable systems.

In early 1958, Defense Secretary Neil McElroy had to make a decision about which program to go ahead with. He finally instructed the Army to step up work on its Nike-Zeus system, and ordered the Air Force to cut back its program and concentrate instead on missile early warning systems. But although the Army was given the go-ahead to continue development, there were a significant number of people in the government who had doubts about the efficacy of the proposed system. One reason for this was that research intended to develop methods for counteracting a Russian ABM had revealed potential areas of weakness that were, in fact, pertinent to the Nike-Zeus as well.

Because of the questions raised, two Defense Department studies were initiated to examine all areas of the Army's program. Both of these studies found what they considered to be serious problems. The President's Science Advisory Committee (PSAC) also ran a study, under my directorship. The study began in January 1958 and ran for over a year. During that time, we prepared several reports that discussed the problems we saw with Nike-Zeus. These were very similar to the problems which the Defense Department studies had pointed to. As a result, McElroy and President Eisenhower finally made the decision not to deploy the system, as the Army was strongly urging, but to continue funding for research and development. At the time of the PSAC study, I also chaired a panel on missile early warning capability, which recommended acceleration of an early warning system.

Although McElroy's decision put off construction of the system for a time, the program was far from dead. There were still many people, including a significant number in Congress, who supported Nike-Zeus and continued to push to have it built. Supporters included the usual military-minded senators, like Henry M. ("Scoop") Jackson, who believed we should build every weapons system we could, no matter how questionable its effectiveness. Many of these senators sat on powerful committees and were able to bring significant pressure to bear on the issue. There were, as well, congressional districts that stood to profit by the construction of the various components of the system. The Army and its contractors lobbied hard among congressional representatives to convince them of the wisdom of deployment.

Combined with the Army's wider public relations program, the continuing support of these congressional groups was responsible for keeping the program alive as a viable possibility when the next administration took office. In 1961, when President Kennedy first began to survey his military problems, his attention was quickly drawn to Nike-Zeus. Almost immediately, the Army began to lobby him for deployment. They were now proposing construction of a huge system, with 7,000 missiles intended to defend 27 areas in the United States and Canada. Kennedy also began to receive a stream of letters from people in industry stressing the importance of deployment.

In the face of this pressure, Kennedy spent many hours trying to learn as much as he could about Nike-Zeus, so that he could make an informed decision. Secretary of Defense Robert McNamara initially was in favor of deployment, though on a reduced scale, with many fewer missiles intended for defense of a smaller number of areas. While he did not believe the system would live up to the Army's claims for it, he thought that it would give the Russians pause for thought and that it might be effective against small-scale attacks or accidental firings. My own conviction, by this time, was decisively against deployment. Because of my belief that it was an all but unworkable system whose deployment would only add fuel to our ongoing competition with the Russians, I spent as much time as I could discussing it with Kennedy, explaining what I believed were its many weaknesses.

The most serious problem we had initially identified in the PSAC study concerned the issue of decoys. As originally designed, the system was supposed to intercept missiles at very high altitudes, out of the atmosphere. This meant that it could be easily confused, because an enemy could mix real missiles with light-weight decoys made to look like missiles and send them in against Nike-Zeus, so it would be totally saturated. To try to correct this problem, a plan was devised to allow the incoming devices to enter the atmosphere, where the difference in weights would allow atmospheric drag to slow down the decoys but not the warheads. This separation tended to work somewhat better, but unfortunately it created other problems. If you allowed missiles down to an altitude low enough to filter the incoming devices, the vulnerability of the ABM system was such that the explosions from the intercept missiles seriously threatened the workings of the other components.

Another problem, something the later systems were subject to as well, was a phenomenon called "blackout." If you set off a nuclear explosion to destroy an incoming missile, you also upset the gas in the air: you "ionize" it, you strip electrons off the molecules, and for a while the gas acts like metal rather than gas, so that radar waves cannot go through it and you cannot see behind it. With the radars blacked out, the entire system is incapacitated.

Added to these issues, there were several other problems pertaining to the system's capacity for population defense. First was the matter of which points in the country would be defended. This was a serious political issue. Would you defend the 50 largest cities? The 25 largest? If so, what would be the reaction of the rest of the population outside these areas? A second matter, related to the first, was that after you chose the sites to defend, there was a good possibility that an intelligent enemy could simply bypass the system, landing his missiles just outside its range but still close enough to generate a lethal fallout attack on the population. Finally, I was convinced that virtually none of the individual components of the system was capable of adequately performing the tasks demanded of them. The missiles could not respond with the necessary speed, the mechanically controlled radars were insufficiently sophisticated for their purpose, and the system's traffic-handling capacity—the number of missiles it could deal with at once—was completely inadequate.

To strengthen my arguments, I arranged for several people who were opposed to the deployment to come and speak with Kennedy. The most important of the meetings I arranged was with Jack Ruina, a colleague of mine from MIT, who was then head of the Advanced Research Projects Agency (ARPA), charged with oversight of the ABM issue, and who had also participated in the earlier Defense Department studies of Nike-Zeus. Jack spoke at length with Kennedy, outlining the many issues involved with the planned deployment and detailing the areas in which he believed Nike-Zeus was most deficient. As director of ARPA, his negative assessment had considerable influence on Kennedy.

In the end, Kennedy decided not to build Nike-Zeus. By the time he made the decision, McNamara had also come around to a negative view of it. As with President Eisenhower and Secretary McElroy, however, Kennedy and McNamara continued funding for further research and development, thus continuing to leave the door open for it to emerge as an issue in the future.

Following the decision, the Army went back to work once again, trying to overcome Nike-Zeus's deficiencies and design a more workable system. They made a good deal of progress in the next few years. With new technical elements, they were able to improve many of the most important of the system's components. They gave the name Nike-X to this new program. Although it was clearly an improvement over Nike-Zeus, there were still a number of problems involved with a defense based on this system. The Defense Department, simultaneously, was sponsoring a series of studies on the overall issue of ABM defense. The general conclusion was that a large-scale system was probably not practicable—that no possible configuration of an ABM could provide a plausible, countrywide population defense. On the other hand, they did find that a smaller-scale system might be of use in some situations against certain limited kinds of threats. One of the participants in the studies referred to the ABM as "a system in search of a mission."

During these years, McNamara's thinking continued to evolve. He became increasingly convinced that deployment of any ABM system would be a mistake—that doing so would upset the strategic balance, forcing the Soviets into a reaction and causing another upward turn in the spiral of the arms race. He also continued to doubt the capacity of the Army's system to work as claimed and believed the cost ratios continued to favor the offense. In addition, he was now concerned that deployment would put another obstacle in the way of meaningful arms talks with the Russians.

Despite McNamara's reservations, however, by 1966 strong political pressure had begun to build on President Johnson to deploy an ABM. The Russians' construction of an anti-missile defense—the Galosh system—around Moscow hardly posed a serious threat to our strategic position, yet Galosh had stirred many people, especially Johnson's Republican opponents in Congress, to push him to take action and to chide him for being weak on defense. Predictably, the Army joined in these calls for deployment.

McNamara, meanwhile, continued to advise Johnson the idea was a mistake. At the same time he worked to enlist the Russians in an agreement to hold talks, believing that the existence of serious negotiations between the two countries, of first importance of their own account, would remove much of the impetus from the calls for immediate deployment. At the Johnson-Kosygin summit in Glassboro in June 1967, McNamara spoke at length with Kosygin, making the case for both sides

Passing the baton—Jerry in conference with President Lyndon B. Johnson and Donald Hornig, Jerry's successor as special assistant to the president for science and technology, ca. January 1964. (Courtesy of the MIT Museum.)

holding back on the deployment of defenses and trying again to get a commitment for negotiations. Kosygin, however, was not forthcoming. He was not convinced on the issue of defenses and he would make no definitive statement on the possibility of holding talks.

Although discouraged, McNamara kept up his efforts to forestall a final decision. He decided to convene a meeting that would include all past presidential science advisers, as well as the present one, and all past and present directors of the defense department's research and engineering program, to present their views on ABM to Johnson. The group of us—including Jim Killian, George Kistiakowsky, myself, and Don Hornig as science advisers; and Herb York, Harold Brown, and John Foster from the defense department; along with the Joint Chiefs of Staff—met with Johnson in the Oval Office. Going around the room, we each presented our views and the thinking that had led us to them. Although there was some less than enthusiastic argument in support of deployment, the clear consensus was opposed, the reasons given being essentially the same as those that had convinced McNamara, with some additional emphasis on the technical issues involved and the improbability of the current system ever working as designed.

I was greatly surprised, then, when only two weeks later, on September 18, 1967, McNamara gave a speech in San Francisco, to the editors and publishers of United Press International, at the end of which he stated the administration's intention to deploy a scaled down or "thin" ABM system aimed at protecting against a threat from the Chinese who, he claimed, were on the verge of having the capability to launch a small-scale but still dangerous nuclear attack on the United States. The speech was a very curious presentation. McNamara began by discussing the reasons for not deploying a large-scale system to protect against the Soviet Union. He articulated the shortcomings of such a system and the political and strategic arguments against its construction. In the process, he made several statements that were pertinent to the deployment of any-sized ABM system and were persuasive as reasons to oppose such a defense. He then made one or two remarks about other conceivable uses for an ABM and enumerated reasons for considering the Chinese as a potentially serious threat to our security, our massively superior strategic posture notwithstanding. Finally, he stated that the decision had been made to deploy the scaled down or "light" system to protect against this possible threat, saying that there were "marginal grounds" to conclude that such a deployment was "prudent."

On first hearing, it was hard to know quite what to make of this speech. The contradictory sense of it—in which he outlined the many reasons to oppose ABM deployment and then, against his own logic, saying that the administration was nonetheless going ahead to protect against a largely concocted threat from the Chinese—was peculiar enough. Clearly, he was being forced against his own judgment to act for the political purposes of the president. To those who knew his true beliefs, this made it a disheartening performance. But in addition to this, he made a reference to our meeting with President Johnson, stating that those present had been opposed to a large, Soviet-oriented system and giving the impression that we had not voiced opposition to any other sort of deployment, at least leaving the matter open as to whether we might be in support of the plan he was announcing.

This was extremely misleading. Having worked closely with McNamara, I was familiar with his ability to fashion the truth for his own purposes. But I had no idea he would go so far as to misrepresent the views of those he had personally requested to give their judgments to the president, in an effort to dissuade him from a mistaken course; or that, having succumbed to political and presidential pressure,

With President Johnson as he congratulates five National Medal of Science recipients, January 13, 1964—Norbert Wiener, John Pierce, Vannevar Bush, Cornelius Van Niel, and Luis Alvarez. This was one of Jerry's final public appearances as a White House official. (Courtesy of the MIT Museum.)

he would exhibit such lack of conscience as to actually name those same people in an effort to lend the prestige of their positions to a plan he knew they did not support.

As I thought about the entire situation, I felt that I could not remain silent about what I believed to be a most egregious action on the part of the administration. In the past, when I had disagreed with a decision concerning military or other issues, I had always confined my criticism to intergovernmental channels. Having been for many years a government adviser—first as a member of PSAC, then as science adviser, and then again with PSAC—I had not felt it was proper for me to publicly disagree with government policies. If I disagreed or had reservations concerning a particular issue, I would voice these feelings either through PSAC or, as science adviser, to the president or other members of the administration. Even when I was no longer in an official position, I continued to feel I could be most effective speaking privately with people in the government, and that for me to publicly argue with administration policy might cause a breech that would diminish the influence I had as a respected adviser and former member of the government. In addition to this, I was also concerned because I had for so long been closely associated with PSAC, as a member and then as its chairman, that any public position I might take that was unpopular with the administration might impact on the current science advisory mechanism and generate a negative reaction against PSAC on the part of the president and others in the administration.

But despite these concerns, the strength of my conviction concerning the deployment of the ABM system was such that I felt to remain silent was to acquiesce in the face of a dangerously ill-considered decision—one that would escalate the arms race, disrupt the strategic equilibrium between ourselves and the Russians, and very likely force a Russian buildup in reaction to it, leaving us ultimately less secure and facing an increased, not lessened, possibility of destruction. For these reasons I decided to write an article that appeared in *Look* magazine in November, discussing some of the issues surrounding the planned deployment and why I believed it was a mistake.[2]

Because I was writing so soon after the announcement and also because it was for a popular magazine, I did not go into an exhaustive discussion of all the ramifications involved or detail the many technical difficulties I believed the system faced. I tried, instead, to outline the most important issues and to suggest some of the potential consequences of the decision. I stated that the most serious issues, in both the political and strategic areas, involved the effect the deployment would have on our relationship with the Soviet Union. Though the Russians had not made a decision to meet with us in formal talks, relations between the two countries had been improving significantly for several years and we were in the final stages of a mutual effort to gain a nonproliferation treaty, designed to reduce the international spread of nuclear weapons. For us to choose to deploy an ABM system could only serve to impede the process of conciliation and to escalate the tensions that we had been working to reduce. The ploy of reorienting the system as an anti-Chinese defense was not likely to nullify it as a concern in the Russians' eyes. Despite the newly invented objective, the issue of an ABM deployment had always been related to our

---

2. Jerome B. Wiesner, "The Case Against an Antiballistic Missile System," *Look* 31 (28 November 1967): 25–27.

military position in regard to the Russians. In an effort to find the least provocative way to give in to political pressure, the administration had decided that a system to protect us—not against the Russians, but against the supposed threat from the Chinese—would be proposed, thus appeasing the president's critics while purportedly giving the Russians no cause to be disturbed.

This attitude seemed to me ill-considered. I believed it wrong to think that the Russians would not regard any deployment of such a defense as having a possible impact on their position. What is more, it was obvious to those of us in the United States who opposed the system that the military and its allies in Congress intended for the current deployment to be the first step towards a greatly expanded system. The Russians, certainly not unaware of this, could hardly afford to wait and see how extensive the system would eventually become, and would be forced to initiate an offensive buildup in order to meet the potential threat to their deterrent position.

Regarding the Chinese, there were two issues that I believed needed to be considered—first, was it realistic to consider the Chinese as a serious threat to our security; and, second, how effective would the proposed system be against that threat if it existed or developed in the future? As the situation stood at the time, the Chinese were in the early stages of development of a nuclear capability and had not yet deployed or tested a long-range missile capable of reaching the United States. They had made considerable strides in their nuclear program, however, and it was believed that the time was not far off when they would have such a capability.

The premise behind the construction of the proposed "light" system was that the Chinese would, at the outset, have a small number of unsophisticated missiles that would not employ decoys and other penetration aids and thus could be thwarted by a relatively limited ABM deployment. Such a deployment, operated by intercepting enemy missiles outside the atmosphere, would in theory make it possible to protect a wide region of the country from attack. The problem with this scenario was that to believe that the Chinese would be able to deploy intercontinental ballistic missiles (ICBMs) capable of reaching our shores, but would not have the capacity to outfit them with penetration aids that would overwhelm the proposed system, made little technical sense. The techniques for designing such aids were neither highly complex nor exceedingly costly; indeed, one could learn all about them in American aerospace journals. In addition, once the Chinese could build an ICBM, the cost to them of producing additional missiles would be relatively small, so that although they would not have a force nearly comparable to our own, they could have enough missiles in a fairly short time to penetrate the administration's planned system.

As I have said, I was very doubtful that any ABM system based on the prevailing approach would ever function at its calculated effectiveness. To give a further feeling for the difficulties involved, no one had then—or has now—ever succeeded in developing an anti-aircraft defense that was more than ten percent effective. An ABM system that was only that effective would be almost worthless. Even if an ABM system were as much as ninety percent effective, it would still not prevent an opponent from inflicting millions of fatalities on us.

Anyone who was at all familiar with military matters knew that virtually no kind of weaponry ever functioned as intended when it was first put in the field. From hard experience during World War II we knew that far simpler devices, such as submarine torpedoes, failed to work when first employed. Yet an ABM system would have to work essentially perfectly the first time in battle conditions, or the results would be catastrophic. And this unlikely degree of perfection would have to be attained without the system's ever having undergone realistic testing, for how could the Army approximate the conditions of a nuclear attack or, in its planning, account for the great number of possible methods of attack that an opponent, once he was familiar with the configuration of our system, might devise? Therefore, I stressed, it was folly to think that we could depend on an ABM to give us increased protection and security.

What, then, of the potential threat from the Chinese? First of all, as matters stood at the time, no one knew exactly when the Chinese would actually be able to deploy an ICBM. Once they had one, it would take time for them to build up a modest-sized force. Even when they had done that—if they were, in fact, willing to commit their material and human resources to that end—the United States would still possess an overwhelming superiority, not only in land-based missiles but in our submarine-based Poseidons, as well as in our bomber force. The U.S. and Russia relied on the deterrent effect of their offensive missiles to keep the peace. I was convinced that we would have to do the same thing with China. Our known ability to retaliate devastatingly if attacked was a potent defense, and the only true one that existed in the circumstances of a nuclear-armed world.

There was no magical or technical escape from the dilemmas of the nuclear age through defense. It was my belief that the most sensible course was to reduce greatly the offensive missile forces on both sides, thereby achieving the deterrence with much less danger to us all. I was convinced that much mutually coordinated disarmament was technically achievable with considerably less risk, effort, and cost than was involved in the existing deterrent position. The blocks to disarmament were political and psychological, not technical. The problem was that disarmament had no effective political support or power base in the government or Congress. Many of the same senators who pressed the president to spend tens of billions of dollars on defense against a missile attack consistently tried to cut the tiny budget of the Arms Control and Disarmament Agency. During that period of armed stand-off, when the fear of nuclear war was a daily reality, the only hope, I felt, was that statesmen would come to take disarmament seriously and fashion international security arrangements appropriate to the existing realities. If they did not, the best we could expect for the foreseeable future was an increasingly nightmarish peace insured only by a balance of terror.

In the period immediately following the administration's announcement, there was not a great deal of vocal criticism of the decision. In the Senate and House there was, as there had been for Nike-Zeus, strong support from the military-minded members, working in unison with the Army and Defense Department. The Joint Committee on Atomic Energy held hearings that, predictably, heard almost exclusively from government spokesmen and known proponents of ABM deployment. One exception was Alice Hsieh, a senior staff member at Rand Corporation, who questioned both the system and China's intention to deploy a missile force that could threaten the United States. In addition, my *Look* article was inserted into the record of the hearings. There was some limited questioning of the administration in the press. In his newspaper column, James Reston asserted that the system was being built for the Republicans, not the Chinese. It was, he said, the opening move in Johnson's 1968 presidential campaign. Some Western diplomats at the UN voiced concern that the decision might complicate the prospects for signing of the non-proliferation treaty, as other countries saw us deploying more nuclear weapons, while they were expected, by the terms of the treaty, to forswear their use.

Despite the claim that it was to protect against the Chinese, much of the talk regarding the system, which the administration had named "Sentinel," continued to center on the threat from the Soviet Union. In Congress and elsewhere, there was considerable concern about the increases the Russians were making to their ICBM force and about the possibility of their outfitting their missiles with multiple independently targetable reentry vehicles (MIRVs). This situation illustrated in a clear way the self-perpetuating nature of the arms race: the United States makes plans to deploy an ABM system; largely because of this, the Russians accelerate their ICBM program and move toward the deployment of MIRVs; in the United States, the resulting concern takes the form of justifying ABM deployment on the grounds of the Russian buildup. This was the dynamic that had operated throughout the whole period of the Cold War and was responsible for bringing us to the dangerous place we then occupied. ABM deployment represented just another step in the irrational progression.

In the middle of November 1967, the Army released a list of places it intended to survey as possible installation sites. Though they had no intimation of it then, over the next several months, public awareness of the fact that a number of these sites were in the vicinity of some of the country's major cities would cause the Army serious problems, creating unanticipated public opposition to the planned deployment. In the period during which this opposition was starting to grow, individuals and groups more traditionally concerned with the issues surrounding arms deployments began, in increasing numbers, to voice their opinions regarding the administration's plans.

In late December 1967, the American Association for the Advancement of Science held a debate on the issue. Hans Bethe, who opposed deployment, discussed the proposed system's deficiencies, including the fact that it could be overcome by China's employment of simple penetration aids. He also stressed the danger of an over-reaction by the Soviet Union. An article he would write with another participant, Richard Garwin, in *Scientific American*, expanded on the issues they had raised at the debate.[3] It had considerable influence in the scientific community, and would be responsible for forcing the Defense Department to rethink certain aspects of Sentinel's design. In contrast to Bethe's stand, Freeman Dyson, whose capacity for consistent thinking I had always found questionable, voiced support for deployment at the same AAAS forum, suggesting it would contribute to a relaxation of tensions between ourselves and the Soviet Union and aid in the detente effort.[4]

President Eisenhower declared his opposition to the plan early in 1968.[5] He doubted the value of the "thin" system and did not believe, he said, that the eventual costs would bear any resemblance to those quoted by the Defense Department.

---

3. Hans A. Bethe and Richard L. Garwin, "Anti-Ballistic Missile Systems," *Scientific American* 218 (March 1968): 21–31.

4. See Walter Sullivan, "Scientists' Parley Debates Missile Defense Merits," *New York Times*, December 27, 1967, p. 27.

5. Mary Kersey Harvey, "Of War and Peace and the United Nations: An Exclusive Interview with Dwight D. Eisenhower," *Vista* 3 (January-February 1968): 13–21, 26–35.

The Department's stated figure was 5 billion dollars. Eisenhower said he believed that, in the end, this would rise to something more like 40 billion.

In Congress, opposition to deployment also was beginning to be heard. Senators Cooper, Nelson, and Hart took the lead in arguing against it. In April, in the first test of its position, the Senate rejected—41–17—an amendment by Senator Nelson to cut 342.7 million dollars from the fiscal 1969 budget in preliminary funds for Sentinel. By June, a similar proposal, introduced as a joint motion, had the backing of 34 senators.

This increase in the votes against funding reflected, to a considerable degree, the growing public opposition to construction of the system. As more and more people in the areas where the installations were going to be placed became aware of the fact that nuclear missiles were to be located in or nearby their cities, the larger and more organized the protests became. A coalition of forces began to develop, consisting of opposing citizens, who formed themselves into action groups; local scientists, who aided by providing them with information; nationally oriented scientists, who were concerned about arms issues; and opposing congressmen and senators. Though concerned scientists and congressmen would have voiced their opposition to the proposed system without the unprecedented popular protest that arose, there would have been no real possibility, otherwise, of having an impact on the administration's plans.

In cities across the country, meetings were held to consider the most effective means to fight the administration's plans. Scientists and others knowledgeable about the issues were asked to speak. I was frequently asked and found myself, for a time, criss-crossing the country from the locale of one planned installation to another. The Army, beginning to sense that its plans were imperiled, started sending representatives to these gatherings to present their side of the issue and to downplay the dangers involved. These spokesmen were frequently received with undisguised skepticism, and faced tough questioning from the citizens in the different cities who often, as in Chicago, were backed by local scientists who openly disputed many of the Army's technical claims about the safety of the system. Once, I even found myself debating an Army representative at a meeting outside my home. As more and more protest meetings were held, the media started to give them increased coverage and the publicity began to force members of Congress who had not given the issue close attention to consider more seriously where they stood on the matter, as well as placing additional pressure on the administration to justify its plans.

During this same period, a hope was beginning to grow that the United States and the Soviet Union might soon enter into arms limitation talks. The Russians had given signs that they were willing to explore the idea and, in this country, there had begun to be a guarded optimism that we might finally have an opportunity to start reducing the nuclear arsenals of the two countries and to work with each other to alleviate the tensions that had brought those arsenals into existence. Side by side with this optimism, however, there continued to be concern over the administration's plans for deployment of the Poseidon and Minuteman III missiles and about both countries' planned testing of MIRVs, which neither was willing to halt or even to postpone in consideration of possible negotiations. One result of this intransigence was that, at the United Nations, a number of the smaller countries who were to be signatories to the Non-Proliferation Treaty insisted that the U.S. and the Soviet Union add to the treaty draft assurances that they would make more urgent efforts to end the arms race.

While these developments were taking place, the presidential primaries had begun. The Vietnam War had produced enormous animosity toward President Johnson, and Eugene McCarthy had mounted an increasingly effective campaign against him—as had Bobby Kennedy, for the brief period he was in the race before being assassinated. Thus, it was of considerable political importance for Johnson when he announced, at the White House signing of the Non-Proliferation Treaty, that the United States and Russia had reached a preliminary agreement to open talks.

To those of us who had been working for many years to curb the arms race, there was encouragement in the events of the time. Not only did it appear that the two superpowers were finally going to sit down and start, at least, to talk together, but in our country the unprecedented challenge to the administration on an issue of weapons deployment, by a public which normally ceded to government the automatic right to make such decisions, gave hope that there might be some awakening to the realities of the arms race and that future defense policy might be affected as a result.

Although I did not formally support his candidacy, I had spoken with Eugene McCarthy several times after he announced his challenge to President Johnson and I had provided him with information on certain scientific and defense issues. In July 1968, George Kistiakowsky and I prepared a position paper for him in which it was proposed that the United States delay all offensive and defensive arms deployments to aid in an accord with the Russians. This paper got considerable attention in the press, and was endorsed by an editorial in the *New York Times*.[6] Not long after it

---

6. "Halting Missile Deployment," *New York Times*, July 31, 1968, p. 40.

was released, I went to New York to attend a fundraiser for McCarthy's campaign. It happened that I was standing next to him when someone complimented him on the paper and asked him a question about a particular section of it. Most politicians in such a circumstance would probably have responded in more or less general terms, depending on how much they had familiarized themselves with the matter, and then, with my standing there, would likely have brought me into the conversation, saying I was a person who gave them advice on such matters and I might be able to clarify the issue in more detail. However, McCarthy's refusal to engage in any kind of political posturing, coupled with his subversive sense of humor, precluded such an approach. He simply pointed in my direction and said, "Jerry here wrote it—ask him."

That summer there was intensified concern over the administration's imminent MIRV testing, which was widely criticized as an endangerment to the pending arms talks. I was part of a group that petitioned President Johnson by telegram, asking him to reconsider the action. These efforts were unavailing, however, and on August 17 the first tests occurred.

Only a few days after this, an event took place that had a considerably larger impact on the prospects for negotiations. The Soviet Union, refusing to tolerate a trend toward liberalization in one of its satellite states, invaded Czechoslovakia, ousting its government and instituting martial law. The reaction in the United States was, naturally, one of condemnation, and there was an immediate awareness that the planned Soviet-American talks had been placed in jeopardy as a result. President Johnson, in his denunciation of the invasion, stated that he was determined that the negotiations would go ahead as planned, but as the Soviet occupation continued, it became clear that the administration had made a decision to postpone them indefinitely.

I was discouraged by these events and fearful that in the period of delay things might shift in such a way that one or the other country might decide it was no longer in its interest to hold talks. By this time, Hubert Humphrey had been nominated as the Democratic candidate for president. Although I did not consider him an ideal candidate, I felt that he had some positive qualities and that his judgment on issues such as the arms talks and the Sentinel deployment were not that far from my own. Humphrey had always been more liberal than it had appeared during his years as Johnson's vice president. While he was unwilling, even during the campaign, to openly dissent from Johnson's policies, I believed that, if elected, he would have altered the approach to military and foreign policy issues followed by the preceding administration.

Both because I hoped that he would make some positive changes and also because I feared the prospect of the alternative, I spent quite a bit of time working on Humphrey's campaign that fall. When the election ended with Humphrey the loser, there was the disheartening prospect of living with a Nixon presidency. This would mean four years of regressive action on social issues and an antagonistic approach to foreign policy. Nixon had already voiced his support for an ABM system and clearly intended to continue the buildup of our missile forces initiated by Johnson.

Shortly after he took office, the announcement was made that Secretary of Defense Melvin Laird would make a full review of Sentinel in order to decide how the new administration would proceed. The situation they faced was a difficult one. If they went ahead with Sentinel, they would face increasingly troublesome opposition which might ultimately end in congressional defeat. Full-scale deployment of a Russian-oriented system, however, was no longer a feasible option because such a system had by then been so widely discredited. And a decision not to deploy any ABM system would cause serious problems with the military and with many of Nixon's supporters.

The solution they reached was to reconfigure the system so that it would serve as a defense of our missile sites against a Russian first-strike attack. To begin with, two out of our six Minuteman sites were to be defended by the system, with a possibility of expanding it to cover more sites as well as the Capitol. In this next phase, there was also the possibility of adding a "light" countrywide population defense. However, unlike the Sentinel, none of the new system's installations would be near any large cities.

In terms of military rationale, this new plan addressed a nominally more valid threat than had the Sentinel. Though I did not believe it, it was argued that Russia was potentially nearing the time when it would have a first-strike capability—that is, the ability to destroy nearly all of our ICBM force using only a percentage of its own missiles. This assertion was based on Russia's deployment of a very large ICBM, the SS-9, which, it was predicted, would be built in large numbers and would soon be outfitted with MIRVs. But although the SS-9 deployments and Russia's progress toward a MIRV capability certainly merited attention by the United States, they did not in my view justify the deployment of an ABM system or pose the level of threat that some people claimed. The fact was that even if Russia gained a theoretical first-strike capability and had enough confidence in the performance of its missiles to believe such an attack could succeed, there were several other factors to consider, including the fact that the United States would still have both its bomber and submarine forces with which to retaliate.

Shortly after Secretary Laird's announcement of the new system, I was asked to attend a meeting with President Nixon to discuss matters related to the space program. When I arrived, Nixon greeted me in a friendly manner and then said, "I understand we have some differences on the ABM." I said that was true, that I didn't believe it was a good idea, and that if he gave me an hour I thought I could explain why. He said he would think about it and then, with the meeting about to begin, the conversation ended.

Afterward, when people were preparing to leave, the president approached me again. "I've been thinking about your suggestion," he said, "and I don't think there's any point in it, because my mind is made up." He said he would like me to reconsider my position. I replied that I could not change my position unless I was told something new that altered my view, adding that I had taken a public stand against it. He paused a moment and then, in a tone intended to impart a sense of frankness and of confidentiality between us, he said, "I need the system as a bargaining chip with the Russians." I said, "That's an awfully expensive bargaining chip." A look of anger came into his eyes. He stared at me a moment, then turned abruptly and moved away.

Over the next three years, I was to find myself the object of several White House-orchestrated attacks. Looking back, it was probably this exchange—which Nixon clearly viewed as personally insulting to him—as much as my continued vocal opposition to the ABM that was responsible for the efforts to have me professionally discredited and to have MIT penalized through the government funding apparatus because of my association with it. These being the early days of his presidency, the extent of the vindictiveness Nixon could feel toward those who opposed him—or those who he believed had slighted him personally—was not yet known. In fact, I was to become one of the first on the list of "enemies" who were targeted for special retribution by the men who kept the accounts for Nixon and assisted him in devising means of retaliation. This, of course, was unknown to me at the time and I continued to protest the administration plan without suspecting the sort of trouble my opposition would cause me.

Not long after the meeting with Nixon, I got a call from Ted Kennedy. Kennedy had become one of the most vocal opponents of ABM in the Senate. Though Nixon and Laird had hoped that by altering the stated objective of the system, and by changing the location of the planned installations so that they were no longer near any large cities, they would be removing the impetus for much of the protest, the opposition had by that time broadened to encompass the entire issue of ABM deployment. In the Senate, the intensity of the debate continued to grow, as more senators joined the opposing side. Kennedy called to ask if I would talk with his legislative assistant, Dunn Gifford, about putting together a book that would be comprehensible for a non-expert, discussing the technical and political issues involved in the controversy. I thought the idea was interesting and said I would speak with Gifford.

It didn't take me long to decide that I would take on the proposed project. I thought the idea a good one, and that it would be a valuable contribution to the public debate. I called Abe Chayes, a close friend of mine who had been legal counsel in the State Department under President Kennedy, and asked if he would be coeditor with me. When he accepted, the two of us got to work, planning out what we felt should be included and deciding on the book's format. When we had a general sense of how it should be organized, we began to contact people we hoped would contribute pieces on specific topics. At the same time, Dunn Gifford kept us informed of what was going on in the Senate, so that if any important new issues arose there, we would be able to address them in the book.

Our idea was to get the book out as quickly as possible, in the hope of having an impact on the public and congressional debates. After about a month, George Rathjens, a specialist on disarmament issues from MIT, and Steven Weinberg, an MIT physicist, joined Abe and me to help organize and edit the material. The list of people who eventually contributed pieces was an impressive one. It included Hans Bethe, who discussed a number of the planned system's vulnerabilities; Marshall Shulman, who wrote about the effect of an ABM deployment on U.S.-Soviet relations; Arthur Goldberg, who discussed ABM in relation to world concerns over nonproliferation; Leonard Rodberg, former chief of policy research in the Science and Technology Bureau of the U.S. Arms Control and Disarmament Agency, who considered questions of the system's reliability; Bill Moyers, who addressed the issue of presidential control over an ABM system; and Theodore Sorensen, who discussed the possible detriment the deployment would cause to our relations with Western Europe. Additional contributors addressed further technical, strategic, and political issues. Chayes, Rathjens, Weinberg, and I wrote an overview of the debate, and there was an introduction by Senator Kennedy.

The project was finished in just under three months, and in early May the book was issued.[7] It was distributed to all members of Congress and to a number of people in the administration, as well as going on sale publicly. The favorable attention it

---

7. Abram Chayes and Jerome B. Wiesner, eds., *ABM: An Evaluation of the Decision to Deploy an Anti-Ballistic Missile System* (New York: Harper and Row, 1969).

was given, especially in the press,[8] prompted a number of refutations by spokesmen for the Defense Department. It received particular criticism from John Foster, who, as the director of research and engineering, was one of the key people in the administration's campaign for the ABM. In testimony before Congress, Foster challenged a number of conclusions reached in the book that ran counter to the Defense Department's position, as well as contesting a number of specific facts. In addition, he devoted an entire speech before the Aviation and Space Writers Association to a point-by-point rebuttal of what he claimed were misinterpretations of relevant intelligence data and faulty conclusions concerning both the Soviet and U.S. technical capabilities. At the same time, he defended the operational and technical assumptions on which the Defense Department based its case.

All in all, the book had a considerable impact, addressing almost all the relevant issues necessary for taking an informed position on the administration plan and clarifying the detailed technical issues on which the scientific criticism of the system was founded. In a sense, the amount of criticism leveled at the book by the administration and other supporters of deployment was the clearest indication of its influence. No other book on the issue—including *Why ABM?*, written by proponents of the system[9]—received nearly the attention or prompted the degree of discussion by people on both sides of the issue as ours did.

In early March, while we were at work putting the book together, an unprecedented series of congressional hearings on the ABM had begun. Never before, when considering deployment of a major weapons system, had Congress taken testimony from so many people from outside the government who opposed the plan. The decision to do so in the case of the ABM reflected both the public concern and the congressional division over the issue.

In all, I was to testify five times—three times that spring and twice the following year. The first time, in early March, was before a House Committee on Foreign Affairs subcommittee that was not intended to specifically inquire into ABM deployment but rather to cover the broad question of national security policy for the 1970s.[10] However, the majority of the questioning concerned the ABM, as this was

---

8. See, for example, the reviews in *New York Times Book Review*, June 29, 1969; *Saturday Review*, July 12, 1969; *National Review*, July 29, 1969; and *Science* 165 (8 August 1969): 576–78.

9. Johan J. Holst and William Schneider, Jr., eds., *Why ABM? Policy Issues in the Missile Defense Controversy* (New York: Pergamon Press, 1969).

10. "Strategy and Science: Toward a National Security Policy for the 1970's," Subcommittee on National Security Policy and Scientific Developments, House Committee on Foreign Affairs, March 11, 1969.

obviously the issue uppermost in the committee's mind. In fact, little important information was elicited by the questioning at this hearing. For my part, I explained what I believed were the ABM's most serious drawbacks and I tried to stress the political ramifications, both in regard to the Soviet Union and to other countries, whose views of the matter I thought needed to be taken into consideration. Testifying along with me was Dr. Charles Herzfeld, who had succeeded Jack Ruina as director of the Advanced Research Projects Agency. Herzfeld was a supporter of the "thin" anti-Chinese system, which was what the discussion revolved around. Because of our opposing views, there was polite argument over a number of points. It was my feeling that this disagreement served to define the issues more clearly, though I don't know if this was the opinion of the committee.

My next testimony was before the House Armed Services Committee on April 24. This hearing specifically concerned the matter of Safeguard's deployment, and the committee heard from a wide range of people for and against the administration's plan.[11] In my testimony, I contested several assertions made by Secretary Laird concerning the potential threat from the Soviet Union to our Minuteman and bomber forces. It was my calculation that even given the optimal capabilities projected for the Soviet ICBM force by Secretary Laird, and assuming the absence of even elementary precautions to protect our own forces, it was possible to show that a significant number of missiles and bombers, capable of delivering a devastating counter-attack, would still survive. Therefore, I did not consider the force levels projected by Laird to constitute a first-strike capability, as was claimed. Regarding the Soviet potential to gain such a capability, I stated that, though not impossible, it would require that a large number of very substantial technical programs all be highly successful, that it was clear these programs had not achieved anything close to such a degree of success at that time, and that there was essentially no reason to believe they would be able to do so by 1975, the time frame of Laird's projections. If we were actually worried about our position, it was my opinion that we could improve it quite readily by a number of simpler means. Moving our bombers from coastal bases to the center of the country would, I pointed out, almost double the number that would survive a submarine-launched attack. An airborne alert would have allowed still more aircraft to survive. If we were still worried, a fire on warning—or firing after the first nuclear explosion—doctrine would have assured that all workable Minuteman missiles were used in retaliation. There were still other steps that could be taken to strengthen the deterrent, but, I said, unless the

11. Safeguard was the name given to the scaled-down ABM system proposed by the Nixon administration as a replacement for Sentinel.

possible threat got more serious than Secretary Laird's projections, I did not believe that such steps were necessary.

After I had finished these remarks, I briefly discussed the difficulties I foresaw regarding two particular components of the proposed system. The first problem concerned Safeguard's radars. I pointed out that, as everyone familiar with the system's design was aware, they were extremely vulnerable to blast effects and, in addition, since there were only a few of them and they were vital to the system's operation, a well-planned attack would concentrate its first fire on them. If successful, this could entirely neutralize the system. The second matter I pointed to involved Safeguard's computer control component. At that time, no computer program of comparable magnitude and complexity to the one being proposed had ever been developed and run. The largest programs developed had all had serious operational trouble when they had been put into use. Even today, when we have much more experience dealing with the inevitable problems that arise in designing and implementing software following extensive development and testing programs, the complex systems always contain many defects that only come to light during the stress of operation, and it is common for them to fail entirely as some new demand is put on the system. As with the other components of Safeguard, there was to be no possibility of testing the computer's functioning in its actual operational environment, which would have been a minimum requirement to have any confidence that it would work as intended. Therefore, I stated my belief that the odds were strongly against the computer adequately performing its crucial role in the overall system.

At the same time that I was called to testify, others on both sides of the issue were appearing as well. The first opponent of the system to appear before one of the committees was Wolfgang Panofsky, a respected physicist and a long-time friend of mine. Partly because he was the first to testify, but even more because of the clear and detailed reasoning of his testimony, his presentation was considered to be among the most effective. Other opponents who testified included Herb York, Hans Bethe, George Rathjens, Jack Ruina, Marshall Shulman, and George Kistiakowsky. Among those who testified in support of the system were Edward Teller, whose prestige was inevitably sought for the backing of every major military program, Eugene Wigner, Frederick Seitz, Donald Brennan, and Albert Wohlstetter. Of these proponents, the one who eventually was to have the most impact on the debate—though not, it should be said, through any persuasiveness in the presentation of his position—was Albert Wohlstetter. Wohlstetter was a mathematician from the University of Chicago who was a long-time advocate of conservative military policies. Much of the research funding he received came from the Department of Defense. I had known him ten years before when we both sat on the Gaither Panel, where he supported the extensive buildup of U.S. nuclear forces.

During the spring of 1969, a conflict arose between Wohlstetter and George Rathjens over some specific matters involved in the debate, regarding which Wohlstetter was extremely adamant about proving Rathjens in error. The dispute originated in their respective testimonies before the Armed Services Committee, and concerned some specific calculations regarding Soviet capabilities that were largely irrelevant to the more important issues of the debate. Wohlstetter wrote a supplement criticizing not only Rathjens but Ralph Lapp, Panofsky, Chayes, Weinberg, and myself. This was followed by an exchange of letters printed in the *New York Times*.[12]

It was a basic strategy of the proponents of deployment to focus on minor points of analysis, particularly those pertaining to the potential capabilities of the Soviets, in order to avoid addressing the matter of Safeguard's effectiveness, on which they were on much weaker ground. Although both issues were open to quibbling on relatively unimportant technical points, the Defense Department's case for Safeguard's effectiveness was so strained that they consistently avoided raising it in their discussions. This was due, in part, to the results of calculations regarding offensive-defensive missile ratios, which made it necessary for proponents of the system to maintain that a quite specific Soviet force level would exist at the time of Safeguard's deployment (something there was not adequate data to predict), in order to make the case that Safeguard was both capable and necessary in providing a defense against a Soviet attack. The range of the force level they were required to project was so narrow because the calculations showed that at levels outside this range, Safeguard served no purpose. If the number of attacking missiles was lower, it was clear that the system was unnecessary because of the quantity of Minutemen that would survive without any defense. If it were very much higher, Safeguard was useless because the Russian missiles would have overwhelmed it.

It was this unpleasant reality, in conjunction with several other demonstrable weaknesses in the proponents' larger case, that caused Wohlstetter to concentrate on discrediting Rathjens and several other opponents, on the grounds that they had

---

12. See William Beecher, "Scientist Rebuts Criticism of ABM; Wohlstetter Sees Mistakes in Some Foes' Arguments," *New York Times*, May 26, 1969, p. 13; "Safeguard Missile System Is Evaluated by Two Scientists," *New York Times*, June 15, 1969, p. E17; and "Calculations on ABM," *New York Times*, June 22, 1969, p. E15.

performed incorrectly some essentially minor mathematical analyses and made some assumptions from data that were contrary to the assumptions he himself had drawn from them. The import of the contested issues was relatively negligible, and the analyses and interpretations reflected disagreement between respected professionals offering opposing judgments on a matter of public debate. Wohlstetter's actions, however, provoked a controversy—still some time off—that threatened to overshadow the real issues. Meanwhile, the opponents of Safeguard continued to contest the shifting data and estimates released by the Defense Department and concentrated their attention on the anticipated Senate vote on the deployment.

On May 22 Secretary Laird, testifying at length before a subcommittee of the House Appropriations Committee, gave a detailed presentation of the Defense Department's position. Considering it the most definitive account to date of that position, Rathjens, Weinberg, and I prepared a response which we issued in June, offering specific refutation of several points asserted by Laird as well as criticizing a number of unwarranted assumptions on which the Defense Department was basing its case. Also in June, a National Sciences Advisory Committee on the ABM was formed, with Donald Hornig and Herb York as cochairmen. This group, which numbered among its members some of the country's outstanding scientists, took as its task the publicizing and dissemination of the case against deployment.

Frequent articles appeared in the press, covering different areas of the debate. One piece, printed in the *Chicago Tribune* (June 1, 1969), was an editorial entitled "Professor Wiesner's Dream World," in which I was portrayed as soft on defense, with a "naive and credulous trust in the peaceful pretensions of the Russians." It listed, in two cases incorrectly, the weapons systems I had opposed over the previous ten years, and then quoted, with a misleading lack of context, a proposal I had made in 1960 for a U.S.-Soviet arms limitation agreement. I responded in a letter to the editor, saying that the editorial did not provide an accurate or complete picture of the positions I had taken, nor did it support the article's implication that I was willing to base arms agreements with the Soviets primarily on trust. After addressing a couple of other points, I then gave a list of the weapons systems I had supported and had helped to develop in the 1950s and 1960s, and explained why I had come to believe that safe alternatives to the arms race were both vitally necessary and possible to achieve. I ended by saying that a safe missile limitation agreement was a dream world that was accessible in 1960, that I believed it still was, and that I thought it was something well worth striving for.

Finally, in August 1969, the Senate vote was held. Though officially a victory for the supporters of Safeguard deployment, the 50–50 tie, broken by Vice-President

Agnew's deciding vote, could hardly be taken as a decisive endorsement of the president's plan. Never before had an administration faced so much questioning or met such opposition from within Congress on a military proposal. The marginal victory was widely perceived as a rebuff to the president, which Nixon and others in the administration did not take with good grace. Though they had publicly stated that they knew the vote would be close, the future difficulties they could anticipate—with so many Senators voting against the program and failing to heed Nixon's calls for support—were cause for serious concern and anger within the White House.

The narrow margin of the congressional vote reflected wide public protest against the deployment, a protest that had been supported and encouraged by outside experts who had contributed their knowledge and insights to the movement. The administration, therefore, in an attempt to shift matters in its favor, tried to discredit the scientists and others who had so vocally expressed their opinions on the drawbacks and deficiencies of the planned system. Although there is no certain evidence linking the actions taken by Albert Wohlstetter to the White House, subsequent events suggested both an awareness and an approval of what was unquestionably an attempt to undermine the influence of certain opponents and to call their professional reputations into question. These suggestions were reinforced both by the aim and the timing of Wohlstetter's action, which coincided with the initiation of the White House's own campaign against a number of individuals.

In early November 1969, Wohlstetter wrote a letter, which had obviously been preceded by earlier communication, to an organization called the Operations Research Society of America, or ORSA, of which he was a member, requesting that they hold an investigation into the professional conduct of a number of the opponents in the debate over Safeguard. ORSA was, as the name indicates, the professional organization of the relatively new discipline known as operations research. Emerging from the wartime need for analysis and projection of weapon systems operation, those in the field use mathematical and analytical methods—further developed since that time—in operational analyses of both military and other complex systems. None of the people whom Wohlstetter specifically named in his letter, nor any of those that ORSA criticized in its eventual report, belonged to the society. Nor were any of them members of the profession, or claiming to practice operational research. It was, therefore, unprecedented for ORSA to investigate and pass judgment on the individuals singled out, professionals from other fields participating in a public debate. ORSA had never held such an investigation into the conduct of one of its own members or of anyone else, had no organizational mechanism for doing so, and obviously had never seen such a task as constituting a part of its function. Indeed, in order not to be subject to accusations of complete arbitrariness, ORSA was forced, simultaneously with its investigation, to formulate a set of guidelines as to how the organization conducted such a proceeding.

In his request for an investigation, Wohlstetter listed four things that he believed any scientific discipline must do to establish its claims as a profession. The first was to establish its area of special competence. The other three related specifically to standards that members of the profession should be required to meet. Because none of the individuals to be investigated were members of the profession, these comments had no relevance. Wohlstetter asserted, however, that many of the questions at issue fell within the domain of operational research—a claim which, whether or not it was true, also was largely irrelevant. All the sciences employ methods and techniques that are either borrowed from other fields or are commonly used within a number of them. This is particularly true of the fields of engineering, physics, chemistry, and of systems analysis, the disciplines that the majority of the scientists with backgrounds in weapons development are from. Wohlstetter's stance was analogous to that of a physicist who, addressing an engineer, says: "In a part of your analysis, you used a technique from my field. You have no right or competence to do so. I disagree with your results, and I'm going to appeal to the Physical Society to have you investigated and censured for unprofessional conduct."

Wohlstetter also charged that the opponents named had failed to admit errors when they were pointed out to them (which was not true) and that they had made abusive remarks about those who disagreed with them—an assertion entirely without foundation, but one which we became convinced he truly believed, particularly in regard to Rathjens. Predictably, Wohlstetter wanted the Society to direct its attention to the issues surrounding Soviet missile capabilities and Minuteman vulnerability, rather than to any matters involving Safeguard itself. Some of the specific issues he mentioned included Rathjens's supposed misestimate of the probability of destroying a Minuteman silo for a specific yield of enemy warhead, one of the main questions involved in their earlier disagreement; reiteration of the assertion regarding Weinberg's and my use of an incorrect estimate in calculating SS-9 performance; and the claim that the opponents as a group had made a number of incorrect assumptions regarding reprogramming of Soviet missiles. In detailing the errors and misinterpretations he believed had been made, the sense of Wohlstetter's remarks was that not only were the results of the calculations in question incorrect, but that they had been arrived at dishonestly, with preformed bias and the intent to misrepresent. On the closing page he made this charge explicit: "The question that I am raising is not whether the ABM decision was good or bad, but a question of professional standards and professional ethics."

After ORSA decided to hold an investigation, they contacted Rathjens, Weinberg, and me to solicit our participation. It was their intention to hold hearings, in which the three of us, as well as anyone else who might become a subject of the inquiry, could appear. They also offered us the opportunity to address in writing any issue we wished to clarify or to respond to the specific charges made by Wohlstetter. The three of us informed the Society that we declined to be involved in any way. We explained, among other things, that we were not operational researchers and thus did not believe we came under their purview, and that we believed it improper to have the questions and parameters of such an inquiry dictated by a partisan participant. It was clear that what they were really trying to do was neutralize the influence of those they were "investigating."

More than a year and a half passed between the time the Society initially contacted us and the completion of its investigation. During this period, a number of matters concerning Safeguard arose. Two, in particular, stood out as important concerning the debate as a whole and my involvement in it. The first matter concerned me personally, but was also indicative of the times.

At one point I received a phone call from Deborah Shapley, a writer for *Science* magazine. She called to tell me that she had received, from some people in the Office of the Budget, copies of an October 1971 memo addressed to George Shultz, John Ehrlichman, and Henry Kissinger (cc'd to H. R. Haldeman) requesting reports on President Nixon's request that MIT's research funding be cut because of my opposition to Safeguard; she also had received a copy of Ehrlichman's follow-up "report." Deborah said she planned to print the memos in *Science*, to which I had no objection.[13]

Over a period of time I learned, from several different sources, a number of the details of what had happened. It turned out that both Haldeman and Nixon had been in contact with Shultz, who was then the director of budget, instructing him to pass on their orders to the Defense Department. Shultz was resistant, both on ethical grounds and because he believed that if such an action ever became known it would politically damage the administration. He may also have been influenced by some time he had spent at MIT, during which he and I had known each other.

---

13. See Deborah Shapley, "White House Foes: Wiesner Target of Proposal to Cut MIT Funds," *Science* 181 (20 July 1973): 244–46.

In any case, it is clear that he postponed doing anything for as long as he could, until Nixon finally grew angry.

On the White House tapes there is a recording of a phone call Nixon made from Camp David, in which he told Shultz, in language requiring several excisions, that when he gave an order he wanted it carried out. It was at this point, presumably, that Shultz finally passed the directive to the Defense Department. However, once the Defense Department received the directive, they were also reluctant to take any action, because of their longstanding relationship with MIT and because the majority of the funds they provided us with were for projects being carried out on their behalf. They, as much as MIT, stood to lose if they were slowed down or halted by a cutback in money. In the end, apparently nothing was done regarding the orders. There were no interruptions in funds for existing projects, nor did we see any indication that MIT was being excluded in the awarding of new research contracts.

The other important development during this period was that there began to be confirmation that the opponents' estimates regarding a number of matters contested in the ABM debate, including the possibility of the Soviets achieving a first-strike capability and other issues surrounding their ICBM force, had been considerably more accurate than the projections issued by the administration and the other proponents of deployment. The proponents had argued that without Safeguard, a force of 420 to 500 Soviet SS-9s would have the capability of destroying 95% of our Minutemen and that they would very likely have this many deployed by 1974–75. The majority of those opposing Safeguard, including myself, were doubtful that they would attain such a force level by that time and believed that, even if they did, it would not pose the degree of threat the administration claimed. The proponents took the position that it was a foregone conclusion that the Soviets would have equipped all their SS-9s with MIRVs by that time, an assumption the opponents also questioned. In fact, the Soviets never deployed MIRVs on the SS-9 and the rate of their buildup also turned out to be much more in line with deployment opponents' estimates. By 1971, it was evident that there was no possibility of the Soviets achieving a first-strike capability in the time frame projected.

Another crucial issue in the debate was whether it was possible for the Soviets to threaten not only the Minutemen but also our bomber and submarine force at the same time. An important part of the opponents' argument concerned the fact that even were the Russians able to destroy a large percentage of our land-based missiles, we would still have our bomber force and our submarine-launched missiles with which to retaliate. Some of the most stressed logic of the debate was employed by the proponents to try to prove that it was feasible for the Soviets to simultaneously knock out all three elements of our deterrent force in one attack. Most of their arguments centered on the bomber force. It was possible, at least, to create scenarios in which the force might be placed in a position of vulnerability at the same time as the Minutemen were being attacked. But given the lack of anti-submarine capabilities existing at the time, it was virtually impossible to argue that the Russians would be capable of neutralizing our submarine force, even if they were not also attacking the Minuteman and bomber forces at the same time.

During the debate, nevertheless, Secretary Laird made the claim that improvements in Russia's anti-submarine warfare capability might make it possible for them to threaten our force in the coming two or three years. He gave no grounds for this assertion and refused to be more informative when questioned about it. But less than a year after the Senate's vote on Safeguard, he backed away from his position, stating that it was unclear when either the Soviets or the U.S. would possess the capability required to seriously jeopardize the other's submarine force.

Finally, in late May of 1971, ORSA sent advanced copies of its finished report to the people it had concentrated its investigation on, including me, Rathjens, Weinberg, Wolfgang Panofsky, and Ralph Lapp. Enclosed was an invitation to submit any comments we wished to make for publication along with the report. In most of our communications, both to and regarding ORSA, Rathjens, Weinberg, and I had worked together, responding as a group. Concerning the offer of publishing our remarks, we wrote back saying, in effect, that we did not see any reason to change our view of the absurdity of their proceeding and had no desire to be associated with it.

The report was officially published in September 1971.[14] It received considerable attention in the press and soon became the main focus of discussion of both the anti- and pro-deployment groups.[15] At the White House, spokesmen congratulated ORSA on their conscientious work. The gist of the report was, predictably, that the opponents had been guilty of numerous errors and transgressions, some of them grievous, in contrast to the calculations and assumptions made by those supporting

---

14. *Operations Research* 19 (September 1971)—"Guidelines for the Practice of Operations Research."

15. See, for example, William Beecher, "Report on Safeguard ABM Testimony Finds Unprofessional and Misleading Comments on Both Sides," *New York Times*, October 1, 1971, p. 23; and Michael Getler, "Colleagues Criticize Anti-ABM Scientists," *Washington Post*, October 1, 1971.

the deployment (particularly Wohlstetter), which were both largely correct and performed with a clear understanding of the range of information needed to reach a valid conclusion. On the first page of Appendix III, dealing specifically with the debate, these two comments are found: "Charges of nonprofessional conduct by scientists and other experts in that debate indicated to the council of ORSA the need for a statement of professional standards" and then, a little further down the page, *"The Committee and the Council also make no judgment on the motives or ethics of any participants in the debate."* A curious juxtaposition.

Among the specific issues addressed by the report were the argument between Wohlstetter and Rathjens concerning Minuteman vulnerability, the accusation that Weinberg and I had no basis for claiming that the administration had changed its figures concerning the SS-9s and that our extrapolations were incorrect, and criticism of Ralph Lapp's calculations concerning the Minuteman issue. Following this, there was a list of ten types of errors made by the opponents. In his exemplary performance, Wohlstetter was said to be guilty of none of them. A quote from this section gives a good summary of the report's findings: "Most of the abuses were committed by those experts on record as opposing the Safeguard program. The Committee is reluctant to draw the conclusion that the opposition was more unprofessional as a group than the supporters, since most supporters outside the Administration did not attempt to buttress their positions with analysis or claims to analysis. It must be noted, however, that the analytical arguments presented by spokesmen for Safeguard within the Administration were carefully examined. While shortcomings were found, as documented below, they nowhere equaled the cumulative mass of inadequacies compiled by the opposition."

Though we had maintained a position of noninvolvement until then, Rathjens, Weinberg, and I made the decision, after reading the advance copy, that some response was called for in light of the extremely slanted and misleading nature of the report. We prepared, therefore, a twenty-five page paper commenting on the report and responding to a number of its specific charges. We released this paper, as a separate document, at the time the report was published.[16] In the opening section, we noted a number of issues that the ORSA committee had ignored in its determination to concentrate on the opponents' involvement in the debate and to ignore the areas where the administration and other proponents had made obviously incorrect assumptions or had been misleading in their presentation of facts.

16. George W. Rathjens, Steven Weinberg, and Jerome B. Wiesner, "Comments on the Ad Hoc ORSA Committee Report on Professional Standards," September 29, 1971.

We noted that: 1) the committee had apparently looked at classified material (including the development of intelligence estimates) very incompletely, and had they gone about their work in a more comprehensive way, it would have been hard to ignore the fact that the Defense Department had released such estimates in a selective and highly questionable manner; 2) they had not commented at all on many of the documents and much of the testimony of those favoring the administration's position, the reason for the committee's focus on us and Drs. Lapp and Panofsky not being obvious in the report, because the section of Wohlstetter's letter and the relevant documents referenced in it, which identified us as the people whose performance he wished to challenge, had been curiously omitted from the published version of his letter; 3) they had restricted themselves to the period from the beginning of 1969 up to September of that year, and had they examined the debate as it continued in 1970, the inadequacies—both of Safeguard and of the administration's defense of it—would have been more apparent.

In addition, we raised a question concerning the propriety of one of the members of ORSA's committee, Dr. Howard Berger, having participated in the inquiry. Berger and Rathjens had previously had a very serious difference of opinion which resulted in Rathjens having to relieve Berger of responsibility for a major study while they were both at the Institute for Defense Analyses. Under the circumstances, we questioned why Berger had not disqualified himself from sitting on the committee or why ORSA had not disallowed him from serving, if in fact they had bothered to look into the qualifications of the members to sit in judgment on the case.

We also noted that the committee had largely avoided examining the area of the debate in which the effectiveness of Safeguard was discussed. We pointed to a number of examples of calculated omissions, misrepresentations, and faulty analyses by the administration and its supporters, and concluded that a number of major questions had not been discussed because they were an obvious embarrassment to the proponents. Then we commented on a number of issues where the committee had cited the opponents without considering the plausibility of the administration's position. One of these issues was the question of the SS-9s and Minuteman vulnerability. We pointed out that the questions of complementarity and vulnerability of the other elements of our deterrent force—at least as important as the vulnerability of the Minutemen—were ignored, as were the issues of whether Safeguard would make an appreciable difference regarding their vulnerability or in the adequacy of the deterrent force as a whole. These were matters which the proponents in general, and Wohlstetter in particular, were largely unwilling to discuss.

Finally, we addressed the issues over which the committee had been most critical of the opponents. These issues almost entirely concerned the Minuteman and SS-9 questions. We stated that we did not claim to be infallible and that we had made some mistakes, but that we believed they were not serious mistakes. Our mistakes, we said, were a reflection of the fact that—with limited time and resources—we had devoted our efforts to the issues of fundamental concern in the debate. We believed, too, that the proponents and the ORSA committee had avoided many of these issues, preferring to dwell on minutiae. We stated that we regretted having had to spend time commenting on the report, but that we had done so both in self-defense and so that the public might be informed as to the character and quality of what we regarded as an extremely regrettable incident.

For a time after the report was issued, there was considerable discussion of both the propriety and the validity of ORSA's inquiry.[17] Many of the opponents of Safeguard, as well as a considerable number of people who were not involved in the debate but felt that ORSA's actions were improper, wrote to the Society condemning the report and citing the numerous inconsistencies, omissions, and biased judgments that the committee had made. Those taking ORSA to task included Philip Morse and Robert Machol, both past presidents of the Society, who stated emphatically that they wished to be disassociated from its actions.

Two comments regarding the report, one made by Senator Hart and the other by Herbert Scoville, in response to a questionnaire on the matter issued by Hart and fellow senators Symington and Cooper, are indicative of the responses generated by the investigation. Senator Hart stated, "A careful reading of the report makes clear that the study was sharply limited to two of the many questions involved, that the study did not take a position on the question of deploying Safeguard (did not really look into this, apparently), and the committee did not have jurisdiction to act as a tribunal over participants in the debate. Unhappily, the broad language of the report does not indicate those limitations and, quite predictably, I think, the conclusions have been used as a general criticism of the overall anti-Safeguard debate."

Scoville, in his reply to the senators' inquiry said, "I share the concern expressed in your letter about the report of the Ad Hoc Committee on Standards of the Operations Research Society of America. Charges of the kind made in this report should

---

17. For published reactions, see Nicholas Wade, "ABM Debate: Learned Society Split by Old Grievance," *Science* 174 (15 October 1971): 276–77; "Letters" [Truman Botts, Walmer E. Strope, and Benjamin L. Schwartz], *Science* 175 (31 March 1972): 1417; and "Judgment," *Scientific American* 225 (November 1971): 48.

never be treated lightly . . . I was very disturbed, therefore, when I read the report, which was so obviously narrow in its approach and biased in its analysis. In fact, one can only reach the conclusion that the Ad Hoc Panel was unduly influenced by one of the protagonists in the debate, the only one who was a member of the ORSA, and the man who requested the investigation in the first place. For a group, under the auspices of a supposed scientific society, to publish a study of this nature is almost unbelievable and raises questions as to its independence from the military-industrial complex. The propriety of this ORSA action was indeed questioned in a minority report of five members of its council."

On the other side of the issue, supporters of the administration took much pleasure in the committee's findings and, as indicated in Senator Hart's comment, their general response was that the report vindicated both the proponents' position and the administration's assertions that those opposed to Safeguard had been unscrupulous in their conduct in the debate. Media backers of the administration plan gave prominent coverage to the most negative areas of the report, and also saw it as a vindication of the pro-Safeguard group. In response to the worst of the articles covering the investigation, letters were written by a number of the opponents in which they contested both ORSA's findings and the conclusions that were being drawn from them.

Eventually, the controversy died down. Despite the clamor it had caused, it had no real or lasting impact. In the end, the facts were left to speak for themselves and, on an overwhelming majority of the issues, the passage of time revealed that the judgments of the opponents had been more sound—and their predictions more accurate—than those of the supporters of deployment. Of the numerous suggestions that the opponents made regarding alternatives to Safeguard, all of which the proponents had discounted as insufficient or ineffective during the debate, a considerable percentage of them were eventually implemented, including dispersal and early warning capability for the bomber force, hardening of the Minuteman silos, and redesign of elements of Safeguard itself, specifically the radar system. In addition, the most crucial issue of all—whether there existed adequate justification for Safeguard's deployment—was implicitly ceded in the opponents' favor.

The entire argument for building the system was finally reduced to the issue of its use as a bargaining chip in negotiations with the Russians. Despite the fact that so many of the administration's predictions were proven to be inaccurate and their policy on deterrent defense was redirected to a posture very much like that advocated by the opponents throughout the debate, no one in the administration or any of the prominent proponents ever publicly conceded that the opponents to

Safeguard had been correct in their assessments, and no one admitted to any mistakes in analysis. The Safeguard issue was finally brought to a conclusion when the United States and the Soviet Union reached an agreement whereby each country would limit its ABM deployment to two installation sites each. In our country only one installation was ever built, and it was eventually dismantled.

Thus, a debate that had begun over four years before, with McNamara's announcement of the Sentinel decision, ended—and, in a sense, satisfactorily for both sides. There would be no deployment of an ABM system, which was the end the opponents had directed their energies to achieve, while at the same time the proponents were able to claim that the threat of such a deployment had been crucial in bringing the Russians to an agreement on defensive weapons limitation. There is no conclusive proof that this was or was not the case. However, those of us who were in the opposition continued to believe that there were less expensive, less disruptive, and less dangerous ways of achieving the same result.

Gorbachev's Revolution[1]

Jerry's personalized account of "opening moments" in the political transformation and, ultimately, dissolution of the Soviet Union. Shortly after taking office as Soviet head of state in 1985, Mikhail Gorbachev initiated policies—popularized in the terms glasnost (openness) and perestroika (restructuring)—that opened the way for liberalization of a system widely perceived as stagnant and repressive. Jerry's feeling of kinship with Gorbachev and his allies, particularly those within the Soviet scientific community, grew stronger after Gorbachev unveiled plans, in 1986, to work towards a nuclear-free world by the end of the century. But Jerry was also interested in the larger social and political consequences of Gorbachev's leadership, and he watched—with as much amazement as the rest of the world—as events rapidly unfolded in the Soviet Union in the late 1980s and early 1990s.

I first heard about Mikhail Gorbachev in the fall of 1985(?)[2] from Dr. Yevgeniy Velikhov, a Soviet physicist, as the result of an incident that took place at a meeting we were both attending in Moscow. I was at a meeting of the CISAC,[3] a disarmament conference sponsored jointly by the Soviet and American Academies of Science.

The conference was one of a continuing series the two Academies were sponsoring, with meetings held twice a year—the spring meeting in Washington, the fall

---

1. A draft written by Jerry in the early 1990s, with edits by Josh Wiesner in 1995 or 1996, and additional edits and notes by editors of this book.

2. Actually, 1983—the Korean airline incident mentioned later as roughly contemporaneous with this meeting occurred on September 1, 1983. Jerry was in Moscow October 16–21, 1983, not at all in 1985.

3. Committee on International Security and Arms Control, founded in 1980 to channel scientific and technical talent into tackling the problems associated with international security and arms control.

one in Moscow. There were eight members, I think, from each country—usually the same people, though the membership changed over time on both sides and both sides were also allowed to bring other people if they wished. I was included in this and subsequent meetings by Dr. Frank Press, who was then the president of the National Academy of Sciences (U.S.). The American group was headed by Dr. Marvin ("Murph") Goldberger, a highly regarded theoretical physicist, who was the president of Caltech. Velikhov, an affable plasma physicist well known in western circles, ran the Soviet side. Though I had not known him at the time, it turned out that Velikhov had actually shared experiments with a group at MIT who were interested in high-powered plasmas. The MIT physicists could make very tough electrodes, while Velikhov had much more powerful electron beams than we had to test them out on. For several years they had had a very productive collaboration, until someone in the United States government shut it down for fear that the Soviets might learn something useful.

The CISAC meeting took place shortly after the Soviet downing of an airliner (Korean Air Lines flight 007) as it flew over the Soviet missile test-range in the Far East. Although there was a prearranged agenda that included discussion of a controversial new long-range radar spotted by a U.S. reconnaissance satellite which our country claimed to be illegal, the Americans in the group could not stay away from discussion of the downing incident. For their part, the Russians were quite willing to talk about the tragedy. They told us that no one in the Soviet Union, including the highest military officials, knew what had actually happened for several days after the incident. As we were aware that the Soviets depended on short-wave radio for communications between Moscow and the Far East, and that this was sometimes blacked out for days at a time, we were not surprised by this admission.

As was widely known, the incident itself contained a number of strange aspects. To begin with, there was the fact that the airliner was so far—several hundred miles—off its course. This was hard to account for, but what was odder was the fact that it was not the first time it had happened; previous Korean airline flights had wandered into Soviet territory in the past. Then, there was the aspect of the incident that had ignited the world outcry—the fact that the interceptor pilot who shot the plane down had evidently made no attempt to warn the airliner's pilot away or to force him to land before firing on him and knocking the plane out of the sky. The incident led one of President Reagan's press assistants to call the Soviet Union "the Evil Empire," a name that Reagan was pleased to take credit for.

The Russian group at the CISAC meeting readily agreed to add discussions about the Korean plane and the radar system to the original agenda, which dealt primarily with missile system force reductions and verification procedures. Since most of the members of the two groups had met before, both in Moscow and Washington, there was none of the tension or mistrust that marked general U.S.-Soviet relations in the aftermath of the disaster.

The leader of the Soviet delegation, Velikhov, was a friendly, slightly heavy-set man with a round face and a starting-to-thin-out head of hair. He was so good-natured and agreeable that he had a reputation for rarely saying no to any suggestion, no matter how impossible it might be to carry out. This characteristic was to cause me considerable grief as our relations became close for a time in the next few years. Eventually, it caused his own associates to stop taking him seriously much of time. Yet, Velikhov had an uncanny knack of being able to turn any idea into a useful one when it grabbed his attention. He was quick to agree to studies that were proposed on all manner of military/technical issues, issues which he understood exceedingly well. Later on, however, when he worked directly for Gorbachev and I worked with him on projects as varied as the International Foundation for the Survival and Development of Humanity, arms control, human rights and computer-based education, I found that his eagerness to say yes so often exceeded his capacity to get things done. Many important projects dragged on forever or sometimes never even got started, despite his good intentions.

One example of this involved an idea that the two of us had for bringing an American business to Russia. On one of my visits to Russia, Velikhov and I sat together through the night on the banks of the Neva River in Leningrad (once again Petrograd) with thousands of local citizens, enjoying the midnight sun at the summer solstice. We spent the time talking about the enormous task of building a modern society. At one point he talked about the lack of electronic supplies available to young would-be experimenters in Russia, who were unable to gain the kind of first-hand experience which comes so naturally to kids in the United States. I suggested that they needed a RadioShack store in Moscow, and we decided to see if that might be possible to arrange. When I got back to Boston, I called John Roach, president of the Tandy Corporation, who was enthusiastic about the idea and thought perhaps they could put several of them in different Soviet cities. I reported this to Velikhov and made a date for him to meet Roach in Washington. That was the last I heard of the project.

Velikhov's deputy, Roald Sagdeev, was an equally interesting and competent individual. He had, for many years, been the head of the Soviet space program and he also shared Velikhov's interest in seeking ways to stop the arms race. The two of them were the Soviet leaders in the dialogue between the two national Academies.

The Soviet Union had communication satellites, so we were puzzled by the fact that they had not used them for important messages. I realized that our Soviet colleagues were not any better connected to operational matters than most of us were. They knew, however, that Soviet fighter planes didn't have the equipment needed to talk to civilian aircraft, and at the CISAC conference we agreed to recommend to the Russian leaders that their fighter planes be equipped with radios that would make such two-way conversations possible if encounters like the one with the Korean airliner happened in the future. The Soviet scientists appeared not to know anything about the radar that was being built on their side and said that they would ask about it.

This meeting of the group was unusual because the Soviet side included two military men who were on active duty. They did not appear to speak English and so had to use interpreters, as the discussion was conducted in English. This conveniently ensured that there would be no spontaneous chit-chat between the Americans. The military men didn't participate much during the discussion, but answered questions addressed to them by both groups. They professed to know nothing about the controversial radar either.

The main topic of the meeting was reports on studies both sides were making about the relationship between missile numbers and risk in a surprise attack, which was for me the most interesting subject. I had not attended a Soviet-American meeting since 1978, and I was amazed at the lack of defensiveness which had been a regular feature of the earlier get-togethers and also the fact that when technical issues were being discussed, it was one meeting, with everyone chiming in. I was also struck by the fact that both the Soviet and American analysts had an innate conservatism that made them shy away from small numbers of missiles which, as I have said, I believed would have constituted a thoroughly adequate deterrent.

Because the conference was hosted by the Soviet Academy, when it ended we went to pay our respects to the Academy's president, Academician A. D. Alexandrov, whose office was in the stately old Presidium of the Academy which serves as the center of all Soviet science (or did until 1991, when some of the Republics chose to have independent Academies). I had known Alexandrov since one of my first trips to Moscow, when I had visited his laboratory. The last time we had interacted was when I received a "Dear friend Wiesner . . ." letter from him a couple of years earlier, explaining why Academician Sakharov was not allowed to return to Moscow from Gorky.

As we went into the conference room, I could see him standing near the center of the large black table that dominated the room. As I walked toward him to say hello, he noticed me and waved his hand and smiled. Meanwhile, the rest of the group came into the room and took places around the table—the Soviets on his side of the table, the Americans on the opposite side. Suddenly, he motioned for me to sit down next to him in what was to have been Velikhov's chair, and, urged by Velikhov, I reluctantly did so. It went through my mind that the more hawkish members of our group probably thought that I rightly belonged there.

Goldberger and Velikhov began by summarizing our talks, paying particular attention to the discussion of how to avoid future man-made air tragedies. As they presented the summaries, Alexandrov seemed to be only half listening. When they were done, he made only a couple of brief remarks on what had been said. The rest of the report was quite perfunctory and no one from either group said much.

Finally, with our presentation finished, Alexandrov stood up with a piece of paper in his hand and started to speak. "It is nice to see so many old friends," he said, "and we welcome you to Moscow. But what is the use of these meetings when your government behaves as it does?" I assumed this comment was a reference to the Korean plane downing and the worldwide protest that the United States had led. But after a moment he started to read from the paper he was holding, which turned out to be a recent U.S. Freedom of Information release of a document from about 1949. It was a memorandum from the Joint Chiefs of Staff to some high official, presumably the president, suggesting—maybe even recommending, I never saw the paper—that the United States bomb the new Soviet nuclear plants before they became operational.

When he finished reading the piece, he stopped and waited for somebody to react. There was an embarrassed silence, which grew louder as no one responded. After what seemed like minutes, he turned to me and said, "You are an old friend—what do you think about this?" I tried to duck a response by saying that I had not come prepared to make a speech. He responded that he hadn't either. "But you had some papers," I said. I was hoping he would let me off, but he continued to push me to make some comment.

Finally, without being entirely conscious of what I was doing, I got to my feet and began speaking. I don't have a transcript of what I said, but what I remember saying went like this: "There are a number of issues involved. First of all, Russia was not bombed, so I imagine that the civilian leaders of the United States vetoed the idea. This is how the system works. The military looks at all the alternatives and they forward them to the civilian leaders for their review. I imagine that things are done more or less the same way in Russia. If the Soviet military isn't constantly looking at problems and proposing possible solutions, they aren't doing their job and should be replaced. I remember what I was doing at that time. I was trying to build air-defense warning systems because we were afraid of Stalin."

I was surprised at what was coming out of my mouth and a bit worried, but nonetheless I continued: "Because we were frightened by Stalin, we built up our defenses. Maybe we built them up more than was necessary—I think we probably did—but because of what we did, Stalin was not able to harm us or our allies. We now know that Stalin harmed and killed millions of your fellow Russians, so I think that we did the right thing in building up our defenses."

As these last words came out, I felt a sense of horror and expected Alexandrov to be very angry. But to my surprise he wasn't. He just looked at me for a long time and then said quietly, "Maybe you are right."

With that, the meeting ended. As we left the Presidium, Velikhov took me aside and said that I shouldn't be upset by Alexandrov because he was one of the old guard and his time was limited. They expected to have new leadership in the Soviet Union before long, and then many things would change. "Many of us," he said, "are working with someone whom we expect to be president soon." And he thought that I would like his ideas. The reference was to Gorbachev, whom he named and told me he was a protégé of Andropov's. Musing, Velikhov said, "You should meet him, you would like him—but there is not enough time now. Why don't you come back for a few days? There won't be time to really get to know him after he's in power."

After I got home, I corresponded with Velikhov and arranged to spend five days traveling with Gorbachev and Velikhov a few weeks from then. But the evening before I was to go to Moscow, I had a gall bladder attack and had to postpone the visit until I was recovered. After that, we had some trouble arranging a new date because Gorbachev had become much busier. Andropov had succeeded to the post of Party chairman and this meant more work for the people around him, including Gorbachev. Then, suddenly it seemed, Andropov was dead and Gorbachev was in charge of the Soviet Union.

High on Gorbachev's priority list, according to Velikhov, was a major effort to improve relations with the West and to give the Eastern Bloc countries more freedom. So it was not a surprise when I began to see some of our Russian friends, particularly Velikhov and Georgiy Arbatov, on television news reports showing the Soviet delegation traveling with the new president. He was, as Velikhov had said, trying hard to thaw the Cold War and with surprising success. The words he spoke were ones the world had long been hoping to hear.

As a man Gorbachev came across as friendly, civilized, and knowledgeable, and his wife, Raisa, reinforced this favorable image. Margaret Thatcher summed it up succinctly very early in their encounter, when she said, "I think we can do business with him." President Reagan and his handlers, fearful of being fooled, were suspicious, even though his first meeting with Gorbachev had gone well and the two men had long private walks and talks. In the Soviet Union, too, there were numerous signs of a new and hopeful spirit, as perestroika and glasnost—freedom and openness—became the order of the day, at first timidly and almost unbelievingly, and then, as people came to believe Gorbachev, with great enthusiasm, particularly among the intelligentsia.

Although Velikhov was working closely with Gorbachev on scientific and military matters, we were told that he still was the Soviet leader of the National Academy-Soviet Academy Arms Control Committee, so I was not surprised when, in January of 1987, I received a telegram from him inviting me to attend a three-day meeting on disarmament to take place in mid-February.[4] I already had a meeting scheduled in Paris on the last of the three days, so I replied that I could only come for the first two. I received a quick message back saying that it was important that I stay for the entire time. I took him at his word, canceled my trip to Paris, and told him that I would stay for the full meeting. I got another quick message thanking me and asking what should be on the agenda. I replied: Star Wars, test ban, and cuts in nuclear force levels. Then I added, "Invite Sakharov," to which I received the terse reply, "Sakharov invited."

Although I had been to Russia many times, I looked forward to this meeting with particular excitement and hope. When I arrived in Moscow, I was met at the main civilian airport by a group of "hosts," a couple of whom I knew, who took me to a VIP waiting room where there was a crowd of other visitors, all in a festive mood. Walking to the waiting room, I had seen a large bright banner that said, "WELCOME TO THE FORUM," which might have alerted me to what was coming but which I paid little attention to. When my passport was returned, I was taken to a limousine where I joined up with my bags and one of the Academy escorts, a young chemist, and we started into the city. The escort didn't seem to know much about what the other people were doing or what was going to happen when we got into the city.

---

4. Forum for a Nuclear-Free World, for the Survival and Development of Humanity—convened in Moscow and attended by several hundred intellectual, political, artistic, and spiritual leaders from around the world.

By the time we began the drive, it was six in the evening and very dark. After leaving the airport, there were few lights except those from our car, which lit a narrow path in the endless sea of birch trees. Occasionally we would pass a piece of the social realism sculpture that graced many of the Soviet highways, and which I rather liked. I always imagined the pleasure it had given some unknown young sculptor to make it.

After about an hour, we reached the hotel—a very large, new structure on the outskirts of town that had been built a few years before for the aborted Olympic games. At the hotel, I was met by more people whom I didn't know but who had obviously been waiting for me. They greeted me effusively and then escorted me and my young chemist—who, he said, was to look out for my needs—into the lobby.

The large room was crowded with people, many of them evidently greeting friends they hadn't expected to see. As we walked to the registration counter, I saw a number of people who looked familiar to me but whom I couldn't identify. Then I saw Yoko Ono, whom I recognized from her pictures. A moment later I saw the Soviet poet Yevtushenko, looking somewhat foolish in a bright red suit. I had met him once in New York, and my face must have lit up as I recognized him because he came over to me with a warm smile. We talked a few moments and we agreed it was going to be a great forum.

Finally, I was registered and found out who I was. The program told me that I was a member of Panel Five, disarmament—one of seven panels which also included economics, business, religion, news, entertainment, and politics. I was one of seven hundred guests, most of whom were staying in the hotel, who were being asked to address the world's problems. My session was to take place in the west conference room next to the lobby, starting the next morning and lasting two days. At the end of that time we, like the other panels, were to compose a twenty-minute summary to present to President Gorbachev on the third day. I was told that if I needed any-thing—such as a car or food or a Moscow telephone book—that was hard to get, or tickets to the ballet or anything else, I was to go to room 1016. The program also said that there was to be a gala entertainment that evening at nine o'clock.

As I went into dinner I met Jeremy Stone of the Federation of American Scientists, who asked me if I wanted to go with him to see Sakharov after dinner. I was delighted to accept, for, although he was well known to several of my physics colleagues and I had written to him several times at their and his request, inviting him to be a visiting professor at MIT, and I had also worked for many years to have his stepchildren allowed to leave the Soviet Union, I had never met him.

I was assigned a spacious room, where we deposited my bags and then went to my assigned dining room where I and my escort had dinner. After dinner I met Jeremy and a young interpreter, whom he knew, and we drove together to Sakharov's apartment.

I was surprised by the small size of the apartment and its run-down appearance. Although I knew that he and his wife Elena had been in disfavor for many years, I also knew that the flat dated from an earlier time when he had been made a Hero of the Soviet Union for his work on the H-bomb. The only Russian homes I had visited before belonged to officials of the Academy of Science, and they were considerably bigger and better furnished.

Despite its size, the apartment seemed to me to have the look of Sakharov and his wife. Books, papers, and letters were everywhere, and there was little space to sit down. In fact, the only place it was possible to sit was the kitchen, which we crowded into. The Sakharovs seemed glad to see me because of our earlier communications. They asked about Elena's children, who lived in Brookline, near Boston, and whom I saw occasionally. Sakharov looked surprisingly well, considering what he had been through—the years of isolation, harassment, hospitalization, forced feeding, and the stress and fear his and Elena's defiance had cost them. His head was slightly bowed and his hair was thinning, almost bald.

He greeted Jeremy as a good friend; Jeremy had helped Sakharov get some of his articles published and also had visited him and Elena since they had returned to Moscow. Though Sakharov spoke no English and Elena very little, and my college Russian didn't go very far, we managed well enough through the translator. We talked about Elena's children and the conference and about a paper that Sakharov was doing for Stone. But mostly we talked about their major work: helping to free the nine hundred political prisoners they believed to still be in the gulags. All of their time, Sakharov said, was taken up corresponding with them and their relatives and friends, and trying to help them by encouragement and advice.

I had read most of Sakharov's nontechnical papers since his famous "Freedom and Democracy," which had been circulated clandestinely through the underground press in Russia and had been published by the *New York Times* in (1972?).[5] I had been impressed by the combination of rationality and passion in the short pamphlet,

---

5. Refers to Sakharov's "Reflections on Progress, Peaceful Coexistence, and Intellectual Freedom," completed in May 1968 and published by the *New York Times* in July 1968, under the headlines "Text of Essay by Russian Nuclear Physicist Urging Soviet-American Cooperation," "Joint Action by Two Nations Viewed as Essential to Avert Perils Facing Mankind," and "Basis for Hope Seen in Rapprochement between Socialist and Capitalist Systems."

and I recognized these same traits as I listened to him speak about their efforts to help those who were still incarcerated.

After talking for more than two hours, Jeremy and I felt it was time for us to go. Bidding the two of them goodnight, we returned to our hotel. When we returned, we went down together to the large auditorium and talked to people, known and unknown, until the festivities started.[6] They were a bit late starting, but about ten o'clock a large group of entertainers gathered and took turns performing. There were Russian rock groups and many Western singers, including Yoko Ono. As the audience warmed up, they joined in the singing—in Russian, English, French, and several other languages—but most of the songs were unknown to me. At one point, Yevtushenko recited poetry and people from the audience began making light-hearted toasts to Gorbachev and the new Soviet freedoms. I joined in the fun until about midnight, then drowsiness won out and I reluctantly left. I was told later that the entertainment had continued till three in the morning. I had never before seen a spontaneous celebration in Moscow. It seemed that the spirit of glasnost was catching, at least for the moment.

I got up early the next morning, still excited by the mood of the evening and anxious to see what the day would hold. After breakfast, I found my group assembling in the west conference room. I saw many friends, including Velikhov and Sagdeev of the Soviet group and many American friends such as Frank von Hippel from Princeton; Ruth Adams, my colleague in the international security and development program of the MacArthur Foundation; and Ken Galbraith.

While I stood chatting, I was approached by a very upset Thomas Corcoran, the project leader of a breakthrough experiment in which a team from the American National Environmental Defense Committee (NRDC) was being allowed to do experiments at one of the Soviet nuclear test sites. The MacArthur Foundation had participated in the funding, so I knew about the experiment. The team's goal was to see how well they could measure U.S. nuclear explosions at the Russian site as a way of learning how good the reciprocal measurements would be. Corcoran wanted to talk to me privately, so we walked down the hall to a quiet spot. With clear agitation, he told me that Velikhov had gone back on his promise to allow him to conduct experiments during the forthcoming Soviet test and he wanted me to protest to someone, suggesting ex-ambassador Dobrynin. I felt I should hear

6. A note in the text indicates a plan to fill in names of other well-known people in attendance at the conference, including Norman Mailer.

Velikhov's side of the matter before doing anything, and so, with Corcoran standing next to me, I repeated his complaint.

As I had assumed, the story was more complicated than Corcoran had said. First of all, Velikhov said there had been no agreement at the start of the experiment concerning the team's presence during a test. The issue had not come up because no one had expected the Soviets to start testing again. After Gorbachev had announced their intention to do so, Velikhov said, Corcoran had approached him to see if the NRDC could record through the test time, and Velikhov said he would see what the military would allow. They had told him that it would not be permitted and he, Velikhov, could do no more. I asked if recording during the Russian tests was important to the basic experiment, and then I decided the answer was no and said so. I later learned that Velikhov had already appealed to Gorbachev, who had been turned down by the Soviet high command. I am not sure that Corcoran ever agreed with me, but as we spoke we realized that we were holding up the start of the meeting, as Velikhov was to make the opening remarks. So we hurried to the conference room.

There were seven panels, according to the scheduled items on our agenda, including discussion of nuclear testing, Star Wars, and reductions in the numbers of ballistic missiles. Velikhov also invited panel members to suggest additional topics for discussion.

The first subject was Star Wars and the linkage the Soviet scientists were insisting had to exist between a ban on Star Wars and cuts in numbers of strategic missiles. Their arguments did not make sense because they insisted at the same time that Star Wars could not work, a position shared by most of the Western participants, that the Soviet Union would not agree to a ban on it without a cut in missile numbers. After I had listened to this argument for about thirty minutes, I stood up and said I didn't understand their logic. Since we all agreed, I said, that anti-missile systems like Star Wars would not work and the Russians were right in being opposed to building them, why were they insisting on putting other conditions on the ban of them? In my view, they would make the world more dangerous because people might fear that they could work and so build even more missiles. With these remarks, I sat down.

Until then Sakharov had been quiet, but after I spoke he stood up. He started by saying that I was right and then he proceeded to read a well-reasoned, short paper that he had prepared beforehand. I was to see him do this many times in the couple of years that we later worked together. In fact, I was to realize that he often had trouble in the give-and-take of a discussion if he had not thought out what he was going to say beforehand. As he spoke, the audience listened with special care to his quiet voice, heard for the first time since the return from exile in Gorky. His slightly stooped figure was the center of attention as he read his arguments about why the Star Wars system couldn't function adequately. When he finished and sat down, everyone recognized that they had been witness to a very special performance. There was general agreement, when he finished, that the group would recommend a ban on Star Wars.

The group more or less agreed on the next several agenda items: a halt to nuclear testing, cuts in various missile systems in both the U.S. and Soviet arsenals, and there was some discussion about cuts in conventional forces. I did not stay for all of the discussions because I was invited to two other meetings, a luncheon meeting with the economists and an afternoon meeting with a UN Committee on Disarmament that just happened to be meeting in Moscow at the time of the forum.

The American scientists thought that a certain building, visited by U.S. congressmen, was designed to house a low-frequency missile warning radar which would have been a violation of the ABM treaty. At our meeting, the Soviet scientists noted that there was a formal way to inquire about the radar, and that was through the control commission which had been established to investigate claims of treaty violations. For some reason the United States was reluctant to use this route, possibly because it feared that the Soviets would complain about the siting of two new radars that the U.S. was just then installing.

We did eventually get to the original agenda, which was about the stability of missile systems in crisis situations. This was the first time that the group had explored this subject, and soon saw after talking about it in a general way that we more or less agreed on general propositions, such as the dangerous instability brought on by the MIRVs. MIRVs make it possible for a single missile to shove several nuclear warheads into orbit, and thus make it possible for a single missile to attack and possibly destroy several of an opponent's missiles at a time, consequently putting a high premium on surprise attack in the advent of war.

As I explained earlier, this was an American invention made initially to confound a Soviet anti-ballistic missile system in the event that they should deploy one, but in the end it seemed to be more useful to get an edge on the Soviets by putting several warheads on one missile. The United States started by having three warheads on many of its Minuteman III missiles. Unfortunately, the Russian scientists had followed with their own MIRVs which, because the Soviet missiles were bigger, carried as many as ten warheads on one missile. By the time of this meeting, both sides now realized that we had made a serious mistake because this great idea made both sides trigger-happy and thus made it more likely that a single accidental firing or even a false alarm would turn into Armageddon.

The proposed American solution to this madness was to build a giant new missile, the MX, which would carry ten warheads. This was not very sensible because it was an even more attractive target than the Minuteman. In fact, it was so target-attractive that many exotic but impractical deployment systems were devised to hide it. One of them, a mobile rail system which shuffled the proposed one hundred missiles between a much larger number of pods—much like the old shell game that covered much of the state of Nevada—was the favorite until the people of the state soundly rejected it. In the end sanity prevailed, only a few of them were built, and they were put in super-hardened silos.

We realized that we would not make any progress on so sensitive and important an issue without adequate analysis, which in any case required a more contemplative environment and a more sustained effort than the meeting allowed. We agreed that a small subset of the CISAC would follow up.

SELECTED SPEECHES AND PAPERS

Convocation Speech

Jerry's remarks delivered at a public forum in Kresge Auditorium, October 15, 1969, as part of MIT's observance of the "October 15th Moratorium." The Moratorium, widely observed on college campuses, called for a day-long cancellation of classes in protest of the Vietnam War. That day, Jerry also joined MIT students and others in an anti-war march and demonstration on the Boston Common.

My concerns about the Vietnam War extend to convocations about that war. It is not because I lack clear views about the Vietnam War or of the course I believe that our country should follow, and certainly not because I am afraid to say what I believe, but because this is an all-Institute convocation. It should be an occasion that contributes to understanding if not to agreement, and, because of the kind of Institute MIT is, it should contribute to the effort to extricate the nation from the Vietnam quagmire.

Yet all I can do is tell you what I believe. The MIT faculty voted overwhelmingly for this convocation to support the October 15th moratorium, whose purpose is to speed the ending of the Vietnam War. That is the question we should examine here: how to terminate the Vietnam War rapidly and without deepening the already great schisms which exist in our society. Never before in our history has a foreign adventure been so deeply unpopular. Never before have our ideas of morality and decency, and our notions of patriotism, been so badly at odds. The tensions in our society which these conflicts create threaten to tear it apart. Unless we can find an acceptable basis for ending this loathsome war quickly, those strains may pass the yield point. There is almost total agreement on the need to end the war and to end it quickly, but not nearly so much agreement on the reasons for wanting to or the means of achieving a peace or even the kind of peace. One's views of these issues obviously affect one's priorities, and what one is willing to do to end the war.

Solidarity in protest—marching with students against the Vietnam War, Boston Common, October 15, 1969.

In his inauguration address, President Nixon asked us to lower our voices. He said, "We cannot learn from one another until we speak quietly enough so that our words can be heard as well as our voices." He went on to say, "For its part, government will listen. We will strive to listen in new ways—to the voices of quiet anguish, the voices that speak without words, the voices of the heart, the injured voices, the anxious voices, the voices that have despaired of being heard."

October 15th is planned in the spirit of the request. When President Nixon and those who back up his view say that October 15th does not help achieve an early peace in Vietnam, they have one kind of peace in mind, one in which appearances play a major role. The voices of October 15th are anguished voices saying that a vast number of us have a different list of priorities, and highest on the list is to stop the senseless killing being done in our name.

The voices say other things, too. The voices of the heart say that opposition to the war is based on deep moral concerns, not fear. The injured voices say that we cannot justify the hundreds of thousands of lives lost, including those of more than 40,000 Americans, in support of goals we don't understand. The voices of despair say that our protest stems from the recent disclosures that the United States involved itself in Vietnam without any request from that country's government and a widely held suspicion that the justification for our vast escalation of the war—the Gulf of Tonkin incident—was at best an incredible intelligence and communications blunder, and possibly even a deliberate deception. The voices of humanity say that it is hard to be proud of our vast power punishing a tiny country that doesn't know how to quit. They say that pride should not compel us to continue the carnage and destruction of the past five years. All of these voices are saying urgently and desperately that we should have the courage to face our mistakes and wrongdoings squarely.

What do we want and what are our options?

Reasoning with student activists at MIT, October 10, 1969. The students, members of Students for a Democratic Society (SDS), had taken over the top floor of the Center for International Studies in protest against war research. (Courtesy of the *Boston Herald*.)

Our fondest hope would be realized if we could return to the situation of 1954 and the pledged elections that our government helped to block. Unfortunately, that option doesn't appear to be available to us, probably not even if we were willing to double our past investment, measured in lives, money, and time. If this be so, what choices do we have? The only clear one is to stop on some reasonably urgent timetable. All other courses have grave uncertainties and, for me, serious questions of propriety. The present favorite is to build up the South Vietnamese army until it can stand by itself, meanwhile slowly or swiftly withdrawing our forces. This is called Vietnamization of the war. Past experience should not make us optimistic about this route, and in any event we would end up with an endless commitment to support a military government of low attractiveness. I don't want that.

Most of the people opposing the goal of quick withdrawal want an "honorable conclusion." The only honor there can be in the end of this illegal, immoral war is to be found in ending it quickly and in ending it with honesty, not with subterfuge.

For me there is one agonizing point in immediate withdrawal, and that is the fate of a large number of South Vietnamese who have cast their lot with us—not the generals and high officials, but the thousands of more junior people, officials in the villages and towns. But their safety is hardly ensured by continuing the war in South Vietnamese hands—that's just a way of hiding the problem. There are many ways to help these people. For example, we could easily finance their resettlement—in the United States, if they desire it, or in a friendly Asian country. We have done this before. The debate should be on this question.

The important message of October 15th is that millions and millions of Americans—a majority of the people—want this war stopped, and stopped now. That is the goal to which we should dedicate all of our energies.

Science, Technology, and the Quality of Life

Jerry's inaugural address as the thirteenth president of the Massachusetts Institute of Technology, Inaugural Convocation, Rockwell Cage, MIT, Cambridge, Mass., October 7, 1971.

There is a decided preference among newly designated university presidents to eschew the traditional pomp and ceremony of an inaugural occasion. Frequently, in recent times, new presidents have taken up their duties almost clandestinely, with essentially no formal recognition of their arrival, and faculties only learn of their presence through a cut in the budget. My own predilection was to propose that we, too, forego the traditional observances. There are many reasons, I suspect, for this almost universally instinctive impulse. One is a strong urge to save money; another factor, I am sure, is the recognition that pomp and circumstance are not seemly at a moment when the society is so seriously troubled.

But, in fact, during these past weeks I have become aware of a deeper intuitive wisdom that counsels that the inaugural occasion offers an opportunity for affirmation—for a rededication of the community to the values and ideals we all share. The characteristic shyness of new presidents is a reflection, no doubt, of a general unwillingness to rehash clichés, a refusal to repeat the tired bromides that are yielding such meager rewards to the current crop of political aspirants.

The times are no longer conducive to speculation. Our burden is that we *know enough* today to make dire, and specific, predictions about the future—and most of us here this afternoon will live to see some of them come true. Nor do the times call for purely expedient commitments to action. We have all memorized the words of ten years ago which conjured visions of great new worlds; our need now is to move practically and painstakingly toward their fulfillment. Our commitment must be to progress in significant and inspiring steps toward solving our local and global

Laya and Jerry, all smiles, at his inauguration as MIT president, October 7, 1971. (Photo by Geo. Dixon, courtesy of the *Boston Herald*.)

problems. In the pursuit of these tasks we cannot afford clichés, and a failure to examine and reexamine ideas will amount to a betrayal of the human race.

In this context, I wish to reiterate what I see as the basic purpose of any university and ours in particular: it is the quest for learning, the nurture of learning, the transmission of learning, the use of learning. We are all gathered here, teachers and students, to expand man's knowledge of his universe. No doctrine, no orthodoxy, no conventional discipline or gust of political passion can be allowed to divert us from this purpose. When this university was founded a century ago, the atom was an irreducible unit, radiation was not understood, the great equations that frame the physical universe were undreamed of; Pasteur was just beginning his work, Einstein was unborn, the moon was more than a lifetime away. As much as any institution of learning in the entire world, we have helped roll back the frontiers of darkness. And we shall continue. Here we shall offer shelter for the search for knowledge to all those who come, at any age, to join in that search. And the only loyalty test we shall impose is that of loyalty to learning.

Informal chat on inauguration day, October 7, 1971.

In this spirit and under the leadership of the three distinguished presidents who are with us here today, our pride of presidents, the faculty, and alumni of MIT have earned us an honored place among the world's great universities. Through the guidance of Drs. Killian, Stratton, and Johnson, the social and behavioral sciences, management, humanities, and the creative arts have taken their place alongside the original activities in science and the "useful arts" (as founder Rogers called them), adding substantially to MIT's intellectual breadth and distinction, and to its record in public service.

The seminars of this inaugural week have reflected the uncertain mood of the times in which we live and have highlighted the necessity for reemphasizing the essential value of research. They also reflect a deep awareness of the threats to the quality of life in our society and the need for increased sensitivity to the dangers arising from the careless exploitation of new technology.

I have been impressed, since being appointed president, by the great concern and affection of people I meet everywhere for the welfare of MIT and for universities in general. The hidden message I decode is that a lot of people, including many with no ties to the academic world, do care about the universities, do look to them for leadership, and, consequently, are very upset when they find their performance disappointing. But I also hear much criticism of MIT specifically, as well as of other universities. The criticism comes from everywhere, old and young, rich and poor, radical and conservative, from all ethnic and minority groups.

For each group, the university is the symbol of its frustrations and fears. The reactionary elements in the society are prone to view the university as a subversive force and believe that its administrators have been too tolerant of student and faculty challenges—some say threats—to the established order. Large numbers of young people and those adults who want more rapid social reform are critical because they consider the university a conservative force whose primary function is to "socialize"—in their words, "co-opt"—students for a role in society which they see as exploitative, unsatisfying, and, to varying degrees, obsolete and designed to support existing institutions and social relationships.

We have achieved the dubious distinction of being regarded, at one and the same time, as the hothouse of revolution and the propagator of the status quo. To the poor and the blacks, the university is the locked gateway to opportunity. And others see the university as an untrustworthy ally whose staffs use knowledge sought at public expense to frustrate government purpose. In other words, to many citizens of our society, the university has become the essence of the enigma that is the future; in it are fused the hopes and disappointments that power the continuing revolution of our times. Academia, with its conflicting constituencies, is at once the intellectual front line and the only neutral meeting ground of that revolution.

The many individual objections to the performance of universities are given coherence and are amplified by a growing wave of anti-intellectualism, mysticism, and primitivism. This new evangelism is fostered by those who feel that the structure and goals of a society which stresses the achievement of material progress through science and technology cannot provide a life of dignity for the individual. For these critics, including many students and faculty, the university is in league with the enemy; for some, it is the enemy. And to those who see uncontrolled technology as the major source of our social dislocations, MIT is the special symbol of their concerns and frequently the object of their anger. They are persuaded that the social and economic forces which propel technological innovation cannot be directed toward the general welfare; that, in fact, technology represents a malignancy which will dominate our civilization and ultimately condemn all men to be slaves of a vast impersonal and all-powerful organization. Their cry is that its onslaught must be stopped.

Jerry's inauguration as MIT president, October 7, 1971—former presidents James Killian and Howard Johnson (in foreground); unidentified individual, Walter Rosenblith, Archibald MacLeish, and Jerry (in background). (Courtesy of the MIT Museum.)

If this vision is correct, we are already doomed, for it is clear to me that we cannot escape technology in some form. In fact, I am convinced that without new scientific knowledge and wise technological investments now and in the future, the problems of mankind will only increase. At the same time, the increasing complexity of society and its capability for control of the individual pose very real hazards, and these matters require our continuous vigilance.

I view the present multi-crisis differently—and hopefully. I see it as a perilous but positive phase in man's continuing evolution—a process now determined largely by his own actions, which he is still learning to manage. At this juncture, it is our obligation to intervene on the side of man. Ironically, the problems we face stem from our success—from efforts to achieve equality and a decent life for all citizens.

Science and technology have helped create our present predicament by extending to most of us options in modes of living and working that were previously reserved for a privileged few. For too long we have been totally hypnotized by what we could do. Until recently, people in the "advanced countries," as we like to call ourselves, have assumed that any application of technology that expanded mastery over nature was desirable, and we have ignored the implications of this power. Rarely before this decade was the relationship between technological change and man's social, biological, and physical environments examined; only obvious benefits were considered and only immediate costs. Little consideration was given to the "ecological" dimensions of innovations—physical, social, or psychological. It is precisely the chasm between our tremendous power to change and our apparent inability to guide these changes for the good of mankind that has led to the feeling of desperation and the loss of confidence in the scientific approach.

But, if we look at recent events with some detachment, we can see some positive responses to these problems. The social feedback systems are working.

Not long ago, the environmental hazards were recognized by only a few experts whose warnings were completely disregarded. I recall how violently Rachel Carson was attacked in 1961 for her statements about the deadly consequences of the indiscriminate use of pesticides, and a panel established merely to look into her allegations was strongly criticized. The use of many of the chemicals she warned against is now prohibited. Likewise, only a decade ago man-made radioactive poison fell from the sky with every rain, doing incalculable damage to living beings everywhere on the planet and jeopardizing hundreds of future generations. The nuclear test-ban treaty of 1963 almost completely stopped that poisoning of the atmosphere. Today, protecting and improving the quality of the environment is a major national goal which almost everyone accepts, and is prepared to pay for, and the human, social, scientific, and political issues involved are receiving concerted academic study.

Another major response to current dissatisfactions with the status quo was that mounted by the country's educational system. As I think of it, it has been the most massive reaction in my memory to a social crisis. At all levels and in every kind of school we see new programs, experimentation, a reaching upward in a continuing search for a "better," more engaging and significant education. However, it's obvious that, to date, the good intentions outrun accomplishments.

Nowhere, I believe, is the fervor for educational innovation and for undertaking inquiries into society's many needs greater than right here at MIT. And, an important reason for this educational ferment has been the students themselves. They are knowledgeable and mature. They insist upon a chance to think about who they are and why they are doing what they are doing and where they are going. They want to develop broadly in all spheres—moral, social, intellectual, and political—and they do not want their lives compartmentalized. They are eager to work hard and anxious to learn, but only in connection with a faculty and an institution they can respect for its values, its commitment to society, and its attention to the individual. To a far greater degree than his counterpart of a decade ago, today's student contemplates a career in some part of the public sector or in an industry that is oriented to social responsibility. This is indeed a heartening sign.

We have begun to break the academic lockstep—to make it possible for a student to learn in a style that suits him, at a pace that he chooses, with the freedom to tailor his own academic program. The project laboratory, the seminars, the undergraduate research involvement, the Experimental Study Group, the Unified Science Studies Program all add new dimensions to undergraduate educational opportunities. These accomplishments have been accompanied by the development of a deep and sustaining interest on the part of students and faculty in the educational process itself as a discipline worthy of investigation and study, in which a regard for subject matter, a broad knowledge of human beings, and an appreciation of the possibilities of technology are joined.

There is still much to learn. How can MIT more fully engage the outstanding young people it attracts? How can it help them discover themselves? How can it organize its programs and utilize the promising new technologies to permit faculty members to spend more of their time and efforts in direct relationships with students? How can MIT make effective use of the educational potential in industry and government? How can it respond to the hopes of many alumni for a more intimate and productive association with the Institute through periodically renewed contacts for learning? And how would such continuing educational programs alter the time and substance of the formal university experience?

This is a unique moment to pause and reexamine our educational policies, for the walls of the professional departments are breaking down to make room for the evolution of new unities. Professional faculties and their students are reaching out to the society—the neighboring community, government, and industry—in order to make a conscious contribution, through understanding and action, in the fields of environment, health, urban studies, architecture, educational innovation, international understanding, and in the management of science and technology. This movement can stimulate a renaissance among the professions in which man will replace machine at the center of the stage. New cooperative ventures involving the social sciences and humanities should draw disparate disciplines closely together, and in so doing provide opportunities to create exciting new forms of professional education. Thus, we can recast the concept of a liberal education in a contemporary mold by integrating science and technology with the study of man and his culture. Perhaps then the history and philosophy of science and technology will become a significant aspect of humanistic studies.

Last year William Arrowsmith, the classics scholar turned educational innovator, surveyed the spreading dissatisfaction within liberal arts institutions and responded with a not dissimilar vision of a new educational synthesis flowing from the impact of current social turmoil on the professions. He said: "We have integrated problems and disintegrated skills. And the alienation of knowledge and the liberal arts from the crisis of the professions is no longer a tolerable luxury. If the liberal arts attempt to maintain their traditional aloofness, their devotion to pure research and contemplation, their subject matters will simply be appropriated. The professionals have no alternative; they are too close to society, to the convulsive chaos around us, to escape responsibility for change, for rational and humane action." And he went on to say: "The professions, I am suggesting, have encountered the 'other'; a new humanism is already taking shape among younger professionals in response to the desperation of those who depend upon the professions. And because the professions cannot do without the arts of knowledge and the liberal arts, their encounter will eventually spread to education too."

Twenty-two years ago, a faculty committee of which Dr. Stratton and I were members concluded its recommendations with the hope that "the Institute may become known as a place where the professional training and the general education necessary for professional leadership are integrated." To assist in achieving this goal, the committee recommended the establishment of the School of Humanities and Social Science. Though the School has become a distinguished and vital component of MIT, the integrated education we dreamed of did not emerge. Partly it was because the goals were not clearly articulated, certainly not generally understood, and perhaps not even quite believed in. Perhaps we didn't appreciate the difficulty of the task—it is easier to teach facts and problem-solving skills than to teach the expressive and appreciative skills. Despite the fact that some of these objectives have eluded our grasp, we know that we have great strengths in the School to support our new initiatives.

What I have explored here today is in the nature of mid-course guidance for our academic flying machine. As I close, I would remind us of our immediate opportunities to enhance the quality of life close to home—on the campus and in the neighboring community.

First, to make careers in science and engineering more attractive and accessible for members of minority groups and women, through opportunities as students, faculty, and as staff employees at MIT.

Second, to contribute through our actions and support to the well-being of the community in which we live.

Third, to seek new ways of collaboration with our sister institutions of the area. Our joint programs with Harvard University, Wellesley College, and the Woods Hole Oceanographic Institution already play a major role in the lives of many students and faculty, both through collaboration and the sharing of resources. The interchange of students and faculty enriches far beyond the scholarly opportunities thus provided.

Lastly, charity, they say, begins at home, and we must remain committed, in spite of severe fiscal constraints, to continue the recent efforts to improve the quality of the campus environment.

Now, let me recapitulate the thread of my thoughts. Our first responsibility, as I have said, is to learning itself. Our second responsibility, since ours is the world's foremost institute of technology, is to understand what our learning and discoveries may do to man and society, and to transmit that knowledge to new generations, to men and leaders who may be wiser than we in applying it, or wiser in judging how slowly or rapidly these technologies may be absorbed.

I conclude, with a humility forced on me by the contemplation of my own experience and the experience of our country in these times, with the realization that our central problem is man himself. If, through our quest for learning, we can help develop wise men; if, by our research and study, we can deliver leaders trained in the study of nature's evidence and nature's promise; if we can shape young people who are fully aware of their own powers of mind, who have the courage to stand alone, who are committed to justice and to humanity, people modest enough to know that men trained in other disciplines may understand America as well as they—if we can do all this, then MIT may face a future as glowing as its past. As an institution within a larger community, we must respond to national needs. We hope to educate men and women here who will help, when they leave and as they mature, to define what those national needs are—who will work not as elitist specialists, but as individuals among the other 200 million Americans to bring about the necessary improvements in our society.

Our country presently is full of public mourners, of dour analysts of the future. I do not count myself among them. The times are hard today; no one would see this as a moment ripe with the full flowering of the American spirit. Yet the times

SPEECH ON A PUBLIC OCCASION
for Jerome Wiesner

Rinsing our mouths with praise ...

                                    The cup

by the limestone spring in the cool of the midday ...

Earlier generations knew this place,
made their way here thronging. We have forgotten it:
we have kept to the street too long, tongues
stale, hearts - thirsty.

                    Oh, to praise!
God's will in the world if we could learn it,
test it on our lips, would taste of praise.
Why else should the world be beautiful? Why should the
leaves look as they do, the light, the water?

Rinsing our mouths with praise of a good man ...

    I say what I mean. I do not say
    a good man in a bad time.
    All times are bad when the man fails them.
    I say:
    a good man in a time when men are
    scarce, when the intelligent forgotten,
    follow each other around in the fog like
    sheep, bleat in the rain, complain
    because Godot never comes, because
    all life is a tragic absurdity — Sisyphus
    sweating away at his rock and the rock
    won't, because freedom and dignity ....

    Weep, they say, for freedom and dignity!
                                          itch
    You're not free: it's your grandfather's ∧ you scratching.
    You have no dignity: you're not a man,
    you're a rat in a vat of rewards and punishments.
    You think you've chosen the rewards. You haven't:
    the rewards have chosen you!

                        Aye, weep!

Rinsing our mouths with praise of a good man
in a time when men are scarce, when the Word
chirps like a cricket on the cellar floor,
or the clang stones — when the mind maunders ...

A good man!
                    Look at him there against the fog!
He saunters along to his place in the world's weather,
hitches his pants, lights his pipe,
talks back to accepted opinion.

Congressional committees hear him say:
"Not what you think: what you haven't thought of."

He addresses Presidents. He say:
" Governments even now still have to govern.
   No one is going to invent a self-governing holocaust."

The Pentagon receives his views:
" Science", he say, " is no substitute for thought".
   Miracle drugs perhaps: not miracle wars".

Advisor to Presidents, the papers call him.
Advisor, I say, to the young.
It's the young who need competent friends, bold
companions, honest men who won't run out —
won't write off mankind, sell up the country,
quit the venture, jibe the ship.

      I love this man. I rinse my mouth with his praise.

Archibald MacLeish's handwritten version of the poem he wrote for Jerry's inauguration as
MIT president, October 7, 1971.

ANTIPHON FARE

for Brass Quintet

by   David   L. Ludwig

A set of antiphonal brass fanfares
composed for the lobby of MIT building 7

Dedicated to Jerome B. Wiesner

upon   his   inauguration
as President   of MIT

5   October 1971

Manuscript title page and a phrase from the opening fanfare of a musical offering by David L. Ludwig, written for Jerry's inauguration as MIT president, October 7, 1971.

have always been hard for men who seek to change, whose occupation and calling is the forecasting and the fostering of change. For those of us who see problems as challenges, these times may be one of the rare opportunities in history when men of our kind may contribute their most. I am thankful to have, at my side, one of those men, Paul Gray, my long-time colleague, as Chancellor. I take pride in this new opportunity; I am hopeful for what lies before this community; I rejoice in the adventure which, all together, we can look forward to sharing.

Many years ago, Mr. MacLeish suggested that civilization would not be healed until people could see and know feelingly. His words should ring in our memories as we go about our tasks, and if he will excuse my presuming this once to invade his craft, I will conclude thus:

No equation can divine the quality of life

    no instrument record,

    no computer conceive it.

Only bit by bit can feeling men,

    lovingly retrieve it.

Commencement Address

Excerpts from Jerry's last commencement address as MIT president, June 2, 1980.

As most of you know, I am also a graduating member of the Class of 1980—no doubt the oldest, at least chronologically. I am not certain how many years it has taken me to graduate because, like some of you, I have occasionally taken time off to see what was going on in other parts of the world. One thing is certain. Life at MIT for me has been a continuous learning process with some of the best possible teachers, both students and faculty members. I face the future with much of the same excitement and wonder that I know most of you feel. I expect to go on learning as long as my neurons will keep firing, and I hope you will too, for the world needs the kind of help that your MIT education has prepared you to give.

For the past several years, I have conducted a mini-poll in March and April to see what besides the normal springtime preoccupations were worrying the about-to-be graduates. This year's concerns were not surprising, just overwhelming. Some, such as the dangers of nuclear war and the role of technology in the society, have been perennial questions. New this year were the issues of the hostages and the growing instability in the Middle East. An increasing number of you seem to have a fatalistic expectation of nuclear war and a feeling of powerlessness to do anything to prevent it. (Incidentally, there is much we can do, as I will try to explain later.) Others of you emphasized the energy crunch and the out-of-control economy. As if these were not enough themes, very many students expressed dismay about the lagging efforts in social equity and still others reflected the growing concern that the United States was losing its technological leadership. Finally, almost everyone questioned why our government was so impotent, why our country no longer

"Roasted" by friends and colleagues at his last regular faculty meeting, May 20, 1980—*left to right*: Hartley Rogers, Paul Gray, Walter Rosenblith, Jerry, and William Ted Martin.

seemed to be able to make critical decisions, and some were even upset because they found it hard to choose a favorite presidential candidate among the many.

Altogether, this list seemed more like an agenda for the new MIT Program in Science, Technology, and Society than the outline for ten minutes of a commencement program. As I puzzled how this all fit together, I received a message, not from heaven, but from a student who told a member of the faculty that the most important thing he had learned at MIT was from a remark I had made at his commencement. I was a bit startled—and obviously somewhat pleased—so I asked what it was that I had said. Apparently, as I handed him his diploma, he stopped to say something to me, but I said, "Keep moving"—advice that he has been following ever since.

That's not bad advice. I would only add that if you follow it, you should pause from time to time to see where you are going, and perhaps even more importantly, where your good sense tells you that you should be going.

It is hardly necessary to point out that the energy crunch and the out-of-control economy are closely related problems. So is the increased danger of nuclear war, for if the United States were more or less energy independent, as it could be if it were able to get its act together and exploit its almost endless energy resources, the very survival of our nation would not depend upon maintaining order in the turbulent Middle East. In fact, if we didn't depend upon that region so completely to keep our industrial system powered, the Middle East would be considerably less turbulent. This perplexing situation provides all of us with two major challenges.

First, to speed the exploitation of the world's plentiful energy resources in order to regain control of our own destiny, and second, to do all we can to slow down the accelerating arms race.

Why is the United States unable to develop its vast indigenous energy resources? It's clearly not for lack of technological ideas or solutions. Rather, it comes from a paralysis due to a mixture of inhibitions on corporate initiatives, regional conflicts, and questions of social equity—how to distribute the costs among us—resulting in an equation we have found impossible to solve. A few years ago, the president suggested that we treat the energy problem as the moral equivalent of war. He never quite explained what he meant. In any event, the response up to now has been more like a pillow fight. Congress has finally designed an energy program for the nation, one good enough to ease *its* concerns—or conscience—but hardly one that will eliminate *our* frightening dependence on other nations' oil in the foreseeable future.

Recently, John Kemeny, president of Dartmouth College, while giving the Compton Lecture here at MIT this spring, described his experience as chairman of the presidential commission investigating the accident at the Three Mile Island nuclear plant. His most telling conclusion was that the nation's decision-making processes were not adequate for the world we had created, and that a system of governance that was designed 200 years ago for an agricultural nation of 20 million people would not work well enough for a highly technological nation of 200 million people. I would agree with Dr. Kemeny—we do need to redo our political system to permit quicker decision making, to create a political process that has a degree of stability and coherence appropriate to the long time constants of contemporary problems and to reassign a degree of decision-making authority to political leaders: in sum, to create a political process better suited to our present condition, one that provides an opportunity for all views to be expressed and still allows the many components of the nation to function expeditiously. I believe that the next president of the United States should create a commission to study these organizational problems of government, as a prelude to a national dialogue on the issues.

The problem, however, is not as simple as designing a new management structure. We must first decide what we want to manage and how much, and that means better understanding of our resources, strengths, and objectives. I am convinced that it means most of all achieving a much better understanding of how a technological industrial society operates, what makes it strong, and why it seems to be less innovative today than it was in the past. In my opinion, it means creating conditions where individual initiatives and rewards can once more be the major driving force in our society. It means, too, reestablishing a degree of national consensus with regard to national objectives. It means better understanding of the aspirations of the poor at home and of the new and developing nations abroad. It means understanding how we must behave if we truly believe that technology has made all the people and all the nations of the world interdependent. It means understanding the limited ability of military forces based on nuclear power to project our will on the world community and especially nuclear-armed antagonists. It means believing once again that we lead best when we lead by *excelling* in social and economic progress based on moral behavior.

My personal graduation exercise has been going on for several weeks now, punctuated by receptions and seminars. One of these, a day-long colloquium that seemed to be patterned on the television program "This Is Your Life," was climaxed by an exciting and insightful reminder of the two cultures theme, suggesting a communications gap between scientists and humanists, that C. P. Snow made so popular by his now famous BBC Rede Lecture in 1959. Like so many others concerned with the impact of technology on society, I have from time to time reflected on Snow's revelation—whether it was indeed true, and if so, what might be done about the problem he highlighted. (Incidentally, one of Snow's criteria for a scientist was a person who understood the second law of thermodynamics. By that definition, most of us here would qualify as humanists.) A decade before Snow's lecture—in 1949, to be precise, here at MIT, recognizing the growing impact of science and technology, a Committee on Educational Survey outlined a program designed to provide an adequate humanistic component to our educational program, and the Institute has been hard at work trying to implement it ever since.

My personal experiences have convinced me that the problem is much more complex than Snow suggested. In our complex times, there are not two but many inadequately communicating cultures forced to live together in an increasingly interdependent and rapidly evolving world community. Little wonder that there are so many strains between them.

As science adviser to Presidents Kennedy and Johnson, and now as president of MIT, I have for years been under heavy pressure to defend science and technology.

At first, I did this with some of the same trepidation one would have in defending one's naughty child, but with each new challenge, whether it was environmental pollution, the appropriate choice of weapon systems, education, privacy in the electronic age, energy, radioactive fallout, the side effects of drugs, or any one of dozens of other issues on which I helped shape policy, I found that I was entering a new culture—or at least subculture—that saw the problem (and the world) through an intellectual filter quite different from mine. Even more troublesome, I frequently found myself trying to understand and reconcile two subcultures, both foreign to me. One of my earliest such experiences was my efforts to bring together environmentalists and the users of agricultural pesticides after Rachel Carson's book, *Silent Spring*, was published.

Most of us live in more than one culture, so to speak. As Americans, for example, we share a common language and many ideals, concerns, and objectives. But we are separated by the differing perceptions of our own subcultures based on background, profession, ethnicity, regionalism, etc. As I began to understand this, I became increasingly aware of the universality of a concept from communication theory: for communications to be possible, there must be shared symbols. Most people and most societies do not appreciate this relativity of the communication process—what they see is the world through a highly specific filter, but nonetheless believe that they possess the only true vision. I am not saying there are no rights or wrongs, or principles that one should live by—and even die for if necessary—but rather that in today's world with its high stakes there is a great premium on each person attempting to understand one's own preconceptions and how they interact or conflict with the many other cultures and subcultures that together produce the world in which we live. I hope that your MIT education has given you the objectivity and breadth to help yourself, your social group, your profession, your region, your country, and the world to bridge the many intellectual and emotional gaps that make understanding difficult.

Doing this is neither easy nor popular. Think for a moment about the current impasse regarding nuclear power. Here we face both technical issues and questions of value, some of them requiring judgmental resolution rather than analysis—as, for example, what risks are to be tolerated, even how much growth is good for a society, a hidden agenda that frequently emerges when you probe deeply enough into the motivation of some nuclear opponents. Neither side has much tolerance for the other or welcomes efforts to close their cultural gap.

Most current domestic problems involve such conflicts. Economic growth and innovation versus tax and regulating policy, energy versus environmental purity, security versus risk taking, money for arms versus the needs of the cities or the elderly. How people see these issues heavily depends on where they are on the economic and power ladder. How many of us understand and accept the frustrations of the minority members of our own country well enough to make removing these frustrations a continuing part of our lives? Every culture and subculture, including the scientific and technological disciplines, has its conventional wisdoms that provide its structure and cohesion. These conventional wisdoms also create a rigidity that resists change. Our colleague, Professor Thomas Kuhn, has described the difficulty of changing scientific structures—paradigms, firmly held beliefs in science—but that the great leaps in understanding resulted from challenging them, from breaking with conventional wisdoms. Such breaks are also required to make social progress, but are even more difficult in the societal setting than in science.

It takes courage to step outside one's own cultural walls, either as professionals or as citizens. Yet doing this is the key to resolving international conflicts, especially those that could plunge us into a catastrophic war. Yet only by doing this can we hope to find solutions to many of our present domestic problems or the growing discord in the international community.

I have found from long personal experience that trying to understand foreign cultures as a way of helping to resolve conflicts between our country and other nations is a particularly unpopular undertaking. But on the other hand, the successes are especially satisfying. I intend to return to that effort after graduation. I hope you too will find time on your agenda to challenge the multicultural conventional wisdoms that must be bypassed to build a better world and have the courage to be a paradigm smasher if necessary.

Communication Theory and the Learning Process

A speech delivered by Jerry at a meeting of CBS management executives (ADCOM), Westchester Country Club, Rye, New York, October 23, 1980. Jerry and Isaac Asimov, the noted science writer, attended as outside "experts" to address a session focusing on "science and technology, moving from the role and effects of science as a general force to the narrower arena of the new communications technology." Jerry wrote to Asimov beforehand, outlining what he would say:

> *I plan to talk about the experimental nature of the research process and how scientific knowledge spawns technology. I want to focus on what I call the third field of science—the information sciences—i.e., communication theory, the nature of the learning process, and how these ideas are leading to new information systems and to understanding of many of society's problems.*

When I began to think about meeting here with you today, I decided that I had committed what must rank as one of the biggest follies of my lifetime—perhaps not as serious as agreeing to become the 13th president of MIT during the student revolution, or defending nuclear power in a debate with the likes of Jane Fonda, but nonetheless a pretty serious error. I am followed on the platform by a truly unique genius, Isaac Asimov, who is not only a well-known scientist, but the Catfish Hunter of science writers.

Actually he is better than Catfish, for he can pitch fast balls with both hands, so to speak.[1] He is the best, and most prolific, of science expositors; and he is a writer of science fiction "par excellence." How can you beat that combination—explain what's understood, and when you come to the end of knowledge, let your

---

1. Jerry later characterized Asimov's talk as "an entertaining glimpse of the world without schools and (I imagined) without teachers . . . pin[ning] his hopes for a more enjoyable and effective educational process on the use of computers."

imagination carry you onward perhaps with even greater confidence and more interesting results. Incidentally, I am not claiming that science-fiction writing of a sort is unknown among scientists or engineers, but professionally it tends to be frowned upon. In fact, being away from home, I intend to take off from what is known in my own field, the information sciences and science policy, into the realm of speculation.

Today I intend mainly to explore our increasing inability to employ science and technology and their societal role by means of some concepts lifted from the closely related fields: communication theory, the theory of automatic control, learning theory, and a field with the awful name of artificial intelligence. I will try to explain why we seem to have so much trouble understanding and managing contemporary affairs, particularly innovation, in a technologically based industrial society like ours. This will not be a highly technical talk. I should also express the hope that my message carries a particular challenge to all of you because my conclusion—if I may tip my hand—is that I have become convinced that a technological society can only exist in a dynamic state, a continuously adapting condition, requiring good communications, good feedback, between all of its segments. How well the system functions, how smoothly it adjusts to changes and shocks depends upon the effectiveness of its feedback systems and especially on its ability to learn. I will elaborate on this later, but I mention it at the start because you—here at CBS, along with your other media colleagues—provide some of the most important feedback signals and undoubtedly should be presenting more.

So you see that I am using this to try out some of the ideas about technology and society that I have been developing during the past three decades. I am anxious to get feedback from you that I am certain follows.

As some of you know, I started life as a communications engineer who during World War II, while working on radar, was forced to think about how people recognized signals and how random noise impaired the human's ability to perceive and communicate. This brought me into close and continuing contact with the CBS Labs on many important military projects. After World War II, I continued my interest in communications processes in man-made and living systems, a field that my MIT mentor, Norbert Wiener, dubbed "cybernetics." And today I am extending that inquiry into communications processes a bit further.

It is frequently said that the information and knowledge industries are replacing the manufacturing industries in importance, that we are becoming an information society. This is foolishness. While it is obvious that evolving industrial societies require ever increasing amounts of knowledge, information and information processing to keep them progressing, manufacturing must remain a key element of an industrial society. Someone has to make the information processing equipment. But the information explosion will make our factories more productive, partially through the use of intelligent robots. It also should provide us with tools to cope with the increasing number of complex issues we face, such as the worries about developing technological gaps between the United States and other nations, energy shortages, risks posed by technology, preventing nuclear war, etc.

The hallmark of the higher forms of life clearly is their superior information processing ability—their greater ability to learn. Much of the advancing knowledge in the life sciences involves understanding living communication processes, ranging from the exquisite design of life transmitted through the DNA code to the exciting discoveries now taking place about language and how the brain functions. The new recombinant DNA technologies and the emerging industries based upon them are just early stages in man's ability to understand and manipulate the information encoded in the genetic material.

For years scientists have been learning about how the nervous system transmits electrical impulses; how microscopic control elements called neurons act as switching elements and modulators in the nervous system, not wholly unlike semiconductor circuit elements in modern electronic systems; and increasingly how these neural elements are organized to convert light, sound, smell, heat, and touch into electrical messages for the brain to assimilate; how neural feedback circuits control our muscles and allow us to maintain balance and walk and talk; how the brain is organized to make language and do the many other miraculous things it does.

Some of the most exciting and hopeful research being carried out today involves understanding of the brain function and especially, at the moment, the literally dozens—if not hundreds—of complex chemicals that control and modulate the way neural networks function and affect moods, the ability to learn, and memory. This work is but the most recent aspect of a rapidly growing understanding of information processes in living systems. Much is yet to be understood, but so much is happening that workers in these sciences are hopeful that they will have enough knowledge within the next decade to provide help with many present mental health problems, ranging from learning disabilities and memory loss to severe mental disorders. In fact, the present successes of psychopharmacology, achieved with only modest understanding, is an indication of the great potential in this field. Understanding information processes in organisms may hold the key to solving many other health problems as well, such as Parkinson's disease. Cancer is another of the major health challenges in which uncontrolled behavior of some aspect of the information system of individual cells undoubtedly plays a major role.

During the years in which scientists have been deciphering the secrets of living systems, there have been equally exciting developments of man-made communications and information processing systems, starting with the telegraph, the telephone, and wireless transmission, which all seem prosaic today but which first allowed communications over large distances; and the phonograph and motion pictures, which permitted storage of information. Then we moved on to complicated electronic systems ranging in sizes from almost invisible microprocessors that are providing "crude intelligence" for many of our most used products and factory robots, to vast machines that make possible more effective design of complex machines and the management of large systems. In fact, the design of microcomputers has become so complex that the next phase in their evolution may depend upon our ability to employ matching intelligence in their design. In my more fanciful moments, I imagine that at this very moment in time we humans are reenacting the evolutionary unfolding of intelligent systems. Man-made systems are still vastly outclassed by nature's accomplishments, but no one has developed any theoretical bounds that tell us that man-made systems cannot be as good or better than the human mind. Computer scientists spend their recreational time debating this issue—and the question of who will then be master.

Back to more immediate problems . . .

Many commentators on the contemporary scene believe that democratically governed industrial societies are doomed. They believe that the combination of growing resource shortages, especially in energy, overly complex systems proven to be failures, and the growing confrontational style of dealing with societal problems condemns us to a declining future, a view with which I strongly disagree. In fact, I believe and want to convince you that much of the worry, turmoil, and confrontation that exists in industrial societies is a healthy response—a learning response—to the wholly unprecedented set of conditions that can be understood and managed. In fact, I have convinced myself that we are struggling to make a mod two industrial society, eliminating many of the things we don't like or that cannot be sustained on a continuing basis.

Perhaps no issue of our times is more puzzling and more controversial than the role of technology, and perhaps no one has had his nose rubbed in it more than I have. As I said at the start, my present position of spokesman and sometimes defender of American science and technology caused me to think hard about those aspects of technology that are worrying people. These activities have made me especially aware of mankind's total dependence upon the continuing availability of new technology for its wellbeing. I am convinced that—given our present state of societal evolution—only through new knowledge, new approaches, and new technologies can we assure the survival of a satisfactory world. To paraphrase the New Hampshire slogan of live free or die—"invent or die!"

But it is increasingly difficult to develop the needed technologies today. I see two reasons for this: the growing concern about the impact of new technologies which cause many people and organizations to fear and oppose them, and so slow down their realization; and the fact that the growing maturity, size, and complexity of many technological systems make it more difficult—and very much more costly—to develop and build replacements for them as they become necessary. These two phenomena interact to create a situation which does seriously threaten the continued viability of industrial societies and mankind's future. It is my belief that just a widespread understanding of the role of technology in society's evolution will both do much to put these worries in perspective and at the same time provide insights into how to moderate or avoid the most destructive impacts of new things, and make possible the continuity and lead time necessary to create needed replacement technologies.

It is my hope that if more people understand the nature of a modern society, their responses to problems will be much more constructive than they have been in the past. This is the main reason that I am pursuing the rather esoteric ideas which I am discussing.

To help you understand my viewpoint, I need to explore three separate aspects of technology. First, a quick review of the major concerns that people have about technology. Second, a cybernetic view of the role of science and technology in a modern, industrial society which tries to explain why "surprises"—new problems—are part of the process. And third, a very brief look at some of the things being done, or that could be done, to improve the situation.

A state of mind akin to schizophrenia exists in advanced societies with regard to the role of technology. People—perhaps I should say "we"—enthusiastically welcome the benefits, the many ways in which science and technology expand our health, capabilities, opportunities, and comforts. At the same time, we have become deeply aware that too often an exciting new technology leaves unpleasant and unanticipated consequences in its wake. The list of cases where this has happened is very long and well known to all of us. The ever-present specter of catastrophic nuclear war, the life support systems that seem to be too complex to be managed by mere mortals, health hazards from some synthetic products and environmental pollutants, the fear of unemployment caused by growing use of automation, the loss of human skills and capabilities as people are replaced by computers and other information devices, the generalized worry that biological science will create possibilities for manipulating life which humanity is not wise enough to use carefully—you can surely add to this list.

While many people are fearful of new technology, others (including me) are very concerned that because of the many technological, political, and economic constraints, *needed* new technology won't be developed rapidly enough, and we feel that the greatest danger lies here. I have been concerned about this for years. It is now surfacing as certainly the pressing need for new and more environmentally compatible energy technologies, and the consequences of not creating them, is obvious. The worldwide need to limit population growth and provide more and better foods is obvious, too. And the overriding need to find ways of providing a functional education to the youth of the world who are now growing up without it is certainly obvious.

These conflicting viewpoints—too much, or too little technology—should make it clear why it is so hard to form a consensus about anything involving new technology.

It is frequently said that the highly industrialized nations of the world have entered a new phase in their evolution, sometimes described as the "post-industrial society." I object to this characterization of the situation, as I implied earlier, for it seems to say that the technological-industrial phase of societal development is behind us and the service and intellectual activities are the only waves of the future. The need for new technologies and new industries to sustain our economy is certainly clear. Yet, whatever the name, something is different in a technologically mature society. During the early stages of industrialization, the introduction of technology created a better life for the typical person along with major unexpected changes in the lifestyle and environment that we are still trying to accommodate. Now in the industrialized nations, new technologies must increasingly be put to work just to maintain the status quo or improve it slowly. Serious discontinuities in advanced societies are more likely to be degenerative in character, and the result of a failure to have such new technologies available when needed, than from the unanticipated results of wholly new technologies.

So, we are engaged in two quite separate, though deeply intertwined efforts. On the one hand, we are attempting to maintain the present level of wellbeing, and on the other we are trying to push forward the quality of life they provide, to improve the physical, environmental, and living conditions of everyone. Much of our current confusion stems from the fact that the two goals are pursued simultaneously and frequently are to some degree in conflict. We see this clearly in the conflict between the goals of assuring adequate energy sources and the preservation of the environment. Almost all of the efforts to provide a better environment conspire to slow down the availability of such new sources. The necessity of working out a compromise is obvious. Better still would be the development of environmentally compatible technologies so that the uneasy compromises are not necessary. We will ultimately do this.

So we have to focus on two goals simultaneously, giving a high priority to societal survival, to maintaining what we have *while* at the same time attempting to improve conditions.

Now for my explanation of what's going on, seen from a communications theory viewpoint. Two concepts derived from man-made information systems have helped me understand the complex set of issues we face and have convinced me that the continuous emergence of unanticipated problems and efforts to solve them is a permanent but manageable aspect of modern life. They also gave me some clues about how to better manage our affairs by providing more timely and appropriate information. In fact, I am convinced that just an explanation of how society works, like that I am struggling to produce, would ease the trauma and help us deal with specific issues.

Here are my propositions: A modern society is a learning machine trying to invent ways, technical and social, to better satisfy the goals and needs of its members and at the same time solve the many unexpected problems that arise as we go along. It is a very complex, dynamic system, needing to evolve continuously in order to maintain an equilibrium with both the natural and the man-made world, much as a person must continuously adjust his muscles to stand erect. Except, once a man has learned to walk, he does it automatically most of the time, at least when he's on familiar ground, while a modern society is exploring new terrain most of the time.

These characteristics of societies are relatively new, having become dominant aspects of life only during the past half century. Though societies have long been evolving in a manner which can be characterized as learning, it is only within the past century that mankind became fully conscious of the opportunities of using machines to multiply his capabilities and created research and development enterprises—research centers—dedicated solely to producing these machines. This has greatly accelerated the learning process, but at the same time amplified the tensions that learning and adjustments always entail.

We now know that process of technical evolution and growth generates many unpleasant side effects that have to be endured or corrected, often by people who had nothing to do with their creation. One example of this is the many chemical dumps left over from a time when we did not understand fully the health hazards of many chemical wastes, or when there were few automobiles or electrical power plants the pollution from them was so small that no one worried about it. Now pollution seriously affects our lives and we must replace the many polluting devices we have built with ones that treat the environment more considerately. It is important to recognize that these problems resulted from ignorance, not malice, and that we are haltingly stressfully learning to prevent such things from happening again.

Furthermore, in our lifetimes the many components of an industrial society have become so large and closely coupled, i.e., interactive, that the behavior of each part seriously affects the others. Only three or four decades ago this was rather unimportant. These situations have developed quickly and, not surprisingly, caused a great deal of turmoil and anxiety. The fact is that we are beginning to understand how to make assessments of the impact of new technologies before they overwhelm us, how to provide early warning of undesired effects so that the responses are not too slow and painful, and we are even now making many of the needed corrections.

I hope that this discussion has convinced you that a technologically based society must evolve continuously, regardless of its social and economic system. It is and must be a dynamic learning system, in a continuing state of change and evolution, requiring new technologies and new organization forms, new relationships, and probably even new lifestyles as it evolves. If we accept this situation, we should spend our time and energies not in recrimination but in seeking ways to manage the processes better, with less strain and trauma—basically trying to improve information handling and learning properties rather than engaging in confrontations and searching for a scapegoat for the problems, as we do now.

Many people, perhaps most, will find this viewpoint troublesome, for they have been hoping that the world might one day—sooner rather than later—approach a steady state in which change, and especially technologically induced change, would cease. Sad to say, we must accept the fact that there is not likely to be—in our lifetimes—a stable state in the sense that new problems and new opportunities will cease to arise or new and better solutions are found to old problems.

The real issue is how to improve the learning properties of our society. This starts with improved education at all levels. It also involves improved processes of recognizing incipient problems and it finally becomes a question of how to create an intelligent public dialogue on the choices that exist.

Can we identify the properties of a good learning system? The work I referred to in my introduction provides us with many clues. The most important fact is that all learning involves trial and error. Start with what we know and do intelligently chosen experiments. But in spite of our best efforts, first tries, second and even third tries will miss the mark to some degree, but that's the only way to learn. In order to judge the outcome of an experiment, one must have goals and standards. If not, it is impossible to judge an outcome except perhaps intuitively.

From the studies of living and man made systems that I reviewed briefly at the beginning, we can get some important guidance about what makes good societal learning strategies. They should be able to carry out many experiments simultaneously so as to gather information quickly. The experiments should be as small as is compatible with the problem, so that potential errors don't cause major dislocations. The error detection system—whatever it is—should be sensitive so that errors don't become large before they are recognized, and the feedback loop should respond quickly so that the corrections are made rapidly. In an automatic control system, such as a power steering device, information that arrives too late actually causes the system to oscillate violently. We can often see this phenomenon in the society.

It is interesting to note that by these criteria, the free market, where profit or loss provides the feedback signal, is a very effective learning machine for those things that are appropriate to the marketplace and responsive to individual initiative, because here decisions are made automatically. Unfortunately, there are few truly free markets today because of government regulation, etc. In the public sector the feedback signals are fuzzy. Rather than simple profit-or-loss, the major feedback signal in business, in the public sector they are ordinarily value judgments that widely vary among the various groups involved. What are the goals of a given agency or program? Who sets them? Who judges the results? When do you change an obviously failing experiment? Can we afford their projects, etc.? Last night George Ball described the economic difficulties of the Soviet Union. Since it is all public sector, the reason should be obvious.

If the vague nature of the feedback signal wasn't trouble enough, in the public sector each experiment tends to be very large and so response times are long; consequently, the number of experiments in search of a solution to a given problem that can be carried out in a given period of time is small. This also slows down the learning process, in contrast to competitive business where the many relatively small competitive units rapidly find out what will work. All of these factors taken together allow (perhaps even require) the public sector errors to become very large before corrective actions are taken. You can see this clearly in the problems of risk, one of our major problems today. What is the risk posed by a new technology? How much risk should we accept? What are people prepared to pay for greater safety? In fact, who makes the choice? These decisions must be made by the political process, and at the moment take much too long.

If we accept these characteristics of modern societies, then the task before us is clear, if not easy. We need to get people to improve the effectiveness of the societal learning and communications processes.

Here, we have two major communications or information tasks. The first, a general one. We must get the public (as well as ourselves) to understand that a technological society by its very nature always encounters problems and challenges, requiring much of our attention and resources. In other words, that science cannot create a steady state, problem-free utopia, and that we must be alert to catch new problems early and seek solutions to them diligently. Right now the process is so poor that problems must become very threatening or annoying before they are given any attention. Second, we must find a way to enhance the effectiveness of the learning process itself so that delays and fluctuations are made smaller.

This task itself will involve research and development, both technical and social. Here again, we have two problems. The first is that of evaluating potential risks so that decisions can be made on a rational basis. The second task is to develop better means of making decisions when the facts exist. Today, we often try to make decisions without the data. Given an adequate understanding, there is then a need to disseminate the knowledge widely to the interested public and to the persons with special responsibilities for decisions. This is perhaps the hardest problem of all, as I am sure you know. Here again we have a complex set of problems, short and long-range.

The public understanding of science and technology is almost non-existent. This is part of the pervasive crisis in education that leaves a large portion of our youth unprepared for work in a modern society, let alone to become enlightened citizens. This is even more of a problem in the third world. I am hopeful that a better understanding of learning processes combined with modern information and computer technologies will provide a major breakthrough in this area—but that's the subject for another talk.

The immediate problem presents challenges on the many fronts—energy, environment, chemical wastes, innovation and productivity, management of the economy, and you could add many to this list. An attempt to understand any one of these areas would show that there are large areas of disagreement about the nature of the problem and what is possible. Energy is perhaps the best example. There are proponents and opponents of almost every option. There is so much noise that no one can recognize the signal. For example, some scientists and economists maintain that conservation alone would solve our energy problems. While conservation would clearly help, we also need new domestic energy sources. The public is bombarded with so much contradictory information that decision making is almost impossible. The networks, including yours, have tried hard to explain the facts and show what can be done.

But, there is a real mismatch between the complicated message and the typical citizen. If you dig just a bit, you find that the technical people don't have adequate answers to many of the questions, and so we must make decisions that have potential risks go away as a consequence of further study and research—or they might loom larger.

The uncertainties of the nuclear power option are now well known. But how many people know that using fossil fuel at the current rate might cause major changes in the weather within the century? There are many similar questions on which we have contradictory voices. Many groups are starting to study the questions and new information is constantly being generated, but there is no adequate process for integrating what we know or communicating it. The congressional Office of Technology Assessment (OTA) is trying to do this. So are the energy policy centers at many universities. Many congressional committees also follow aspects of this issue, but in a fragmented way.

I leave you with a question not an answer—WE NEED A PROCESS.

Disenthralling Ourselves

A speech given by Jerry at the National Academy of Sciences, Washington, D. C., April 28, 1984.

✳

For this talk I have taken a title from Lincoln, who led us in a crisis where the issues of slavery and freedom had the same desperate meaning for those times as nuclear weapons have for ours. In his famous message to Congress on December 1, 1862, Lincoln wrote "the dogmas of the quiet past are inadequate to the stormy present. The occasion is piled high with difficulty, and we must rise with the occasion. As our case is new, so we must think anew and act anew. We must disenthrall ourselves."

Lincoln's advice is very relevant today. Disenthrall ourselves we must, not from old dogmas, but from new ones that some of us here tonight even helped create.

I have been worrying a lot about what I would say tonight and how to say it. For one thing, there is the problem of compressing almost 40 years of learning about the arms race into 30 minutes. But that's not really the problem. How do I convey a message that might seem to go against the grain of a deep feeling we all share— a passionate loyalty to the United States as a land of freedom and equality—while at the same time conveying my deeply held conviction that as a first step in moving ourselves from the brink of annihilation, we must discard several notions deeply etched in our collective minds? Doing this, as difficult and unpopular as it may be, represents the ultimate test of dedication to our American ideals.

We must first of all appreciate the extent to which the United States has been running an arms race with itself and in the process has become a military culture. This and what we might do about it are my messages for tonight. In the anarchistic world in which we live, there remains the need for a strong, effective military to defend our country and its freedoms, so our difficult task is the one of finding the balance between that which is essential and the infinite demands of a self-stimulating nuclear arms race.

We need to accept the fact that despite President Eisenhower's 1961 warning about the growing influence of the military-industrial complex in our society, it has grown even more powerful in the years since then. President Eisenhower's talk reflected his frustration and inability to control the combined impact of the military, industrial, congressional, journalistic, and veterans organizations' pressure on issues of military procurement or efforts to seek accommodations with the Russians.

As a member of the President's Science Advisory Committee, I saw firsthand how individuals from government and industrial military establishments collaborated with members of Congress to defeat the president's efforts. The neutron bomb, peaceful uses of nuclear explosions, and cheating by testing behind the moon and even the sun were just a few of the arguments used to kill the nuclear test-ban negotiations. Exaggerated estimates of the Soviet nuclear bomb stockpile and delivery system strength were also used several times to justify unneeded U.S. strategic forces. Interestingly, at no time when the truth was discovered did the creators of those distorted predictions show any concern about the unnecessary buildup they had stimulated or propose that the United States revise its objectives so as to limit the level of the U.S. and USSR nuclear threats.

Last summer I spoke to an individual who had been one of the most articulate alarmists about the bomber gap and asked him why he hadn't revised his view of the Soviet threat when the facts became known. He answered that he had always been certain that they would eventually present a nuclear threat to the U.S., and he didn't want to make it too easy for them. He, even now, isn't willing to admit that our enormous buildup had anything to do with that of the Soviet Union.

President Kennedy, too, had to contend with much opposition when he continued President Eisenhower's effort to achieve a halt to nuclear testing. In fact, the opposition to his efforts was much more intense than that faced by President Eisenhower, because it appeared that his efforts might just succeed. Similar pressure caused Kennedy to build a much larger Minuteman missile force than was necessary even after photo reconnaissance made it clear that the feared "missile gap" did not exist.

I can document similar pressures on subsequent presidents. For example, President Johnson attempted to buy a modest-sized ABM system to protect the country from a Chinese missile attack and, incidentally, himself from an increasing attack by Republicans during the 1968 presidential election. President Carter yielded on the MX in the hope of getting the SALT II treaty through the Congress.

But such pressure groups no longer operate on the president at the present time. The current president not only accepts the ideas of the groups that Eisenhower warned us against, he has become their most articulate spokesman—espousing an enormous buildup in U.S. military power, especially nuclear fighting power, while making a shambles of arms-control efforts. What's more, his administration is largely made up of like-minded people, so he is not apt to hear a dissenting voice from within.

Yet a large number of people continue to worry about the militarization of the nation. For example, recently two respected West Coast newspapers examined the influence of the weapons industry on U.S. defense policy and had some harsh things to say. In July of 1983, the *Los Angeles Times* published a sixteen-page special report entitled "Servants or Masters." In an accompanying editorial, the newspaper said: "Two decades ago Dwight D. Eisenhower warned Americans not to let what he called the military-industrial complex come to dominate their lives and dictate their futures. The nation was not listening. And today a network of defense producers, the Pentagon, and Congress bends policy to its will, as he said it would. In every city, every statehouse, every office of the federal government." It went on to say: "What would surprise Eisenhower, as it does us, is the findings of the Times investigators that the military-industrial complex has burrowed so deeply into the very fabric of America without even producing reliable and affordable weapons for defense against aggression."

In a more recent report (April 7, 1984) the *San Francisco Examiner*, reporting on the successful effort to sell the B-1 bomber, details a history of fraud by the manufacturer in which funds for space shuttle and other government projects were used to keep the project alive after it had been shut off by the Carter administration. The story went on to outline the company's strategy of placing contracts so widely that almost every state and hamlet had a stake in the B-1's future. Even though it is generally agreed to be unneeded, the campaign succeeded. According to the paper, the average take per state on the B-1 was $700 million, and the states of the twenty senators who lobbied hardest for the aircraft were scheduled to get sums ranging from $1 to $9 billion. Even more disturbing to me is the fact that labor unions and chamber of commerce groups lobby vigorously for the unneeded and marginally useful aircraft at a time when budget deficits are destroying our economy and the infrastructure of the society.

This mad action is only possible because we, the citizens of the nation, permit it. It's no longer a question of controlling a military-industrial complex, but rather, how to keep the United States from becoming a totally military culture. That's why we must take Lincoln's advice to heart and reexamine the fundamental assumptions that motivate us, challenge the dogmas that account for our fatalistic acceptance of the arms race, and in doing so, recognize the significant role that the United States has played in its existence.

I have collected some data which compares the relative sizes of the opposing nuclear weapons and delivery systems since the early days of the Cold War, so that you can see the distortions I have been talking about. I will first run through the slides quickly so you can see the trends from the early days until the present, and then I will examine in detail significant points at each end, noting in passing significant turning points along the way.

These slides, that show the relative force levels through the years, perhaps best illustrate the extent to which the United States has been setting the pace of the nuclear arms race. For our first look, let's examine the bomber gap. I used to believe that our misestimate of Soviet bomber capability was the result of poor intelligence

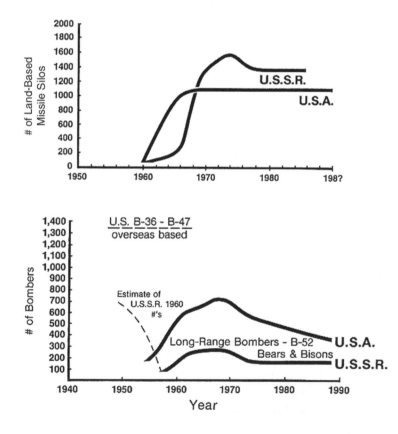

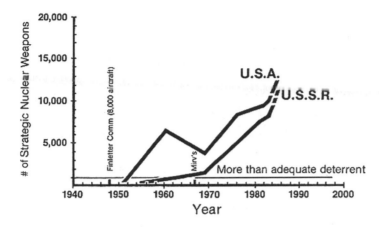

estimates. Recent information now makes it seem more like a case of deliberate deception.

In 1950 the Air Force, after a study of the aircraft industry, concluded that it would require 18 million pounds of aircraft production per year to maintain adequate military production readiness. Soon thereafter, on April 19, 1951, Secretary Stuart Symington told Congress that "the Russians possess air equipment capable of delivering a surprise attack against any part of the United States, and this country has no adequate defense against such an assault." He said that the USSR "has an airforce whose strength in nearly all categories is now the largest in the world and growing larger month by month." Such statements mobilized many of us for work on U.S. defenses. On July 14, a Senate Appropriations Subcommittee was urged to drive toward a 150-group air force in 3 years instead of the 87 groups it already had at an estimated cost of $96 billion. Secretary Finletter not only supported the buildup but urged a major buildup in the production of fissionable material. *The Congressional Record* reported that "the testimony of all witnesses except those speaking for the Department of the Navy was so uniformly of a classified nature that it does not lend itself to publication in any form." Yet most of the testimony regarding the extent of the threat quickly found itself into the *New York Times* and *Washington Post*.

At the other end of the time scale, let's look at the recent "window of vulnerability" scare which served as the rationale for building the MX missile. A careful examination of the arguments put forth by the Committee on the Present Danger showed that their scenario was wrong in many ways. They concerned themselves with only the land-based portion of the U.S. strategic triad. Furthermore, they assumed that a massive Soviet first strike involving the accurate coordination of hundreds of missiles and thousands of warheads in an attack that had never been practiced would work as predicted. The experimenters in this group know how likely that is.

But the crowning absurdity showed up when I made some calculations about the proposed attack. The attack presumed a two-for-one attack on each of the U.S. land-based missile sites, which therefore required 2,200 Soviet warheads. If the attack was entirely successful, it would have destroyed about 2,000 U.S. nuclear weapons, thus putting the Soviet Union in a somewhat worse position regarding the nuclear weapons balance than they had been in before. I know that if a member of the committee I am criticizing were here he would argue that the Soviets would still have more highly accurate missiles than the United States and that the USSR's weapons were larger, etc.; but he could hardly argue that the many thousands of U.S. weapons left would not be able to decimate the initiators of such an attack many times over.

More than 35 years of confrontational language has created a situation in which it is difficult to talk rationally about how we got here even among ourselves. A combination of new-speak words, false information, half-baked ideas about successful preemptive attacks, winning nuclear wars, and clairvoyant projections of Soviet forces and objectives mask the opportunities for experimenting with alternatives. Dependence upon such ideas as worst-case analysis, for example, supported by controlled leaks of secret information have made possible the manipulation of what we think and made it easy for Americans to deny any responsibility for the arms race, to believe that the Russians are relentless and reckless aggressors and thus choose to conclude that there is nothing we can do to stop the catastrophe we see coming.

In spite of this history, we obviously have to deal with the problem in terms of today's reality, but I would hope with more understanding and openness. First of all, as I said earlier, we need to disenthrall ourselves of a sense of innocence and appreciate the extent to which our combination of fears and overwhelming technical and economic strength have caused our country to be a leading force in the arms race, and therefore find ways of using these same strengths and energies to take the lead in ending it. We need to abandon the hope that innovative technology can make it possible to win a nuclear war or protect a nation involved in one from annihilation. We must also abandon the belief that there are no reasonable alternatives to the arms race. We must disabuse ourselves of the belief that understanding the forces driving the arms race and the alternatives to the arms race is beyond the comprehension of non-expert citizens. Most of all we must become convinced that at this moment in the history of our truly democratic nation, it has been overtaken by a social cancer from which only mass understanding and action can save it. Only through the continuing involvement of great numbers of informed and dedicated individuals do we have any hope of rescuing ourselves and all of humanity from ultimate destruction.

It is encouraging to see that a large number of people recognize this. In recent years there has been a growing involvement of people in all walks of life in the efforts to find alternate national security measures. There is an explosion of anti-nuclear groups whose strength flows from an inner conviction that the present course is wrong and dangerous. Perhaps most important of all, we are witnessing the emergence, as dissenters, of increasing numbers of former insiders and experts whose professional loyalty to the "establishment" has, until recently, made them reluctant to speak out against policies that worried them. More and more civilian and military officials of the past are expressing disagreement with the current national defense policies. This development is very important because the uninformed citizen needs the information and intellectual support that such insiders provide—support, that is, for their commonsense judgments and intuitions.

You've been listening all day to discussion about fantastically elaborate and overwhelmingly powerful systems of thermonuclear weapons and counter-weapons that now dominate our thinking, our actions, and our psyches. But at the end of the story it must be obvious to you that survival is not primarily a technological story at all, even though we recognize the technological component to be the problem and that it began with technological challenges, the nuclear bomb, and intercontinental delivery systems. If we are going to get out of the tragic, frightening, appalling situation which we and the Russians have created for ourselves and all of our companions on this globe, we are going to have to change our mode of thinking to include issues that lie at the root of human behavior and are basically social, cultural, historical, moral, ethical, economic, and psychological.

The nuclear bomb stubbornly remains the terror weapon wise men saw it to be at its birth. The default solution of the frustrated hordes of so-called experts has been to continue the arms race in the futile hope that a magic solution will appear. Einstein once said that God would not shoot dice with the universe. Man should not play such games either. That's why we need so desperately to rethink our premises and priorities, why we need to stop amassing nuclear destructive power.

When I talk about this subject, I am often told that it is too complicated for the average person to understand, and so even though they are frightened by what they see and hear, they have no choice but to accept what the "experts" say. These people are wrong on two counts. First, on the issues that really matter, there are no experts. Second, those issues can indeed be understood by almost everyone. Anyone can understand the important facts if he is willing to make a sustained effort to do so.

Just a few hours of study and discussion a week can make a person knowledgeable, if not expert, and a truly knowledgeable citizenry will lead to sounder national policies.

People should realize that there are no experts on nuclear war. No one knows how to use nuclear weapons. While there are thousands of experts on technical matters and on military hardware, on the critical issues of strategy, tactics, deterrents, war-winning, etc., there are truly no experts. *None*! No one knows for sure about the actual field performance of missiles, their reliability, or their accuracy. Because it is impossible to test nuclear weapons systems in realistic conditions, uncertainty about their performance in combat predominates even more than for individual components.

There has never been a war, even a tiny one, in which tactical or strategic weapons were used by both sides. Planners are, therefore, completely dependent on theory to support their strategies. Analysts and military officers who plan for the use of conventional weapons can draw on past experience as well as conduct more or less realistic field exercises to test their ideas about the use of new weapons or tactics. Because there has never been a nuclear war, or even one nuclear weapon fired at another, all scenarios discussed with such solemnity by so-called "experts" are based entirely on speculation.

To be sure, the analysts use computer models as a substitute to real experience, but the predictions from such models are totally dependent on the assumptions— guesses—put into models by the analysts. Such questions as the reliability of missiles when operated by soldiers instead of trained technicians and fired by hundreds or thousands instead of singly, the reliability of the command and control system, the accuracy of guidance systems, certain knowledge of the location of the targets, and estimates of the target vulnerability are among the many unknowable factors.

Even when computers are used to design comparatively simple physical systems, such as power systems or aircraft or computers, a certain amount of trial and error is necessary to correct for unanticipated deficiencies. But how can this technique be applied to modeling a massive nuclear war in which there can only be one trial? I doubt that anyone would agree to rerun it to take advantage of the lessons learned the first time.

The layman who argues for a nuclear freeze or a test ban or some other logical arms-limitation measure is frequently put down because he lacks secret information. There are no secrets on the vital issues that determine the course of the arms race. Each citizen should realize that on the critical issues of what constitutes enough, what is a deterrent, etc., his or her judgments are as good as those of a

The Board of Directors
of the **ARMS CONTROL
ASSOCIATION** hereby bestows the
WILLIAM C. FOSTER AWARD
on

Dr. Jerome B. Wiesner

For his longtime service, as a public official, scientist, and private citizen, toward the goal of peace. Dr. Wiesner has long been an eloquent spokesman on behalf of international nuclear arms control negotiations. His active role in the establishment of the Arms Control and Disarmament Agency, the achievement of the Limited Test Ban Treaty and the successful effort in the past to restrict the deployment of antiballistic missile systems will long be remembered with respect and admiration. The Arms Control Association is privileged to present this commendation to a man who has devoted his life's work to achieve a world of peace, Dr. Jerome B. Wiesner.

Presented this day, the twenty-ninth of November, nineteen hundred and eighty four.

Gerard C. Smith
CHAIRMAN

Herbert Scoville, Jr.
PRESIDENT

Barry E. Carter
VICE PRESIDENT AND TREASURER

Betty Lall
SECRETARY

Marjorie Benton
William T. Coleman, Jr.
Lloyd Cutler
Sidney D. Drell
Randall Forsberg
Noel Gayler
Benjamin Huberman
Thomas L. Hughes

Bobby R. Inman
Robert C. Johansen
Henry Kendall
Arthur Krim
Robert S. McNamara
William F. McSweeny
Joseph Martin, Jr.
Saul H. Mendlovitz

Edward P. Morgan
Stanley R. Resor
John B. Rhinelander
Sargent Shriver
Marshall Shulman
Barbara Stuhler
Paul C. Warnke
Daniel Yankelovich

president or secretary of defense, perhaps even better since he or she is not subjected to all of the confusing pressures that impinge on people in official positions. It is important for citizens to realize that their government has no monopoly on wisdom or special knowledge that changes the commonsense conclusion that nuclear weapons have only one purpose—namely, to prevent their use. But realization is not enough. It must become informed conviction based on personal study.

Many people express a hopelessness because the situation seems too complicated to understand or act upon. They frequently ask how they can become better informed so that they develop confidence in their intuitive judgments. My suggestion is that they involve a few close friends or relatives, say six or eight, in a continuing study group that spends a few hours a week reading and listening to the arguments about the major issues, one at a time, and learn as much as can be known about it before moving on. It won't be long before such a group will be expert enough to understand the arcane language of the expert and have some judgment about what is reasonable and what is exaggeration or untruth in the vital debate about the arms race. At that stage, the group will be in a position to fission—if that expression is permissible here—and begin new groups, continuing until there is a critical mass of citizens to help lead our leaders out of the trap they have dragged us into.

Creating with Computing

In a speech given at the Wiesner Building Dedication Luncheon, October 2, 1985, Jerry explored the complex relationship between human creativity and electronic computation, and how his own perspective on this theme evolved over the years. The Jerome and Laya Wiesner Building—housing the MIT Media Laboratory and the List Visual Arts Center—was named for Jerry and his wife in recognition of their dedicated service to the Institute and their sustained advocacy of communications technologies and the arts.

✷

This day and the event from yesterday keep reminding me of a television program called "This Is Your Life." And I keep wanting to correct the exaggerations that you are hearing, but I will do that another time. There are a few things I would like to say, though. Even those who know us well do not know how important Laya was to my existence at MIT. I was working in Washington for Archibald MacLeish and alternately happy and unhappy in the job of Chief Engineer of the Library of Congress. When World War II began, I began to feel that my job—even though it was helping to set up the Office of Facts and Figures, the U.S. propaganda agency for World War II—was not an adequate technical challenge. All I was doing was signing requisitions to purchase RCA equipment, and I figured anyone could do it because you either bought their equipment or you did not buy anything. Then you did not have any choice, quite a change from today.

One afternoon I received a letter from Sam Goudsmit, a former professor of mine at Michigan, inviting me to join the staff of the MIT Radiation Laboratory. His invitation was stimulated by Professor Louis Smullin, a fellow student with me at Michigan. I wrote a letter saying that I would love to come, but that I was extraordinarily busy. Fortunately, I did not actually send it. I dictated it, so it did not get mailed that afternoon.

Jerry and Laya at the dedication of MIT's Wiesner Building, named "in recognition of their inspired devotion to the Institute and their advocacy of the arts and communications technologies," October 2, 1985. In the background (left to right) are Robert Mann, Kathryn Willmore, and Paul Gray. (Courtesy of the MIT Museum.)

That evening I told Laya about it, and she looked at me with that scowl she can get when she knows what I am doing is foolish, and said, "I thought you wanted to get back to something that was more technical." I only said, "Yes." In the morning I tore up that letter and wrote another to Sam, saying that I would love to come, and here I am. You should all know how important Laya has been to MIT and me since then.

My talk today, "Creating with Computing," started out as "Thinking with Computing," but after a bit of reflection I decided that "Creating with Computing" was more interesting and an easier subject to deal with. Actually, I have concluded that you really cannot deal adequately with either, but I will try. I have written many drafts of this paper. I first wrote it on a computer, and toward the end the young ladies in my office interacted with it to make English out of it. Each time we went through a cycle, they gave it a new name so that we could tell one draft from the other. The one that was put in my briefcase last night had the title "Let's Hope." I suspect that that's not a bad idea for this topic.

The title "Creating with Computing" obviously raises an infinity of questions, such as: "who is creating what and why?" and before that, "what is really meant by the word 'creating'"? I could spend an hour or more researching just that one word—"creating"—a simple word which we have all heard many times and use almost as often. There is no simple definition, however, because it applies to the activities of so many people, each with his or her own idiosyncratic way of working, creating, and thinking. The word includes activities of ingenious, untutored craftsmen and inventors who think in terms of the world in which they have been brought up. This includes varieties of scientists, engineers, and other intellectuals who think in the images and ideas of their very specialized worlds. A chemist, for example, who lives in a world of chemicals, molecular symbols, and spinning atoms thinks and creates in that world. This same perspective also applies to writers, filmmakers, scholars, and just plain human beings. Together they are always creating the future.

Sociologists say that we are living through a second industrial revolution propelled by communications, computers, and control systems. Actually, we have been living through this since the invention of the telegraph and the railroad, but the pace is changing and so is the capability of our machines.

This revolution is basically an information revolution, in contrast with the first industrial revolution in which man expanded his physical capacities, i.e., amplified his muscle power by creating machines that harnessed energy from natural sources—ranging from water power to atomic power—to do much of his work and to vastly expand his mobility. Now we are expanding brain power. The basic goal is the same—to increase human productivity.

The result of these inventions has been a liberation from drudgery and poverty because of this increase in productivity. As I implied earlier, I do not like the word "revolution" because our present industry evolved over a long period of time, and what we are doing is using information processing systems to enhance our skills. When people use the word "revolution," it is because things have happened fast. But the information revolution began more than 100 years ago and is far from exhausted. I think that the most visionary things that we predict now will fall short of what will actually happen. And they will be different. If Tom Watson, the man whose genius made IBM what it is, was here—and I'm sorry he could not come—I would tell you about his prediction in 1947 that the world could probably absorb five computers, but since he's not here I won't mention it.

Today's symposium is examining a facet of that second phase of the continuing industrial revolution. We are leaving out of our discussions such things as robots, bookkeeping machines, and many other computers that have become so important to our society, to concentrate on how we can use them to enhance human creative capabilities. Like the Media Laboratory itself, today's symposium is intended to explore the scope and potential of the emerging areas of information technology, broadly speaking, in communications and computing.

Because Walter Rosenblith has already told you about our interaction with Norbert Wiener at the end of World War II, I will save a little time and mention him only briefly. Our eyes were opened to the central role of communications by Norbert. I began to see the whole world as a communication process. Even the electron circling the proton, after all, needs information to keep it there.

"The Thinking Machine"—David Wayne interviews Jerry for a program on developments in computer science, presented by CBS Television in association with MIT, October 26, 1960. "I hope," Jerry told Wayne, "that through [computers] we will learn to understand the working of man's brain . . . and that with this understanding, we can help mankind to make a better world than we've made muddling through without thinking—by machine, or much by people, for that matter." (Courtesy of the MIT Museum.)

This was an upsetting thing for me when I worked in Washington, because I came to see that all social processes were communication processes. One day President Kennedy said to me, "Why were you smiling when we were talking about that terrible disaster we were facing?" I said, "I didn't realize that I was smiling," and he said, "What were you thinking about?" I told him my view, that individuals and all societies are really communicating systems. I repeated Wiener's phrase, "If it wasn't for communications and information, life itself could not exist." I guess I was dreaming about how we were dealing with an information process that was inadequate. It had too much delay and we were two years too late to find an adequate solution. The feedback had been so slow that the government was now trying to contend with a problem that was impossible to solve, so we just had to live with the disaster—similar to today's situation with South Africa. We were not perceptive enough to notice it early enough to do something about it in time.

I think that illustrates the problem of our society. It has become more complex as the scale of all of its parts has grown, and as faster transportation and communication have effectively shrunk it. The world is struggling to somehow learn how to keep the magnitude of the error excursions down.

The Media Laboratory is a product of the MIT culture. In the Institute's tradition, it is exploring the creative tools and ideas of the future. The Media Lab is a place where creative and curious people are exploring uses of electronic and other media. The Laboratory facility is a direct consequence of the establishment of the Council for the Arts by alumni and friends over a decade ago to nourish the arts at MIT. At its initial meeting, two distinguished poets—Stanley Kunitz and Archibald MacLeish—challenged us to see science and the arts as a part of the total human experience. Kunitz said, "There are many disciplines, but only one imagination." That statement has continued to resonate in my head as we talked about what we were doing in the Laboratory about educational reform, and as we explore the goals of a good education. What he implied was that the head can store many different kinds of information, but somehow it has only one organ for bringing it all together. To me, that means that the more you have—the more different things you have in your head—the more you understand the totality of life's potential experiences, and the greater chance you have of being a creative, contributing citizen. Archibald MacLeish pushed us further, when he argued that humanity could only be saved by bringing science and the arts together again. That's a big order. He was obviously looking back to the 19th-century humanist-scientist who was able to encompass all that was known. We will have to do a lot of consolidating and learning to recapture that ideal state. Maybe the Media Laboratory will move us toward that goal.

The electronic information revolution started rather innocently with the invention of the telegraph with its dots and dashes. Then came the telephone and electrical transmission of voice, followed by the wireless and picture transmission devices including television. These systems have provided humans with global communication capabilities. But these were all passive devices, primarily able to transmit a telegraph signal, an image, or a voice from one place to another to extend the range of the human senses.

The electronic computer provided a very different capability which some people recognized very early. With its information manipulation capability, it provided a means to expand mental powers and to do many mental-like tasks. That is what is meant by the term "the second industrial revolution." Without the ability to manipulate, store, and find information, we would have a very different and simpler information industry.

We are just at the beginning of the development of information systems. We face the challenge of creating much more effective and powerful systems, and also adapting them to the many industrial, educational, and social opportunities, changes, and problems that they will leave in their wake.

One of the aspects of information and computing developments which is particularly intriguing to me, which I first learned about through Norbert Wiener's interests, is that many of the technical developments in information systems mimic living systems so that, in a sense, we are retracing nature's invention of information and control systems, but with different components. Twenty years ago, nature's were better; now the man-made elements may be. One should not be surprised that we are mimicking living systems, not only because they are the only systems that we know, but because information systems must be compatible with human systems.

Some people may be offended when I say that I think that man-made components are better than biological elements. But consider the facts; electrical signals travel a million times faster than signals on nerve fibers, and semiconductors operate millions of times faster than neurons—the biological information processing elements—and they are also more reliable. But nature has one large edge—maybe a decisive edge—in design complexity, involving both the individual elements and the number of elements that it can effectively organize in a system. Man may never match these elements in an electrical system. We may never match the systems' complexity either. Nature may always retain this edge, who knows? But, the man-made systems enhance human creative capacities, that is all they do, they cannot displace them.

Some cognitive and computer scientists are having an exciting time trying to understand and imitate human reasoning with computing systems, and though they can do a few things that would be regarded as thinking if done by a human, they differ among themselves about whether or not machines with human thinking and creative ability are ever possible. Even in the so-called "artificial intelligence" field, which prompted Walter Rosenblith to say that he preferred "natural stupidity," people usually only try to capture the knowledge and skills of humans. I do not think that that is what Marvin Minsky had in mind when he began his work. It is perfectly clear that such machines—thinking machines, creative machines—do not exist now.

Many people—perhaps many of you—worry about the day when machines are better thinkers than the best humans, and whether they will then displace humans in their most advanced roles, perhaps even telling humans what to do. That possibility seems remote at the moment.

I believe that I am on safe ground if I say that, for the moment, neither the process of thinking nor the act of creation is really understood. So, I can simplify this discussion by eliminating any attempt to explore either the act of creation itself or machines that can think and concentrate on the many ways in which the combination of computing and communication, as we know it, may evolve in the decades ahead and, in the process, expand the human creative capacity.

Arthur Koestler, in his book *The Act of Creation*, argued quite convincingly that novel creations of the mind required the intersection of two normally unrelated sets of ideas or mental fields. And that is why, he says, most creative products from puns and jokes to great music, art, scientific discoveries, or engineering creations, share one feature—they all provide an element of joy when they are experienced. I believe that the role of man-machine systems, and thus the role of the Media Laboratory, is to increase the mental fields available to an individual and so increase the probability that the exploring human mind will find productive intersections.

This morning Sherry Turkle expanded my vision of the problem by pointing out that human beings have mismatched input and output systems. The visual system takes in information at a fantastic rate, and when we try to record that same information or put it out, we use the part of the human system that did not evolve for rapid transmission of information. In fact, the untrained individual cannot transmit the visual images he stores, and even the most skilled artist takes much longer to transmit than to receive an image. Similarly, the human mind is limited in the amount of data on which it can focus or manipulate. So, in a sense, we are trying to connect that mismatch and make it possible for the human creative mind to get information faster, use it more effectively, and by graphic systems make it possible to share images with others. Seymour Papert, in exploring computer-based education, is also trying to enhance the ability of individuals to learn to use their natural information processing capability.

Koestler's insight into the creative process is supported by an examination of creativity in most areas from the work of artists, writers, scientists, or engineers, and is based upon familiar themes and available information. Most novels have, I believe, an element of autobiography, or at least biography. Artists have styles from which they find it hard to escape. In a sense, these are transfer functions that are their signatures. Scientists tend to use the same techniques and approaches that were successful on earlier problems even when the new ones are very different, even when their efforts fail.

It should be clear by now why I avoided any extensive attempt to explore the act of creation itself or machines that can think. There is a big enough challenge in just exploring the ways in which the combination of computing and communications—as we know it and expect it to evolve—can vastly expand the individual human creative capacity.

Computing can aid the creative process in several distinct ways. First, by vastly expanding the scope of the traditional creative activities (for example, by making possible calculations that far exceed unaided human capacity, by searching indexes and storing and retrieving large information sets, and so on). Anyone as old as I am remembers the computing room, full of faculty wives who manually turned cranks of mechanical calculators to the tune of handwritten programs prepared by scientists or engineers who were trying to get information out of numbers provided by their experiments or theories. That process drastically limited the scope of scientific inquiry and scientific design. That limitation was accepted as a fact of life. Today it has almost disappeared, but not quite. That is why there will always be super-computers. The human mind will always devise a problem that is bigger than the tools available. And I am sure that the computer inventors and manufacturers will always respond happily. But the fact is that very few scientific analysis or engineering design problems are now limited by computing power. The limitation today is more at the conceptual stage—organizing the complex problems.

The second contribution of the information sciences, one I have already alluded to, is providing new cognitive tools and new models for thinking about problems that involve information such as understanding speech, or genetic codes, or the functioning of complex living systems—including, for example, thinking and creative processes themselves. There are many other examples of this, such as the economic models that so many economists make which provide a basis for thinking about problems where symbols and their relationship—their identity, rather than their physical properties—are significant.

And, finally, computers encourage new media and techniques to be used in the creative processes with an open-ended future. The computer gives us opportunities to explore information processes and challenges us to understand how to use them more effectively in expanding the human creative power.

The Rise and Fall of the President's Science Advisory Committee

A speech given by Jerry at the Cosmos Club, Washington, D.C., April 27, 1987, when he received the Cosmos Club Award, for "leadership in communications technology, federal science policy, and science and technology education."

Few institutions of the federal government have had as rapid a rise to prominence and lapse into oblivion as the President's Science Advisory Committee (PSAC). Few institutions have been punished as thoroughly for doing a good job. And few institutions are needed more right now. The position of the president's special assistant for science and technology still exists, but it has been reduced to a meaningless role. Recent administrations have rejected the use of a formal science advisory committee altogether, and have made other arrangements to assist the president on technical matters. The current administration, for example, depends more upon the agencies that sponsor individual programs to evaluate them, and on an inchoate collection of informal advisors.

In this talk, I am going to examine the costs to the nation of the rise and demise of the President's Science Advisory Committee and the diminished role of the president's science adviser with regard to presidential decision-making, and show why some form of thorough institutionalized review process is necessary to assist the president in the management of the nation's scientific enterprise. In our form of government, the president is the only official who represents the nation as a whole. He must play a central role in balancing the priorities of the nation and especially those aspects that are dominated by the federal government, as is the case with science and technology. The kind of assistance he has in making these decisions determines the thrust and the quality of the scientific and technical programs. It is vital that it be sound and, as far as possible, objective.

A flood of recent events and problems are directly traceable to the absence of a presidential advisory group: the Challenger disaster, the unproven and exaggerated claims about military inferiority and need for excessive amounts of new military technology and hardware, the exaggerated claims of Soviet cheating on arms agreements, the disregard by the responsible agencies of serious environmental and public health problems, and the loss of competitiveness of much of American industry. Vital decisions that will not only shape the long-range future of the U.S. but of the world are being deferred or undertaken without adequate debate or regard for their impact on other programs. Environmental destruction is an example of decisions deferred; vast expenditures for SDI, decisions inadequately considered. Many technical programs are operating without careful, knowledgeable supervision, and thus fail or at least waste large sums of money. The Packard Commission, appointed by President Reagan to examine Pentagon operations, made these points emphatically.

It may be sheer coincidence, but the disintegration of the U.S. space program, sliding from a position of world leadership to one of embarrassment, has paralleled the decline of presidential science advising. Last year American space scientists had to send their instruments for investigating Halley's Comet on Soviet space probes, and American companies wanting to launch communication satellites are looking to European companies for launchings. Even more serious in the long run than the deterioration of the space program, much of U.S. industry, both low- and high-tech, has gradually slipped out of competitive range of industries in other nations, most notably in price, but often in quality as well. And this is despite the fact that U.S. research activities remain among the world's best. While many factors helped bring the world's strongest industrial complex to its present dilemma, presidential actions and inactions played a major role.

The problem clearly lies in a national inability to allocate and manage our resources rather than in technological incompetence. I believe that an over-emphasis on government financing for space and military technology, without supervision or adequate consideration of the costs or need, is at the root of the problem. The federal government has inadequate processes for setting priorities among the vast demands made on it for technological innovations, development, and production. It has not set priorities for balancing resources between government requirements and the needs of civilian industries. For example, the expensive space shuttle went on—and went under!—in spite of ample evidence that it was not needed for any contemplated space activity. In the area of national defense, too, many unnecessary defense programs have been pursued. The result has been a systematic, decades-long diversion of manpower from productive civilian industry and education. Lest someone else point it out first, I should also note that much of the basic research that has given the United States its leadership position was undertaken for defense purposes. But we are not getting that lift from our defense research today. Quite the reverse, in fact. We now have a crisis which we must face squarely if the United States is to recover the momentum of its scientific enterprise.

Tonight I want to focus on PSAC and the office of the science adviser, and examine why our recent presidents and their advisers have been so opposed to the mechanism developed by Presidents Truman and Eisenhower to provide assistance in their efforts to understand and be in control of the federal role in funding and encouraging science and technology. And then I want to suggest how to recover from the present difficulty.

The demise of the President's Science Advisory Committee parallels a growing U.S. tendency to disregard inconvenient facts in arriving at decisions. This tendency is particularly strong on matters of defense. The fear of the Soviet Union has long provided an excuse for exaggerating the threat in order to justify many unnecessary technical developments and military purchases, and to hide the damage being done to the U.S. science and technological enterprise by the Pentagon control of employment for many technically trained persons and of funding for much advanced research. But forty years of priorities tilted heavily towards the military, even taking into account the positive achievements, have overall brought U.S. civilian technology to its present position and, ironically, have had the net effect of continuously increasing our real national danger.

Because of the dominance of federal funding, the ability of the United States to manage effectively the wide-ranging and complex issues raised by the rapid advance of technology rests on the government, and thus ultimately with the president. This has been true since the end of World War II. Before the war, science and technology were primarily private activities. Technological decisions were made by play of market forces and research decisions were dictated by intellectual curiosity. Since the war, bureaucratic objectives and military profits have invaded a once benign scene. In addition, increased technical complexity and the imposition of military secrecy have shut out public understanding and participation from decision-making. Thus, many technological choices—particularly the major ones—became the sole responsibility of a well-informed president.

It is my observation, based on personal experience with the scientific advisory apparatus used by four presidents, that scientific advisory groups always generate major anxieties among other groups in the government, as well as industrial firms looking for work. It is often said that PSAC had undue influence in the Eisenhower and Kennedy years. But the fact is that this fear of undue influence of science advisers on the president did not start with the creation of the office; it has existed ever since science and technology became a vital aspect of national life. Witness the concerns about the role of Vannevar Bush, Karl Compton, Robert Oppenheimer, and many other scientists during World War II.

Basically, the question of who provides the advice boils down to a competition for control of presidential decisions. For a president, the task is to adjudicate the rivalries among many contenders who join together only to confront him. The challenge is to retain control of his information sources and thus his freedom of decision. I watched at close range the game played by the Pentagon against four presidents; for example, practically the only times the members of the Joint Chiefs agreed was when they were attempting to persuade the secretary of defense or the president to accept their proposals. Otherwise, in their advisory capacity, one could always predict their position on any subject by identifying the vested interest of their individual service. Because, as I said earlier, so many of the dominant issues of our times involved military technology, the perceived need for secrecy has been added to the obvious barrier of technical complexity, and the combination has led most citizens to shy away from sticking to strong views that contradict those of a president, even when the facts appear to support their position. Edward Teller has long argued that secrecy in technical fields does much more harm than good and should be eliminated. I agree with him completely.

President Truman faced the question of technical decision-making as soon as World War II ended. Troubled by inter-service battling over which of them should have the responsibility for the many new technologies that were evolving, and especially by the continuing controversies about nuclear weapons, Truman commissioned a study of how to get himself better information and advice. He persuaded Mr. William Golden, a prominent lawyer who had had considerable experience with the wartime navy department's research and development efforts, and who afterward had been an assistant to Lewis Strauss, the chairman of the Atomic Energy Commission, to study the problem and make recommendations about what to do.

In the fall of 1950, Golden filed a report that proposed a full-time Scientific Adviser to the president, to be assisted by a Scientific Advisory Committee of highly qualified scientists.[1] Golden's recommendation was opposed in varying degrees by

---

1. Jerry planned to refer here to books by James R. Killian (*Missile Czar*) and William Golden (*Science Advice to the President*) for "a detailed history of this activity." Killian did not, however, write a book entitled *Missile Czar*. Jerry may have been thinking of *Sputnik, Scientists, and Eisenhower: A Memoir of the First Special Assistant to the President for Science and Technology* (MIT Press, 1977).

the heads of most governmental agencies and by many individuals working directly for the president. Lewis Strauss, among others, opposed the Golden proposal.[2] In fact, during most of the Eisenhower presidency, Lewis Strauss struggled to control the technical information channels to the president. I know from personal experience that on occasion he privately contradicted the advice of other officials and even gave erroneous information to President Eisenhower.

After months of debate, despite the opposition, Truman and his White House assistants decided to accept Golden's recommendations—in principle—to appoint a presidential science adviser and to establish a scientific advisory committee. But the opponents of Golden's plan succeeded in weakening it. The new committee, established in 1951 by President Truman, was placed under the director of the Office of Defense Mobilization instead of reporting directly to the president. To make matters worse, the director of Defense Mobilization, General Lucius Clay, was not particularly interested in the problems the committee was created to address, and he did not give it much attention. His successor Arthur Flemming, however, did appreciate the important role of science and technology and did involve the committee in his efforts to help the president understand the national security problems of the period.

These compromise decisions badly undercut Golden's plan for a technical advisory system. The most serious problem that resulted was the separation of the functions of the adviser and the advisory committee. The quality of the advisers was high. Dr. Oliver Buckley, a distinguished scientist just recently retired as president of the Bell Telephone Laboratories, was appointed science adviser, and a distinguished group of scientists—among them I. I. Rabi, Lee DuBridge, Jerrold Zacharias, Robert Bacher, James Fisk, George Kistiakowsky, Edwin Land, and others of similar international fame—became members of the initial committee. Members of this early group shared an important characteristic in addition to their outstanding scientific reputations—they had all been deeply involved in the wartime research and development effort. Many of them had worked together on the atomic bomb project and on radar. So they brought a vast fund of knowledge about nuclear and other military matters to the committee. They were undoubtedly the most knowledgeable group in the government regarding the new military technologies.

Buckley and the science advisory committee functioned more or less independently. The committee had its own chairman, I. I. Rabi of Columbia University. The

---

2. Jerry included a reference note here on Lewis Strauss as a member of the Atomic Energy Commission (AEC), 1946–1950; financial adviser to the Rockefellers, 1950–1953; chairman of the AEC, 1953–1958.

Science advisers to the US president, 1957–77—*left to right*: James R. Killian (Eisenhower, 1957–59), George B. Kistiakowsky (Eisenhower, 1959–61), Jerry (Kennedy and Johnson, 1961–64), H. Guyford Stever (Nixon and Ford, 1973–77), Donald Hornig (Johnson, 1964–69), Lee A. DuBridge (Nixon, 1969–70), Edward E. David, Jr. (Nixon, 1970–73). (Courtesy of the MIT Museum.)

compromise arrangement of responsibility and agency oversight was further handicapped by the fact that Buckley was not very active. He was in failing health and, in addition, believing that the role of science adviser should be primarily a responsive one, he did not undertake any personal initiatives. Later science advisers made a practice of alerting their employer to potential problems. The Rabi Science Advisory Committee was somewhat more active than the Buckley, but because it had not been given any specific assignments and because it did not meet often and had little staff help, it did not provide much assistance to President Truman either.

Dwight Eisenhower made somewhat greater use of this original Committee, perhaps because of the close personal relationship between the president and Dr. Rabi that went back to Eisenhower's term as president of Columbia University. For example, the committee sponsored the 1954 Technological Capabilities Panel that gave direction to the U.S. missile and reconnaissance program, and the famous 1957 Gaither Committee study on civil defense. Both of these studies were undertaken in response to the president's growing concern about the Soviet missile program and the increasing danger to the American people.

It took the shock of the Soviet Sputnik in 1957 to realize the Golden proposals. President Eisenhower was upset by how little he had been told about the difficulties of the American satellite, Vanguard. He had earlier been persuaded to announce that the United States was going to launch the world's first artificial moon, and so the Soviet accomplishment and the world's response was a source of major embarrassment to him. The Russian feat led to a widespread belief that the Soviet Union had surpassed the United States in technological strength. The entire scientific and educational system came under fire, and Eisenhower faced a rising clamor for decisive actions to correct the situation. Although he doubted that the allegations were true, he did not believe that the same individuals who had allowed the situation to develop should be asked how to correct it. He also realized how isolated he was and began to search for a way to obtain his own information about technical problems.

His solution, used soon after the launching of Sputnik in the fall of 1957, was to appoint Dr. James Killian as his Special Assistant for Science and Technology and move the Advisory Committee into the Executive Office of the president, where it could provide him with independent evaluation of the government's many scientific programs. Its members quickly developed a close rapport with the president, who turned to it frequently for help. President Eisenhower provided Dr. Killian with a letter of appointment spelling out, in great detail, his responsibilities and giving him wide-ranging authority. So encompassing was this letter that when I became science adviser to President Kennedy in 1961, he used this same letter to define my responsibilities. This essentially gave me total oversight for all science and technology programs in the government and in related education programs. Because of this enormous range of responsibilities, PSAC and I were very careful in our selection of programs and I always checked with the president before starting any major new projects.

The new team of science advisers and the president's science advisory committee responded with a frenzy of activities. I became a member of the committee in the spring of 1958. PSAC's first tasks were to bring order to the space program and sort out the conflicting allegations about relative positions of the U.S. and Soviet science and education programs. An operating procedure rapidly developed based on the ad-hoc committee study process of earlier times, but changing it to a continuing process. As its main source of information, the committee used advisory panels. Typically, a panel would be chaired by a member of the PSAC and would include scientists and engineers from universities, industry, and government, selected for their expertise in the field under review. Sometimes other PSAC members, in addition to the chairman, would be included in the membership.

In the Eisenhower-Kennedy period, a major role of PSAC and the president's special assistant for science and technology was to screen the avalanche of military and space projects confronting the president and attempt to provide sufficiency within a manageable budget. Such a task can only be done by a technically competent group with a nonvested interest. Advisors from industry and the defense laboratories are usually competent but hardly unbiased, so that PSAC depended heavily upon university-based experts plus those from industrial laboratories such as the Bell Telephone Laboratory, whose duties gave them a high degree of independence.

PSAC quickly showed the value of continuity in following individual programs. It also provided another important feature. Because PSAC often met as a group, it was able to provide perspective and balance on the many programs and fields contending for attention. Each panel reported its progress to the monthly meetings of the full Advisory Committee, bringing it up to date and generating questions that needed further clarification. The collective knowledge and experience of the whole Committee contributed significantly to the ultimate recommendations that were made to the president. Dr. Killian and the PSAC members who prepared the plan approved by the president then played a major role in its implementation. The president had a major influence on the focus of the PSAC studies. For example, he wanted to establish a civilian space program and the committee worked toward that end. They worked hard to develop the proposal for an agency that ultimately became NASA.

As President Eisenhower became increasingly involved with military R&D and space programs, PSAC did too. A 1956 Chiefs of Staff study predicted massive carnage and destruction in the United States if a nuclear war occurred. The report stimulated the 1957 Gaither Panel study, which confirmed the conclusion of the military study that even with extensive defenses, both passive and active, many tens of millions of Americans would be killed in a major nuclear war. The Gaither Panel also voiced serious alarm about the speed and scale of the Soviet missile deployment effort. These reports gave a sense of urgency to the U.S. missile program and also heightened Eisenhower's determination to moderate the arms race. He became particularly committed to exchanges of military information to lessen tensions, and to a test ban treaty to halt the development of new weapons.

In 1958, as he became increasingly dedicated to halting the arms race, President Eisenhower asked the Science Advisory Committee to help him. I vividly recall the drama of the moment. Referring to the Gaither Panel's report, he pounded his desk and said, "You can't have that war. There aren't enough bulldozers in the country to scrape the bodies off the streets. Why don't you help me prevent it? Neither the Defense Department nor AEC will give me any help. They have other interests."

With this challenge, many of us on the PSAC turned our attention to the technical questions of the test ban and other disarmament efforts. That moment changed the focus of the rest of my life, though I didn't realize it at the time. This switch had major repercussions for the committee, too. It made PSAC the president's main source of technical information on arms control and also, which was important to its ultimate fate, the target of the weapons advocates' wrath, a situation that continued as long as PSAC survived.

In 1960, after President Kennedy asked me to be his Special Assistant and I agreed, he approved the committee setup as it was operating and, in fact, at my suggestion he retained the members. In this way it was my hope to give the committee a non-political character, so that it could be maintained intact—with the exception of the Special Assistant—through subsequent presidential transitions. And actually, President Nixon followed this practice too, at the start of his administration.

I said earlier that I am convinced that if there had been adequate presidential-level overview of technical programs in recent times, similar to that provided by PSAC, the Challenger explosion would not have happened. The PSAC Space Panel would certainly have detected the problems with the booster rocket early on and alerted the administrators of NASA and the president. PSAC also had developed a source of information in addition to its own reviews that might have alerted it to the shuttle troubles. The science adviser's staff had acquired an unanticipated and important role in the overall science management process. Without planning to do so, PSAC became the ombudsman for federal science and technology programs. The staff became a group to whom workers on government programs, aware of faulty designs, poor manufacturing, inadequate performance, unnecessary programs, or other problems could appeal when their concerns were ignored within their own organization. Scientists and engineers realized that the PSAC staff provided a channel that they could use with the confidence that they were not risking the traditional fate of the whistleblower. We made no effort to encourage this channel, but neither did we discourage it. Robert McNamara once asked me how it was that the few people in my office knew much more about Department of Defense R&D and procurement difficulties than he did, with his large staff.

Although the immediate cause of the Challenger disaster was the explosion of a solid-fueled rocket, the real reason for the failure was that President Reagan did not have his own technical review team. All the groups involved were under extreme pressure to maintain a launch schedule at all costs. They ignored numerous warning signals. In technical jargon, the president had no feedback. He received no independent information or advice to help him judge Challenger or any other technical program for which he was responsible, or for that matter the soundness or need for any of the proposed new programs that flow into the White House continuously, such as most notably the Strategic Defense Initiative (SDI).

It may well be that President Reagan did not want such help. Attempts by individuals to give him access to other views on the existence of the now discredited "window of vulnerability," for example, were certainly repulsed. Nor has the president given opponents of the SDI a hearing. Perhaps Oliver Buckley was right after all, when he said, "You can only give advice to someone who wants it."

In all fairness, I should make it clear that President Reagan did not create this situation, he inherited it. But some of his closest advisors were among those who helped bring it about. It was President Nixon who abolished the Science Advisory Committee and the post of Special Assistant to the President for Science and Technology. He got rid of them because he did not like the advice that they were providing on issues ranging from the controversial antiballistic missile system and the proposed supersonic transport aircraft to the performance of military equipment in Vietnam. Their evaluations were negative, while he was getting more optimistic information from other sources. He finally abolished PSAC and the post of science adviser after a few frustrated members of PSAC—wrongly, I believe—publicly opposed the ABM and supersonic transport. In doing this, they violated the long-standing and proud tradition of confidentiality of the Science Advisory Committee. Previous Science Advisory Committees and science advisers had frequently given advice that was not followed because of nontechnical factors the president chose to emphasize, usually financial or political, but always in the past they had been given a thorough hearing and they remained publicly silent.

President Nixon upset some of the PSAC members by refusing to hear their views. He did not want to hear the facts. In a sense, he chose to kill the messenger. In later years, Presidents Ford and Carter made arrangements to get their own assistance on technical questions. President Ford faced an anti-PSAC bias that lingered on after President Nixon, and so never was able to create an adequate advisory system. President Carter appointed a Special Assistant for Science, but didn't reestablish a Presidential Science Advisory Committee with anything like the extensive capabilities of the original committee. Dr. Frank Press, Carter's science adviser, made extensive use of advisory panels, but did not use a PSAC-style group to achieve integration and continuity.

President Reagan's operating style dictates altogether different ways of making technical decisions. He uses the buddy system, which in the end proved disastrous. Reagan has made no effort to get independent advice about technical questions such as the shuttle or SDI, perhaps because he did not know that he needed it. He trusted the advocates who had surrounded him during his campaign for the presidency, and heeded their advice.

It is true that a number of very good scientists who might have had some influence in the position of science adviser turned Reagan down. They drew back when they learned about the limited role they were going to have, and especially that their information and advice would flow to the president mainly through his Chief of Staff; that, in fact, they were being asked to be an adviser to a presidential aide. George Keyworth accepted the position despite the limitations, and thus served the president and the country poorly.

Much of the Reagan defense and disarmament policy stems from the views of Dr. Edward Teller and the nuclear bomb laboratory staffs. The intense lobbying efforts of Teller and his like-minded colleagues with members of Congress blocked Eisenhower completely in his quest for a total nuclear test ban and forced President Kennedy to settle for a partial nuclear test ban instead of the comprehensive ban that he wanted. Though their efforts did not stop President Nixon's achievement of a limitation on antiballistic missile systems, they did fight it, and their contemporary counterparts are doing their best to undercut it now, fifteen years later. They and their advocates, representative of a particular interested point of view, now dominate whatever scientific decision-making occurs at the White House level.

In addition to wasting money and increasing the danger of nuclear war, the continuing weapons programs, both R&D and manufacturing, have diverted resources from productive efforts, especially technical manpower, which is badly needed in the civilian sector. The lure for industry of the easy profits available on military programs plus the intense concentration of the leadership and the public on defense issues have been an important factor in the decay of the nation's civilian industry. The problem today is not missile balances with the Soviet Union; it is reclaiming American independence from what we were warned about, the military-industrial complex.

Rapid changes in technology mean that there is never a stable moment. Some observers of the military scene hope for a time when the opportunity for new and more fantastic weapons will not exist and a nonthreatening world will just happen. A political expert on the arms race calls himself a short-term hawk, a middle-range owl, and a long-term dove. He does not understand the flow of technology. Its course does not change direction by itself. In technical development, one idea engenders another. This vicious cycle can only be broken by human intervention—not by another invention—by people limiting weapon development and choosing more benign uses of technology. Otherwise, the scale of technical activity devoted to arms will continue to grow until it transforms all society into a military camp. The civilian economy, the true basis of our national security, will decline, thus increasing the fraction of our resources devoted to arms, with a continuing loss of civilian technical leadership.

The tradition in the federal government is for the various executive branch agencies to propose their most ambitious programs to the president with the expectation that they will be pruned back. Usually, the total requests far exceed the financial resources available, and it becomes the president's task to choose those that appear most important and in the best interest of the nation. Obviously, a president cannot be expected to understand all of these highly complex demands or even have much time for them. So for the initial choices, a president must depend upon the Cabinet officers and other agency heads and their staffs, as well as the Office of Budget and Management, which works with the departments to prepare their budgets. But ultimately it is properly the president, as the one official responsible for the welfare of the country as a whole, who must choose.

As the scientific problems that face the various agencies have expanded, so have their funding needs, and the problem of selecting among them grows more difficult. I have estimated that, left to normal growth, technical programs double in cost in approximately six years. The GNP, at its best, used to double in twelve years. So the president's difficulty in making choices increases each year. This is why budgets grow so continuously.

What can be done to reverse the decline in U.S. technological well-being? We are faced with two separate challenges. First, the president must resume control of the federal scientific enterprise. He must take back control and oversight of these vast resources from the military-industrial complex. Second, we must simultaneously revitalize the civilian science and technology enterprise, all of it—education, basic research, and civilian application of technology. We should buy only the few military systems needed to ensure national security and direct the rest of our vast technical resources to rebuilding the nation's civilian industrial base. An essential part of this task is to build the presidential science advisory mechanism back up in a way that would regain the confidence of the Congress and general public in the government's decision-making process. This will not be easy, given the recent history. But it must be done.

An independent investigation is needed to explore the overall problem posed by science and technology for the future well being of the nation. To make a start, we need to reestablish PSAC and utilize the position of the science adviser as it was in the past.

Some scientists who have been involved with the presidential advisory process believe that the president's Special Assistant for Science and Technology should be a member of the Cabinet, a member without portfolio. She or he would thus be subject to Congressional approval, so as to provide a check and a degree of public exposure. Others propose that the entire Science Advisory Committee also be subject to Congressional approval, and that PSAC should be answerable to Congress. Such steps would institutionalize the activity and probably give it obviously needed status. On the other hand, it is probable that exposing the science advisory function to political processes in such a manner would deprive the president of an opportunity for the intimate, confidential relationship that existed under Eisenhower and Kennedy. Such a relationship can be the best guarantee of objective, politically uncontaminated advice and information.

I believe that several additional steps could be taken quickly to improve the presidential process and the quality of the U.S. technical establishment. First among these would be to relax the secrecy imposed on military/technical matters. Secrecy is ostensibly imposed to keep information of military systems from potential opponents. Experience shows that its main role is to keep the American public in the dark. Too often secrecy is applied selectively, more to win debates than to protect information. Some of the best analysis of military technology has been provided by independent studies based upon fundamental physical facts, not secret knowledge.

A new PSAC should give equal attention to the problems of civilian or private-sector science and technology. This would be a new task. During my term as science adviser, a PSAC panel began to examine the problems of civilian technology. In retrospect, I can see that our focus was too narrow. Our concern was for those industries that were not employing R&D effectively. But some of the panel's observations were on the mark. For example, it expressed concern about the lack of R&D in the steel industry. Not only was that industry not doing any significant R&D, it was ignoring what was being done overseas. It was fast becoming obsolete. That was long ago, in 1962. A member of my staff predicted that the American steel industry would be dead in twenty years.

Actually, we did not know how to stimulate civilian industries' uses of R&D. The National Science Foundation has had some modest successes with its experiments in this area, but we really do not know what to do to restore the U.S. position of leadership. Tax credits for R&D seem also to have helped. But the basic problem of maintaining a competitive industrial base obviously needs more than just better R&D, although this is essential. This is a problem that the PSAC process will not solve, except to the degree that it can stimulate science education and basic research. But regular PSAC review could clear the biggest obstacle from the path. It could prevent the colossal waste of technical manpower that the federal government now subsidizes, drawing too many of the best technical people into working on high-tech weapons of war that are not needed, are not productive, and with luck will never be used. We need to give a healthy peace that same priority.

If a study committee were to be set to work on the problem, public consideration and debate on its findings would in itself improve our position in scientific and technological research, development, and deployment; and the economic, social, and security benefits to the nation as a whole, and to the entire international community, would be commensurate. Perhaps such a study would suggest a more effective presidential advisory system. If so, it could be adopted after appropriate consideration. But we should not allow the hope for an ideal solution to leave the president and the nation floundering and at the mercy of random and unidentified forces. We have an effective model. Let's use it. Let's get our technological priorities straight.

Survival, the Moral Equivalent of the Arms Race

An address delivered by Jerry at a week-long symposium held in Washington, D.C., January 1988, to commemorate the centennial of the National Geographic Society. Participants discussed the evolution and interaction of science, technology, and exploration in the century since the Society was founded, focusing on the future quality of life on planet Earth.

Jerry's paper went through several revisions, the last of which was published as "How Societies Learn" in Earth '88, Changing Geographic Perspectives: Proceedings of the Centennial Symposium *(National Geographic Society, 1988), pp. 350–57. The version below is closer to what Jerry actually said at the symposium, although somewhat polished with a view toward publication (addition of subheadings, etc.). He summarized his thrust this way:*

> *In this paper I use cybernetic and information theory concepts to explain society's inability to adequately manage the impact of technologically induced changes in the physical and human worlds and the inability to limit the dangers inherent for humanity if these trends are allowed to continue unchecked. Starting with the premise that humanity has substituted machines for biological adaptation as a means of accommodating to the environment, I argue that the process remains nonetheless one of trial and error in which individual technological initiatives have unpredictable consequences, often destructive. Although this involves random responses to problems as they arise, it is a learning process. I argue that this process must be vastly improved if the current environmental destruction and decline in human well-being is to be reversed. An especially important example is the arms race, a major threat to human survival and a consumer of resources essential for other survival efforts. National security for the superpowers could be increased by massive reductions in military research, production, and deployment, and the freed-up resources used to create constructive human conditions. An alternative of a global development effort using the resources now wasted on the arms race, as well as currently underused capital and human resources, is conceptually feasible.*

Introduction

The world with its billions of people and countless other living creatures, and the complex ecosystem and social systems that supports them, is in chaos. The extent of the global disarray is only dimly perceived because individuals everywhere tend to regard the troubles they face as local or national phenomena rather than as world-wide problems. Scientists are just beginning to realize that the earth is, in reality, a single complex organism made up of living creatures—the land, the sea, and the sky woven together in delicate balance by a combination of natural and man-made links. The recognition of this oneness, this interdependence, is so recent that we don't have a name for the collective "us." We are also just beginning to realize that this wonderful oneness is critically ill. How ill? No one knows.

Bluntly, humanity is suffering from a series of diseases most of which have no ethology, no previous history, and few well-informed doctors. Many concerned individuals believe that the world is approaching a point of no return where conditions will run relentlessly downward. Fortunately, people are also beginning to sense the extent of the threats we face. Unlike the nuclear danger, which promises sudden and total devastation, these global diseases may create extremely inhospitable environments and declining conditions of life, but life will probably go on. At what stage the problem crosses the threshold into a state of steady decline is not yet obvious.

There is a growing awareness that although large-scale applications of technology are responsible for most of the threats to survival, I believe that the only solutions will be found in a judicious mixture of restraint and new technologies focused on improved life-support systems and global resource management.

So the challenge is for us, those now alive, to mobilize; to start building a world that is in ecological and human equilibrium. The resources exist, but not the desire and knowledge to do it. Scientists and engineers can, I believe, provide the "how to." Only an informed and dedicated population can provide the "want to"—a response that needs to be the moral equivalent of the nuclear arms race in its intensity and dedication, a response that starts by eliminating the arms race.

None of this can be done without an adequate understanding of the processes at work, how the applications of technology occur, and how they could be moderated, and equally important, how human beings fit into the process.

When I agreed to prepare this paper, I intended to develop some ideas that I have long harbored about society as a learning system which are based on cybernetic concepts. As I proceeded, I also realized that the understandings that this provided could also indicate how it might be possible to begin a rescue mission for the planet and arrangements for a better world. I started to outline how this might be done and soon discovered two things: first, that I had begun what should be a major interdisciplinary study; and second, that I was far exceeding the space allocated me. Rather than omit the second part, I have shortened the entire paper by eliminating some details and examples. I also realize that the plan I present in the second half of the paper is incomplete and controversial. But because I believe that there is great merit in having a proposal to criticize and debate, I have decided to include it here.

My original intention was to use information and learning theory concepts to merely explore why these problems, what we might call man-made plagues, occur and why the emergence of corrective measures is so slow and inadequate. These ideas can help us to understand why so many inventions and discoveries that are so promising initially lead to the kind of difficulties we are exploring, and why both capitalist and socialist states have become increasingly unmanageable as the extent of their technologies has grown.

Evolution and Learning

This paper is based on two concepts: technology as a basis of social evolution, and a technological society as a learning system.

Obviously, a society with technological ambitions requires a large body of well-trained engineers, scientists, and managers. But they don't perform in isolation. Their effectiveness is determined by characteristics of the system in which they are involved and how they perceive their role in it. How free and motivated they feel to do creative work is determined, to a considerable degree, by how well they regard the system in which they are involved (whether, for example, recognition comes because of personal accomplishments or through winning bureaucratic battles). For those that have supervisory roles, the belief that they have some voice in the overall decisions of their enterprise is also important. In other words, how well these individuals function as nodes in the system is strongly influenced by their judgment about its effectiveness, responsiveness, and fairness. We all know many organizations that have a deadening effect on individuals' creativity and productivity.

Intervening in Evolution

In this model, the role of feedback in the functioning and evolution of the technological state plays a central role. In fact, goal seeking and learning are the characteristics which distinguish living creatures from inanimate objects. This analysis begins with the proposition that the growing challenge to the survival of civilization is the consequence of large-scale uncontrolled human intervention in the evolutionary process that causes overloads in both the ecosystem and the human capacity to understand and cope with resulting problems. This intervention, though not new, began to be serious as a result of the industrial revolution with its exploitation of science and technology. The resulting large-scale intervention in the evolutionary process could be called the meta-problem of our times, for it is at the root of most of the effects that collectively seem to be beyond control. It has brought enormous changes and discontinuities in the physical and social environments by simultaneously speeding up and distorting the course and character of the human evolutionary process. The task in the years ahead is to get the process under control.

Basically, I believe that the use of technology to improve the human condition is an experimental process—i.e., one of trial and error—that needs to be better understood if applications of technology are to be properly directed. For too long we took advantage of the positive contributions of technology and ignored the dark side. In fact, the dark side wasn't always evident, perhaps didn't even exist. When there were only a few thousand automobiles, for example, pollution was not a problem and those who projected the adverse environmental and social impact of their mass deployment were regarded as cranks. But there has been growth in many dimensions, and with it an exponential increase in the destructive impacts of technology which has brought humanity to this crisis point.

All developmental activities are learning processes, inherently involving trial and error. Because this is not understood, many unanticipated problems arise as societies evolve that would be recognized and countered more rapidly if the nature of the learning process were understood. Even in those societies that appear to be traditional and untouched by technology, it has often had a disruptive effect. For example, just a small dose of public health information was enough to cause a dramatic increase in populations in many traditional societies.

Charles Darwin's theory of biological evolution, by now very well established, maintains that living organisms adapt to their environment as a consequence of random changes, mostly small changes of genetic origin, in which natural selection bestows dominance on those species that are best adapted for life in the prevailing environment. This process of random selection occurs over many generations. Man-made interventions via technology have displaced the eons-long natural process, vastly speeding up the rate of change, leaving biological adaptation unable to compensate for the effects of technological change, at least in the short term.

Cultural anthropologists maintain that there is a parallel cultural adaptation through which individuals and social groups learn to adapt to many man-made changes and could obviously continue to do this in the face of deteriorating conditions. The extent to which this is true remains a question of considerable controversy.

Humans have a singular advantage in the evolutionary trek—intelligence—which confers the ability to adapt quickly, particularly through the invention of mental models, tools, and techniques. As providential as this gift has been, it must also be regarded as dangerous because such purposeful adaptive activities until now have left a trail of ever more difficult problems.

General Discussion of Information Systems: Problem Solving and Learning in a Social System

How well a learning system functions is determined by its information processing arrangements, especially how well its feedback systems function to guide it toward its goals. By a society's information processing capability, I don't mean its communication technology, but rather the way in which its groups are organized to do their work and the ease with which they can interact and learn and change based on their experiences.

The two concepts—technology as the source of a man-made evolutionary process and a technological society as a learning system—together help to explain why problems arise from the deployment of new technologies. Seeing the problems in this light helps understand how, with better feedback, they could be minimized or even avoided. These ideas also make evident why the steady stream of new technologies shapes and reshapes civilization, altering the physical environment, and constantly posing new intellectual and psychological hurdles for people.

The state of the world at any given moment is the condition created by the millions, perhaps billions, of independent actions using old and new techniques to accomplish a multitude of individual aims. Individuals and groups use the best tools available to them to achieve their goals, totally unaware of the fact that they are having any effect on the global system. No single automobile, incinerator, chemical dump in the ocean, fluorocarbon can, or chopped down tree seems to matter. Repeated on a global scale by a rapidly growing population, the result is an unpredictably changing physical and psychological world in which the changes are likely to be large, uncongenial, and frequently irreversible.

The collective task, then, is that of *steering* the man-made evolutionary process, one of such complexity that its future state cannot be predicted.

In contrast to nature, the use of technology to enhance human capabilities is not entirely a random process, but neither is it entirely a logical process. In fact, it appears to be a combination of the two. At the micro level, new initiatives or experiments can be well ordered, but even then the outcomes often contain surprises.

Well done scientific research clearly demonstrates this point. The goal is usually obvious. So may be the path to follow. But rarely do the beginning ideas remain invariant, and some of the most important scientific discoveries have been the consequence of switching to very different goals. This is usually the case in other human activities as well, including business and government, and particularly the quest for more effective social arrangements.

Each sub-group in a society has tasks on which it focuses and which it strives to fulfill. Sometimes a task is organizationally simple and relatively independent of the rest of the system, as in the case of a piece of scientific research; sometimes the task is hopelessly dominated by the conflicting demands of the complex social system. The overall performance of a society as a learning machine is determined by the combined performance of all of its pieces, interacting and influencing each other. Little wonder that outcomes, large and small, have a substantial degree of uncertainty and surprise. While it is impossible to predict with confidence the actual outcome of any initiative in this complicated, interactive world, it is possible to judge qualitatively the effectiveness of organizations involved in creative tasks by determining how well they satisfy the conditions for an effective learning system.

Properties of a Good Learning System

What makes a good learning system? Experience with man-made learning systems such as computers in adaptive systems, automata built to pursue prescribed goals such as aircraft autopilots, robots on an assembly line, computers programmed to solve problems, and studies of human cognitive behavior provide a wealth of information regarding the desirable properties of good learning systems. An adequate discussion of this subject is obviously impossible here, but some key characteristics for effective learning systems, regarded as an experimental process, can be stated.

1. *Feedback.* An essential element in any learning system is feedback. In fact, any goal-seeking system, living or man-made, must have a means for comparing the present state of the system with its ultimate goal, i.e., a means of measuring the error between the present situation and the ultimate goal. Consider a person reaching for an object. As his arm moves toward the object, the eyes constantly compare the position of the hand as it moves and adjusts the muscle forces to lead to ultimate closure. In the same way, a robot whose task is to orient parts on a machine compares the position of the part with the desired position—usually using a camera system for determining the error on location—and then with feedback through an

actuating device takes corrective action until the error is as small as the system is capable of detecting and adjusting to. All learning systems require these elements— a goal, a means of comparing the present situation with that goal, and a method for moving toward the correct situation. Intellectual activities that we call "learning" also involve this process. That is true whether the goal is learning the contents of a textbook or involves an effort to gain a new piece of information about nature. In the robot I have described, the task is clearly defined, but the path followed to the objective will depend upon the starting conditions, so in a very primitive sense the machine is learning to do one task over and over. Unlike living systems, the robot cannot change its basic method of operation although some machines can indeed adapt to changing task conditions. A sophisticated telephone network is an example of this.

It is evident that for optimum performance the feedback system should be as responsive as it is possible to make it, i.e., its measuring system and its computer together determine the appropriate path and should be able to detect small errors. In practice there are limits to the degree to which this goal can be met without generating troubles, i.e., noise in the communication channels might be regarded as error signals if the system is too sensitive. In social systems, public opinion, new media, voting, public interest study and action groups, special interest lobbyists, the performance of the economic system, and many other matters serve as feedback. The social organization determines the responsiveness of the system to each of the feedback signals.

2. *Size of experiments.* Experiments should be as small as is consistent with effective learning. Because most learning systems combine elements of directed or logical behavior with trial-and-error learning activities, a number of course changes will undoubtedly be needed to reach a satisfactory goal. New initiatives should be arranged to perform individual experiments quickly or, alternatively, do many of them at the same time. The more urgent the need for an answer, the larger the number of experiments that should be done at the same time. (It is important to realize that a scale change for an old technology is also an experiment; factors of two often totally change the performance or response of human systems.)

It is quite common for hundreds of people to be working independently on a major scientific question at the same time. To spur the development of socially relevant technology, many independent groups should be encouraged to seek solutions to the problems. To my knowledge, this factor has never deliberately taken into account the design of social experiments. In fact, most of the time people involved in making social innovations don't appreciate the degree to which their experiments have the possibility of going wrong more often than right.

Multiple experiments occur automatically in the private sector of a capitalist society where the market forces bring large numbers of competitors into any promising field. The experiments are essentially the products they develop, and the measure of success is the market response. Typical of this phenomenon is the situation in the computer industry at the moment, where hundreds of independent companies are producing small computers and those that satisfy a sufficient need will survive, while many of them will fade away. The situation is very different in the socialist countries, where a few large organizations are responsible for meeting the society's need for such machines. An important element of Chairman Gorbachev's "perestroika" is the encouragement of independence in individual enterprises.

3. *Noise*. Noise in the feedback system introduces random responses. Consequently, every effort should be made to keep it to a minimum so that a sensitive error-detecting system can be employed without the danger of provoking unwanted fluctuations in the system's behavior. The problem is tractable and manageable in man-made systems, but has not been systematically considered in the study of societal problems.

4. *Time constant*. A very important aspect of any feedback or control system is its time constant—the time it takes for it to detect an error, send a message about this error to the computer, which then computes what corrective action should be taken, and sends a command signal to the operating mechanism, which initiates the corrective action. In artificial systems this corrective process is usually continuous. In general, the goal of an equipment designer is to keep this time as short as possible to ensure effective corrective action. If the time constant is too great, the error signal may come too late to initiate corrective actions. In this situation the response to errors will be sluggish, and under certain conditions may even cause the mechanism to amplify rather than correct the error.

These criteria show why very large systems, whether governmental or private, tend to be very inefficient. The feedback loops are very long and slow, error detection is poor and requires large errors to stimulate a correction. In government, the ultimate feedback system is the citizen's response, and this tends to be a very ineffective process because even deciding what issues should be used for the feedback signal is difficult, whether it is the quality of government provided services, or military budgets, or economic decisions, or ethics, or many other issues of public concern.

People Issues

A serious shortcoming of this analysis is the lack of an adequate understanding of the role of individuals in the communication networks of the learning system. Obviously, the abilities, individual goals, interrelationships between individuals and their physical and mental health are vital aspects of a human network. Just as a man-made system will not function properly with defective or inappropriate components, a human system will perform badly if the individuals in it are miscast in their positions. For example, if a person who habitually procrastinates has the responsibility for approving actions, the system's time constants will be long. If a person in charge of an operation does not understand it he will introduce noise in the system. Likewise, if a person adverse to risk-taking is given the responsibility for innovation, little new will result. One can see many individuals miscast in such ways and also observe their destructive effects on the system in which they function. This is a fascinating issue, but beyond the scope of this paper.

With regard to the survival issues we are considering, the majority of the feedback signals have come from the efforts of individuals and private groups who typically go into action only after situations become relatively threatening, in other words when the error signals become big. Furthermore, the messages from such groups have no place to go. That is, the error correction focused on the survival issues is not an integral part of an organized society and has to be created de novo whenever a significant problem arises. This is a slow and ineffective process. That is why the problems we are concerned about have become so serious.

Technological Responses

The best, perhaps the only, response to the problems we now face because of past deployment of technology would, I believe, be a world-wide recognition of the warning signals and a commitment to redeploy a significant portion of the available political, scientific, and technological resources to their solution. But to start, we need to understand the dangers more thoroughly and then develop procedures and technologies that would move toward a sustainable planet. By redeploying the world's resources, I particularly intend to imply the need for the superpowers to stop the arms race and redirect the energies and resources now locked up in this dangerous enterprise. This may appear to be a hopeless task. All the tendencies have been in the other direction—toward more and newer weapon systems. *It is here that we must make a*

*choice, join weapons anonymous and put technology to work on constructive
projects or let civilization slip past the threshold of repairable destruction.*

Halting the Arms Race

Not only does the arms race waste resources, but the longer it continues, the greater
the danger of the ultimate catastrophe. Fortunately, more and more people are
beginning to believe that it can be stopped without jeopardizing the national security of either side. Even our government seems to be realizing this. Most people who
understand the nature of the arms race—with its imagined, delicate balance of terror,
its frantic search for decisive superiority, and control systems so complex that their
interactive behavior is not predictable—are convinced that unless it is stopped it
will eventually end in a global debacle.

From the very days of the invention of the atom bomb, knowledgeable people
like Dwight D. Eisenhower and Winston Churchill realized and said publicly that
there was no military use for nuclear weapons and that the only way to protect the
world from them was to eliminate them. But instead of doing that, after the Soviet
Union produced its bomb American planners decided that they could best ensure
national security through more and better bombs and delivery systems. The ratio-
nalization for nuclear arsenals became deterrence—security under a nuclear
umbrella. Even the Reagan administration agrees with this proposition in its public
statements, though it still seeks funds for a war-fighting capability.

Repeated studies in the United States and elsewhere have shown that a single
nuclear weapon would suffice to devastate functioning society. For most people, the
destruction of a single city would be a deterrent against any form of aggression.
Joseph Stalin's behavior in the Berlin crisis was restrained by the knowledge that
the United States had a few (primitive) nuclear weapons. But that was *before* the
explosion of the first Soviet atomic bomb. With that, an increased fear of Stalin and
intelligence information that enormously exaggerated the Soviet bomber force
caused a large buildup in the American nuclear forces. Since then, both participants
in the arms race have continued to add weapon system to weapon system until the
enormous stockpiles defy all understanding. Why is this? Because the military strategies of the superpowers have built in positive feedback.

Traditionally, nuclear forces have been designed to satisfy what is called
worst-case analysis, i.e., in the case of the American forces, this means to have the
capability to deter an insane opponent bent on dominating the world even if the

cost were the destruction of his country. This leads to sophisticated strategies and arcane analyses based upon pure imagination, like the conclusions that it requires the capacity to destroy forty or fifty percent of the potential aggressor's population and property to constitute an adequate deterrent. Unfortunately, there are two players in this game. Why should a Soviet leader believe that an enormous American arsenal is designed to prevent something he has neither the capability nor the intention of doing? So his worst-case analysis requires him to match the original buildup. Because of the positive feedback nature of this encounter, there is no end to the spiral it generates until one or the other, or both, run out of resources or interest. If civilization is lucky, this may be happening.

But suppose we ask, "Is this really the worst case?" The answer is clearly no. To protect against a very unlikely event—the leader willing to destroy his own country—the worst-case scenario requires a very costly competition which gets increasingly dangerous. A worst-case strategy is actually the worst strategy for humanity and for each nation.

The solution is simple. Abandon worst-case analysis and its positive feedback syndrome and substitute a less dangerous strategic objective, a small secure deterrent force. Actually, President Reagan and Chairman Gorbachev both articulated such goals in their talks at the Reykjavik summit meeting. Their objectives were correct. Drastically reduce the strategic nuclear forces and substitute information, i.e., feedback, to provide the needed security. I believe that they are actually moving in that direction; 50% cuts are in the air.

But, one can still go much further than this with safety. This is easier to do than most people believe. The nuclear forces are so large that either side could unilaterally make substantial force reductions without violating the requirements of a prudent deterrent. Such an action would in fact be very stabilizing. Only after very major reductions would intensive monitoring of each other be necessary.

There is one particularly difficult hurdle to be overcome on both sides, that is, the vested interests that have enormous stakes in the continued development, deployment, and operation of the military forces. To overcome this obstacle, there are two things that I have thought of. First, one could involve the military-industrial-research community in the survival problems. The scientific, technological, production, and operational challenges in this field will prove to be greater, more interesting, more satisfying, and probably equally profitable to those of the arms race, and have even more growth potential. The second is that we can begin building up the verification organization that will be needed to supervise the peace race. This organization should be started now—probably as a responsibility of the Department of Defense. There are many technical challenges here too, but I don't have time to explain them.

Changing the Global Agenda

At this point, I want to merge these ideas into a proposal that points the way to a positive world agenda. As I do this, I remain mindful of my most important premise, that social progress is the result of evolutionary processes involving continuing social, scientific, and technological experiments, so that the best one should expect to do without contradicting my basic premise of social evolution as an unpredictable journey is to outline a process for refocusing of national and global priorities and perhaps set the initial conditions for hopeful new directions. A survival agenda has to meet two requirements: it has to be physically possible and politically achievable.

To see if my proposal was physically possible, I decided to do a "gedunken" (thought) experiment conceptualizing an all-out plan aimed at turning the world toward a sustainable future. This effort convinced me that it was possible to satisfy conditions for a healthy world. To achieve this outcome required a few assumptions. I optimistically assumed that as the plight of the human race became obvious the political processes would accommodate to the survival needs. I made the equally optimistic assumption that civilization had fifty years to make the transition. This comes from current estimates of the doubling time of atmospheric carbon dioxide. Fifty years is, I believe, long enough to allow major changes in the political and economic relationships among nations if they are going to occur. Hopefully, it is still short enough to keep the destructive forces the world faces within acceptable bounds. Physically, the transition could be made much more quickly.

I also assumed that if the arms race is halted some form of super-national authority will emerge to monitor the arms-limitation agreements and to provide the degree of cooperation and mutual assistance between nations required to successfully cope with the remaining survival problems. I did not explore what form that international authority should take. I think that perhaps it must *evolve* with time, perhaps out of the United Nations, as the arms race waxes and international cooperation to save civilization becomes a major effort of the global community. I implicitly assumed that in this case hatred, which paralyzes nations and continents, would give way to tolerance. This is perhaps the most optimistic assumption of all.

Many of the problems that must be faced can and should only be handled through global cooperation. The task of providing replacement and new infrastructures will strain the available research, development, and production capacity of the world. Some obvious examples are: providing adequate and universally available educational systems, health care facilities, efficient and nonpolluting fossil fuel power plants, safe nuclear plants, energy-efficient machines, and alternate energy sources. Ultra-supercomputers to model global climate, pollution, and even social problems, efficient solar cells, education technologies and software, and large-scale desalinization systems must also be provided. Actually, without this demand, the industrial nations will be faced with a growing surplus, a growing manufacturing capacity and labor force, as well as a deep depression as the current market for fancy consumer goods becomes saturated. Advancing technology has brought the world to the point where its continued evolution requires the challenge of the global rescue project.

Do I think this can happen? Not yet, I fear. Perhaps when the dangers are more evident, when it is obvious to all that the world is approaching the irreversible thresholds of the natural systems that sustain the human family. But by then it may be too late. In spite of this small attack of reality, I began to list the things that should be started now and in the not too distant future, so that if civilization survives, and we meet again in one hundred years, there will be general agreement that the present time was indeed the low point in man's irresponsible use of his great powers of mind and its handmaidens, science and technology. As I said at the start, this won't be an operational plan for making this dream come true. I will only, in effect, provide some road signs.

I propose that this effort be planned and managed by a group of new agencies in all the countries: the Departments of Development, or the DOD's. In the early stages, much of their effort and resources would support research and policy studies to provide the basis for the subsequent action programs.

Are there adequate resources to sustain the action programs? I don't know, but a quick estimate shows that there is the potential for financing vast efforts. If one assumes that the nations will just make a transition from the present level of spending for military programs—i.e., between 5 and 8 percent of national GNP's to a security force costing perhaps 2 or 3 percent, while the funds for the survival tasks including the appropriate research and development would increase to 5 or 6 percent—this would make available more than one-half-trillion dollars worldwide. If one further assumes that worldwide excess production capacity would be used to help provide the new infrastructure, perhaps fifty billion dollars per year could be made available for research and development and at least two trillion dollars for new infrastructure. Some of these funds would be used by governments, but much of it could be used to build new capabilities in the private sector as well.

One problem I will carefully avoid is how to distribute the resources, i.e., how to share the large economic burden. In World War II, such problems were avoided by the straightforward recognition that the Allies would survive or perish together. While the situation the world faces today may be similar, this is not recognized. Today we are not even able to use surplus food, goods, or manufacturing capacity to help the poor nations.

This is a political and economic problem, not one of resource limitations. Perhaps the overriding necessity of the task will lead to ingenious solutions and even a survival mentality. Some of this is already occurring. For example, experts believe that one of the major causes of the greenhouse effect is the destruction of the rain forests caused by the desperate energy and land needs of the people who have access to them. Imaginative environmentalists have suggested that the more affluent nations of the world pay their owners fees to leave the forests in their natural condition. This is a wonderful example of an experiment that could easily be done. The rent would provide the needed food, fuel, and equipment for the country that owned the forests. It would be a steady source of income. The local people would be given employment maintaining and improving the forests. Perhaps as a one-world mentality develops, the nations, functioning together, will buy and preserve the essential lands around the world just as many of them do now within their own boundaries. Once a dedication to maintaining the ecosystem develops, there will be many such needs or opportunities around the globe.

Changing Directions

The first move of a new Department of Development should be to start coordinated planning efforts and joint research, development, and operational efforts. Within each nation there should be started many separate programs, focused on different tasks already outlined.

To oversee, support, and evaluate this major new effort in the United States, the Congress should probably establish a joint committee, not unlike the Joint Committee on Atomic Energy that guided the U.S. nuclear program for so many years. A comparable international oversight group should also be created. This level of attention and priority is needed to sustain this massive undertaking and to protect it from inevitable bureaucratic diseases. Because there will be no visible enemy to keep the world's attention and commitment focused on building a sustainable planet, there will be a need for such groups to keep reminding us of the urgency of the task.

As basic knowledge is accumulated and new ideas for coping with the problems emerge, it will undoubtedly be necessary to experiment with new technical solutions just as is done in the present DOD. Great new industries will be needed, and competition for both research and production contracts will be fierce. It will be *proud work*, and students will *once again* flock to study science and engineering. The excitement will again come from making things that improve the quality of life. As indicated earlier, the complex nature of the interaction of new technology with the already existing infrastructure of a society precludes making a detailed plan for solving these many global or local problems, or even for organizing the new DOD's. So humanity's task for the foreseeable future will be that of creating systems for focusing the man-made evolutionary process with its major elements of chance. Since there can be no comprehensive blueprint for the future, citizens and their governments will have to do a balancing act, continuously monitoring the state of their world, detecting problems and then developing new technologies and institutions to meet the changing conditions.

Just appreciating the uncertain prospect of the interactions and being prepared to change means and even goals will permit the emerging difficulties to be recognized and addressed more quickly. Currently, neither individuals nor governments approach a new enterprise with an adequate degree of tentativeness or alertness for signs of unanticipated effects. They are conditioned to believe that deviations from plans are human mistakes rather than inherent in life. Thus, rather than watch for errors, they try not to see them. Rather than look for corrective changes, they look for excuses until the errors become glaring and destructive. Although many nations, including the United States, have established agencies to detect and prevent environmental abuses, until now these groups have not even been able to slow down, halt, or reverse the damage being done.

A new world order is needed, one that focuses on the quality of life. International, interdisciplinary study activities should be started now to raise the level of concern and to point the way. If this happens, the day will come when a meeting such as this one will focus on needs and possibilities and concentrate on solutions, not a catalog of threats with their output of despair.

A Department of Development

A talk given by Jerry at an informal gathering hosted by Professor and Mrs. John Kenneth Galbraith at their home in Cambridge, Mass., May 17, 1988. Among the guests were Emma Rothschild, David Baltimore, Michael Dertouzos, John Gibbons, Penny Janeway, Richard Lester, Amartya Sen, and Sheila Widnall. The aim was to discuss ways to take advantage of reduced Cold War tensions as a "window of opportunity" to redirect military spending for civilian uses, particularly in science and technology.

✳

The purpose of this meeting is to identify a group of research, development, and production needs related to social and environmental problems. In a recent paper,[1] I proposed the creation and massive funding of a Department of Development which would have the responsibility for the continued evolution of civilian technology. In that paper, my focus was on those technologies which were essential to the salvation of civilization in the face of the accelerating erosion of the global ecosystem and the condition of life for vast numbers of the human race.

Although my suggestion was not motivated by the need to have tasks that would aid in the conversion from a military-driven economic system to one more civilian-oriented, this need could become an important economic issue in the years ahead. I believe that it is essential to initiate a major civilian R&D program, whether or not we slow down the military effort. Incidentally, I don't believe that a transition from a military to a civilian focus will be an easy transition. The needs will be very different, and unless R&D programs for civilian purposes have existed for some

---

1. "Survival, the Moral Equivalent of the Arms Race," presented at the Centennial Symposium of the National Geographic Society, Washington, D.C., January 29, 1988; published as "How Societies Learn," in *Earth'88, Changing Geographic Perspectives: Proceedings of the Centennial Symposium* (Washington, D.C.: National Geographic Society, 1988), pp. 350–357.

time, one will not know what to convert to. Experience bears this out. When military R&D slowed down in the 1960s, there was large-scale unemployment in the technical community. No one knew how to use the capabilities that were made available for civilian purposes.

There is an increasing awareness that the solution to the growing multi-crises facing humanity will be found in a judicious mixture of restraint and science and technology focused on improved life-support systems and global resource management. Although large-scale applications of technology are blamed for most of the threats to survival, there is also substantial agreement that only by concentrating on the development and use of more sophisticated technologies can the present degenerative trends be reversed. In fact, it is unlikely that even with an all-out effort will it be possible to undo all of the damage already done. For example, even if no additional carbon dioxide was added to the atmosphere, and destruction of forests stopped, the CO_2 already present would continue to change the global climate for a long time to come.

I believe that it is necessary to begin a coordinated program of research, development, and application for the myriad of ideas needed to reverse the destructive effects of large-scale technologies, the impact of population growth, and the misuse and destruction of much of the planet. Time is running out on several fronts. Such a program can only be created through a sustained, coherent effort that has the purposefulness and scale of the U.S. and Soviet military programs. The reason there has been a continuing parade of new weapons is because the Department of Defense has a complete system for developing weapons that includes basic research, an applied research program, a process for recognizing evolving needs, and a means of creating large-scale development and testing programs which in the end lead to new weapon systems and ultimately to large procurement programs. The present military system is the result of fifty years of evolution and development that began at the start of World War II. A similar effort is needed to create the system that will bring the human family into a stable and happy equilibrium.

With the exception of medical technologies and some chemical and energy developments, much of the recent high-tech progress in the civilian economy of the world has resulted from the application of research and development done for military purposes. In its early post–World War II phase, most military developments had direct civilian applications. The jet aircraft, radar, the transistor, the computer, and improved materials are examples of this. Over time this has changed. Now contemporary military developments are less applicable to civilian use. In addition, the military R&D programs are lopsided. Civilian problems such as pollution, hunger, mental health, the greenhouse effect, or the need for more effective educational means are not likely to be solved by the results of military R&D.

A central theme of my National Geographic paper was that the haphazard application of new developments for civilian purposes failed to anticipate their frequent destructive impacts. In particular, the global ecological impacts were ignored until recently, as were the spillover effects of industrialization on the people and countries not directly involved. Because of this neglect, the need for corrective action is very urgent. For this reason a large-scale early-warning system to anticipate major impacts of technological initiative should be an integral element of the organization.

Earlier, I excepted medical technologies in my discussion of need for large-scale R&D and applications. In this area there has been in effect a Department of Development—the Department of Health, Education, and Welfare—which supports large-scale R&D through the National Institutes of Health. As a consequence, there has been steady progress in the understanding of living systems, of disease, and of how to improve human health. The NIH has many individual Institutes charged with the responsibility for specific diseases and other problems, such as toxic effects of materials, as well as the basic research that is needed to understand the issues.

The HEW is a model for what I am suggesting, a Department of Development whose charter would be broad enough to allow it to mobilize research and development to cope with survival problems by producing technologies that would halt the destructive effects of current practices, expand the base of education worldwide, and make possible a global economy that opened up opportunities for people everywhere. There do exist federal agencies with responsibility for doing something about some of the problems I have mentioned—for example, the Department of Energy, the Environmental Protection Agency, the Food and Drug Administration, and the Department of Agriculture. But each of these is inadequate in many ways. Most important, both the agencies and their missions are too small. They have neither a sense of urgency nor a respect for the value of R&D in their long-term efforts.

Perhaps the Department of Development can be created by a consolidation of the existing agencies. This is dangerous because the task I am seeking to fulfill must be based on quality, persistence, and a full spectrum of scientific, technical, and social activities. I see an opportunity for a network of DODs in the industrialized nations, and in the developing nations too, with a diversity of tasks relevant to the needs of the individual countries and regions.

In their early stages, much of the effort of such groups should be concentrated on research and policy studies to provide a sound basis for the action programs needed to counter the individual problems on the world survival agenda. This effort will need the participation of all of the major industrial nations. Indeed, many of the problems that must be faced can only be handled through global cooperation. The production load of replacement and new infrastructure includes more efficient and less polluting fossil fuel power plants, including plants that consume coal without emitting CO_2, safe nuclear plants, super-computers to model global climate and pollution problems, efficient solar cells, educational technologies and software, large-scale desalinization systems, and unimagined new devices, materials, and techniques.

The purpose of this evening's meeting, as I said at the beginning, is to identify areas of research that would be appropriate for such an effort. We hope that this evening's discussion will stimulate each of you to think of technological needs that would contribute to social, environmental, and cultural progress in the future.

In Memory of Andrei Sakharov

Remarks by Jerry at a memorial ceremony in honor of Andrei Sakharov, leader of the Soviet dissident movement and Nobel laureate (Peace Prize, 1975), who died on December 14, 1989. Held at the American Academy of Arts and Sciences in Cambridge, Mass., on April 27, 1990, the ceremony was presided over by MIT physicist Herman Feshbach. Other speakers included Sidney Drell, Stanley Hoffmann, Robert Marshak, Yurii Orlov, and Valentin Turchin.

Jerry had corresponded with Sakharov since the late 1960s and went on to become a key supporter in the years that followed. "I want to emphasize," Sakharov wrote to him in 1974, "that all of us here are anxious to have open public statements supporting us. The only thing that protects us in our personal faith and in public affairs is to have wide publicity." Jerry invited him to come to MIT in the late 1970s, an invitation that Sakharov appreciated but knew was unrealistic—indeed, shortly thereafter, he was exiled to Gorky. Jerry finally met Sakharov in Moscow in February 1987.

I had some difficulty beginning this remembrance of Andrei Sakharov because I am not at all certain that he would have been comfortable with the only word my mind can find to describe him. I believe that Andrei Sakharov was one of the most heroic men of our time, and I do not think that he would care for that characterization of himself. He was basically a very modest person—modest, but at the same time very determined and strong-willed. It was one of the great privileges of my life to have had an opportunity to work with him for a short time on the International Foundation for the Survival and Development of Humanity, and particularly on his human rights activities in the Soviet Union. As a consequence, I got to know him a little bit. Along with many people all over the world, I share the feeling that his untimely death was a deep tragedy for all of us that we share with his family.

We live in a time which breeds heroic people, a time when states wield enormous, one might say, total power to subjugate the individual human being. To most people it seems hopeless to fight back, but a few individuals did—and do—nonetheless. Sakharov was one of those few. Such people usually struggle against great odds and face serious danger as well, usually using no weapon but their dignity. Andrei Sakharov used all of his powers and especially his extraordinary intellect, as well as his dignity and his courage, to wage his long campaign for a progressive world.

I first heard of Andrei Sakharov's campaign from Harrison Salisbury when, in 1966, he was writing the foreword and afterword to the *New York Times* translation of Sakharov's *Progress, Coexistence, and Intellectual Freedom.* Salisbury told me that he thought that the work was the most important statement about the current human dilemma that had been written. I agreed completely, for it not only spelled out convincingly the collision course that the superpowers were speeding down but, more important, Sakharov had a persuasive basis for hope essentially spelled out in the title of the book.

The book was widely hailed when it was released in 1968 because of the power and lucidity of Sakharov's arguments. More than that, the last chapter, entitled "The Basis for Hope," elaborates on his simple strategy for making a better world. The super-power leaders even tried parts of the prescription, what they understood of coexistence, but the essential ingredient—"Intellectual Freedom"—was too frightening for the Soviet Union's leaders. Though the book was issued in the Russian language in the West, it circulated only in the underground inside the Soviet Union.

Sakharov's and Elena Bonner's experiences since 1966 undoubtedly expanded his understanding of society's dilemmas. He has written a new book about them, which I understand is soon to appear,[1] and will certainly be as important to all of us who shared his hopes and dreams in his first work.

Sakharov was as dedicated to people as he was to his ideals. He and his wife spent much of their time and energy helping their fellow citizens who were in trouble. I recall his tireless effort to free his fellow prisoners of conscience. The first time I heard him talk about them, there were many hundreds still in prisons. Then, thanks to his efforts, there were only two hundred. After much hard work, speaking about their plight whenever he could, including to Gorbachev who pledged to do more about it, there were only nine. Andrei worked just as hard for the nine as he did for the many hundreds, and I remember, when there were just two, they still had his total commitment. I hope that these last two are now also free.

In an article written many years ago, Sakharov summed up humanity's situation with a mathematical analogy. He said that we were living in a very special time, a

---

1. Probably refers to Andrei Sakharov's *Memoirs* (Knopf, 1990).

saddle point in history. Close your eyes and see an ordinary riding saddle. Then look at some random points on its surface and note that there are many more ways to go down than to go up. Also, the further down one goes, the harder it will be to reverse direction. Until recently, history went ever downward. Our lifetime has been punctuated by the horrors of Stalin, Hitler, Mao and their successors, the Japanese Rape of China, the Ayatollah Khomeini, Pinochet, Vietnam, Afghanistan, Idi Amin, and countless other minor tyrants—and always present, the mind-numbing atom-bombing of Nagasaki and Hiroshima, with the even more incomprehensible possibility of a man-made Armageddon at any moment.

Many scientists tried to use their analytical skills to find a way out of humanity's march to a dead end; they used all the passion they could muster to awaken others to the danger. Sakharov's actions were a continuing inspiration to them.

When the Soviets invaded Afghanistan, Sakharov crusaded against it and became the most effective spokesman against the military action. As a consequence, he and his wife were exiled to Gorky where they had no access to the press or little to like-minded people. There they were subjected to inhuman conditions, including physical suffering for five years. Their response, combining the tradition of pacifism and the power of the intellect, excited and gave hope to oppressed people the world over.

Progress, as Sakharov said, requires first of all an end to wars and the threat of wars, and at the same time intellectual freedom. After Gorbachev came to power, new freedoms erupted in many countries in greater Europe. They were as welcome as they were unexpected, particularly in the Soviet Union.

Andrei Sakharov saw many dangers to the growing intellectual freedom from the shortcuts that were being taken, and his last speeches warned about them. The crisis he foresaw is now here. What will now be history's trajectory along the saddle? Will our leaders, beset by troubles, continue to heed his conviction of the central role of intellectual freedom to a better life?

President Eisenhower's Changing Search for Peace

A paper that Jerry wrote for a conference, "Eisenhower's World Legacy: Reappraisal of the Man and the Issues," held in Moscow, November 12–17, 1990. The conference was cosponsored by the Soviet Academy of Sciences, the Soviet Ministry of Foreign Affairs, the Institute of Military History, the Committee of Soviet Scientists in Defense of Peace Against the Nuclear Threat, and the Eisenhower Institute. Its purpose, according to chairman Georgiy Arbatov, was to recognize the achievement of "an American President who exercised wisdom and restraint throughout the crisis of the Cold War and launched the first projects of Soviet-American cooperation in culture and sciences."

When I was asked to write a piece for the Moscow celebration honoring President Eisenhower, I quickly said "yes" because I had so many pleasant memories of the times when I worked for him during his presidency. Now that I am faced with the task of writing something, I realize that a host of good writers have written all about his term in office and I am hesitant to add to that collection. So I have decided to write a little bit about what I think he thought about nuclear weapons, the arms race, the Soviet Union, and disarmament. The early years were gleaned mostly from speeches and what I heard from friends who knew him. What I have to say from 1953 on came increasingly from my own observations. In 1957 I was chairman of a group of the Gaither Panel that President Eisenhower initiated and, starting in 1958, I was a member of the President's Science Advisory Committee and chairman of its disarmament panel. In those roles I had an opportunity to observe his hopes, fears, and frustrations, as well as see how his views and priorities changed through time.

In 1957, while working in the White House, I received a letter from Lord Bertrand Russell inviting me to the second Pugwash meeting in Nova Scotia with a delegation of scientists from the Soviet Union. I showed the letter to Dr. James Killian,

Eisenhower's science adviser, and he showed it to the president, who said I should go because it might be interesting. He added, as an afterthought, that if I got into trouble they could always disown me! The meeting was indeed very interesting because the Soviet group was intent on talking about disarmament measures, and they were anxious to hear what we had to say. While there I met Academician Aleksandr Topchiev, the foreign secretary of the Soviet Academy of Sciences, who later invited me to the Soviet Union. Again, I had to ask the president's permission and again I was encouraged to go, with the same understanding.

Dwight Eisenhower became the president of the United States after a long career as the military leader of the Western forces in World War II and later as the first Supreme Commander of NATO. Between these two military commands, he served for a time as the president of Columbia University, where he befriended many members of the faculty, including I. I. Rabi, a Nobel Prize-winning physicist who had a major role in helping Eisenhower, the president, rally the support of the scientific community.

At the end of the war, the Western countries, including the United States, had demobilized their armies while Stalin had kept a large land force in place, possibly to counter the atomic bomb possessed by the United States and Britain. NATO was created as an answer to Stalin's behavior in the zones he controlled in Eastern Europe, the many threats to countries in the West, and to the Berlin blockade in which Stalin attempted to shut off supplies to Berlin. Eisenhower's experience as Supreme Commander of NATO led him to believe that the only language that Stalin understood was force, and when he became president his speeches and writings reflected that view. This feeling was reinforced by the belief that Stalin was helping the Chinese in the Korean conflict.

My experiences, starting in 1942, qualified me very well to help the president with the confusing technical policy issues that were vexing him. During World War II, I had been a staff member of the MIT Radiation Laboratory, where I had worked on microwave radar components and large airborne early warning radars, the ancestors of the AWACS. At the end of the war, I went to the Los Alamos Laboratory at the University of California (atomic bomb laboratory), where I helped set up an engineering division and was in charge of instrumentation for the Bikini test in the Pacific Ocean. After that I became a member of the faculty of MIT and an associate director of the Research Laboratory of Electronics, where I worked with the famed Norbert Wiener on information theory.

My attitude, like that of most Americans, was to forget world problems and get on with my life. Even so, from time to time I would join a group studying a military/technical problem, as President Truman and his staff worried about the threat that Stalin posed to Europe. Many of my colleagues from Los Alamos and the Radiation Laboratory joined in this effort. For example, when the U.S. Department of Defense became fearful of the long-range Soviet bombers, I helped conceive of the Distant Early Warning Line and the Continental Defense System. Even while I was willing to help defend the country from Soviet bombers, I had a visceral belief that the threat was exaggerated. In 1954, I was invited to be a member of a group called the Von Neumann Panel whose mission was to examine the state of ballistic missile development in the United States. This group formed because of persistent reports from the RAND Corporation of a major missile development in the Soviet Union. Andrei Sakharov discusses the origins of this program in his recent memoir. The Von Neumann Panel recommended a new design of missile, the Minuteman, propelled by a huge solid-fuelled rocket. This experience was the most complete engagement in military technology I had had since the war, and led to my becoming a part-time adviser to the White House.

When Eisenhower became president in 1952, his first goal was to end the Korean War, which he did promptly. At the same time, he undertook a continuing review of the American strategic position, a review that now seems to have been based on a Soviet threat that was in fact a reflection of the U.S. bomber force buildup rather than on any real facts about the Russian long-range attack capability. The first of this series of reviews was made by the Defense Department. Even using an optimistic performance by the U.S. air defense system, the study predicted that more than eighty million casualties would result from a full-scale Soviet attack. The president said, "We can't have that war."

After Stalin died in 1953, there was hope that the Cold War could be moderated, so Eisenhower followed two policies simultaneously: the strengthening of U.S. and NATO forces and beginning attempts to work out arms-control agreements with the Soviet Union. The first course was a response to the vastly superior Soviet land army and resulted in Secretary of State Dulles's policy of "massive retaliation."

The second effort was undertaken by a team led by Governor Harold Stassen, the president's personal assistant for disarmament. He and his Soviet counterpart, Andrei Gromyko, seemed to be making real progress when he encountered serious opposition at home both from the hawkish Democrats in Congress and the Secretary of State, who apparently regarded Stassen as a threat to his dominance in foreign affairs.

Later, when I became involved in arms-control negotiations with the Warsaw Pact nations, I learned how difficult it was to achieve a reasonable negotiating position because of various vested interests in our own government. We used to joke that negotiating with the Soviet delegates was easy compared to what we went through at home. From the team representing the Warsaw Pact, I developed the impression that they felt the same relief when they finally could begin to look for common ground between us. Both of us were required to request new instructions before we could make any significant change in our positions. This made it virtually impossible to make any progress toward an understanding. Even before we got together, it was possible to guess what the two sides would ask for—the Russians always wanted elimination of weapons to be followed by inspection, while the United States wanted the opposite, inspection followed by reduction of weapons. Each side wanted what was best for it, and until recently this remained so.

Each of the three branches of the military was vying for a place in the new missile era, so that a major task for President Eisenhower was to fight the duplication of the very costly facilities and missile research and development programs. His judgment was that the Soviet threat was greatly exaggerated, while at the same time he was worried about a threatening budget deficit. But two of the most powerful members of the Senate, Symington and Jackson, believed that he was wrong and that the country was completely exposed to a Russian first strike. History proved Eisenhower right on his assessment of both dangers.

To resolve the continuing uncertainty, Eisenhower engaged a study group—the Technological Capabilities Panel, chaired by Dr. James Killian of MIT—that, among other things, concluded that the intelligence information which underlay all of the attempts to predict what would happen to the country in the event of a nuclear war, was not to be believed. To cope with this problem, the group designed and had built a special aircraft, the U-2, that flew so high that it was invulnerable to Russian anti-aircraft defenses—for a while.

This aircraft played a decisive role in the course of the Cold War in the years that it was operational, sometimes in unexpected ways. Its use gave Eisenhower some assurance that his estimate of Soviet strength, not that of the "cold worriers," was closer to right. When one of the U-2s was intercepted in 1959, the incident derailed an Eisenhower-Khrushchev summit meeting which the president hoped would ease the super-power confrontation.

Even after the Soviet Union launched its Sputnik in 1957, thus showing an intercontinental missile capability, Eisenhower was not alarmed. But the country was. It was in a panic. The "missile gap" became the main issue in the next presidential election. When the dust settled, facts again proved the president right.

In 1959, Chairman Khrushchev proposed that the two super-powers agree to a moratorium in nuclear testing, and for a little while both countries agreed to it. I know from personal experience that President Eisenhower was pleased to join in it, but at the same time it worried him. Many people in the government and the press accused him of being naïve for trusting the Russians and thus putting the country in danger. He was especially troubled when the chairman of the Atomic Energy Commission, Lewis Strauss, and Dr. Edward Teller told him that a testing moratorium made it impossible to develop peaceful uses of nuclear explosions, essential for digging a sea-level canal to replace the Panama Canal, and the development of the neutron or clean bomb, necessary to the defense of Europe. At the same time, they also told him that it would be easy for the Soviets to develop new nuclear weapons clandestinely by hiding explosions in large holes. These claims were the basis of the incessant charges that eventually caused him to announce in the winter of 1960 that the United States government was no longer bound by the moratorium and was free to resume testing when it was in its interest to do so.

Though Eisenhower felt compelled to make this move because of the many pressures he was exposed to, he obviously was troubled enough by it to warn the nation about dangers of the Military-Industrial-Educational Complex, as he said in his valedictory speech at the end of his presidency.

I regarded President Eisenhower as a great leader, a willing learner, and a wonderful person to work for and with. When he realized that it was impossible to protect the American people from devastation by any military means, he had the courage to take a very unpopular position in favor of a nuclear test ban and arms limitations. Although he was not able to realize these goals, he was able to make them into serious and respectable aims for world leaders who would follow him. Though it was a long time coming, the present end to the Cold War began with his efforts.

The World Needs a Better Security System

An article written by Jerry in the context of unfolding world events in the early 1990s, particularly the Gulf War and rising tension in the Balkans. It went through several permutations, and was called "The New World Order" and "The World Needs a Common Security System" before Jerry settled on the final title. An earlier version was submitted to the Washington Post *in November 1991, but the editors declined to publish it. The present (final) version, dated December 1991 and apparently never published, was distributed in manuscript to agencies interested in issues of war and peace—such as the Carnegie Commission on Preventing Deadly Conflict and the Winston Foundation for World Peace—where it was favorably received, and called by one reader "timely and visionary."*

This is a unique moment in history when a Common Security System encompassing most of the United Nations' members is both necessary and possible. This would include bold new steps that eliminate exorbitant military expenditures, start to resolve the economic difficulties much of the world now faces, and quell the ethnic and other conflicts that continue to plague many nations. For a short time, such steps are now possible. The Carnegie Commission could recommend a new study of steps that would lead toward the goal of a proper new world order.

At the beginning of the Gulf War, as President Bush rounded up allies in the United Nations to drive Iraq from Kuwait, he said that "this is the beginning of the new world order." This was a very exciting idea to people all over the globe. They are still waiting to hear what the president meant.

If the world community fails to achieve a global security system, it will face a very dangerous future. Individual states, including the newly independent Soviet Republics, will feel compelled to continue to arm themselves and their military-industrial complexes will continue to flourish, making ever more high-tech weapons while their citizens' lives will continue to deteriorate. In the absence of a reassuring security system, Germany and Japan will feel increasingly insecure and rethink their commitment to the arms constraints that they were made to accept after World War II, and become large scale arms builders too.

Fortunately, there are alternatives. In 1980, at the height of the Cold War, Swedish Prime Minister Olof Palme organized an independent Commission on Disarmament and Security Issues to study alternatives to existing military policies. The Palme Commission report, crafted by a group of experts from many countries, including the Soviet Union and the United States, provides an outline of the major characteristics of a workable common security system. At that time, few were interested in the Commission's ideas. Today, it matches the needs of global security very well. In an extension of the Palme plan, the military forces permitted to exist in each nation would be set by formula as part of the proposed UN common security system. Weapons of mass destruction such as most nuclear weapons, poison gas, ballistic missiles, and bombers would be outlawed. A portion of a nation's force would be committed to the Security Council for its use in keeping the peace.

If implemented resolutely, such a system would make aggression a very unattractive option. It would function as an effective deterrent, for its very existence would make the use of force mostly unnecessary. It is doubtful, for example, if Iraq would have invaded Kuwait if it had been faced with the certain reaction of worldwide force, such as would have been the essence of the common security system the Palme Commission recommended. In addition to making the world a much more secure place, this system would make large sums of money available for other purposes.

The Palme Commission further suggested that it might be desirable for different regions of the world to have special arrangements with their neighbors for assuring their own security. This might be very useful in some areas and not at all functional in others. It is now possible to imagine such arrangements even in the Middle East. A stable Middle East peace agreement would be much more likely if it was assured by a common security system that included nations outside the region. Such an arrangement could also ameliorate a security problem the Palme group failed to foresee—the virulence of the ethnic conflicts in Eastern Europe, the Balkans, and many other places that would accompany self-determination.

The Palme Commission's recommendations should lead to proposals not only for a common security system to protect states and people against direct attack, but also for a legal system that would have binding power to adjudicate disputes between nations.

The European states have been exploring a common security system for the nations in their area. Very recently, the members of NATO agreed to decrease their stockpile of tactical nuclear weapons, while at the same time searching for a rationale to continue its existence with a continued U.S. involvement. Indeed, at the NATO Council meeting of June 1991, NATO ministers spoke of the need for "common and cooperative security." A visionary possibility would be to merge the European plans and NATO into a common security system for the European Community and any other nations that wanted to join, operating under the leadership of the United Nations.

To explore this, the United Nations should be given a mandate to make plans for the many aspects of the new world order, starting quickly with the Common Security System. It could move on to other global needs, including vital nonmilitary matters. As we make progress on these issues, we will develop the institutions, the protocols, and most important, the WILL to start to resolve the more difficult issues of human rights, full nuclear disarmament, and control of population growth. Best of all, progress on these issues will lead to increased prosperity everywhere and an invigorated human spirit.

Lillian

A talk given by Jerry at a forum on Lillian Hellman's life and work. While the sponsor and venue remain undetermined, the event probably happened in 1993 and may have been organized by Robert B. Silvers, cochair (with Hellman) of the executive committee of the Committee for Public Justice. The committee, a civil-liberties advocacy group, had been founded in 1970 to defend the integrity of the Bill of Rights against abuses by the U.S. government; Hellman had been a prime mover, and Jerry a charter member.

Jerry's friendship with Hellman extended from the mid-1960s until her death in 1985. They shared a number of political interests and values, and Jerry was instrumental in bringing her to MIT as a visiting professor on more than one occasion in the late 1960s and early 1970s.

When Bob asked me to participate in this panel, my first thought was, why me? But, as I thought about it, I realized that there were many reasons why I wanted to do it. First of all, Laya and I became dear friends of hers. Lillian had hosts of friends, as well as some well-worn enemies too. But I like to think that for each other we were special, perhaps the better word is unusual, intimates.

For her, I was an entry point to the mysteries of science and machines. For us, she and her friends on the Vineyard made us part of the liberal literary set which spent much of its time trying to right the many wrongs of the world, something I found very special after three-and-a-half years in Washington where so many people consumed their time ensuring the status quo and their happy place in it, and worse yet, sometimes doing it for money. I had watched John Kennedy's many attempts to slow down the arms race and give more equality to our black citizens, and seen how hard it had been to do what was obviously right and in the best interests of the nation. It reminds me of Hillary and Bill Clinton's current battles.

We met Lillian Hellman through John and Barbara Hersey, who spent much of their time looking after her in the twenty or so years that we knew her. She had difficulties with her sight and was living alone except for the steady flow of visitors that kept her from being too lonesome—a stream that ranged from Joe Alsop, who came one or two weeks each year so that they could carry on their long-running intellectual wrestling match, to close friends such as Peter Feibleman, the author of *Cakewalk*, who is a member of this panel.

The first thing that attracted me to her was her total honesty when it mattered. She was fearless, and how often she was right. As we got to know her well, we realized that she was also the best storyteller we had ever known. Not surprising, I suppose, for one of the world's best playwrights, she could enchant her listeners for half a dinner time with her troubles with the postmaster or the difficulty of getting a Japanese beetle off of one of her beautiful and precious rose plants.

Someone recently raised the question of whether or not Lillian, in giving these rather regular dinners—for mostly the same people, plus the guest of the week—was conducting a salon. The dictionary says that "a salon is an assemblage of persons, usually of social or intellectual distinction, who frequent the home of a particular person." I guess we were guilty. I doubt that Lillian knew that this was what she was doing.

Often some tangible action resulted from these salons. Maybe that is why it was not a salon. The most enduring venture that I remember was the "Committee for Public Justice," whose membership I have forgotten beyond Lillian, John Hersey, and myself. Maybe Bob is a member. I say "is" because I don't think that we ever disbanded. This committee is a good example of Lillian's prescience, for our target was just one person, J. Edgar Hoover. I doubt that even she could have imagined the total depravity of the man, or it would have ended up in "scoundrel time." The committee almost cost me the presidency of MIT, because we had the audacity to run an ad in the *New York Times* that said, "Protect Your Bill of Rights," and an alumnus member of the search committee came to one of its meetings waving the ad and shouting that he had proof that Wiesner was a communist. I guess someone must have explained to him what it said, for he eventually voted for me.

Lillian and I had a longstanding dispute which she eventually won. She wanted to be buried in the Chilmark Cemetery that stands on a hill overlooking the Atlantic Ocean, for the view was so nice. To own a plot there you had to be a resident of Chilmark, which she was not, so I offered to sell her a piece of my land if she would deed it back to me in her will. Somehow this seemed unreasonable to her and it never was done.

One night about 1 A.M., I received a phone call from Lillian's secretary saying Miss Hellman had just died and her last words were that "John and Jerry would know what to do." I called John Hersey and asked him if he had ever run a funeral, because I hadn't and didn't know what to do. John was as innocent as I, so we decided that in the morning John would call Lillian's lawyer and ask if she had left any instructions. John received just two instructions. Lillian wanted to be buried in the Chilmark Cemetery and we were to buy the least expensive casket. Beyond that, we were on our own.

Our first call was to the undertaker, who had expectations of selling a four-thousand-dollar casket for his famous client. John explained that we were under orders to buy the cheapest one, which cost seven hundred dollars. The undertaker kept saying, "You can't bury her in that." Actually, we thought that it was the nicest one in the parlor. When he finally consummated the transaction, we were asked for the details of the internment—the place, the time, and the other details that we hadn't thought about—so John and I divided the chores. I was to see about the Chilmark plot and John took over the rest of the arrangements.

After a bit of searching, I found the cemetery manager, who told me something that I already knew—that he was only allowed to give space to town residents. My pleading was to no avail. When I asked whether the cemetery wouldn't like someone of Lillian's distinction, he said "Not particularly." They already had Belushi and his admirers tramping over the flowers and leaving beer cans on the grounds. We seemed to be at an impasse, when he suddenly had an inspiration. He unfolded the large roll of blueprints that he had been carrying, looked at them for a while, and finally said, "You have a couple of extra plots—why don't you use one of them?" I realized that Lillian had won as I said, "I guess so."

The next day was sunny, blowy, beautiful, and one could see forever over the ocean—the kind of day Lillian had dreamed of. At two o'clock a couple of hundred of Lillian's admirers stood to listen to some of her closest friends say a public goodbye.

In the years since, we have planted flowers on her grave. When I leave, I often imagine that I hear her hearty laugh whistling in the winds. In whimsical moments, I think I will hear that laugh through all eternity.

Award Speech

Prepared by Jerry for the ceremony at which he was awarded the Public Welfare Medal of the National Academy of Sciences, April 24, 1993. The medal is the academy's highest honor, and was bestowed on Jerry "for his devoted and successful efforts in science policy, education, and nuclear disarmament and world peace."

Receiving the National Academy Public Service Award and the words that accompany it are humbling. Thank you, Frank Press, and thank you colleagues. Thank you, also, to all of my friends who gathered here to watch me receive it. My only regret is that Laya can't be here with us, since most of you are her friends, too.

As I have been pondering what I might say as a summing up, I have realized that my active lifetime has spanned much of what we might call the scientific industrial revolution, the period when large-scale scientific discovery has been used as the basis for new technology. Much of the time the driving force came from our military efforts over all of those years as we strove to be a super-power racing with the Soviet Union. This created a funding imbalance in science that President Clinton must now try to correct.

When World War II led me to MIT in 1942, more than fifty years ago, I was one of 4,000 people who made radar a reality to help win the war. We were quite sure we had done just that and were proud of it. At the end of the war, I went to Los Alamos with colleagues from the MIT Radiation Lab with the unrealistic goal of redesigning the atomic bomb. When the enormity of that job sank in, we started Sandia and then I was given another assignment.

While at Los Alamos, I found the local scientists arguing about whether or not the bomb should have been used against Japan, and fighting against the Army's control on nuclear energy. They ultimately had their way. The Federation of

American Scientists and the *Bulletin of the Atomic Scientists* were born during this struggle.

My new task was overseeing the instrumentation of the bomb tests against ships at the Bikini Atoll. The damage to the ships was much greater than had been expected, and so was the long-lasting radiation. This, coming after the annihilation of Hiroshima and Nagasaki, made an indelible impression on my mind that is still there. These experiences made me conscious of the enormous danger of nuclear weapons, their destructiveness, and their uselessness in war. How to get rid of them has been an important part of my life ever since.

At MIT, I worked with Jerrold Zacharias on a series of defense studies motivated by fear of the Soviet Union. In time, I was invited to participate in more and more of such studies around the country. The more I learned, the more I worried that much of what we did made the country more, not less, vulnerable. Finally, when I was a member of the Gaither Panel on Civil Defense in 1957, working in the White House under President Eisenhower, much of what I saw first-hand convinced me that most U.S. military intelligence was a reflection of our own plans and that we were mostly running an arms race with ourselves. The one exception to this was the development of missiles, which the Air Force didn't like. In fact, I once heard General LeMay say that he didn't like missiles because they had no loyalty. Of course, he had many other reasons for not liking them, such as his own bombers.

Many other people, some of them here tonight, had the same experience I had, discovering the hard way that almost any weapon that was invented would be procured, and the more we raced, the more dangerous life became for all of us, as well as for our opponents. Two examples are the tactical nuclear weapons that were a great menace with no redeeming properties, and the multi-warhead missile which started out as a system for confusing anti-missile defenses and became a means of threatening missiles in their silos with a first strike. In the end, many of us spent part of our time trying to slow down or shut down the arms race in order to make the country more secure. We had three threats: the Soviet Union, our own inventiveness, and the military analysts' penchant for always doing worst-case analyses.

In 1958, I was made a member of the Eisenhower Science Advisory Committee and chairman of the Disarmament Panel. When Jack Kennedy became president, he chose me to be his science adviser. When I demurred, saying that people thought I was too wedded to disarmament, he told me that was the reason he wanted me. He had his heart set on stopping nuclear testing. During his term, we managed to achieve a partial test ban, and it is my belief that had he lived, we would also have succeeded in getting a comprehensive ban in spite of the great opposition to it by the military, the Joint Committee of the Congress, and the many mistakes that we made.

Now that the Soviet Union is no more and the United States is the world's only military super-power, It has been impossible so far to get a consensus on what that should mean. But it is clear that the president needs some fiscal breathing room which can come from the oversized military budget. That was the reason my colleagues, Philip Morrison and Kosta Tsipis, and I made our alternate defense budget. Unfortunately, not many people have rushed to embrace it, probably because most people, even those in the Administration, have no clear-cut understanding or authority over the defense budget. As we puzzled about the situation, we decided that the new military needs and the budget for them can only be determined with the help of the Congress. For that reason, we concluded that one of the armed services committees, in the House or Senate, should hold hearings on the future military needs of the military services.

After the Vietnam War, Senator McIntyre led the Senate Arms Services Committee in two sets of interweaving hearings to assess the defense needs as that war ended. One of the hearings examined weapons systems, their capabilities and limitations, and the second dealt with military missions. Each of the hearings heard from each of the branches of the Armed Services, the Joint Chiefs, retired officers, defense scholars, Congressional agencies, industry, labor, representatives of the executive branch of the government, and a miscellaneous group of interested citizens. There was an urgency then because we had to judge the threats posed by the Soviet Union and its wars of liberation, and decide the best way to proceed. The result of this matrix of hearings was a clarification of what was required and what was necessary and sufficient to insure the security of the country.

Similar hearings are badly needed now as we enter a new era of undetermined security needs. The military has not offered a coherent, reasoned set of requirements based on probable threats, but rather only some vague generalizations that add up to the present missions of the four services. Also, the new Administration has a series of handicaps that make it unlikely that the leadership can ever come from there. The president's unfamiliarity with military matters will make him reticent to strike out boldly. In addition, the Administration's and Congress's view on what is needed is distorted by the politics of local job retention. Similarly, industry and labor can only offer extremely parochial advice. Witness the debacles: the new Seawolf submarine, a totally unneeded multi-billion dollar public works program; the never-needed B–2 stealth bombers that cost somewhere between one and a half and two billion dollars apiece; the Star Wars anti-missile program that was started without any idea of how to do it and certainly isn't needed now, even if it could be built; or the giant C-17 transport plane that isn't needed and is in so much technical trouble.

This waste of money is very serious at a time of growing mega-debts. It is easy, as Tsipis, Morrison, and I—and many others, too—have shown, how to save thirty billion dollars more than is now contemplated in the next year alone. But equally serious is the lack of planning for the U.S. forces for the year 2000 and beyond that will be acceptable to all (to us and our allies), helpful to the economic recovery of the country, and yet fair to taxpayers and the military personnel who have devoted their lives and careers in service to the nation.

While it is not possible even to outline such a set of comprehensive hearings in the limited time I have now, I can provide a few broad questions to indicate the nature of the inquiry:

1. Force structure: should we retain the traditional four services, move to a functional basis, or have a hybrid system?
2. What should be our nuclear deterrent or should there even be one: How many warheads are needed past the year 2000 and what should be their carriers?
3. How do we accommodate international forces devoted to providing common security?
4. How do we assure necessary and sufficient research, development, testing, and engineering in the new world order to ensure our military security?
5. What is the nature of dual-use technologies that could satisfy both military and civilian needs?
6. What is the need, if any, for nuclear testing?

I have a much longer list but no time to discuss it, so these are but a few of the many topics that need to be examined in a coherent set of hearings to provide a road map for the military of the future.

Once again, I want to tell you how proud and honored I am for receiving this prestigious award, and thank you very much.

SELECTED LETTERS AND DOCUMENTS

Letter to Theodore Sorensen, December 19, 1960

J. B. Wiesner to Theodore Sorensen, December 19, 1960, written about three weeks before the announcement of Jerry's appointment as JFK's special assistant for science and technology. Jerry outlines a number of complex technical, political, managerial, and financial issues for the incoming U.S. president to consider as he plans directions for the nation's fledgling space program.

We had the first meeting of the Ad Hoc Space Panel in New York last Friday, and while we barely scratched the surface of this problem, there are a number of things I can report at this time, particularly with respect to matters that should be promptly brought to the attention of the Senator.[1]

The two most urgent problems which must be faced are:

a. The Government mechanism for effectively managing the United States space program, and

b. The factual details of the man-in-space program and the possible embarrassment that could accompany a premature attempt to orbit man.

With regard to the management problem, we are confronted with a very large (about 2 billion dollars) program divided more or less equally between the Department of Defense and NASA. When the civilian space agency, NASA, was established certain guidelines for the division of responsibility were set up, NASA to have programs of purely scientific and exploratory nature, while the military programs were to be limited to those which clearly had relevance to our military posture.

In addition to NASA, the Congress established the National Aeronautics and Space Council to coordinate the two programs and resolve the inevitable

---

1. I.e., Senator Kennedy, U.S. president-elect.

jurisdictional conflicts. So far, this mechanism has failed to function effectively and, in fact, the Space Council has been almost totally dormant for the past year. Before making any recommendations regarding this structure, we want to determine whether it can be made to function effectively under the present law. In view of the continuing emergence of a large number of proposed space programs, both military and nonmilitary, there is a clear need for decisive management. We feel that the new Administration must face up to this critical management problem promptly, even now, or we will soon be confronted by an even more complex situation.

There is a rather considerable spectrum of opinion with regard to possible changes in the management structure ranging all the way from giving the military total responsibility for space—a position which I would oppose vigorously—to the integration of all space in a new civilian Department of Security Research, a proposal that Tom Finletter made during the Symington Committee study. The management problem is, in itself, a sufficient task for a good committee, and I would like to raise the question as to whether our present panel, attempting as it is to look at the full range of space problems, will be able to give sufficient attention to this difficult problem.

As I am sure you are aware, the U.S. man-in-space program is regarded by most knowledgeable observers to be definitely marginal. This comes about not as a result of the lack of resources, though I am not sure we couldn't use slightly more support, but because of the lack of adequate boosters for this mission. We are having to make a number of compromises in the man-in-space system in order to have any hope of an early success. For example, it would probably be 1965 at the very earliest on the present program before we would be able to have a much more substantial man-in-space program. It is possible that large increases in financial support could change this date somewhat, but I would be surprised if it would make any significant change so we are simply stuck with the situation I have described. On the other hand, the Soviet Union has available considerably bigger boosters so that the task of putting a man in space is somewhat simpler for them. I would be very surprised if the Russians do not succeed with their man-in-space program within the next year.[2]

We must therefore prepare now to meet the propaganda psychological impact of such a success any time after the Senator assumes office. The recent Soviet re-entry failure probably has slowed their program down a little bit, but from discussions I had with key Soviet scientists on my recent trip, I got the impression that they are

---

2. A prophetic statement—Yuri Gagarin's pioneering orbital space flight took place on April 12, 1961.

expecting to make an attempt soon. The question of what to do with our own program will be even more confusing if the Russians do succeed in putting a man in space, because then every failure of our program will be more glaring in the face of the Russian success, and yet it would probably be unwise to stop our program after the Soviets have launched their man-in-space program. Probably the right approach is to make a hero of the Soviet astronaut and offer him a movie contract. I say this facetiously, but it does seem to me that it would be wise to think a little bit now about how we ought to handle this potentially embarrassing situation.

In addition to the short-range problem of man-in-space, there are a number of painful long-range problems to be faced. The most important of these is the level at which we intend to fund the follow-on programs. I understand that it would be necessary to commit somewhere between 30 and 40 billion dollars over the next decade if we should allow the natural evolution of these programs.

It is hard to justify these expenditures for any imaginable military or scientific objective. Obviously if we continue in the race with the Russians, it would be justified by prestige arguments and possibly as a great adventure or as exploration which man can enjoy if he wants to. Certainly manned or unmanned reconnaissance of the planets Venus and Mars would be the great adventures of the century. On the other hand, while most of this is called science, I do not know a scientist who would support even the present level of space exploration—called science—solely for the purely scientific goals. The decision of how much or how little to do in this field is critical not only because of the competition with the Soviets in space, but because these vast sums of money if spent on space ventures will undoubtedly impair our ability to support other areas of governmental activity, including real science. A possible solution to this problem would be to embark on international projects of space exploration supported by a cooperating group of nations to avoid the waste incurred by a race and duplication. In other words, we might attempt to make this the great adventure of all mankind rather than a race between two competing groups.

While a superficial view of the space race would lead one to conclude that the U.S. has not caught up with the Soviet Union, the fact of the matter is that in every area not requiring the use of large payloads we have moved steadily and decisively ahead of the Soviet Union. Our meteorological satellites, our broad spectrum of scientific investigation in space, passive communications satellites, reconnaissance satellites, etc. have demonstrated a United States capability and versatility which the Soviet Union cannot approach. We should appreciate and publicize these achievements. Moreover, we should now undertake certain obviously achievable and desirable space developments, as for example, communication relayings FM broad-casting from satellites, regular navigational satellite service, etc. In this way we could make a genuine contribution to technological progress and direct the drive for achievements in space into those areas where we can take advantage of our real technical superiority.

There are a number of other problems which our group intends to examine in detail when we meet next, including the balance of science and technology in the space program, the means of using the data now being obtained by satellites, etc., the question of what should be said about U.S. space activities in the State of the Union message, and a review of a variety of military space activities.

Now for miscellaneous comments, I would like to stress the desirability of appointing the NASA Administrator soon, if possible. The present incumbent is trying his best to hold the line in the various conflicts in which his agency finds itself, but because his term is obviously limited he is at rather a considerable disadvantage.

Letter to John F. Kennedy, February 20, 1961

J. B. Wiesner to the president, February 20, 1961; an unclassified memorandum written three weeks after assuming his duties as special assistant for science and technology. Jerry assesses the Soviet and American space and ballistic programs, and, more broadly, the relative strengths and weaknesses of Soviet and American science, along with their political implications.

✵

Following up on our conversation of the other evening, I would like to elaborate on the questions posed by the Russian Venus shot and our relative positions in the general fields of space exploration and science.[1] The most significant factor, as we have said many times, is that the Soviets have developed a rocket as part of their ballistic missile program with considerably more thrust or lifting power than anything we have available. We know that the Soviet booster can put payloads of the order of several tons (the most recent one was announced to be seven tons) in a low orbit, while the best we can do at the present time, using our latest combination rocket Atlas-Agena, is approximately 5,000 pounds. This combination was used to launch the recent Samoa shot. These figures indicate that the Soviets have approximately a three-to-one advantage in weight-lifting capability at this time. This corresponds roughly to the difference we believe to exist in the payload capability of the USSR vs. U.S. ballistic missiles.

We do not fully understand why the Soviets chose to make so large a ballistic missile, because it is undoubtedly a nuisance to operate. We suspect that the design was well under way before the feasibility of thermonuclear bombs was proven and that it was probably designed to carry ordinary nuclear weapons which are much

---

1. The Soviets' first Venus probe was launched February 12, 1961.

heavier. Also, the Soviet Union has been developing ballistic missiles for a considerably longer period of time than has the U.S., so they have had the advantage of an orderly evolutionary program. They began with a relatively short-range missile (200 to 300-mile range), went to a 600-mile missile, then a 900-mile missile, and on up to the IRBM stage,[2] and finally to the present long-range missile. By doing this they were in a position to use many of the components developed in one stage for successive stages, possibly making only minor changes and improvements. We, on the other hand, because of our late entry in the missile field, have found it necessary to develop complete missile systems with entirely new components. This has resulted in more duplications in our experimental program than has been the case in the Soviet program. It is my personal opinion, as a matter of fact, that some of this duplication and accompanying difficulty could have been avoided had our program been somewhat better integrated.

We do not expect to have boosters comparable to the present Soviet booster for approximately three years, though I believe we should be able to speed this up with hard work, so that we must expect continued embarrassments of the present type for some time, because in any space exploit requiring large payload capability the Soviet Union is ahead. On the other hand, as we have frequently said, the U.S. has done by all odds the most impressive job of exploiting its payload capability for scientific purposes. The Soviets have done surprisingly little with the opportunities they have had. The most impressive things that they have done were photographing the back side of the moon and transmitting the photographs back to earth (and this was a superb technical performance) and the return of the dogs from orbit. The U.S. has to its credit the discovery and definition of the Van Allen belts; the first precise geodetic use of an artificial earth satellite to obtain refined information on the size and shape of the earth; the first achievement of both active and passive communications satellites; discovery of a large electrical current system about the earth; successful use of weather satellites with cloud cover pictures and earth heat balance measurements; the first measurements of interplanetary magnetic fields; radio communication at inter-planetary distances; and the first simultaneous observation of solar disturbances and associated magnetic storms from interplanetary space and on earth. Unfortunately, it is much more difficult to dramatize these things than it is the massive performances by the Soviet Union.

One of the things we must realize is that in dramatizing the space race we are playing into the Soviet's strongest suit. They are using this accomplishment at home

---

2. Intermediate-Range Ballistic Missile.

A tour of the Marshall Space Flight Center, Huntsville, Alabama, September 11, 1962—*from left to right*: President Kennedy, Wernher von Braun, James Webb, Vice President Johnson, Robert McNamara, Jerry, and Harold Brown. JFK witnessed a heated debate on this occasion between Jerry and von Braun, director of the Center. Jerry argued the value of unmanned space missions, von Braun the value of sending a man to the moon. (Courtesy of NASA.)

and around the world to prove the superiority of Soviet science and technology and to divert attention from many of their more mundane difficulties. The fact of the matter is that Western science, and particularly American science, is still vastly superior in most fields to Soviet science and they know this as well as we do. Furthermore, in almost any other arena in which we would elect to compete, food, housing, recreation, medical research, basic technological competence, general consumer goods production, etc., they would look very bad. We should attempt to point this out rather than assist them by an official and press reaction which supports their propaganda.

Letter to John F. Kennedy, December 18, 1961

Jerome B. Wiesner to the president, December 18, 1961, a memorandum written nearly a year into his appointment as JFK's science adviser. Jerry captures a complex range of themes in U.S.-Soviet relations—disarmament prospects, scientific exchanges, political tensions, and civil liberties—in a forceful, concise way. Both JFK and LBJ were known to have appreciated the brevity and directness of Jerry's writing style.

As you know, Ambassador Menshikov recently invited me to lunch with him, and I did on Wednesday, December 13th. I will put down a few of the more interesting points of our conversation for your information.

Menshikov began the conversation with a bit of flattery, saying that I was well known to Soviet scientists and that they had often expressed high regard for my work. I told him that I knew a great many Soviet scientists, both as a result of their visits here and my two visits to the Soviet Union; and that I knew a few of them, such as Topchiev, reasonably well. I said that I also had followed the work of their computer specialists, communications engineers, and radio astronomers rather closely, and thought that they did good work.

I used this opportunity to say that we had hoped to be able to work out some cooperative research activities with the Soviet Union and regretted the fact that so far we had been unable to do so. He said the Soviet Union was also anxious to do this. I responded that while their scientists often expressed an interest in such programs, when pressed they always retreated to the position that such things had to be worked out in the political department, to which they had no access. Menshikov suggested that if we had specific proposals to make, we do so either through him or through Ambassador Thompson in Moscow, and I agreed to see if there are any specific projects that we would like to propose at this time.

He then brought up the question of disarmament and nuclear testing, and we had the usual East-West disagreement about inspection versus disarmament. We spent 15 or 20 minutes arguing the point and concluded the debate with a draw. In fact, he seems to know little about the subject, and I was left with the impression that he was just repeating well-known slogans such as "the important thing is to inspect disarmament, not armaments," etc.

On the matter of nuclear testing, I said that I thought the matter could be resolved if they would just agree to the proposals they themselves had backed prior to the Summer of 1960, including the Geneva Inspection System and control machinery. He said that they were no longer willing to accept the on-site inspection system because they had become convinced that it wasn't needed to control nuclear testing and that it would offer opportunities for espionage. Incidentally, during the earlier discussion about disarmament he had said that there was very little need for inspection since our intelligence system was undoubtedly good enough to tell us what we needed to know, a remark which I had ignored the first time, but when he repeated it in the testing context, I asked what they were trying to hide, and he said it was just a matter of principle. I disagreed with his statement about the lack of need for an underground test detection system and actually got him to admit that it was probably needed if we wanted to be sure that clandestine testing was not taking place. His view was that it didn't make any difference anyway, because both sides now had sufficiently well developed weapons so that further progress was unnecessary. In defense of their recent testing program, he said that it was well known that Western nuclear weapons were far superior to those of the Soviet Union prior to their tests, and that they had reluctantly concluded that the balance had to be redressed. He went on to say, quite explicitly, that if we continued testing, even underground, they would resume, and that he didn't think the world would be a better place for either of us if this happened. I said that while I agreed that an accelerated arms race was a bad thing, there was general feeling in this country that the recent unilateral Soviet actions might be repeated in the future, and that we should not participate in any moratorium unless accompanied by firm agreements including adequate inspection. I told him that whatever were their reasons for resuming testing, their actions seriously set back prospects for any agreement because of the almost universal belief that they are not serious.

We had an interesting discussion about which country offered the most freedom of opportunity for workers, the U.S. or the USSR, in the course of which I made the statement that the workers in the United States had already achieved most of the objectives which the Soviet leaders were promising their workers. This annoyed

Menshikov somewhat, and he said that the workers in this country had no political voice in government. In fact, he went on to say that there wasn't a worker in our Congress, to which I took exception, saying that I knew a great number of Congressmen who had been laborers of various kinds and he said, "Ah, yes, but now they are Congressmen, they are no longer workers." I asked how he could expect them to be both, and he said in the Soviet Union actual workers were delegates to their Congress. I asked how they carried on both jobs, and he pointed out that they only had to meet in Congress every two years. When I laughed at this, he shook his head sadly and said, what hope was there if even the scientists didn't understand. On this delightful note we parted.

Incidentally, he asked why Mac Bundy was anti-Soviet. I replied that I didn't know that he was and asked why Menshikov thought so. He said that this was the impression that people had formed at Berlin. I told him that it would not be surprising, considering Mac's job, to find him exasperated by Soviet actions. I have repeated this to Mac.

Report on Meeting with Soviet Ambassador Anatoly Dobrynin, March 1967

Part of an internal memorandum "to file," summarizing a meeting between Jerry and Anatoly Dobrynin at the Soviet Embassy, Washington, D.C., March 1967. Jerry had known Dobrynin since March 1962, when Dobrynin arrived in Washington as Soviet Ambassador to the United States. They met regularly during Jerry's White House years and remained cordial acquaintances afterward. Jerry arranged for Dobrynin to pay an official visit to MIT in October 1967, and continued corresponding with him into the late 1970s.

⚛

This is a report of my luncheon meeting with Soviet Ambassador Dobrynin, which took place after he had called me relaying the invitation to Laya and me to spend two weeks in the Soviet Union at our convenience. I had tried to get from him over the telephone some indication of whether there was any significance to the invitation other than goodwill, and in particular, whether there was any interest on the part of the Soviet government to have me come early in order to discuss such things as the antiballistic missile moratorium.

When I arrived, I was shown into the living room where he normally receives guests and we talked there for about 15 or 20 minutes before going into the dining room. He started by asking whether I had really made up my mind about the trip and when I could go. I told him that I was trying to decide whether it made more sense to try to go soon for a relatively short trip of one week rather than think about something more leisurely during the summer, and he said that it really didn't matter. He gave no indication at all of any feeling on his part. He did say, of course, that they would be interested in talking with me about various arms control measures that I have been recommending. He also reminded me that I had a standing invitation to give some disarmament lectures at the request of the Soviet-American Society. I told him that I knew that and it was one of the things I planned to do if I went.

Soviet Ambassador Anatoly Dobrynin (center) chats with Jerry, Charles Stark Draper (to Dobrynin's left), and others during a visit to MIT, October 1967. (Courtesy of the MIT Museum.)

He then asked whether I had anything very definite that I wanted to see in the Soviet Union. I said "no," but that I had many friends I would like to make sure that I saw—such as Millionshchikov, whom he reminded me had been in Paris, and many others whom he said would be glad to see me whenever I came. I also told him that I was continuing my interest in data processing, radioastronomy, and cybernetics in general.

Following a general discussion about my trip, the Ambassador asked me what I thought about the nonproliferation treaty and its possibilities. I told him that I hadn't been following it carefully, but that it seemed to be making progress. I asked what he thought, and he said that it would probably have a certain amount of difficulty among the Europeans because of inspections but that the United States and the Soviet Union, by means of the preamble, have succeeded in ironing out their own difficulties, and that this was an important step forward.

We then turned to a discussion of other measures, and he asked me whether I still believed that an antiballistic missile ban should be considered. I told him the view that I had expressed in the IGY Report a year or so ago and discussed with him at great lengths was still my view. I said that I knew that the Soviet view was somewhat different, but that I had been heartened by their willingness to at least talk about it. He said that he thought he believed pretty much as Kosygin did that it was better to spend your money on defense than on offense, to which I agreed but that I didn't think that this was possible. If I felt that it were possible to have large-scale production of defensive systems without inducing another round of offensive deployment, I would certainly not disagree. But I said I didn't think it was possible to have either the United States or the Soviet Union deploy what appears to be partially effective defensive systems without the other feeling compelled to increase its deterrent force back to somewhere near the point where it had been before in terms of effectiveness.

This, it seemed to me, sort of vitiated the whole idea. In other words, if it were possible to suggest some way to build defenses and not let the other side fear that its deterrent had been completely vitiated, then I would agree with Kosygin and the Ambassador, but I didn't think that it was reliable and, in fact, I felt that the same thing that had happened in the air defense business would happen in the case of the antiballistic missile. I felt that the United States and the Soviet Union actually were more vulnerable after they had each spent rather considerable amounts of money on defense than they had been before, because of the over-response of the strategic forces. I said that I had watched with interest for a number of years the growth of their air force and ours in response to the construction of defense systems, and while I didn't know much about the build-up of the Soviet force, I was convinced that the U.S. response to the Soviet air defenses had created a situation where the Soviet Union would have been more seriously damaged than less if war had occurred.

I asked him whether he thought that were so. He maintained that he didn't know very much about air defenses. I said that I had worked on them long and hard and thought I had a pretty good assessment of them, and felt that neither of us had succeeded in building air defense capable of stopping the other's strategic forces completely. We talked about this general theme for quite a while, and he asked me whether I thought that this really would happen again with ballistic missiles. I said I thought it would because we now had so many more options in defense when it came to playing the game of surprises. I also pointed out something that most people lose track of; he admitted it was so—namely, that they could build a defense against ballistic missiles and still be vulnerable to aircraft, so that one had to consider that in deciding whether or not a defense was really worthwhile.

After a considerable discussion of this kind, he said that he thought it would make sense if one could restrict strategic weapons well. I told him that I thought a strategic weapons freeze or cutback made a great deal of sense, but in the past the Soviet

Union had not been willing to talk about percentage cuts in defense at the time of the conferences in the mid 1950s. I also said that I didn't think that to drastically lead to a very small number of weapons was feasible at this stage, and that one had to approach any strategic cutbacks gradually.

He then asked what other things I felt were important. I said that I still felt that strengthening the United Nations peacekeeping machinery was an important thing, to which he essentially didn't respond except that there were problems there. I went on to say that I thought the United States and the Soviet Union should show more restraint in the distribution of conventional weapons we have, as I already indicated in our IGY Report, and that I noted they had signed another agreement to deliver another $100,000,000 worth of weapons in the Middle East. His reply was simply "that we were helping you by doing this."

We then turned again to discussion of my trip. He asked me what cities in Eastern Siberia we would like to go to. I said I didn't really care so much, but that I just wanted to have the feeling for that part of the Soviet Union, whether we went from Delhi or wherever we happened to be beforehand to a point where we could ride the China-Siberia Railroad a couple of days and then fly on to Moscow. He said he would investigate.[1]

---

1. The memorandum ends abruptly here, but a letter from Jerry to Dobrynin (March 6, 1967) indicates that their discussion also included the possibility of an exhibition of pre-Revolutionary Russian impressionist artists at MIT. While the plan was for Jerry and Laya to visit the Soviet Union in the summer of 1967, he did not go until December 1967—and without Laya, who was in poor health at the time.

Letter to Howard W. Johnson, April 3, 1967

Jerome B. Wiesner to Howard W. Johnson, April 3, 1967, written about a year into his term as MIT's provost. While the plans to which Jerry alludes for purchase and development of the Watertown Arsenal never materialized, many of the ideas he lays out here took shape later in other guises, such as the Undergraduate Research Opportunities Program (UROP); the Harvard-MIT Division of Health Sciences and Technology; the Program in Science, Technology, and Society; the Experimental Study Group; and the Media Laboratory. The proposal, addressed to MIT's president, shows Jerry characteristically thinking "outside the box," pressing his case for the centrality of innovative interdisciplinary teaching and research in MIT's mission.

I have given some thought to possible uses of the Watertown Arsenal site, and I have come to the conclusion that we could build an extremely exciting experimental college at the site—one in which we could attempt to incorporate the innovative notions that are emerging at such a rapid rate on the campus today, but which are unlikely to be accepted quickly on a large, well established campus such as ours. The exciting thing is that we could at the same time stimulate a number of important research and development activities, such as those in the biomedical engineering field, which we have not yet been able to bring into focus.

Among the possible resources which could be brought together at the Watertown site are the biomedical systems development center that the Bay State Foundation, MIT, and the Harvard Medical School have been discussing; the facilities of the Educational Development Center now located in Waltham; the communications sciences center which we have never been able to get launched effectively here on the campus; Project MAC and possibly other components of the Electrical Engineering Department, or some basic research activities from the Lincoln Laboratory. In addition, we would want to consider academic facilities, housing for students and faculty.

By combining these various resources, it would be possible to create the setting for a very unusual university-level educational experiment. In fact, it is the ideal setting for a variation on the college idea that Din Land, Elting and I were talking about last Spring. As you recall, Elting wanted to create a separate college with a good mixture of science, engineering and the humanities and political science all together. But as we talked about it, it didn't seem possible to do this on the MIT campus where the traditional mode of operating was so dominant. On the Watertown site, one could start fresh and create a setting in which experimentation could be more easily undertaken.

I would like to see us start a new campus on which the traditional boundaries and disciplines were essentially non-existent; that is, I would like to ignore the distinctions between pure science, applied science and engineering in the technical areas. And similarly, in the humanities and political science fields, I would attempt to keep the disciplinary segregation to a minimum, encouraging both scientific and nonscientific groupings by intellectual interests rather than by professional credentials.

The most important feature of the new campus would be the opportunity for educational experimentation which a small, independent academic center or college would provide. During the past decade, we have developed a large number of exciting ideas which we have not been able to try out or implement on the MIT campus for a variety of reasons. Among these ideas are an earlier and deeper association of students with research, more flexible packaging of subject matter, more individual collaboration between faculty and students, arrangements whereby students can go at different paces depending on their own interests and abilities, more effective experimentation with teaching aids, the involvement of the students in the teaching process, etc.

The college should include graduate as well as undergraduate activities, and an important part of the experiment should be an attempt to reduce the total time required from matriculation through the Ph.D. by the early planning of the learning process. Because the research activities will be a central part of the teaching program, they will, in a large measure, control the character of the institution. Fortunately, there are a series of research needs which are almost ideal for this endeavor. Among them are the interdisciplinary biomedical research institute about which we have been talking, a center for educational research and experimentation including a very substantial component of psychological and psychiatric research. As part of this, I would like to see the EDC, now in Waltham, become a part of this complex so that there would be a close interaction between the faculty and students of our new college and the staff of the EDC.

Several other components are needed to provide a balanced research environment. We should add a program of research in science and public policy problems and provide a focus for the humanities and the creative arts by creating a center for motion pictures and television. For mathematics, I would propose an activity both of a pure and applied nature that would be built around the area of the computation sciences. Finally, I would have a large general purpose research center patterned very much on the RLE where scientists, applied scientists, engineers, humanists, political scientists would work and live together.

I would consider seriously building up the communications sciences activities which we have not been able to pull together on the campus. In fact, we could use communications sciences as a central theme for much of what we would do at the new college. A bold step which would help us start the new school with a bang would be to use the existing activities in electrical engineering, including Project MAC,[1] linguistics, the related activities in biology and psychology, for these all would relate to the research activities I discussed earlier. If one wanted to include the solid-state activities of the Electrical Engineering Department, we would then have the basis of a broad and effective college built around applied science. The fact of the matter is that the Department has long been a school of applied science.

While this seems like radical surgery, I don't believe that it would do any harm to the things remaining on the campus.

---

1. Founded in 1963, Project MAC (for Multiple Access Computer and Machine-Aided Cognition) was the predecessor to MIT's Laboratory for Computer Science.

Letter to Edward M. Kennedy, June 25, 1968

Jerome B. Wiesner to Edward M. Kennedy, June 25, 1968. Writing just three weeks after Robert F. Kennedy's assassination, Jerry proposes that the Kennedy family consider spearheading a drive to establish a network of day care centers as a memorial to RFK. A couple of weeks earlier, in a speech to the MIT community, Jerry had eulogized RFK as a civil rights champion, the single most important force in JFK's cabinet to press "a commitment to the poor and particularly to the black members of our society, who were not only poor but oppressed as well."

I have a suggestion for a memorial to Bob which I think meets all your criteria and which is particularly relevant to Bob and his family. The idea grows out of Laya's involvement with efforts to deal with the hard-core problems in Boston and Cambridge. I would propose that the family either create a mechanism or be the sponsors for the establishment of day care centers throughout the United States, and most particularly in the cities.

The need is overwhelming. More than six million children between the ages of six and 11 have working mothers, and in 1967 there were licensed day care facilities for a total of less than 350,000 children from all socioeconomic levels. There are an estimated two to three million more children whose mothers are not now working (and may need to, or wish to), because they have no one to care for their children. Many of the children of those women now working are cared for under very poor conditions: by older siblings (8-year olds minding 2-year olds); by older neighbors, more often than not ill, untrained in child care, and living in miserable and unsanitary quarters; or not really cared for at all, but simply have their names written on a tag and hung around their neck, and set loose for the day.

Other women who need licensed, qualified care for their young are students and students' wives (often working to put their husbands through college); professional

SENATOR EDWARD KENNEDY   JEROME B. WIESNER

On a panel with Senator Edward M. Kennedy, ca. 1969. (Courtesy of the MIT Museum.)

women of all races and economic levels; and women who have an emergency situation in the home which suddenly demands their presence elsewhere.

The greatest need for this service is among the poor of our cities and towns—those on welfare and immediately above the welfare level. If an ADC [Aid to Dependent Children] mother had a place to leave her child, she could go back to school or start on-the-job-training to prepare herself for employment, steady wages, and a chance to get off the welfare lists. And the mother who now earns only $3,000 should be able to send her children to a well run center with the best of facilities and staff and pay a fee commensurate with her earnings.

Day care centers can and should play a key role in the whole development of the child. Under properly trained personnel, many underprivileged youngsters can be read to for the first time in their lives, have toys to play with and be exposed to a world around them which otherwise would never be part of their experience. Their mental and physical health is a major concern. For some of these children it offers the only loving care and concern they can get. We can try to stop the "cycle of poverty," and all it implies in crippled personality, at the start by preparing these youngsters for a competitive position in learning, earning, and living which they cannot now possibly obtain at home.

Industries and institutions of the nation are desperate for skilled and semi-skilled workers. Women are an underutilized labor source. Hospitals need doctors and nurses and maintenance staff; colleges need instructors; schools all over the country need more teachers; business and industry are searching for new labor sources. By establishing day care centers for their children, we could free many women who both need to and want to work, and begin to make a dent on this large and economically crippling labor deficit.

The first purpose of day care centers is to serve children—and the children's welfare is the prime consideration. To this purpose, the number and quality of the personnel is of first importance. There are not enough people now trained for these jobs. Centers in the cities could recruit and train high school students, mothers who are now at home with children, and older citizens able and eager to be useful, to augment the inadequate ranks of the professionals. Universities can contribute with child development experts, dieticians, play and school specialists, and help train the paraprofessionals at the same time.

The three absolute essentials for an adequate day care program are buildings to house the centers, qualified personnel, and the money to establish and maintain continuing operation. There aren't enough of any of these. All the federal, state, and local programs combined cannot take care of the need, and besides, they are mostly for demonstration programs, and offer no sustaining funds. There is no one group or institution in the country which has the day care needs as its central focus and at the same time the knowledge and ability to put together all parts, including the main one of raising money, and get the program rolling.

I am therefore proposing that you be the sponsors of a drive that would help to develop a national program of child care centers; stimulate the growth of these centers in local communities; train and recruit personnel; do research in child development and education and health; stimulate effective legislation for government support of such centers; and encourage private, foundation, institutional, and industrial financial support.

We already have all the parts for a successful day care program in the United States. Scores of excellent people have labored for years to initiate and maintain those facilities that do exist, and to devise and lobby for appropriate legislation. What's lacking is the one central coordinating thrust that your family can so well provide. If the idea appeals to you at all, we would be glad to talk to Ethel and yourself.

Letter to Henry A. Kissinger, April 23, 1970

Jerome B. Wiesner to Henry A. Kissinger, April 23, 1970, suggesting a youth summer jobs program with a focus on environmental conservation. While Jerry differed politically with Henry Kissinger on many (likely most) issues, they had had a cordial professional relationship since the 1950s in various forums and debates on national security policy. Jerry was aware, too, that one of the Nixon administration's first acts on assuming office in 1969 had been to mandate environmental impact statements for all federal projects, thus potentially laying the stage for environmental reforms nationwide.

This is a short note to put in writing for the President my suggestion that we attempt to find the means to put a substantial number of college and high school students to work next summer on problems related to the environment. There is every indication that there will be far fewer summer jobs for young people this year than at any time in the past decade, and many of them who depend on summer employment to earn part of their college expense are going to be in serious trouble. In addition, the prospect of having large numbers of unhappy youngsters loafing in the cities and adding to their bitterness is not a pleasant thought.

On the positive side, there is the national awakening to the problems of the environment which the President has stimulated which has exposed endless opportunities for useful work, in the cities, in the woods, on the roadsides, on the lakes and streams, and in the countryside generally. I believe that it would be possible to organize a very exciting and productive program of environmental housekeeping and ecological rebuilding which could create many useful, educational jobs in the cities and also get a large number of the vacationing students and other young people.

There are many signs that lead me to believe that this is going to be a particularly troublesome summer for the young, and so I believe that any move that could give them something important and constructive to do should be considered seriously. It is not only important for the particular young people who would otherwise be idle, but it would also serve to help preserve the hopeful mood for the entire country in regard to the prospects of arresting the environmental decline. The concern with the condition of life on the planet is one of the few positive themes that has struck a wholesome response in recent months. It has brought young and old together on problems on which they could collaborate rather than fight. A prompt move to engage some of these people who have been mostly talking about the problems of the environment on really constructive activities would capitalize on the interest that the President has succeeded in generating. There is a danger otherwise that just the opposite will happen, that after all of the excitement and discussion about the environment and the creation of the hope of doing something about it, in the end the concerned young people will not be able to find any way in which they can make a personal contribution.

There is also a special problem to be worried about this coming summer. There is considerable evidence that the extreme radicals, not having been able to create any base of support for their causes, will turn to more and more destructive tactics aimed more at the community than at the university. As you know, there has been some of this already.

I am told by Professor Jerome Lettvin, who as you undoubtedly know has been following the student drug scene, that we are likely to see a major push of heroin this summer as part of an attempt to cause further chaos in the cities.[1] He believes that even though government efforts to halt the flow of narcotics into the country have been reasonably successful, sufficient stocks of heroin are available to cause major problems this summer if they are used as he fears. This alone would be reason for trying to reduce the number of under-employed young people, and for trying to get some of them out of the cities.

I recognize that time is short and that it would take a major effort to set up such a program in a short time, and that it will be quite expensive if we attempt to engage very large numbers of young people in it. Nonetheless, I do think that it is still pos-

---

1. A few years earlier, Professor Jerome Lettvin (MIT) had taken on LSD advocate Timothy Leary in a much-publicized debate over the benefits and dangers of hallucinatory drugs.

sible to do something useful and it should be given serious consideration. I would be willing to help with this if the President wanted me to, though I believe that there are many other people in the country much more experienced with action programs of the kind I am talking about.

I imagine that it would be possible to get help from a number of groups such as those interested in the environment and in conservation, youth groups, university administrations, the OEO,[2] and many social work groups if one wanted to organize a program of this kind.

---

2. U.S. Office of Equal Opportunity.

Letter to Richard M. Nixon, January 3, 1973

Jerome B. Wiesner to Richard M. Nixon, January 3, 1973, expressing support for "affirmative action" as a national policy. In 1967, the U.S. Department of Health, Education and Welfare (HEW) had begun requiring colleges and universities receiving federal funds to establish goals for hiring women and minority faculty, and the 1972 HEW guidelines required detailed documentation of such efforts. Jerry's letter to the President was prompted by the erosion of political support for affirmative action—both within Congress and the White House—as a result of widely publicized complaints by university faculty and administrators that the program threatened to undermine scholarly standards.

I would like to express my personal support of your administration's efforts in spurring universities toward greater progress in equal opportunity in education and employment. This letter is to amplify my views of the Federal Affirmative Action Program about which a number of university presidents, including myself, are writing to you.

There has been criticism from within the university community, on the part of both faculty and administration, raising the difficult issues of implied quota systems and possible dilution in the quality of university personnel. In addition, some universities have experienced difficulties as the result of sometimes vague guidelines and uneven quality in compliance reviews. We at MIT have also experienced difficulties in these areas. On balance, however, the Federal Affirmative Action Program has been a constructive force in stimulating the universities, including my own, to greater and more positive efforts to provide educational and employment opportunities at all levels for women and members of minority groups.

Hopefully your administration will continue to maintain a posture of support for these goals. I have heard of some concern within the White House that the reactions of the universities have been largely negative, and that this concern may lead to a review of the wisdom of the Affirmative Action Program. Whatever their particular problems with the Program administration, the universities have an obligation to provide national leadership toward equal opportunity. They are just beginning to gain momentum, pressed by the Federal initiatives.

I urge that no action now be taken which may signal a lessened concern on the part of your administration for progress toward equal opportunity goals. Perhaps an appeals committee, where institutions could have HEW actions reviewed, would allay the concerns regarding arbitrary decisions.

Letter to Robert M. Fano, December 9, 1981

Jerome B. Wiesner to Robert M. Fano, December 9, 1981, suggesting points of possible focus in planning a centennial celebration of the electrical engineering program at MIT. It was typical of Jerry, as here, to emphasize future challenge over past achievement.

We have not had a chance to talk about the thoughts that underlay my suggestion that we make "lifelong education" the theme of the Electrical Engineering Department's one hundredth anniversary celebration.[1] Since I will be away at the time of the next meeting of the planning committee, I will put some of my ideas down for you.

I actually had in mind several different problems and opportunities which I think are both emerging and converging at this time. They add up to a need for a comprehensive look at the educational system from beginning to end. One might well agree and still ask, "Why do this via the EE department?" Two reasons appeal to me. First of all, the EE education is affected both by the preparation students have when they arrive at MIT and the world they are going into. Second is that new information and communication technologies, together with the understandings emerging in the cognitive and brain sciences, will make possible educational avenues that we can only dimly perceive but will, I believe, make revolutionary opportunities quite possible. The information revolution could be as important to society as the invention of type.

The nation has been living through a decline in quality education in the elementary and secondary school system which promises to continue for the foreseeable

---

1. The Department of Electrical Engineering at MIT was not established until 1902. Jerry meant to refer here to the centennial of the course in electrical engineering, which had its start as part of the Department of Physics in 1882.

future unless something is done about it. This is a trend which might be turned around by decisive efforts on the part of academic institutions like MIT, if we could get a group working on the problem. To all of this, one must add the fact that technology is changing the nature of work in the industrial world and, therefore, imposing the need for a very different educational base for most people.

There is increasing evidence that manufacturing industries will ultimately use a small fraction of the total work force, as agriculture now does. Increasingly, the population will be engaged in what is called the service industries, including intellectual activities, i.e., medicine, education, maintenance, and general management of the society. These activities call for a high degree of education and training as well as continuing intellectual renewal, and are highly dependent on good information systems for their maximum effectiveness.

Finally, we must consider the problem of the Third World where more and better education and new industries are a major need and where, again, the only hope lies in the information technologies.

Gordon Brown used to emphasize the fact that the only constant was change and that the only appropriate education was one that prepared an individual for lifelong learning. While we have responded somewhat to this challenge, it has been primarily through efforts we made to change the content of our formal education, not by a rethinking of the entire educational process. Continuing education has helped to some degree in this process, but the evidence is that it tends to be too little, too late.

So, what I am suggesting for our look into the next century of the electrical engineering department is a thorough review of the entire educational process, starting with the earliest years, and continuing through university graduate education, and going on forever. I would hope, as you suggest, that we might involve many other academic institutions and, possibly, some individuals who view education in a nonconformist way. Perhaps we could be so ambitious as to outline what one should like to see as a modern education and specify some possible means for providing it, including appropriate educational opportunities for youngsters growing up in today's world.

I hope that we could involve a range of engineers, scientists, educators, and people from industry in our celebration. Perhaps the whole School of Engineering, possibly all of MIT, would be willing to join in this affair. We should lean heavily on the cognitive scientists, as well as on computer scientists who have focused on the educational potential of computers and people like Nick Negroponte whose principal interest has been in how to use modern information technology to enhance the individual's creative and learning opportunities.

All of this sounds like a mighty big order, but then we at MIT have been working up to it for a century and have more people with deep commitments to information and learning than can be found at most other institutions. It seems to be the fate of the electrical engineering profession to have the needed new technologies in its hands at each stage of the industrial society's evolution. It is also very important to the department's future—we have not responded fully to the challenge of the new information technologies. I believe there is a new profession in the making, one that might be called "knowledge engineering," and we do not fully appreciate it.

Incidentally, have you ever heard Asimov's description of the education of the future? He's a bit extreme, but might be the ideal kickoff speaker presenting a challenge to which the rest of the celebration could respond. I suspect that it would take three or four days minimum—possibly a week—to really do full justice to all the questions that we should examine. Perhaps, too, we can propose for the final sessions working groups as was done for the Alexander Graham Bell Centennial. Good Luck!

Letter to Charles Smith, March 14, 1984

Jerome B. Wiesner to Charles Smith, director of programs, System Development Foundation, Palo Alto, Calif., March 14, 1984. As part of the effort to raise funds for MIT's new Media Laboratory, Jerry outlined his vision for the Lab in the context of his own research on problems of communication, dating back more than 30 years. The Media Laboratory opened in 1985, in a building designed by I. M. Pei and named in honor of Jerry and his wife Laya.

✳

You asked Nicholas Negroponte and me to tell you what propelled us in our enthusiasm for the work we want to do in our new Media Technology Laboratory. In fact, your request was to tell you a bit about where we come from. For me this requires writing a brief autobiography, for I see the things we are trying to do as a continuation of my life-long interest and involvement in information processes. My enthusiasm for the work that Nick Negroponte was doing, when I first became aware of it as president of MIT, stemmed from his vision of bringing together understanding of human sensory and cognitive systems with knowledge of man-made systems to enhance the interface between the two. That is also why when I was trying to decide what to do after I stepped down as president of MIT, I asked him to let me team up with him. I saw that his interests and mine were closely related and complementary. As you will see as I write on, I have spent most of my professional career involved in understanding, building, or encouraging the implementation of communication and information processing systems.

Under the spell of Norbert Wiener I became convinced that many of the fundamental problems that were being studied in living systems—ranging from speech communication, perception, and cognition to genetic coding and those in man-made systems—were essentially the same except for enormous differences in complexity. I came to believe that in some amazing way the evolution of man-made systems was repeating the development of the cognitive and communication features of humans with nonbiological components. Finally, I also became convinced that both the study of manmade and living systems would prosper in an environment where they could nurture each other. But I have gotten way ahead of myself.

As I look back on what I have done, I see that these two aspects have always been part of my career path. I began my professional life at the University of Michigan where I studied both mathematics and communications engineering and got degrees in both. As a student I earned my living running the University broadcasting studios, experimenting with television, building equipment, and doing experiments in a speech laboratory concerned with teaching deaf children to speak while trying at the same time to learn something about the speech and hearing mechanisms. This was my first exposure to a set of problems I have encountered repeatedly in the 47 years since then.

My graduate work involved a theoretical analysis of complex antenna systems combining my mathematical and electrical engineering interests. This research ultimately led to my being invited to the MIT Radiation Laboratory, where I initially worked on microwave component development. An important aspect of this work involved trying to understand the effects of random electrical noise in receivers and display systems. Toward the end of the War, I became the director of a radar system project that involved putting a very large radar in an aircraft and relaying its information to aircraft carriers. This system was later used for sea-based early warning when the United States developed an air-defense system in the 1950s.

After World War II, I became assistant professor in the Department of Electrical Engineering and assistant director of the newly formed Research Laboratory of Electronics, sponsored by three military services to exploit the microwave technology of the Radiation Laboratory and to continue some of the basic research of that laboratory. I was given the responsibility of organizing the communications research program for the laboratory, and I continued my own research on noise and signal-detection problems. Many other people at MIT were interested in the same problems. During the war, Wiener had developed mathematical methods of dealing with random noise problems. Claude Shannon had just published his classic papers on information and coding theory which caused a major stir among people interested in information systems.

Wiener had long been interested in feedback systems in humans, and he inspired a Cambridge supper seminar that brought together individuals involved in many local groups, especially at Harvard. This included individuals interested in speech, neurophysiology, vision, and the brain. The digital computer was just emerging as a machine of great interest, and the seminar group spent a substantial part of its time discussing it and speculating about what it might be good for.

Many graduate students and young faculty were drawn to the RLE group, including many who were interested in living systems. Wiener attracted McCulloch, Lettvin, Pitts, and Wald, then at the University of Illinois, to spend part of their time at the RLE, and they eventually joined the MIT staff full time. Individuals from Harvard including Walter Rosenblith, George Miller, and Peter Elias also became part of the supper group and the RLE communications group. These people brought to the group a strong research program in neurophysiology and psychology.

Three separate sensory research programs emerged in the Laboratory focusing on speech analysis and synthesis, on vision, and the tactile senses. The speech work included research on both the character of speech as a communication mode or code, on the physiological structure of the ear and how the ear analyzes acoustical signals. Not surprisingly, the coexistence of speech research and a growing interest in the potential of the programmed computer generated an interest among people in the language department, and a language project was begun. The group started by exploring the possibility of computer translation of languages, but it wasn't long before they realized that effective translation was an impossible task, not primarily because of computer limitations but because so little was known about language structure and how the brain processed language. Rather rapidly, the group that included Halle, Chomsky, and Roman Jakobson (who was then a professor at Harvard but eventually moved to MIT) shifted their attention to a study of linguistics.

My own research continued to focus on noise and signal-detection problems, and in collaboration with Professor Y. W. Lee we exploited Wiener's random function theory and used the concept of correlation to create highly sensitive signal-detection systems, signal analysis methods, and spread-spectrum communications systems. During the same period (1952–53) I became involved in an effort to develop an air-defense system for the United States and proposed that we use the Whirlwind Computer as a central computer to tie together the many radars and intercept control centers that were required to create an effective defensive system. This system became the prototype for the SAGE system. We were making a timesharing system but didn't realize it. A few years later when we were planning a new computer installation for the RLE, we recalled this experience and asked Professors McCarthy and Minsky who had formed an AI group in the Lab whether they thought it would be possible to develop a remote-terminal machine for general service for the lab staff. Their answer was yes, and they designed a machine for us that was built by IBM as the 7094.

Awaiting output from the autocorrelator, ca. 1949. The autocorrelator, among other things, analyzed speech patterns for predictability and correlation. (Courtesy of the MIT Museum.)

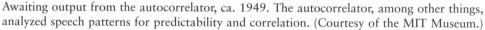

Along the way, Wiener and I began to experiment with tactile inputs for deaf-blind children and actually had a graduate student build and try out a prototype machine that we used at the Perkins School for the Blind. While it worked after a fashion, it was a monstrous collection of vacuum tubes that was impossible to keep running. Colleagues in the laboratory were experiencing similar frustrations with schemes for reducing bandwidth by removing redundancy and various coding systems for taking advantage of the encoding algorithms that were being developed. At that time our theories and ideas had far outrun our technical capabilities. Today the situation is just the reverse; we can make reliably the most elaborate systems that we can conceive. Understanding is now the limitation.

The communications group in the laboratory eventually involved faculty and students from eight departments, including Electrical Engineering, Mathematics,

With Norbert Wiener (left) and Yuk-Wing Lee, discussing output from the "MIT autocorrelator," ca. 1949. (Courtesy of the MIT Museum.)

Modern Languages, Physics, Humanities, and Biology. To give you a glimpse of the scope of the communications-science activities that existed in the Research Laboratory of Electronics in 1960, I have dug out an old quarterly progress report from that period in which you will find a description of the on-going activities.

During 1959 and 1960 a group of us began to plan for a new interdepartmental Information Sciences Center based on the RLE communications activities. MIT encouraged this development and committed a large sum of money ($12 million) that came from a patent settlement to it. At the last minute the money was diverted to meet a current budget crisis, and the project floundered. After that, several of the groups grew into separate departments or laboratories. I was rescued from my frustration by an appointment as science adviser to President Kennedy. The Department of Linguistics and the Department of Psychology, as well as the Computer Science Lab and the AI Lab, trace their origins to the Research Laboratory of Electronics. Descendants of those earlier groups still carry on in the RLE, however much related work is carried on in the new entities with only modest interaction with other groups.

There are a couple of other threads to my story which are relevant to our current interests and goals. From about 1965 to 1978 I was a member of the IBM Scientific Committee, and until I became president of MIT I served on the SRA Advisory Committee under Ralph Tyler. During the same period I became involved in efforts to do something about inner-city school problems in Boston. These simultaneous experiences convinced me that the computer had much to contribute to elementary and secondary education, but before this could happen machines had to improve and we would have to achieve a much better understanding of the learning process. The first has happened. I hope the second is happening. A major goal of our new center is to contribute to this problem by our own work and by drawing in individuals from the many groups at MIT whose work has something to contribute toward this objective.

As I see my role during the next five years, my first task is to complete the funding for the Arts & Media Technology building. We are close to the end on that task. In parallel, I will participate with Nicholas in planning the center's program and help to select the six young faculty members we are searching for. I also intend to be involved in some of the teaching and research programs. In addition, we are planning a seminar on information processes in living and man-made systems and related topics which I will supervise. We hope that this seminar will appeal to faculty and students in the many related departments, as well as to people in our center. We are doing this to reinforce the interdisciplinary spirit which we believe is essential for the educational and research activities we are pursuing.

With regard to my own research, I hope to return to one of my old interests—the learning patterns of sensory-deprived youngsters—because I believe that this type of inquiry can tell us much about cognitive processes. This approach is similar to that employed by physiologists and psychologists who are investigating localization of function in the brain and the interconnections between areas by studying the cognitive deficiencies created by various brain injuries. I hope, too, that I will be able to look over the shoulder at the research on computer-based education because I believe that this work and my specific interest can be mutually reinforcing. In this connection, I have some vague thoughts about the possibility of using a student's computer memory track, made as he/she solves a problem, as a means of assessing problem-solving competence and the understanding of the specific substantive subject involved.

When I say that I hope to do these things, I obviously mean to engage students

Model of downtown Boston tested for structural integrity in the MIT "wind tunnel," ca. 1975.

and, hopefully, some of the young faculty members in specific research projects while I concentrate on a small subset and also work at a more general level.

This may be too ambitious a program, but for a number of years it has been my hope to ultimately get back to the study of information processes. This is the reason for the course that I have followed in recent years and, in particular, one of the reasons why I decided to withdraw from administrative duties.

This is probably more autobiography than you wanted, but it all seems relevant to your question.

Letter to Thomas R. Odhiambo, June 1, 1986

Jerome B. Wiesner to Thomas R. Odhiambo, June 1, 1986, apparently a cable message intended to be read to participants at the Symposium on the Utilization of Indigenous Scientists in National Development, Nairobi, Kenya, June 1, 1986. A year earlier, Jerry had cochaired a steering committee to organize a study of water resource management in Africa and had sought funding for this purpose from the MacArthur Foundation and Schlumberger, on whose governing boards he sat. The June 1986 symposium was the project's pilot event.

Jerry's interest in emerging nations in Africa and elsewhere remained high, even after his stroke in 1989. When asked in 1990 to serve as an adviser to the Third World Academy of Sciences, for example, he responded that although his health would likely preclude his attendance at meetings, he would be happy to try to be "useful in my limited capacity."

I send my warmest greetings to your group and to the African Academy of Science on this very important day. I had hoped to be with you for the beginning of your efforts to employ scientific knowledge and skills to improve agriculture and water resource conditions in Africa. Unfortunately, personal complications have made it impossible for me to be present. Nonetheless, you have my pledge of any assistance that I am able to provide.

In his message, Professor Abdus Salam has described how, twenty-five years ago, our chance meeting led us to initiate a project to improve water and agricultural conditions in Pakistan. This project made a major difference in the food resources of Pakistan and stands as one of our proudest accomplishments. Professor Salam has also described the strong encouragement we received at the UN meeting of the Third World Foundation last year to explore whether or not a similar scientific undertaking could make a contribution to the agricultural problems of Africa. We pledged to try, and your meeting should be an important step in pointing the way for such an effort.

I believe that the present task will be more difficult, require more determination and effort and more resources. In the Pakistan project, Salam and I were very fortunate. First of all, we were concerned with the problems of one nation, Pakistan. Second, we had two leaders—Ayub Khan and John F. Kennedy—who backed our project completely with resources and unpopular political decisions when they were needed. Finally, we had the inspiring leadership of Roger Revelle, who was able to formulate the scientific questions and assemble the scientists, engineers, and other professional help that was needed to understand the problems and formulate solutions. Fortunately, too, we had the opportunity to model the aquifers on a computer, one of the first times this had been done on a large scale. When we were finished and had recommendations for coping with the many problems that were uncovered, President Kennedy, through the U.S. Aid Organization, pledged the even more scarce resource—his personal political capital—to make the necessary technical, agricultural, and organizational reforms possible. Professor Salam has already described our success.

There are many differences between the two projects. First of all, in Pakistan we were facing the dilemma of too much water. Here that is hardly the case. Then, the spirit among the people was one of optimism and between nations that of helping. Today that is hardly the norm—partially because the world has not become a better place as fast as we had hoped, partly because of cultural and political strains, but perhaps mostly because of fear and greed.

In spite of these reasons for caution, we should make a major attempt along the lines being discussed. First of all, scientists can and continually do bridge difficult cultural and political barriers because natural phenomena provide a common language, an arena where knowledge and experience can breed confidence that can make it possible to put aside suspicions and political disagreements. For almost thirty years, I have been able to communicate with Soviet scientists in spite of the often bitter antagonisms between our countries. Often our joint efforts have helped to modify the disagreements. As the power and reach of technology grows, our countries become ever more mutually dependent. The world is becoming Marshall McLuhan's global village. Carbon dioxide and other pollutants recognize no boundaries, neither does radioactivity. And the same will be true of deprivation. And the same will be true of hunger unless we learn to cope with these issues.

Global collaboration is necessary for humanity to survive. We have here a scientific and educational challenge, actually not quite global but so large that it can only be helped by regional and global collaboration. It is for scientists working together to define potential solutions and then for each of us to communicate what is required to make them work for all the nations of the world.

Humanity will only survive the next century if collaboration and caring replace the current confrontational behavior. Scientists have a foundation of international collaboration and trust on which to build. Each of us and our Academies of Science have participated in global scientific activities such as the International Geophysical Year. Perhaps they were possible because their purpose was primarily scientific. Here we are confronting both the rewards of success for all of civilization, not just Africa, and striving to make the rewards dramatic.

Good luck, and please excuse my absence. I will be thinking of you and hoping that the deliberations generate much work for all of us.

Letter to Alvin M. Weinberg, January 14, 1987

Jerome B. Wiesner to Alvin M. Weinberg, January 14, 1987. Weinberg, himself a pioneer in the field of nuclear energy and former head of the Oak Ridge National Laboratory, had taken issue with the characterization of Edward Teller in a New York Times *op-ed, "Put 'Star Wars' Before a Panel" (November 11, 1986) coauthored by Jerry and Kosta Tsipis. Jerry and Tsipis had argued:*

> *If the folly of Star Wars is so obvious to many of us, why does it have such strong backing? There are many reasons, starting with support for the Commander in Chief—a very strong motivation—and ranging from business to political motives to personal career ambitions. Among a few scientists, there is also the strong belief that any technical idea that surfaces should be backed.*
>
> *This is what we might call the Edward Teller syndrome. Dr. Teller is an enthusiastic supporter of Star Wars and his endorsement carries weight because he is popularly known as the father of the hydrogen bomb. But his technical track record is not perfect. One example was his support for the idea of using nuclear explosives to dig a sea-level canal. Other scientists calculated that the radioactive fallout from such a project would be prohibitively heavy, yet the idea was kept alive and helped block President Dwight D. Eisenhower's nuclear test ban effort.*
>
> *Dr. Teller's technical judgment in the case of the fusion or hydrogen bomb was similarly flawed. When Dr. Robert Oppenheimer—whose top priority in the 1940s was the development of a workable fission weapon, or atomic bomb—reluctantly consented to allow his colleague to continue independent work on a fusion bomb, Dr. Teller delayed the bomb's development by insisting on his own unworkable design. The necessary technical insight was finally provided by Stanislaus Ulam. Dr. Teller provided the political support to build the bomb, and for that he is known as the father of the bomb.*

The exchange of letters between Jerry and Weinberg illustrates deep divisions in scientific and academic circles over the Reagan administration's plan, first announced in March 1983, to develop a space-based system of missile defense—the so-called Strategic Defense Initiative, or SDI.

I am writing in response to your recent letter in which you take me to task for my statement about Edward Teller in his role on the H-bomb.

First of all, I did not claim that his only role was political but that in the final analysis it was his political pressure that brought it about. In fact, I mentioned the fact that he worked on the H-bomb at Los Alamos while other people were working on the fusion bomb. The point was that the original conception was not right and it took development by others to make the H-bomb succeed. In fact, it is my recollection, based on what I heard since I was not directly involved, that the history was somewhat as follows: The first fusion device developed by Los Alamos worked. The second, Teller's, built by Livermore, did not. Perhaps you know more about this. My point was merely that Edward is not always right, and I have seen him argue many times for things which didn't make a lot of sense, such as the nuclear excavation of a sea-level canal.

I personally had a confrontation with Edward and Johnny Foster regarding the feasibility of conductivity of large underground explosions. It always happens that his arguments coincide with his political objectives. SDI is an interesting example where he argued for it in general but when he's confronted with a specific issue he'll often say "no, I never said that would work."

You also wanted my comments on your attack on what you call "academia" for the position on SDI. First of all, I don't think there is such a thing as academia. If you mean a monolithic position on SDI, I know a number of people in universities around the country who believe that SDI might work at least to some degree. In fact, that would be my position. I would imagine that one could make a 30–40 percent system if one went all out, but that is stretching the bounds of what I believe to be possible in a give and take between offense and defense. There are people in the universities who feel more positive about SDI, but most people, I think, would feel less hopeful than I about its possibility. But, you miss the real point of the academic argument with the Defense Department over SDI. The consolidated academic position was against DOD's effort to sweep many ongoing research programs that have little or no relevance to SDI under the SDI funding umbrella in order to give the impression that universities were gladly accepting SDI research money. It was that act that caused normally reticent university presidents to speak out in a single voice against SDI's effort. There are still arguments in every university about whether or not to accept research support for things like computer science and super-computers, which people would like to do. I could give you other arguments, pro and con, vis-a-vis SDI involvement on the campus, to prove to you that there is no single academic position, but I suspect I have given you enough examples.

Perhaps we will bump into each other somewhere and have a chance to talk about this at greater length.

Letter to Georgiy Arbatov, March 18, 1987

Jerome B. Wiesner to Georgiy Arbatov, March 18, 1987, regarding myths, perceptions, and stereotypes as barriers to communication and understanding between the Soviet Union and the United States. Arbatov—along with Yevgeniy Velikhov, Roald Sagdeev, and others—was part of a group of academicians closely allied with Mikhail Gorbachev and the Soviet political reform movement.

The encounter between Jerry and Gorbachev referred to below took place at the Forum for a Nuclear-Free World, for the Survival and Development of Humanity (February 1987), attended—on Gorbachev's invitation—by several hundred intellectual, political, artistic, and spiritual leaders from around the world. Right afterwards, a small group of participants met to discuss the possibility of forming a western-style foundation to support research and action on issues raised at the forum—what became, a year later, the International Foundation for the Survival and Development of Humanity, based in Moscow.

When I was talking with Chairman Gorbachev at the World Peace and Development meeting luncheon, he asked me why Americans were so afraid of the Russians, and I gave a very partial and unsatisfactory answer before we were interrupted by others who wanted to speak to the chairman. As I thought about it afterwards, I decided that he deserved a better answer than I had given, and I undertook to try to provide one. . . .[1]

. . . [O]ne of the most serious problems we have to face in both nations is the slowness with which perceptions change, except for the worse. Both sides must recognize this fact and work hard to overcome this information gap and lag. People

---

1. Omitted here are details concerning Jerry's request that Daniel Yankelovich of the Public Agenda Foundation supply relevant background information for transmittal to Gorbachev; Jerry enclosed in this letter a memorandum by Yankelovich, apparently summarizing recent polling data on Americans' attitudes towards the Soviets.

exchanges, satellite television exchanges, and much more exchange of literature and information of all kinds work towards this end.

I would also like to add a few thoughts that have occurred to me since the conversation. As you know, I have been working hard for almost thirty years to end the arms race, and I have frequently encountered the kind of fear and even hostility that the chairman accurately recognizes. I am sure that in your many visits to the United States you frequently encountered these attitudes.

Before 1957, I spent my time developing military equipment, first for World War II use and later as part of the U.S. cold war effort. In 1957–58, while working in the White House for President Eisenhower, I recognized that our two nations were on a dangerous path on which neither wanted to be but, because of the history, vested interests, public attitudes, at least in the United States, and political realities in both countries, it was difficult to change to a more rational course. Since then, I have tried to understand what motivated me to participate in the cold-war effort. I have concluded that I shared my countrymen's fear of Stalin, something that I am sure you can understand, and I lacked a basis for distinguishing truth from propaganda.

Many people were also frightened by the Comintern's activities in the prewar years, which in the United States appeared to be attempting to overthrow our government. That appears to be the experience that has so colored President Reagan's attitudes. Once the cold war started, many people acquired a vested interest in keeping it going. This was what President Eisenhower called "the military-industrial complex." It is my impression that this factor also existed in the Soviet Union.

One difficulty that I have encountered in trying to bring better understanding between our two countries is that perceptions change so slowly because there is so little information exchanged between our two peoples. This situation has been changing rapidly since Chairman Gorbachev assumed leadership, and we must work very hard to continue to improve it. When there is little information, those that have a vested interest in keeping the tensions high are free to say what they want. You may recall that I explored this situation in a talk that I gave to the National Academy of Sciences about three years ago.[2]

---

2. "Disenthralling Ourselves," National Academy of Sciences, Washington, D.C., April 28, 1984.

In closing, I want to say how heartened I was by what I heard and saw while I was in Moscow for the symposium. I hope that I will be able to return in the not-too-distant future to continue our discussion of the writing project I have been talking about. I have been so busy since I returned home that I have not had the time to write the letter I promised to send you

Seweryn Bialer has arranged to have this letter and Yankelovich's piece translated, and he will take them when he goes to Moscow in two weeks.

Letter to the Nobel Committee, April 3, 1987

Jerome B. Wiesner to the Nobel Committee of the Norwegian Storting, April 3, 1987, recommending the Pugwash Group for the Nobel Peace Prize. The Peace Prize was eventually awarded jointly to the Pugwash Conferences on Science and World Affairs and its prime mover Joseph Rotblat in 1995, "for their efforts to diminish the part played by nuclear arms in international politics and in the longer run to eliminate such arms."

It has come to my attention that the Pugwash Group has been nominated for the Nobel Peace Prize. I would like to strongly endorse that nomination. I know from firsthand experiences how important Pugwash has been in moderating the arms race. During the first years of its existence, Pugwash provided the only link between the Soviet bloc and the West. Its technical interventions kept the test ban aspirations alive and helped achieve the partial nuclear test-ban. Its forum provided opportunities for developing countries to understand the arms race and to increase awareness of their predicament among the industrial nations.

I first began what has been a very positive association with Soviet scientists in 1958 via a Pugwash meeting.[1] From that and subsequent Pugwash meetings, I developed very good relationships and a good rapport with Soviet scientists as well as people from China and many other countries. While working as science adviser to President Kennedy, these contacts were very important to me in my efforts to achieve a nuclear test-ban and reduce sources of international friction.

I hope that you do honor this dedicated group.

---

1. Second Pugwash Conference on Science and World Affairs, Lac Beauport, Quebec, March-April 1958.

Diary Entry on Recovering from His Stroke, 1989

Fragment of a diary kept by Jerry over the course of several months in 1989, recounting his struggle to regain cognitive and manual skills after the stroke he suffered on January 12 of that year. Murray Gell-Mann, a fellow member of the MacArthur Foundation board of directors, had urged him to continue this "writing therapy." A note in the margin indicates that Jerry intended to send the diary fragment to syndicated radio commentator Paul Harvey, also a fellow member of the MacArthur Foundation board.[1]

✳

This is my first attempt at writing anything and I am having a lot of trouble with my spelling. I am trying to use the spelling checker as a way of getting around the problem and except for the fact that this approach is very slow, it seems to work. I am recovering from a stroke that left me with my speech systems not working. In fact my whole left side of my body was paralyzed including my left arm, left leg, and the left side of my mouth.

On the third day after my stroke I was able to list the various things that were wrong and I was startled by the realization that I did not know the alphabet. Rather automatically I began to learn to memorize it again. Every time someone came to visit me I would ask them what came after d or g or p or y. After a while I knew all of the letters but did not have the order right. After a while I learned to get the order more or less right too. Then I realized that a few letters called vowels had a special role and that there were combinations of these, taken two at a time, com-

---

1. Donna Coveney paraphrased and quoted parts of the diary fragment in her article, "Jerome Wiesner's Greatest Experiment Was His Stroke Recovery," *Technology Review*, April 1993, pp. 7–10. Another article about Jerry's struggle is Richard Saltus, "When the Words Won't Come: New Therapies Strive to Overcome Language Loss," *Boston Globe*, June 3, 1991, pp. 29, 31.

pound vowels, that were very important too. These were confusing to me because not all of the combinations were used and, of those that were, the letter order was important.

At the same time I was learning to talk, not that there was ever a time when I couldn't communicate a bit, but at first my speech was slurred and the words often would not be the ones that I intended to generate. In fact when I became conscious approximately four hours after I had my stroke I realized that my blood sugar was uncomfortably low and I was desperate to get something to drink. I could only say one word, "education," which I repeated with increasing volume. Somehow my son Zachary who was with me finally deciphered my shout and brought me some orange juice.

This was my situation roughly the second week after I had the stroke. In fact I still have much trouble when I try to read aloud. My visitors seemed to be pleased by what they heard and always commented on the progress that they could see from visit to visit. I was not conscious of these daily improvements. I was more aware of the trouble that I was having with the articulation of multi-syllabic words than any other problem. In fact that is true today. It seems that I have trouble only when I am trying to speak out loud and then it appears that I don't always make the right connections between the stored words and sound-producing mechanism. When this happens it is very hard to get on to the right placement of the mouth and tongue.[2] One thing that seemed to help was to raise my voice. We have had many explanations about why this happened but none of them are really convincing. The explanation I find most reasonable is that shouting shakes things up and eventually they come out right.

This is hardly an explanation.

Roughly two weeks after I had the stroke, I was transferred to the Spaulding Rehabilitation Hospital and I was given daily speech therapy by Karen Haring who helped me a lot in all kind of ways. First of all she put some order into my eager but unstructured activities by systematically exploring my speech problems. She did this by carrying out a series of diagnostic tests that put my problems into some focus. For example, she was able to show that in spite of the fact that I couldn't spell and so couldn't write I was able recognize all of the words I was shown including knowing all of their meanings. This seemed to say that my library was intact but I wasn't able make a connection between the library and the voice or arm or

---

2. A note added later indicates "this was written after approximately one month of recovery."

whatever had to make the letters. Since the same motions were used to print and type, typing was not a way out of the difficulty.

Karen began by telling me that there was no systematic process for rebuilding my language skills. We would, she said, just have to experiment until we found things that worked. So we worked on learning to spell the hard way with some success, combining lots of spelling, mixed-up words, words with missing letters, and a variety of trial and error methods. Then quite by accident I found that if I traced the letters of the word while I said the word I frequently would spell it correctly. Sometimes this works better than others. I haven't any real clue as to why this is. Sometimes it seems to be a function of my peace of mind. I think that there is memory in my arm (the right arm) or rather, the part of the brain connected to the arm. I got a big surprise when I was given a hundred words that Karen had dictated for me to write. I found that I got most of them right. In fact I did better writing by hand than I did when I was working on the computer. Karen thinks that the reason is because I am listening and possibly using my fingers to trace the words out. Karen is going to dictate some more words to see if we can find out what is going on. I realized I always wrote the words down as I heard them and when I was typing I was watching the keyboard, not tracing the words. To complicate the matter more I frequently spell best when I am responding to dictation.

Now we have begun to work on my speech which often gets confused apparently because I use the wrong first letter. Karen has me saying single words, even hard ones, quite well by making sure of the first letter. This actually works even when I am reading out loud until I forget to say the first letter. One of the troubles that dogs me is that I don't always know how to spell the word that I want to say— psychiatry, for example, is a word that I don't know how to spell so I would have trouble with it.

This is my first try at using the spelling checker. I have two of them, one in the IBM computer and a little portable one that is made by the Franklin company for people who are poor spellers. Even though this spelling looks good it is the result of much work because I have to look up roughly one word in three and sometimes it takes me several minutes to find the right spelling for a word.

The previous writing was done when I had been in the Spaulding Rehabilitation Hospital three weeks. Unfortunately I did not continue this diary because I began to work on some other writing that I had wanted to do for a long time. I am sorry now that I did not continue this diary about my continuing experiences after Murray urged me to write down more of it. I will now try to fill in what I have done since

I stopped writing. I would dictate but I still have to write to continue learning to spell.

In June Karen left Spaulding and I continued language learning by myself. The start she gave me augmented by the computers makes it possible to learn alone. The only problem I have is that of having to type with one hand.

Two occupational therapists spent an hour a day trying to get a response from my left arm without any result whatsoever. In fact I thought that they were trying to get me used to the fact that there was little hope of it ever being useful.

Laya and I spent the month of August on Martha's Vineyard where I had therapy on my arm three times a week dispensed by a local therapist, Virginia Randall, who

Four years after his stroke, the year before his death—"still learning to manage the many strands of my life that were unraveled," February 3, 1993. (Photo by Donna Coveney. Courtesy of the MIT Museum.)

had been practicing thirty or thirty-five years on patients who suffered from a variety of muscle and limb problems including polio, arthritis, many different war injuries as well as stroke. She may have some formal training but by now it was buried deep beneath the lore of a lifetime of experience that she depended upon. She gave me hope as she talked endlessly about the many people she knew who, after years of hard work and frustration, found that they were rewarded by the return of useful function of a hand. She worked hard and though my fingers got more limber they did not move.

About two weeks after we began to work together I had a quite remarkable experience, one that I almost did not believe. At that time I tired quickly and went to bed before eight o'clock in a bedroom were I was all alone so it was unusually still and all I heard were a few bull frogs, the Menemsha harbor bell 2 miles away and my heart pulsing in my eardrums. As I lay there half awake, half asleep, I realized that I could feel a pulsing sensation in the fingers of my paralyzed hand that was synchronized with a slight but similar pulsing on the right side of my head. As I played with it I found that I could make the sensation move from one finger to another and at the same time the focus of feeling in my head moved too. And I soon saw that there was a unique spot in the head for each finger. I decided that this must mean that there was some nerve conduction between the muscles and my brain though not enough to move the fingers.

Paul, I began to write other things and never finished this. I forgot about it and now I will get back to it. My spelling is good enough that I haven't had to look up anything as I typed this little piece. I have to type with one hand which I now do quite well.

Letter to William J. Clinton, May 18, 1993

Jerome B. Wiesner to William J. Clinton, May 18, 1993, urging opposition to the resumption of nuclear testing by the United States. Earlier, Jerry had sent Clinton—and others in his administration, including Secretary of Defense William J. Perry—a copy of his pamphlet, Beyond the Looking Glass *(coauthored with Kosta Tsipis and Philip Morrison), pressing for "radical reform of America's giant military enterprise."*

⚛

Please forgive me for writing you again so soon but the issue I write about now is of the highest importance to world security, including ours. I understand that you are under considerable pressure to allow the resumption of underground nuclear testing when the current test moratorium expires later this year. I believe that if you do that it will most likely begin a new round of testing by most nuclear powers, and will diminish the chance of a successful renegotiation of the Non-Proliferation Treaty in 1995. If there were any important reason for testing, you should consider it, but there is not even a mild need to test any more. Testing, in the absence of visible national need, will weaken the nonproliferation efforts of this country.

It is greatly in our interest to have all of the industrial nations forego nuclear tests and exert great pressure on any others such as North Korea and Iran that might be tempted to develop nuclear bombs. I also fear that if testing resumes and continues, Germany and Japan will be drawn into wanting bombs of their own, and Ukraine may not be willing to give up the nuclear weapons it presently controls.

We are about to celebrate the thirtieth anniversary of the limited test ban which many people think was President Kennedy's greatest triumph. I know that not achieving a comprehensive test ban was his greatest disappointment. More than that, I do not believe that anything important was really achieved by the hundreds of billions of dollars that have been spent since then in nuclear weapons development and testing. Actually, the continued testing made our country and others more vulnerable. The only reason for continued testing then, as now, is to give work to the nuclear weapons laboratories.

Please, Mr. President, do all you can to end these fifty years of horror.

APPENDIXES

Chronology

1915
Jerome Bert Wiesner born in Detroit, Michigan (May 30), the son of Joseph and Ida (Friedman) Wiesner, first-generation European immigrants; Joseph, a native of Vienna, Austria, had migrated to the United States around 1894, at the age of 20; Ida was born in Romania.

1918
Family moves to Dearborn, Michigan, where his father runs a small drygoods store catering largely to employees of the local Ford motor car plant.

1920–1932
Attends public schools in Dearborn, Michigan.

1929
Tinkers with radios and telephones; builds apparatus for his school's physics laboratory and an automatic scoreboard for the gymnasium.

1930
Travels abroad for the first time—spends a month touring Holland, Austria, and Romania.

1932–1933
Attends Michigan State Normal School, Ypsilanti, Michigan.

1933
Enters the University of Michigan as an undergraduate.

1937
Becomes associate director in charge of technical and recording equipment at WUOM, the university's radio station.

Earns bachelor's degree in mathematics and electrical engineering.

Elected to membership in Eta Kappa Nu, national electrical engineering honor society, Phi Kappa Phi, and Sigma Xi; becomes a member of the Institute of Radio Engineers (IRE).

1938
Earns master's degree in electrical engineering.

Begins doctoral studies; teaches an undergraduate course in broadcasting techniques at the University of Michigan.

1939

Engineers the remote live broadcast of a talk by Archibald MacLeish, librarian of Congress, at the University of Michigan—a major technical undertaking at the time.

Teaches in an 8-week course at the Radio Workshop of the National Music Camp, Interlochen, Michigan—curriculum includes production technique, sound effects, elementary engineering, music balance, and script and continuity writing.

1940

Marries Laya Wainger of Johnstown, Pennsylvania, a fellow student and mathematics major at the University of Michigan, daughter of Louis H. and Amelia (Claster) Wainger.

Becomes a member of the Acoustical Society of America.

Appointed chief engineer, Acoustical and Record Library, Library of Congress (Sept.); for next two years, helps develop facilities and equipment; results now preserved and documented in the collections of the Library of Congress and the Smithsonian Institution's Center for Folklife and Cultural Heritage.

1941

As part of his work with the Library of Congress Radio Research Project, travels in the summer with Alan Lomax, Glenn Gildersleeve, and Joseph Liss to record interviews, songs, and harmonica tunes in Delaware and Maryland; also North Carolina and Virginia performers, including the Asheville (NC) Mountain Dance and Song Festival and the Galax (Va.) Old Fiddlers' Convention; interviews with Tennessee Valley Authority (TVA) workers on the Cherokee Dam project at Blairsville, Georgia; with workers at the TVA fertilizer plant in Muscle Shoals, Alabama; and with Tennessee residents whose lives were impacted by the TVA project.

1942

Joins the staff of MIT's Radiation Laboratory (May), established two years earlier to conduct defense-related research on microwaves, radar, and aircraft navigation; works on the development of radar and signal processing; later serves as an associate member of the Laboratory's steering committee.

Birth of son, Stephen J.

1944

Appointed group leader of Project Cadillac, concerned with development of airborne radar, forerunner of the Airborne Warning and Control System (AWACS).

1945

Receives an offer of a faculty appointment at MIT—James R. Killian, Jr. (MIT vice president) urges him to accept because "opportunities here over the coming years in your field of interest will be of ample scope to your work."

Becomes a member of the Federation of Atomic Scientists (later the Federation of American Scientists).

1945–1946

Works at Los Alamos National Laboratory developing electronic components used in atomic bomb tests at Bikini Atoll (1946).

1946

Birth of son, Zachary K.

Starts duties as an assistant professor of electrical engineering at MIT; joins MIT's Research Laboratory of Electronics (RLE), the peace-time sequel to the Radiation Laboratory.

Becomes a consultant to the Raytheon Company.

1947

Promoted to associate professor of electrical engineering at MIT.

Appointed assistant director, Research Laboratory of Electronics.

Master's degrees awarded to two of his first graduate students, Edward E. David, Jr., and Raymond A. Glaser.

Appointed to serve on an auxiliary committee—the Committee on Staff Environment—of the Committee on Educational Survey (Lewis Commission), which leads to a sweeping overhaul of the status of the humanities and social sciences at MIT, and to the establishment of the School of Humanities and Social Studies (now the School of Humanities, Arts, and Social Sciences).

Receives high-level ("Q") security clearance from the Atomic Energy Commission.

1948

Awarded (by Harry S. Truman) the President's Certificate of Merit, the second highest civilian award for outstanding service to the country; award made for war-time services.

Joins a weekly dinner seminar founded by distinguished MIT mathematician Norbert Wiener, bringing together representatives of a wide range of disciplines—engineering, acoustics, medicine, mathematics, neurophysiology, philosophy, and others—to discuss common research and intellectual interests.

Appointed to the Committee on Nuclear Studies, Institute of Radio Engineers (IRE).

1949

Birth of daughter, Elizabeth A. (Lisa).

First doctoral degree (Sc.D.) awarded to one of his graduate students, Ernest R. Kretzmer.

Appointed associate director, Research Laboratory of Electronics.

Coauthors, with a student and Norbert Wiener, an article in *Science* (Nov.)—"Some Problems in Sensory Prosynthesis"; goes on to work with Wiener in stimulating a major MIT research and teaching effort in living and man-made information systems.

Along with RLE colleagues Y. W. Lee and Robert M. Fano, develops the "autocorrelator"— a machine whose purpose is to analyze communications for predictability.

1950

Awarded doctorate in electrical engineering, University of Michigan, with a thesis entitled "Pre-Ignition Phenomena in Gas Switching Tubes and Related Rectifier Burnout Problems."

Signs a statement, "The Strategy of American Defense," with a number of scholars voicing concern about U.S. military policies, especially the "present entangling alliance with atomic warfare" (May 1).

Second trip to Europe—England and Switzerland (Sept.–Oct.).

Promoted to professor of electrical engineering at MIT.

Receives "top secret" security clearance from the U.S. Signal Corps and the Office of Naval Research.

1951
Third trip to Europe—England, France, Scotland (July).

1952
Appointed director, Research Laboratory of Electronics (RLE); is RLE's third director, succeeding Julius A. Stratton and Albert G. Hill.

Cofounder, MIT's Lincoln Laboratory.

Appointed to chair the Graduate Committee, MIT's Department of Electrical Engineering.

Elected a Fellow of the Institute of Radio Engineers (IRE).

Elected a member of the Cosmos Club, Washington, D.C.

Meets Congressman John F. Kennedy for the first time.

Proposes (with colleagues) the use of forward scattering from the troposphere for reliable, narrow band communication.

1953
Birth of son, Joshua A.

Refuses a request by Senator Joseph McCarthy to testify that the Voice of America has been sabotaged by "Communist" staff members; is accused by McCarthy of giving VOA "bad advice."

Appointed a member of the Scientific Advisory Board, U.S. Air Force.

Appointed to the U.S. Air Force Strategic Missiles Evaluation Committee, often referred to as the Von Neumann Committee (after its chairman, John von Neumann); the committee advises and makes recommendations to the secretary of the Air Force on all missile projects under that branch's jurisdiction.

Attends meetings of the International Union of Radio Science in Paris.

Elected a fellow, American Academy of Arts and Sciences; speaks on "radio propagation" at his inaugural Academy meeting.

1954
Becomes a member of the Technological Capabilities Panel (TCP) (chair, MIT president James R. Killian, Jr.), established by the Eisenhower administration to study the capabilities of the Air Force and how the United States can defend itself against surprise attack; is appointed to head the TCP's Overseas Military Communications group.

Patent No. 2,682,034, "Apparatus for applying high-intensity pulses to crystal rectifiers," issued to him and Henry C. Torrey with title assigned to the U.S. government (June 22; original application filed 15 Jan. 1946).

Receives "outstanding engineering graduate" award, University of Michigan.

Appointed to the Committee on Awards, Institute of Radio Engineers (IRE).

Supports J. Robert Oppenheimer in his unsuccessful appeal for reinstatement of his U.S. Atomic Energy Commission security clearance.

1954–1955
Serves as a consultant to the McDonnell Aircraft Corporation.

1955
Establishes Hycon Electronics Company (later known as Hermes Electronic Company), jointly with Jerrold R. Zacharias, I. I. Rabi, and other physicists and engineers; the company specializes in developing and marketing electronic equipment, and takes on government research contracts.

Becomes a member of the American Association of University Professors and the Geophysical Union.

Appointed a consultant to the Kerr-McGee Oil Company.

Appointed a member of the advisory board, American Foundation for the Blind.

1956
Receives the Alfred P. Sloan Award for outstanding service at MIT.

Appointed to serve on several MIT committees—Committee on Undergraduate Policy, Special Committee on Faculty Responsibility, Arthur D. Little Lecture Committee (chair), and Committee on Engineering Education.

1957
Appointed by President Eisenhower to the Gaither Panel (chair, H. Rowan Gaither, Jr.), studying the country's ability to defend large populations during nuclear attack; serves as the panel's technical director.

Elected to Tau Beta Pi honor society, in recognition of "high attainments in engineering and scientific knowledge" (April).

Appointed a consultant to the Sprague Electric Company.

Warns about the Soviet Union moving rapidly toward overall superiority over the United States (Nov. 21 meeting, Committee for Economic Development).

Discusses arms control and the Soviet threat with former Democratic presidential candidate Adlai Stevenson, who suggests that the Eisenhower administration does not have "an adequate feeling of urgency" in this regard.

Invited by Bertrand Russell to attend the second Pugwash Conference on Science and World Affairs, a series of meetings on problems of nuclear weapons and world security, attended by scientists from different countries; receives President Eisenhower's approval to attend.

Appointed to the President's Science Advisory Committee (PSAC) (Dec. 1).

Supports the Soviet proposal for a temporary ban on atmospheric nuclear testing.

1958
Establishes the Center for Communication Sciences at MIT—a place, he observes, for "collaborative work between mathematicians, electrical engineers, linguists, psychologists, physiologists, and others [that] should lead to a new understanding of communications and to more effective use of machines."

Staff director, U.S. delegation to the Geneva Conference on the Prevention of Surprise Attack.

Attends the second Pugwash Conference on Science and World Affairs, Lac Beauport, Quebec; special interest in improving lines of communication between American and Soviet scientists.

Guest speaker at the Harvard Summer School Conference on National Security Policy.

Joins two other government advisers in appearing on a telecast, sponsored by NBC and Educational Television, to criticize the U.S. defense program for ineffective management and excessive security controls on information.

Elected to the Watertown (Mass.) Planning Board.

Receives "top secret" White House security clearance.

Serves on the visiting committee of the Graduate School of Education, Harvard University.

1959

Interviewed, along with scientists Detlev Bronk and J. Robert Oppenheimer, in a televised program called "Where Is Science Taking Us?" part of CBS's "Great Challenge Series."

Appointed acting head, Department of Electrical Engineering, MIT, a post he holds for one year.

First visit to Israel.

Appointed chair, ABM Panel, President's Science Advisory Committee.

1960

Elected to the National Academy of Sciences.

Visits Moscow on the invitation of the Soviet Academy of Sciences (March); tours the country for three weeks; attends the Pugwash conference in Moscow, presenting an analysis of the consequences of the arms race, "Comprehensive Arms-Limitation Systems"; introduces what becomes known as the "Wiesner Curve," the relationship between numbers of weapons deployed and levels of verification advisable under a disarmament treaty.

Informal science adviser in John F. Kennedy's presidential campaign; member, JFK's foreign affairs/defense advisory committee.

Purchases a home on Martha's Vineyard, which he visits every summer thereafter with his family; becomes part of a community of intellectuals, artists, writers, actors, and musicians on the island, including playwright Lillian Hellman, novelist John Hersey, and conductor Leonard Bernstein.

Appointed to the board of directors, Aerospace Corporation, established to manage missile and satellite research and development.

Appointed to the board of directors, World Peace Foundation.

Speaks on "the relationship of military technology, strategy, and arms control" at the Conference to Plan a Strategy for Peace, Arden House, Harriman, New York.

Appears on a CBS television show called "The Thinking Machine," explaining the process by which a computer at MIT was programmed to "write" a teleplay; the teleplay is produced as part of the show (Oct.).

Contributor and chair of the guest editorial board, special issue of *Daedalus* (quarterly journal of the American Academy of Arts and Sciences) devoted to arms control.

Appears with Eleanor Roosevelt, C. P. Snow, and others on a television program, "The Scientist and World Politics," the fourth in the WGBH series "Prospects of Mankind"; discussion includes communication between science and government, scientists and the arms race, government careers, science curricula, and scientists' influence on government.

1961

Appears on WGBH with Walt Rostow, Alexander Rich, Paul Doty, and others in a discussion of the 1960 Pugwash conference—"Report from Moscow on Disarmament and World Security."

Takes a leave from MIT to become President John F. Kennedy's special assistant for science and technology (appointed Jan. 11, effective Feb.); also chair, President's Science Advisory Committee (PSAC).

At the start of the Kennedy presidency, initiates (with economist John Kenneth Galbraith) a major effort to persuade the U.S. government to recognize its responsibility for industrial technology; President Kennedy recommends, in his first State of the Union address, that the federal government inaugurate a program in support of civilian industrial technology.

Expresses reservations about manned lunar missions, but President Kennedy decides to proceed with the goal "before this decade is out, of landing a man on the moon and returning him safely to Earth" (May 25).

Called "as much a crusader for ideas as . . . a researcher for scientific knowledge," in a profile published in the *New York Times* (John Finney, "Top Scientist on the New Frontier," Sept. 3).

Awarded an honorary doctorate by the Polytechnic Institute of Brooklyn.

Elected an honorary fellow of the Weizmann Institute, Rehovot, Israel.

Publication of his first book, *Where Science and Politics Meet* (McGraw-Hill).

Awarded the Medal of Honor, Electronic Industries Association.

Visits England, Pakistan, and India on government business; vacations in Jamaica.

Described by President Kennedy as "a good friend and trusted advisor . . . one of those rare individuals . . . who can work effectively to relate the complexities and the opportunities of science to the needs of a nation, to its culture, its security, its influence and its humanity" (letter to Arthur B. Krim, Dec. 1).

1962

Helps persuade President Kennedy to establish an Office of Science and Technology (OST) in the executive office of the president, with the president's special assistant for science and technology as director.

Awarded honorary doctorates by the Lowell Technological Institute, Rensselaer Polytechnic Institute, and University of Michigan.

Undergoes U.S. Senate confirmation hearing to serve as OST director (July 17).

Testifies on three occasions before U.S. House and Senate committees on issues relating to science organization and government contracting for research and development, OST budget, and scientific and technical information (July–Sept.).

Visits the Marshall Space Flight Center in Huntsville, Alabama, with President Kennedy, Vice President Lyndon B. Johnson, and others (Sept.); engages in heated debate over lunar rendezvous strategy, with space center director Wernher von Braun.

Elected Institute Professor, MIT's highest faculty rank.

Visits England and Switzerland on government business.

1963

Visits Switzerland on government business; in Geneva, delivers an address—"Education and the Promise of Science and Technology"—at the United Nations Conference on the Application of Science and Technology for the Benefit of Less Developed Areas.

Testifies on more than twenty occasions before U.S. House and Senate committees on issues relating to water and energy resources, patent policy, education, use of pesticides, health research and training, federal research and development policies and prospects, supersonic transport, the NASA program, and technical resources in the national economy.

Speaks on "Living with Science," at a meeting of the Federation of American Scientists, Washington, D.C.

At President Kennedy's request, leads a delegation to the United States-Japan commission exploring possible U.S. assistance in the development of Japanese technology (May).

Delivers the commencement address, "Making the Most of Your Opportunities," at the Georgia Institute of Technology.

On his initiative, a high-profile seminar to discuss the problem of improving music education in the nation's public schools is convened at Yale University (June); among the well-known composers in attendance are Lukas Foss and Leon Kirchner.

Awarded a citation from the Massachusetts Committee, Catholics, Protestants and Jews, for "outstanding contribution . . . to the cause of human brotherhood."

Nearly dies in a boating accident (with son Josh) in Menemsha Pond, Martha's Vineyard (Sept.); passion for sailing continues unabated.

Delivers an address, "Science in the Affluent Society," at the Centennial Celebration of the National Academy of Sciences (Oct. 23).

Receives an award—Sitara-i-Pakistan (Star of Pakistan)—from the Pakistan government, in recognition of services to Pakistan in the area of world peace, particularly his assistance as JFK's science adviser in developing the country's irrigation and agricultural resources.

Serves on the Committee of Public Higher Education in the District of Columbia (appointed by President Kennedy), exploring ways to provide higher educational opportunities to young people traditionally denied such opportunities.

Appears on a Voice of America program, "Science and the Emerging Nations," to discuss issues relating to the recent UN conference on science for new nations.

Receives the Man of the Year Award, New England Hebrew Academy.

Plays an important role in negotiations over the partial Nuclear Test Ban Treaty, signed with the Soviet Union; suggests, following the assassination of President Kennedy (Nov. 22), that the treaty "can inspire us to persist in the efforts to avoid the nuclear holocaust that so haunted him."

Reflects on JFK for an article published in *Science*—"John F. Kennedy: A Remembrance."

1964

Steps down as President Lyndon B. Johnson's special assistant for science and technology, and returns to MIT as dean of the School of Science (Feb.).

Is interviewed on WGBH-TV's "Great Decisions Series" on issues relating to nuclear weapons, deterrents, and arms control.

Argues, in an article coauthored with Herbert F. York and published in *Scientific American* (Oct.), that the partial Nuclear Test Ban Treaty has increased U.S. security and that a comprehensive test ban treaty may be feasible.

Active in the presidential election campaign with the group Scientists and Engineers for Johnson, later Scientists, Engineers and Physicians for Johnson and Humphrey.

Appointed to the board of governors, Weizmann Institute, Rehovot, Israel.

Second visit to Israel; first visit to Egypt; third visit to the Soviet Union.

Delivers the keynote address at a conference, "Computers '64: Problem-Solving in a Changing World," exploring the technical, social, and economic impact of electronic data.

1965

Agrees, on request of the White House, to head the Citizens Committee on Arms Control and Disarmament, to make policy recommendations to President Johnson as part of the UN International Cooperation Year.

Wife Laya becomes a member of the founding group and board of trustees of the Metropolitan Council for Educational Opportunity (METCO), focused on improving the quality of education for inner city black children by volunteer attendance in suburban school systems.

Appointed (by President Johnson) as consultant-at-large to the President's Science Advisory Committee (Jan.).

Publishes (with Walter Rosenblith) an article—"From Philosophy to Mathematics to Biology"—in *The Journal of Nervous and Mental Disease*.

Awarded honorary doctorates by Brandeis University and Lehigh University.

Visits India on government business; vacations in Ireland, England, Italy, France, and Denmark; third visit to Israel.

1966

Elected to the National Academy of Engineering.

Elected to the Watertown (Mass.) School Committee (March), focusing on issues of academic standards.

Appointed by MIT president Howard W. Johnson to serve as provost, the Institute's chief academic officer (appointment announced in May, effective July 1).

Appointed a member of the Advisory Committee to the director of the National Institutes of Health; serves four years.

Appointed to the board of directors and scientific and technical board of Celanese Corporation.

Launches (with George Kistiakowsky) the Cambridge Discussion Group, "to clarify, through discussions, our understanding of the problem of the peaceful settlement of the South Vietnamese war and *possibly* to reach a consensus leading to some agreed-upon group action."

Third visit to India.

1967

Delivers the Arthur Holly Compton Memorial Lecture at Washington University, St. Louis—address entitled "Disarmament and National Security."

Hosts a visit to MIT by Anatoly Dobrynin, Soviet ambassador to the United States.

Testifies before a Congressional committee on "urban problems in the light of technological opportunities."

Receives the Sesquicentennial Award, University of Michigan.

Appears with Eugene Skolnikoff and others in a joint WGBH-BBC televised discussion of anti-ballistic missiles; also appears on the WGBH-TV series, "Science and Foreign Policy," in a discussion that includes a review of Dwight Eisenhower's views on the importance of the Special Assistant for Science and Technology in advising the U.S. president.

Fourth, fifth, and sixth visits to Israel, for meetings of the Weizmann Institute board of governors; fourth visit to the Soviet Union.

Delivers an address at the Cultural Institute of America, Mexico.

1968

Urges President Johnson to postpone an imminent nuclear test, lest it interfere with efforts to pass the United Nations' proposed nonproliferation treaty (April).

Helps organize at MIT a series of "public discussions of social issues of special relevance to our times"; persuades eminent black psychologist Kenneth B. Clark to participate with a talk on racism, and subsequently to accept an appointment as "visiting Institute professor in urban affairs."

Awarded an honorary doctorate by Williams College.

Testifies in support of HR 875, Institutional Grants Bill, in support of fundamental research in higher education, before the Subcommittee on Science, Research, and Development, U.S. House Committee on Science and Astronautics.

Joins chemist George Kistiakowsky and other scientists in pressing the U.S. to accept a coalition government in South Vietnam, including members of the National Liberation Front.

Announces, as part of what he calls "[MIT's] determination . . . to help black America obtain its rightful place in society," several special projects—student-run community tutoring programs, Upward Bound, and others—"designed to permit black youth and members of other underprivileged minority groups to have access to more adequate educational opportunities, including an MIT education."

Participates in a conference entitled "Racism and American Education: Imperatives for Change," Martha's Vineyard, Massachusetts.

Speaks on "The Meaning of Science" at the Temple Dedication, Congregation B'nai Jeshurun, Short Hills, New Jersey.

Receives the National Human Relations Award, National Conference of Christians and Jews.

Advises U.S. Democratic presidential candidate Eugene McCarthy on McCarthy's proposal to delay deployment of ABM's and new Poseidon and Minuteman missile systems in order to promote an arms control agreement with the USSR.

Founding member and cochair, Committee of Scientists and Engineers for Humphrey-Muskie, whom the committee calls "the candidates most qualified to lead our country in its quest for world peace and in the resolution of problems which beset our own society"; chair, science advisory panel for Hubert H. Humphrey's presidential campaign.

Appears with students on Youth Forum, WNBC-TV, discussing the topic "Nuclear Energy for Peace or Destruction?"

1969

Agrees to President Richard Nixon's request (Jan.) to continue as consultant-at-large to the President's Science Advisory Committee until 30 Dec. 1971.

Arranges for his friend, playwright Lillian Hellman, to teach a course at MIT on reading and writing (spring semester).

Coauthor (with Abram Chayes), *A.B.M.: An Evaluation of the Decision to Deploy an Anti-Ballistic Missile System* (Harper and Row); appears with Chayes on NBC-TV's "Meet the Press" to outline their opposition to ABM deployment.

Testifies several times before U.S. House and Senate committees on environmental, defense, and security issues, including deployment of the ABM.

Joins with Abram Chayes and others to form the New England Citizens Committee on ABM; states at a press conference that to build the system would be "to start a mad arms race with ourselves with no hope of buying true defense."

Elected a member of the American Philosophical Society.

Speaks at the Madison Square Garden Rally Against the ABM, New York, NY (June 25).

Awarded an honorary doctorate by Oklahoma City University.

Speaks on "The Scientist in a Rapidly Evolving Society," before the American Psychological Association (Sept.).

Is chosen by the editors of *Playboy* magazine (along with Supreme Court Justice William O. Douglas, New York mayor John Lindsay, and others) as one of "eleven men of realistic vision" to highlight in the magazine's 15th-anniversary issue "specific reforms that they think can and must be undertaken today in order to achieve a more decent and humane society."

Delivers an address, "Current Prospects and Problems in Arms Control and Disarmament," at the annual conference of the American Association for the Advancement of Science, Boston, Massachusetts (Dec. 26).

1970

Cofounder and charter board member, Massachusetts Science and Technology Foundation, providing advice to the governor and other state officials on scientific and technical matters, and on the development of technical industries.

Active in creating the Harvard-MIT Division of Health Sciences and Technology.

Speaks before the American Philosophical Society, Philadelphia, Pa.—"Can the University Continue to Be an Important Source of Scientific Research?"

Testifies on several occasions before U.S. House and Senate committees on defense, security, nuclear, and science policy issues, including establishment of the Office of Technology Assessment.

Urges the Nixon White House to support a nationwide summer jobs program, as "this is going to be a particularly troublesome summer for the young."

Awarded an honorary doctorate by Yeshiva University.

Charter member of the Committee for Public Justice, a civil-liberties advocacy group founded by Lillian Hellman and others to defend the integrity of the Bill of Rights against abuses by the U.S. government.

1971

Assumes office as MIT's 13th president (July 1; official inauguration, Oct. 7); delivers an inaugural address entitled "Science, Technology, and the Quality of Life."

Oversees the creation of MIT's Council for the Arts, a volunteer group of alumni and others working to develop the creative arts at MIT.

Elected to honorary membership, MIT Alumni Association.

Encourages MIT faculty to participate in consortia of "visiting scholars" programs at historically black colleges and universities; argues "it is important to help these struggling institutions as much as we can."

Appeals to Massachusetts governor Francis W. Sargent for clemency on behalf of Stephen Krasner, the only felony indictment and conviction stemming from the Vietnam war protest takeover of the president's office at MIT.

Testifies before U.S. House and Senate committees on issues relating to controls on the use of information technology and prospects for a comprehensive nuclear test ban.

Becomes a director *ex officio* of WGBH, and goes on to serve nine years in that capacity.

Appoints a Task Force on Continuing Education, exploring directions and opportunities for MIT to enlarge its contribution to society.

One-week visit to Yugoslavia.

Awarded the Migel Medal, American Foundation for the Blind, "for spurring technology research of aids to the blind"; speaks on "Making Sensory Aids a Reality."

Congratulates President Nixon on his "courageous steps . . . regarding the economy and the nation's relations with China" (Oct.); Nixon replies "how deeply I appreciate your support for the initiatives we are taking in both the domestic and international spheres."

Addresses the winter meeting of the American Physical Society—"What Is Science Policy?"

1972

Invites Pablo Picasso to create a sculpture for MIT, conveying Picasso's qualities as "the model for the behavior of the creative man combining . . . a fight for a decent world and a concern for the individual with a restless creative expression . . . inspir[ing] the young people and stir[ring] them to stretch, to reach up, to be courageous individuals, to use their talents and their science imaginatively for peace and for the benefit of people everywhere and, finally, to have their mind's eye opened to beauty."

Congratulates President Nixon for his "outstanding achievement in bringing about the first phase of the SALT agreement . . . a landmark achievement in the long, slow process of building a more stable and secure world order."

Delivers the commencement address at the General Motors Institute, Flint, Michigan.

Is invited to serve on Democratic presidential candidate George McGovern's Panel on National Security, but declines because "when I became president of MIT, I decided that I should forgo the pleasures of partisan politics for the duration."

Elected councilor, American Philosophical Society; serves three years.

Expresses the need for a policy group at MIT to examine technology and engineering problems and their interaction with social issues; the Center for Policy Alternatives is established.

1973

Urges President Nixon to continue support for the Federal Affirmative Action Program, which has been "a constructive force in stimulating the universities . . . to greater and more positive efforts to provide educational and employment opportunities at all levels for women and members of minority groups."

Influential in establishing the Division for Study and Research in Education (DSRE) at MIT, an interdisciplinary program focused on knowledge structures, individual learning, and the concept of public learning.

Appears on President Richard Nixon's "enemies list," released during the U.S. Senate's Watergate hearings (June); is mentioned as having an "anti-defense bias," with President Nixon urging punitive action against MIT through government funding agencies.

Addresses a reception at the National Academy of Sciences, Washington, D.C.—"In Memory of the Office of Science and Technology."

1974

Appointed to the Technology Advisory Council, U.S. Congress's Office of Technology Assessment (OTA).

Appointed to the Science Advisory Committee, Massachusetts General Hospital.

Awarded honorary doctorates from Harvard University and the University of Notre Dame.

One-week visit to Teheran, Iran; three-week visit to the People's Republic of China.

1975

Testifies before Congress on constitutional issues relating to electronic surveillance, data banks, communications, and their potential impact on privacy.

Addresses the gathering at the Black Students' Conference on Science and Technology, MIT—"Science and Technology: Strategies for Educational, Economic, and Political Development."

Speaks on "The Response of Research Universities to National Problems" before the National Research Council Commission on Human Resources, Cambridge, Massachusetts.

Attends a forum of the Naval War College, Newport, Rhode Island, where he speaks on "The Morality of Science."

1976

Elected chair, OTA's technology advisory council (Jan.).

Speaks on "Science Policy and the Political Process" at a meeting of the American Association for the Advancement of Science, Boston, Massachusetts (Feb.).

Delivers an address at the Celebration of the Centennial of the Telephone, MIT, Cambridge, Massachusetts (March 9).

Accepts appointment to the science policy task force advising Democratic presidential candidate Jimmy Carter.

1977

Develops a keen interest in the pioneering work of MIT's Architecture Machine Group (ArchMac), headed by Nicholas Negroponte; becomes the intellectual champion of efforts to develop new relationships between people and computers, which later blossoms into a field known as "media arts and sciences."

In the wake of the Vietnam war, urges President Carter "to upgrade to honorable discharges the less-than-honorable discharges of those who committed no serious crimes and to pardon deserters still fugitive and civilian resisters."

Supports establishment of the Program in Science, Technology, and Society (STS) at MIT as a way to integrate humanities into the education of scientists and engineers.

Awarded the Founders Medal of the Institute of Electrical & Electronics Engineers (IEEE), "for leadership and service to the nation and the engineering and scientific professions in matters of technical developments, public policy, and education."

Appointed to the board of trustees, Solar Energy Research Institute.

1979

MIT's Council for the Arts establishes the Laya W. and Jerome B. Wiesner Student Art Awards, in honor of the Wiesners' contributions to the creative and performing arts at MIT.

Receives the MIT Alumni Association's Bronze Beaver Award, for distinguished service.

Appointed to the board of the John D. and Catherine T. MacArthur Foundation.

The Jerome B. Wiesner Scholarship Fund, "for scholarship assistance to undergraduate students at the Institute," established at MIT in his honor.

Receives the Award of Merit, American Consulting Engineers Council.

Counsels President Carter, who observes that "your guidance has helped me set forth clearly such national goals as energy security, and will be important in developing the policies we need to meet these goals."

1980

Retires as MIT president (June 30).

Becomes a life member, MIT Corporation.

Outlines (with Nicholas Negroponte) a plan to establish a Media Laboratory, building on disciplines ranging from cognition and learning to electronic music and holography.

The Jerome B. Wiesner Professorship is established at MIT by Schlumberger Technology Corporation of Houston, a subsidiary of Schlumberger Ltd., on whose board he served for many years.

Visits the People's Republic of China; second and third visits to Japan.

Receives the Public Service Award, Federation of American Scientists.

Awarded the Order of Bocaya, government of Colombia's highest distinction "in recognition of distinguished service to humankind."

Elected vice chairman, Technology Assessment Advisory Council (TAAC), of the Congressional Office of Technology Assessment (OTA).

Appointed to the board of directors of Raychem Corporation.

Receives the Delmar S. Fahrney Medal, Franklin Institute.

Honored as a "Jubilee Bostonian," as part of the city of Boston's 350th celebration.

1981

Quoted in an interview on the arms race, published in the *New York Times*, that "we desperately need to break this cycle of escalation before it becomes totally unmanageable."

As the U.S. begins a new arms buildup, joins 10 other scientists (including 4 Nobel laureates) in urging President Ronald Reagan to seriously consider the "awesome threat" of nuclear destruction.

Testifies against the U.S. Department of Justice plan for breakup of the Bell System, which he believes "will almost certainly deprive Bell Laboratories of the unique characteristics that have made it the best research and development center in the world."

Appointed to the advisory committee of the Science Policy Fellowship Program, Brookings Institution.

Fourth visit to Japan.

Urges President Reagan not to implement his proposal to curtail the federal government's synthetic fuels program.

First offering of a course that he taught for five years at MIT with Emma Rothschild—STS 560, "Arms Races in Industrial Society."

1982

Awarded an honorary doctorate by the University of Pennsylvania.

Urges President Reagan to reconsider his proposed executive order restricting the free publication of basic research on national security grounds.

Organizes a visit to MIT of Swedish prime minister Olof Palme, chair of the Independent Commission on Disarmament and Security Issues, to speak on questions of disarmament and security.

1983

Heads the MacArthur Foundation board's committee to explore prospects for an international program on security issues.

Receives First Class of the Order of the Sacred Treasure, awarded by the Emperor of Japan for extraordinary service in promoting scientific and technical exchanges between Japan and the United States.

Fifth visit to the Soviet Union; fifth visit to Japan.

1984

Three-week visit to Nairobi, Kenya.

Awarded the IEEE Centennial Medal.

Dedication of the Jerome B. Wiesner Student Art Gallery, Julius Stratton Student Center, MIT (April 7).

Speaks on "the power of creative philanthropy" at the dedication of the Whitehead Institute for Biomedical Research, MIT, Cambridge, Massachusetts (Dec. 5).

1985

Comments, on the announcement of the MacArthur Foundation's new International Security Program (Jan.), that the program's goal is to "strengthen the intellectual roots" of civilian leadership in the field.

Speaks on "creating with computing" at the dedication of the Wiesner Building, housing the MIT Media Laboratory and the List Visual Arts Center, dedicated to himself and his wife,

Laya, in recognition of their inspired devotion to the Institute and their advocacy of the arts and communications technologies (Oct. 2).

Becomes a nonresident fellow, Salk Institute.

Speaks on "world security and the arms race" at a United Nations symposium—Survival in the Nuclear Age—in New York, N.Y.

Sixth visit to Japan.

Speaks to an MIT jazz history class on "recording black jazz," harking back to his work at the Library of Congress in the early 1940s.

Visits Chancellor Willy Brandt in Bonn, Germany.

1986
Receives the National Academy of Engineering's Arthur M. Bueche Award, "for long-term contributions to public understanding of the risks of the nuclear age and to efforts to reduce those risks, including the Atmospheric Test Ban Treaty and arms reduction programs, and for personal leadership at the highest levels in the areas of high-performance communications systems, science policy in the federal government, and scientific and engineering education"; at the award ceremony, speaks on "Engineering and the Public Welfare" (Jan. 21).

Pledges assistance to the newly founded African Academy of Science, in its efforts to use scientific knowledge and skills to improve agriculture and water resource conditions on the African continent.

Awarded an honorary doctorate by Tufts University.

Awarded the C & C Foundation Prize (Tokyo, Japan), for contributions to the establishment, development, and growth of the fields of computer science and media technology; seventh visit to Japan.

Begins work on an autobiography.

1987
Sixth and seventh visits to the Soviet Union; attends a meeting of scientists, artists, and scholars in Moscow—the Forum for a Nuclear-Free World, for the Survival and Development of Humanity—organized by Mikhail Gorbachev; proposes (with Yevgeniy Velikhov, vice president of the Soviet Academy of Sciences, and others) establishment of the International Foundation for the Survival and Development of Humanity, to promote collaborative international research on global problems such as environmental pollution, arms control, and economic development; serves as vice chair, with Velikhov as chair.

Endorses nomination of the Pugwash Group for the Nobel Peace Prize, in recognition of its role in moderating the arms race.

Testifies before the U.S. House Science, Research and Technology Subcommittee (Committee on Science, Space and Technology) that federal funding for science and technology is "too focused on applied goals instead of on the discovery of fundamental knowledge."

Receives the Cosmos Club Award; speaks at the ceremony on "The Rise and Fall of the President's Science Advisory Committee."

Receives the Aging in America Prize, for contributions to a better world for mankind.

Speaks on the "beginnings of radio astronomy at MIT" at a Harvard symposium on astrophysics.

Eighth visit to Japan.

1988
Advocates admission of women to the exclusive, all-male St. Botolph Club in Boston, "to contribute our bit to the continuing emancipation of women and in doing so contribute even more to our own self-respect."

Delivers an address entitled "Survival, the Moral Equivalent of the Arms Race," at the National Geographic Society Centennial Symposium (Jan. 29).

Eighth, ninth, and tenth visits to Moscow; ninth visit to Japan.

Welcomes and exchanges views with Soviet physicist and human rights activist Andrei Sakharov, during Sakharov's visit to the United States (Nov.).

Criticizes certain U.S. government science initiatives, such as the proposed space station: "I'd put it under adventure and exploration. If the country can afford it, fine, but I would first want to make sure that real science was adequately funded."

1989
Suffers a severe thrombotic stroke; begins a rehabilitation effort that inspires other stroke victims and raises physicians' expectations about levels of recovery possible after a stroke.

Resumes work on an autobiography, stimulated by reading David Bradley's *No Place to Hide*.

1990
Becomes a life member, American Geophysical Union.

Becomes a life member emeritus, MIT Corporation.

Signs an international appeal, prepared and circulated by astronomer and popular science writer Carl Sagan, entitled "Preserving and Cherishing the Earth: An Appeal for Joint Commitment in Science and Religion"—outlining environmental problems such as the depletion of the protective ozone layer, global warming, deforestation, species extinction, possible global nuclear war, and exponential increase of the world population.

Prepares a paper, "President Eisenhower's Changing Search for Peace," for a Soviet-American Conference on Dwight D. Eisenhower—Eisenhower's World Legacy: Reappraisal of the Man and the Issues, Soviet Academy of Science, Moscow.

1991
Nominated, along with Jimmy Carter, Nelson Mandela, and others, for the Albert Einstein Peace Prize.

1992
Receives the National Science Board's Vannevar Bush Award, "for pioneering with vision, boldness and drive, the exploration, mapping, and settlement of new frontiers in research, education and public service" (April).

1993
Co-author (with Philip Morrison and Kosta Tsipis), *Beyond the Looking Glass: The United*

States Military in 2000 and Later, calling for deep cuts in American military procurement and spending.

Visits Washington, D.C. (with Morrison and Tsipis) to try and draw the attention of President Bill Clinton to the need for further cuts in the U.S. defense budget (February).

Receives the Public Welfare Medal, highest honor of the National Academy of Sciences, "for his devoted and successful efforts in science policy, education, and nuclear disarmament and world peace" (April 24).

Urges President Clinton to resist pressure to resume underground nuclear testing.

1994
Dies of heart failure at his home in Watertown, Massachusetts (Oct. 21).

A Note on Sources

Philip N. Alexander

At my first meeting with Walter and Judy Rosenblith in July 2001, we talked about who would write essays for this book. Walter already had prospects in mind—and they all sounded excellent to me—but, being the rigorous scientist that he was, he insisted on submitting his list to an empirical test. Fine, I said, and started on a survey of the vast collection of Jerry's papers at the MIT Archives, including both his personal and administrative files. The goal was to create a list of the major players in Jerry's enormous sphere of activity—government, education, engineering, philanthropy, and on and on—and from that list to choose a dozen or so potential essayists, ranging across the spectrum of Jerry's universe.

After a few weeks, we came up with several hundred names and developed a list of prospects from among surviving members of that group. It was a bit of a surprise to me—but, I think, no surprise to Walter—that the list pretty much mirrored the one he had started out with. Then, with help from the group that Walter assembled to serve as advisers for the project, we came up with the essayists represented here.

The initial survey of archives was important in other ways as well. It provided clues to the key events and activities in Jerry's life; raw material for a detailed chronology; a factual, contextual basis for his wide-ranging experiences and perspectives; and a resource for essayists whose memories might need jogging after the lapse of many years, half a century in some cases.

Philip N. Alexander, historian, editor, and archivist, is a research associate in the Program in Writing and Humanistic Studies at MIT, and has also been connected with MIT's Program in Science, Technology, and Society. He works mostly in the history of science and medicine, African-American studies, archival history, and West Indian history. He has published in several journals and encyclopedias, including *Jamaica Journal*, *American Archivist*, *Primary Sources and Original Works*, and *Encyclopedia of African-American Culture and History* (Macmillan, 1996).

Family Materials

Jerry began writing his memoirs in the mid-1980s. The project came to a halt after he suffered a stroke in 1989, but his son Josh, eager to help him continue, audio-taped more than 30 interviews with him in the early 1990s, mostly 1991–93. These interviews provided a basis for several chapters, as well as supplementary information to fill gaps in chapters that Jerry had already drafted.

The first interview (April 14, 1991) focused on Jerry's relationship with his close friend and colleague, Jerrold Zacharias; the last (May 15, 1994) dealt with Jerry's experience at Los Alamos, New Mexico, in the mid-1940s. Subjects covered in the intervening interviews include the Radiation Laboratory at MIT, early reactions to the atomic bomb, the Von Neumann Committee, Project Troy, the Technological Capabilities Panel (TCP), the President's Science Advisory Committee, the nuclear test ban treaty and the Kennedy years, Kennedy and Khrushchev, Russian views on the test ban, Pugwash conferences, Lyndon B. Johnson, anti-ballistic missiles (ABM), "current" policies in arms control (i.e., early 1990s), Jerry's political views, and key figures in the large cast of characters whose paths crossed Jerry's in important ways—Bernard Feld, Paul Doty, Trevor Gardner, Lloyd Berkner, Edward Purcell, George Kistiakowsky, Henry Kissinger, Albert Hill, and James Killian, among others. The interviews provide a rich overview of Jerry's perspectives on central issues, concerns, and personalities over a fifty-year period, and some of this material found its way into drafts of the proposed memoir (specifically, the chapters printed in this book).

Josh also supplied several family photographs reproduced here—in particular, the images of Jerry's father, mother, and other relatives, as well as scenes from his childhood.

Archival Collections at MIT

Two core collections relating to Jerry's life and career (filling nearly 300 record center cartons) are at the Institute Archives and Special Collections, MIT. The first—*AC 8, Massachusetts Institute of Technology, Office of the President and Chancellor, Records of the President, 1965–1983*—contains mostly records generated during his period as MIT provost (1966–71) and president (1971–80). The second—*MC 420, Jerome Bert Wiesner Papers, 1949–1983*—contains personal papers and manuscripts relating to broader aspects of his role in education, government, industry, and international affairs.

AC 8 reflects some of the turbulence of a university administrator's life in the late 1960s and 1970s. A number of Jerry's activities, as revealed through these records, were shaped by the sheer drama of the time (student strikes, riots, and bomb threats) as well as by legislative pressures (affirmative action, equal opportunity, and urban affairs). But his own special interests shine through—the emphasis, for example, on issues relating to social justice, pollution and the environment, the arts, and international affairs.

MC 420 is broader in scope, including material on Jerry's MIT and outside activities from the late 1940s to the 1990s (although nothing, unfortunately, from his time at the Library of Congress or his early MIT years, including his work at the Radiation Laboratory). The collection, pieced together from several accessions, is not yet well arranged or described; its organization is rudimentary at best. Scattered here and there are several draft chapters of Jerry's proposed memoir. The earliest, dated June 1986, is a prospectus entitled "A Personal History of JBW and the Arms Race," transcribed from audiotape for further development as a narrative. Also found here are the memoir's opening chapter, "A Random Walk Through the Twentieth Century," and initial drafts of the chapter about the Radiation Laboratory and Research Laboratory of Electronics ("Remembering"); the latest versions of both chapters are printed in this book. Early versions of two other chapters printed here—"Up the Ladder to the White House" (originally called "Working in the White House") and "Kennedy" (originally called "Backing Into the Kennedy Administration")—reveal much about Jerry's writing and revision process, particularly as he and Josh worked together to craft a "final" product.

Files from the 1940s to mid-1960s in MC 420 focus on Jerry's teaching, administrative, scientific, and committee work at MIT, as well as his growing involvement as an industry consultant, government adviser, and advocate for international arms control. Particularly noteworthy are files relating to the President's Science Advisory Committee (PSAC), the Pugwash Conferences, disarmament, antiballistic missiles, and the 1960 special issue of *Daedalus* (American Academy of Arts and Sciences) on arms control. Files from the White House years include correspondence with John F. Kennedy, Theodore Sorensen, McGeorge Bundy, Lyndon B. Johnson, and others in the executive and legislative branches. Among the other notable correspondents are Adlai Stevenson, Bertrand Russell, Robert F. Kennedy, and Henry Kissinger.

The collection includes notes and/or full texts of literally hundreds of Jerry's speeches, given both in the United States and abroad on a wide range of topics—technical (especially in the fields of electronics and the communication sciences, space sciences, energy, and the environment), national security and defense policy, arts and culture, arms control, health care, scientific information and secrecy, university research and education, university-industry relations, the public impact of science and technology, educational broadcasting, the role of women and minorities in science, and foreign policy (especially U.S.-Soviet relations). Along with the speeches are correspondence, programs, and notes about the particular forums or events at which Jerry spoke. The earliest speech is "Source Noise and Its Effect Upon Electronic Systems," dated November 1954 and delivered at a Symposium on Fluctuation Phenomena in Microwave Sources of the Institute of Radio Engineers. The latest, dated April 1993, is the text of his prepared talk on the occasion of his receiving the Public Welfare Medal of the National Academy of Sciences. Most of the speeches date from the 1960s and 1970s, at the peak of Jerry's activity in government and academic life. An additional flurry crops up in the 1980s, when he was deeply involved in public debates over arms control and détente with the Soviet Union. A few examples are printed in this book.

In addition to speeches, there are transcripts, correspondence, notes, and other materials relating to media forums that Jerry took part in beginning in the late 1950s, a time when he was first widely recognized as an influential figure in U.S. domestic and foreign policy. One of the earliest of these forums is a discussion about the Soviet Union for the Educational Television Foundation, June 12, 1958. In February 1959, Jerry was interviewed by Eric Sevareid for CBS's "Great Challenge" series, along with scientists Detlev Bronk and J. Robert Oppenheimer, on the subject—"Where Is Science Taking Us?" In December 1960, Eleanor Roosevelt interviewed him and others for WGBH-TV—a program called "The Scientist and World Politics," part of the series "Prospects of Mankind." The media events in which Jerry participated were sponsored, produced, and aired by public networks such as WGBH, the Educational Broadcasting Corporation, and National Educational Television; commercial networks such as CBS, NBC, and ABC; government outlets such as the Voice of America; and foreign stations such as the BBC and Canadian Television Network. The events were organized around topics as varied as nuclear disarmament, science and emerging nations, the arms race, space science, foreign affairs, technology and survival, and higher education. There are a few unusual curiosities as well, e.g. the transcript of a 1964 videotape critical of U.S. presidential candidate Barry Goldwater, produced by Scientists and Engineers for Johnson and Humphrey with the participation of Jerry and scientists Herbert York, George Kistiakowsky, Harold Urey, and Benjamin Spock.

Some of Jerry's rough drafts and manuscripts are intriguing, because they reveal what little survives of a number of writing and other projects that he started and did not always carry to completion. One typescript entitled "Growing Up With the Arms Race" (dated April 1986), for example, is a series of notes evidently intended to stimulate him to work on his personal memoir. There are also proposals for an international arms compliance center (1991), reflections on technology and the future of the postal service (1990), achieving nuclear security, civilian technology policy (1992), a proposed microwave-powered rocket (1991), the electronic battle-field (1972), technology and the U.S. presidential election (1988), commentary on what constitutes a strong national defense, and many other topics—sometimes cryptically conveyed, but always reflecting the sweep of Jerry's interests. He almost invariably brought scientific and technical topics back to his primary concern: the impact of science and technology on people, institutions, and the environment.

Jerry's life touched so many people and institutions that a listing of his voluminous correspondence in MC 420 reads rather like a *Who's Who of the World*. Among the individuals whose correspondence with Jerry survives here are prominent figures from the academic world, such as John Kenneth Galbraith, Archibald Cox, Theodore Hesburgh, Roman Jakobson, Noam Chomsky, Paul Samuelson, and Arthur Schlesinger, Jr.; politicians and government officials such as Edward Kennedy, Hubert Humphrey, Walter Mondale, Richard Nixon, William Clinton, Albert Gore, Jr., Edward Brooke, Jimmy Carter, Emilio Daddario, Eugene McCarthy, Edmund Muskie, and Thomas P. (Tip) O'Neill, Jr.; writers, artists, and musicians such as Archibald MacLeish, Lillian Hellman, Ann Landers, and Leonard Bernstein; American scientists such as Jerrold Zacharias, Leo Szilard, George Kistiakowsky, Victor Weisskopf, Salvador Luria, Edward Teller, Jonas Salk, Linus Pauling, and David Baltimore; British scientists such as Victor Rothschild and Solly Zuckerman; Russian scientists such as Andrei Sakharov, Yevgeniy Velikhov, and Roald Sagdeev; Russian government officials such as Anatoly Dobrynin and Jermen Gvishiani; international heads of state such as King Hussein and the Shah of Iran; media figures such as Bill Moyers; international peace activists such as Alva Myrdal and Olof Palme; and African-American scholars and community activists, such as Herman Branson, Kenneth Clark, and Elma Lewis. This list gives a sense of the range of Jerry's correspondents, but it is just a tiny sample.

The topics covered, likewise, are numerous and varied—ranging from the American political scene, including Vietnam and Watergate, to Jerry's role as a consultant to multinational corporations such as Schlumberger; in professional organizations such as the National Academy of Sciences, National Academy of Engineering, and Institute of Electrical & Electronics Engineers; in civil rights advocacy, through groups such as the Committee for Public Justice, Americans for Amnesty, and American Civil Liberties Union; as an adviser to the federal government, including the President's Science Advisory Committee, Office of Technology Assessment, and Office of Science and Technology, a number of the federal "departments" (energy, commerce, defense, etc.), and congressional offices; on Massachusetts state boards such as the Governor's Advisory Committee on Science and Technology and Governor's Task Force on Economy; and with broadcasting concerns—PBS, WGBH, ABC, and other media outlets. Jerry's role in international affairs is especially well documented, including his activities relating to the Weizmann Institute, Third World Academy of Sciences, CISAC (Committee on International Security and Arms Control), and the International Foundation for the Survival and Development of Humanity, which Jerry helped organize and administer. Other important material relates to Jerry's role at MIT, including his interest in conceptualizing, planning, and promoting innovative educational, cultural, and research programs—the Council for the Arts; the Program in Science, Technology, and Society; the Harvard-MIT Health Sciences and Technology Program; and the Media Laboratory, for example.

Also among the materials in MC 420 are several boxes of "declassified government archives," gathered by Jerry as part of a plan conceived in the early to mid-1980s—probably around 1984—to write a book about U.S. defense policy in the 1950s. There are many government files, reports, and other records relating to the development and deployment of satellites, ballistic missiles, and other military and civilian hardware over a 30-year period (1940s–70s), as well as agendas, minutes, and papers on arms control, disarmament, the Geneva Conference on Surprise Attack (1958), meetings of the President's Science Advisory Committee, and similar forums and discussions relating to technology and public policy mostly during the Eisenhower and Kennedy presidential administrations. Jerry gathered these materials from the John F. Kennedy Library, Dwight D. Eisenhower Library, and National Archives, often through a series of Freedom of Information Act requests that were cumbersome, frustratingly slow, and not always successful (some of the requests were still being answered a year after Jerry died in 1994). He never got very far with the book, possibly because the government's security review process was so complicated that access issues—rather than writing—threatened to consume most of his time. He mapped out a number of "possible writing projects," and some of these—the Technology Capabilities Panel, the Gaither Panel, and ABM, for example—carried over almost intact when he began his personal memoirs. The memoirs gradually superseded the defense history project as a manageable goal in Jerry's mind, although those, too, remained incomplete at the time of his death.

A number of other collections at the MIT Archives include significant documentation relating to Jerry's life and career. In addition to the standard administrative record groups (too numerous to list here), also of interest are the Bernard T. Feld Papers (1943–76), James R. Killian Papers (1923–85), William Ted Martin Papers (1961–80), and Norbert Wiener Papers (1898–1966). Correspondence with Jerry is scattered throughout other manuscript collections as well.

Jerry's wife, Laya, who shared many of his interests, particularly in the arts and community service, also shows up in the archival collections. AC 307, the Laya and Jerome B. Wiesner Student Art Awards, includes copies of award certificates signed by Laya and Jerry in the mid-1980s. The awards were established in 1979 by the Council for the Arts in recognition of the Wiesners' contribution to the arts at MIT. Laya's involvement with women's issues at MIT is documented in AC 381, MIT Women's League Records (1917–82). Material on Laya also appears in Jerry's own papers, especially in MC 420. AC 8 includes material on MIT's first Workshop on Women in Science and Technology, a series that Laya helped organize in 1973 to address challenges for women in scientific and technical fields.

The MIT Museum

The MIT Museum's rich collection of photographs focuses on MIT history, and includes more than 200 images of Jerry, both individual portraits and group shots. A number of these images are reproduced in this book. Also at the museum, but not studied for the purposes of this project, are audiotapes and videotapes showing Jerry at different points in his career. Of special note are: an oral history on the Kennedy years, conducted for the Kennedy Library, 4 December 1964; assorted speeches, including one given by Jerry at Punjab University (India), 5 October 1961; Jerry's commencement addresses at MIT and elsewhere, various dates; his inaugural address as MIT president, 7 October 1971; a talk to MIT alumni as he approached his retirement as president, "Reminiscences of Years at MIT" (January 1980), in which he placed his Institute experience in the context of his larger career in engineering, government, and other spheres of activity; and selected television interviews, including panel discussions on disarmament and arms control. There is also a computer optical disk, put together by Glorianna Davenport and Cheryl Morse as part of the tenth anniversary of the MIT Media Laboratory, that was one of the first systematic efforts to construct a detailed biography of Jerry, and that benefited from his direct input. Called "A Random Walk through the Twentieth Century" (clearly a favorite title of Jerry's—he continued to use it for his own prospective memoir), the content is also available on-line.

The museum also has artifacts—posters and programs, for example, relating to Jerry's inaugural concert, retirement reception and colloquium, and other events, as well as a number of certificates awarded to Jerry for services to the Arms Control Association, U.S. Army Scientific Advisory Board, U.S. Department of State, and other organizations.

Outside Archival Collections

We did not consult repositories outside of MIT, but a few key ones are worth listing here for future reference. The John Fitzgerald Kennedy Library in Boston has two important collections: the Jerome B. Wiesner Papers (1961–73) and U.S. Office of Science and Technology Records (1961–63). The Wiesner Papers, relating primarily to Jerry's role as President Kennedy's special assistant for science and technology, are currently closed to researchers; however, MC 420 (MIT Archives) probably includes duplicates of at least some materials. The Office of Science and Technology Records are comprised of microfilm copies (73 rolls) of selected subject files on defense, space, limited war, nuclear propulsion and weapons, radiation, civilian technology, disarmament, education, international affairs, life sciences, the President's Science Advisory Committee (PSAC), and other topics. These files are partially open for research, and may also be duplicated to some extent in MC 420.

Among the relevant items at the Lyndon Baines Johnson Library in Austin, Texas, are recordings of telephone conversations, speeches, media programs, and other events. One recording, for example, is of a conversation between Jerry and LBJ (11 December 1963) about press briefings on Donald Hornig as Jerry's replacement as special assistant to the president for science and technology; another includes secretary of defense Robert McNamara (25 January 1964) outlining for LBJ, among other things, Jerry's concerns about certain budget cuts. There is also tape of a discussion (30 January 1963) aired on Voice of America, part of its "New Horizons in Science" series, in which Jerry and others outlined the forthcoming United Nations Conference on the Application of Science and Technology for the Benefit of Less Developed Areas (Geneva); a tape of Jerry's Geneva conference speech, "Education and the Promise of Science and Technology," 4 February 1963; and a tape of his memorial tribute to JFK, broadcast on Voice of America, 5 December

1963. These are just a few readily identifiable nuggets; the collections include quite extensive documentation of Jerry's role at the White House and as a federal government official during the early to mid-1960s.

Documents by and about Jerry appear in a number of collections at other repositories. Examples include: Eugene Rabinowitch Papers, University Archives, University of Illinois at Urbana Champaign; George B. Kistiakowsky Papers, Harvard University Archives; Harriet Louise Hardy Papers, Schlesinger Library on the History of Women in America, Radcliffe Institute for Advanced Study; and Herbert F. York Papers, Mandeville Special Collections Library, University of California at San Diego. This list, of course, is far from exhaustive, and a thorough identification of primary sources for scholarship on Jerry Wiesner's life and career remains to be done.

Published Sources

Jerry was the subject of a number of articles published in his lifetime. The earliest of these appeared during his years connected to the White House, when his public profile both broadened and deepened. A number are informative and some, particularly those based on interviews with Jerry, are quite probing.[1] Other accounts followed after Jerry's return to MIT in 1964. Several focus on Jerry's MIT years, a topic frequently overwhelmed by the scope of his activities in government, arms control, and international affairs. Constitutionally shy, Jerry sometimes opened up to the media and was always careful about nuances of meaning—evidenced, in part, by his detailed marginalia on drafts submitted to him by journalists and other writers for review and comment.[2]

---

1. Examples include J. Lear, "Chief of the Expedition: Prof. Jerome B. Wiesner, of MIT," *Saturday Review*, 10 December 1960, pp. 53–54; "Mr. Kennedy's Scientist: Space, Where We Are," *Newsweek*, 23 January 1961, pp. 60–61; John W. Finney, "Top Scientist on the New Frontier: Dr. Jerome Wiesner, the President's science adviser, is in some respects as much a crusader for ideas as he is a researcher for scientific knowledge," *New York Times Magazine*, 3 September 1961, p. 8 ff.; "Thinking Ahead With . . . Jerome Wiesner," *International Science and Technology* (February 1962), no. 2: 28–33; a two-part portrait by Daniel Lang, "Profiles: A Scientist's Advice," *New Yorker*, 19 January 1963, p. 39 ff., and 26 January 1963, p. 38 ff.; and "16 Billions for Science—Where the Money Goes: Interview with Jerome B. Wiesner, the President's Science Adviser," *US News & World Report*, 3 February 1964, pp. 72–76.
2.   "Wiesner Opens Up," *Boston Globe*, 17 April 1966, pp. 2–3; Elinor Langer, "After the Pentagon Papers: Talk with Kistiakowsky, Wiesner," *Science* 174 (26 November 1971):

The dozens of obituaries that appeared following Jerry's death vary in scope and depth. Some are detailed, some sketchy, some reflective. Notices appearing overseas were unusually insightful and comprehensive, perhaps not surprisingly so, considering Jerry's global reach.[3] In MIT-related publications, the memorials tend to be relatively thorough, covering Jerry's career in ample detail but also conveying personal reminiscences. The same is true for memorials published in the professional literature.[4]

We did not carry out a systematic survey of secondary sources, but dipped in selectively when the need arose. Jerry's role in the Eisenhower administration was brief and not very central, but some of the specialized studies focusing on science and arms control refer to his contributions there.[5] The literature on the Kennedy

---

923–28; Paul Schindler, "A Day in the Life of a Busy Man, or What Jerry Wiesner Does for a Living," *The Tech*, 11 February 1972, pp. 6–7; Paul Schindler, "On Being President of MIT, or How Jerry Wiesner Runs the Institute," *The Tech*, 15 February 1972, pp. 14–15; "Making Education Responsive to 'the Current Needs of Man'," *Technology Review* 76 (May 1974): 72–74; J. Tevere MacFadyen, "Retiring, But Not Shy: A Conversation with Jerome Wiesner of MIT," *Boston Monthly*, April 1980; Carl Oglesby, "Jerome Wiesner Says Goodbye," *Boston Magazine* (June 1980): 98, 138–44; and Steven J. Marcus, "The Level of Might That's Right: An Interview with Jerome B. Wiesner," *Technology Review* 83 (January 1981): 58–67.

3. Among the best of the U.S. examples are Eric Pace, "Jerome B. Wiesner, President of MIT, Is Dead at 79," *New York Times*, 23 October 1994; and Anthony Lewis, "Abroad at Home; The Public Citizen," *New York Times*, 28 October 1994. The best British obituaries are Frank Barnaby, "Science with Political Clout; Obituary: Jerome B. Wiesner," *Guardian*, 25 October 1994; and Tam Dalyell, "Obituary: Jerome Wiesner," *Independent*, 27 October 1994.

4. The MIT-based memorials include Howard W. Johnson, "Jerry Wiesner," *MIT Faculty Newsletter* 7 (November/December 1994): 1, 18–19; "Resolutions of the Corporation of the Massachusetts Institute of Technology on the death of Jerome Bert Wiesner, 1915–1994" [6 pp., signed by Corporation chair Paul E. Gray and president Charles M. Vest]; and Robert Byers, "Jerome Wiesner 1915–1994: A Renaissance Engineer," *MITnews* [from the Association of Alumni and Alumnae of MIT] (January 1995): 1–8, in *Technology Review* 98 (January 1995). For the professional literature, see especially Walter C. Clemens, Jr. in *Bulletin of the Atomic Scientists* (January-February 1995): 10; Herman Feshbach and Kosta Tsipis in *Physics Today* 48 (April 1995): 104–5; Walter Rosenblith in *Journal of the Acoustical Society of America* 98 (July 1995): 4; Paul E. Gray in *National Academy of Engineering Memorial Tributes* 8 (1996): 291–95; David S. Saxon in *Proceedings of the American Philosophical Society* 140 (June 1996): 254–62; and Louis D. Smullin in *National Academy of Sciences Biographical Memoirs* 78 (2000): 335–53.

5. See, for example, James R. Killian, Jr., *Sputnik, Scientists, and Eisenhower: A Memoir of the First Special Assistant to the President for Science and Technology* (MIT Press, 1977); and David L. Snead, *The Gaither Committee, Eisenhower, and the Cold War* (Ohio State University Press, 1999).

administration includes numerous references to Jerry, including the classic early studies by Sorensen and Schlesinger. Also important are the documentary collections edited by Zelikow and May, which reveal Jerry's central role in advising JFK on momentous issues ranging from communications in Latin America to the federal budget to national security questions to negotiations, testing, monitoring, and research and development for nuclear weapons.[6] Daniel Lang's book, *An Inquiry into Enoughness: Of Bombs and Men and Staying Alive* (McGraw-Hill, 1965) includes an entire chapter on Jerry—"A Scientist's Advice," pp. 71–132—essentially a reprint of his *New Yorker* articles referred to earlier. For Jerry's role in arms control, two books by Herbert York are good places to begin: *Making Weapons, Talking Peace: A Physicist's Odyssey from Hiroshima to Geneva* (Basic Books, 1987) and *Arms and the Physicist* (American Institute of Physics, 1995). The first of these provided background for Josh as he interviewed Jerry and helped draft certain sections of the memoir printed here.

Jerry's work and career are cited regularly in the scholarly and popular literature. The emphasis is generally on broader aspects—his contributions, for example, to science in its social, political, and humanistic contexts. Topics include international scientific cooperation, the Cold War, U.S. foreign policy, environmental protection and sustainability, U.S. presidential administrations, military strategy, arms control and nuclear weapons, U.S.-Soviet détente, national security, openness vs. secrecy in research and development, privacy and data surveillance, information and freedom, creativity in research, university-industry cooperation, educational quality, and the role and responsibility of university faculty. The citations are centered primarily in the social sciences literature, including standard journals in the fields of history, strategic studies, interdisciplinary science, military studies, and public policy.

⚛

This brief overview of primary and secondary sources underscores the extraordinary breadth, depth, and richness of Jerry's life and career: scientist, engineer,

---

6. Theodore C. Sorensen, *Kennedy* (Harper & Row, 1965); Arthur M. Schlesinger, Jr., *A Thousand Days* (Houghton-Mifflin, 1965); Philip Zelikow and Ernest May, *The Kennedy Tapes: Inside the White House During the Cuban Missile Crisis* (Harvard University Press, 1997) and *The Presidential Recordings: John F. Kennedy: The Great Crises* (Norton, 2001, 3 vols.).

educator, statesman, academic executive, social activist, peace advocate . . . along with a number of other portfolios, functions, and qualities that defy easy categorization. Walter Rosenblith hoped that this book would fill a gap in our knowledge and appreciation of his close friend and colleague—his "brother," as he liked to say—and while it does that to some extent, much remains to be explored, much to say and write about. Walter would have been the first to observe that this book is more a starting point than a final word.

Selected Bibliography[1]

"The Recording Laboratory in the Library of Congress," *Journal of the Acoustical Society of America* 13 (January 1942): 288–293.

"3 cm. Magnetron Test Bench Construction and Operation," Radiation Laboratory, Massachusetts Institute of Technology, Report no. M-114, 22 August 1942.

"Microwave Wattmeter II, 3 cm. and 1 cm.," Radiation Laboratory, Massachusetts Institute of Technology, Report no. 246, 21 January 1943 [with M. H. Johnson].

"Pre-ignition Transmission through Gas-switching Tubes, and Its Contribution to Crystal Failures," Radiation Laboratory, Massachusetts Institute of Technology, Report no. 254, 3 July 1943 [with F. L. McMillan].

"Details of an X-band High Level TR Tube Test Bench Construction and Operation," Radiation Laboratory, Massachusetts Institute of Technology, Report no. 417, 3 February 1944.

"The Application of Correlation Functions in the Detection of Small Signals in Noise," Research Laboratory of Electronics, Massachusetts Institute of Technology, Technical Report no. 141, 13 October 1949 [with Y. W. Lee and T. P. Cheatham, Jr.].

"Statistical Theory of Communications," *Proceedings of the National Electronics Conference* 5 (September 1949): 334–341.

"Some Problems in Sensory Prosynthesis," *Science* 110 (November 1949): 512 [with Norbert Wiener and L. Levine].

"Correlation Functions and Communication Applications," *Electronics* 23 (June 1950): 86–92 [with Y. W. Lee].

"Application of Correlation Analysis to the Detection of Periodic Signals in Noise," *Proceedings of the IRE* [Institute of Radio Engineers] 38 (October 1950): 1165–1171 [with Y. W. Lee and T. P. Cheatham, Jr.].

"Speech-Reinforcement System Evaluation," *Proceedings of the IRE* [Institute of Radio Engineers] 39 (November 1951): 1401–1408 [with L. L. Beranek, W. H. Radford, and J. A. Kessler].

"A New Kind of Radio Propagation at Very High Frequencies Observable over Long

---

1. A chronological list of selected published writings by Jerry. For a survey of relevant primary and secondary sources, see "A Note on Sources" (above).

Distances," *Physical Review* 86 (15 April 1952): 141–145 [with D. K. Bailey, R. Bateman, L. V. Berkner, H. G. Booker, G. F. Montgomery, E. M. Purcell, and W. W. Salisbury].

"M.I.T. and the Electron," *Industry* [Associated Industries of Massachusetts], September 1952, pp. 17–19, 84–85.

"Noise in CW Magnetrons," *Journal of Applied Physics* 24 (August 1953): 1065–1066 [with David Middleton and W. M. Gottschalk].

"Communication Theory and the Transmission of Information," in *Modern Physics for the Engineer,* ed. Louis N. Ridenour (New York: McGraw-Hill, 1954), pp. 427–454.

"UHF Long-Range Communication Systems," *Proceedings of the IRE* [Institute of Radio Engineers] 43 (October 1955): 1269–1281 [with G. L. Mellen, W. E. Morrow, A. J. Poté, and W. H. Radford].

"New Methods of Radio Transmission," *Scientific American* 196 (January 1957): 46–51.

"Liaisons radioélectriques au moyen de la propagation par diffusion troposphérique," *L'Onde Électrique* 37 (May 1957): 456–461 [with A. J. Poté].

"Are Research and Technology the Soviets' Secret Weapon?" in *Soviet Progress vs. American Enterprise: Report of a Confidential Briefing Session Held at the Fifteenth Anniversary Meeting of the Committee for Economic Development on November 21, 1957, in Washington, DC* (Garden City: Doubleday, 1958), pp. 63–78.

"Electronics and the Missile," *Astronautics* 3 (May 1958): 20–21, 114.

"Communication Sciences in a University Environment," *IBM Journal of Research and Development* 2 (October 1958): 268–275.

Twelve Years of Basic Research: A Brief History of the Research Laboratory of Electronics (Cambridge, Mass.: Research Laboratory of Electronics, 1958) [with G. G. Harvey, H. J. Zimmermann, and R. A. Sayers].

"Communication Using Earth Satellites," *IRE Transactions on Military Electronics*, MIL-4, no. 1 (January 1960): 51–58.

"Foreword to the Issue 'Arms Control,'" *Daedalus* 89 (Fall 1960): 677–680.

"Comprehensive Arms-Limitations Systems," *Daedalus* 89 (Fall 1960): 915–950.

"Comprehensive Arms-Limitations Systems," in *Arms Control, Disarmament, and National Security,* ed. Donald G. Brennan (New York: George Braziller, 1961), pp. 198–233.

Where Science and Politics Meet (New York: McGraw-Hill, 1961).

"Inspection for Disarmament," in The American Assembly, Columbia University, *Arms Control: Issues for the Public* (Englewood Cliffs, N.J.: Prentice-Hall, 1961), pp. 112–140.

"Communication Using Earth Satellites," in *Lectures on Communication System Theory,* ed. Elie J. Baghdady (New York: McGraw-Hill, 1961), pp. 577–593.

"Electronics and Evolution," *Proceedings of the IRE* [Institute of Radio Engineers] 50 (May 1962): 653–654.

"An Age of Great Discoveries," *Star Magazine*, 19 August 1962.

"Education for Productivity in the Sciences," *Analytical Chemistry* 35 (September 1963): 27A–39A.

"John F. Kennedy: A Remembrance," *Science* 142 (29 November 1963): 1147–1154.

"National Security and the Nuclear-Test Ban," *Scientific American* 211 (October 1964): 27–35 [with Herbert F. York].

"Technology and Society," in *Science As a Cultural Force*, ed. Harry Woolf (Baltimore: Johns Hopkins University Press, 1964), pp. 35–53.

"Innovation and Experimentation in Education" [Xerox Corporation, 1964].

"The Role of Science in Universities, Government, and Industry: Science and Public Policy," *The Scientific Endeavor: Centennial Celebration of the National Academy of Sciences* (New York: Rockefeller University Press, 1965), pp. 279–292.

"From Philosophy to Mathematics to Biology: The Life Sciences and Cybernetics," *Journal of Nervous and Mental Disease* 140 (January 1965): 3–8 [with Walter Rosenblith].

"Engineering in an Evolving World," in *Listen to Leaders in Engineering*, ed. Albert Love and James Saxon Childers (New York: David McKay Company, 1965), pp. 323–338.

"Prometheus Unbound: How Shall We Harness the New-Found Powers of Science to Win a Better World?" [review of Ralph E. Lapp, *The New Priesthood*], *New York Herald Tribune*, 6 June 1965, pp. 1, 8–10.

"Society as a Learning Machine," *New York Times*, 24 April 1966, p. 15.

"RLE . . . Those Early Days," *Technology Review* 68 (May 1966): 44–45, 68.

"A Successful Experiment," *Naval Research Reviews*, July 1966, pp. 1–4, 11.

Foreword to Jeremy Stone, *Containing the Arms Race: Some Specific Proposals* (Cambridge, Mass.: MIT Press, 1966), pp. vii–xi.

"National Security and the Nuclear-Test Ban," in *The Strategy of World Order: Volume 4: Disarmament and Economic Development*, ed. Richard A. Falk and Saul H. Mendlovitz (New York: World Law Fund, 1966), pp. 33–47 [with Herbert F. York].

"We Can Curb World Arms Race Now," *Congressional Record*, 23 January 1967, pp. 1201–1202.

"A Strategy for Arms Control," *Saturday Review*, 4 March 1967, pp. 17–20.

"The Federal Presence at MIT," *Technology Review* 69 (April 1967): 65–72.

"The Cold War Is Dead, but the Arms Race Rumbles On," *Bulletin of the Atomic Scientists* 23 (June 1967): 6–9.

"The Case Against an Antiballistic Missile System," *Look* 31 (28 November 1967): 25–27.

"Education for Creativity in the Sciences," in *Creativity and Learning*, ed. Jerome Kagan (Boston: Houghton Mifflin, 1967), pp. 92–102.

"Hope for GCD?" *Bulletin of the Atomic Scientists* 24 (January 1968): 10–15.

ABM: An Evaluation of the Decision to Deploy an Antiballistic Missile System (New York: Harper and Row, 1969) [with Abram Chayes, coeditor].

"The Decent Society: Science and Technology," *Playboy* 16 (January 1969): 90, 277–278, 280.

"Arms Control: Current Prospects and Problems," *Bulletin of the Atomic Scientists* 26 (May 1970): 6–8, 38–39.

"Memorandum to a Vienna Negotiator," *Technology Review* 72 (May 1970): 38–43.

"Danse Macabre," *Vista* 5 (May-June 1970): 77–79, 150, 153.

"Reflections on Identity," *Technique* [MIT student yearbook], 1970, pp. 16–21.

"Amos de-Shalit," *Rehovot* 5, no. 4 (Spring 1970): 41–45 [with Herman Feshbach].

"Can the University Continue to Be an Important Source of Scientific Research?" *Proceedings of the American Philosophical Society* 115 (January 1971): 22–27.

"The Information Revolution—and the Bill of Rights," *Computers and Automation* 20 (May 1971): 8–10.

"Leveling-off of Economy, Inflation Pose Challenge," *Boston Sunday Advertiser*, 22 August 1971, p. 10.

"Science, Technology, and the Quality of Life," *Technology Review* 74 (December 1971): 15–18.

"Making Sensory Aids a Reality," in *Science and Blindness: Retrospective and Prospective*, ed. Milton D. Graham (New York: American Foundation for the Blind, 1972), pp. 188–193.

"Can Technological Assessment Be Effective?" *Tech Engineering News* 55 (May 1973): 13–14.

"Technology Is for Mankind," *Technology Review* 75 (May 1973): 10–13.

"While We Applaud Technology, '1984' Could Arrive Unnoticed," *National Observer*, 4 August 1973, p. 11.

"The Prospects of Information Tyranny," *Computers and Automation* 22 (December 1973): 1–4.

"Human Communications," *Jurimetrics Journal* 14 (Spring 1974): 179–182.

"Information and a Free Society," *Technology Review* 76 (July/August 1974): 15–17.

"Freedom of Information," *Computers and People* 23, no. 8 (1974): 26–27.

Foreword to David D. Rutstein, *Blueprint for Medical Care* (Cambridge, Mass.: MIT Press, 1974), pp. xi–xvii.

"Has the United States Lost Its Initiative in Technological Innovation?" *Technology Review* 78 (July-August 1976): 54–60.

[Review of George B. Kistiakowsky, *A Scientist in the White House*], *New Republic*, 22 January 1977, pp. 66–68, 70.

World Change and World Security (Cambridge, Mass.: MIT Press, 1978) [with Norman C. Dahl].

"The Case for Basic Research," *Boston Globe*, 20 February 1978, p. 19.

"Universities and the Federal Government: A Troubled Relationship," *Chemical & Engineering News* 56 (11 December 1978): 31–36.

"Vannevar Bush, March 11, 1890-June 28, 1974," *Biographical Memoirs of the National Academy of Sciences* 50 (1979): 89–117.

"Is Innovation in Decline?" *McKinsey Quarterly*, Winter 1979, pp. 54–65.

"Warning: America Can't Turn Back the Technology Clock," *Inc.*, May 1979, pp. 10, 14.

"Can Society Survive the Energy Crunch?" *Energy in America: Fifteen Views* (Center for the Study of American Experience, 1980), pp. 13–26.

"Science and Technology: Government and Politics," *Technology in Society* 2 (1980): 33–40 [special issue: "Science Advice to the President"].

"MIT Ten Years Later," *Technique* [MIT student yearbook], 1980, pp. 64–68.

"We're Hearing It Again: Reds' Sails in the Sunset," *New York Times*, 14 October 1980, p. 19.

"Odd Ways the MX Arguments Don't Add Up," *Washington Post*, 13 September 1981, pp. C1, C3.

"Concerned Physicists," *Bulletin of the Atomic Scientists* 37 (October 1981): 65 [with Owen Chamberlain, Herman Feshbach, Donald Glaser, Sheldon Glashow, Leon Lederman, Francis E. Low, Philip Morrison, Edward Purcell, Victor Weisskopf, and Robert R. Wilson].

"This Is the Way the World Ends" [review of Jonathan Schell, *The Fate of the Earth*], *Washington Post*, 18 April 1982, "book world" section, pp. 1–2, 4–5.

"A Way to Halt the Arms-Race," *New York Times*, 13 June 1982, section IV, p. 23; also, *Bulletin of Peace Proposals* 13 (1982): 259–260; reprinted as "How to Halt the Nuclear Arms Race," *Herald Tribune*, 2 July 1982.

"Russian and American Capabilities," *Atlantic Monthly*, July 1982, pp. 50–53.

"What Is a Comprehensive Test Ban?" *Bulletin of the Atomic Scientists* 38 (June 1982): 13.

"Is a Moratorium Safe?" *Bulletin of the Atomic Scientists* 38 (September 1982): 6–7.

"George Kennan's Case for Ending the Arms Race" [review of George Kennan, *The Nuclear Delusion: Soviet-American Relations in the Atomic Age*], *Washington Post*, 21 November 1982, "book world" section, p. 5.

"The Nuclear Debate: Russian and American Capabilities," *Parameters: Journal of the US Army War College* 12 (December 1982): 85–89.

"George Kistiakowsky," *Physics Today* 36 (April 1983): 70–72.

"MX, the Danger," *New York Times*, 12 April 1983, section I, p. 23.

Foreword to David Bradley, *No Place to Hide 1946/1984* (Hanover, NH: University Press of New England, 1983), pp. ix–xvi.

"Stockpile to Junkpile," *New York Times*, 11 July 1983, section I, p. 15.

"Understanding the Arms Race," *Wellesley College Alumnae Magazine* 68 (Fall 1983): 10–14.

"Expand the Arms Talks," *New York Times*, 11 November 1983, p. A31 [with Emma Rothschild].

Foreword to Jennifer Leaning and Langley Keyes, eds., *Counterfeit Ark: Crisis Location for Nuclear War* (Cambridge, Mass: Ballinger, 1984), pp. xiii–xv.

"Unilateral Confidence Building," *Bulletin of the Atomic Scientists* 40 (January 1984): 45–47.

"Should a Jokester Control Our Fate?" *Los Angeles Times*, 30 August 1984.

"An Attack on 'Nuclear Mythology'," *Los Angeles Times*, 7 October 1984, section IV, pp. 1–2.

"A Perilous Sense of Security," *Boston Globe*, 7 October 1984, "magazine" section, pp. 1, 10–12, 19, 23–24, 26, 28, 30, 34, 36.

"A Militarized Society," *Bulletin of the Atomic Scientists* 41 (August 1985): 102–105.

Introduction to Kosta Tsipis, David W. Hafemeister, and Penny Janeway, *Arms Control Verification: The Technologies That Make It Possible* (Cambridge, Mass.: Pergamon Press, 1986), pp. xv–xviii.

Foreword to Koji Kobayashi, *Computers and Communications: A Vision of C & C* (Cambridge, Mass.: MIT Press, 1986), pp. ix–xii.

"Setting the Moratorium Record Straight," *New York Times*, 3 January 1986, p. A23.

"Europe Questions Our Will on Test Ban Treaty: End of Moratorium," *New York Times*, 30 March 1986, p. E18.

"Commentary," *Science, Technology and Human Values* 11 (Spring 1986): 20–23.

"Engineering and the Public Welfare," *The Bridge* [National Academy of Engineering], Spring 1986, pp. 2–4.

"Soviet 'Cheating' Shouldn't Hinder a Nuclear Test Ban," *Washington Post*, 7 October 1986, p. A18 [with Kosta Tsipis].

"Remarks on Technology, Nuclear Security, and Individual Responsibility," *Technology in Society* 8 (1986): 341–346.

"Put 'Star Wars' Before a Panel," *New York Times*, 11 November 1986, p. A25 [with Kosta Tsipis].

"What Role for Engineers?" *Agricultural Engineering* 67 (November–December 1986): 19–20.

[Letter to the editor], *Reflector* [Boston Section of the Institute of Electrical and Electronics Engineers] 35 (1 February 1987): 3 [with Louis D. Smullin and William F. Schreiber].

"Why We Need a Tough National Science Adviser," *Washington Post*, 24 May 1987, pp. D1, D4.

"More R & D in the Right Places," *Issues in Science and Technology* 4 (Fall 1987): 13–15.

"How Societies Learn," *Earth '88, Changing Geographic Perspectives: Proceedings of the Centennial Symposium* (Washington, D.C.: National Geographic Society, 1988), pp. 350–357.

"The Glory and Tragedy of the Partial Test Ban," *New York Times*, 11 April 1988, p. A19.

"On Science Advice to the President," *Scientific American* 260 (January 1989): 34–39.

"Why Don't We Stop Testing the Bomb?" *New York Times*, 23 December 1990, p. E11.

"Technology Transcends the Borders of Nations," *New York Times*, 8 January 1991, p. A20.

"Ending Overkill," *Bulletin of the Atomic Scientists* 49 (March 1993): 12–23 [with Philip Morrison and Kosta Tsipis].

"7 Percent Solution," *New York Times*, 4 March 1993, p. A25 [with Kosta Tsipis].

Beyond the Looking Glass: The United States Military in 2000 and Later (Cambridge, Mass.: Program in Science and Technology for International Security, MIT, 1993) [with Philip Morrison and Kosta Tsipis].

"The Budget Impediments to an Energetic Government . . . Could Be Eased with Overdue Cuts in the Military," *Boston Globe*, 10 February 1994, p. 19 [with Kosta Tsipis].

"The Future of American Defense," *Scientific American* 270 (February 1994): 38–45 [with Philip Morrison and Kosta Tsipis].

"The Best Defense—A Reply," *Scientific American* 270 (June 1994): 10 [with Philip Morrison and Kosta Tsipis].

Registry of Names[1]

Ruth S. Adams see her essay in this book.

Sherman Adams (1899–1986) Republican legislator in New Hampshire, 1941–44; U.S. congressman (R-N.H.), 1945–47; state governor, 1949–53; key adviser and chief of staff to President Eisenhower, 1953–58.

Jihei Akita president and chief executive officer, Asahi Telescan Broadcasting; chairman and chief executive officer, InterVista Communications, Inc., Japan; executive director, Planetary Society, Japan; senior fellow and Japan representative, MIT Media Laboratory.

Michael A. Albert SB (mathematics) MIT, 1969; president, MIT Undergraduate Association; a leader among campus student radicals.

Alexander D. Alexandrov (1912–1999) Soviet mathematician; rector, Leningrad University, 1952–64; member, Communist Party, beginning in 1951; elected to the Soviet Academy of Sciences in 1964.

Joseph Alsop (1910–1989) journalist; contributor to *Washington Post*, *New Yorker*, *New York Review of Books*, and other periodicals.

Idi Amin (1925?–) president, Uganda, 1971–80.

Wayne V. Andersen (1930–) from associate professor to professor of the history of art, MIT, 1964–86; professor emeritus, 1986; director of exhibitions and chairman, Art Acquisitions Committee.

Clinton P. Anderson (1895–1975) U.S. congressman (D-N.Mex.), 1940–45; secretary of agriculture, Truman administration, 1945–48; U.S. senator (D-N.Mex.), 1949–73;

---

1. Notes on a number of individuals cited in the text. The aim is to clarify the context in which these individuals appear, or their relationship to Jerry, rather than to supply full biographical summaries.

The following organizations are referred to here by their standard acronyms: Atomic Energy Commission (AEC), Central Intelligence Agency (CIA), Department of Defense Advanced Research Projects Agency (DARPA), Institute for Defense Analyses (IDA), National Aeronautics and Space Administration (NASA), North Atlantic Treaty Organization (NATO), President's Science Advisory Committee (PSAC), and U.S. Arms Control and Disarmament Agency (ACDA).

chairman, Joint Committee on Atomic Energy, 1955–56, 1959–60; Senate Committee on Aeronautical and Space Sciences, 1963–72.

Yuri Andropov (1914–1984)   Soviet premier, 1982–84; advocate of nuclear weapons control.

Georgiy Arbatov (1923–)   editor and leading Soviet specialist in American studies; director, Institute of U.S. and Canadian Studies, Soviet Academy of Sciences, starting in 1967; elected vice president, U.S.–USSR Friendship Society, 1972; deputy, USSR Supreme Soviet, and member, presidium of Soviet Peace Committee, starting in 1974; member, Independent Commission on Disarmament and Security Issues (Palme Commission), starting in 1980; central committee, Soviet Communist Party, starting in 1981.

William A. Arrowsmith (1924–1992)   professor of classics, University of Texas, Austin, 1959–70; visiting professor of humanities, MIT, 1971; later taught at Boston University; delivered a famous speech in 1966 critical of higher education, blaming university bureaucracy for the failure of graduate education in the humanities.

Isaac Asimov (1920–1992)   prolific science and science fiction writer.

Robert F. Bacher (1905–)   first head, Division 6 (Receiver Components), Radiation Laboratory, MIT, 1941–43; head, experimental physics division, Los Alamos Laboratory, 1943–44, and bomb physics division, 1944–45; scientific adviser to the U.S. representative on the United Nations AEC, 1946–49; professor of physics, California Institute of Technology, 1949–76; chairman, Division of Physics, Mathematics & Astronomy, 1949–62; provost, 1962–70; member, PSAC, 1953–55, 1957–60.

William O. Baker (1915–)   vice president for research, AT&T Bell Labs, 1953–73; president, 1973–79; member, PSAC, 1957–60; science advisory board, National Security Agency, 1959–76.

George W. Ball (1909–1994)   lawyer, government official, investment banker; U.S. undersecretary of state for economic affairs, 1961; deputy secretary of state, 1961–66; U.S. representative to the United Nations, 1968; later chairman and senior partner, Lehman Brothers.

David Baltimore (1938–)   microbiologist; professor of biology, MIT, 1972–95; Institute professor, 1995–97; director, Whitehead Institute for Biomedical Research, MIT, 1982–90; president, Rockefeller University, 1990–95, and California Institute of Technology, beginning in 1997; member, board of governors, Weizmann Institute, Rehovot, Israel; Nobel Prize (physiology or medicine), 1975; National Medal of Science, 1999.

Ruth M. Batson   community leader and civil rights activist; member, Massachusetts Commission Against Discrimination, 1963–66; executive director, Metropolitan Council for Educational Opportunity (METCO), 1966–70; faculty member, Boston University; president and director, Museum of Afro-American History, Boston, 1987–90; founder, Ruth M. Batson Educational Foundation.

James Phinney Baxter, III (1893–1975)   president, Williams College, 1937–61; president emeritus, 1961–75; senior fellow, Council on Foreign Relations, 1961–65; member, MIT Corporation, 1956–61; author of *Scientists Against Time* (1946), a Pulitzer Prize-winning history of the U.S. Office of Scientific Research and Development.

David Z. Beckler (1918–)   assistant director, industrial development office, AEC, 1952–53; executive officer, PSAC, 1953–73.

David E. Bell (1919–2000) administrative assistant to President Truman, 1951–53; head, Harvard University economic advisory group to Pakistan, 1954–57; director, U.S. Budget Bureau, 1961–62; administrator, Agency for International Development, 1962–66; vice president for international activities, Ford Foundation, 1966–69; executive vice president, 1969–81; appointed director, Harvard Center for Population Studies, 1981; also, professor of population studies and international health.

Walter R. Bender (1956–) senior research scientist and director, Media Laboratory, MIT.

David Ben-Gurion (1886–1973) political leader, proclaimed the independent state of Israel, May 14, 1948; acting prime minister of Israel, 1948–49; Knesset member, 1948–70; prime minister and minister of defense, 1949–53, 1955–63.

Stephen A. Benton (1941–) senior scientist, Polaroid Corporation, 1961–85; joined the MIT faculty in 1985; professor of media arts and sciences, MIT.

Ingrid Bergman (1915–1982) Swedish actress; Academy Award recipient, 1944, 1956, 1974.

Lloyd V. Berkner (1906–1967) physicist and engineer known for his research on the ionosphere and radio propagation; first to measure height and density of the ionosphere; helped develop radar systems, especially the Distant Early Warning System; head, section for exploratory physics of the atmosphere, Carnegie Institution of Washington, 1947–51; special assistant to the U.S. secretary of state, 1950; president, Associated Universities, Inc., 1951–60; director, Brookhaven National Laboratory, 1951–60; president, Graduate Research Center of the Southwest, 1960–65; member, PSAC, 1956–59.

Leonard Bernstein (1918–1990) composer and conductor; faculty member, Berkshire Music Center, 1948–55; professor of music, Brandeis University, 1951–56; music director, New York Philharmonic, 1958–69; conductor laureate, 1969–90; Charles Eliot Norton professor of poetry, Harvard University, 1972–73; a committed civil libertarian interested in a number of social and political causes.

Hans A. Bethe (1906–) physicist, taught at universities in Germany and England before joining the Cornell University faculty in 1935; professor emeritus, 1975; director, Theoretical Physics Division, Los Alamos Laboratory, 1943–46; specialist in nuclear fusion; member, PSAC, 1956–60; panel member, Presidential Study of Disarmament, 1958; Nobel Prize in physics, 1967; National Medal of Science, 1970; Compton lecturer, MIT, 1975.

Seweryn Bialer (1926–) professor of political science, Columbia University, starting in 1974; Renee and Robert Belfer professor of international relations, starting in 1987; specialist in Soviet foreign and military policy.

Grete L. Bibring (1899–1977) psychiatrist, joined the faculty of Harvard Medical School in 1950; clinical professor of psychiatry, 1961–65; clinical professor emeritus, 1965–77; psychiatrist-in-chief, Beth Israel Hospital, Boston, 1955–65.

Richard M. Bissell, Jr. (1909–1994) associate professor of economics, MIT, 1942–48; professor of economics, 1948–52; special assistant to the CIA director, 1954–59; deputy director of plans, CIA, 1959–62; president, IDA, 1962–64; executive with United Aircraft Corporation, 1964–74.

Elena G. Bonner (1923–) Russian human rights activist; wife of Andrei Sakharov; founder of Moscow group to monitor observation of 1975 Helsinki accords; chairman, committee to perpetuate memory of Andrei Sakharov.

David Bradley (1915–)   newspaper reporter, author, and political science educator, taught at Dartmouth College, 1965–81; author of *No Place to Hide* (1948), a best-selling eyewitness account of the nuclear weapons test at Bikini Atoll in 1946.

Louis D. Brandeis (1856–1941)   associate justice, U.S. Supreme Court, 1916–39; noted for his arguments in defense of free speech.

Donald G. Brennan (1926–1980)   mathematician and communications theorist; staff, Lincoln Laboratory, MIT, 1953–62; president, Hudson Institute, 1962–64; director of national security studies, Hudson Institute, 1964–80.

Ayers Brinser (d. 1967)   helped establish at Harvard University the first graduate program in the United States to train government employees in the administration of natural resources.

Detlev W. Bronk (1897–1975)   chairman, National Research Council, 1946–50; president, Johns Hopkins University, 1949–53; National Academy of Sciences, 1950–62; Rockefeller Institute for Medical Research, starting in 1953; chairman, National Science Foundation, 1955–64; delivered the fourth annual Arthur D. Little memorial lecture, MIT, 1949, entitled "The Unity of the Sciences and the Humanities."

Gordon S. Brown (1907–1996)   joined the MIT faculty in 1939; founder, Servomechanisms Laboratory, MIT, 1940; consultant, National Defense Research Committee and U.S. War Department, 1942–45; professor of electrical engineering, MIT, 1946–74; Dugald C. Jackson professor of engineering, 1968–71; elected Institute professor, 1971; professor emeritus, 1974–96; chairman, MIT faculty, 1951–52; dean, School of Engineering, MIT, 1959–68.

Harold Brown (1927–)   member, PSAC, 1960–61; director of defense research and engineering, U.S. Department of Defense, 1961–65; secretary, U.S. Air Force, 1965–69; president, California Institute of Technology, 1969–77; U.S. delegate, Strategic Arms Limitation Treaty (SALT), 1969–77; U.S. secretary of defense, 1977–81.

Oliver E. Buckley (1887–1959)   physicist and research engineer; director of research, Bell Telephone Laboratories, 1933–36; executive vice president, 1936–40; president, 1940–52; appointed science adviser to President Truman, 1950.

Warren Buffett (1930–)   business executive; chairman, Berkshire, Hathaway, Inc., since 1969.

McGeorge Bundy (1919–1996)   taught at Harvard University before serving as national security adviser (special assistant for national security affairs) to Presidents John F. Kennedy and Lyndon B. Johnson, 1961–66; president, Ford Foundation, 1966–79; professor of history, New York University, 1979–89; professor emeritus, 1989–96; chair, Carnegie Corporation Committee on Reducing Nuclear Danger, 1990–93; author of *Danger and Survival: Choices About the Bomb in the First Fifty Years* (1988) and *Reducing Nuclear Danger: The Road Away from the Brink* (1993, with William J. Crowe and Sidney D. Drell).

Vannevar Bush (1890–1974)   joined the MIT faculty in electrical engineering, 1919; inventor of the electronic calculating machine and differential analyzer; vice president and dean of the School of Engineering, MIT, 1932–38; president, Carnegie Institution of Washington, 1939–55; chair, National Defense Research Committee, 1940–41; director, U.S. Office of Scientific Research and Development, 1941–47; chair, MIT Corporation, 1957–59 (honorary chair, 1959–71); author of *Science, the Endless Frontier* (1945), arguing the case for substantial federal investment in scientific research; recipient, National Medal of Science, 1964.

Robert D. Calkins (1903–1992)   professor of economics, University of California, Berkeley; director, General Education Board, Rockefeller Foundation; president, Brookings Institution, 1952–67; vice chancellor, University of California at Santa Cruz, 1967–70.

Alexander Calder (1898–1976) artist well known for his kinetic sculpture "mobiles."

Robert B. Carney (1895–1990) career naval officer; member, Joint Chiefs of Staff and head, Naval Operations, 1953–55; president, U.S. Naval Institute.

Rachel Carson (1907–1964) biologist and environmentalist; author of *Silent Spring* (1962), a study of the dangerous impact of chemical fertilizers on human health and the environment.

James Earl (Jimmy) Carter (1924–) U.S. president, 1977–81; recipient, Nobel Prize for peace, 2002.

Marc Chagall (1887–1985) French painter of Russian origin; influenced by cubism and surrealism; known for his work in stained glass.

Abram Chayes (1922–2000) legal scholar, joined the faculty of Harvard University in 1955; retired in 1993 as Felix Frankfurter professor of law emeritus; legal adviser to the assistant U.S. secretary of state, 1961–64; coeditor (with Jerry Wiesner), *ABM: An Evaluation of the Decision to Deploy an Anti-Ballistic Missile System* (1969); author, *The Cuban Missile Crisis: International Crises and the Role of Law* (1974); coauthor (with J. P. Ruina and G. W. Rathjens), *Nuclear Arms Control Agreements: Process and Impact* (1974).

Noam Chomsky (1928–) linguist, educator, philosopher, social critic, and political commentator, joined the MIT faculty in 1955; revolutionized linguistics with his theory of transformational-generative grammar; elected Institute professor, 1976; professor emeritus, 2002; author of numerous works in linguistics, including the classic *Syntactic Structures* (1957); also, critiques of U.S. domestic and foreign policy, starting with *American Power and the New Mandarins* (1969).

Pei-Yuan Chou (1902–1993) scientist known for his work in the fields of fluid turbulence and general relativity theory; founder, mechanics and engineering science department, Peking University; president, Peking University; president, Chinese Association for Science and Technology.

Winston S. Churchill (1874–1965) English statesman and political leader; UK prime minister, 1940–45, 1951–55; gave "iron curtain" speech at Fulton, Missouri, 1946; principal speaker, MIT Convocation on the Social Implications of Scientific Progress at the Mid-Century Point, March-April 1949; recipient, Nobel Prize in literature, 1953.

Kenneth B. Clark (1914–) developmental psychologist; founder and research director, Northside Center for Child Development, 1946–66; Harlem Youth Opportunities Unlimited, 1962–64; professor of psychology, City College of the City University of New York, 1942–75; president and board chairman, Clark, Phipps, Clark & Harris, 1975–86; visiting Institute professor, MIT, late 1960s and early 1970s; author of *Desegregation: An Appraisal of the Evidence* (1953) and *Prejudice and Your Child* (1955); his research played an important role in the U.S. Supreme Court *Brown* v. *Board of Education* decision (1954), voiding the "separate but equal" doctrine.

Lucius D. Clay (1897–1978) career military officer; retired as four-star general in 1949; military governor of Germany after World War II; U.S. ambassador to Germany under President Kennedy, 1961–62.

Chester V. Clifton, Jr. (1913–) from second lieutenant to major general, U.S. Army, 1936–61; assistant to Joint Chiefs of Staff, 1940–53; military aide to President Kennedy, 1961–63, and President Johnson, 1963–65.

Hillary Rodham Clinton (1947–) partner, Rose Law Firm, 1977–92; U.S. first lady, 1993–2001; U.S. senator (D-N.Y.), 2001–.

William J. (Bill) Clinton (1946–) governor of Arkansas, 1979–81, 1983–92; U.S. president, 1993–2001.

Karl Taylor Compton (1887–1954) physicist; taught at Princeton University before serving as president of MIT, 1930–48; chairman, MIT Corporation, 1948–54.

James B. Conant (1893–1978) president, Harvard University, 1933–53; chairman, National Defense Research Committee, 1941–46; member, general advisory committee, AEC, 1947–52.

Muriel R. Cooper (1926–1994) graphic designer and book designer; director, Office of Publications, MIT, 1952–58; appointed first art director, MIT Press, 1967; appointed to the MIT faculty, 1977; professor of interactive media design and director of the Visible Language Workshop, MIT.

Thomas J. Corcoran (1920–) U.S. foreign service officer; served in Vietnam, Laos, Haiti, and other countries; ambassador to Burundi, 1977–80.

John J. Corson III (1905–1990) held various U.S. federal and United Nations positions before serving as an executive with the *Washington Post*, 1945–51; director, McKinsey & Company, Inc., 1951–65; professor of public and international affairs, Princeton University, 1963–66; adviser to several foreign governments in the 1970s, including Tanzania, Panama, and Iran.

Michael Crichton (1942–) postdoctoral fellow, Salk Institute, 1969–70; novelist, particularly in the techno-thriller genre; creator of the NBC-TV series *ER*.

Richard J. Cushing (1895–1970) became Roman Catholic archbishop of Boston in 1944; appointed cardinal, 1958; close friend of the Kennedy family.

Robert (Bobbie) Cutler (1895–1974) brigadier general, U.S. Army (retired 1945); President Eisenhower's special assistant for national security affairs, 1953–55, 1957–58.

Wilbur B. Davenport, Jr. (1920–) member, MIT faculty in electrical engineering, 1949–82; associate director, Research Laboratory of Electronics, MIT, 1961–63; assistant director, Lincoln Laboratory, MIT, 1963–65; head, department of electrical engineering and computer science, MIT, 1974–78; consultant to government and industry; member, National Academy of Engineering.

John P. de Monchaux dean, School of Architecture and Planning, MIT, 1981–92; professor of architecture and planning; director, Special Program for Urban and Regional Studies in Developing Countries (SPURS), MIT; founding chair, Boston Civic Design Commission.

Michael L. Dertouzos (1936–2001) computer scientist, joined the MIT faculty in 1964; appointed director of MIT's Laboratory for Computer Science in 1974; author of *The Unfinished Revolution: Human-Centered Computers and What They Can Do for Us* (2001).

Amos de-Shalit (1926–1969) Israeli physicist; postdoctoral appointment at MIT, early 1950s; head, physics department, Weizmann Institute; director general, 1966–68; president, Israel Physical Society, 1958.

Everett M. Dirksen (1896–1969) conservative U.S. congressman (R-Ill.), 1933–48; U.S. senator, 1950–69; U.S. Senate Republican leader, 1959–69.

Anatoly F. Dobrynin (1919–)   Soviet diplomat; deputy secretary-general, United Nations, 1957–60; Soviet ambassador to the United States, 1962–86; deputy, Supreme Soviet, 1986–91; consultant to foreign ministry of the Russian Federation, beginning in 1991.

James H. Doolittle (1896–1993)   World War II aviator and commander; vice president, Shell Oil, 1946–58; board chairman, aerospace division, TRW, 1958–61; subsequently with Mutual of Omaha, member, MIT Corporation; recipient, Presidential Medal of Freedom and Congressional Medal of Honor.

Robert Dorfman (1916–2002)   economist, taught at Harvard University, 1955–87; held several posts in the Kennedy presidential administration, including membership on the Presidential Commission on Employment and Unemployment Statistics and the Presidential Commission on Waterlogging and Salinity in West Pakistan; member, environmental studies board, National Research Council, 1974–77; clean air advisory committee, U.S. Environmental Protection Agency, 1978–84.

Thomas A. Dorsey (1899–1993)   blues and gospel musician; recorded under the name "Georgia Tom," starting in the 1920s; choral director, Pilgrim Baptist Church, Chicago, 1932–72.

Paul M. Doty (1920–)   biochemist and arms control specialist; professor of chemistry, Harvard University, 1950–68; professor of biochemistry, 1968–88; professor of public policy, 1988–90; director, Center for Science and International Affairs, Harvard University, 1973–85; member, PSAC, 1961–64; President's general advisory committee on arms control, 1976–80; author of *Defending Deterrence: Managing the ABM Treaty* (1989).

Sidney D. Drell (1926–)   physicist; research associate, MIT, 1952–53; assistant professor of physics, 1953–56; joined the faculty of Stanford University in 1956; executive head of theoretical physics, Stanford Linear Accelerator Center, 1969–86; deputy director, 1969–98; consultant to the U.S. Office of Science and Technology, 1961–73; Office of Science and Technology Policy, 1977–82; ACDA, 1969–81; codirector, Stanford University Center for International Security and Arms Control, 1983–89.

Hugh L. Dryden (1898–1965)   physicist; long-time service with the U.S. National Bureau of Standards; director, National Advisory Committee for Aeronautics, 1947–58; deputy administrator, NASA, 1958–65; U.S. delegate to the advisory group on aeronautical research and development, NATO; recipient, National Medal of Science, 1965.

Lee A. DuBridge (1901–1994)   physicist; director, Radiation Laboratory, MIT, 1940–45; president, California Institute of Technology, 1946–69; president emeritus, 1970–94; member, general advisory committee, AEC, 1946–52; chair, science advisory committee, Office of Defense Mobilization, 1952–56; member, board of directors, National Educational Television, 1962–69; PSAC, 1970–72.

Renato Dulbecco (1914–)   virologist; senior research fellow, Salk Institute, 1963–71; appointed distinguished research professor in 1977; president, 1982–92; corecipient Nobel Prize (physiology or medicine), 1975.

John Foster Dulles (1888–1959)   drafted foreign policy planks of the Republican platform leading up to the 1952 U.S. presidential election; served as secretary of state under President Eisenhower, 1953–59.

Frederick G. Dutton (1923–)   lawyer; deputy national chairman, Citizens for Kennedy and Johnson, 1960; special assistant to President Kennedy, 1961; assistant secretary of state for congressional relations; organizing director, Kennedy Memorial Library oral history project, 1964–65.

Freeman J. Dyson (1923–) professor of physics, Institute for Advanced Study, Princeton, NJ; member, nuclear reactor design team, General Dynamics, beginning in 1956; nuclear weapons designer, Lawrence Livermore National Laboratory, 1959; consultant, ACDA, 1962–63.

Cyrus S. Eaton (1883–1979) industrialist and businessman; supported President Roosevelt's economic policies in the 1930s; early proponent of improved relations with the Soviet Union, 1950s; sponsored the first Pugwash meetings, bringing together scientists from Western and Communist countries; outspoken advocate of nuclear disarmament and opponent of the Vietnam War; endorsed U.S.–Soviet détente in the early 1970s, and pressed for normalized relations with China and Cuba.

Harold E. (Doc) Edgerton (1903–1990) developer of the modern stroboscope; joined the MIT faculty in 1932; professor of electrical engineering, 1948–66; elected Institute professor, 1966; recipient, National Medal of Science, 1973; National Medal of Technology, 1988.

John D. Ehrlichman (1925–1999) counsel to President Nixon, 1968–69; assistant to the president for domestic affairs, 1969–73; resigned as chief presidential adviser in the midst of the Watergate investigation; convicted of conspiracy, obstruction of justice, and two counts of perjury relating to Watergate, 1975.

Albert Einstein (1879–1955) physicist, was active in efforts to promote international peace following World War II and critical of efforts to limit free speech in the name of internal security; coauthor (with Bertrand Russell) of the Russell-Einstein Manifesto (1955), warning of the danger of nuclear war.

Herman N. Eisen (1918–) microbiologist and immunologist; joined the MIT faculty in 1973 after many years at New York University and Washington University, St. Louis; professor of immunology, Whitehead Institute, MIT; retired in 1989.

Carola Eisenberg see her essay in this book.

Dwight D. Eisenhower (1890–1969) commander in chief of Allied Forces, World War II; president, Columbia University, 1948–53; U.S. president, 1953–61.

Peter Elias (1923–2001) joined the MIT faculty in 1953; conducted research at the Research Laboratory of Electronics in information theory and its applications to problems in communication, data processing, and computation; head, Department of Electrical Engineering, 1960–66; joined the Laboratory of Computer Science in 1976; associate head of computer science, 1981–83; professor emeritus, 1992–2001.

M. C. Escher (1898–1972) Dutch graphic artist known for lithographs and woodcuts; recognized for his spatial illusions and repeating geometric patterns.

Robert M. Fano (1917–) electrical engineer and educator; staff member, microwave components group, Radiation Laboratory, MIT, 1944–46; assistant professor to professor of electrical communications, MIT, 1947–84; professor emeritus, 1984; group leader, radar techniques group, Lincoln Laboratory, 1950–53; director, Project MAC, 1963–68; associate head, Department of Electrical Engineering and Computer Science, MIT, 1971–74.

James Farmer (1920–1999) civil rights activist; founder, Congress of Racial Equality, 1942; national director, 1961–66; assistant secretary, U.S. Department of Health, Education, and Welfare, 1969–70; later a professor at Antioch University and Mary Washington College.

Myer Feldman (1917–)   legislative assistant to U.S. senator John F. Kennedy, 1958–61; deputy special counsel to President Kennedy, 1961–63, and President Johnson, 1963–64; counsel to President Johnson, 1964–65; member, board of directors, Kennedy Memorial Library.

Enrico Fermi (1901–1954)   Nobel laureate in physics in 1938, immigrated from Italy to the United States in 1939, when he joined the faculty of Columbia University; worked on the Manhattan Project at the Chicago, Hanford, and Los Alamos sites; research scientist, Argonne National Laboratory; professor of physics, University of Chicago, 1942–54.

Luis A. Ferré (1904–)   SB (mechanical engineering) MIT, 1924; established Ponce Museum of Art, 1959; elected governor of Puerto Rico, 1968; member, MIT Council for the Arts; MIT Corporation.

Richard P. Feynman (1918–1988)   physicist, writer, and popular lecturer, worked on the Manhattan Project at Princeton, 1942–43, and Los Alamos Laboratory, 1943–46; professor of theoretical physics, Cornell University, 1946–51, and California Institute of Technology, 1951–88; Nobel Prize in physics, 1965, for work in quantum electrodynamics; member, Presidential commission investigating the 1986 space shuttle *Challenger* disaster.

Thomas K. Finletter (1893–1980)   lawyer and government official; director of the Marshall Plan in England after World War II; served as secretary of the Air Force under President Truman; became an advocate of nuclear disarmament.

James B. Fisk (1910–1981)   assistant director of physics research, Bell Telephone Laboratories, 1939–47; director, 1949–51; director for research in the physical sciences, 1952–54; vice president for research, 1954–55; executive vice president, 1955–58; president, 1959–73; chairman of the board, 1973–74; member, general advisory committee, AEC, 1952–58; PSAC, 1957–60; consultant to the PSAC, 1960–73; member, several MIT visiting committees, 1945–63; member, MIT Corporation, 1959–63; life member, 1963–81.

Arthur S. Flemming (1905–1996)   director, U.S. Office of Defense Mobilization, and member, National Security Council, 1953–57; U.S. secretary of health, education, and welfare, 1958–61; president, University of Oregon, 1961–69, and Macalester College, 1969–71; chairman, U.S. Commission on Civil Rights, 1975–82.

John S. Foster, Jr. (1922–)   physicist and defense industry executive; director, Lawrence Livermore National Laboratory, 1961–65; defense research and engineering, U.S. Department of Defense, 1965–73; chairman, Defense Science Board, 1989–93.

William C. Foster (1897–1984)   business executive and government official; U.S. deputy secretary of defense, 1951–53; director, ACDA, 1961–69; U.S. delegate to the United Nations, 1964–66, 1968; U.S. representative to the United Nations Disarmament Commission, 1965; chairman of the board, U.S. Arms Control Association.

Gloria L. Fox (1942–)   state legislator, Massachusetts (7th Suffolk District); elected 1985.

Gaylord Freeman (1910–)   bank executive; board chairman, First Chicago Corporation, 1969–75; honorary board chairman and director, First National Bank of Chicago and First Chicago Corporation, 1975–80.

Francis L. Friedman (1918–1962)   group leader in theoretical physics, Manhattan District; from assistant professor to professor of physics, MIT, 1950–62; director, Science Teaching Center, MIT, 1960–62; consultant, AEC.

Harald T. Friis (1893–1976)   electrical engineer and pioneer in radio communications; research engineer, Bell Telephone Laboratories, 1924–45; director of radio research, 1946–51; director of research in high frequency electronics, 1952–57; independent consultant, 1958–69.

David H. Frisch (1918–1991)   staff member, Manhattan Project at Los Alamos Laboratory, 1943–45; research associate, MIT, 1945–48; from assistant professor to professor of physics, MIT, 1948–88; professor emeritus, 1988–91; active interest in nuclear disarmament; attended Pugwash conference in Moscow, 1960; editor, *Arms Reduction—Program and Issues* (1961).

Robert Frost (1874–1963)   poet, read his poems "Dedication" and "The Gift Outright" at John F. Kennedy's presidential inauguration; U.S. poet laureate, 1958–59.

Yuri A. Gagarin (1934–1968)   Russian cosmonaut; first human in space, 1961.

Edmund B. Gaither (1944–)   director and curator, National Museum of Afro-American Artists; special consultant, Museum of Fine Arts, Boston.

H. Rowan Gaither, Jr. (1909–1961)   banker, foundation executive, and government consultant; member of steering committee and head of business administration, Radiation Laboratory, MIT, 1942–45; associate director, Ford Foundation, 1951; president, 1953–56; chairman, 1956–58; board chairman, Rand Corporation, 1948–59.

John Kenneth Galbraith   see his essay in this book.

Trevor Gardner (1915–1963)   assistant secretary for research and development, U.S. Air Force, 1953–55; chairman and president, Hycon Manufacturing Company, 1956–63; member, President's Space Task Force, 1961; general advisory committee, ACDA; consultant-at-large, U.S. Air Force Scientific Advisory Board.

Marcus Garvey (1887–1940)   black nationalist leader; founder, Universal Negro Improvement Association, 1914; promoted the "Back to Africa" movement.

Richard L. Garwin (1928–)   physicist, played a role in creating the hydrogen bomb and subsequently became an outspoken advocate of arms control; consultant, Los Alamos Scientific Laboratory, 1950–93; consultant, PSAC, 1958–62; member, PSAC, 1962–65, 1969–72; member, Defense Science Board.

Murray Gell-Mann (1929–)   professor of theoretical physics, California Institute of Technology, 1956–93; professor emeritus, 1993; consultant, IDA, 1961–70; visiting professor, MIT, 1963; member, PSAC, 1969–72; Nobel Prize in physics, 1969; member, board of directors, John D. and Catherine T. MacArthur Foundation, beginning in 1979; California Nature Conservancy, 1984–93.

Roswell L. Gilpatric (1904–1996)   under secretary of the U.S. Air Force, Truman administration, 1951–53; deputy secretary of defense, Kennedy and Johnson administrations, 1961–64.

Arthur J. Goldberg (1908–1990)   lawyer and law professor focusing on labor issues; U.S. secretary of labor, 1961–62; associate justice of the U.S. Supreme Court, 1962–65; U.S. ambassador to the United Nations, 1965–68; ambassador at large, 1977–78; chairman, Truman Center for the Advancement of Peace, 1968–90; ex officio member and ad hoc participant, National Security Council.

Marvin L. (Murph) Goldberger (1922–)   physicist; research associate, MIT, 1949–50; faculty member, University of Chicago, 1950–57, and Princeton University, 1957–78; member, PSAC, 1965–69; president, Federation of American Scientists, 1971–73; president, California Institute of Technology, 1978–87; director, Institute for Advanced Study, Princeton, 1987–91; subsequently at University of California, Los Angeles, and University of California, San Diego.

William T. Golden (1909–)   assistant to the commissioner, AEC, 1946–50; special adviser to President Truman on reviewing government science activities, 1950–51; consultant, AEC, 1950–58; member, advisory committee on private enterprise in foreign aid, U.S. State Department, 1964–65; Hudson Institute, 1964–94; founder, Carnegie Group of Ministers of Science and Science Advisers to Heads of G8 countries, Russia, and the European Union, 1991; guest editor, *Science Advice to the President* (1980).

Nicholas E. Golovin (1912–1969)   associate director for administration, U.S. National Bureau of Standards, 1953–55; associate director for planning, 1955–58; chief scientist, White Sands Missile Range, New Mexico, 1958; director of the technical operators division, DARPA, 1959; deputy associate director, NASA, 1960; director, NASA-Department of Defense large launch vehicle planning group, 1961–62; technical adviser, Office of the Special Assistant to the President for Science and Technology, 1962–69.

Wladislaw Gomulka (1905–1982)   Polish political leader, governed Poland as first secretary of the Communist party, 1956–70.

Andrew J. Goodpaster (1915–)   career officer, U.S. Army, 1939–74; defense liaison officer and staff secretary to President Eisenhower, 1954–61; special assistant for policy to chair of Joint Chiefs of Staff, 1962–64; assistant to chair, 1964–66; director, Joint Chiefs of Staff, 1966–67; deputy commander of U.S. forces, Vietnam, 1968–69; commander-in-chief of U.S. forces, Europe, 1969–74; superintendent, U.S. Military Academy, 1977–81; president, IDA, 1983–85.

Richard N. Goodwin (1931–)   speechwriter for John F. Kennedy, 1959–60; assistant special counsel to the U.S. president, 1961; deputy assistant secretary of state for inter-American affairs, 1961–63; secretary-general, International Peace Corps Secretariat, 1963–64; special assistant to the U.S. president, 1964–65; visiting professor of public affairs, MIT, 1968.

Mikhail Gorbachev (1931–)   Soviet statesman and politician, held several local, regional, and national Communist Party positions before becoming a full member of the Politburo in 1980; general secretary, 1985–91; chair, Presidium of the Supreme Soviet, 1988–91; president of the USSR, 1990–91; head, International Foundation for Social, Economic, and Political Research, Moscow, beginning in 1992; awarded Nobel Prize for peace, 1990.

Raisa Gorbachev (1932–1999)   educator, author, and wife of Mikhail Gorbachev; member of the Soviet Presidium beginning in 1987.

Samuel A. Goudsmit (1902–1978)   authority on atomic energy and nuclear research; codiscoverer of the electron spin; faculty member in physics, University of Michigan, 1925–40; first leader of Group 43 (Theory), Radiation Laboratory, MIT, 1940; later connected to Northwestern University and Brookhaven National Laboratory; chair of physics department, Brookhaven, 1950–78; active in defending science against attack during the McCarthy period, 1950s; editor, *Physical Review*, 1952–74; distinguished visiting professor, University of Nevada, Reno, 1974–78.

Gordon Gray (1909–1982)   secretary of the Army under President Truman, 1949–50; served in the Eisenhower administration as assistant secretary of defense, director of the Office of Defense Mobilization, and special assistant for national security affairs; was later chair, Summit Communications, Inc.

Paul E. Gray   see his essay in this book.

Priscilla King Gray   first lady of MIT, 1980–90; cochair, steering committee, MIT Public Service Center; volunteer, Children's Hospital, Boston; active with MIT Women's League; wife of Paul E. Gray.

Cecil H. Green (1900–2003)   geophysicist and (with his wife, Ida) philanthropist; president, Geophysical Service Inc. (later Texas Instruments), Dallas, Texas; member, MIT Corporation; donated funds for the construction of MIT's earth and planetary sciences building (1964), named the Green Building in honor of him and his wife, Ida M. (Flansburgh) Green.

Andrei Gromyko (1909–1989)   Soviet first deputy foreign minister, 1949–57; foreign minister, 1957–85; president, 1985–88.

Leslie R. Groves, Jr. (1896–1970)   army officer and director of the Manhattan Project during World War II; based at Los Alamos; left the army in 1948; vice president in charge of research, Remington division of Sperry Rand, 1948–61; retired in 1961.

Woodrow Wilson (Woody) Guthrie (1912–1967)   singer and songwriter; taped as part of the Library of Congress Archive of American Folk Song project, 1939–40; appeared on Alan Lomax's CBS network show, "Folk School of the Air."

Jermen M. Gvishiani (1928–)   deputy chairman, Soviet State Committee for Science and Technology, 1965–85; chairman, Committee for Systems Analysis, Presidium of the Soviet Academy of Sciences, 1971–86; deputy chairman, International Council for New Initiatives in East-West Cooperation, 1985–93; became honorary chairman, 1993.

Dimitri Hadzi (1921–)   sculptor and educator; professor at Harvard University, 1977–89.

Kathy Halbreich (1949–)   director, committee on visual arts, Hayden Gallery and List Visual Arts Center, MIT, 1976–86; curator of contemporary art, Museum of Fine Arts, Boston, 1988–90; director, Walker Art Center, Minneapolis, starting in 1991.

H. R. Haldeman (1926–1993)   chief of staff, Richard Nixon's presidential campaign, 1968; assistant to the president and chief of White House staff, 1969–73; resigned during the Watergate investigation and was later convicted of perjury.

Morris Halle (1923–)   linguist and educator, joined the MIT faculty in 1951; Ferrari P. Ward professor of modern languages and linguistics, 1976–81; elected Institute professor, 1981; professor emeritus, 1996; member, National Academy of Sciences; president, Linguistic Society of America, 1974.

David A. Hamburg (1925–)   psychiatrist and foundation executive; president, Institute of Medicine, National Academy of Sciences, 1975–80; Carnegie Corporation of New York, 1983–97; member, committee on international security and arms control, National Academy of Sciences, 1981–86; U.S. president's committee of advisers on science and technology, 1994.

Henry Hampton (1940–1998)   film producer; founder of Blackside Inc., 1968; executive producer, *Eyes on the Prize*; visiting professor of film, Tufts University; board chairman, Museum of Afro-American History, Boston.

Philip A. Hart (1912–1976)   U.S. senator (D-Mich.), 1959–76; a leader among liberal Democrats.

George G. Harvey (1908–1988?)   joined the physics department at MIT in 1938; from assistant professor to professor of physics, 1938–1973; professor of physics emeritus, 1973; from assistant to associate director, Research Laboratory of Electronics, 1950–73; executive officer, physics department, MIT, 1952–70; academic officer, 1970–73.

Paul Harvey (1918–)   award-winning syndicated news commentator and columnist; selections from his broadcasts and columns have been printed in the *Congressional Record* over a hundred times; member, board of directors, John D. and Catherine T. MacArthur Foundation.

Caryl P. Haskins (1908–2001)   research associate (physics and biology), MIT, 1935–45; president and research director, Haskins Labs, Inc., 1935–55; consultant to secretary of defense and secretary of state, 1950–60; member, PSAC, 1955–58 (consultant, 1959–70); president, Carnegie Institution of Washington, 1956–71.

Leland J. Haworth (1904–1979)   physicist; group leader and later head, Division 6 (Receiver Components), Radiation Laboratory, MIT, 1941–46; vice president, Associated Universities, Inc., 1951–60; member, Technological Capabilities Panel, PSAC, 1954–55; appointed a commissioner, AEC, 1961; coauthor, *Civilian Nuclear Power—A Report to the President—1962*; president, National Science Foundation, 1963–69; married Jerry Wiesner's White House secretary, Irene Benik, in 1963.

Harold L. Hazen (1901–1980)   a pioneer in the field of machine computation and automatic control, joined the MIT faculty in electrical engineering, 1925; department head, 1938–52; dean of the Graduate School, 1952–67; professor and dean emeritus, 1967–80.

Lillian Hellman (1906–1984)   playwright and voice of social consciousness in American letters; taught and conducted seminars at MIT, Yale University, and Harvard University, 1960s–70s; recipient, National Book Award in Arts and Letters, 1969; cofounder, Committee for Public Justice, a civil-liberties advocacy group, 1970; sometime resident of Martha's Vineyard.

John Hersey (1914–1993)   Pulitzer Prize-winning fiction writer; also a noted non-fiction writer and journalist, e.g. his book about the bombing of Hiroshima, 1945; deep interest in social issues in America, including education and race relations; taught writing at Yale and other universities; visiting professor, MIT, 1975; sometime resident of Martha's Vineyard.

Charles M. Herzfeld (1925–)   physicist; assistant director, DARPA, 1961–63; deputy director, 1963–65; director, 1965–67; later with ITT Corporation; consultant, U.S. Office of Science and Technology Policy, 1990–91.

Calvin L. Hicks   director, Third World Studies Program, Goddard College; Third World Center, Brown University; division chair and dean, Roxbury College; cofounder, Black Educators' Roundtable; also, Community Collaborations, New England Conservatory of Music.

Albert G. Hill (1910–1996)   physicist and educator; a leader in the development of radar during World War II; instructor in physics, MIT, 1937–41; headed the Radio Frequency Group, MIT Radiation Lab, 1942–46; joined the MIT physics faculty in 1946; director, Research Laboratory of Electronics, MIT, 1949–52; director, Lincoln Laboratory, MIT, 1952–55; vice president and director of research, IDA, Washington, D.C., 1956–59; trustee, 1956–61; lecturer in political science, MIT, 1965–75; vice president for research, 1970–75; chairman of the board of directors, Charles Stark Draper Laboratory, 1970–82.

Sidney Hillman (1887–1946)   labor leader, important figure in shaping national labor and welfare legislation during the 1930s.

Charles J. Hitch (1910–1995)   assistant U.S. secretary of defense (comptroller), 1961–65; president, University of California, 1968–75.

Stanley Hoffmann (1928–)   political scientist; professor at Harvard University; chairman, Center for European Studies, Harvard University.

J. Edgar Hoover (1895–1972)   director, Federal Bureau of Investigation, 1924–72; targeted liberal activists for special government scrutiny.

Donald F. Hornig (1920–)   group leader, Los Alamos Laboratory, 1944–46; taught at Brown University and Princeton University; member, PSAC, 1960–69; special assistant for science and technology to the U.S. president, and director, Office of Science and Technology, and chairman, Federal Council on Science and Technology, 1964–69; president, Brown University, 1970–76; professor of chemistry in public health, Harvard University, 1977–90; chairman, department of environmental sciences and physiology, 1988–90; president, Water Board, Cambridge, Mass., 1985–94.

Alice Langley Hsieh (1922–1979)   political scientist specializing in nuclear weaponry and military capabilities of the People's Republic of China; international relations officer and foreign services officer, Bureau of Far Eastern Affairs, U.S. State Department, 1945–55; consultant, RAND Corporation, 1955–58; senior staff member, RAND, 1958–69; member, IDA, 1969–71.

Robert I. Hulsizer, Jr.   see his essay in this book.

Hubert H. Humphrey (1911–1978)   U.S. senator (D-Minn.), 1948–64, 1970–78; U.S. vice president, 1964–68; Democratic candidate for U.S. president, 1968; active in the area of arms control, particularly work on the Nuclear Test Ban Treaty (1963) and ACDA.

James A. (Catfish) Hunter (1946–1999)   Major League baseball pitcher for the Kansas City Royals, Oakland Athletics, and New York Yankees; named to Baseball Hall of Fame, 1987.

John D. Isaacs (1913–1980)   associate oceanographer, Scripps Institution of Oceanography, 1951–55; associate professor of oceanography, 1955–58; professor and director of marine life research, 1961–80; director, Institute for Marine Resources, 1971–80; consultant to the White House, 1962–67.

Henry M. (Scoop) Jackson (1912–1983)   U.S. congressman (1941–53) and senator (1953–83) (D-Wash.); authority on defense, energy, and environmental issues; ranking Democrat on Senate Armed Services Committee; chair, Energy and Natural Resources Committee; conservative on foreign policy and national security issues; a leader among Democratic neoconservatives.

Jesse Jackson (1941–)   civil rights leader; president, Operation PUSH, 1972–83; National Rainbow Coalition, beginning in 1984; candidate for Democratic nomination for U.S. president, 1983–84, 1987–88; special presidential envoy to Africa, 1997.

Shirley Ann Jackson   see her essay in this book.

Roman Jakobson (1896–1982)   sometimes called the father of modern structural linguistics; professor of Slavic languages, literatures, and general linguistics, Harvard University, 1949–66; Institute professor and professor of linguistics, MIT, 1958–66; professor emeritus, MIT and Harvard, 1966–82.

Steven Jobs (1955–)   founder and chief executive officer of Apple Computer Company, 1976.

Clarence L. (Kelly) Johnson (1910–1990) chief research engineer, Lockheed Aircraft Corporation, 1938–52; chief engineer, 1952–56; vice president, 1956–74; senior vice president, 1974–90; creator of the "Skunk Works," a division within Lockheed that designed secret military aviation projects; recipient, National Medal of Science, 1966.

Howard W. Johnson see his essay in this book.

Vivian Johnson senior researcher, Center on Families, Communities, Schools and Children's Learning, 1990–96; clinical associate professor of administration, training, and policy studies, Boston University School of Education; coauthor (with her husband, Willard R. Johnson), *West African Governments and Volunteer Development Organizations: Priorities for Partnership* (1990).

Willard R. Johnson see his essay in this book.

Frank S. Jones (1928–) executive director, Urban Systems Laboratory, MIT, 1968–69; Ford professor of urban affairs, 1970–92; professor emeritus, 1992; director, Community Fellows Program, 1971–75, and HUD Minority Intern Program, MIT, 1976–85.

Herman Kahn (1922–1983) mathematician, physicist, and political scientist; staff, Rand Corporation, 1948–60; founder and director, Hudson Institute, 1961; author of the controversial books *On Thermonuclear War* (1959) and *Thinking About the Unthinkable* (1962), which proposed the probability and survivability of nuclear war.

Carl Kaysen see his essay in this book.

Spurgeon M. Keeny, Jr. see his essay in this book.

John G. Kemeny (1926–1992) mathematician and academic executive; assistant in the theoretical division, Los Alamos Laboratory, 1945–46; professor of mathematics, Dartmouth College, 1953–70, 1981–90; president, 1970–81; chair, commission to investigate the Three Mile Island nuclear power plant accident, 1979.

Edward M. (Ted) Kennedy see his foreword to this book.

Ethel Skakel Kennedy (1928–) wife of Robert F. Kennedy.

Jacqueline Bouvier Kennedy (later Onassis) (1929–1994) married John F. Kennedy in 1953; Aristotle Onassis in 1968; editor, Doubleday.

John F. Kennedy (1917–1963) U.S. congressman (D-Mass.), 1946–52; U.S. senator (D-Mass.), 1952–60; president of the United States, 1961–63.

Joseph P. Kennedy (1888–1969) financier, entrepreneur, government official; served in both houses of the Massachusetts legislature; first chairman, U.S. Securities and Exchange Commission, 1934–35; U.S. ambassador to Great Britain, 1938–40, espousing isolationist views that implied agreement with policies designed to appease Hitler; U.S. Senate appointee to the Hoover Commission, 1953, 1957; father of John F. Kennedy, Robert F. Kennedy, Edward M. Kennedy, and six other children.

Robert F. Kennedy (1925–1968) brother of John F. Kennedy and manager of his presidential campaign, 1960; U.S. attorney general, 1960–64; U.S. senator (D-N.Y.), 1964–68; assassinated in 1968 while campaigning as a potential Democratic nominee for U.S. president.

Gyorgy Kepes (1906–2001) joined the MIT faculty in 1946; associate professor of visual design, 1946–49; professor, beginning in 1949; elected Institute professor, 1970; founder and director, Center for Advanced Visual Studies, MIT, 1967–72; also an artist (painter, photographer, and designer), with numerous one-man shows to his credit.

George A. Keyworth (1939–)   physicist, Los Alamos National Laboratory, 1968–81; science adviser to President Reagan and director, Office of Science and Technology Policy, 1981–85; afterwards director of research and distinguished fellow, Hudson Institute.

Mohammad Ayub Khan (1907–1974)   president of Pakistan, 1958–69.

Ruhollah Khomeini (1900?–1989)   Iranian cleric and political leader; established a constitutional theocracy in Iran, 1979.

Nikita Khrushchev (1894–1971)   chair, Council of Ministers of the USSR; premier, 1957–64.

James R. Killian, Jr. (1904–1988)   educator and university administrator; executive assistant to the president, MIT, 1939–43; executive vice president, 1943–45; vice president, 1945–49; president, 1949–59; chair, MIT Corporation, 1959–71; honorary chair, 1971–79; held several posts in government service, including special assistant for science and technology to President Eisenhower and chair, PSAC, 1957–59; member, Foreign Intelligence Advisory Board, 1961–63; advisory board member, ACDA, 1969–73; chair, Carnegie Commission on Educational Television, 1965–67, and Corporation for Public Broadcasting, 1968–75; recipient, Public Welfare Medal, National Academy of Sciences, 1957; author of *Sputnik, Scientists, and Eisenhower* (1977).

Martin Luther King, Jr. (1929–1968)   civil rights leader; founder and president, Southern Christian Leadership Conference, 1957–68; recipient, Nobel Prize for peace, 1964.

Melvin H. (Mel) King   see his essay in this book.

Henry A. Kissinger (1923–)   political scientist and government official, taught at Harvard University, 1954–69; executive director, Harvard's International Studies Seminar, 1951–69, and director of the Defense Studies Program, 1958–69; consultant, ACDA, 1961–68; director of the National Security Council and special assistant to President Nixon, 1969–75; U.S. secretary of state, 1973–77; founder and chairman, Kissinger Associates, Inc; author of *Nuclear Weapons and Foreign Policy* (1957); recipient, Nobel Prize for peace, 1973.

George B. Kistiakowsky (1900–1982)   Russian-born chemist and educator, taught at Harvard University for most of his career, beginning in 1930; chair, Harvard chemistry department, 1947–50; worked on the Manhattan Project, 1941–43; member, ballistic missiles advisory committee, U.S. Department of Defense, 1953–58, and the U.S. delegation, Conference for Prevention of Surprise Attack, Geneva, 1958; joined PSAC in 1958, and succeeded James Killian as Eisenhower's special assistant for science and technology in 1959; author of *A Scientist at the White House* (1976).

Koji Kobayashi (1907–1996)   senior vice president, NEC Corporation, Japan, 1956–61; executive vice president, 1961–62; senior executive vice president, 1962–64; president, 1964–76; chairman and chief executive officer, 1976–88.

Arthur Koestler (1905–1983)   Hungarian-born writer on politics and philosophy; author of *The Act of Creation* (1964), a study of the human creative process.

Alexei N. Kosygin (1904–1980)   deputy Soviet premier under Nikita Khrushchev; Soviet premier, 1964–80.

Robert N. Kreidler (1929–1992)   White House staff member, 1958–61; staff, U.S. Office of Science and Technology, 1961–62; later a foundation executive with the Alfred P. Sloan Foundation, Carnegie Institution of Washington, and Charles A. Dana Foundation.

Arthur B. Krim (1910–1994)   lawyer and motion picture executive; chairman, United Artists Corporation, 1951–78; Orion Pictures Corporation, 1978–94; member, board of directors, Weizmann Institute, 1948–94; John F. Kennedy Library Foundation, 1964–94; special counsel to the U.S. president, 1968–69; member, President's general advisory committee on arms control, 1977–80; Arms Control Association, 1985–94.

Stanley Kunitz (1905–)   poet; named U.S. poet laureate, 2000.

Vasily V. Kuznetsov (1901–1990)   Soviet ambassador to the People's Republic of China, 1953; deputy Soviet minister of foreign affairs, 1953–55; first deputy foreign minister, 1955–77; first deputy chairman, Presidium of the Supreme Soviet, 1977–86; acting head of state, 1982–83, 1984–85.

Melvin R. Laird (1922–)   U.S. congressman (R-Wis.), 1953–69; U.S. secretary of defense, 1969–73; domestic adviser to President Nixon, 1973–74.

Roy Lamson (1908–1986)   taught at Williams College before joining the MIT faculty in 1958; professor of English, MIT, 1958–73; professor emeritus, 1973–86; helped found MIT's Council for the Arts; director, MIT's interdisciplinary humanities, science, and engineering program; president's special assistant for the arts, beginning in 1971.

Edwin H. (Din) Land (1909–1991)   college dropout, inventor, and physicist; founded the Polaroid Corporation, Cambridge, Mass., 1937; president, chairman, CEO, and director of research, 1937–80; developed optical systems for the military, World War II; appointed by President Eisenhower in 1954 to head an intelligence committee studying how to prevent a future Pearl Harbor-like attack; visiting Institute professor, MIT, 1956–91; member, PSAC, 1957–59, and consultant-at-large, 1960–73; president, American Academy of Arts and Sciences, 1951–53; recipient, Presidential Medal of Freedom, 1963; National Medal of Science, 1967.

Ann Landers (Esther P. Lederer) (1918–2002)   syndicated advice columnist, *Chicago Sun-Times*, 1955–2002; member, advisory committee on better health, American Medical Association; visiting committee, board of overseers, Harvard Medical School; known for consulting experts (Jerry among them) before giving technical advice; numerous awards from medical and mental health groups, including the humanitarianism award of the International Lions Clubs, 1967; established a chair in immunology at the Weizmann Institute, 1974; summer resident of Martha's Vineyard.

Ralph E. Lapp (1917–)   staff, Manhattan Project, University of Chicago, 1943–45; consulting scientist for Bikini bomb tests, 1946; executive director for atomic energy, Research and Development Board, Washington, D.C., 1947–48; consulting physicist, Nuclear Science Service, Washington, D.C., beginning in 1950; scientific adviser to the Pentagon; activist on the dangers of radiation and uncontrolled arms proliferation.

Leo S. Lavatelli (1917–1998)   physicist; research assistant, Manhattan Project, Princeton, NJ, 1942–43; junior staff member, Los Alamos Laboratory, 1943–46; member of measurement groups and witness, Trinity atomic bomb test, 1945; research assistant, Harvard University, 1946–50; faculty member in physics, University of Illinois, Urbana, 1950–79; professor emeritus, 1979–98; consultant to Illinois group, Physical Sciences Study Committee, 1956–57, and Science Teaching Center, MIT, 1966.

Richard Leacock (1921–)   cinematographer, producer, and director; joined the MIT faculty in 1969 as professor and head of the film section, Department of Architecture.

Bertram M. Lee (1939–)   media executive; president, Dudley Station Corporation, Roxbury, Mass., 1969–81; president, New England Television Corporation, 1982–86; president, Kellee Communications Group, Inc., starting in 1986; chairman, TransAfrica Forum; trustee, Martin Luther King, Jr. Center for Non-Violent Social Change.

Yuk-Wing Lee (1904–1989)   visiting professor of electrical engineering, MIT, 1946–48; associate professor of electrical engineering, 1948–60; professor, 1960–69; author of *Statistical Theory of Communication* (1960).

Curtis E. LeMay (1906–1990)   U.S. Air Force general who directed the bombing of Japan during World War II; commanding general, Strategic Air Command during the Cold War; vice chief of staff, U.S. Air Force, 1957–61; chief of staff, 1961–65; urged military strike on Cuba during the missile crisis of 1962, and later, during the Johnson administration, escalation of bombing in Vietnam; vice presidential running mate of George C. Wallace on the American Independent Party ticket, 1968.

Richard K. Lester (1954–)   joined the MIT faculty in 1979; professor of nuclear engineering; director, Industrial Performance Center, MIT; author of *The Productive Edge: How U.S. Industries Are Pointing the Way to a New Era of Economic Growth* (1998).

Jerome Y. Lettvin (1920–)   neurophysiologist; joined the staff of the Research Laboratory of Electronics, MIT, 1951; professor of electrical and bioengineering and communications physiology, MIT, 1966–88; professor emeritus, 1988.

Anthony Lewis   see his essay in this book.

Elma Lewis   see her essay in this book.

Warren K. Lewis (1882–1975)   chemical engineer, joined the MIT faculty in 1910; professor of chemical engineering, 1915–48; professor emeritus, 1948–75; chairman, Committee on Educational Survey (the Lewis Committee), MIT, 1947–49, conducting a major review of the Institute's educational policies and procedures.

Klaus Liepmann (1907–1990)   conductor and educator; professor of music, MIT, 1947–72; professor emeritus, 1972–90.

Evelyn Lincoln (1910–1995)   personal secretary to John F. Kennedy as U.S. congressman, senator, and president.

Jacques Lipchitz (1891–1973)   French sculptor of Lithuanian descent; early experimenter in cubism; married Yulla Halberstadt in 1947.

Andrew Lippman   senior research scientist, Media Laboratory, MIT; director, Digital Life consortium.

Albert A. List (1901–1987)   industrialist, businessman, and philanthropist; donated funds for construction of MIT's art gallery, named in honor of him and his wife, Vera (Glaser) List.

William N. Locke (1909–2000)   linguist and educator, joined the MIT faculty as head of modern languages in 1945; initiated study of linguistics at MIT, including projects in speech analysis and machine translation; director, MIT Libraries, 1956–74; early advocate of wide-ranging uses of computers in linguistics research and library practices.

Alan Lomax   see his essay in this book.

Francis Wheeler Loomis (1889–1976)   professor of physics, University of Illinois, 1929–57; associate director, Radiation Laboratory, MIT, 1941–45; member, board of governors, Argonne National Laboratory, 1946–48.

Robert A. Lovett (1895–1986)   lawyer and government official; U.S. secretary of defense, 1951–53; consultant on foreign intelligence to the Eisenhower administration; declined three Cabinet posts in President Kennedy's administration; served on JFK's executive committee during the Cuban missile crisis, 1962; adviser on war issues to President Lyndon Johnson.

Salvador E. Luria (1912–1991)   Italian-born microbiologist, taught at the University of Illinois before joining the MIT faculty in 1959; professor of microbiology, MIT, 1959–64; Sedgwick professor of biology, 1964–91; Institute professor, 1970–91; director, Center for Cancer Research, MIT, 1972–91; recipient, Nobel Prize (physiology or medicine), 1969; active in world peace movements.

J. Roderick (Rod) MacArthur (1920–1984)   son of John D. MacArthur, philanthropist; trustee, John D. and Catherine T. MacArthur Foundation.

Angus N. MacDonald   SB (aeronautics and astronautics) MIT, 1946; SM 1947; member, Council for the Arts, MIT; MIT Corporation.

Robert E. Machol (1917–1998)   electrical engineer and educator; taught at Purdue University, University of Illinois (Chicago), and Northwestern University; president, Operations Research Society of America, 1971–72; chief scientist, Federal Aviation Administration, 1985–95.

Archibald MacLeish (1892–1982)   poet, dramatist, and statesman, served as Librarian of Congress, 1939–44; director, Office of Facts and Figures, 1941–42; assistant U.S. secretary of state, 1944–45; helped draft a constitution for UNESCO, 1945; Boylston professor of rhetoric and oratory, Harvard University, 1949–62; professor emeritus, 1962–82.

Harold Macmillan (1894–1986)   British prime minister and first lord of the treasury, 1957–63; chancellor, Oxford University, 1960–86.

Margaret L. A. MacVicar (1943–1991)   MIT's first dean for undergraduate education, joined the MIT physics faculty in 1969; devised the Undergraduate Research Opportunities Program (UROP); vice president, Carnegie Institution of Washington, 1983–87; the MacVicar Faculty Fellow program was established in her honor at MIT in 1992, to recognize outstanding contributions to undergraduate education.

Thomas S. Maddock (1928–)   civil engineer and company executive; with U.S. Navy, 1952–55; project manager for domestic and international water resource projects.

Malcolm X (1925–1965)   civil rights leader; minister, Black Muslims, 1952–64; founder, Organization of Afro-American Unity, 1964.

Nelson R. Mandela (1918–)   organizer and leader, African National Congress, 1944; South African political prisoner, 1962–90; elected first president of post-apartheid South Africa, 1994.

Mao Tse-tung (1893–1976)   chairman, Communist Party of China, 1949–76; People's Republic of China, 1949–59.

Robert E. Marshak (1916–1992)   staff, Radiation Laboratory, MIT, 1942–43; deputy group leader in theoretical physics, Los Alamos Laboratory, 1944–46; professor of physics, University of Rochester, 1949–70; president, City College of New York, 1970–79.

Hugh Masekela (1939–)   South African jazz trumpeter and civil rights activist; banned from South Africa, 1960s–1990.

Charles M. Mathias (1922–)   U.S. senator (R-Md.), 1969–87.

Jean Mayer (1920–1993)   nutritionist and university administrator; taught at Harvard University before serving as president, Tufts University, 1976–93; member, board of directors, Action for Boston Community Development, 1964–70; vice chairman, President's Commission on World Food Problems, 1978–80.

Eugene J. McCarthy (1916–)   political leader; public school teacher, 1935–40; college teacher; U.S. congressman (D-Minn.), 1949–58; U.S. senator, 1958–70; Democratic candidate for U.S. president, 1968; vocal opponent of Vietnam war; independent candidate for U.S. president, 1976.

John McCarthy (1927–)   pioneer in artificial intelligence; connected to the computer center and electrical engineering department, MIT, 1957–62; inventor of the LISP computer language; professor of computer science, Stanford University; professor emeritus, 2001; recipient, IEEE computer pioneer award, 1985.

John J. McCloy (1895–1989)   diplomat and lawyer; assistant secretary of war, 1941–45; president, World Bank, 1947–49; high commissioner for Germany, 1949–52; chairman, Ford Foundation, 1953–65; presidential envoy under Presidents Eisenhower, Kennedy, and Johnson; disarmament and arms control adviser to Presidents Kennedy, Johnson, and Nixon, 1961–74, as chair, President's General Advisory Committee on Disarmament; special negotiator with the Soviets during the Cuban missile crisis, 1962; recipient, Presidential Medal of Freedom, 1981.

Elizabeth J. McCormack (1922–)   foundation administrator; assistant to the president, Rockefeller Brothers Fund, 1974–76; thereafter, philanthropic adviser and associate, Rockefeller Family and Associates.

Warren S. McCulloch (1898–1969)   member, Laboratory for Neurophysiology, Yale University, 1934–41; professor of psychiatry and clinical professor of physiology, 1945–52; joined the Research Laboratory of Electronics, MIT, in 1952; active in the cybernetics movement.

Eugene McDermott (1899–1973)   cofounder and president, Texas Instruments Inc.; life member, MIT Corporation; active in the arts at MIT, with his wife Margaret (Milam) McDermott; McDermott Court at MIT named in their honor.

Neil H. McElroy (1904–1972)   U.S. secretary of defense under President Eisenhower; first government official to raise the Cold War issue of a "missile gap" with the Soviet Union; chairman, Procter and Gamble, 1959–72.

Thomas J. McIntyre (1915–)   U.S. senator (D-N.H.), 1962–78; member of the Armed Services Committee; Banking, Housing, and Urban Affairs Committee; and Select Committee on Small Business.

Marshall McLuhan (1911–1980)   director, Center for Culture and Technology, University of Toronto, 1963–80; expert on the media.

Robert S. McNamara (1916–)   served in the U.S. Air Force, 1943–46; secretary of defense for Presidents John F. Kennedy and Lyndon B. Johnson, 1961–68; resigned in 1968 over the Johnson administration's hawkish Vietnam policy; president, the World Bank, 1968–81, after which he lobbied worldwide on behalf of arms limitation, East-West détente, and anti-poverty efforts; author of *Blundering into Disaster: Surviving the First Century of the Nuclear Age* (1986), a history of the U.S.–Soviet arms race; and *In Retrospect: The Tragedy and Lessons of Vietnam* (1995, with Brian Van de Mark), a memoir of the Vietnam War era.

Vincent V. McRae (1918–) operations research officer, Johns Hopkins University, 1952–60; senior staff member, Research Analysis Corporation, 1961–64; technical assistant, U.S. Office of Science and Technology, 1964–74; director of strategic planning, IBM, 1974–87; member of technical staff, Gaither Panel, 1957; adviser to delegates and member of the U.S. delegation, Surprise Attack Conference, Geneva, 1958; consultant, National Security Council, 1973 78; member, Defense Science Board, 1973–80.

Mikhail A. Menshikov (1902–1976) Soviet ambassador to India, 1953–57; Nepal, 1957; United States, 1957–62; Soviet foreign minister, 1962–68.

Charles L. Miller (1929–2000) joined the MIT faculty in civil engineering in 1955; director, Urban Systems Laboratory, MIT, 1968–77; left MIT in 1977 to run his own company, CLM/Systems, Inc. in Tampa, Florida.

Mikhail D. Millionshchikov (1913–1973) Russian nuclear physicist; Soviet representative at early Pugwash meetings; became an activist in arms control efforts; participant, Soviet-American Disarmament Study, 1960s; vice president, Soviet Academy of Sciences.

Marvin L. Minsky (1927–) mathematician; leading authority on artificial intelligence; cofounder, Artificial Intelligence Laboratory, MIT; Toshiba professor of media arts and sciences, MIT; professor emeritus, 1996; recipient, Japan Prize, 1990.

Joan Miro (1893–1983) Spanish surrealist painter.

Carroll G. Montgomery associate leader, Group 41 (Fundamental Developments), Radiation Laboratory, MIT, World War II.

Dorothy Montgomery member, Group 41 (Fundamental Developments), Radiation Laboratory, MIT, World War II.

Henry Moore (1898–1986) English abstract sculptor.

Elting E. Morison (1909–1995) historian, joined the MIT faculty in 1946; assistant professor of English, 1946–49; associate professor, 1949–53; professor of industrial history, Sloan School of Management, MIT, 1953–66; professor of history and American studies, Yale University, 1966–72; returned to MIT in 1972 as Elizabeth and James R. Killian Class of 1926 professor; helped found MIT's interdisciplinary Program in Science, Technology, and Society; author of *From Know-How to Nowhere: The Development of American Technology* (1974).

Philip Morrison see his essay in this book.

Phylis Morrison (1927–2002) science teacher and writer; curriculum developer, Educational Development Corporation, Newton, Mass., 1962–68; museum developer, Children's Museum, Boston, 1965–70; coauthor (with her husband Philip Morrison), *Powers of Ten* (1983).

Philip M. Morse (1903–1985) joined the MIT faculty in 1931; professor of physics, 1939–73; professor emeritus, 1973–85; director, Brookhaven National Laboratory, 1946–48; deputy director and director of research, Weapons Systems Evaluation Group, 1949–50; president, Operations Research Society of America, 1952–53; member, IDA, 1956–61.

Bill Moyers (1934–) journalist; special assistant to Lyndon B. Johnson, 1959–60, 1963–65; associate director, Peace Corps, 1961–62; White House press secretary, 1965–67; television executive and series host successively with National Educational Television, CBS, NBC, and PBS.

David G. Mugar   businessman and philanthropist; chairman and chief executive officer, New England Television Corporation; Mugar Enterprises, Inc.

Mitrofan I. Nedelin (1902–1960)   Soviet field marshal connected to space and military programs; perished, along with scores of others, in a missile testing accident.

Nicholas Negroponte   see his essay in this book.

Jawaharlal Nehru (1889–1964)   first prime minister of independent India, 1947–64.

Gaylord A. Nelson (1916–)   lawyer and political leader; governor of Wisconsin, 1958–62; U.S. senator (D-Wis.), 1963–81; special interest in environmental issues; originator of Earth Day, 1970.

Carl Nesjar (1920–)   Norwegian painter, sculptor, and graphic artist; associate and colleague of Pablo Picasso.

Paul H. Nitze (1907–)   vice chairman, Strategic Banking Survey, 1944–46; president, Foreign Service Education Foundation, 1953–61; assistant secretary for international security affairs, U.S. Department of Defense, 1961–63; secretary of the Navy, 1963–67; deputy secretary of defense, 1967–69; representative of the secretary of defense on the U.S. delegation to the Strategic Arms Limitation Talks (SALT) with the Soviet Union, 1969–74; consultant on defense policy and U.S./Soviet strategic relationship for government departments and private firms, 1975–81; coauthor of *From Hiroshima to Glasnost: At the Center of Decision—A Memoir* (1989).

Richard M. Nixon (1913–1994)   U.S. congressman (R-Calif.), 1947–50, serving on the House Committee on Un-American Activities; U.S. senator (R-Calif.), 1950–53; U.S. vice president under President Dwight D. Eisenhower, 1953–61; Republican candidate for U.S. president, 1960, losing to John F. Kennedy; U.S. president, 1969–74; resigned under threat of impeachment in 1974.

Kenneth Noland (1924–)   abstract expressionist painter.

Lawrence F. (Larry) O'Brien (1917–1990)   state director for John F. Kennedy's senatorial campaigns in the 1950s; director, Kennedy-Johnson presidential campaign, 1960; special assistant (for congressional relations) to Presidents Kennedy and Johnson, 1961–65.

Thomas R. Odhiambo (1931–2003)   professor of entomology and department head, University of Nairobi, 1970–77; dean, faculty of agriculture, 1970–71; first director, International Centre of Insect Physiology and Ecology, Nairobi, Kenya, starting in 1970; chairman, Kenya National Academy of Sciences, 1977–85; founding fellow and president, African Academy of Sciences, 1985; Africa Prize for Leadership, 1987.

Kenneth O'Donnell (1924–1977)   helped manage John F. Kennedy's senatorial and presidential campaigns; appointments secretary to JFK, 1961–63; aide to Lyndon B. Johnson, 1963–65; assisted in Hubert H. Humphrey's presidential campaign, 1968.

Yoko Ono (1933–)   artist, musician, and peace activist; widow of "Beatle" John Lennon.

J. Robert Oppenheimer (1904–1967)   physicist at University of California, Berkeley, and California Institute of Technology, 1929–47; director, Los Alamos Laboratory, 1942–45; sometimes referred to as "the father of the atom bomb"; later declared a security risk by the U.S. government, for his leftist connections; chairman, general advisory committee, United Nations AEC, 1946–52; director, Institute for Advanced Study, Princeton, NJ, 1947–66.

Yuri F. Orlov (1924–) high energy physicist; founder, Moscow chapter, Amnesty International, 1973; founder and chair, Moscow Helsinki Watch Group; senior scientist in nuclear studies, Cornell University, starting in 1986.

Olof Palme (1927–1986) prime minister of Sweden, 1969–76, 1982; member, Independent Commission on International Development Issues; Independent Commission on Disarmament and Security Issues.

Wolfgang K. H. Panofsky (1919–) participated in national defense research at Los Alamos, 1942–45; professor of physics, Stanford University; director, High Energy Physics Laboratory, Stanford Linear Accelerator Center, 1962–84; member, PSAC, 1960–65; consultant, U.S. Office of Science and Technology, 1965–73; ACDA, 1968–81; recipient, National Medal of Science, 1969.

Seymour A. Papert (1928–) pioneer in artificial intelligence; cofounder and codirector, Artificial Intelligence Laboratory, MIT; joined the MIT faculty as professor of applied mathematics, 1968; later professor of education and media technology; professor emeritus.

Louis Pasteur (1822–1895) French chemist and bacteriologist; developed the process of food sterilization known as "pasteurization."

Linus Pauling (1901–1994) professor of chemistry, California Institute of Technology, 1931–64; research professor, Center for the Study of Democratic Institutions, 1963–67; professor of chemistry, University of California, San Diego, 1967–69, and Stanford University, 1969–74; subsequently president and research professor, Linus Pauling Institute for Science and Medicine; Nobel Prize in chemistry, 1954; Nobel Prize for peace, 1962, for warning of dangers in radioactive weapons.

Vladimir Pavlichenko Soviet official who attended many of the early Pugwash conferences as a Russian-English translator and manager of the Soviet delegates.

I. M. Pei (1917–) SB (architecture), MIT, 1940; architect noted for a number of prominent buildings worldwide; in the Boston area, his designs include the John F. Kennedy Library, the west wing of the Museum of Fine Arts, and the Christian Science Church center; his designs at MIT include the Cecil and Ida Green Center for Earth Sciences, the Ralph Landau Building for Chemical Engineering, and the Arts and Media Technology Building (Wiesner Building).

Shimon Peres (1923–) Israeli political leader; long-time Knesset member; minister with various portfolios in several Israeli cabinets.

William J. Perry (1927–) technical consultant, U.S. Department of Defense, 1967–77; U.S. under-secretary of defense for research and engineering, 1977–81; codirector, Center for International Security and Arms Control, Stanford University, 1989–93; U.S. deputy secretary of defense, 1993–94; U.S. secretary of defense, 1994–97; recipient, Presidential Medal of Freedom, 1997.

Pablo Picasso (1881–1973) Spanish painter and sculptor; a pioneer in cubist art.

Augusto Pinochet (1915–) Chilean military and political leader; ousted the elected president (Salvador Allende) in a bloody coup, 1973; president of Chile, 1973–90.

Emanuel R. (Manny) Piore (1908–2000) physicist; head, electronics board, U.S. Office of Naval Research, 1946–47; director for physical sciences, 1947–48; deputy director for natural sciences, 1949–51; chief scientist and deputy director, 1951–55; visiting researcher, Research

Laboratory of Electronics, MIT, 1948–49; member, board of directors, Draper Laboratory, MIT; member, visiting committee, Department of Electrical Engineering, MIT, 1956–57; PSAC, 1959–62; held research and executive positions with IBM Corporation, 1956–75.

Walter H. Pitts (1923–1969)   neuroscientist; member, Group 84 (Theory), Radiation Laboratory, MIT; joined the staff of the Research Laboratory of Electronics in 1947.

Dave Powers (1911–1998)   worked on John F. Kennedy's U.S. congressional, senatorial, and presidential campaigns; special assistant to JFK in the White House; curator, John F. Kennedy Library and Museum.

Francis Gary Powers (1929–1977)   American aviator captured when shot down in U–2 aircraft on reconnaissance mission over the Soviet Union, 1960; exchanged in 1962 for Russian spy Rudolf Abel.

Frank Press (1924–)   geophysicist, taught at Columbia University and the California Institute of Technology before joining the MIT faculty in 1965; professor of geology and geophysics, MIT, 1965–77; member, U.S. delegations to Nuclear Test Ban Conferences in Geneva, 1959–61, and Moscow, 1963; PSAC, 1961–64; United Nations Conference on Science and Technology for Underdeveloped Nations, 1963; science adviser to the U.S. president and director, Office of Science and Technology Policy, 1977–80; president, National Academy of Sciences, 1981–93; private consultant, 1993–.

Melvin Price (1905–1988)   U.S. congressman (D-Ill.), 1945–88; first chairman, U.S. House Ethics Committee; known for support of the military.

Robert C. Prim, III (1921–)   engineer and mathematician, U.S. Naval Ordnance Laboratory, 1944–49; research mathematician, Bell Telephone Laboratories, 1949–58; director of mathematical and mechanical research, 1958–61; from special assistant to director, Defense Research and Engineering, 1961–63; vice president for research, Sandia Corporation, 1963–64; Litton Industries, 1966–69; executive research associate, Bell Laboratories, 1969–71; executive director of research, 1971–80.

Edward M. Purcell (1912–1997)   physicist and educator with interests in nuclear magnetism, radio astronomy, astrophysics, and biophysics; leader, Group 41 (Fundamental Developments), Radiation Laboratory, MIT, 1941–46; faculty member in physics, Harvard University, 1946–1977; Gerhard Gade University Professor, 1960–77; professor emeritus, 1977–97; member, U.S. Air Force Scientific Advisory Board, 1947–48, 1953–57; PSAC, 1957–60, 1962–66; Nobel Prize in physics, 1952; recipient, National Medal of Science, 1980.

I. I. Rabi (1898–1988)   taught physics at Columbia University, 1929–67; Nobel Prize in physics (1944) for his work on measuring the spin of subatomic particles; associate director and head of Division 4 (Research), Radiation Laboratory, MIT, 1940–45, helping to perfect radar and advise developers of the atomic bomb; subsequently joined fellow physicists J. Robert Oppenheimer and Enrico Fermi in efforts to limit the nuclear arms race; vice president, International Conference on the Peaceful Uses of Atomic Energy; member, general advisory committee of the AEC, 1946–56 (chair, 1952–56); member, PSAC and its predecessor, 1952–68.

Eugene Rabinowitch (1901–1973)   instructor in chemistry, MIT, 1938–44; senior chemist, Manhattan Project, University of Chicago, 1944–46; professor of botany and biophysics, University of Illinois, Urbana, 1947–68; editor, *Bulletin of the Atomic Scientists*; organizer, Pugwash Conferences, 1957–73; professor of chemistry and biology and director of the

Center for Science and the Future of Human Affairs, State University of New York, Albany, 1968–73.

William H. Radford (1909–1966)   specialist in electrical communications and electronic computers, research assistant in electrical engineering, MIT, 1932–39; instructor, 1939–41; assistant professor, 1941–44; associate professor of electrical communications, 1944–51; appointed professor of electrical communications, 1951; division head, Lincoln Laboratory, MIT, 1952–57; associate director, 1957–64; director, 1964–66; member, U.S. Air Force Scientific Advisory Board, 1957–66.

George W. Rathjens (1925–)   member, weapons systems evaluation group, U.S. Department of Defense, 1953–58; staff to the special assistant to the U.S. President for science and technology, 1959–60; deputy director, DARPA, 1961–62; staff, ACDA, 1962–65; director, weapons systems evaluation division, IDA, 1965–68; professor of political science, MIT, 1968–96; professor emeritus, 1996; secretary general, Pugwash Conferences on Science and World Affairs.

James Reston (1909–1995)   American journalist and foreign correspondent; Pulitzer Prize-winning political columnist for the *New York Times*, 1945–87; copublisher, *Vineyard Gazette*, starting in 1968; author of *The Artillery of the Press: Its Influence on American Foreign Policy* (1967).

Roger Revelle (1909–1991)   science adviser to the U.S. secretary of the interior, 1961–63; professor of population policy, 1964–79, and director of the Center for Population Studies, Harvard University, 1964–75; U.S. delegate to UNESCO; author of many environmental studies, including *Land and Water Development in the Indus Plain* (1964); member, National Academy of Sciences.

Jean Riboud (1919–)   executive vice president, Schlumberger Limited, 1963–65; president and chief executive officer, 1965–75; board chairman, president, and chief executive officer, 1975–83; board chairman and chief executive officer, 1983–85.

Alexander Rich (1924–)   molecular biologist; associate professor of biophysics, MIT, 1958–61; professor since 1961; member, visiting committee, Weizmann Institute of Science, 1965–66; senior consultant, U.S. Office of Science and Technology, 1977–81; member, USA-USSR Joint Commission on Science and Technology, U.S. Department of State, 1977–82; recipient, National Medal of Science, 1995.

John V. Roach, II (1938–)   retail company executive; vice president of RadioShack, 1972–80; subsequently president and chairman of the Tandy Corporation, Fort Worth, Texas.

Chalmers M. Roberts (1910–)   chief diplomatic correspondent, *Washington Post*, 1953–71; columnist, beginning in 1971; author of *The Nuclear Years: The Arms Race and Arms Control* (1970).

Nathaniel Rochester (1919–)   SB (electrical engineering), MIT, 1941, worked on crystals in Group 53 (Radio Frequency), Radiation Laboratory, MIT, 1941–43; engineer, Sylvania Electric Products, Inc. 1943–48; joined the electronics staff of IBM in 1948; manager, IBM's department of information research; visiting professor of communication sciences, MIT, 1958–59.

Nelson A. Rockefeller (1908–1979)   governor of New York, 1958–73; U.S. vice president, 1974–77.

Leonard S. Rodberg (1932–)   research associate in physics, MIT, 1956–57; consultant, Los Alamos Scientific Laboratory, beginning in 1959; science policy officer and then chief of policy research, ACDA, 1961–66.

Lloyd Rodwin (1919–1999)   joined the MIT faculty in 1947; professor of land economics, 1959–73; Ford professor of international affairs, 1973–87; professor emeritus, 1987–99; chairman, faculty committee, Joint Center for Urban Studies, 1959–69; founder and director, Special Program for Urban and Regional Studies of Developing Areas (SPURS), 1967–88; head, Department of Urban Studies and Planning, 1969–73.

William Barton Rogers (1804–1882)   geologist and educator; first president of MIT, 1862–1870, 1878–81; president, National Academy of Sciences, 1878–82.

Walter A. Rosenblith (1913–2002)   see his essay in this book.

Bruno Rossi (1905–1993)   staff, Los Alamos Laboratory, 1943–46; professor of physics, MIT, 1946–66; Institute professor, 1966–70; professor emeritus, 1970–93; expert on cosmic x-rays research; member, National Academy of Sciences and American Philosophical Society; Rumford Prize, American Academy of Arts and Sciences, 1976.

Walt W. Rostow (1916–)   joined the MIT faculty in 1950 as professor of economic history; staff, Center for International Studies, MIT, 1951–61; consultant to the Eisenhower administration before joining the Kennedy administration as deputy special assistant for national security affairs in 1961; chairman, policy planning council, U.S. Department of State, 1961–66; special assistant to the president on national security, 1966–69; concern among MIT faculty members and students about his role in the Johnson administration (particularly his support of U.S. involvement in the Vietnam war) led to his not returning to the MIT faculty in 1969; professor of economics and history, University of Texas at Austin, starting in 1969.

Joseph Rotblat (1908–)   physicist, worked on the atomic bomb project at Los Alamos, World War II; long-time secretary-general, Pugwash Conferences on Science and World Affairs; president, 1988–97; author and editor of numerous works on arms control, including *Scientists, the Arms Race, and Disarmament* (1982); Nobel Prize for peace, 1995.

Emma Rothschild   see her essay in this book.

Nathaniel Mayer Victor Rothschild (1910–1990)   zoologist, British government official, and company executive; chairman, Agricultural Research Council, 1948–58; executive, Shell Research, 1961–70; director-general, central policy review staff, British government, 1971–74; head of firm, N. M. Rothschild & Sons, 1974–90; father of Emma Rothschild.

Ida Ely Rubin (1923–)   art consultant and writer; member, executive committee, and chair, acquisitions committee, MIT Council for the Arts, 1972–86; adviser to private collectors, including the Rockefeller family; vice chair, visual arts committee, New York City Cultural Council, 1969–72.

Jack P. Ruina (1923–)   electrical engineer and educator; assistant director for defense research, Office of the U.S. Secretary of Defense, 1960–61; director, DARPA, 1961–63; panel member, PSAC, 1963–72; joined the MIT faculty in 1963, retiring in 1995; president, IDA, 1964–66; vice president for special laboratories, MIT, 1966–70; director and principal investigator, research program on communications policy, MIT Center for Technology, Policy, and Industrial Development; senior consultant, White House Office of Science and Technology Policy, 1977–80.

Byron D. Rushing (1942–) director, Community Voter Registration Project, 1964–66; president, Museum of Afro-American History, 1972–84; state legislator, Massachusetts, 1983–.

Dean Rusk (1909–1994) educator and government official; special assistant to the U.S. secretary of war, 1946–47; director, office of United Nations affairs, U.S. State Department, 1947–49; deputy under secretary of state, 1949–50; president, Rockefeller Foundation, 1952–60; U.S. secretary of state, 1961–69.

Bertrand Russell (1872–1970) mathematician, philosopher, and social reformer; fellow, Trinity College, Cambridge; active in the post-World War II peace movement, including the "Ban the Bomb" effort; coauthor (with Albert Einstein) of the Russell-Einstein Manifesto, seeking to curtail and eventually eliminate weapons of mass destruction; cofounder, Pugwash Conferences on Science and World Affairs, 1957; first president, Campaign for Nuclear Disarmament, 1958; vigorously opposed U.S. involvement in Vietnam; recipient, Nobel Prize for literature, 1950.

Roald Z. Sagdeev physicist; member, Institute of High-Temperature Physics, Moscow, USSR, 1971–73; director, Institute of Space Research, Moscow, USSR, 1973–90; active in the arms control movement; appointed distinguished professor of physics, University of Maryland, College Park, 1990; also, director of the East-West Space Science Center; editor (with Frank von Hippel), *Reversing the Arms Race: How to Achieve and Verify Deep Reductions in the Nuclear Arsenals* (New York, 1990); married to Susan Eisenhower, daughter of Dwight D. Eisenhower.

Andrei D. Sakharov (1921–1989) Russian nuclear physicist, political dissident, and human rights activist; helped develop the Soviet hydrogen bomb, 1945–63; later advocated for nuclear disarmament and USSR–U.S. détente; joined other Soviet scientists in forming the Committee for Human Rights, 1970; awarded Nobel Prize for peace, 1975; exiled to Gorky for his outspokenness, 1980; returned to Moscow in 1986.

Abdus Salam (1926–1996) physicist who began work in his native Pakistan and moved to England in the 1950s; professor of theoretical physics, Imperial College of Science and Technology, London, 1957–93; member, science and technology advisory committee, United Nations, 1964–75; founder and director, International Center for Theoretical Physics, 1964–93; appointed president in 1993; founder and president, Third World Academy of Sciences, 1983–94; shared Nobel Prize in physics with Steven Weinberg (below) and Sheldon Glashow, 1979.

Pierre Salinger (1925–) press secretary to U.S. senator John F. Kennedy, 1959–60, and to Presidents Kennedy, 1961–63, and Lyndon B. Johnson, 1963–64; later chief foreign correspondent, ABC News.

Harrison E. Salisbury (1908–1993) journalist who specialized in reporting on developments in the Soviet Union and China; Moscow correspondent for the *New York Times*, 1949–54; reporter in New York City, 1955–61; national editor, 1962–64; assistant managing editor, 1964–70; associate editor and editor of opinion-editorial page, 1971–75.

Jonas Salk (1914–1995) consultant in epidemic diseases to the U.S. secretary of war, 1944–46, and the secretary of the Army, 1946–54; developer of the polio vaccine, 1954; director, Salk Institute for Biological Studies, 1963–75.

Paul A. Samuelson (1915–) joined the MIT economics faculty in 1940; assistant professor to professor of economics, 1940–86; elected Institute professor, 1966; professor emeritus,

1986; member, President's Council of Economic Advisers, 1960–68; chair, President's task force on maintaining American prosperity, 1964; Nobel Prize in economics, 1970; National Medal of Science, 1996.

David S. Saxon (1920–) research physicist, Radiation Laboratory, MIT, 1943–46; faculty member, University of California, Los Angeles, 1947–75; president, 1975–83; member of the MIT Corporation, 1977–90; chairman, 1983–90; honorary chairman, 1990–95.

Edgar H. Schein (1928–) management educator, joined the MIT faculty in 1956; appointed professor of organizational psychology and management, 1964; Sloan Fellows professor of management, 1978–93; professor emeritus, 1993.

Thomas C. Schelling (1921–) professor of economics, Yale University, 1953–58; Harvard University, 1958–90; University of Maryland, beginning in 1990; member, U.S. Air Force scientific advisory board, 1960–64; author of *Arms and Influence* (1966).

Arthur M. Schlesinger, Jr. (1917–) historian, taught at Harvard University before serving as special assistant to the U.S. President, 1961–64; author of numerous books, including *The Age of Jackson* (1946) and *A Thousand Days: John F. Kennedy in the White House* (1965), both Pulitzer-award winners.

Christopher Schmandt principal research scientist, Media Laboratory, MIT; director, speech interfaces group.

Donald A. Schon (1930–1997) director, Institute for Applied Technology, National Bureau of Standards, 1961–66; cofounder and director, Organization for Social and Technological Innovation, Boston, 1966–73; Ford professor of urban studies and education, MIT, 1972–92; department chair, 1990–92; professor emeritus, 1992–97.

Herbert (Pete) Scoville (1915–1985) senior scientist, AEC, 1946–48; technical director, U.S. Armed Forces special weapons project, 1948–55; assistant director of scientific intelligence, then deputy director for research, CIA, 1955–63; member, Technological Capabilities Panel, 1955; U.S. delegation to the Geneva Conference on Surprise Attack, 1958; assistant director for science and technology, ACDA, 1963–69; director of arms control program, Carnegie Endowment for International Peace, 1969–71; chair, U.S. delegation to NATO disarmament experts' meetings, 1966–68, and U.S. delegations to various countries on the nuclear non-proliferation treaty, 1967–68; consultant, PSAC, 1969–73; cofounder, Arms Control Association.

Glenn T. Seaborg (1912–1979) chemist, was director of plutonium work for the Manhattan Project at the University of Chicago, 1942–46; member, first general advisory committee, AEC, 1946–50; head of nuclear chemistry division, Lawrence Berkeley Laboratory, 1946–58; first scientist appointed to head the AEC, 1961–71; wide interests in the public understanding of science, science education, peaceful uses of atomic energy, and international cooperation in science and technology.

Frederick Seitz (1911–) faculty member in physics at the University of Pennsylvania, Carnegie Institute of Technology, and the University of Illinois; president, National Academy of Sciences, 1962–69; president, Rockefeller University, 1968–78; University of Miami, 1989; chairman, Naval Research Advisory Committee, 1960–62; vice chairman, Defense Science Board, 1961–62; chairman, 1964–68; member, advisory board, Center for Strategic and International Studies, 1975–81; recipient, National Medal of Science, 1973.

Michael Sela see his essay in this book.

Amartya K. Sen (1933–) economist and educator; professor of economics at Jadavpur University, 1956–58; Delhi University, 1963–71; London School of Economics, 1971–77; Oxford University, 1977–88; Harvard University, 1987–98; appointed master, Trinity College, Cambridge, 1998; Nobel Prize in economics, 1998.

Leopold Sedar Senghor (1906–2001) poet and political leader; president of Senegal, 1960–80.

Claude E. Shannon (1916–2001) mathematician and computer scientist sometimes called "father of the information sciences"; first scientist to apply Boolean logic to electrical systems, thus laying groundwork for the computer industry, telecommunications, and a new communications theory; cryptanalyst during World War II; research mathematician, Bell Telephone Laboratories, 1941–72; joined the MIT faculty in 1957; Donner professor of science, MIT, 1958–78; professor emeritus, 1978–2001.

James A. Shannon (1904–1994) medical investigator and research administrator; consultant on tropical diseases to the U.S. secretary of war, 1943–46; assistant U.S. surgeon general and associate director, National Institutes of Health, 1952–55; director, National Institutes of Health, 1955–68; consultant, PSAC, 1959–65; member, National Academies of Science and Engineering; founding member, National Institute of Medicine; recipient, National Medal of Science, 1974.

Deborah Shapley (1945–) reporter, *Technology Review* (MIT), 1968–71; *Science* magazine, 1971–79; senior associate, Carnegie Foundation for International Peace, 1979–81; member, editorial board, *Bulletin of the Atomic Scientists*, 1984–89.

Marshall D. Shulman (1916–) political scientist; special assistant to the U.S. secretary of state, 1950–53; associate director, Russian Research Center, Harvard University, 1954–62; later professor of international relations at Tufts University and Columbia University; director, Russian Institute, Columbia University, 1967–74; Harriman Institute for Advanced Study of the Soviet Union, Columbia University, 1982–86; special adviser on Soviet affairs to the U.S. secretary of state, 1977–80.

George P. Shultz (1920–) economist and government official; earned his Ph.D. in industrial economics at MIT in 1949; faculty member, MIT, 1949–57; then a professor and dean at the University of Chicago; U.S. secretary of labor, 1969–70; director, Office of Management and Budget, 1970–72; U.S. secretary of the treasury and special assistant to President Nixon, 1972–74; professor of management and public policy, Stanford University, and executive with the Bechtel Corporation, 1974–82; chairman, President's Economic Policy Advisory Board, 1981–82; U.S. secretary of state, 1982–89; professor of international economics, Stanford University, 1989–91.

John Silber (1926–) philosopher and university administrator; taught at the University of Texas, Austin, and Boston University; president, Boston University, 1971–96; Democratic gubernatorial candidate for governor of Massachusetts, 1990.

Beverly Sills (1929–) opera singer; council member, National Endowment for the Arts, 1970–76; member, Carnegie Commission on the Future of Public Broadcasting.

Robert B. Silvers (1929–) assistant editor, *Harper's Magazine*, 1959–63; thereafter coeditor, *New York Review of Books*.

Constantine B. Simonides (1934–1994) assistant director, International Programs in the Sloan School of Management, MIT, 1962–64; assistant dean, Sloan School, 1964–66;

assistant to the MIT president, 1966–70; vice president, 1970–94; secretary of the MIT Corporation, 1985–94.

Hector R. Skifter (1901–1964)   associate director, Airborne Instruments Laboratory, 1942–45; president, 1945–64; consultant to the assistant secretary of defense for research and development, 1957–60; assistant director of defense research and engineering, U.S. Department of Defense, 1959–60.

Eugene B. Skolnikoff   see his essay in this book.

John C. Slater (1900–1976)   theoretical physicist, began his academic career at Harvard University and joined the MIT faculty in 1930 as chairman of the physics department; leader, Group 57 (Special Problems), Radiation Laboratory, MIT, World War II; also worked on magnetrons at Bell Telephone Laboratories during the war; helped shape the Research Laboratory of Electronics at MIT in the postwar period; also, the Laboratories for Nuclear Science and Acoustics, and the Solid-State and Molecular Theory Group, a precursor to the interdisciplinary materials science and engineering program; professor, Brookhaven National Laboratory, 1951–65; research professor, University of Florida, 1965–76.

Louis Slotin (1912–1946)   physicist who worked in radiobiology and specialized in triggering devices; staff, Manhattan Project, Los Alamos; died of radiation poisoning in May 1946 at Los Alamos.

Louis D. Smullin   see his essay in this book.

Henry DeWolf (Harry) Smyth (1898–1986)   physicist, author, and educator; member, physics faculty, Princeton University, 1924–66; professor emeritus, 1966–86; consultant on war research projects to the National Research Council and Office of Scientific Research and Development, 1940–45; Manhattan Project, 1943–45; member, AEC, 1949–54; U.S. representative, International Atomic Energy Agency, 1961–70; author of *Atomic Energy for Military Purposes: The Official Report on the Development of the Atomic Bomb Under the Auspices of the United States Government, 1940–1945*, also known as the "Smyth Report"; outspoken critic of government secrecy on atomic energy.

C. P. Snow (1905–1980)   physicist, writer, and government official; author of *The Two Cultures and the Scientific Revolution* (1959).

Benson R. Snyder (1923–)   psychiatrist-in-chief, MIT, 1959–69; professor of psychiatry, 1967–90; dean for institute relations, 1969–73; professor of urban studies and education, 1973–77; director, Division for Study and Research in Education (DSRE), MIT, 1975–90.

Robert M. Solow   see his essay in this book.

Theodore C. (Ted) Sorensen   see his essay in this book.

Percy LeBaron Spencer (1894–1970)   inventor and radio engineer; director of development and engineering, Raytheon, 1925–40; manager and chief engineer, microwave and power tube division, 1940–55; senior vice president and director, 1955–65; director and consultant, 1965–70.

Philip Sporn (1896–1978)   electric company executive; president, American Gas and Electric Company (later, American Electric Power).

Robert C. Sprague (1900–1991)   pioneer in radio and television electronics; founder, Sprague Electric Company; member, MIT Corporation, 1953–55; life member, 1955–75; life member emeritus, 1975–91; director, Gaither Panel, PSAC, 1957–58; trustee, MITRE

Corporation, 1958–81; member, board of governors, Massachusetts Science and Technology Foundation, 1970–78; Draper Laboratory, 1970–78.

Elmer B. Staats (1914–) deputy director, U.S. Bureau of the Budget, 1950–53, 1958–66; executive director of operations, National Security Council, 1953–58; U.S. comptroller-general, 1966–81; president, Harry S. Truman Scholarship Foundation, 1981–84.

Harold E. Stassen (1907–2001) Republican governor of Minnesota, 1938–45; president, University of Pennsylvania, 1948–53; member, National Security Council, 1953–58; in private law practice thereafter.

Adlai E. Stevenson (1900–1965) political leader, was U.S. minister and chief of the U.S. delegation to the Preparatory Commission on the United Nations, 1945; governor of Illinois, 1948–52; Democratic candidate for U.S. president, 1952 and 1956, losing on both occasions to Dwight D. Eisenhower; U.S. ambassador to the United Nations, 1960–65.

Jeremy J. Stone (1935–) research associate, arms control and disarmament, Harvard University Center for International Affairs, 1964–66; president, Federation of American Scientists, 1970–2000; author of *Containing the Arms Race* (1966) and *Adventures of a Public Interest Activist* (1999).

Catherine N. Stratton see her essay in this book.

Julius A. (Jay) Stratton (1901–1994) physicist and electrical engineer, joined the MIT faculty in 1928; staff member, Radiation Laboratory, MIT, 1940–45; head, Basic Research Division, Radiation Laboratory, 1946; founding director, Research Laboratory of Electronics, MIT, 1946–49; MIT provost, 1949–51; vice president, 1951–55; chancellor, 1955–57; acting president, 1957–59; president, 1959–66; consultant to the U.S. secretary of war, 1942–45; member, U.S. Army Scientific Panel, 1954–56; Naval Research Advisory Committee, 1956–59; National Science Board, 1956–62, 1964–67; vice president, National Academy of Sciences, 1961–65; board chairman, Ford Foundation, 1966–71; author of *Science and the Educated Man* (1966); husband of Catherine N. Stratton.

Lewis L. Strauss (1896–1974) was appointed a member of the AEC in 1946; advocate of development of hydrogen bomb in response to the first Soviet atomic explosion in 1949; supporter of Edward Teller, opponent of J. Robert Oppenheimer; special assistant on atomic energy to President Eisenhower and chair, AEC, 1953–58; nominated by Eisenhower as secretary of commerce in 1958, but rejected by the U.S. Senate.

William Styron (1925–) Pulitzer Prize-winning novelist with a deep interest in social issues, e.g. slavery (*The Confessions of Nat Turner*) and the Holocaust (*Sophie's Choice*, winner of the National Book Award); married Rose Burgunder (poet) in 1953.

Lawrence E. Susskind (1947–) urban and environmental planner, joined the MIT faculty in 1971; professor of urban affairs and environmental planning, 1982–95; appointed Ford professor, 1995; department head, 1978–82.

Stuart Symington, II (1901–1988) government official and banker; surplus property administrator, Washington, D.C., 1945–46; assistant secretary of war, 1946–47; first secretary of the U.S. Air Force, 1947–51; U.S. senator (D-Mo.), 1953–76; his primary legislative interests were in defense and foreign policy, and he served simultaneously on the Senate arms services and foreign relations committees.

Norman H. Taylor (1916–) was involved in several computer projects at MIT, including Project Whirlwind, beginning in 1948; associate division head, Lincoln Laboratory, MIT, until 1958; member, Gaither Panel, 1957–58; vice president, Itek Corporation, 1958–62; executive consultant, Arthur D. Little Company, 1965–69; later president, Corporate Tech Planning, Inc.

Edward Teller (1908–2003)   physicist and educator, taught at Columbia University and other institutions before joining the Manhattan Project in Chicago and Los Alamos, 1942–46; helped develop the atomic bomb, and later (over Robert Oppenheimer's objections) the hydrogen bomb; professor of physics, University of Chicago, 1946–52, and University of California, Berkeley, 1953–75, when he became professor emeritus; advocate of arms buildup throughout the Cold War and proposer of the Strategic Defense Initiative (SDI), under President Ronald Reagan; author of *Better a Shield than a Sword: Perspectives on Defense and Technology* (1987), his rationale for SDI.

Margaret Thatcher (1925–)   member of parliament for the district of Finchley, UK; secretary of state for education and science, 1970–74; opposition leader, 1975–79; prime minister and first lord of the treasury, 1979–90.

Harold A. Thomas, Jr. (1913–)   Gordon McKay professor of civil and sanitary engineering, Harvard University, 1956–84; consultant, executive office of the U.S. president and U.S. Department of Interior; member, science board for the Middle East and Southeast Asia, National Academy of Sciences, 1964–66.

Llewellyn E. Thompson, Jr. (1904–1972)   U.S. ambassador to the Soviet Union, 1957–1962, 1967–69.

Lester C. Thurow (1938–)   economist, joined the MIT faculty in 1968; dean, Sloan School of Management, 1987–93; staff member, President's Council of Economic Advisers, 1964–65.

Paul Tishman   SB (civil engineering) MIT, 1924; chairman, Council for the Arts, MIT.

James Tobin (1918–2002)   economist, joined the Yale University faculty in 1955; Sterling professor of economics, 1957–88; professor emeritus, 1988–2002; member, President's Council of Economic Advisers, 1961–62, and consultant, 1962–68; recipient, Nobel Prize in economics, 1981.

Alexsandr V. Topchiev (1907–1962)   organic chemist active in nuclear research; scientific secretary, Soviet Academy of Sciences; delegate to the Geneva Conference on the Peaceful Uses of Atomic Energy, 1958; attended each of the Pugwash Conferences on Science and World Affairs, 1957–62.

Kosta Tsipis (1934–)   experimental particle physicist; research associate, 1966–68, and then assistant professor of physics, MIT, 1968–71; visiting senior researcher, Stockholm International Peace Research Institute, 1973–75; senior research fellow, Center for International Studies, MIT, 1973–77; senior research physicist, 1977–83; director, Program in Science and Technology for International Security, MIT; coauthor (with Philip Morrison and Jerry), *Beyond the Looking Glass: The United States Military in 2000 & Later* (1993).

Valentin F. Turchin (1931–)   a leading Soviet human rights activist; scientist, Physics and Energy Institute, Obninsk, 1953–64; senior scientist, Institute for Applied Mathematics, Moscow, 1964–73; appointed professor of computer science, City College of the City University of New York, 1979.

Sherry Turkle (1948–)   sociologist, psychologist, and educator; joined the MIT faculty in 1976; Abby Rockefeller Mauze professor of the sociology of science; author of *The Second Self: Computers and the Human Spirit* (1984).

Charles (Chuck) Turner civil rights activist; Boston city councilor, elected 1999; chairman, education committee, Boston City Council.

James M. Turner physicist; research assistant, MIT, 1966–71; program manager and international collaborations manager, U.S. Department of Energy (DOE) Office of Fusion Energy, 1977–88; director, Office of Weapons Surety, 1988–94; deputy U.S. negotiator for dismantlement of nuclear weapons in the former Soviet Union, 1991–94; manager, DOE Oakland Operations Office, starting in 1994.

Ralph W. Tyler (1902–1994) dean, Division of Social Sciences, University of Chicago, 1948–53; founder and director, Center for Advanced Study in the Behavioral Sciences, Palo Alto, California, 1953–67; president, Social Science Research Council, 1971–72.

Paul Valéry (1871–1945) French poet, philosopher, dramatist, and essayist; president, League of Nations Committee for Intellectual Cooperation, 1936.

George Valley (1913–1991) physicist and air defense specialist; staff, Radiation Laboratory, MIT, 1940–46; appointed professor of physics, MIT, 1946; member, U.S. Air Force scientific advisory board, 1946–64; associate director, Lincoln Laboratory, MIT, 1953–57; chief scientist, U.S. Air Force, 1957–58; founder, Experimental Study Group (ESG), MIT, 1969.

Yevgeniy P. Velikhov (1935–) physicist, joined the staff of the Kurchatov Institute of Atomic Energy in 1958; laboratory head, 1962–70; deputy director, 1971–89; appointed director, Russian Scientific Center, Kurchatov Institute, 1989; professor, Moscow University, starting in 1973; elected to the Soviet Academy of Sciences, 1974; vice president, 1978–96; cofounder, International Foundation for the Survival and Development of Humanity, 1987; chairman, Committee of Soviet Scientists for Peace against Nuclear Threat.

Barry Vercoe (1937–) composer and computer-music specialist, joined the MIT faculty in 1971; professor of media arts and sciences since 1985; head of the music, mind, and machine group, Media Laboratory, MIT.

Frank von Hippel (1937–) physicist; taught at Stanford University and Princeton University; senior research physicist, Center for Energy and Environmental Studies, beginning in 1978; member, risk assessment review group, U.S. Nuclear Regulatory Commission, 1977–78; subcommittee on science for citizens, National Science Foundation, beginning in 1977; member, editorial advisory board, *Bulletin of the Atomic Scientists*; editor (with Roald Z. Sagdeev), *Reversing the Arms Race: How to Achieve and Verify Deep Reductions in the Nuclear Arsenals* (New York, 1990).

Henry A. Wallace (1888–1965) U.S. secretary of agriculture, 1933–40; U.S. vice president, 1941–45; U.S. secretary of commerce, 1945–46; U.S. presidential candidate on the Progressive ticket, 1948.

Mike Wallace (1918–) award-winning broadcast journalist, began his career at the University of Michigan radio station while he was a student there in the 1930s; coeditor and presenter, *60 Minutes* (CBS), beginning in 1968.

Roger S. Warner (1907–1976) coordinating engineer and division head, Manhattan Project, Los Alamos, 1944–47; director of engineering, AEC, 1947–49; joined engineering staff of Arthur D. Little, Inc., 1949; later, staff member, DARPA, Washington, D.C.

Earl Warren (1891–1974) conservative Republican governor of California, 1943–53; chief justice, U.S. Supreme Court, where he became known for his liberal or activist judicial philosophy; chair, President's Commission on the Assassination of President John F. Kennedy (the Warren Commission).

Booker T. Washington (1856–1915) spokesman for conservative viewpoint among American blacks opposed to agitation for social and political ends; founder and president, Tuskegee Institute; author of *Up from Slavery* (1901).

Lew Wasserman (1913–) film, recording, and publishing company executive.

Alan T. Waterman (1892–1967) physicist; faculty member, Yale University, 1923–48; deputy chief and chief scientist, U.S. Office of Naval Research, 1946–51; director, National Science Foundation, 1951–63; member, Defense Science Board, 1956–63; Federal Council for Science and Technology, 1958–63; consultant, PSAC; trustee, Atoms for Peace Awards; recipient, Presidential Medal of Freedom, 1963.

Muddy Waters (1915–1983) blues musician.

James D. Watson (1928–) molecular biologist; codiscoverer (with Francis Crick) of the double-helical structure of DNA; consultant, PSAC, during the Kennedy administration; recipient, Nobel Prize (physiology or medicine), 1962.

Thomas J. Watson, Jr. (1914–1993) vice president in charge of sales, IBM, 1946–49; executive vice president, 1949–52; president, 1952–61; chief executive officer, 1956–71; chairman, 1961–71; member, MIT Corporation, 1957–62; President's Task Force on the War Against Poverty; Presidential Commission on Arms Control and Disarmament, 1978–89; U.S. ambassador to the Soviet Union, 1979–81.

Robert Watson-Watt (1892–1973) chief developer of radar; deputy chairman, Radio Board, UK War Cabinet, 1943–45.

William Webster (1900–1972) executive vice president and director, New England Electric System, 1950–59; president, 1959–63; chairman and chief executive officer, 1963–70; appointed chairman, research and development board, U.S. Department of Defense, 1950; deputy secretary of defense for atomic energy; member, MIT Corporation.

Alvin M. Weinberg (1915–) held various administrative and research positions (director of the physics division, research director, and director), Oak Ridge National Laboratory, starting in 1945; member, PSAC, 1960–62; President's Medal of Science Committee, 1979–82.

Steven Weinberg (1933–) visiting professor at MIT, 1967–69, before joining the faculty as professor of physics, 1969–73; later at Harvard University and University of Texas, Austin; consultant, IDA, 1960–73, and ACDA, 1973; shared Nobel Prize in physics with Abdus Salam (above) and Sheldon Glashow, 1979.

Meyer W. Weisgal (1894–1977) editor, theatrical producer, and Zionist leader; member, Zionist Organization of America; president, Weizmann Institute of Science, Rehovot, Israel, 1966–69; chancellor, 1969–77.

Herbert G. Weiss (1918–) electronics researcher; staff member, Radiation Laboratory, MIT, 1941–45; group leader in charge of electronics research section, Los Alamos Laboratory, 1945–48; senior engineer, Raytheon, 1948–52; group leader, radar systems, Lincoln Laboratory, MIT, 1952–60; division head, 1960–79; vice president, Windpower, Inc., beginning in 1980; appointed a member of the strategic military panel, PSAC, 1971.

Victor (Viki) Weisskopf (1908–2002) physicist noted for his theoretical work in quantum electrodynamics; group leader and associate head of the theory division, Manhattan Project, Los Alamos, 1943–46; cofounder, Federation of Atomic Scientists, 1945; joined the MIT physics faculty in 1945; department chair, 1967–73; director-general, European Center for Nuclear Research (CERN), 1961–65; elected Institute professor, MIT, 1966; professor emeritus, 1974–2002; outspoken advocate of arms control; president, American Academy of Arts and Sciences, 1975–79; recipient, National Medal of Science, 1980; Public Welfare Medal, National Academy of Sciences, 1991.

Lee C. White (1923–)   lawyer; legislative assistant to U.S. senator John F. Kennedy, 1954–57; assistant special counsel to President Kennedy, 1961–63; associate counsel to President Lyndon B. Johnson, 1963–65; special counsel to President Johnson, 1965–66; chairman, Federal Power Commission, 1966–69.

Sheila E. Widnall (1938–)   aeronautical educator; joined the MIT faculty in 1964; professor of aeronautics and astronautics, 1974–93; chairman of the faculty, 1979–80; associate provost, 1992–93; secretary, U.S. Air Force, 1993–97; elected Institute professor, MIT, 1997.

Norbert Wiener (1894–1964)   mathematician and educator, taught at MIT, 1919–60; professor emeritus, 1960–64; known as the founder of cybernetics (a term he coined), focusing on the relationship between cognitive processes and mechanical-electrical communications systems; established a weekly supper seminar in Cambridge, Mass., bringing together representatives of a wide range of disciplines to discuss common research and intellectual interests; recipient, National Medal of Science, 1964.

Edna Wiesner   sister of Jerry Wiesner.

Ida (Friedman) Wiesner   mother of Jerry Wiesner.

Joseph Wiesner (1874–1954)   father of Jerry Wiesner.

Laya W. Wiesner (1918–1998)   wife of Jerry Wiesner; met Jerry when they were fellow students at the University of Michigan in the 1930s; cofounder and trustee, Metropolitan Council for Educational Opportunity (METCO), bringing minority children from Boston to suburban schools starting in the early 1960s; chair, human resources committee, Massachusetts League of Women Voters, 1964–66; member, Governor's Advisory Committee on Child Development in Massachusetts and the Massachusetts Advisory Council for Vocational-Technical Education; board member, Cambridge School of Weston (Mass.); coorganizer (with Edith Ruina) of the 1973 MIT Workshop on Women in Science and Technology, a pioneering effort to bring together leaders from government, industry, and education to explore ways to encourage the participation of women in non-traditional careers.

Elizabeth A. (Lisa) Wiesner (1949–)   daughter of Jerry and Laya Wiesner.

Joshua A. Wiesner   see his preface to this book.

Stephen J. Wiesner (1942–)   son of Jerry and Laya Wiesner; research physicist, Mizpeh Ramon (Israel) Yishiva; Tel Aviv University, Ramat-Aviv, 1995.

Zachary K. Wiesner (1946–)   son of Jerry and Laya Wiesner.

Eugene P. Wigner (1902–1995)   staff, metallurgical laboratory, University of Chicago, World War II; professor of mathematical physics, Princeton University, 1938–71; professor emeritus, 1971–95; member, general advisory committee, AEC, 1952–57, 1959–64; director, civil defense research project, Oak Ridge, 1964–65; editor and contributor, *Survival and the Bomb: Methods of Civil Defense* (1969); recipient, Nobel Prize in physics, 1963; National Medal of Science, 1969.

Carroll L. Wilson (1910–1983)   assistant to the president, MIT, 1932–36; executive assistant to the director, Office of Scientific Research and Development, Washington, D.C., 1940–46; general manager, AEC, 1947–51; professor of management, MIT, 1959–77; director of workshop on alternative energy strategies, 1974–77; director of Fellows in Africa program, Sloan School of Management, MIT; chairman of governing board, International Centre for Insect Physiology and Ecology, Nairobi, 1968–74; trustee, World Peace Foundation; senior adviser, United Nations Conference on Human Environment.

Thomas Winship (1920–2002)   editor, *Boston Globe*, 1965–85.

Albert J. Wohlstetter (1913–1997)   strategic analyst on nuclear arms control and foreign policy; researcher, Rand Corporation, where he conducted studies for the U.S. Department of Defense, 1950–64; adviser, Geneva Conference on Surprise Attack, 1958; adviser to President Kennedy during the Cuban missile crisis, 1962; taught at the University of Chicago, 1964–80.

Thomas H. (Tom) Wolf (1916–1996)   executive producer, CBS News, 1960–62; producer of the CBS series *Tomorrow*; news executive, ABC News, beginning in 1963; president, Wolf Communications, 1981–96; consultant, Smithsonian Institution.

Daniel Yankelovich (1924–)   social researcher and pollster; president, Yankelovich, Skelly & White (business and social research), 1958–81; chairman, starting in 1981; cofounder and president, Public Agenda Foundation; known for his analyses of contemporary American culture.

Adam Yarmolinksy (1922–2000)   special assistant to the U.S. secretary of defense, 1961–64; deputy director, President's Task Force on the War Against Poverty, 1964; later taught at Harvard University and the University of Massachusetts, Boston; counselor, ACDA, beginning in 1977.

Yevgeny Yevtushenko (1933–)   Russian poet, filmmaker, and actor; recipient, USSR Commission for the Defense of Peace award, 1965.

Herbert F. York (1921–)   physicist; staff member, Radiation Laboratory, University of California, Berkeley, 1943–54; director, Livermore Weapon Development Laboratory, 1954–58; member, ballistic missile advisory committee, U.S. secretary of defense, 1955–58; director of defense research and engineering, DARPA, 1958–61; member, PSAC, 1957–58, 1964–68; general advisory committee, ACDA, 1961–69; author of *Race to Oblivion: A Participant's View of the Arms Race* (1970) and *Making Weapons, Talking Peace: A Physicist's Odyssey from Hiroshima to Geneva* (1987).

Jerrold R. Zacharias (1905–1986)   physicist and educator, worked on microwave radar at MIT's Radiation Laboratory, World War II; head, Transmitter Components Division; later head, Ordnance Engineering Division, Los Alamos; joined the MIT faculty as professor of physics in 1945; director, Laboratory for Nuclear Science until 1955; member, PSAC, 1952–64; founder, Physical Sciences Study Committee (PSSC) and Educational Services, Inc. (ESI); elected to the National Academy of Sciences in 1957.

Solly Zuckerman (1904–1993)   British anatomist and educator; scientific adviser to British military organizations, 1939–46; deputy chairman, Advisory Council on Scientific Policy, 1948–64; chairman, British Committee on Scientific Manpower, 1950–64; Defense Research Policy Committee, 1960–64; chief scientific adviser to the British Secretary of State for Defense, 1960–66, and to Her Majesty's Government, 1966–71; president, Parliamentary and Scientific Committee, 1973–76; author of *Scientists and War: The Impact of Science on Military and Civil Affairs* (1966) and *Nuclear Illusion and Reality* (1982); knighted in 1956.

Acknowledgments

This book might never have come about had it not been for Lawrence S. Bacow. Larry's interest in Walter's idea for a book on Jerry gave Walter the impetus to go ahead. Larry explored, jointly with Walter and Judy, the possible interest of the MIT Press. Before he left his post as MIT's chancellor to become president of Tufts University, he arranged funding for the project. Since then, he has continued to be supportive.

Before moving to Tufts, Larry arranged for Philip S. Khoury, dean of the School of Humanities, Arts, and Social Sciences at MIT, to oversee the project. We are deeply indebted to Philip for assuming this role, for providing key logistical support, and for being supportive in a variety of ways.

Members of the advisory group assembled by Walter also deserve special credit. The group consisted of Philip N. Alexander, Paul E. Gray, Carl Kaysen, Philip S. Khoury, Kenneth R. Manning, Judy F. Rosenblith, Eugene B. Skolnikoff, Louis D. Smullin, and Joshua A. Wiesner. We met at the beginning to discuss possible contributors, and on occasion thereafter to assess progress. Members volunteered to ascertain the willingness of particular essayists, served as liaison with essayists who accepted our invitation, and in some cases helped with editing and feedback on the essays. Their support and encouragement throughout was extremely valuable.

Jerry's youngest son, Josh, not only served on the advisory group, but also provided a wealth of material from unpublished memoir chapters by Jerry—and some by Josh himself—based on his intensive interviews with Jerry in the early 1990s. A good portion of that material appears in this book. In addition, Josh supplied some family photographs for reproduction here.

One member of the advisory group, Kenneth Manning, initiated contact and interviewed Elma Lewis, who was unable to write an essay. An edited transcript of their interview appears in this book. One other contribution, that by Ruth Adams, was obtained in this way. Adele Simmons rose to the last-minute challenge of conducting the interview with Ruth, an edited transcript of which also appears here.

Special thanks go to the staff of the Institute Archives and Special Collections, especially Nora Murphy; the staff of the MIT Museum, especially Jennifer O'Neill; and to the staff of the MIT Press, especially former editor in chief Larry Cohen and managing editor Michael Sims, for their diligence, patience, and good humor throughout.

Last, but by no means least, we acknowledge the invaluable work of Philip Alexander. Philip served as liaison between Walter and the essayists, did invaluable work in the MIT Archives, MIT Museum, and other repositories and sources to obtain relevant material on Jerry; maintained contacts with all involved; and provided a number of essayists with needed help. After working closely with Walter on the chronology, he continued to work with Judy to select and edit all materials. He prepared the explanatory preambles, footnotes, and bibliography, and assembled and captioned the photographs. In short, Judy could never have finished Walter's book without him. Philip was dedicated, thoughtful, and provided needed expertise.

Index

Page numbers in boldface refer to essays by the cited individuals.